ARCHITECTURAL
TECHNOLOGY

ARCHITECTURAL TECHNOLOGY

THOMAS OBERMEYER

Registered Architect
Instructor
Dakota County Area Vocational Technical Institute
Rosemount, Minnesota

Gregg Division
McGraw-Hill Book Company

New York   St. Louis   Dallas   San Francisco   Auckland
Düsseldorf   Johannesburg   Kuala Lumpur   London
Mexico   Montreal   New Delhi   Panama   Paris
São Paulo   Singapore   Sydney   Tokyo   Toronto

Library of Congress Cataloging in Publication Data

Obermeyer, Thomas
  Architectural technology.

  1. Architecture—Study and teaching—United States.
2. Architectural technicians—United States.
I. Title.
NA2108.O23   720'.7'1073   75-42134
ISBN 0-07-047496-6

ARCHITECTURAL TECHNOLOGY

234567890 BABA 7832109876

The editors for this book were William K. Fallon and
Myrna W. Breskin, the designer was Victoria Wong, the
art supervisor was George T. Resch, and the production
supervisor was Iris Levy. It was set in Caledonia by
Progressive Typographers.
Printed and bound by George Banta Company, Inc.

CONTENTS

PREFACE   vii

ONE   BASIC ARCHITECTURAL SKILLS   1

TWO   FUNDAMENTALS OF DRAFTING   13

THREE   PRODUCTION OF WORKING DRAWINGS   63

FOUR   BUILDING CONSTRUCTION AND TECHNOLOGY   119

FIVE   BUILDING EQUIPMENT AND SERVICES   163

SIX   STRUCTURAL DESIGN   191

SEVEN   PROFESSIONAL PRACTICE   223

EIGHT   ARCHITECTURAL HISTORY   279

NINE   SITE PLANNING AND DESIGN   315

TEN   LAWS AND PRACTICES   327

INDEX   341

PREFACE

Architecture has been a vital part of civilization for more than six thousand years. While twentieth-century skyscrapers hardly resemble the Egyptian pyramids, modern and ancient architecture do have several points in common. They both incorporate design, they are both dependent on technology, and they are both functional.

Over the same period of time, the role of the architect has not changed appreciably, but the complexity of the job has increased. For this reason, there is an increasing need for architectural technicians—people with two years of post-secondary training who can assist architects and work meaningfully with structural engineers and other members of the architectural team.

Architectural Technology has been written for students in two-year building trades programs that primarily involve architecture, construction management, and building inspection. The text gives students a well-rounded knowledge of architectural practice and helps teach them to assemble graphically the necessary construction elements to meet the needs of clients. While it is not meant to be a beginning reader in architecture, the book does provide the fundamental knowledge necessary to begin a career. The primary goal of this text is to give a student the information needed to work *with* an architect rather than *for* an architect.

ORGANIZATION OF THE TEXT

Essentially, the first half of the book concentrates on the assembly of a working drawing package, taking the reader through the "nuts and bolts" of putting a building together. The second half of the book is presented to extend the architectural knowledge of the reader.

The text is divided into ten chapters. Chapter 1, "Basic Architectural Skills," introduces the student to the skills and knowledge necessary for the architectural technician to acquire. It also discusses the types of architectural projects and the people involved, including the architectural staff and the client. Chapter 2, "Fundamentals of Drafting," deals with basic drafting, including equipment, symbols and abbreviations, reference materials, and drafting procedures and techniques. An extremely important part of this chapter is the 25-page presentation of architects' large-scale details. This material is intended to be a "dictionary" for a student to use in determining the assembly of a building. Chapter 3, "Production of Working Drawings," outlines and discusses the main categories of working drawings. Chapter 4, "Building Construction and Technology," includes a discussion on each of the major materials of construction as well as methods and systems of structural detailing.

Chapter 5, "Building Equipment and Services," describes each of the support systems that a building must have to meet its needs. The systems covered are water distribution, plumbing disposal, heating, cooling, electricity, lighting and acoustics. Methods of designing and detailing such systems are also discussed. Chapter 6, "Structural Design," is presented to give the student a basic understanding of building structures. Even though architectural technicians are not usually called upon to design any structure beyond a wooden frame, they should have sufficient knowledge to work productively with structural engineers. In Chapter 7, "Professional Practice," the reader is shown by a step-by-step procedure exactly what takes place in an architect's office. A typical job comes in and is followed through to completion. Sample filled-out forms are illustrated to give the student an idea of the documentation involved in architectural practice. Chapter 8, "Architectural History," gives the student a condensed version of the evolution of architectural style and contains illustrations of the most significant styles through the ages. Chapter 9, "Site Planning and Design," covers the methods used to plan a building site in the most functional manner. Chapter 10, "Laws and Practices," contains valuable information on national and local building codes as well as instruction on architectural techniques such as isometric and perspective drawing, rendering and model building.

INSTRUCTOR'S MANUAL

A separate instructor's manual is available. This manual contains teaching suggestions as well as projects and exercises that the instructor may use in conjunction with the text.

CONCLUSION

The writing of a textbook is a marked departure from the usual work of an architect. My goal in this book has been to blend my collegiate experience with knowledge gained in architectural practice to give an accurate view of what is expected of an architectural technician. This undertaking would not have been possible without the moral support, editing, and typing assistance from my wife, Beth, and the understanding of my children, Mark and Kristin. The book is greatly enhanced by the number of drawings generously shared by the offices listed below. I would like to thank them for their assistance.

ACKNOWLEDGMENTS

Fredrick Bentz, Milo Thompson
Bentz-Thompson, Architects

William Anderson
Design Partnership, Architects

Roger Johnson
Johnson, Sheldon and Sorensen,
Architects, Inc.

The Cerny Associates, Architects, Inc.

Miller, Hanson, Westerbeck, Bell, Architects

Winsor Faricy, Architects

John Flad and Associates, Architects

Gerald Mazzara, Architect

Dennis LaFrance, Architect

Inter Design, Architects

The American Institute of Architects

Rauenhorst Corporation

Acorn Structures, Inc.

ONE

BASIC ARCHITECTURAL SKILLS

THE SKILLS NEEDED FOR ARCHITECTURE

Architecture is a complex and exciting profession. Architectural technicians need to know both how to assemble buildings and how to use materials; they also need to know about many related areas, such as contract administration and planning. The intent of this book is to give information on *detailing* (the ability to draw all the data necessary to tell a builder exactly how to construct a project). It also will provide fair working knowledge of other areas of architectural practice. Students will begin to appreciate the breadth of the profession more and may decide to obtain further information on the subject.

A course in architectural technology is one way to become involved in architecture. A five- or six-year college program stresses the theories of design, planning, and structural and architectural history. It places less emphasis on detailing a building. Architectural technicians spend most of their two-year learning experience in the technology of building construction. We will discuss eight areas of study in which technicians need to display varying degrees of proficiency. These topics are covered in greater detail later in the book, but they are mentioned here to orient students new to the subject.

Building Construction and Technology

Building construction refers to the manner in which materials are assembled. Certain standard construction techniques and typical dimensioning systems must be familiar to architectural technicians. Unique detailing may never have been encountered on prior projects of a particular firm. Thus, technicians must depend on their knowledge and past experience for the solution to a variety of problems. Building construction is always changing. Increased experience improves technicians' ability to comprehend and solve most problems that might arise.

Building technology is a general term including all processes and materials used to assemble a building. Architectural technicians first must learn the language of architecture. In addition to all the terms, it is vital for technicians to become familiar with the thousands of building materials and to know which is best in each particular situation. An example might be the anchoring of an aluminum window frame to a poured-concrete wall. A weak galvanic (battery) action causes the aluminum to corrode. Thus, the aluminum should be painted first with bitumen, which acts as a barrier between the reacting materials. Items like this—and the thousands of possible errors that could be detailed into a building—can be caught and corrected in several ways. Obviously, the least acceptable method is by trial and error. In the case of the corroded aluminum frame, it would have to be replaced upon discovery, probably at the architect's expense. A better approach is for the technician to recognize problems when drawing the project and to find acceptable solutions.

The language that technicians use to detail buildings is highly technical and communicates to a skilled builder how the structure is to be assembled. The plans tell the excavating contractor where to dig, the mason how to lay brick, and the glazier how to install a window. Architectural technicians must speak intelligently to skilled workers in many occupations, from those who place copper flashings on a roof to those who install elevators. The problem is that an elevator installer is not simply going to ask how to push the down button. More likely, the installer will want a solution to a highly technical problem. It is certainly advantageous to solve these problems in the office before the job is even begun. This saves time for the architect as well as for the contractor. Since major building companies supply architectural firms with detailed information on particular products, the task is not hopeless.

Of the eight fields covered in this book, building technology is the most important.

Building Equipment

Building equipment includes the great variety of mechanical and electrical apparatus that makes a structure livable. The equipment includes lighting, electrical outlets, telephone and television connections, heating and cooling, dust and odor removal, hot and cold water, sewage removal, and even lightning protection.

A technician is not expected to have working knowledge in all related fields in building equipment. For this reason, architectural firms require the services of mechanical and electrical engineers. Some firms have engineers on the payroll (in-house engineers). Other firms retain private engineering firms for each specific job (engineering consultant firms). Working with professional engineers certainly simplifies the process of assembling a building, but architectural technicians still must gain general familiarity with the engineer's profession in order to solve problems in the design.

To a great extent, the demands of the mechanical and electrical systems will affect the entire design and assembly of the building. Take, for example, the air-supply system in a building. The requirements might include five complete air changes per hour in a room 30′ wide, 30′ long, and 9′ high. The room has 8100 cu ft of air; with five air changes per hour, the total air requirement is 40,500 cu ft. Assuming the air duct provides 500 cu ft of air per minute, the size of the duct must be about 1′-4″ × 1′-0″. While the duct size may seem insignificant, it is accompanied by a return air duct as well, usually located between the ceiling and the underside of the roof deck. More importantly, it is the air supply for one classroom-sized space (900 sq ft) that could occur in a 250,000 sq ft school. With requirements of this proportion, the mechanical system becomes a significant part of building design.

Structures

Perhaps the most difficult related technical field for technicians is structures. Architectural firms retain the services of structural engineers to ensure the proper assembly of a building frame. A technician's knowledge of structures must be sufficient for her or him to talk intelligently with engineers about matters pertaining to the building.

Structures play an extremely important role in building design, and structural engineers are in-volved very early in the initial design concept. Their primary functions during design are to counsel the architect on what can be done and to inform her or him of the limitations imposed on the building.

The study of structures gives technicians a certain intuition about structural concepts. The initial concept of column spacing or the type of connection between the beam and column is as complex as any structural information the technician needs to provide. Typically, an architectural firm does not, and cannot, have architectural personnel involved with the actual structural design. First, it is too costly on a part-time basis to get an architect with the highly specialized skill needed to design structures. The remainder of the architect's time would be spent on detailing architectural portions of the building. Second, the legality of an architectural firm's trusting structural drawings to a person with limited background is questionable. All states require drawings and calculations to be prepared under the direct supervision of a licensed architect; he or she is liable for any structural failure that could occur. Few architects will risk the consequences of an improper design.

This raises an important question. Why is there a strong emphasis on structures both in schools and in examinations for architectural registration if technicians do not use this talent in practice? A practical answer is that the study of structures imparts a certain intuitive approach to the real problem of supporting a building. Obviously, a structural engineer is not going to be available for consultation every time a question arises. However, knowing where to find information on lintel sizes (the structural support over an opening) or realizing that the depth of a bar joist can be found in the structural design development set, makes the technician a more valuable member of an architectural firm.

Professional Practice

Professional practice is an all-encompassing term applied to the legal items that transpire in architectural practice. It includes the various contracts that an architect must sign, the legal documents that are processed to properly administer the building changes, and the architect-approved payments to the contractor. Knowledge of this area increases greatly with practical experience and as a result of demands placed upon the technician.

Every building has unique problems that must be documented for reference. The following is a description of the normal sequence of events that occurs in an architect's office in processing a building.

Initially, when the owner chooses an architect, a contractual agreement is drawn up. The agreement stipulates the services to be provided and the payments to be made. Then the architect prepares the building concept and actual construction drawings. When these drawings and specifications are finished, the architect sends the set to contractors to receive bid prices. The successful bidder (usually the one with the lowest price) then signs a contract with the owner agreeing to follow the architectural documents and to finish the building in a prescribed length of time. The architect determines whether the contractor has the proper bonds, insurance, and contracts before issuing a notice to proceed.

While the project is under construction, the architect approves the contractor's monthly request for payment, documents any change in construction that alters the price with a change order, and issues periodic inspection reports to the owner. When the project is completed, the architect makes a final inspection and, if satisfied, issues notification to the owner that the project is substantially complete.

Training obtained in areas of professional practice could be considered academic. Experience received while handling a job covers many areas that cannot possibly be touched in a text. The broad areas covered in general discussion throughout this book provide some background against which to view most problems that might arise.

Architectural History

This phase of study requires some justification. Why dwell on what was done in the past? What can modern architecture and its detailing possibly share with a Gothic cathedral built 700 years ago? If the answer is limited strictly to a view of architectural drafting, then there is little, if any, connection between modern architecture and detailing in the past.

Technology has changed building materials. From 3000 B.C. to A.D. 1800, the singular building material was loadbearing stone. Some variations were made in using it with other materials. The

Romans backed it with concrete, and the Greeks used metal ties. However, the one permanent material for a span of almost 5000 years was stone. Today stone is one of many exterior building materials used, but it is seldom used to support a structure's weight.

The purpose, then, in studying history is obviously not to improve drafting skills. The less obvious, perhaps more important reason is to begin to understand, appreciate, and enjoy architecture more. When you learn that the Great Pyramid of Cheops is 480 ft high and 756 ft square and was built 4500 years ago by a civilization that didn't even know about the wheel, it becomes apparent that someone must have known something about building before Frank Lloyd Wright happened on the scene. There is a fairly well-defined progression of architectural style that followed the centuries of humanity's need to create an artificial environment. The study of architectural history will reveal more than a culture's building form. It shows the lifestyle, religion, recreation, and habits of a civilization. While there is a strong relationship between the styles of Greek and Roman architecture, the Romans actually used the Greek style after they conquered Greece. When the two styles are studied in depth, the Greek sense of order and philosophy is strongly carried through to their architecture, while the Roman engineering mind dominated their building form.

In short, the study of the history of architecture probably isn't going to make you draw better plans, but it will make your profession more interesting and enjoyable.

Site Planning

Site planning is an integral part of architecture, involving both design and technology. Its technical points, such as drainage and parking-lot design, have ground rules that define the limits within which the architect can work. Obviously, set rules can be learned. They provide answers to most technical problems encountered in site planning.

The other area of planning involves design, which is the nonstatic part of preparing a site. The scope of a project can range from a single lot to an entire city. Many areas considered in site planning have dramatic effects on the final building. Some obvious features to be considered are the automobile access to and parking on the site. The building is also located with a consideration as to the best view, weather conditions, relation to other buildings, proper site grading for drainage, and pedestrian circulation. The strong influence site planning has on the overall design of a building generally places it under the direct supervision of the design department. What this means to an architectural technician is that most of the site planning is either previously conceived or drawn before it gets to the working drawing stage.

Even though the technician may not be asked immediately to do site planning, he or she certainly should be aware of the designer's approach and the many problems that must be solved to place the area surrounding the building in harmony with the structure. This can involve moving earth, planting trees, or building a lake. Whatever the approach, it must be fully detailed and specified so that a contractor can understand and build what the site planner intended. In effect, the technician is taking the concept of the site planner and translating it into technical information that the builder needs.

Design

Design is the glamor area of architecture; it's the primary attraction for students of the profession. A popular conception of the designer is the architect who draws many pretty pictures of the exteriors of buildings with a loaf of French bread in one hand and a bottle of wine on the table. But like many things, in reality design is not at all this glamorous.

Indeed, most good architectural offices have a well-established design philosophy that reflects itself in the buildings they produce. Designers do not "sit back and create." Most often they act as the chief coordinator of a team of architects and technicians. If a formula could be written to create an architectural designer, it would read:

Architectural designer = 25% talent + 5% luck + 60% hard work + 15% perseverance

And that's 105 percent! This description is meant to introduce a realistic view of the profession, not to frighten potential architects from attempting to design a building.

There are nearly 100 accredited schools of architecture in the United States. Roughly one-quarter of the students who start the architecture curriculum graduate. Perhaps one in ten becomes a designer. Yet this does not close the door to those who want to pursue design.

Before you rush to the bookstore that sold you three tubes of HB lead to demand your money back, let's further define design. Design never really stops when an architectural firm produces a building. It ranges from the floor plans that reflect the design circulation pattern to an item as small as a handrail. Somewhere along this line, each technician finds a place as a designer. Even the layout detail of plumbing fixtures in a lavatory requires a designer. While this may seem menial, if the lavatory isn't laid out properly, the overall building cannot be termed a success. An architectural technician works with a designer on various details, mainly in the capacity of doing hard-line scale drawings of the designer's details in an effort to find out if the plan will work. The draftsman's position, therefore, can be classified as that of an *architectural technician* whose job it is to make a design into a workable detail. If more assurance is needed that the technician is indeed involved in design in an architectural firm, a well-done set of working drawings should be inspected. Each detail is designed to work. It is drawn with great skill and laid out on the sheet to be clear and orderly. This is the kind of design an architectural technician is likely to be involved with. Great pride can be taken in detailing, as the drawing is a personal creation. When placed with other drawings, each detail will help to complete a building.

Design training is necessary for several reasons. To communicate with an architectural designer, the technician must obviously know something about the subject. Perhaps a more important personal reason is that design helps develop an appreciation and understanding of the architectural profession. Do not consider architecture a job that starts at 9:00 a.m. and ends at 5:00 p.m. It is a profession that deals with all of our culture. People eat, sleep, shop, work, play, are born, and even die surrounded by architecture. Thus, a building which a technician details will, to a varying degree, affect the environment of many people. A great sense of accomplishment is derived from the end product of architecture.

Miscellaneous Skills

Each place of employment stresses, to varying degrees, several miscellaneous skills. These may include the following abilities:

Using a calculator
Surveying
Interpreting building codes
Construction observation
Client interviews
Photography

Learning something about these fields cannot be a waste of time. Actually, some knowledge of each skill is a great help to any architectural career. A small amount of information in each area should be enough to make a workable situation. A more thorough knowledge in any particular area can be gained through study while on the job.

TYPES OF ARCHITECTURAL PROJECTS

Most architectural firms become involved in projects as a result of chance, not choice. Although this statement needs some qualification, it is generally true. Nearly all architectural commissions result from competitive interviews between an owner and several architects. A major exception is when competition is sponsored by a client and each competing firm is compensated for its time. When a client interviews for an architect, he or she usually contacts several firms and listens to each presentation. The client must decide on the basis of this meeting and on the architect's past work. It is considered unethical for an architect to perform any work for a client before he or she is hired. Thus a client has no preview of how the project will look until the schematic phase of the contract.

From the five or six architects interviewed, only one is selected and given a contract. Competition is usually keen. For this reason most architectural firms do not specialize in a particular type of building. A more common type of specialization is to limit interviews to a particular price range (say $1 million to $7 million). This method does not narrow the field as much as picking one building type would. There are more new buildings in a particular price range than there are unique projects being built. An unfortunate consequence of this lack of specialization is the amount of research time that must be devoted by each firm to each new commission. If an architectural firm does nothing but schools, obviously a new school job isn't going to require much study on the concepts and theories of education, because the data have already accumulated from prior school projects.

The cost of the project and the building type determine the necessity of an owner's retaining an architect. A typical state requirement stipulates that all buildings, except single- and two-family dwellings, public buildings under $2000, or any private building under $30,000 must be done under the direct supervision of a registered architect. This makes it unnecessary for a person who is building a home to commission an architect unless such services are wanted. The minimum recommended fee in the same state for an architect to design a $50,000 house is 13 percent of the construction cost, or $6500, which eliminates most homeowners' desire to hire an architect.

Residences

Most people consider it uneconomical to commission an architect to design houses. Less than 1 percent of houses built in the United States are built by architects. A valid question should now be: If architects don't concentrate on housing, why learn residential construction techniques? It is certainly valid to learn residential construction (wood frame) but it should not be considered the only course of study in architecture. There is little similarity between house construction and commercial building techniques, both in materials and in details. If an architect's main source of employment leans away from house design, obviously a student of drafting could put his or her time to much better advantage by concentrating on larger and more difficult types of building.

Now that a rule has been stated, it is only fair to give the exceptions. Some architects do houses, and a few even specialize in them. Most of these firms have a small staff or a single person who can afford to devote time to such a project since they do not have a large staff to pay. As a smaller firm grows, it will tend to do fewer residences and to concentrate on larger building types. An architect's fee to do a house could be twice as high, by percentage, as to do a commercial project (like a bank) with about the same construction value. For its size, a house design demands more time to coordinate and detail. Beginning architects or technicians could easily find their first residential job outside their place of employment. This can prove to be a workable option. It allows a beginner to express talent as well as to earn extra money. Because the job does not have to be processed through an office, the client also can save consider-

Figure 1-1. The Johnson residence in Minneapolis, Minnesota discussed in Chapter 3.

able money. (A typical office fee is 2½ times an employee's salary when billing a client.) If the project is handled properly, both parties benefit, and the experience will help the technician on larger projects. A large office that would decline to do a typical residence probably has no objection to their members' working on the side. Most will even refer inquiries that come into the office to competent staff members. If the office is small and specializes in residential construction, a moonlighting staff member might have to work under a pen name, since his or her employer would probably take a dim view of employees who go into competition with the firm.

Not only is residential construction good experience, but it is fun to do as well. It is probably the only type of construction that is limited only by an architect's imagination and a client's acceptance. It is designing for a single personality rather than for a group. Building materials can range from poured concrete to goose feathers applied to the ceiling or to sprayed urethane foam walls.

The advantage of learning while working on a project the size of a house is that it usually is small enough not to pose many serious problems. Also, the designer of a house does not have to be registered. The structure generally is simple, and many suppliers can be used as consultants in unfamiliar areas. A mechanical contractor can assist in the heating and cooling system once a general contractor has been selected. The circulation patterns for people occupying the house are typically not complex, and standard residential building materials are fairly easy to detail. In short, a house is a good place to start an individual career in architecture because it poses fewer problems and liabilities than other types of construction. It is still an excellent idea to have office experience before attempting the first project.

The primary point to be followed is that the administration of a house should not deviate from how a standard architectural project is handled. A client hires an architect to perform a service that he or she cannot do. The project should be executed in a professional manner. A house project should include the five phases of an architect's practice:

1. *Schematics*—schematics is the phase dealing with the formation of a design idea. The needs of the client together with the imagination of the architect produce rough floor plans and elevations of the building.
2. Design development—design development is the phase in which the design is arrived at in schematics and refined into a more complete set of drawings.
3. Working drawings—the working drawing phase is the one in which the architect draws the building in enough detail to tell a contractor how to construct the project. Specifications are also prepared to define the quality of workmanship.
4. Bidding—bidding is the point where the architect assists the owner in obtaining cost estimates from contractors.
5. Construction—construction is the stage during building where the architect verifies that the project is constructed according to his or her drawings.

The contractor should submit a monthly bill for approval before it is forwarded to the owner. All changes in the project should be handled by a change order. Standard procedures require extra time to expedite, but this effort more than compensates for the problems it eliminates.

Commercial Construction

Since residential construction holds a secondary position in most architectural firms, the other major building type could be labeled *commercial construction*. Most architects concentrate their practices in this building category. It includes, but is not limited to, schools, office buildings, multiple housing, transportation centers, public buildings, libraries, medical buildings, museums, churches, and recreational facilities. Architects work with all these building types frequently; it is not uncommon for a medium-sized firm (10 to 20 staff members) to have completed at least one of each of the above buildings within a five-year period. The variety of commissions in an architect's office provide the firm with a background of projects that help to generate new jobs. Since it is unethical for an architect to advertise, the best way for a firm to

display its talents is in the projects it completes. An architect or technician could assume that he or she would participate in a project for an average of three to six months and then work on a new job.

The variety of construction materials that occur in major commercial projects are more numerous than those used in typical residences. Some of the diverse forms of building types are:

Aluminum curtain walls	Exposed concrete
Zipper wall	Porcelainized metal
Weathering steel	panel
Brick panel	Stone
Brick with block	Sprayed concrete
back-up	Wood

All these building types are used in commercial construction, and all have unique systems of detailing. Several factors determine what the exterior skin will be. Certainly the architect's design concept is of primary importance, but many secondary factors affect this decision. Is a view important? Is durability and ease of maintenance necessary? What are the insulating qualities of the material, and is the material compatible with surrounding buildings?

The intended function and purpose of construction has a strong effect on its overall design. It is an accepted practice to allow the requirements of the project to direct the design. Louis Sullivan, a nineteenth-century architect, made the important statement, "Form follows function." Obviously, no two designers will evolve the same form for the same function. Even the materials will differ. However, a good design will reflect the building's purpose.

If a count were made of the various materials used in large construction and their combinations, the result would be staggering. Preliminary data for material assembly are decided in the development of the design, but the working drawings finally resolve their assembly. This places the responsibility for knowledge of how individual pieces will fit together to make a building on the architects and drafting technicians doing the construction drawings. With so many different building materials and types, several factors are involved in providing a detail that fits the design concept, that can be constructed easily, and that meets the budget. The most important objective is the ability of the technician to perceive the detail and to assemble it in a drawing. This challenges

Figure 1-2. The Driver's License Training Center discussed in Chapter 3.

the detailer to deal with all the conditions unique to a certain building.

Every commission an architect receives requires planning. Some specific projects are concerned primarily with the location and relationship of building groups rather than with the design of one building. Such a job could include the entire replanning of a downtown area with emphasis on vehicular and pedestrian traffic patterns, buildings located by type (supermarket, drugstore, etc.), and housing shown in the area. A project of this size could be sponsored by a group of property owners or a city governmental body; the master plan might be done by one firm, and individual building projects completed by other architects. To see that the original master-plan concept is carried out, the planning firm usually is retained in an advisory capacity while individual buildings are presented. Some firms specialize in planning and carry a project through only to the design development phase of the master plan. Such firms generally drop the title of architect and assume the role of city planner. Their staff is composed mainly of architects or people with similar backgrounds, since the jobs are closely related. The main differences between the city planner's work and the architect's is in the scope of their projects and the degree of building completeness. A planner usually works on a larger community scale, while an architect generally carries a project to a final set of construction documents.

An architect also may be commissioned to prepare a report, such as a *feasibility study*, which provides an owner with enough professional data to assess the value of a proposed project. Generally this is an economic study to allow a property owner to attain the highest return on land invest-

ment. Most of a feasibility study could be obtained instead in schematics, but this is another step that lets an owner study the advantages of a proposed project without spending too much money. An architect's fee for this report is generally a fixed sum.

An example of this commission would be a client who has a 20-acre parcel of land adjacent to a tract that has many office buildings. The owner wants to know which alternative building type would give the greatest monetary return and most benefit the community. (Unfortunately, the latter point is generally secondary.) The architect's task is to weigh the factors of zoning limits, traffic patterns, soil conditions, topography, and the surrounding population requirements to render a professional opinion. The recommendations could range from providing additional office space to building high- and medium-density housing for the people working in existing offices. Obviously, office policies and staff dictate which projects a firm will select, but generally a feasibility study will be done less often than city planning, residential, and commercial construction. Most clients have a definite idea of their building needs before they seek an architect's services.

THE PEOPLE INVOLVED

The key to a well-run architectural project is *coordination*. Actually, the higher positions in an architect's office generally are given to people with the ability to handle data and assemble information—in short, to people who can coordinate. For our discussion, five general people or groups serve as sources of information to properly design and build a project. If any of these five people do not perform the tasks, the job could face serious problems. The five groups are

1. Client
2. Architectural staff
3. Engineers
4. Consultants
5. Specification writer

These categories are listed in the order in which they are met on a project. One point should be clear from looking at the list: All the groups, except the architectural staff, know more about a particular subject than the architect. It thus becomes the architect's job to filter data and assemble the project.

Client

While architects may argue the point, clients usually do know more about their own needs than the architect does. The key to a successful project lies in satisfying the client with the finished product. This is almost impossible if a client's building needs have not been met. For this reason, successful architects have learned to use their clients as a primary source of information.

An owner hires an architect to get a building that is custom-built to individual requirements. This is why so many typical building types, such as senior high schools, have different floor plans. The individual needs of the client have been combined with the architect's knowledge of building and ingenuity of design. An architect can use the client as a consultant by learning the client's needs, likes, and dislikes. This usually is accomplished during schematics by meeting with the owner and those who will be closely associated with the building when it is completed. On a school project it could include the school board, the faculty by departments, the administration, the students, the kitchen staff, the janitors, and possibly a citizens' committee that is concerned with the new building. All these various groups can contribute to the architectural design concept to produce a custom building. The architect's task is to weigh all the data that accumulate during schematics and produce a workable, cohesive plan which fits the budget.

It is extremely important that the architect document all important items discussed in these meetings for the office job file and the client's opinion. Subcommittees can make as many and as varied demands as they like, but it is the owner's decision whether or not to implement the demands.

Using the client as a prime consultant has advantages. He or she must be satisfied with the finished project. However, there is a point in the project when the client should no longer be considered the main source of data. His or her greatest help to the project will occur during the schematic phase, when the architect is formulating an idea. The client continues to supply materials and ideas in design development, but at a reduced rate. When the project reaches construction documents, the client is no longer a consultant. After this point the client assumes the role of approving detailed drawings.

Architectural Staff

The most important place to coordinate construction lies within the architect's office among the staff members. This coordination must be present at the beginning of the project and continue through the final dealings with the client. Major items are written in memo form and distributed to the people involved. However, the thousands of minor items that occur in a project cannot possibly be recorded in memo form. These items are recorded by various methods depending upon the phase of production. In the schematic phase, the material obtained from the client is organized in the program, while technical data are assembled in various checklists. (These include preliminary building-code studies, engineering data checks, and site survey requirements, to name a few.) Most firms assemble these checklists because the necessary preliminary data for a project are much the same for most projects.

The pattern changes when the project reaches the working drawing stage. Now the many technical items that affect how each team member assembles a particular sheet of drawings must be coordinated. An architectural firm organizes the items in the working drawings by having the person in charge of production (the job captain) correct a check set. A *check set* is a set of prints of all in-progress architectural sheets. It usually is dated and periodically rerun to remain current with the progress of the job.

A check set allows the job captain to make comments on the sheets pertaining to incorrect detailing or the need to coordinate one detail with another. The usual procedure is for each drafting technician to pick up all the check-set remarks on his or her own sheets of drawings. Upon changing each point on the original drawing, the technician crosses out the comment on the check-set print.

Most of the other information accumulated during the period of working drawings is recorded in memo form and distributed to staff members. This could include information derived from meeting with public building-code enforcement officials, decisions made during client conferences, or data received from meeting with product salespeople pertaining to the inclusion of a particular product. Every member of the architectural staff concerned with the project should be kept up to date on matters concerning work in which he or she is involved. A constant knowledge of the project's current status makes it possible to assemble a set of drawings with the team approach.

When a project reaches the bidding stage, the responsibility for coordination changes to the architect. He or she must keep all the bidding contractors informed of the progress of the job. The office must make certain that all contractors who request copies of construction documents receive them and that they all be informed of any changes that occur between the time when the job is sent out for bid and when bids are received. Usually changes in details, bid opening dates, acceptable products, etc., are handled by addenda and subsequently sent by registered mail to every party checking construction documents. This also involves providing subbidders (subcontractors) with an up-to-date list of bidders so that they can submit a price to each bidder. The type of coordination and certainly the amount of time involved makes this phase much less difficult to organize and administer than the other subdivisions of architectural practice. It takes an extremely large project ($5 million to $10 million) to involve more than one staff member on a full-time basis.

The construction phase of an architect's contract demands a new type of organization and communication. Contact between the architect and contractor, dealing with exact methods of installation, are handled by shop drawings. The architect receives these drawings after the contractor checks them and makes corrections on the sheets as they relate to the design. This coordinates all major construction items between the architect and contractor in that these items cannot be started without the architect's approval. This is stated in the contract (the general conditions of the specifications). The usual means of approval is a rubber stamp stating:

This approval is for design only and does not in any way imply responsibility for the correctness of any figures on the drawings.

The contractor usually is required to submit six copies of each shop drawing—one for the architect's file, one for the contractor's file, and four for distribution to the fabricator. If the shop drawings are not acceptable to the architect, he or she has another rubber stamp stating, "Not approved; correct, resubmit."

The second point of necessary coordination during construction is to keep the architect and owner informed of current progress at the job site. The architect's field representative makes periodic visits to the site and files a report of his or her observations each time. The report advises the architect about the progress being made by each trade, any discrepancies between the construction documents, and how the project is being built. It also mentions incidental items such as weather conditions, the number of workers on the job, and who the field representative met with. These data plus frequent conversations with the field representative allow the architect to control the construction phase from the office. Supplemented with occasional visits to the site with the owner, the architect in charge of the job (project manager) can coordinate most problems that might be encountered on a job.

The architect also must coordinate the contractor's request for payment so that the monthly payment relates to the job's actual progress. It is indirectly the architect's responsibility to test materials and see that they meet the minimum allowable standards established in the specifications. The most common item that it is necessary to test is concrete, which, at the time of pouring, must meet proper requirements for slump and air entrainment. After 28 days the concrete must meet certain strength requirements. The owner usually hires an independent testing company to make the analysis, and if it proves below the specified amount, the contractor could be required to replace the work. The architect acts as the owner's representative in administering test results.

The last major point in construction involves the final coordination of finishing small details. This is a meeting in which the architect compiles a punch list of every small item that must be completed before the project is finished. The owner and each prime contractor is supplied with the punch list and asked to respond to the architect with a date when all items will be completed. The system of organization in an architectural firm hinges on several important points that allow jobs to run properly and smoothly. By and large these have been established through knowledge gained on past projects. They can take the form of a series of checks or tests that each stage of a job should meet or an actual review committee that is made up of experienced staff members who pass judgment on the job's progress.

Another factor directly affecting the coordination of a job lies in the personnel assigned to the project. Experience again determines what role a staff member will play on a project. The following section spells out the chain of command found in a typical architect's office. The organization of staff members in an office offers a means of coordination by placing experienced personnel in charge of projects.

Engineers

The work that an engineer accomplishes for an architect has been mentioned briefly. The architect must coordinate all engineering data. The structural, mechanical, and electrical engineers become involved in a project early in schematics and follow the same general pattern as the architect through the five phases of the project. The only difference is that the architect goes through each stage with the owner's approval, while the engineers receive the architect's approval. To ensure proper coordination, the engineering data must lag slightly behind the architectural work.

Preliminary data are assembled in meetings among the architect and the engineers; early schematic drawings form the basis of discussion. Most vital points established during these meetings are recorded in memo form. More than likely the architect exchanges check sets with the engineers each time they meet so that they can all follow the job's progress. This pattern is followed and intensified starting with schematics through design development and ending at the completion of construction documents. Obviously, if all engineering

drawings are not coordinated precisely with the architectural drawings, the building will not work. The usual structural tolerances for beams are within $1/16''$. Plumbing and mechanical duct work must fit in the walls indicated on architectural drawings, while all electrical systems must fit the designed plan.

During bidding and construction engineers follow the same basic steps as the architectural staff did. It is a standard procedure to have engineering field representatives observe their specific areas while the project is under construction. Copies of the field data reports are sent to the architect for his or her information and ultimate coordination of the job.

Consultants

So many technical trades are involved in designing a specific building that an architect is compelled to retain a consultant to provide the client with a proper design when the expert knowledge is not within his or her own experience. Some fields in which an architect would occasionally use a consultant are

Acoustics	Professional model of
Cost analysis	the project
Hospital design	Kitchen design
Roofing	Hardware layout
Interior design	Aluminum curtain-wall
Theater design	design
Professional rendering	Landscaping
(artist's painting of	Educational techniques
the proposed build-	Science equipment lay-
ing)	out

The size, type, and complexity of the commission determine whether or not an architect will need a consultant. If consultant services are needed, they usually are provided early in the design stages so that the architect's scheme reflects the consultant's assistance. The physical means of obtaining consultants' data may range from a written report in the case of a cost analysis to the consultant's actually preparing sheets of drawings that are bound into the construction documents, as could happen with the layout of kitchen equipment. The architect meets with each consultant and provides the data needed to begin the study. The architect also spells out the exact form and the detail in which the finished consulting report should be presented. Typically a consultant is retained by an architect and is paid out of the fee the owner pays the architect.

Specification Writer

Two separate items constitute the set of construction documents that the architect issues at the time of bidding. Basically, the working drawings indicate the quantity of materials to be used, and the specifications detail the quality. These two factors depend upon each other to the point that both are necessary for construction. Every material indicated on the working drawing set is described in full detail by the specification writer, ranging from concrete-reinforcing steel to roofing nails. The detailed quality requirements guarantees the owner that the finished product will be what the architect intended and allows the contractors to bid competitively against each other with identical quality standards.

A specification writer is generally a member of the architectural staff and, depending upon the size of the office, could write specifications full time. Not only must every material used in the project be described exactly in the specifications, but the method of installation and the need to submit shop drawings must be fully explained.

Specification writing, unlike other work, starts late in the project, usually not until the working drawings are 50 to 75 percent complete. The data needed to write the specifications are again assembled mainly by using check sets of the project. The specification writer is able to coordinate most of the material by looking at the intent of the drawings and applying the proper written description. Most offices adopt an office standard on major specification items, and so the job of the writer on many points is to check with the architect in charge of the job to see whether the project deviates from the norm. If it does not, a prewritten section of the specification is included. This system, and meeting with the job captain frequently to discuss specific points, and referring to the materials, methods, and equipment outline (prepared by the job captain) allows the specifications to echo the working drawing exactly.

TWO

FUNDAMENTALS OF DRAFTING

An architectural firm has one basic medium with which it puts across a building concept—drafting. The two general patterns of drafting are presentation and production. The *presentation* of an architect's ideas gives building information to a client. During *production*, the more technical of the two phases, an architect directs a contractor through working drawings. This chapter describes the method and tools to be used for the production phase of the contract. The presentation phase is covered in Chapter 10.

DRAFTING EQUIPMENT

Individual offices adopt varying policies on whether the employer or employee is to provide drafting equipment. Even though many employers supply equipment for office use, a draftsman would be wise to own some equipment so that he or she can set up shop at home.

Two points are important when buying drafting equipment: Don't buy too much, and don't buy the least expensive material available. Also, specialty and novelty drafting equipment is used so seldom that it is not really useful to own such materials. First buy the minimum amount of quality equipment you need. Then add to the collection as the need arises. Good-quality drafting equipment probably will outlast you, so consider the money well spent.

Table 2-1 lists the minimum amount of quality equipment you need to get started. It also indicates brand or type of product and suggests the quantity needed. These brand names are readily available at most drafting-supply stores. Figure 2-1 shows some of this equipment.

Although Table 2-1 lists a sufficient amount of material with which to start, some of the following items could be added as the need arises. Figure 2-2 illustrates some of these items.

Beam compass
18″, 30°–60° triangle
Castell TG technical
    drawing ink pens

TABLE 2-1 DRAFTING SUPPLIES

ITEM	BRAND NAME OR TYPE	QUANTITY
Lead holders (pencils)	Dietzgen #3162	2
Lead	A. W. Faber Castell; types HB, 2H	1 tube each
Lead pointer	Eagle Turquoise 17	1
Eraser	Magic Rub	1
Erasing shield	Typically $2^3/8″ \times 3^3/4″$ (Many technicians prefer a very thin metal shield with at least one long, skinny slit and a circle.)	1
12″ architects' scale	Dietzgen #1656-BG	1
12″ engineers' scale	Dietzgen #1667-BG	1
Drafting tape	3M, $^3/4″$	1 roll
Drafting brush	Dietzgen	1
Compass	6″ bow compass with an interchangeable point that can double as a divider*	1
Adjustable triangle	10″ Tacro #4456 (Many technicians prefer an adjustable triangle over separate 45° and 30°–60° triangles because only one triangle is needed and the adjustment knob doubles as a handle for moving the instrument on the drawing board.)	1
Felt-tipped pen	Flair, several colors	2–3
Toilet plan template	American Standard #9383-A	1
Toilet elevation template	American Standard 387-3	1
Circle template	8″ × 5″ with holes graded from $1^1/2″$ to $^1/16″$	1

* Many drafting students are required by the school or feel a need to purchase a $25 drafting set containing four or five compasses. Most experienced technicians consider this expenditure unnecessary, since an architect rarely uses anything other than a 6″ bow compass.

French curve
Rechargeable electric
    eraser
Tree and car rubber
    stamp set with ink pad

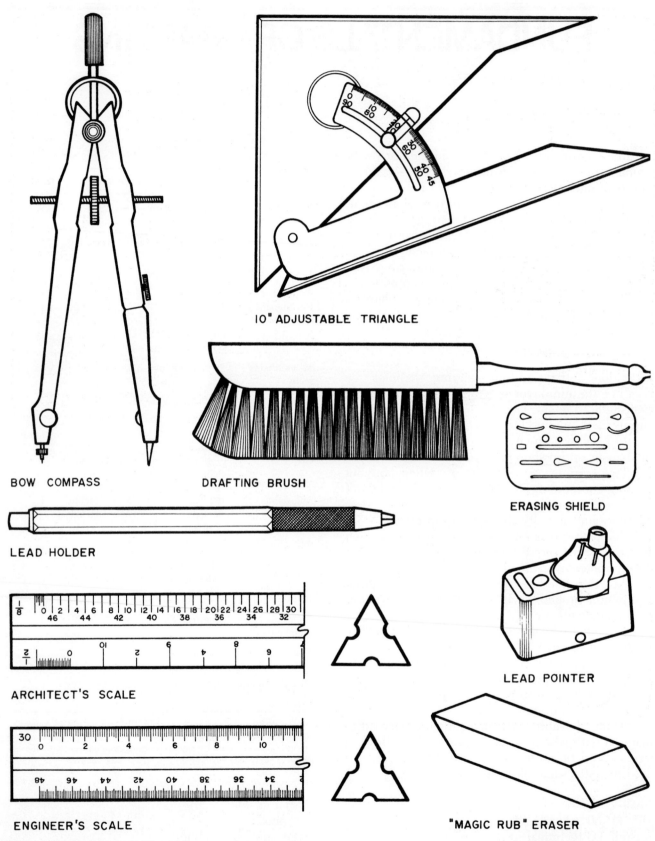

BOW COMPASS

10" ADJUSTABLE TRIANGLE

DRAFTING BRUSH

ERASING SHIELD

LEAD HOLDER

ARCHITECT'S SCALE

LEAD POINTER

ENGINEER'S SCALE

"MAGIC RUB" ERASER

Figure 2-1.   Some basic drafting tools.

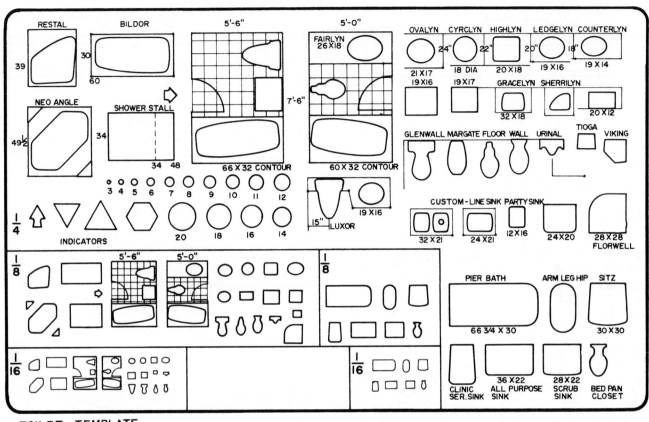

TOILET TEMPLATE

CIRCLE TEMPLATE

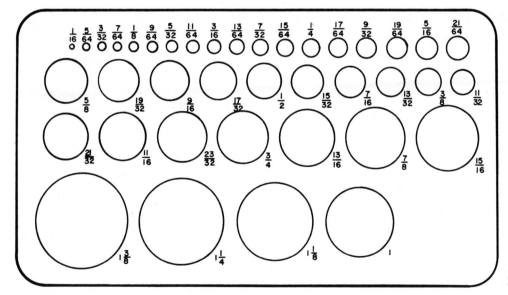

Figure 2-1 (continued).

Adjustable curve
Perspective charts
Press-on letters
Mat knife
Isometric circle
   template

A drafting board is a wise expenditure, and it is possible to economize on it. The least expensive but acceptable solution is to buy a 3′ × 4′ sheet of ¾″ A-C plywood; the A-C designation indicates the quality of each face of the plywood. Also purchase a 3′ × 4′ drawing-board surface, either a drafting

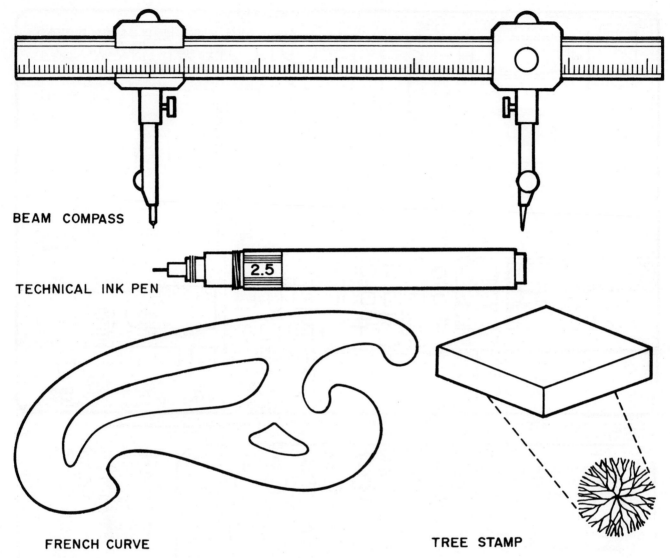

BEAM COMPASS

TECHNICAL INK PEN

2.5

FRENCH CURVE

TREE STAMP

Figure 2-2. Drafting equipment.

quality linoleum material or a laminated vinyl surface such as Borco. The linoleum is harder and considered by many to give a better line quality. Each is available at a drafting equipment supply store. The surface material can be attached to the plywood either by contact cement or with a double-adhesive tape for carpet installation.

The third item necessary to assemble a self-made drafting board is a good 48″ parallel bar, Mayline Mobile or equal. A T-square is not a substitute for a parallel bar. (See Figure 2-3.)

The total cost of these three items is approximately $50, about one-third the cost of a commercial drawing board. The plywood and applied surface can be put on top of another desk with bricks stacked under the far end of the board to prop it at an angle.

In addition to these three items, another good, inexpensive addition is a 3′ × 7′ hollow-core door, purchased at a lumber yard. When the door is lain level on four legs, it provides a place to fasten securely the drawing board at a slant. Since the board is only 3′ × 4′, the door also provides a 3′ × 3′ flat layout space.

A drafting technician should be familiar with certain pieces of office equipment and their operation. Office equipment might include the items listed below. A print machine is a common item; other items on the list are more specialized, and their use will vary from office to office.

• **Print machine** Most offices have a print machine for use when copies are needed. Print machines can vary in size but usually follow the same basic

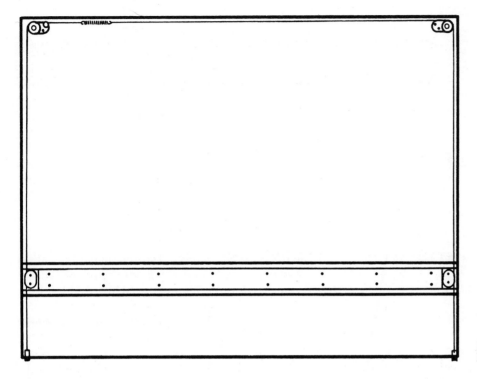

Figure 2-3. Drafting board and parallel bar.

idea. A special light-sensitive paper is placed on the backside of the drawing and put in the print machine. The drawing and print pass through a light source; then the original drawing comes out of the machine, and the print passes through concentrated ammonia vapors that develop the print. (See Figure 2-4.) The darkness of the print is gauged by how fast the print and the original pass the light source—the faster the speed, the darker the print.

This is a fast, economical method of getting a reproduction of an original, either in blue line or black line (depending on the paper) with a light-colored background. The prints are opaque, and so additional prints cannot be made in the same way. If reproduction of a print becomes necessary, a sepia print paper is used as an original from which to run additional prints.

Prints of plans are often incorrectly referred to as blueprints. *Blueprints* are photographic reproductions on a blue background. This process is used very seldom.

• *Perspective chart* A perspective chart is a printed graphlike chart used as an underlay to draw a building in perspective.

• *Electronic slide rule calculator* An electronic slide rule calculator is used to figure areas, costs, and quantities of materials. The relatively low price and variety of uses make this a most valuable tool (Figure 2-5).

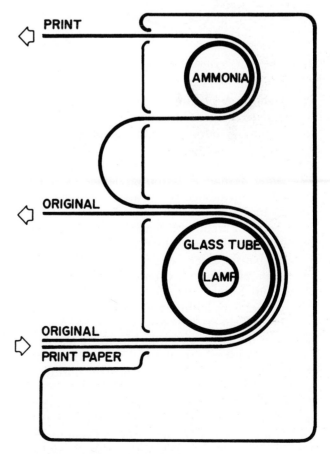

Figure 2-4. An office print machine.

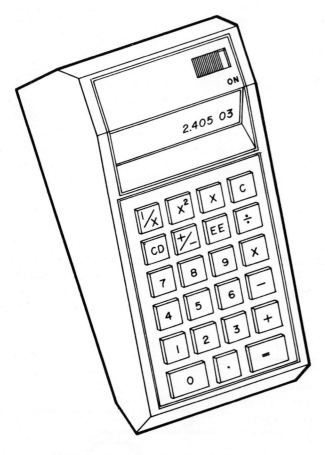

Figure 2-5. An electronic slide rule calculator.

• **Planimeter** A planimeter is an instrument used to calculate the area of an irregular shape, such as the amount of soil in a site topography.

• **Air brush** An air brush is a very small spray gun used to apply color on a presentation perspective.

• **Lettering device** A lettering device is a three-point ink-pen device that uses a template to mechanically letter a drawing (used more by an engineer than an architect). Some companies have an extremely small typewriter that attaches to a special parallel bar for mechanical printing.

• **Press-on lettering** Press-on lettering is a sheet of plastic with letters on the back. By rubbing the front of the sheet with a blunt tool, the letter transfers to the drawing sheet. This procedure is used for presentation drawings and title blocks. A less formal (and inexpensive) use of press-on letters is to place the sheet under the paper and trace the outline with a felt-tipped pen or soft lead.

• **Computer** The complexities of designing and producing a building have opened the way to several types of computer operations. Computers are being used to program building spaces; to select

the best building materials; to schedule the various jobs in an office by providing critical dates for completion of stages; to design portions of structural, mechanical, and electrical systems; to compute architects' cost estimates; to estimate construction time; and even to draw a building instantly in perspective on a television screen for the designer.

• **"Paper"** Four basic materials are used for drawing, only two of which are actually paper. The usual sheet size is 30″ × 42″ for fairly large projects and 24″ × 36″ for smaller jobs. Some architectural firms use sheets up to 30″ × 60″, but unless the job warrants this size (such as a 60-story high-rise office building), it proves difficult to handle.

1. *Utility-grade paper* Interchangeably called *cedar paper*, *bum wad*, or *canary paper* (all the same material). This material is a light-yellow transparent paper, available in rolls 12″, 18″, 24″, or 36″ wide. It is used to sketch designs and details from schematics through working drawings. It is inexpensive. Since it also is transparent, parts of details may be traced; felt-tipped pens do not bleed through it. It can be run through a print machine, and, although the paper is used seldom for client presentation, it is easily Photostatted, a process that improves its appearance.

2. *Drafting paper* The least expensive of the three materials used for final working drawings. It has the qualities of providing a fairly good drafting surface and yielding a quality print, but it does not erase as well as other materials, nor does it offer the permanence so necessary for working drawings.

3. *Linen or pencil cloth* Probably the most widely used drawing material in architectural practice. It has an excellent surface for drawing, it prints well, it erases without a trace, and it takes the heavy handling a sheet receives during the working drawing stage. The material is actually cloth with a plastic or resin surface. Most firms have the sheets cut to size and printed with a border containing the firm's name in the title block. Standard drafting lead and ink can be used with linen.

4. *Plastic film* The newest drawing material in architectural practice. It is a thin sheet with an abrasive surface. It is more durable than linen. Draftsmen have strong opinions about whether it has a better or worse drawing surface than linen. Special lead and erasers are used to get best results.

5. *Paper pad* An 8½″ × 11″ pad gridded in ⅛″ squares. This paper is available in the same material as print paper so that it may be run through a print machine. Rough sketches of details are drawn to scale with this graph paper.

SYMBOLS AND ABBREVIATIONS

A great deal of data must be put on a working drawing sheet. An architect looks for ways to reduce the size and amount of data on drawings. Certain standard abbreviations approved by each office help in making drawings easier to read. Table 2-2 shows a list of such abbreviations. In addition, symbols are used to show materials when cut in section on a working drawing. This is referred to as *hatching* the material, which we will discuss in detail. Table 2-3 shows some typical symbols for materials.

The key to using short cuts is to follow the office-approved standard. If the office does not abbreviate the words "ceramic tile" to C.T., you are required to spell them out. This is not merely a whim of the office manager. It is technically a legal point. The working drawings and specifications are a part of the legal contract signed between an owner and a contractor. An architect puts an outline of approved abbreviations and a materials legend in the specifications. Thus, all the material hatching and abbreviated terms are part of the contract documents available to the contractor for reference.

Not all abbreviations in an office standard are used on each project. This would only add to the problems encountered by a contractor in reading drawings. The job captain selects the appropriate abbreviations for the job, keeping them to a reasonable number. If a term appears infrequently on the

TABLE 2-2 STANDARD ABBREVIATIONS

Note: Single-word abbreviations may change when combined with other abbreviations, but only as here listed. An example is the change from FL. (floor) to F.D.S. (floor divider strip).

A	A.	air		C.B.	concrete block	**E**	EA.	each
	ABR.	abrasive		C.B.C.	concrete block courses		ED.	edging
	A.B.	anchor bolts		CEM.	cement		E.F.	each face
	ACO.	acoustic		CER.	ceramic		EL.	elevation
	ACO. T.	acoustic tile		C.I.	cast iron		ELEC.	electric (or electrical)
	ADJ.	adjustable		C.J.	construction joint		ELEV.	elevator
	A.D.	area drain		℄	centerline		ENCL.	enclosure (or enclose)
	ALT.	alternate		CL.	closet		E.P.	electrical panel
	ALUM.	aluminum		CLG.	ceiling		EQ.	equal
	APPROX.	approximately		COL.	column		EQUIP.	equipment
	A.P.	access panel		CONC.	concrete		E.W.	each way
	ARCH.	architectural		CONN.	connection		E.W.C.	electric water cooler
	ASB.	asbestos		CONST.	construction		EXC.	excavated
	ASPH.	asphalt		CONT.	continuous		EX. GR.	existing grade
	A.T.	asphalt tile		CONTR.	contractor		EXH.	exhaust
	@	at		CONV.	convector		EXIST.	existing
	∠	angle		CSK.	countersink		EXP. JT.	expansion joint
				C.T.	ceramic tile		EXT.	exterior
				CU. FT.	cubic feet			
B	B.C.	brick courses		C.W.	cold water	**F**	F.A.	fresh air
	BD.	board		[or ⌐	channel		F.A.S.	fire alarm station
	B.F.E.	bottom footing elevation					F.D.	floor drain
	B.L.	brick ledge					FDN.	foundation
	BM.	beam	**D**	DEG. (or °)	degree		F.D.S.	floor divider strip
	B.M.	bench mark		DET.	detail		F.E.	fire extinguisher
	BLDG.	building		D.F.	drinking fountain		F.E.C.	fire extinguisher cabinet
	BLK.	block		DIA.	diameter		F.H.	fire hose
	BOT.	bottom		DIM.	dimension		F.H.R.	fire hose and rack
	BR.	brick		DMPR.	damper		F.H.C.	fire hose cabinet
	BSMT.	basement		DN.	down		FIN.	finish (or finished)
	BTWN.	between		DO.	ditto		FL.	floor
	B.W.V.	back water valve		DP.	dampproofing		FLDG.	folding
				DR.	drain		F.P.	fireproof
				D.S.	downspout		F.S.	full size
C	C.	clock		DWG.	drawing			
	CAB.	cabinet						

TABLE 2-2 *Continued*

	FSP.	fire standpipe	M.O.	masonry opening	SIM.	similar
	FT. (or ′)	foot	MLDG.	molding	S.J.	steel joist
	FTG.	footing	MR.	marble	SLR.	sealer
			MR. T.	marble threshold	S.M.	section modular
G	G.	gas	M.S.	mop sink	SPECS.	specifications
	GA.	gauge	M.T.	metal threshold	SQ. (or □)	square
	G.B.	grab bar	MTG.	mounting	S.R.	soap retainer
	GEN.	general	MULL.	mullion	S.S.	service sink
	G.I.	galvanized iron			S/S	stainless steel
	GL.	glass	**N** NO.	number	STA.	stainless
	G.S.T.	glazed structural tile	NOM.	nominal	STIFF.	stiffeners
	GR.	grade	N.I.C.	not in contract	STD.	standard
	GRL.	grill	N.T.S.	not to scale	STL.	steel
					STRUCT.	structural
H	H.B.	hose bibb			SUSP.	suspended
	H.C.	hose cabinet	**O** O.	oxygen	SYM.	symmetrical
	HDWD.	hardwood	OB. GL.	obscure glass	STG.	storage
	HDWE.	hardware	O.C.	on center		
	HGT.	height	O.D.	outside diameter		
	H.M.	hollow metal	OPN'G	opening	**T** T.	tread (or treads)
	HOR.	horizontal	ORN.	ornamental	T & B	top and bottom
	HTR.	heater	OZ.	ounce	T & G	tongue and groove
					T.B.	towel bar
I	I.D.	inside diameter	**P** P.A.	public address	T.C.S.	top of concrete slab
	IN. (or ″)	inch (or inches)	P.H.	paper holder	TEL.	telephone
	INSUL.	insulation	PL.	plate	TER.	terrazzo
	INT.	interior	PLAS.	plaster	T.H.	test hole
	INV.	invert	PLBG.	plumbing	THRU.	through
			PLSTC.	plastic	TL.	tile
J	JAN.	janitor	PLY'D	plywood	TRAN.	transom
	JT.	joint	POL.	polished	TYP.	typical
			PORC. ENAM.	porcelain enamel		
K	K.C.	keone's cement	PR.	pair	**U** U.H.	unit heater
	KIT.	kitchen	P.S.I.	pounds per square inch	UR.	urinal
	KIP (or K)	thousand pounds	P.S.F.	pounds per square foot	U.V.	unit ventilator
			PT.	paint		
			PTN.	partition		
L	L.	line	%	percent	**V** V.O.P.	vitrified clay tile pipe
	LAB.	laboratory			VERT.	vertical
	LAD.	ladder	**Q** Q.T.	quarry tile	VEST.	vestibule
	LAM.	laminated			VOL.	volume
	LAV.	lavatory	**R** R.	risers (stair)	VT.	vent
	LB.	pound	R.A.	return air	V.A.	vinyl asbestos
	LIN.	linear	RADN.	radiation	V.A.T.	vinyl asbestos tile
	LINO.	linoleum	R.D.	roof drain		
	L.F.	lawn faucet	REF.	refrigerator	**W** W.	waste
	LTG.	lighting	REG.	register	W.C.	water closet
	LWCB.	lightweight concrete block	REINF.	reinforcing	WD.	wood
			REQD.	required	WDW.	window
			RF.	roof	W.F. (or WF.)	wide flange beam
M	MACH. RM.	machine room	RM.	room	W. GL.	wire glass
	MAT'L	material	RND.	round	W.H.	water heater
	MAX.	maximum	RUB.	rubber	W.I.	wrought iron
	MECH.	mechanical	R.W.L.	rain water leader	W. MES.	wire mesh
	MED. CAB.	medicine cabinet	RADR.	radiator	W.P.	waterproof
	MET.	metal			WSCT.	wainscot
	MEZ.	mezzanine			WT.	weight
	MFGR.	manufacturer	**S** S.	miscellaneous sink	W/	with
	M.H.	manhole	S.D.	soap dispenser	W/O	without
	MIN.	minimum	SECT.	section		
	MIR.	mirror	S.F.T.	structural facing tile		
	MIR. & S.	mirror and shelf	SH.	shower	**X** X	by (as 6′ × 8′)
	MISC.	miscellaneous	SHT.	sheet	X	with (hardware)

TABLE 2-3   MATERIALS LEGEND

This materials legend has been established as a standard to indicate symbols. This hatching is used only if the building material is to be seen in section.

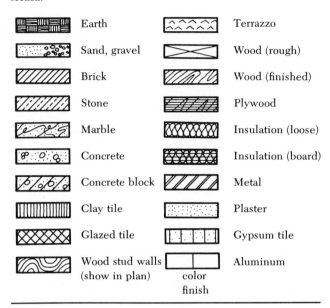

	Earth		Terrazzo
	Sand, gravel		Wood (rough)
	Brick		Wood (finished)
	Stone		Plywood
	Marble		Insulation (loose)
	Concrete		Insulation (board)
	Concrete block		Metal
	Clay tile		Plaster
	Glazed tile		Gypsum tile
	Wood stud walls (show in plan)		Aluminum, color finish

drawings, it is advisable not to abbreviate. Abbreviations may be combined, such as FL. (floor) and DR. (drain) to FL. DR. (floor drain).

Material Hatching

When a floor plan is drawn or a wall section is detailed, a section is shown cut through the wall material. The floor plan is drawn as though a large knife were cut through the building approximately 3′ above the floor and parallel to it. This means that the open floor area is drawn as though you were standing in the room and looking down, showing the first several steps on a stair, the door openings, window locations, floor patterns, to name a few. Architects can label materials quite easily until a section plane cuts through a wall. At the scale at which most floor plans are drawn, it would not be practical to spell out all the materials that make up the wall. A standard solution is to indicate wall materials by hatching them in accordance with an office standard. This allows a draftsman to indicate different wall materials without labeling each one.

One rule to remember when graphically delineating wall materials is *hatch only the material through which a section is cut*. All other materials beyond the section that are necessary to the detail are shown in elevation (the way a building would look in a photograph).

REFERENCE MATERIALS

The reference data used by students in architectural drafting are very similar to the material used by architectural firms. A building contains many complex materials. An architect's detailing shows what materials will be included in a project; and detailing depends strongly on how an architect uses and understands reference data.

The sources of material relating to construction are so numerous that a book could be filled with the names and addresses of the references. Some more valuable data for students follow:

• ***Architectural Graphic Standards*** (6th ed., John Wiley) If an architect has a Bible, this book comes closer than any other. It is a source for practically every method of construction ranging from adobes to acrylic plastic zipper-curtain walls. It gives architects pertinent dimensions, ranging from the height of a riding horse to the size of a teakettle. This book could very easily be considered the best source available for studying details and obtaining data. Not only are the data valuable, but they are graphically presented as well as in any source. Chapters are assembled to correspond with numerical headings in specifications.

• ***Time Savers Standards*** (McGraw-Hill) This book has a similar format to *Graphic Standards*; it has much valuable information, and most offices have a copy to supplement *Graphic Standards*.

• ***Sweet's File*** (F. W. Dodge) This is available free to qualifying architectural firms. The bound volumes in *Sweet's File* are, in effect, one big advertisement. The volumes, when stacked, are 3′ to 4′ high and contain manufacturer's data on particular products. Nearly every building supplier is represented with a file of technical data. The material differs from *Graphic Standards* and *Time Savers Standards* in that it pertains to specific products. Each volume of *Sweet's File* is indexed in three ways: by product, by manufacturer, and by trade name. Numbering corresponds with the numerical system in specifications. The entire set is free to architectural firms that qualify, depending on the type and size of the business, and is renewed yearly. Schools generally obtain a year-old volume of *Sweet's File* from an architectural firm in their area.

• ***Manufacturers' technical data*** Along with material found in Sweet's, most suppliers provide more complete brochures of their products for architects' reference. These data are assembled by specification writers and usually fill the bookshelves of a fairly good-sized room. In addition to this material, samples of actual products are stored for draftsmen to inspect during working drawings.

• *Past projects* One of the best sources of understanding the assembly of a building is to carefully study the plans of a previously constructed building project. This process has definite advantages. It allows an architectural draftsman to use similar details with some variation, while students have the chance to observe all the details necessary to build a project. Several pitfalls, however, are to be avoided. A great deal of knowledge and experience are needed to determine whether a detail from another project is used in proper context on a current job. Using solutions from jobs that have not been completed and tested by use may be risky in that there is no guarantee that the original solution will be the most successful or the most economical. On the other hand, if a detail is known to work, it both is economical for an architect to use because it eliminates research time, and it ensures the client of a properly built building. The success of solutions on earlier projects should be verified before they are reused in order to avoid perpetuating errors. The common rule in an office is to refrain from using earlier work as a reference unless directed to do so by the job captain. The usual practice is to rely on former project details that are known to work.

• *Other personnel* A definite hierarchy of responsibility exists in an office. The degree of each employee's responsibility depends in large part on his or her experience. A job captain has earned the position because, among other qualities, he or she knows more about putting a building together than the people he or she supervises. The job captain assists each draftsman with unfamiliar details or finds the proper source of reference.

Most offices have personnel with a great variety of experience in architecture. In fact, it would be unusual to find a problem in detailing that some other member of the firm has not experienced. Thus, these people can advise you. The proper procedure is for you to seek this information through the job captain. This system of relating first-hand knowledge frequently goes beyond a particular office to jobs handled by other architects.

• *Trade associations* Many trade associations, such as The National Bureau for Lathing and Plastering

and The California Redwood Association, have data prepared on their particular products. Trade associations usually present extremely well-detailed materials, most of which are either free or low in price. These publications contain very technical data, mostly pertaining to the engineering qualities of products.

• *Underwriters' Laboratories, Inc. (UL)* Underwriters' Laboratories, Inc., is a nonprofit organization that, among other things, tests and certifies various building materials. The most common service performed for architects by Underwriters' Laboratories, Inc., is to rate the fire value (in hourly classifications) of building components vital to the safety of occupants or the structural integrity of buildings. The UL label is required on doors and door frames for safety exiting and on structural steel columns, among others. Underwriters' Laboratories, Inc., offers several publications that list the hourly classifications of various design systems and the performance of each manufacturer's product. Underwriters' Laboratories, Inc., is intended strictly as a technical source.

• *American Society for Testing and Materials (ASTM)* The American Society for Testing and Materials is a nonprofit organization that tests and certifies materials, not only for fire-retardant characteristics but also for the strength and quality of performance on which data are compiled.

• *Trade publications* Several professional magazines are excellent sources of the latest architectural designs and details. The best United States publications are *Architectural Record*, *Progressive Architecture*, and *The A.I.A. Journal*. Of this group, *Progressive Architecture* and *Architectural Record* are probably the best sources for students. They are well put together, have many articles of interest to new members of the profession, and offer architecture students a reduced subscription rate. Magazines are probably the best way to keep informed of current trends in architecture. The *Architectural Index* is a yearly publication which alphabetically lists articles under building type, location, and architect.

• *The American Institute of Architects (AIA)* The AIA is a professional organization for architects which provides many publications necessary to the practice of architecture. These publications deal with the wide range of data needed to run an architectural office properly and efficiently. The best publication explaining office procedures is an AIA loose-leaf notebook entitled the *Handbook of Professional Practice*. This document covers a great variety of circumstances likely to arise in architectural firms, varying from contractual agreements between architects and their consultants to partnership-agreement suggestions for establishing a new firm. The AIA has information available on practically every area of architecture.

• *Sales representatives* Most major building-supply manufacturers have sales representatives in larger cities to promote and explain products to architects. Suppliers invest considerable time and money in training representatives in the technical capabilities of their products. It is definitely to an architect's advantage to use these consultants when designing and detailing projects.

Since sales representatives primarily are interested in selling particular products, their information should be placed in proper perspective with other products in the field. However, good sales representatives know competing products as well as their own and often give a fair opinion of the entire field. This is the person whom architects trust and use frequently. As a rule, specification writers see all sales representatives when they come into an office, but if a job captain has a specific question, he or she personally contacts a representative.

• *Professional associations* Drafting technicians or architects in an office may join a professional organization, such as the local chapter of the American Institute of Architects. This allows them to attend architectural seminars, receive AIA publications, sit in on committees, and, most importantly, meet staff members from other offices, allowing an interchange of ideas.

• *Building codes* Most state and local governments adopt laws, referred to as *codes*, to govern the safety requirements of all buildings built in their jurisdiction. The intent of a building code is to establish the minimum exiting, safety, and fire-resistant qualities rather than to control design.

Codes that apply in the location of a building site must be followed. If they are not followed, the building can be closed until the proper corrective measures have been taken. This closing is referred to as *red-tagging* a building.

DRAFTING PROCEDURES

Drafting is a mechanical process that requires very little technical explanation. It does, however, require a great deal of fundamental knowledge of construction. Basic drafting equipment includes a lead holder, a straightedge, and a scale. The best way to learn drafting technique is to develop a draft-

ing style that is natural, neat, and accurate. Do not attempt to follow an elaborate set of rules which tell you how to move a pencil across a drawing sheet. If it feels correct for right-handed draftsmen to move their pencils from left to right along a parallel bar for horizontal lines and from top to bottom along a triangle for vertical lines, this is the natural style they should follow.

Neatness

Neatness is essential in good drafting. One sheet of working drawings can require 40 or more hours of drafting time, which means that much graphite has been deposited on the sheet, both in the form of lines and loose dust. When a parallel bar or triangle is moved across the surface, the sheet can easily become dirty. One remedy is to brush off the surface of the sheet frequently, eliminating any graphite buildup. A commercial product made of finely ground eraser crumbs can be sprinkled on the drawing, and the sheet is cleaned simply by moving drawing equipment over the surface. The main objection to the use of this material is that the small particles of eraser may dull a sharp, crisp line. Some technicians pick up the habit of blowing off the sheet after each line is drawn. These techniques, plus extreme care, result in neatness.

Erasing errors or making changes in a drawing do not require a special technique, but care is again essential. An eraser shield is used to avoid erasing lines around the area to be changed. A beginning technician may have difficulty developing a habit of using this tool. It is, however, an excellent way to increase neatness and reduce drafting time.

Drawing to Scale

Portions of a building are drawn to scale because it would not be practical to provide a contractor with full-size drawings. The typical scales used in architecture are, from small to large: $1/16'' = 1'-0''$, $1/8'' = 1'-0''$, $1/4'' = 1'-0''$, $1/2'' = 1'-0''$, $3/4'' = 1'-0''$, $1^{1/2}'' = 1'-0''$, $3'' = 1'-0''$.

To scale off the dimension $10'-8''$ on an architect's scale, mark one point at $10'$ on the $1/4''$ scale and put the other mark at the $8''$ increment on the other side of zero. (See Figure 2-6.)

An engineer's scale differs from an architect's scale in that it is scaled into $1'' = X$ number of feet,

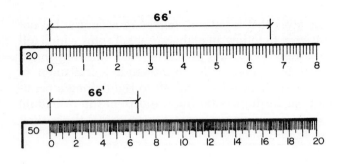

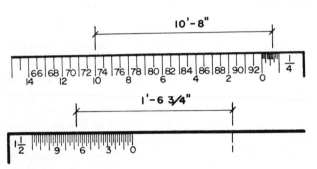

Figure 2-6.   The top two scales are engineer's scales and the bottom two are architect's scales.

and it is divided into tenths of a foot rather than inches.

Dimensions

Every critical distance in a set of working drawings must be dimensioned for a contractor's information. An architect's specification commonly states that the contractor is not to scale the drawing to determine any dimension or wall location. This rule gives the architect control over dimensions in all construction phases rather than opening up the possibility of error in the scaling of a drawing.

Dimensions for walls are given to the outside face of the block but to the center of each stud wall. Typically, wood and metal stud walls are dimensioned to their center, while all other walls are dimensioned face to face.

Dimension lines are referred to as *strings*. In some cases three-dimension strings are needed to give sufficient measurements. The outer string gives the overall building length, the center string indicates the major corners, and the inward string shows the contractor where to locate doors and windows.

Interior partitions and walls are not dimensioned with exterior strings but are instead handled with strings inside the building. Dimensions should be shown only on the drawings the con-

tractor will use to construct a particular work. Since the structural drawings indicate all structural dimensions, it is not necessary to repeat these on an architectural drawing. The contractor will refer to larger-scale drawings for construction of window openings, parapets, and other highly detailed areas of a building. Thus, pertinent dimensions are shown on a large-scale drawing rather than attempting to dimension small details.

Dimensions on architectural drawings up to but not including 1' should be in inches and fractions. If the dimension is 1' and over, it should be given in feet and inches. For example, 1'-6", not 18"; 1'-0", not 12"; 9¾", not 0'-9¾". Major exceptions to this rule would be dimensions for furniture and for beam sizes, which usually are given in inches.

It is acceptable to change the dimension of a line without erasing the entire detail and redrawing it to scale if it does not appreciably affect the proportions of the detail. If the dimension is not drawn to scale, the following note should be given:

22'-6" (N.T.S.)

If the dimension of an opening is given by note rather than by dimension string, the width should be given first. An example would be an air louver in a wall: 6'-8" × 4'-0". This indicates that the louver is 6'-8" wide.

Figure 2-7 shows masonry dimensioning. Note the following characteristics:

1. The dimension strings are run to the *outside face of the walls*.
2. The inside string locates masonry openings (a 2'-8" door and a 4'-0" window).
3. The center string shows corners.
4. The outside string gives the overall building length. In this case the whole building isn't shown, and so the 50'-0" dimension has a double arrowhead.
5. Interior walls are dimensioned on the inside of the building.
6. The entire building is dimensioned using modular planning. Standard block size is 8" × 8" × 16", and so if every dimension is divisible by 8", it eliminates cutting each block to fit.

Figure 2-8 shows wood-frame dimensioning. Note the following characteristics:

1. Brick-veneer (at left) and exterior-frame walls (at right) are dimensioned to the outside face of

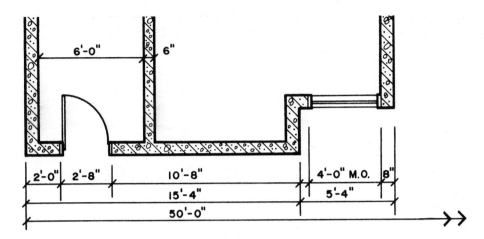

Figure 2-7. Masonry dimensioning.

the wood stud, not to the outside face of the wall.

2. Interior partitions are dimensioned from the center of the partition wall to the outside face of the stud on an exterior wall, or center of interior wall to center of interior wall.

3. Doors and windows are dimensioned to the center of the opening with the size of the door or window either called out on the plan or in a schedule.

Plans, Elevations, and Sections

An architect uses three types of two-dimensional drawings to show a contractor how to build—plans, elevations, and sections. A *plan* is the view looking down on the site or the building. A floor plan shows the building's length and width. An *elevation* of a building is a view indicating the length

and height of the walls. A *section* is a view of a cut through the building walls showing the materials that are used in construction. Sections show height and width.

References and Cross-References

Many references and cross-references are used in drafting. The references shown here are typical of what you are likely to come across in a drafting job.

For the most part you will be executing *detail drawings* or *working drawings*, which are drawings of a building or part done to scale. Each detail must be numbered. The typical symbol is a circle ½″ in diameter, with the number of the detail in the top half of the circle and the number of the sheet in the bottom half. Here is a typical detail drawing label.

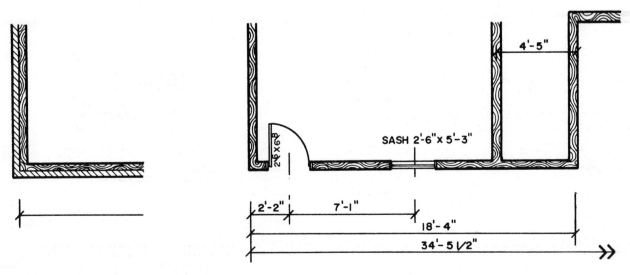

Figure 2-8. Wood frame dimensioning.

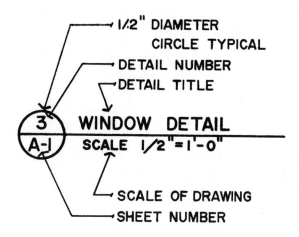

The numbering on an elevation drawing would look like this:

The numbering on a section drawing would look like this:

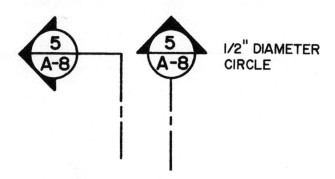

For the number on a floor elevation, a circle ¼″ in diameter is used, as shown here:

1/4″ DIAMETER CIRCLE

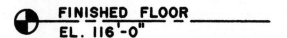

Whenever a detail is revised after the set has been given to the contractor, a revision number such as the one shown here is included:

A room number is shown as follows. For this shape, use the sink from the toilet template to trace the outline:

A door number is shown as follows:

When laying out a plan grid, number lines run horizontally, and letter lines run vertically—preferably starting at the upper left-hand corner. The numbers go from left to right, and the letters go from top to bottom, as shown on the following floor plan:

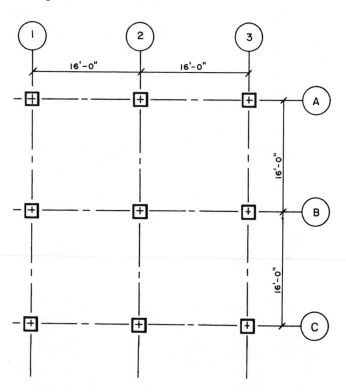

Exterior elevations are noted by the points of the compass—north, south, east, and west:

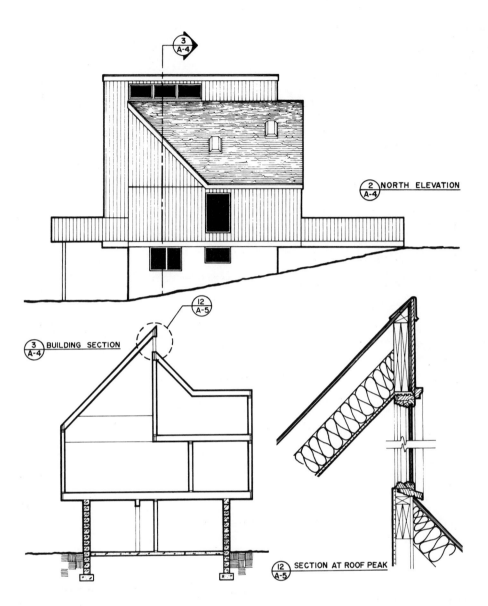

3/A-4

2/A-4 NORTH ELEVATION

12/A-5

3/A-4 BUILDING SECTION

12/A-5 SECTION AT ROOF PEAK

The combination of the three types of drawings (plan, elevation, and section) gives a three-dimensional picture of a building. The relationship of the three types of drawings is shown in Figure 2-9. It is a wall condition for a small community building. Reference bubble 1/A-1 refers to the first-floor plan in Figures 2-9 and 2-10. Details 1/A-2 and 2/A-2 refer to Figure 2-11, the elevation and wall-section drawing. Reference symbols and abbreviations used on the first-floor plan are listed in Table 2-4. The isometric view is included in the text mainly as a reference for the other drawings. The plan, elevation, and section drawings, however, could be part of the working drawings.

The place to begin in drawing a *plan*, such as the first-floor plan in Figure 2-10, is to lay out the perimeter walls to scale, followed by the interior walls and doors and windows.

At this point, the walls are darkened (with 2H lead) and additional facilities (door swings, windows, toilets, stairs) are added. The next step is to hatch the wall material in various places. Note that a representative indication can be given without hatching every wall.

After the room names and numbers are noted, the dimension strings are drawn. Each wall and opening should be dimensioned only once. Any additional notation is redundant and takes up valu-

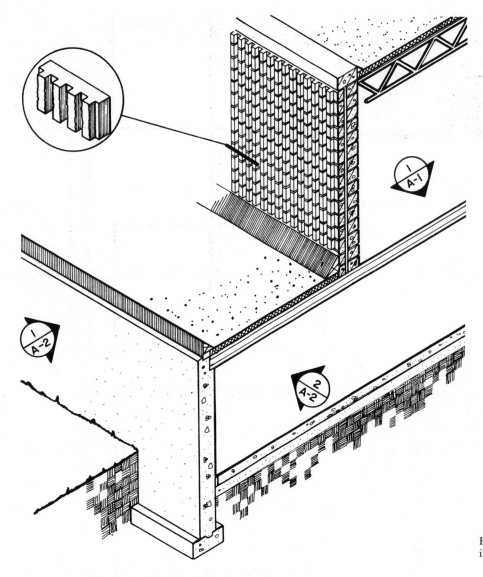

Figure 2-9. An isometric drawing showing a plan, an elevation, and a section.

able space on the plan. For example, the east and west walls in the kitchen, Room 102, are not given because they obviously line up with the office, Room 108. The center of the west stud wall is 10′-8″ from the west face of the building, while the east wall is flush with the inside face of the block wall in Room 108.

A short cut to laying out an *elevation*, such as the east elevation in Figure 2-11, is to place a print of the floor plan under the drawing sheet as a guide for locating walls and openings and then scale off their height. The outline of the elevation should be laid out in light pencil first along with the openings and lines showing changes in material. The major lines are then darkened, and the building material as seen in elevation is drawn. It

is not hatched because it is not drawn in section.

The material shown on the second floor in Figure 2-10 is called break-off block and is indicated in elevation by 2″ vertical lines. The remainder of the building material is either exposed poured concrete or smooth-finish concrete block. The spiral stair going out of Room 100 is drawn in elevation.

A wall *section*, such as the one in Figure 2-11, is started by drawing the floor and roof height to scale in light pencil. Note that the walls on both floors in detail 2/A-2 have break lines indicating that the full height of the wall is not drawn to scale. This is done to reduce the size of the drawing.

The next step is to locate the walls and widths of materials within the wall and mark them lightly.

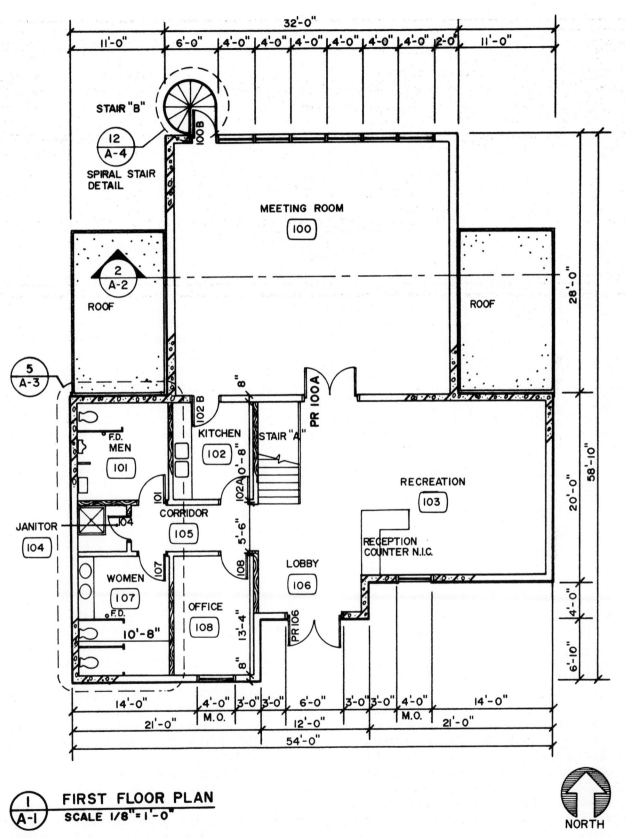

Figure 2-10. First floor plan.

TABLE 2-4 KEY TO REFERENCES AND CROSS-REFERENCES ON FIRST-FLOOR PLAN

SYMBOL	MEANING
	Block wall.
	Wood-stud wall.
①/A-1	This is the first drawing on sheet A-1.
⑤/A-3	Rooms 101, 104, and 107 are drawn at a larger scale in detail 5 on sheet A-3.
⑫/A-4	Stair B is detailed on sheet A-4 in detail 12. (Stair A is near Lobby Rm. 106.)
②/A-2	A section through the building is detailed on 6/A-12.
RECEPTION COUNTER N.I.C.	The counter in Room 103 is drawn on the plan, but the contractor is not to figure it in the bid or install it. N.I.C. (not in contract).
4'-0" M.O.	The 4' dimension for windows is a masonry opening (M.O.); the block mason is to leave a 4'-0" opening in the wall.
NORTH	North is up on the sheet.
PR 100	Door 100A is a pair of doors (PR.), the letter A follows the door number because there is more than one door in Room 100. (100B is leading outside to the spiral stair.)

After the major elements have been located, the lines for walls and roofs are darkened, and the various building materials are hatched.

There are some additional drafting procedures you will be required to know.

Equal Proportioning

To divide a line into equal proportions, choose a scale that is slightly longer than the actual distance. The stair in Figure 2-12 scales 10'-10" at the scale used. The stair is shown divided into 13 equal treads. Angle the scale until the 0 touches the projected end of the line and 13 touches the other end. Each foot increment is then marked lightly, and the marks are projected up to the stair treads parallel to the line that was projected for the end of the line.

French Curve

A French curve is used to draw the irregular pattern of a line that cannot be drawn with a compass. A smooth line can be drawn by first locating as many points of the curve as possible. To draw a continuous curve, a segment of the French curve is chosen that will give the longest line connecting the points. The smoothness of the curve is greatly affected by the care taken to make each setting of the curve tangent to the next.

Delineation

Good working drawings depend on four major points: sheet layout, line quality, lettering, and technical knowledge. A drafting technician must have a working command in each of these areas before a sheet can be competently prepared. It is equally fair to say that it is impossible to properly execute a set of drawings with one of the points lacking.

Two points, line quality and lettering, can be learned with practice by a student. Sheet layout involves the placement of individual details on a sheet so that they are compact and orderly and so that they make the most sense to a contractor. This skill is acquired through knowledge of architectural detailing and construction detailing. Architectural detailing requires not only a complete knowledge of building materials and their capabilities but also the ability to visualize design conditions and build them.

Lettering Architects have developed a unique stylized form of printing that is common to the profession. It is mandatory that this style be adopted. Any great variance from this standard will cause confusion. Several rules are helpful:

1. Always use guidelines at both the top and bottom of the lettering.
2. All architectural lettering is uppercase.
3. Use a straightforward technique. The development of an unusual style is time-consuming and against most office standards.

Figure 2-13 shows some architectural lettering styles that should be avoided.

A softer, duller lead (H, F) is used more often for lettering than for line work.

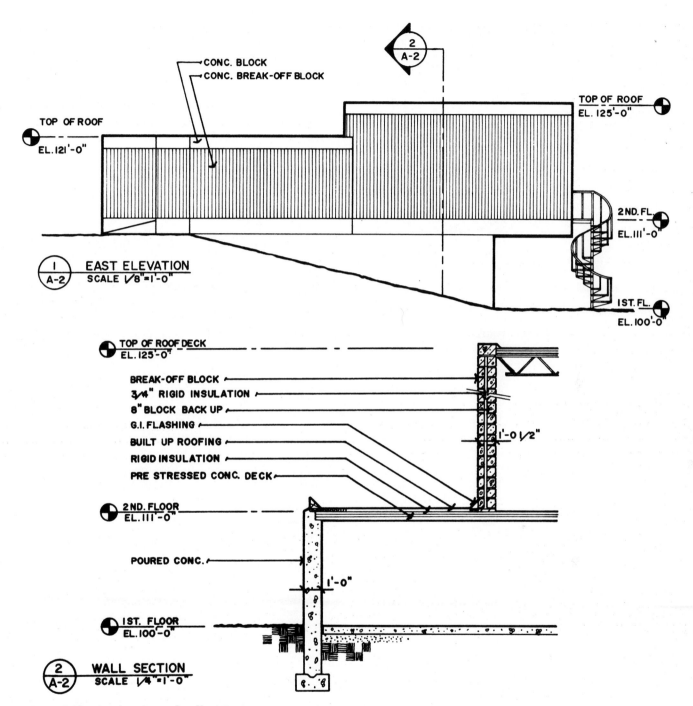

Figure 2-11. An elevation and wall section.

Offices adopt a standard of lettering size so that continuity is preserved when more than one person is doing the drafting on a project. A usual standard is to show notes at $3/32''$ and titles at $3/16''$. The standard given in Figure 2-14 should be copied and practiced until the style is learned.

Several tips for lettering may prove helpful:

1. It is generally more difficult to letter at a large size than a small one since you would have to follow the $3/32''$ space between guidelines so closely.

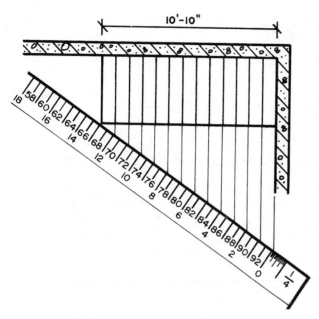

Figure 2-12.   A stair divided into equal proportions.

Mixed Letter Sizes

Accented Letters

lowercase letters

Compressed Letters

Wide Letters

Figure 2-13.   Architectural lettering sizes to be avoided.

2. To develop skill and speed, print everything (such as class notes and letters) instead of writing.

3. In standard architectural printing, vertical and horizontal lines should be straight, not slanted. One method of getting straight vertical lines is to use a triangle under the parallel blade to make all vertical lines (as the vertical line for B, D, E, F, H, etc.). This method could prove helpful once the technique of handling a triangle is mastered (see Figure 2-15).

The purpose of lettering on a working drawing sheet is to identify dimensions and describe details. As we said earlier, the drawings indicate quantity, and the specifications indicate quality. The notes on the drawings should also reflect this by being general in nature rather than specific. The following points tell you just what the drawings should and should not indicate:

1. The drawings should indicate a material such as concrete, but let the specifications determine whether it is to be 2500 or 3000 P.S.I. for strength.

2. The drawings should not indicate structural sizes that are shown in the structural set of drawings. A note calling out a shelf angle should read "shelf ∠ (see struct.)," rather than "2½" × 2½" × ¼" shelf ∠."

3. The drawings should not define color, texture, cost range, quality, etc. These items are part of the specifications. An example is brick: The notes on the drawing should be limited to face brick, common brick, or fire brick. The points dealing with the color or the cost of the brick would be covered in the specification.

4. Materials such as wood should be given a general note calling out only what the material is. The specifications will indicate such characteristics as "clear heart redwood," "No. 3 grade channel rustic 1" × 6" cedar," "kiln dried," etc. If confusion arises because more than one type of wood material is used on the job, the note could indicate "Type 1 wood siding," or "Type 2 wood siding." Types 1 and 2 wood siding would then be explained in the specification.

5. Metal flashing is typically called out by type but not by size: "copper flashing," not "16-oz copper flashing"; "painted G.I." (galvanized iron), not "28-GA. painted G.I."

6. Brand names should not be used in notes, the reason being that the brand noted may not be the one eventually used by a contractor. Technically, a brand name on a note, without several options, eliminates the contractor's options and thus competitive bidding. Unfortunately, some brands have become almost "household" terms for a whole product line, and so care must be taken to identify them properly. Some more common brand names are

ABCDEFGHIJKLMNOPQRST —|— 1/4"
UVWXYZ 1234567890 ABCD

ALL LETTERING SHOULD BE SINGLE-STROKE VERTICAL LETERS IN CAPITALS.
THE PROJECT NAME AND TITLE BLOCKS SHOULD BE DRAWN 1/4" HIGH.

ABCDEFGHIJKLMNOPQRSTUVWXYZ 12 —|— 3/16"
34567890 ABCDEFGHIJKLMNOPQRST

TITLES OF DETAILS, PLANS, ELEVATIONS, AND SECTIONS SHOULD BE DRAWN
3/16" HIGH.

ABCDEFGHIJKLMNOPQRSTUVWXYZ 1234567890 ABC —|— 3/32"
DEFGHIJKLMNOPQRSTUVWXYZ 1234567890 ABCDEFG

ALL OTHER LETTERING NOTES SHOULD BE DRAWN 3/32" HIGH.

HORIZONTAL DIMENSIONS SHOULD READ FROM THE
BOTTOM OF THE SHEET.

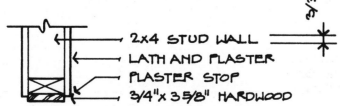

NOTES SHOULD BE KEPT IN A LINE
MAINLY TO ADD TO THE NEATNESS
AND COMPOSITION OF THE DETAIL.

VERTICAL DIMENSIONS
SHOULD READ FROM THE
RIGHT SIDE OF THE
SHEET.

LINES DRAWN FROM NOTES
SHOULD BE DONE WITH A
STRAIGHTEDGE OR FRENCH
CURVE

Figure 2-14.   Some standard lettering sizes.

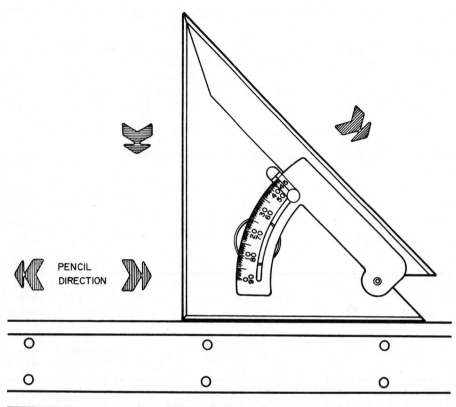

PENCIL
DIRECTION

Figure 2-15.   Using a triangle and a parallel blade to get a straight vertical line.

Use	Don't Use
batt insulation	Fiberglas
plastic laminate	Formica
insulating glass	Thermopane
heat-reducing glass	Solarbronze glass
gypsum board	Sheetrock
gypsum block	Pyrobar
self-weathering steel	Cor-ten steel
cellular glass insulation	Foamglas
cellular insulation	Styrofoam
tempered glass	Herculite
cement asbestos board	Transite
rod stock back-up	Ethafoam
fiberboard	Masonite
rigid insulation	Celotex

One possible exception to the rule of not using trademarks is on a small private project, such as a house. In this case, a client may predetermine the quality of products and be willing to pay a premium for the elimination of competitive bidding. This also eliminates the necessity of describing the material in the specification. The note "Anderson Permashield Window C26" needs no further specifying.

Line quality Line quality refers to the darkness, line weight, and crispness that draftsmen achieve in their drawing styles. The line produced depends on four main points, to be discussed separately: (1) weight of lead, (2) pressure applied in drawing, (3) sharpness of lead point, and (4) angle of pencil to straightedge.

Lead weight is graded from a very hard 9H to a very soft 6B, as shown below.

Working drawing range

9H	8H	7H	6H	5H	4H	3H	2H	H	F	HB	B	2B	3B	4B	5B	6B

Hard   Soft

The weight selected for drafting depends greatly on personal preference. To start, 2H is considered a good lead weight, but experiment with several grades on either side to establish a preference. A lead much harder than 2H gives an extremely crisp line, but it is too thin and light. Lead in the B range makes a wide, dark, fuzzy line that smears easily.

Most technicians prefer to draw with one lead weight and print with a softer weight. Lead holders usually have different-colored tops so that you can tell pencils apart.

The *pressure* applied to a pencil controls the darkness of the line produced. A uniform pressure yields a line with equal gradation. A close study of a good sheet of working drawings shows that several variations in line darkness are deliberately used to achieve an effect. Generally, the darker the line, the more important it is to the total detail. Lines are generally placed in the following groups:

- **Heavy**   Exterior walls are drawn dark to make the building profile stand out. Interior walls are drawn slightly lighter, but they still stand out.
- **Medium**   Grid lines and other reference keys, dimension lines, and wall hatching.
- **Medium to light**   Floor materials, such as brick pavers.
- **Light**   Guidelines for lettering.

The line categories could continue, but the pattern should be evident: The darkness of a line is related to its importance. It takes time to develop a drafting technique, but it is a sign of a professional. Since most lines will more than likely be drawn with the same lead weight, the basic factor contributing to the difference is the pressure applied to the lead holder.

The *sharpness* of the lead determines the crispness of the line. The only time a draftsman does not draw with a reasonably sharp pencil is when he or she is lettering.

The best point to use for line drawing is one that has a sharp point, but not so sharp that it breaks when pressure is applied. It is possible to get a needle-sharp point with a pencil pointer, but any pressure snaps the point off. The other extreme is a rounded point that is so dull it gives a broad, fuzzy line. Some draftsmen use a paper scratch pad on which to slightly dull the point after sharpening.

The "chisel" that develops on one side of the lead the first time a line is drawn causes a broad, fuzzy line (Figure 2-16). To avoid dulling lead, develop the drafting technique of gradually twisting the pencil while drawing a line. This causes the lead to wear evenly into a conical point rather than into a chisel. The point lasts longer, and lines stay crisp.

Practice is the only way to develop this skill. On a long line the pencil should be rotated once about every 2′ of line. The total procedure than becomes a task of slowly twisting the pencil clockwise between the thumb and index finger and applying a uniform pressure while drawing the lead across the paper.

The angle of the pencil to the straightedge is the least critical of the four points, but it can affect the straightness of a line. If the angle between the pencil and straightedge is less than 90°, the lead rides along the top edge of the triangle or parallel bar instead of the bottom edge (Figure 2-17). Any variance in the angle when the line is drawn results in an uneven line. The correct procedure is simply to use the lower side of the straightedge as a guide or to be certain the same angle under 90° is maintained for the full length.

Several other points relate to drawing a detail. Lines that intersect at a corner should not cross each other or barely meet. Also, the lines should be of even quality until they meet. Some experienced technicians prefer the effect of slightly

CHISEL POINT

DULL POINT

(GOOD FOR PRINTING)

POINT TOO SHARP

SLIGHTLY DULL

(GOOD LINE QUALITY)

Figure 2-16.   Lead points.

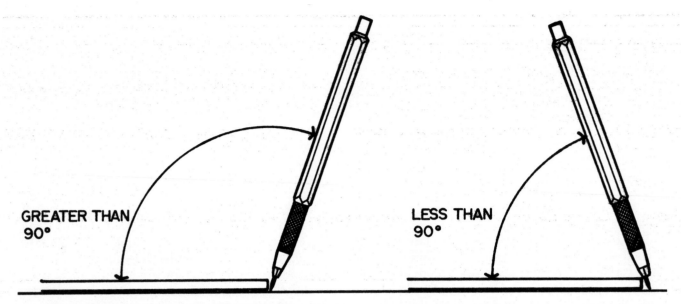

GREATER THAN 90°

LESS THAN 90°

Figure 2-17.   The angle of the pencil to the straightedge.

crossing intersecting lines (example 2 in Figure 2-18), but it is not a standard to be used by beginning technicians.

Another procedure sometimes used is to accent the outer lines around a detail to make it stand out (Figure 2-19). This can be done simply by darkening the outside lines of materials around the detail. This technique should not be attempted until a technician has confidence that his or her drafting skill is good enough to try extra work.

Sheet layout   The orderly location of plans and details on a working drawing sheet will result in an economical use of space. It also will allow a contractor to understand the drawing set better and to produce a better-looking sheet of drawings. Chapter 3 covers the drawing sequence to be followed in assembling a set of drawings and the layout of each individual sheet.

Before any working drawing sheet is started, you should know exactly where everything is to be located. A rough sketch can be done at full scale on an overlay of cedar paper.

Since the plans and a good share of the details have been laid out previously in the design development phase of the project, a part of the job is already laid out for the technician's approval or change. Sheet layout somewhat resembles a puzzle with interchangeable pieces. The goal is to design a cohesive sheet with little wasted space and yet to make the assembly of the building easy to understand.

The best guide to follow in laying out a sheet is common sense, along with an understanding of construction procedures. The following points are helpful:

1. Locate similar details, drawn at the same scale, together. Six separate wall sections, all drawn at ½" = 1'-0", should be drawn together in a block if at all possible.

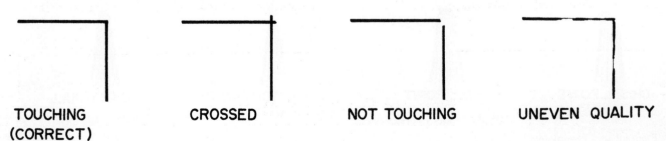

TOUCHING (CORRECT)   **CROSSED**   **NOT TOUCHING**   **UNEVEN QUALITY**

Figure 2-18.   Cornering lines.

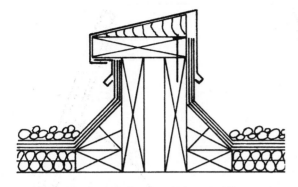

UNACCENTED DETAIL

ACCENTED DETAIL

Figure 2-19. Accent lines can make a detail stand out.

2. Details with similar reference points, such as floors, should be drawn with these points lined up. If the six wall sections mentioned above have the same floor and roof height, they should be drawn side by side with the floor and roof of each lined up. Similarly, if the head (top) and sill (bottom) of a window are drawn in separate details, the head detail should be drawn directly above the sill with the glass in each detail lined up.

3. One way to assemble a large group of small details on a sheet is to divide the sheet with light pencil lines into evenly spaced rectangles that are about the size of an average detail. If a detail larger than one rectangle occurs, several rectangles may be used. Upon completion of a sheet, you have the option of darkening the grid lines to block in each detail

4. Any time more than one drawing occurs on a sheet, you should concern yourself with how the details relate to each other. The relationship improves if the notes, dimension strings, and titles of the details line up.

TECHNICAL KNOWLEDGE

Some sources for acquiring technical knowledge have been discussed in this chapter. They range from observing construction to studying completed working drawings. Chapter 4, "Building Construction and Technology," briefly shows some more common solutions used in construction, but it is impossible to cover the many conditions that may be unique to a particular job.

Obviously, a natural talent in drafting is of little value if a student lacks a technical knowledge of what to draw. The prime consideration of this text is to provide a substantial base of technical material in both commercial and residential architecture. The details illustrated in this chapter are "workable" architectural conditions used in actual construction. They were selected both because they represent frequently encountered building details and because they are well drawn.

This chapter should be considered as an index of details which can be typical conditions when assembling a package of working drawings. Unlike Chapter 3, no explanation is given for each detail here. Rather, the detail should be studied to determine the assembly of various materials and its adaptability in the particular condition you might find. No set of universal building details pertains to every piece of architecture. While these details were proper for their particular building, they could not be used to assemble another building without first ascertaining their appropriateness.

Sample Details Follow

DETAIL INDEX

NUMBER

1-7	Site
8-21	Wood Frame
22-31	Exterior Walls
32-42	Roof Conditions
43-50	Stair Details
51-66	Window
67-71	Door
72-75	Interior
76-83	Miscellaneous

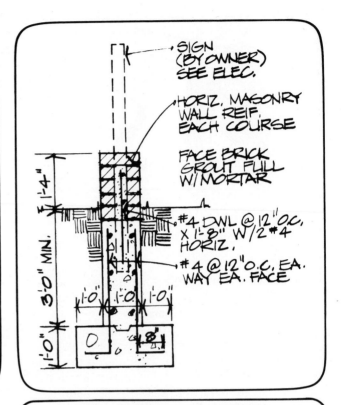

SIGN (BY OWNER) SEE ELEC.

HORIZ. MASONRY WALL REIF. EACH COURSE

FACE BRICK GROUT FULL W/ MORTAR

#4 DWL @ 12" O.C. X 1'-8" W/2 #4 HORIZ.

#4 @ 12" O.C. EA. WAY EA. FACE

1'-4"

3'-0" MIN.

1'-0"

1'-0" 1'-0" 1'-0"

8"

1 SIGN BASE SECTION

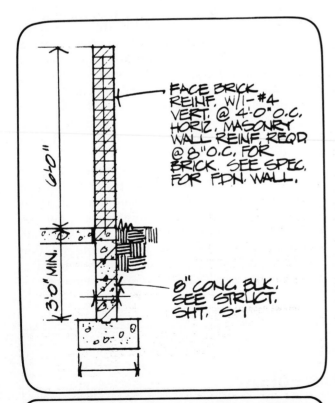

FACE BRICK REINF. W/1-#4 VERT. @ 4'-0" O.C. HORIZ. MASONRY WALL REINF. REQD @ 8" O.C. FOR BRICK. SEE SPEC. FOR FDN. WALL.

8" CONC. BLK. SEE STRUCT. SHT. S-1

6'-0"

3'-0" MIN.

2 EXTERIOR SCREEN WALL

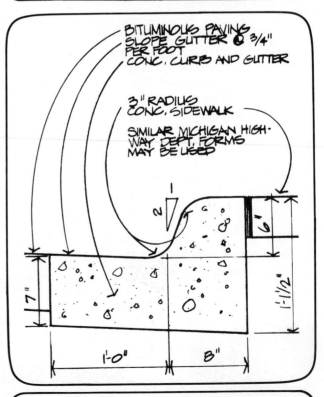

BITUMINOUS PAVING SLOPE GUTTER @ 3/4" PER FOOT CONC. CURB AND GUTTER

3" RADIUS CONC. SIDEWALK

SIMILAR MICHIGAN HIGH- WAY DEPT. FORMS MAY BE USED

1
2

6"

7"

1'-1 1/2"

1'-0" 8"

3 CONC. CURB & GUTTER

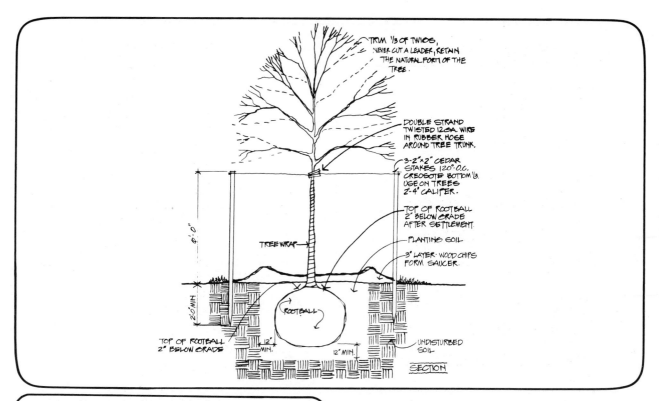

TRIM 1/3 OF TWIGS, NEVER CUT A LEADER, RETAIN THE NATURAL FORM OF THE TREE.

DOUBLE STRAND TWISTED 12 GA. WIRE IN RUBBER HOSE AROUND TREE TRUNK.

3-2"x2" CEDAR STAKES 120° O.C. CREOSOTE BOTTOM 1/3. USE ON TREES 2-4" CALIPER.

TOP OF ROOTBALL 2" BELOW GRADE AFTER SETTLEMENT.

PLANTING SOIL

3" LAYER WOOD CHIPS FORM SAUCER.

8'-0"

TREE WRAP

2'-0" MIN.

ROOTBALL

TOP OF ROOTBALL 2" BELOW GRADE

12" MIN.

12" MIN.

UNDISTURBED SOIL

SECTION

4 TREE STAKING

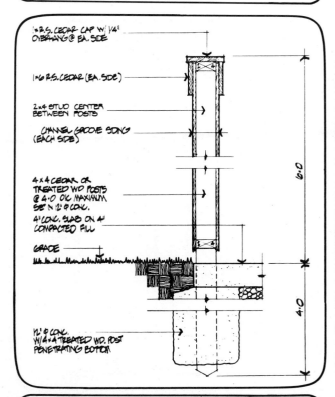

1"R.S. CEDAR CAP W/ 1/4" OVERHANG @ EA. SIDE

1"x6 R.S. CEDAR (EA. SIDE)

2x4 STUD CENTER BETWEEN POSTS

CHANNEL GROOVE SIDING (EACH SIDE)

4x4 CEDAR OR TREATED WD. POSTS @ 4'-0 O.C. MAXIMUM SET IN 12' Ø CONC.

4" CONC. SLAB ON 4" COMPACTED FILL

GRADE

6'-0

4'-0

12' Ø CONC. W/ 4x4 TREATED WD. POST PENETRATING BOTTOM

5 WOOD FENCE

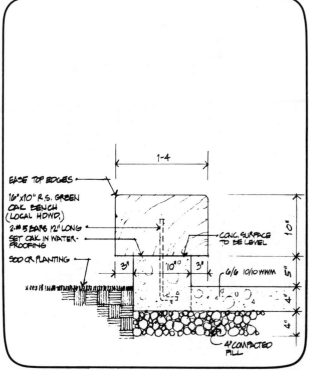

EASE TOP EDGES

16"x10" R.S. GREEN OAK BENCH (LOCAL HDWD.)

2-#5 BARS 12" LONG SET OAK IN WATER-PROOFING

SOD OR PLANTING

1-4

3"

10"

3"

CONC. SURFACE TO BE LEVEL

6/6 10/10 WWM

10"

5"

4"

4"

4" COMPACTED FILL

6 BENCH SECTION

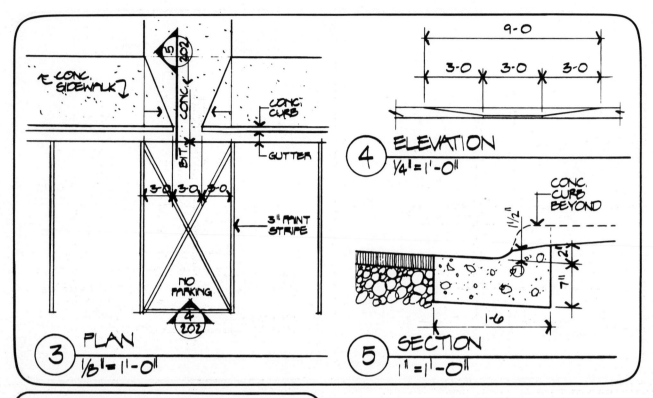

CONC. SIDEWALK

CONC. CURB

GUTTER

3" PAINT STRIPE

3-0 3-0 3-0

NO PARKING

③ PLAN
1/8" = 1'-0"

9-0

3-0 3-0 3-0

④ ELEVATION
1/4" = 1'-0"

CONC. CURB BEYOND

1 1/2"

7" 2"

1-6

⑤ SECTION
1" = 1'-0"

7 PARKING LOT DETAILS

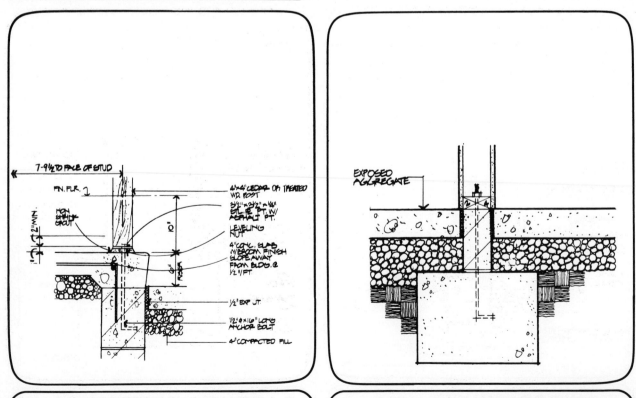

7-9 1/2 TO FACE OF STUD

FIN. FLR.

NON SHRINK GROUT

2" MIN

4"x4" CEDAR OR TREATED WD. POST

3 1/2" x 3 1/2" x 1/4" BTL. PL. PT. W/ ASPHALT PT.

LEVELING NUTS

4" CONC. SLAB W/BROOM FINISH SLOPE AWAY FROM BLDG. @ 1/2"/FT.

1/2" EXP. JT.

1/2"Ø x16" LONG ANCHOR BOLT

4" COMPACTED FILL

8 EXT. WOOD COLUMN

EXPOSED AGGREGATE

9 INT. LOAD BEARING WALL

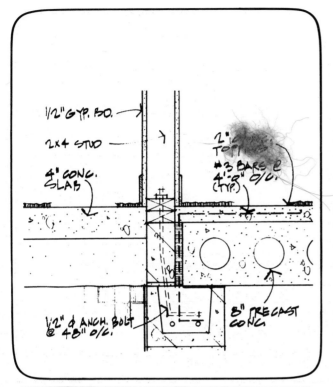

1/2" GYP. BD.

2X4 STUD

4" CONC. SLAB

2" TOP.

#3 BARS @ 4'-8" O/C. (TYP.)

1/2" Ø ANCH. BOLT @ 48" O/C.

8" PRECAST CONC.

10 SILL DETAIL

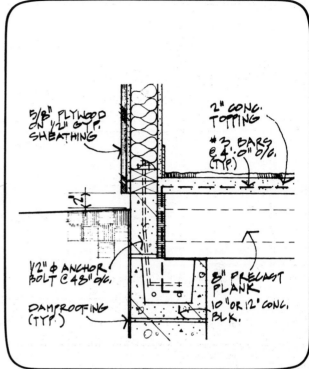

5/8" PLYWOOD SHEATHING

1/2" GYP. BD.

2" CONC. TOPPING

#3 BARS @ 4'-0" O/C. (TYP.)

1/2" Ø ANCHOR BOLT @ 48" O/C.

DAMPROOFING (TYP.)

8" PRECAST PLANK

10" OR 12" CONC. BLK.

11 SILL DETAIL

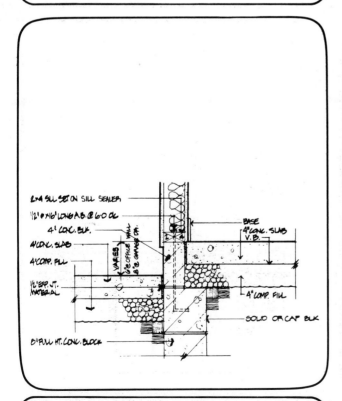

2X4 SILL SET ON SILL SEALER

1/2" Ø X16" LONG A.B. @ 6'-0 OC

4" CONC. BLK.

4" CONC. SLAB

4" COMP. FILL

1/2" EXP. JT. MATERIAL

0" FULL HT. CONC. BLOCK

BASE 4" CONC. SLAB V.B.

4" COMP. FILL

SOLID OR CAP BLK

12 FLOOR SLAB

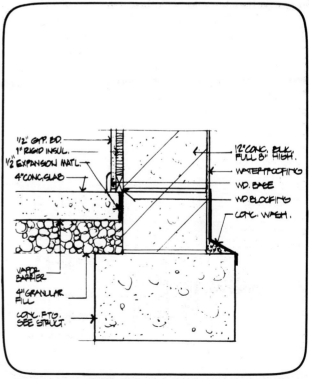

1/2" GYP. BD.

1" RIGID INSUL.

1/2" EXPANSION MATL.

4" CONC. SLAB

12" CONC. BLK. FULL 8" HIGH.

WATERPROOFING

WD. BASE

WD. BLOCKING

CONC. WASH.

VAPOR BARRIER

4" GRANULAR FILL

CONC. FTG. SEE STRUCT.

13 FLOOR SLAB BELOW GRADE

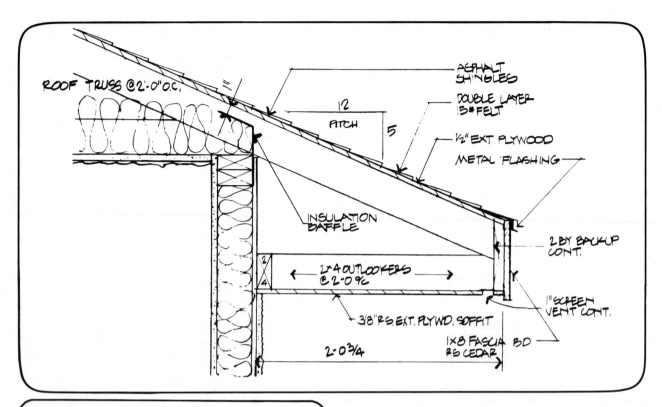

ROOF TRUSS @ 2'-0" O.C.

ASPHALT SHINGLES

DOUBLE LAYER 15# FELT

12 / 5 PITCH

1/2" EXT. PLYWOOD

METAL FLASHING

INSULATION BAFFLE

2 BY BACKUP CONT.

2x4 OUTLOOKERS @ 2'-0" OC

1" SCREEN VENT CONT.

3/8" RS. EXT. PLYWD. SOFFIT

1x8 FASCIA BD RS CEDAR

2'-0 3/4"

14 ROOF AT SOFFIT

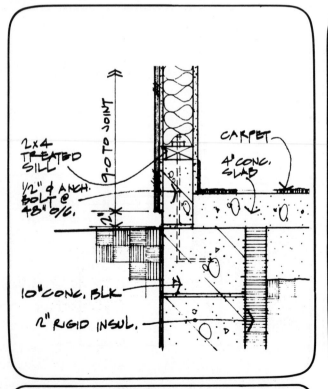

2x4 TREATED SILL

CARPET

4" CONC. SLAB

1/2" Ø ANCH. BOLT @ 48" O.C.

9'-0 TO JOINT

2"

10" CONC. BLK.

2" RIGID INSUL.

15 SILL DETAIL

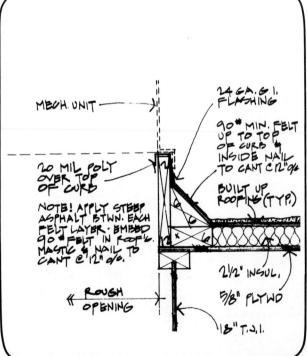

MECH. UNIT

24 GA. G.I. FLASHING

90# MIN. FELT UP TO TOP OF CURB & INSIDE NAIL TO CANT @ 12" OC

20 MIL POLY OVER TOP OF CURB

NOTE! APPLY STEEP ASPHALT BTWN. EACH FELT LAYER · EMBED 90# FELT IN ROOF'G. MASTIC & NAIL TO CANT @ 12" OC.

BUILT UP ROOFING (TYP.)

2 1/2" INSUL.

5/8" PLYWD

ROUGH OPENING

18" T.J.I.

16 ROOF CURB

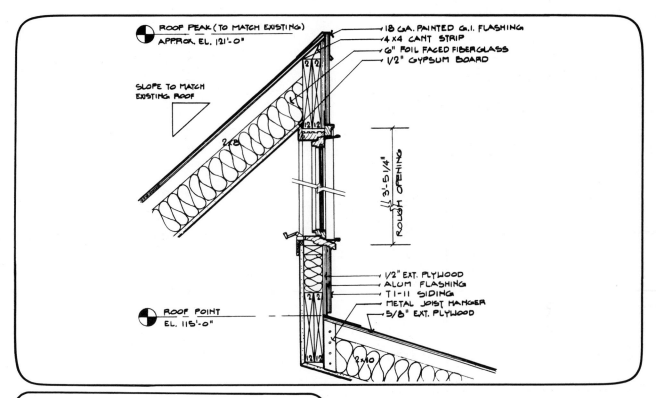

● ROOF PEAK (TO MATCH EXISTING)
APPROX. EL. 121'-0"

SLOPE TO MATCH
EXISTING ROOF

2x8

18 GA. PAINTED G.I. FLASHING
4 x 4 CANT STRIP
6" FOIL FACED FIBERGLASS
1/2" GYPSUM BOARD

3'-5 1/4" ROUGH OPENING

● ROOF POINT
EL. 115'-0"

1/2" EXT. PLYWOOD
ALUM FLASHING
TI-11 SIDING
METAL JOIST HANGER
5/8" EXT. PLYWOOD

2x10

17 ROOF PEAK

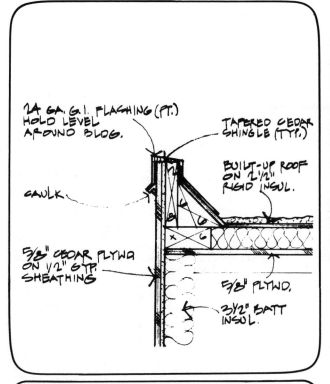

14 GA. G.I. FLASHING (PT.)
HOLD LEVEL
AROUND BLDG.

CAULK

TAPERED CEDAR
SHINGLE (TYP.)

BUILT-UP ROOF
ON 2 1/2"
RIGID INSUL.

5/8" CEDAR PLYWD
ON 1/2" GYP.
SHEATHING

5/8" PLYWD.

3 1/2" BATT
INSUL.

18 ROOF CANT

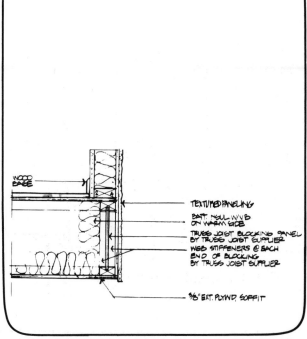

WOOD
BASE

TEXTURED PANELING
BATT. INSUL. W/VB
ON WARM SIDE
TRUSS JOIST BLOCKING PANEL
BY TRUSS JOIST SUPPLIER
WEB STIFFENERS @ EACH
END OF BLOCKING
BY TRUSS JOIST SUPPLIER

3/8" EXT. PLYWD. SOFFIT

19 WOOD SOFFIT

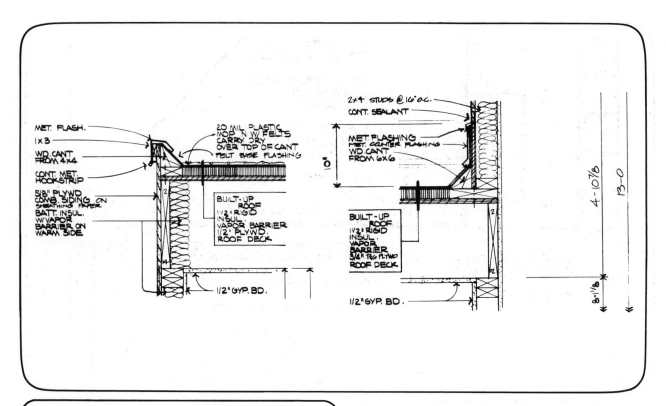

MET. FLASH.
1x3
WD. CANT.
FROM 4x4
CONT. MET.
HOOKSTRIP
5/8" PLYWD.
COMB. SIDING ON
SHEATHING PAPER
BATT. INSUL.
W/VAPOR
BARRIER ON
WARM SIDE

20 MIL PLASTIC
MOP'N W/ FELTS
CARRY DRY
OVER TOP OF CANT
FELT BASE FLASHING

BUILT-UP
ROOF
1/2" RIGID
INSUL.
VAPOR BARRIER
1/2" PLYWD.
ROOF DECK

1/2" GYP. BD.

2x4 STUDS @ 16" O.C.
CONT. SEALANT

MET. FLASHING
MET. COUNTER FLASHING
WD. CANT
FROM 6x6

BUILT-UP
ROOF.
1/2" RIGID
INSUL.
VAPOR
BARRIER
3/4" P&G PLYWD
ROOF DECK

1/2" GYP. BD.

10"
4'-10⅞"
13'-0"
8'-1⅛"

20 ROOF FRAMING

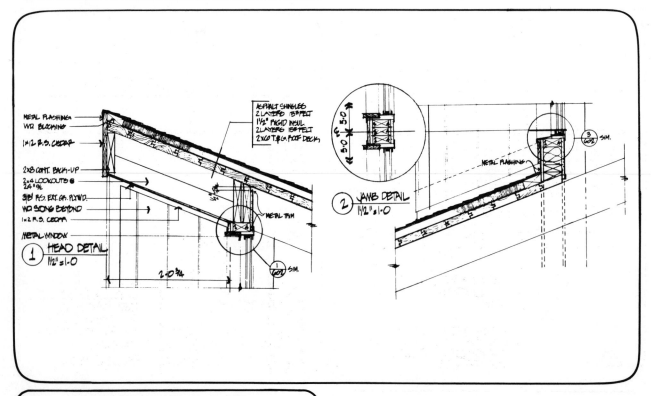

METAL FLASHING
WD. BLOCKING
1x12 R.S. CEDAR
2x8 CONT. BACK-UP
2x4 LOOKOUTS @
24" OC
3/8" P.S. EXT. GR. PLYWD.
WD. SIDING BEYOND
1x2 R.S. CEDAR
METAL WINDOW

ASPHALT SHINGLES
2 LAYERS 15# FELT
1½" RIGID INSUL
2 LAYERS 15# FELT
2x6 T.&G. ROOF DECK

METAL TRIM

① **HEAD DETAIL**
1½" = 1'-0"

2'-0 ¾"

① SIM.
601

② **JAMB DETAIL**
1½" = 1'-0"

5'-0
5'-0

METAL FLASHING

③ SIM.
601

21 WINDOW AT ROOF

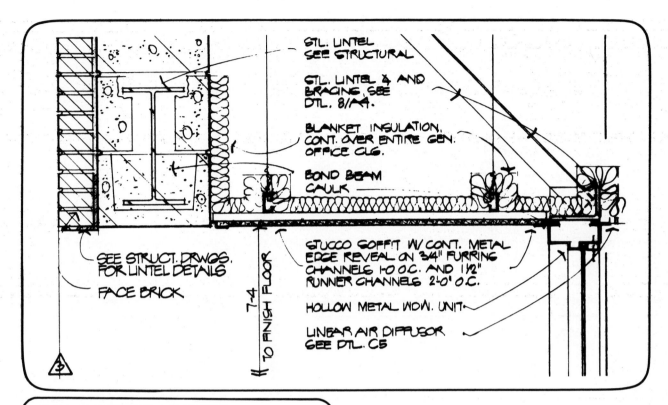

STL. LINTEL
SEE STRUCTURAL

STL. LINTEL & AND
BRACING, SEE
DTL. 8/A4.

BLANKET INSULATION,
CONT. OVER ENTIRE GEN.
OFFICE CLG.

BOND BEAM
CAULK

SEE STRUCT. DRWGS.
FOR LINTEL DETAILS

FACE BRICK

7'-4" TO FINISH FLOOR

STUCCO SOFFIT W/ CONT. METAL
EDGE REVEAL ON 3/4" FURRING
CHANNELS 1'-0 O.C. AND 1½"
RUNNER CHANNELS 2'-0" O.C.

HOLLOW METAL WDW. UNIT.

LINEAR AIR DIFFUSOR
SEE DTL. C5

22 SOFFIT DETAIL

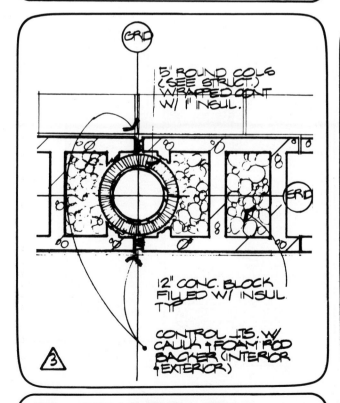

GRID

5" ROUND COLS
(SEE STRUCT.)
WRAPPED CONT.
W/ 1" INSUL.

GRID

12" CONC. BLOCK
FILLED W/ INSUL.
TYP

CONTROL JTS. W/
CAULK & FOAM ROD
BACKER (INTERIOR
& EXTERIOR)

23   COLUMN IN WALL

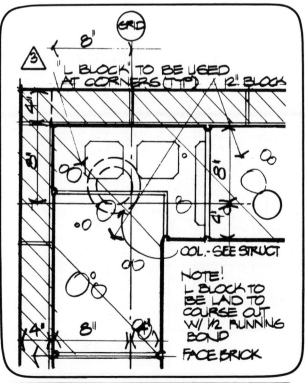

GRID

8"

"L BLOCK" TO BE USED
AT CORNERS (TYP)   12" BLOCK

8"

8"

4"

COL.- SEE STRUCT

NOTE!
L BLOCK TO
BE LAID TO
COURSE OUT
W/ ½ RUNNING
BOND

FACE BRICK

4"   8"

24   BRICK CORNER

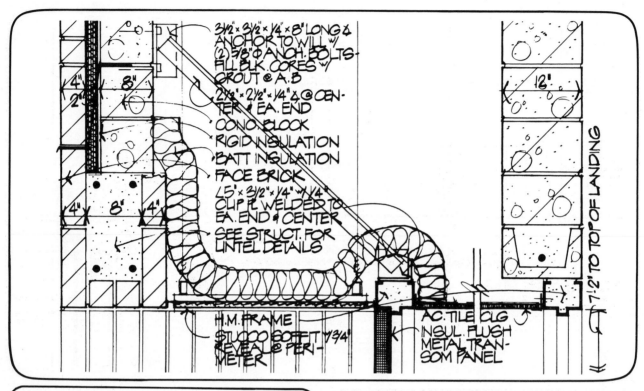

3½" × 3½" × ¼" × 8" LONG & ANCHOR TO WILL W/ (2) ⅝" ∅ ANCH. BOLTS - FILL BLK. CORES W/ GROUT @ A.B

2½" × 2½" × ¼" ∠ @ CENTER & EA. END

CONC. BLOCK

RIGID INSULATION

BATT INSULATION

FACE BRICK

∠ 5" × 3½" × ¼" × ¼" CLIP ℓ WELDED TO EA. END & CENTER

SEE STRUCT. FOR LINTEL DETAILS

H.M. FRAME

STUCCO SOFFIT ¼"/¾" REVEAL @ PERI-METER

AC. TILE CLG

INSUL. FLUSH METAL TRAN-SOM PANEL

7'-2" TO TOP OF LANDING

25 SOFFIT & LINTEL

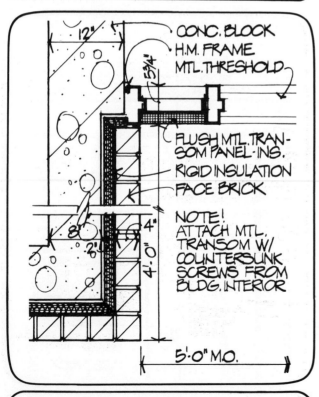

CONC. BLOCK
H.M. FRAME
MTL. THRESHOLD

FLUSH MTL. TRAN-SOM PANEL - INS.

RIGID INSULATION

FACE BRICK

NOTE!
ATTACH MTL. TRANSOM W/ COUNTERSUNK SCREWS FROM BLDG. INTERIOR

5'-0" M.O.

26 JAMB DETAIL

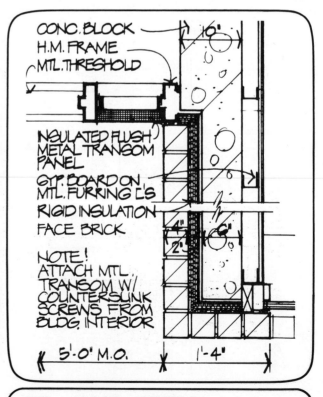

CONC. BLOCK
H.M. FRAME
MTL. THRESHOLD

INSULATED FLUSH METAL TRANSOM PANEL

GYP. BOARD ON MTL. FURRING C'S

RIGID INSULATION

FACE BRICK

NOTE!
ATTACH MTL. TRANSOM W/ COUNTERSUNK SCREWS FROM BLDG. INTERIOR

5'-0" M.O.

1'-4"

27 JAMB DETAIL

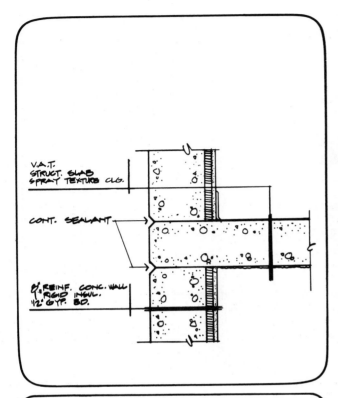

V.A.T.
STRUCT. SLAB
SPRAY TEXTURE CLG.

CONT. SEALANT

8" REINF. CONC. WALL
1" RIGID INSUL.
1½" GYP. BD.

28 FLOOR SLAB

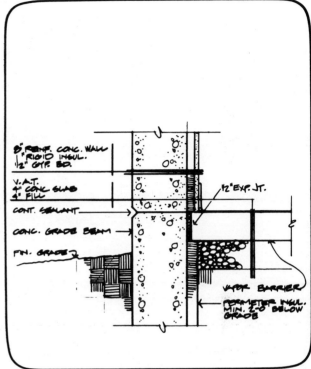

8" REINF. CONC. WALL
1" RIGID INSUL.
1½" GYP. BD.

V.A.T.
4" CONC. SLAB
4" FILL

CONT. SEALANT

CONC. GRADE BEAM

FIN. GRADE

½" EXP. JT.

VAPOR BARRIER

PERIMETER INSUL.
MIN. 2'-0 BELOW
GRADE

29 SLAB ON GRADE

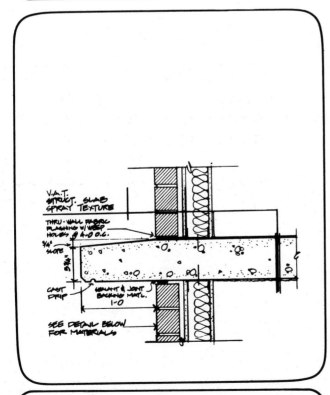

V.A.T.
STRUCT. SLAB
SPRAY TEXTURE

THRU-WALL FABRIC
FLASHING W/ WEEP
HOLES @ 4'-0 O.C.

¾" SLOPE

5¾"

CAST DRIP

SEALANT & JOINT
BACKING MATL.
1'-0

SEE DETAIL BELOW
FOR MATERIALS

30 BRICK WALL AT FLOOR

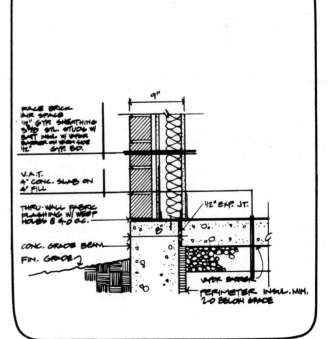

9"

FACE BRICK
AIR SPACE
½" GYP. SHEATHING
3⅝" STL. STUDS W/
BATT INSUL. W/ VAPOR
BARRIER ON WARM SIDE
½" GYP. BD.

V.A.T.
4" CONC. SLAB ON
4" FILL

THRU-WALL FABRIC
FLASHING W/ WEEP
HOLES @ 4'-0 O.C.

CONC. GRADE BEAM

FIN. GRADE

½" EXP. JT.

VAPOR BARRIER

PERIMETER INSUL. MIN.
2'-0 BELOW GRADE

31 BRICK WALL AT GRADE

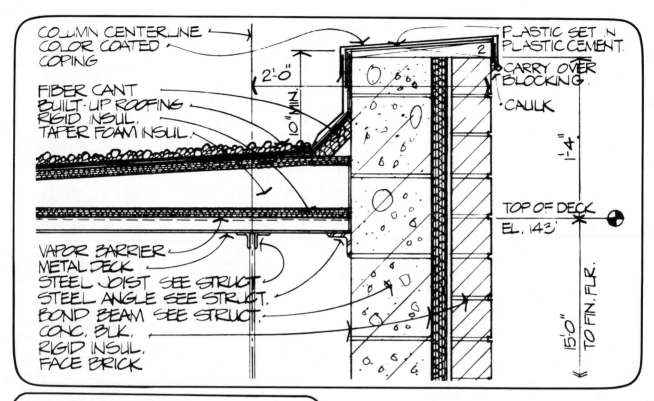

COLUMN CENTERLINE
COLOR COATED
COPING

2'-0"

PLASTIC SET IN
PLASTIC CEMENT.

CARRY OVER
BLOCKING.

CAULK

FIBER CANT
BUILT-UP ROOFING
RIGID INSUL.
TAPER FOAM INSUL.

10" MIN.

1'-4"

VAPOR BARRIER
METAL DECK
STEEL JOIST SEE STRUCT.
STEEL ANGLE SEE STRUCT.
BOND BEAM SEE STRUCT.
CONC. BLK.
RIGID INSUL.
FACE BRICK

TOP OF DECK
EL. 143'

15'-0" TO FIN. FLR.

32 ROOF EDGE

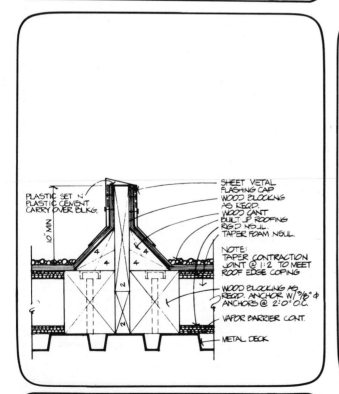

PLASTIC SET IN
PLASTIC CEMENT
CARRY OVER BLKG.

10" MIN.

SHEET METAL
FLASHING CAP
WOOD BLOCKING
AS REQD.
WOOD CANT
BUILT UP ROOFING
RIGID INSUL.
TAPER FOAM INSUL.

NOTE:
TAPER CONTRACTION
JOINT @ 1:2 TO MEET
ROOF EDGE COPING

WOOD BLOCKING AS
REQD. ANCHOR W/3/8" Ø
ANCHORS @ 2'-0" O.C.

VAPOR BARRIER CONT.

METAL DECK

33 CONTRACTION JOINT

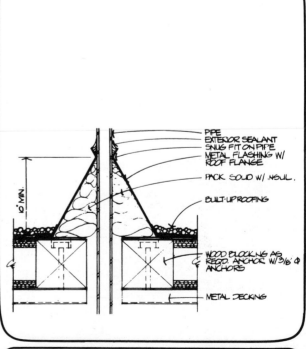

PIPE
EXTERIOR SEALANT
SNUG FIT ON PIPE
METAL FLASHING W/
ROOF FLANGE

PACK SOLID W/ INSUL.

BUILT-UP ROOFING

10" MIN.

WOOD BLOCKING AS
REQD. ANCHOR W/3/8" Ø
ANCHORS

METAL DECKING

34 FLASHING AT PIPE

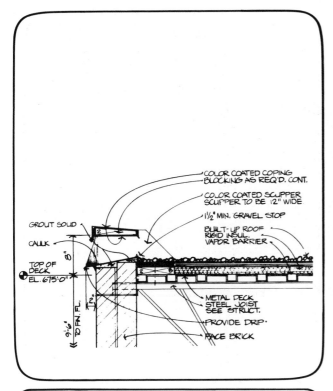

COLOR COATED COPING
BLOCKING AS REQ'D. CONT.

COLOR COATED SCUPPER
SCUPPER TO BE 12" WIDE

1½" MIN. GRAVEL STOP

BUILT-UP ROOF
RIGID INSUL.
VAPOR BARRIER.

GROUT SOLID

CAULK

TOP OF
DECK
EL. 675'-0"

8"

2"

9'-6"
TO FIN. FL.

METAL DECK
STEEL JOIST
SEE STRUCT.

PROVIDE DRIP.

FACE BRICK

35 OVERFLOW SCUPPER

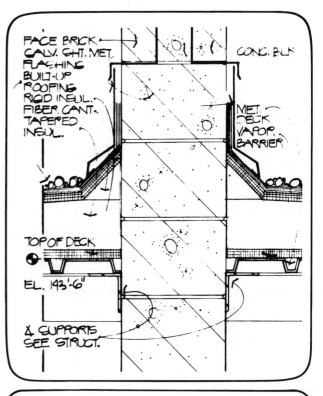

FACE BRICK
GALV. SHT. MET.
FLASHING
BUILT-UP
ROOFING
RIGID INSUL.
FIBER CANT.
TAPERED
INSUL.

CONC. BLK.

MET.
DECK
VAPOR
BARRIER.

TOP OF DECK

EL. 143'-6"

& SUPPORTS
SEE STRUCT.

36 PARAPET WALL FLASHING

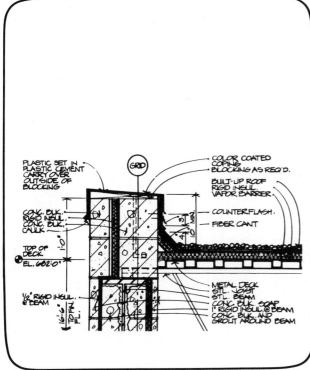

PLASTIC SET IN
PLASTIC CEMENT
CARRY OVER
OUTSIDE OF
BLOCKING

GRID

COLOR COATED
COPING
BLOCKING AS REQ'D.

BUILT-UP ROOF
RIGID INSUL.
VAPOR BARRIER.

COUNTERFLASH.

FIBER CANT

CONC. BLK.
RIGID INSUL.
CONC. BLK.
CAULK

TOP OF
DECK
EL. 682'-0"

½" RIGID INSUL.
@ BEAM

1'-0"

3" MIN.

4"

16'-6"
TO FIN.
FL.

METAL DECK
STL. JOIST
STL. BEAM
CONC. BLK. SOAP
1" RIGID INSUL. @ BEAM
CONC. BLK. AND
GROUT AROUND BEAM

37 ROOF EDGE

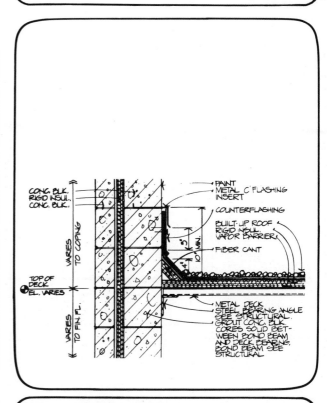

CONC. BLK.
RIGID INSUL.
CONC. BLK.

PAINT
METAL 'C' FLASHING
INSERT

COUNTERFLASHING

BUILT-UP ROOF
RIGID INSUL.
VAPOR BARRIER.

FIBER CANT

VARIES
TO COPING

5" MIN.

12" MIN.

TOP OF
DECK
EL. VARIES

VARIES
TO FIN. FL.

METAL DECK
STEEL BEARING ANGLE
SEE STRUCTURAL.
GROUT CONC. BLK.
CORES SOLID BET-
WEEN BOND BEAM
AND DECK BEARING.
BOND BEAM SEE
STRUCTURAL

38 PARAPET FLASHING

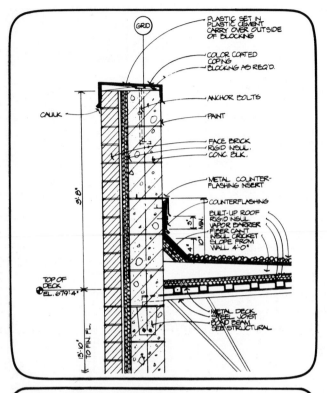

PLASTIC SET IN
PLASTIC CEMENT
CARRY OVER OUTSIDE
OF BLOCKING

GRID

COLOR COATED
COPING
BLOCKING AS REQ'D.

ANCHOR BOLTS

CAULK

PAINT

FACE BRICK
RIGID INSUL.
CONC. BLK.

METAL COUNTER-
FLASHING INSERT

COUNTERFLASHING

BUILT-UP ROOF
RIGID INSUL.
VAPOR BARRIER
FIBER CANT
INSUL. CRICKET
SLOPE FROM
WALL 4'-0"

3'-0"

TOP OF
DECK
EL. 679'-4"

15'-0"
TO FIN. FL.

METAL DECK
STEEL JOIST
BOND BEAM
SEE STRUCTURAL

39 ROOF EDGE

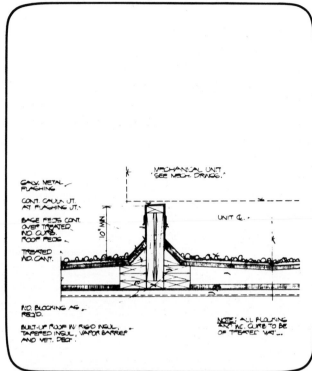

MECHANICAL UNIT
SEE MECH. DRWGS.

GALV. METAL
FLASHING

CONT. CAULK JT.
AT FLASHING JT.

BASE FLGS CONT.
OVER TREATED
WD. CURB.
ROOF FELTS.

UNIT ℄

10" MIN

TREATED
WD. CANT.

WD. BLOCKING AS
REQ'D.

NOTE: ALL FLASHING
ANY WD. CURB TO BE
OF TREATED WD'...

BUILT-UP ROOF W/ RIGID INSUL,
TAPERED INSUL., VAPOR BARRIER
AND MET. DECK.

40 CONTRACTION JOINT

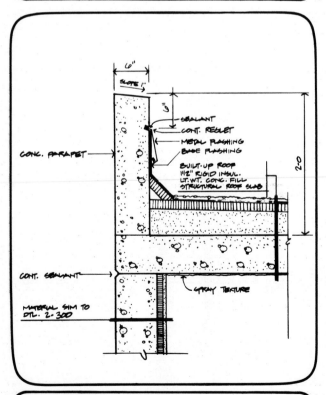

6"

SLOPE 1"

6"

SEALANT

CONT. REGLET

METAL FLASHING

BASE FLASHING

CONC. PARAPET

BUILT-UP ROOF
1½" RIGID INSUL.
LT. WT. CONC. FILL
STRUCTURAL ROOF SLAB

2'-0

CONT. SEALANT

GRAY TEXTURE

MATERIAL SIM. TO
DTL. 2-300

41 ROOF EDGE

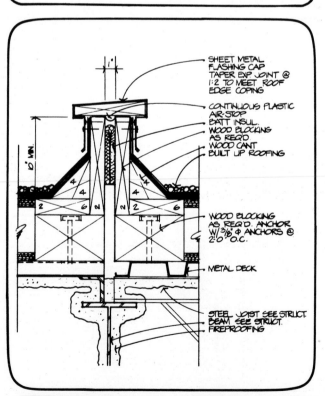

1"

SHEET METAL
FLASHING CAP
TAPER EXP JOINT @
1:2 TO MEET ROOF
EDGE COPING

CONTINUOUS PLASTIC
AIR-STOP
BATT INSUL.
WOOD BLOCKING
AS REQ'D
WOOD CANT
BUILT UP ROOFING

6" MIN

WOOD BLOCKING
AS REQ'D. ANCHOR
W/ ⅜" Ø ANCHORS @
2'-0 O.C.

METAL DECK

STEEL JOIST SEE STRUCT.
BEAM SEE STRUCT.
FIREPROOFING

42 EXPANSION JOINT

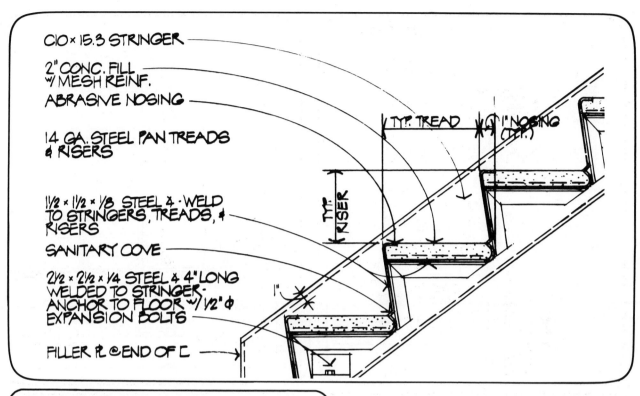

C10 × 15.3 STRINGER

2" CONC. FILL
w/ MESH REINF.

ABRASIVE NOSING

14 GA. STEEL PAN TREADS
& RISERS

1½ × 1½ × ⅛ STEEL ∠ · WELD
TO STRINGERS, TREADS, &
RISERS

SANITARY COVE

2½ × 2½ × ¼ STEEL ∠ 4" LONG
WELDED TO STRINGER ·
ANCHOR TO FLOOR w/ ½" ∅
EXPANSION BOLTS

FILLER ℞ @ END OF ⊏

TYP. TREAD   1" NOSING
                (TYP.)

TYP. RISER

1"

43 STAIR AT BASE

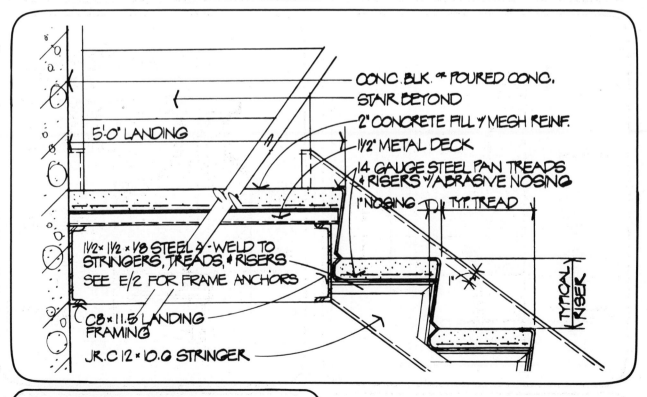

CONC. BLK. or POURED CONC.
STAIR BEYOND

2" CONCRETE FILL w/ MESH REINF.

1½" METAL DECK

14 GAUGE STEEL PAN TREADS
& RISERS w/ ABRASIVE NOSING

1" NOSING   TYP. TREAD

5'-0" LANDING

1½ × 1½ × ⅛ STEEL ∠ · WELD TO
STRINGERS, TREADS & RISERS

SEE E/2 FOR FRAME ANCHORS

C8 × 11.5 LANDING
FRAMING

JR. C 12 × 10.6 STRINGER

1"

TYPICAL RISER

44 STAIR LANDING

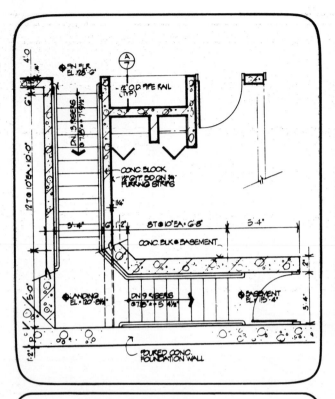

45 STAIR PLAN

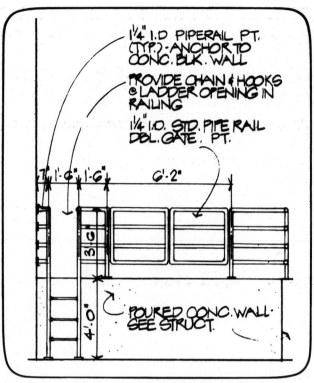

46 LADDER ELEVATION

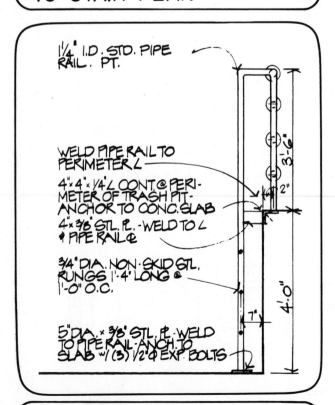

47 LADDER (SIDE)

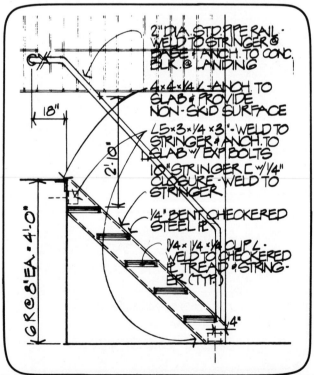

48 STEEL STAIR

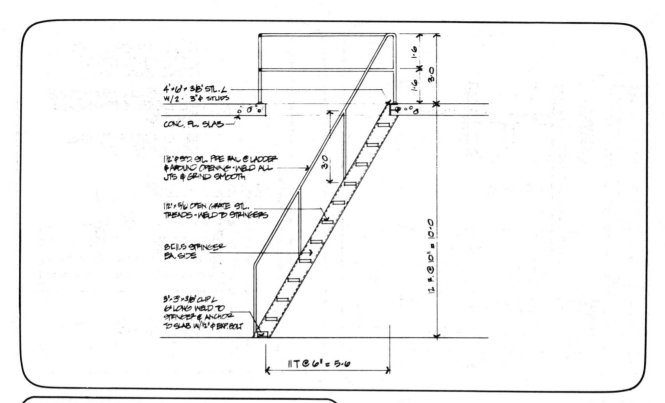

49 SHIPS LADDER

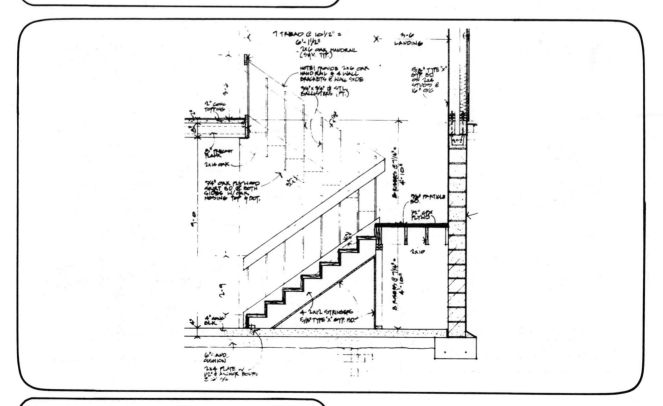

50 WOOD STAIR

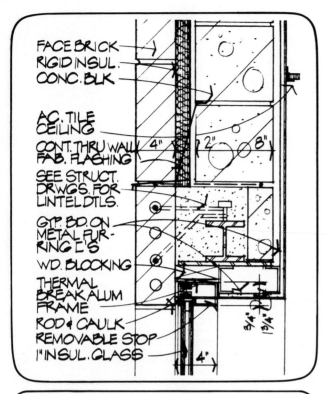

FACE BRICK
RIGID INSUL.
CONC. BLK

A.C. TILE
CEILING
CONT. THRU WALL
FAB. FLASHING
SEE STRUCT.
DRWGS. FOR
LINTEL DTLS.
GYP. BD. ON
METAL FUR-
RING L'S
WD. BLOCKING
THERMAL
BREAK ALUM
FRAME
ROD & CAULK
REMOVABLE STOP
1" INSUL. GLASS

4" 2" 8"

3/4" 1 3/4" 4"

51 WINDOW HEAD

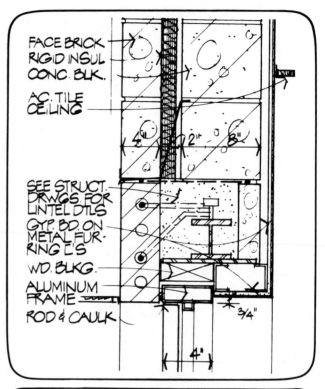

FACE BRICK
RIGID INSUL
CONC. BLK.

A.C. TILE
CEILING

SEE STRUCT.
DRWGS. FOR
LINTEL DTLS
GYP. BD. ON
METAL FUR-
RING L'S
WD. BLKG.
ALUMINUM
FRAME
ROD & CAULK

4" 2" 8"

3/4"

4"

52 DOOR HEAD

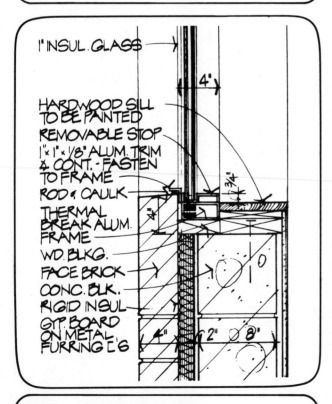

1" INSUL. GLASS

4"

HARDWOOD SILL
TO BE PAINTED
REMOVABLE STOP
1" x 1" x 1/8" ALUM. TRIM
& CONT. - FASTEN
TO FRAME
ROD & CAULK
THERMAL
BREAK ALUM.
FRAME
WD. BLKG.
FACE BRICK
CONC. BLK.
RIGID INSUL
GYP. BOARD
ON METAL
FURRING L'S

3/4"

4"

4" 2" 8"

53 WINDOW SILL

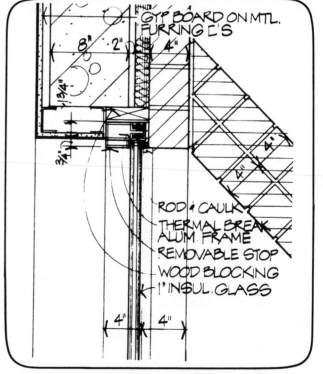

GYP. BOARD ON MTL.
FURRING L'S

8" 2" 4"

1 3/4"

3/4"

4"

4"

ROD & CAULK
THERMAL BREAK
ALUM. FRAME
REMOVABLE STOP
WOOD BLOCKING
1" INSUL. GLASS

4" 4"

54 WINDOW JAMB

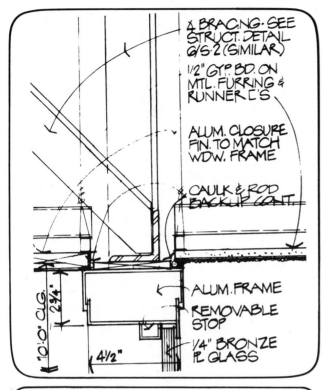

& BRACING · SEE
STRUCT. DETAIL
6/S·2 (SIMILAR)

1/2" GYP. BD. ON
MTL. FURRING &
RUNNER C'S

ALUM. CLOSURE
FIN. TO MATCH
WDW. FRAME

CAULK & ROD
BACKUP CONT.

ALUM. FRAME

REMOVABLE
STOP

1/4" BRONZE
PL. GLASS

10'-0" CLG.
2¾"
4½"

55 WINDOW HEAD

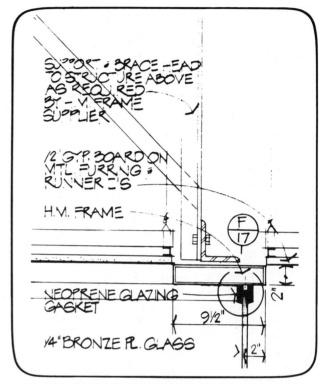

SUPPORT & BRACE HEAD
TO STRUCTURE ABOVE
AS REQUIRED
BY WDW FRAME
SUPPLIER

1/2" GYP. BOARD ON
MTL. FURRING &
RUNNER C'S

H.M. FRAME

F
17

NEOPRENE GLAZING
GASKET

9½"

1/4" BRONZE PL. GLASS

2"
2"

56 WINDOW HEAD

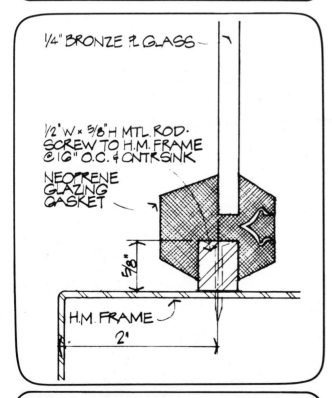

1/4" BRONZE PL. GLASS

1/2" W × 5/8" H MTL. ROD.
SCREW TO H.M. FRAME
@ 16" O.C. & CNTRSINK

NEOPRENE
GLAZING
GASKET

5/8"

H.M. FRAME
2"

57 ZIPPER WALL GASKET

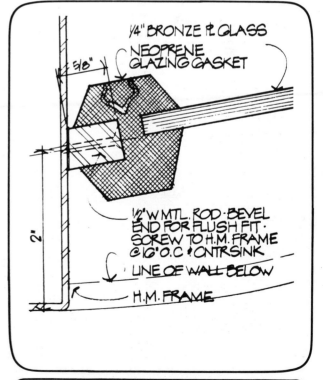

1/4" BRONZE PL. GLASS

NEOPRENE
GLAZING GASKET

5/8"

2"

1/2" W MTL. ROD · BEVEL
END FOR FLUSH FIT ·
SCREW TO H.M. FRAME
@ 16" O.C. & CNTRSINK

LINE OF WALL BELOW

H.M. FRAME

58 GASKET AT JAMB

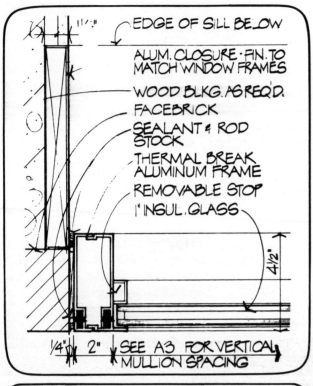

EDGE OF SILL BELOW

ALUM. CLOSURE · FIN. TO MATCH WINDOW FRAMES

WOOD BLKG. AS REQ'D.

FACEBRICK

SEALANT & ROD STOCK

THERMAL BREAK ALUMINUM FRAME

REMOVABLE STOP

1" INSUL. GLASS

4½"

¼" 2" SEE A3 FOR VERTICAL MULLION SPACING

59 WINDOW JAMB

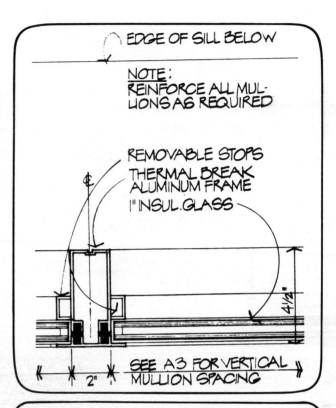

EDGE OF SILL BELOW

NOTE: REINFORCE ALL MUL-LIONS AS REQUIRED

REMOVABLE STOPS

THERMAL BREAK ALUMINUM FRAME

1" INSUL. GLASS

4½"

2" SEE A3 FOR VERTICAL MULLION SPACING

60 WINDOW JAMB

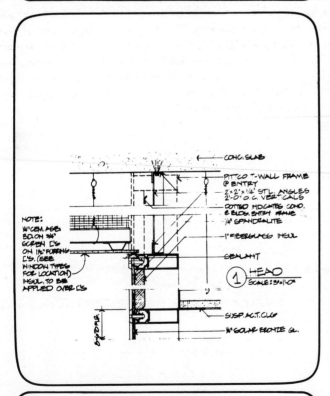

NOTE: ¼" CEM. ASB BD. ON ¾" SCREEN C's ON 1⅝" FURRING C's (SEE WINDOW TYPES FOR LOCATION) INSUL. TO BE APPLIED OVER C's

CONC. SLAB

PITTCO T-WALL FRAME @ ENTRY

2"×2"×¼" ST'L. ANGLES 2'-0" O.C. VERTICALS

DOTTED INDICATES COND. @ BLDG. ENTRY FRAME

¼" SPANDRALITE

1" FIBERGLASS INSUL.

SEALANT

① HEAD SCALE: 3"=1'-0"

SUSP. AC.T. CLG.

¼" SOLAR BRONZE GL.

61 WINDOW HEAD

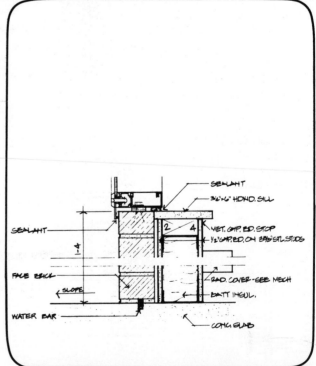

SEALANT

3½"×6" HDWD. SILL

MET. GYP. BD. STOP

½" GYP. BD. ON 3⅝" ST'L STUDS

RAD. COVER - SEE MECH.

BATT INSUL.

SEALANT

2   4

FACE BRICK

SLOPE

WATER BAR

CONC. SLAB

62 WINDOW SILL

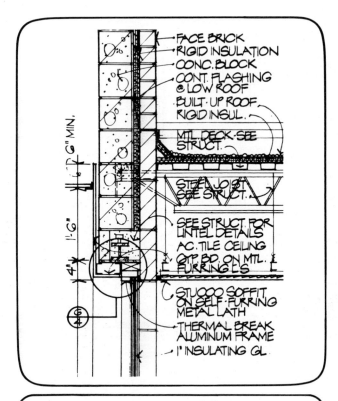

FACE BRICK
RIGID INSULATION
CONC. BLOCK
CONT. FLASHING @ LOW ROOF
BUILT-UP ROOF RIGID INSUL.
MTL. DECK-SEE STRUCT.
STEEL JOIST SEE STRUCT.
SEE STRUCT FOR LINTEL DETAILS
AC. TILE CEILING
GYP. BD. ON MTL. FURRING Ls
STUCCO SOFFIT ON SELF-FURRING METAL LATH
THERMAL BREAK ALUMINUM FRAME
1" INSULATING GL.

63 WINDOW HEAD

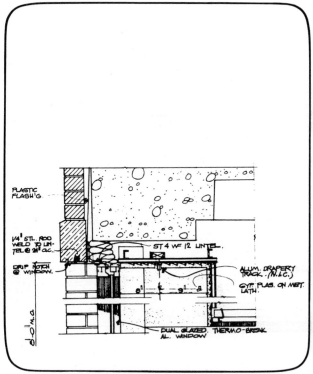

PLASTIC FLASH'G
¼" STL. ROD WELD TO LINTEL @ 24" O.C.
DRIP NOTCH @ WINDOW.
ST 4 WF 12 LINTEL
ALUM. DRAPERY TRACK. (N.I.C.)
GYP. PLAS. ON MET. LATH.
DUAL GLAZED, THERMO-BREAK AL. WINDOW

64 WINDOW HEAD

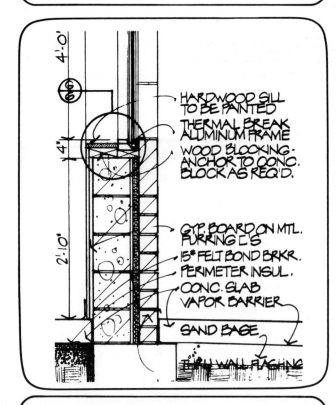

HARDWOOD SILL TO BE PAINTED
THERMAL BREAK ALUMINUM FRAME
WOOD BLOCKING. ANCHOR TO CONC. BLOCK AS REQ'D.
GYP. BOARD ON MTL. FURRING Ls
15# FELT BOND BRKR.
PERIMETER INSUL.
CONC. SLAB
VAPOR BARRIER
SAND BASE
THRU WALL FLASHING

65 WINDOW SILL

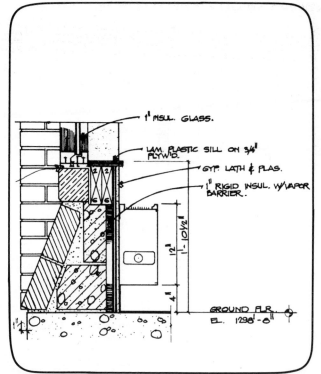

1" INSUL. GLASS.
LAM. PLASTIC SILL ON ¾" PLYW'D.
GYP. LATH & PLAS.
1" RIGID INSUL. W/VAPOR BARRIER.
GROUND FLR. EL. 1298'-8"

66 WINDOW SILL

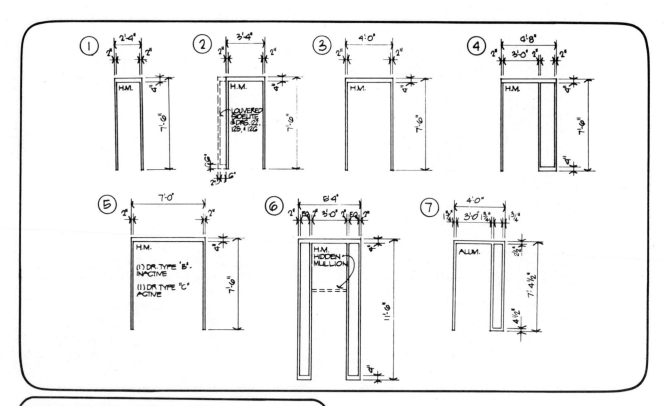

67 DOOR FRAMES

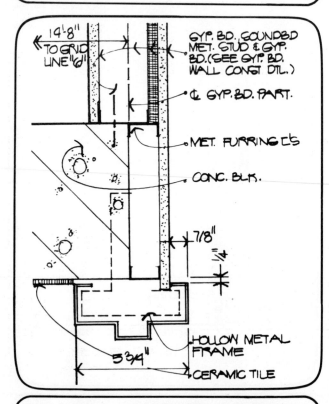

68 HOLLOW METAL FRAME

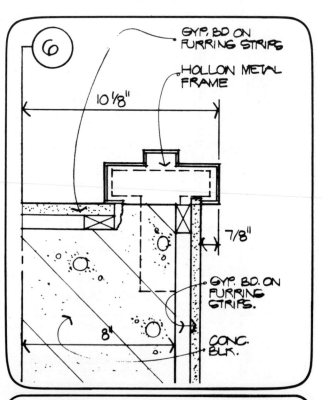

69 HOLLOW METAL FRAME

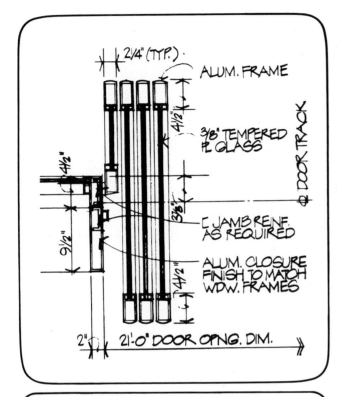

2¼" (TYP.)
ALUM. FRAME
4½"
3/8" TEMPERED PL GLASS
Ⓒ DOOR TRACK
4½"
3/8"
9½"
C JAMB REINF. AS REQUIRED
4½"
ALUM. CLOSURE FINISH TO MATCH WDW. FRAMES
2"
21'-0" DOOR OPNG. DIM.

70 FOLDING DOOR PLAN

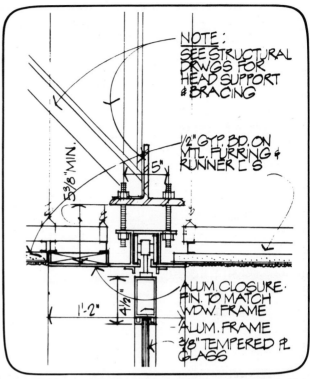

NOTE: SEE STRUCTURAL DRWGS FOR HEAD SUPPORT & BRACING

½" GYP. BD. ON MTL. FURRING & RUNNER C'S

5⅜" MIN

5"

ALUM. CLOSURE. FIN. TO MATCH WDW. FRAME
ALUM. FRAME
3/8" TEMPERED PL GLASS

1'-2"

4½"

71 SLIDING DOOR AT HEAD

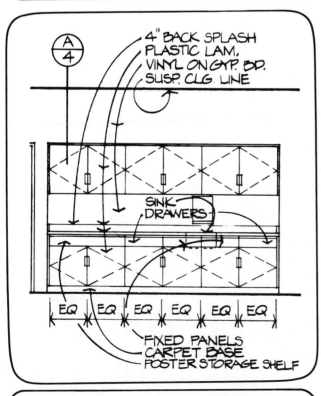

A/4

4" BACK SPLASH PLASTIC LAM.
VINYL ON GYP. BD.
SUSP. CLG. LINE

SINK DRAWERS

EQ | EQ | EQ | EQ | EQ | EQ

FIXED PANELS
CARPET BASE
POSTER STORAGE SHELF

72 CABINET ELEVATION

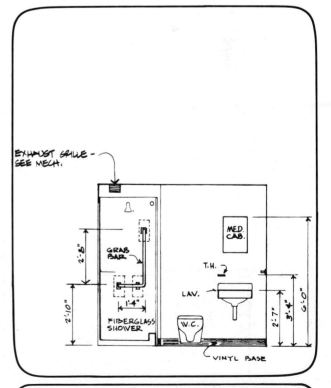

EXHAUST GRILLE – SEE MECH.

MED. CAB.

2'-8"

GRAB BAR

T.H.

LAV.

2'-10"

1'-4"

FIBERGLASS SHOWER

W.C.

VINYL BASE

2'-7"

3'-4"

6'-0"

73 TOILET ELEVATION

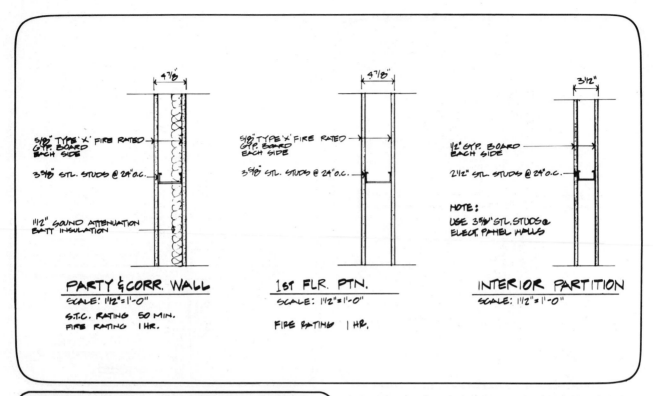

5/8" TYPE 'X' FIRE RATED
GYP. BOARD
EACH SIDE

3 5/8" STL. STUDS @ 24" O.C.

1 1/2" SOUND ATTENUATION
BATT INSULATION

4 7/8"

PARTY & CORR. WALL
SCALE: 1 1/2" = 1'-0"

S.T.C. RATING   50 MIN.
FIRE RATING   1 HR.

5/8" TYPE 'X' FIRE RATED
GYP. BOARD
EACH SIDE

3 5/8" STL. STUDS @ 24" O.C.

4 7/8"

1ST FLR. PTN.
SCALE: 1 1/2" = 1'-0"

FIRE RATING   1 HR.

1/2" GYP. BOARD
EACH SIDE

2 1/2" STL. STUDS @ 24" O.C.

NOTE:
USE 3 5/8" STL. STUDS @
ELECT. PANEL WALLS

3 1/2"

INTERIOR PARTITION
SCALE: 1 1/2" = 1'-0"

74 PLAN OF INTERIOR WALLS

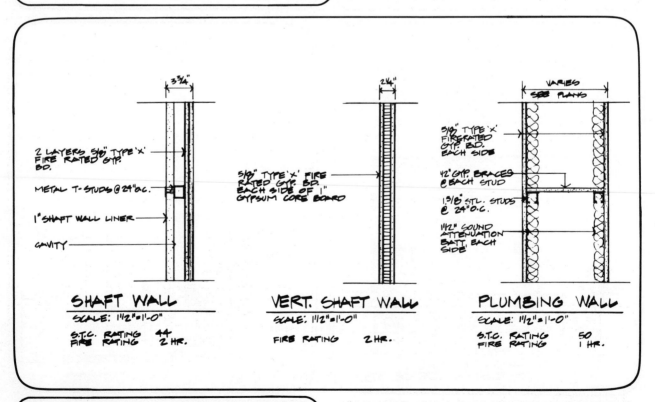

2 LAYERS 5/8" TYPE 'X'
FIRE RATED GYP.
BD.

METAL T-STUDS @ 24" O.C.

1" SHAFT WALL LINER

CAVITY

3 3/4"

SHAFT WALL
SCALE: 1 1/2" = 1'-0"

S.T.C. RATING   44
FIRE RATING   2 HR.

5/8" TYPE 'X' FIRE
RATED GYP. BD.
EACH SIDE OF 1"
GYPSUM CORE BOARD

2 1/4"

VERT. SHAFT WALL
SCALE: 1 1/2" = 1'-0"

FIRE RATING   2 HR.

5/8" TYPE 'X'
FIRE RATED
GYP. BD.
EACH SIDE

1/2" GYP. BRACES
@ EACH STUD

1 5/8" STL. STUDS
@ 24" O.C.

1 1/2" SOUND
ATTENUATION
BATT. EACH
SIDE

VARIES
SEE PLANS

PLUMBING WALL
SCALE: 1 1/2" = 1'-0"

S.T.C. RATING   50
FIRE RATING   1 HR.

75 PLAN OF INTERIOR WALLS

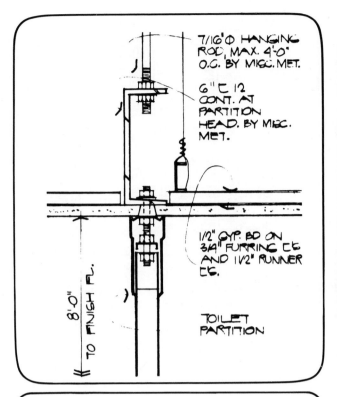

7/16" Ø HANGING ROD, MAX. 4'-0" O.C. BY MISC. MET.

6" C 12 CONT. AT PARTITION HEAD. BY MISC. MET.

1/2" GYP. BD ON 3/4" FURRING CS AND 1 1/2" RUNNER CS.

TOILET PARTITION

8'-0" TO FINISH FL.

76 TOILET PARTITION HEAD

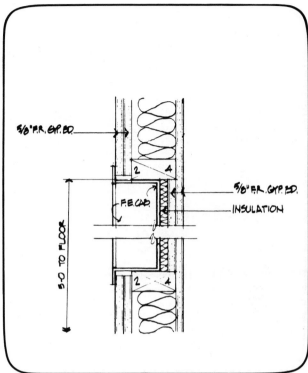

5/8" F.R. GYP. BD.

5/8" F.R. GYP. BD.

INSULATION

F.E. CAB.

5'-0 TO FLOOR

2   4

2   4

77 FIRE EXTINGUISHER CAB.

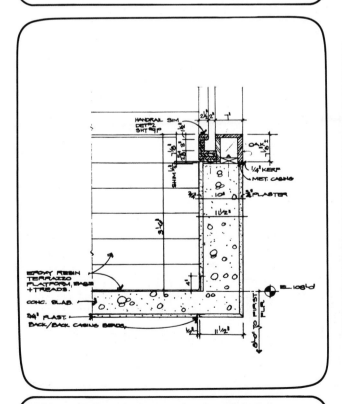

HANDRAIL SIM DET. SHT 91P

2 1/2" 2"   1"

OAK

1/4" KERF MET. CASING

3/4" PLASTER

1 1/2"

3'-2"

EPOXY RESIN TERRAZZO PLATFORM, BASE + TREADS.

CONC. SLAB.

3/4" PLAST. BACK/BACK CASING BEADS

EL. 108'-0"

TO FIRST FLR.

1/2"   1 1/2"

78 HANDRAIL AT LANDING

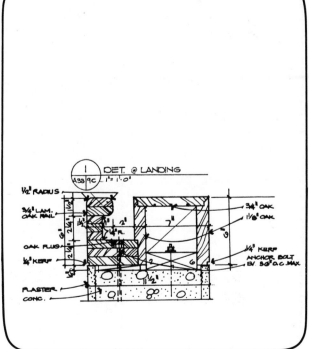

1   DET. @ LANDING
A38 91C   1" = 1'-0"

1/2" RADIUS

3/4" LAM. OAK RAIL

OAK PLUG

1/4" KERF

PLASTER

CONC.

3/4" OAK

1 1/8" OAK

1/4" KERF ANCHOR BOLT BY 36" O.C. MAX.

7"

79 HANDRAIL BLOW UP

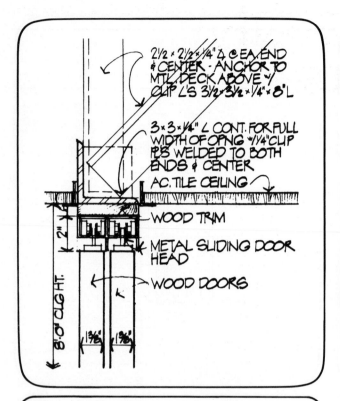

2½ × 2½ × ¼" ∠ @ EA. END & CENTER · ANCHOR TO MTL. DECK ABOVE W/ CLIP ∠'S 3½ × 3½ × ¼" × 8' L

3 × 3 × ¼" ∠ CONT. FOR FULL WIDTH OF OP'NG W/ ¼" CLIP R'S WELDED TO BOTH ENDS & CENTER

AC. TILE CEILING

WOOD TRIM

METAL SLIDING DOOR HEAD

WOOD DOORS

2"

8'·0" CL. HT.

1⅜" 1⅜"

80 SLIDING DOOR HEAD

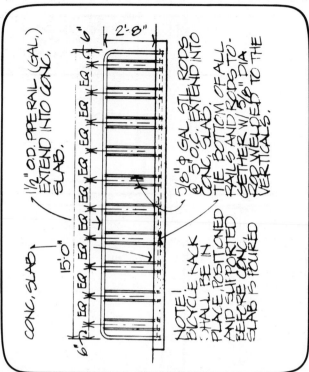

2'·8"

6"

1½" O.D. PIPE RAIL (GAL.) EXTEND INTO CONC. SLAB.

5/8" ∅ GAL. ST'L RODS @ 5" O.C. EXTEND INTO CONC. SLAB.

TIE BOTTOM OF ALL RAILS AND RODS TO-GETHER W/ 5/8" DIA. ROD WELDED TO THE VERTICALS.

CONC. SLAB.

15'·0"

EQ EQ EQ EQ EQ EQ EQ EQ EQ EQ EQ

6"

NOTE! BICYCLE RACK SHALL BE IN PLACE. POSITIONED AND SUPPORTED BEFORE CONC. SLAB IS POURED

81 BICYCLE RACK

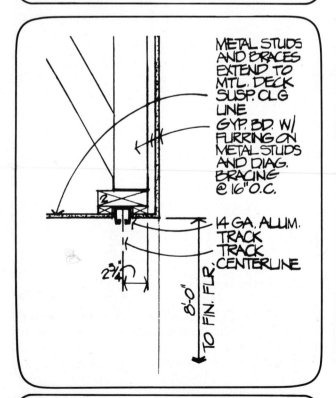

METAL STUDS AND BRACES EXTEND TO MTL. DECK SUSP. CLG LINE

GYP. BD. W/ FURRING ON METAL STUDS AND DIAG. BRACING @ 16" O.C.

14 GA. ALUM. TRACK

TRACK CENTERLINE

2¾"

8'·0" TO FIN. FLR.

82 FOLDING PARTITION HEAD

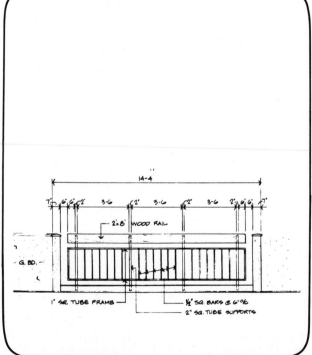

14-4

7" 6" 6" 2"   3-6   2"   3-6   2"   3-6   2" 6" 6" 7"

2×8" WOOD RAIL

G. BD.

1" SQ. TUBE FRAME

½" SQ. BARS @ 6" O.C.

2" SQ. TUBE SUPPORTS

83 HANDRAIL ELEVATION

THREE

PRODUCTION OF WORKING DRAWINGS

A definite system has been established for producing a well-ordered set of working drawings. The order generally follows the pattern in which a building project is constructed. If it is possible to summarize this logical progression of steps, it would be that the drawings show the building from the ground up and in progressively more detail.

By the time a job reaches the stage of working drawings, a considerable amount of groundwork has been laid to come up with the design-development package. The building has been designed by the architect and accepted by the owner. The site plan has been detailed to the point of showing all roads and parking. The exact building location is known, and any changes in grade have been calculated. The floor plans have been drawn to scale, and wall thicknesses and materials have been indicated. The exterior building elevations are drawn to scale showing windows, doors, and materials.

The design-development set commonly includes several wall sections through portions of the building to represent the wall conditions and interior space. The design package is actually the last document that an architect specifically prepares for a client's information. Thus, the drawings are accurate but not technically or fully detailed. The working drawing phase follows the intent of the design-development package, but it is technical in nature and gives all information needed for construction.

Architectural working drawings can be placed in five main categories. It is mandatory that each section be keyed to the next. The five categories are exterior plans, architectural plans, architectural elevations, architectural sections, and architectural details.

• **Exterior plans** (Generally shown in an engineer's scale) The exterior plans show the site conditions and the location of the building system within the construction limits.

• **Architectural plans** ($1/8'' = 1'$ - $0''$ is the standard scale used but some special plans may warrant $1/16'' = 1'$-$0''$, as in the case of a very large plan without much detail; or $1/4'' = 1'$-$0''$, as in the case of a highly detailed area such as plans for a small building or a residence.) The architectural plans show every floor area. They are the main set of working drawings, and most other groups are keyed from them.

• **Architectural elevations** (Usually the same scale as the plan, typically $1/8'' = 1'$-$0''$) Architectural elevations show the exterior of the building and indicate the proportion of windows, doors, etc. If the architectural plans are the best source of information, the elevations contain the least amount of material. They are necessary, certainly, but mainly as a key to other details.

• **Architectural sections** (Generally the same scale as the floor plans) Architectural sections are typically cut through the most complex areas in a building to show the relationship of spaces. As in exterior elevations, few dimensions except the floor-to-floor heights are shown on the building sections.

• **Architectural details** (The scale of detail drawings ranges from $1/2'' = 1'$-$0''$ to $3'' = 1'$-$0''$, usually starting at a small scale of the whole detail and progressing to a larger-scale drawing of a portion of the detail.) The architectural details are either blow-up drawings of plans or sections of conditions shown in another group at a smaller scale. Architectural details spell out exactly how a difficult portion of the building is to be constructed.

The intent of an architect's working drawings is simply to tell a contractor exactly how to build. The drawings make up the major part of the contract between the owner and the contractor. Any error in the plans becomes a flaw in the contract. Obviously, then, drawings with insufficient details can cause the owner and contractor real problems, while too much detail results in a waste of time and money for the architect.

By the time a project has passed through schematics and design development, the design concept has been firmly established, and the working drawings are the technical details that reflect the design of the building. The ideal design-development package is so finely detailed that there can be no question about the intent of the design during the working drawings. However, many technical questions about design are raised in working drawings. In reality, the design phase ends only when the job goes out for bid.

The following is a system for laying out working drawings. Although it is fairly standard in most architectural firms, the system adopted by individual offices may vary slightly.

The first sheet in a set of working drawings is the *title and index.* It usually contains the full project title and address (in press-on letters) and the numerical list of the architectural, structural, mechanical, and electrical drawings bound in the set.

The usual procedure is to label the architectural sheets A-1, A-2, etc.; the structural sheets S-1, S-2, etc.; with the mechanical (M-1) and electrical (E-1) sets following suit. Any special sheets such as large and complex kitchen-equipment layouts (K-1, K-2, etc.) or an extremely detailed curtain wall (W-1, W-2, etc.) are typically given separate letters on very large jobs. The size of the job determines if the first sheet is to contain more than just the title and index.

The next sheet in the set is the *site survey,* provided by the owner. It must be prepared and signed by a registered land surveyor. (It is the only drawing in the architectural set that is not directly supervised and signed by the architect.) The survey contains all physical data on the site as the contractor would find it before the project is begun. Some of the features necessary on this drawing are

Existing streets and walks	Utilities (sewer, water, gas)
Power lines	Easements through the property
Existing topography	
Fences	Location of existing buildings
Property lines	
Trees (size and type)	Bench marks

If an architect wants to ensure receipt of all necessary data, a checklist of required information is usually sent to the surveyor. The architect uses the material received from the surveyor to make a prime technical decision in the working drawings—that of where to place the building and what grading should be done. Although this sheet is not changed from the way it is received from the surveyor, it is the base for all remaining site details. The survey is included in the package of construction documents because many state laws require it and because it allows the contractor to check existing site conditions, along with the soil-boring data that is bound in the specifications.

The survey drawing does not include the building location or any other proposed building that, at the time of bid opening, does not exist on the site. Generally the survey is drawn at an engineer's scale rather than an architectural scale (the range is from 1″ = 10′ to 1″ = 100′, with 1″ = 50′ being most common). The scale depends on the size of the site (if the site will fit on the drawing sheet) and the complexity of the existing site details.

SITE PLANS

The *site plan* (or *plot plan*) is next in order. It contains much of the same information shown on the survey, but it includes the total amount of planned changes. The exact building location is given, all roads and walks are detailed, any proposed changes in grade are indicated, and miscellaneous exterior details are located.

The building is dimensioned not only from the boundary but also from the up-and-down level of the first floor, which is given in relation to a bench mark. The distance from the boundary to the building must be given exactly so that the contractor has no questions. If a grid system has been established on the floor plan, it becomes fairly easy to indicate the distance from the boundary lines to grids ① and Ⓐ. Grids ① and Ⓐ should then be shown on the site plan. If grids are not used, two perpendicular exterior walls should be dimensioned from the boundary. A further safeguard is to indicate in a large wall detail on a later drawing the exact point on the wall to which the dimension was run.

The purpose of dimensioning the building is to pinpoint a major corner, not to run dimension strings to every nook and cranny of the building. Once this corner has been located on the site, the contractor can refer to the floor plans for further dimensions.

One problem arises in locating only the corner of a building. If the two boundaries from which the dimensions are run are not at right angles to each other, which wall is to be parallel to the boundary? If this situation arises, either a note indicating the wall to be parallel or two dimensions from the boundary to the wall at opposite ends is sufficient. In the case of a circular building, the radius points are generally dimensioned from the boundary lines.

North arrows should be shown on all the exterior plans. If a major axis of the building does not run exactly north-south, two north arrows are shown on each plan. One arrow points to "true north" (and is so marked), while the other runs parallel to the closest north-south axis of the building and is marked "assumed north." This leaves no confusion as to which side of the building is north, because the assumed-north arrow properly orients the building. Most offices adopt a standard north arrow that incorporates both true north and assumed north.

Once the building has been located, roads and walks can be dimensioned either from exterior walls or from the boundary lines, whichever is easier. The width of every road and walk must be indicated, along with the material and its thickness—for example, 4″ concrete or 2″ crushed granite gravel.

When roads meet at a 90° angle, they generally are curved by including a quarter circle between the lines. This circle is given on the drawing by indicating the radius of the curve, for example, 15′ radius. Generally, a hard-surface road is accompanied by a curb or integral curb and gutter. It is necessary to detail the curb in section, and so the site plan should include the detail bubble through each curb.

One of the most difficult problems in site work is the topography. If the grades are to be changed, the topographic lines are the only means of indicating this change to the contractor. To avoid confusion, the existing topographic lines are dotted, and the proposed grade changes are shown solid. Some reasons for changing the grade are to provide drainage, allow a better movement of vehicles and pedestrian traffic, and to provide a good place for the building to be located.

The contour lines represent the elevation of the site at every point. Every place along a particular contour line is at the same elevation. Contours 314′ and 316′ indicate by their spacing that the ground between them is going uphill 2′. The closer the contour lines are together, the steeper the slope. The accuracy to which the site is to be graded will determine the horizontal increment chosen for the contour.

If the grade around a building requires precision, the draftsman will probably show the location of every 1′ change in grade, while the grading of a large, relatively flat area could require showing only every 5′ or 10′ contour. For accuracy, most architects require that the survey data received from the owner show contours every 2′ on the site plan, except around the building, which usually is broken into 1′ increments.

Contour numbers refer to the number of feet the point is above sea level. It is a common practice to drop the first digit or the first two digits of the elevation. Thus, if the actual height above sea level of a site in Denver is 5156′, the contour number could be shortened to elevation 156′ or just 56′. Obviously, care must be taken in reducing the elevation number. If the Denver site changes more than 100′, a two-digit number could cause the contractor some difficulty in reading because two contours 100′ apart would have the same number. In all cases, the contours must be related to a known elevation that could not possibly be moved or disturbed during construction. This is referred to as a *bench mark*. It could be an x on a large boulder, the top of a fire hydrant, or a spike driven partially into a power pole. This is the starting point for the survey and the reference key for determining the floor elevations.

To simplify the whole system, some architects select a first-floor elevation of 100′-0″ and adjust the bench-mark reading accordingly. This allows the floor elevations to be in more readable dimensions. The fourth floor of a building using a first-floor elevation of 100′-0″ would be at 139′-0″ if each floor-to-floor height is 13′-0″. If the same building uses the actual sea-level elevation, the first floor could be at 1281′-9″, and the fourth floor would be 1320′-9″.

In addition to the ground elevation, a site plan must also show the elevations of walks and roads. In most cases, a contour every foot is not accurate enough to show the grade of a road, and so the topography lines are supplemented by spot elevations.

Several rules for establishing contours must be followed to produce a workable site plan:

1. Always slope the grade away from the building for proper drainage.
2. Even though the contours are being changed, they must remain at the same point at all

boundary lines so the grade of adjacent properties remains unchanged.

3. If the natural drainage of water occurs through the site from adjacent property, it must be allowed to continue through the site.

4. Low points on a site that have no natural run-off should not be created (unless storm sewer drainage is provided).

5. A numerical progression of contour lines is necessary at 2' intervals; for example, 214' must be adjacent to 212' before 210' can occur.

6. Existing trees cannot be expected to survive if the contours around them are changed.

7. Roads and walks should be given at least a minimum slope for drainage that must lead to a system designed to take the water away.

A variety of additional miscellaneous items are normally included in the site plan, all pertaining to physical features on the site that the architect intends to change, build, or protect. Since this is the only group of drawings that shows the total land area to be developed, all exterior details should be shown, including items such as flagpoles, benches, fountains, and new plantings (trees, bushes, grass).

Site drawings should also contain notes about protecting certain existing items on the site from damage during construction, ranging from trees to buildings. While the soil-boring data are generally contained in the specifications, the location of the boring and its number is indicated on the site plan for the contractor's reference. Similarly, if trees are to be removed or buildings demolished, it is noted on the site plan.

The contractor is allowed a reasonable area around the building for storing materials and equipment and for access to the project. Some building sites are so large that the area of the land is in great excess of the "reasonable area" for storage. In this event, the owner can establish construction limits to keep the contractor's activities to the proximity of the project. These limits are shown on the site plan and lie anywhere within the owner's property line. It simply means that the contractor should restrict activities to the confines of the construction limits.

Either an engineering or an architectural scale is used for the site plan. The size of the site and its degree of complexity determines the scale. An engineering scale could be 1" = 60', 1" = 50', or 1" = 40'. An architectural scale is usually $^1/_{16}$" = 1'-0" or $^1/_{32}$" = 1'-0".

It might be necessary to go one step further in developing the exterior plans and include a *roof plan*. This plan, as the title implies, shows the layout of all penthouses, mechanical stacks, roof drains, scuppers (overflows for rain on the roof), control joints, and various equipment on the roof. The plan is usually drawn at a scale larger than the site plan but smaller than the floor plans. Because the roof plan is larger than the site plan it can include a greater degree of detail of the site around the building. Thus, it can double as a site detail sheet. It could dimension roads (making it unnecessary to do so on the site plan), detail planters, and show grading, steps, and ramps. The usual scale for this plan is $^1/_{16}$" = 1'-0".

Many variations are employed in presenting the site information. One architect may elect to place the topographic data (the information received from the surveyor), the site details, and the roof plan all in one drawing. (This would be a fairly small project and would probably be drawn at $^1/_8$" = 1'-0".) A large project with a complex site could warrant a survey sheet, a site-plan sheet, a layout for the street parking lot, a grading plan, a roof plan, and several exterior-detail sheets. A project with a comparable cost but relatively simple site conditions could be done with two sheets. The exterior plan serves two purposes. First, it shows the contractor what the site is like before the project is started. Second, it spells out exactly what the contractor must do to complete the contract. A single site drawing may be adequate for one job, while six architectural sheets may be required for another. The rule of thumb is to give the contractor accurate and complete information without repetition. (This rule applies to the entire set of working drawings.)

The first group of drawings establishes a recognizable pattern. The system of graphic presentation starts on the broadest level and progresses to the most complete detail. The group of exterior plans differs from the others in that it is more self-contained. The majority of the site details are kept within this group rather than keyed to other areas in the set.

The last drawing in this set, the roof plan, is generally at half the scale of the floor plans. The transition between this plan and the larger-scale floor plans flows quite easily.

A final rule for the site-plan sheets—and for all plan sheets—is to determine the best direction north can point on the sheet. North may point down if this is the best orientation. Do not change the direction the plan faces on any subsequent plan sheets. When north points the same direction on all plan sheets, proper orientation is much easier on every plan in the set.

Another logical pattern for the assembly of drawings is to follow the order in which the contractor accomplishes construction. Obviously, the site must be roughly developed before construction begins. Thus, the first group of drawings in this method would also be the site plan.

ARCHITECTURAL FLOOR PLANS

Architectural floor plans are the most important group in the working drawings because they dimension all walls and act as a key to the remainder of the set. Major items shown on the floor plans include make-up of walls, doors, rooms, stairways, windows, and spaces for special equipment.

The material, location, and thickness of all walls in the project are dimensioned. The material is hatched, the location of the walls is dimensioned to other walls or to a grid line, and the overall thickness of each wall in the project is dimensioned.

Doors and rooms are numbered. The first-floor rooms are 100 numbers, second-floor rooms are 200 numbers, etc. Room numbers are started in the upper left-hand corner of the building and progress from left to right and from top to bottom. Every corridor, janitor's closet, and toilet is assigned a room number so that it can be referred to without confusion.

Most architects relate the door numbers to the room numbers. The usual procedure is to assign the door the same number as the room into which it swings. If there is more than one door opening into a room, an alphabetical designation is used along with the room number. The only general exception to this system is that an out-swinging exterior door is assigned the number of the room from which it swings because the exterior space has no number. If room 151 has three doors swinging in, they are labeled 151A, 151B, and 151C. Each member of a pair of doors is given the abbreviation "PR." and a number (and a letter if more than one pair enters into the room). The swing of the door is indicated on the plan by a quarter circle with a line drawn from the hinge point to the circle, with the door number printed along the line.

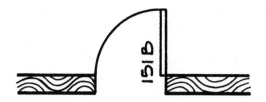

This door number is then keyed back to a door schedule later in the set. The schedule then defines the specific details of each door.

Another way to handle the doors shown on the plan is to eliminate the door number and substitute a three-part identification code in its place. The first part indicates the size of the door frame. The second specifies the type of door, and the third specifies the hardware. This code eliminates the door schedule, which is why some architects choose this concept. The code is then identified in the drawings.

Several items should be taken into account when locating doors:

1. The door frame must be designed to fit the wall.
2. The door and frame must comply with the building code.
3. The door swing should not interfere with either pedestrian circulation or equipment location.
4. An adequate wall space needs to be provided adjacent to the door so that it may remain in an open position without blocking other access.

Stairways are shown on the plan with their treads, landings, and handrails drawn to scale. Because there is no third dimension on the plan, it is necessary to indicate whether a stairway is going in an upward or downward direction from the floor. Thus, the stair is marked with an arrow, and "up" or "down" is placed after the arrow. Stairs are assigned letters of the alphabet (stair A, stair B, etc.) to differentiate them from room numbers. This system differs from room numbers in that stair A is labeled "A" on the first floor, the second floor, etc., for as high as the stair runs.

It is difficult to detail and dimension stairs properly at ⅛″ = 1′-0″. They are generally keyed to a ¼″ = 1′-0″ detail in the architectural details. The walls surrounding the stair are located on the floor plan, but the actual dimensioning of the stair is done on the larger-scale drawing.

An accepted standard for laying out a floor plan is to follow a *grid* that is determined by running imaginary lines through each structural column. The structural engineer on the job makes every effort to space the structural system uniformly for ease of fabrication, also allowing the grids to be evenly spaced.

A good system to follow is to number the grids along the top of the sheet starting from the left, and to letter the grids along the side of the sheet starting from the top. Establishing a grid system may not work for every building, but it does provide an excellent system of orientation if it can be adopted. The grids are dimensioned on the sheet, which allows the walls of the building to be dimensioned from each grid rather than from another wall. (This eliminates many dimension strings and saves time.) Grids in a building should be run from the lowest floor to the top floor so that the point formed by the intersection of grids D and 14 would be at the same spot on every floor. The use of grid lines is not limited to square or rectangular buildings. Grid lines can work with any project that has a fairly uniform structural system.

Window patterns are shown and dimensioned in the walls on the plan. At the ⅛″ scale in which the typical floor plan is drawn, little more than basic dimensions can be shown. Floor plans are drawn to show a view looking down at the building after a cut was made through all walls. The cut is parallel to and about 3′ above the floor. When the slice is made through the window, the jamb and mullions are shown in section, and the sill is shown in plan.

The general system used in dimensioning windows is to give the overall window-opening size. In the case of brick or block construction, the abbreviation "M.O." (masonry opening) is given after the window dimensions. A secondary dimension string is then run to the centerline of mullion to the centerline of mullion spacing. This system is usually not complete enough to give a contractor all the necessary information, and so it is keyed to a detail (possibly a plan and elevation) ¼″ = 1′-0″ or larger which is located later in the set. Most buildings have window patterns that repeat many times throughout the plan, and so it is not necessary to detail and dimension every window if it is apparent they are the same. This is particularly true in curtain-wall construction, where repetition is not only common but necessary. A good system that is used to inform the contractor of similar window units is to assign a letter to each window panel so that equal window patterns have the same letter. The general notes for the windows on the plan could include the type of glass and the material and finish of the window frame.

The amount of equipment and degree of detail in a *toilet room* make it difficult to show at the standard floor-plan scale. For this reason, toilet rooms are usually keyed over to a ¼″ = 1′-0″ enlarged plan that can show more detail. The overall floor plan shows lavatories and counters, water closets, urinals, floor drains, and toilet partitions. Since the entire plan will be drawn at a larger scale, it is not necessary to dimension the equipment on the small-scale plan. The toilet-partition doors do not need to be numbered. They are part of a manufactured product, and the specifications on toilet partitions cover all the necessary items.

It is economical to cluster toilet rooms. A larger-scale plan generally encompasses an entire cluster of rooms, such as mens' and womens' toilets, lounges, and janitors' closets.

Areas that might possibly have an excessive amount of water on the floor (such as the toilet room) are best provided with a floor drain and a slightly sloped floor. The floor drain is indicated by drawing a small circle and putting the abbreviation "F.D." next to it. The slope is indicated by drawing a line from each of the four corners of the sloped area to the floor drain. A note indicating the amount of slope is usually included, such as "slope floor ½″ per foot to drain."

The space for mechanical and electrical equipment is shown on the floor plan but generally is not detailed except for special conditions that must be taken into consideration by the general contractor. Rooms for mechanical equipment can contain the boiler, electrical transformers, telephone equipment, and water heaters, to name a few. Unless special provisions such as a raised concrete floor slab or a floor drain are required, the room is simply given a name, such as "transformer vault" or "boiler room," and a number.

If a mechanical duct shaft is passing through one floor slab to the next, the floor plan shows the duct in section. This is indicated on the plan by drawing a line from each corner of the shaft, forming an X. Heating equipment located on the floor, such as radiators or floor grills, are drawn on the plan.

Items either attached to or recessed into a wall generally are shown and labeled on the plan, showing their location in relation to the floor plan.

The mounting height, however, must be either noted or detailed in an interior wall elevation. Typical equipment in this category includes drinking fountains, fire extinguishers, clocks, chalkboards, mop hook strips (in janitors' closets), and coat racks.

Although the architect-owner contract does not usually include equipment or furniture, some special or built-in equipment, such as basketball bleachers or laboratory tables, may be included and drawn on the plan to show location. Other equipment, such as a vending machine, may be drawn on the plan even though it is not included in the contract, in order to show the contractor where to locate the electrical outlet and water supply. Such equipment is drawn on the plan with the abbreviation "N.I.C." (not in contract) next to the equipment's name.

If something special occurs on the ceiling above the floor plan, it is not going to be shown on the plan. Items such as a canopy, a roof overhang on the exterior, a change in ceiling height, a balcony edge, or a skylight in the interior, however, can be located in relation to the plan by dotting the boundary line and noting on the floor plan that the item will be further detailed later in the set.

Construction features of items located close to the outside of the building can be indicated on the floor plan, along with all items and material within the confines of the building. Walks, ramps, drives, and light poles have been indicated on the site plan, but the scale of the floor plan allows them to be shown in greater detail. This also permits the draftsman to indicate any relationship between interior and exterior details, such as showing that sidewalk scoring joints line up with window mullions. One important point to keep in mind is that the area shown outside of the building should correspond with the floor level shown. Exterior walks and roads shown on the plan for the third floor would only be confusing.

It is not uncommon to find that, because of size, the building does not fit on one sheet when it is drawn at ⅛″ = 1′-0″. Two options are open: Either reduce the scale of the plan to ¹/₁₆″ = 1′-0″, or divide each floor into parts and draw the parts at ⅛″ = 1′-0″. Of the two solutions, the more standard approach is to divide the building and draw it at ⅛″ = 1′-0″. To eliminate confusion caused by showing parts of the building on different sheets, orientation is usually aided by placing a key plan on the lower right corner of each sheet. The key plan is a very small plan (not more than 2 or 3 inches square) which shows the total building project. The portion of the building that is drawn at ⅛″ = 1′-0″ on the sheet is then shaded in on the key plan.

Floor materials generally are not shown on the floor plan, but the line showing the transition between materials is usually drawn and noted. If an entrance floor is to be made of quarry tile and the rest of the room is to be carpeted, the line where the materials change would be drawn and a note such as the following would be shown.

A north arrow is shown on every floor-plan sheet, and north should always be pointing the same direction on the sheet.

The floor plans are used as a key plan to the remaining details in the set. All details given to the contractor to build the project originate from the floor plans. The ⅛″ = 1′-0″ floor plan then becomes an index for larger-scale plans, sections, and elevations.

An indication of the elevation of each floor is helpful. Usually, the elevation is only indicated once per floor, next to the room name of the most prominent room on the floor. If the floor changes elevation from room to room on the same floor (with stairs or ramps between rooms), each floor height must be given an elevation number.

Every building has different conditions and therefore has unique details that must be shown on the plan. If a rule of thumb could be established for the data to be presented on the floor-plan sheets, it would be that everything that can be seen by looking down on a building cut horizontally 3′ above the floor should not only be shown but exactly located. Certainly the items we have already discussed fall into this category; but, in addition, many miscellaneous details will appear on every project that goes beyond a list of general items.

A long list of material has been defined for inclusion into the plan sheets thus far. The next task is the assembly of details. The place to start, on this and on every other sheet, is to make a sheet layout showing the approximate size and location of the drawing and how it relates to other details on the sheet. In the case of the plan sheets, a building over 15,000 or 20,000 sq ft generally fills the entire sheet. The only task is to center the plan to fit the sheet.

Any exterior area around the building to be detailed should be considered when centrally locating the plan on the sheet. If the building has an established grid system, the first lines on the paper should be an accurate layout of every grid. An easy, time-saving step is to draw the grid lines on the back of the transparent sheet with a blue pencil. The blue lines print the same as the other lines. They stand out on the original because of the color and do not erase if a wall on the grid must be changed. If the building does not have grid lines, the first step is to lay out the exterior walls lightly, showing the exact length, size, and material of each wall.

The general procedure, once the exterior walls have been laid out, is to scale and draw the remainder of the interior walls, locating the door and window openings. Then the process of dimensioning and locating all items to be included in the project begins. Keying an item off the floor plan to a larger-scale detail of the same item happens only when that detail is drawn. This means that the floor plans can never be complete until all large-scale details have been drawn and referenced back to the plan. The floor plans are so necessary to the remainder of the project that they should be 90 percent complete when the remainder of the working drawings are 25 to 50 percent complete.

Several additional minor points are necessary to the proper execution of the working drawing floor plans. The choice of the scale at which floor plans are drawn depends mostly on the type of project being done. Obviously, the more complex the project, the larger the scale at which it should be drawn. An extremely large but uncomplicated project, such as a convention center or warehouse, can be drawn at $\frac{1}{16}'' = 1'-0''$, this is large enough to cover most items necessary on the plan. A relatively small and complex plan, such as a house, is generally drawn at $\frac{1}{4}'' = 1'-0''$, to allow more notes and dimensions in the confines of fairly small rooms.

Several exceptions to this system are quite common. A $\frac{1}{16}''$ plan would have $\frac{1}{8}''$ details of complex areas. A $\frac{1}{8}''$ floor plan typically has $\frac{1}{4}''$ blow-ups of toilet rooms and stairs. Another fairly obvious point is that floor plans should follow a numerical order in the set. The basement would be drawn first, then the first floor, second floor, etc. A building with many floors, such as a high-rise apartment, often has several floors that have identical floor plans. Rather than draw the same plan more than once, the common practice is to note the identical floors on the title of the plan (5th, 7th, 9th, and 11th Floor Plan).

ROOM FINISH SCHEDULE AND DOOR SCHEDULE

The *room finish schedule* and the *door schedule* are the next standard items found in a set of working drawings. They are actually continuations of the floor plans, since every door and room finish shown on the plan is described.

Most architectural firms using schedules set them up in box form, with the room names and numbers running down the left side and the possible materials running across the top. Four basic items are spelled out in the room finish schedule—floor, base, walls, and ceiling. The quality of the material is not given (this is indicated in the specifications), but the type of material in each room is specifically called out. Large buildings generally have a great repetition of materials. Thus the schedule can cover all room finishes with a relatively few number of entries in each of the four groups. The following are finishes included in the schedule of floors:

Exposed concrete	Carpet
Vinyl asbestos tile (V.A.T.)	Hardwood
Ceramic tile	Brick pavers
Quarry tile	Slate
Terrazzo	

The base of a room is the strip of material attached to the wall at the intersection of the wall and floor and is generally 4″ to 6″ high. It serves as a protection device for the wall from mops, chair legs, etc. Some standard materials found in the finish schedule are

No base	Vinyl
Ceramic tile	Quarry tile
Glazed tile	Carpet
Wood	Metal
Terrazzo	

The walls in a building probably require more space in the schedule than the other three groups combined. Some typical architectural materials are

Concrete block (painted or exposed)	Wood paneling
Painted gypsum board	Vinyl wall covering
Painted plaster	Exposed concrete
Ceramic tile	Glazed tile
Brick	Movable partitions
Keene's cement plaster (for high-humidity areas)	Stone
Glass	Cork
Glazed concrete block	Burnished block (concrete block with an exposed face that is ground smooth)

The ceiling materials commonly included in buildings are

Painted plaster or gypsum board	Sprayed plaster
Exposed-painted structure and mechanical system above	Keene's cement plaster (for high-humidity areas)
Acoustical tile (ACO.T.)	Lay-in panels
Wood	Metal panels

The room finish schedule (Figure 3-1) is set up to have every room name and number running down the left side of the grid and every building material in each group running along the top of the grid. To indicate the finish of a room, a check is placed in the box that meets at the intersection of the room and the finish. If more than one finish is used in a room, each finish is checked on the schedule. If the stairs are enclosed, the stair letter is included in the schedule, and appropriate data are filled in.

Two other pieces of information typically are included in the schedule: the ceiling height of each room and a column headed "Remarks," under which any unusual room finishes are noted.

The door schedule (Figure 3-2) closely approximates the room finish schedule, both in layout and in purpose. Each is set up as a system that eliminates a great deal of notes from the floor plan. Every door in the project is included in the schedule. The door number is given in the first column. Then all necessary data about the door are given. The column headings are

1. **Door size** 3′-0″ × 6′-8″ × 1¾″
2. **Door type** This is usually a letter that refers to a ¼″ = 1′-0″ scale elevation of the door, indicating whether the door is solid or has glass, a grill, etc. A note next to each elevation shows the material of the door, such as plastic-laminated face, gypsum core, hollow metal aluminum, or solid core wood. If the code check indicates that the door is to have a fire rating, the label requirements would be contained in the note. Each separate condition has an individual letter.
3. **Frame elevation** This could be a detail number that refers to a ¼″ = 1′-0″ elevation of all possible door frames. As opposed to the

ROOM FINISH SCHEDULE

ROOM NAME	RM. NO.	FLOOR					BASE			WALL				CEILING		REMARKS
		EXPOSED CONC.	CERAMIC TILE	VINYL TILE	CARPET		VINYL	CERAMIC TILE		PAINTED GYP BD.	VINYL WALL FABRIC	CERAMIC TILE		EXPOSED	LAYIN A.C. TILE	
		1	2	3	4	5	6	7	8	9	10	11	12	13	14	
MEETING ROOM	100			3			6			9				13		NORTH WALL 1" INS. GLASS
MEN'S TOILET	101		2					7				11			14	
KITCHEN	102			3			6			9					14	SEE SH 4 FOR CABINET ELEV.
RECREATION	103			3			6				10				14	
JANITOR	104	1					6			9				13		
CORRIDOR	105				4		6				10					

Figure 3-1. Room finish schedule.

DOOR   SCHEDULE

DOOR NO.	DOOR SIZE	DOOR TYPE	FRAME TYPE	HDWE.	LINTEL	REMARKS
301	3'-0"x7'-0" x 1 3/4"	A	1A	16	3	24" x 6" LOUVER
302	3'-0"x7'-0"x 1 3/4"	C	1A	16	3	
303	3'-4"x7'-0"x 1 3/4"	B	7A	11	————	
304A	2'-8"x7'-0"x 1 3/4"	E	4D	4	7	UNDERCUT 1"
304B	2'-8"x 7'-0"x1 3/4"	E	2	4	2	UNDERCUT 1"
304C	3'-0"x 7'-0"x1 3/4"	C	1B	16	3	
305	3'-4"x 7'-0"x1 3/4"	D	2C	9	2	'B' LABEL
306	3'-0"x 7'-0"x1 3/4"	C	2E	6	2	PAIR SLIDING SEE DETAIL SH 9

DOOR TYPES   FRAME TYPES   FRAME CONDITIONS

Figure 3-2. Door finish schedule.

door types, each frame is dimensioned for the height, width, and frame depth. The reason for not dimensioning the door type is that several doors of different sizes with the same elevation would only have to be detailed once.

4. **Jamb detail** (the head is similar) The condition that exists when the door jamb intersects the wall must be detailed. The detail number is shown in the schedule and also keyed off the frame elevations. The jamb detail, drawn at 3″ = 1'-0″, shows the dimensions and method of attachment of the wall and frame.

5. **Hardware** A number in the door schedule after each door refers to its hardware package in the specifications. If the door has hardware group 10, it could be a group that has a panic-bar device and an outdoor lock that can be opened by the master key. (This package is indicated only in the specifications.)

6. **Lintel detail** Most doors require a structural support in the wall above the opening. This

support is called a *lintel*. A number designation in the schedule refers to the lintel type that is detailed at 3″ = 1'-0″ in the set. Lintel types range from a steel angle or combination of angles to a U-shaped concrete lintel block that has reinforcing bars and poured concrete in the center. The type of lintel depends on the wall condition, and the lintel size is decided by the width of the door opening.

7. **Transom** Some doors have a transom panel above that can be either a continuation of the same material as the door or a material such as glass. The transom panel is fixed in the door frame, which in this case extends to the top of the panel instead of stopping at the top of the door. The number in the schedule refers to a transom detail.

8. **Door grill** Fresh air must be supplied to a room, and exhaust air must be evacuated. It is sometimes easier to exhaust the air in a room through a grill in the door rather than through

a return air duct. If this is the case, the mechanical engineers give the location and size of each door grill to the architest for inclusion in the plan. The schedule designates the width and height of the grill. A note showing 24/16 indicates that a 2'-0" × 1'-4" grill is to be placed in the door.

9. **Remarks** A condition peculiar to a door could be noted in this column. Notes could include the information that the door should be undercut 1" in order that it might pass over deep carpet or that a unique jamb condition exists.

If the detail does not apply to the particular door, a line is drawn through the appropriate box. The column boundary lines are drawn dark, while the ³/₃₂" guidelines for lettering within the column are drawn light. A short cut for drafting is to draw the lines for the schedule on the back of the transparent sheet. This allows any necessary erasures (which occur often on a schedule) without redrawing the schedule. Another timesaver is to put ten doors or rooms on a schedule and then leave one or two spaces blank before the next ten entries are lettered. Then, if several doors or rooms are added to the project during the working drawing stage, as is often the case, the additions can be placed in the correct numerical order rather than at the end of the schedule where the contractor might overlook them. If extra spaces are not provided in the schedule after every ten entries, an added door or room would mean that the entire schedule would have to be erased after the addition. If the blank spaces are provided, an addition could only cause a maximum of five erased entries.

The above system is very descriptive, accurate, and easily read by the contractor. Several other techniques are used by architects. All have the singular purpose of informing the contractor of the exact room finish and door type without cluttering the floor plan.

Another system is to assign each room and door a code designation, thus eliminating the need for a door and room finish schedule. The room code is relatively simple in that each combination of floor, base, wall, and ceiling finish is assigned a number. Thus, the room finish code number "R.F. 28" could mean carpeted floor, hardwood base, painted gypsum board walls, and a lay-in acoustic-tile ceiling. Every room in the building that has these exact material conditions will then have the code "R.F. 28" placed under the room number.

This system still requires a schedule defining each number and letter. However, if a project has a considerable amount of exact repetition of room finishes, the code definition schedule is much shorter than the room schedule would be.

The door schedule code has four basic categories spelled out:

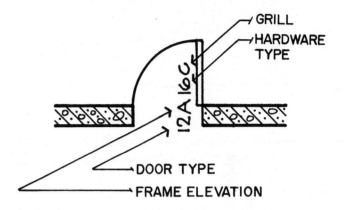

Each number or letter refers to a detail on the sheet. The code eliminates the necessity of the door schedule but can sometimes be confusing because the various door numbers are scattered around the floor plan and coordination can be difficult.

EXTERIOR ELEVATIONS

The next item in the set is the *exterior elevations*. Every exterior wall is shown on the elevations and generally is drawn at the same scale as the floor plans (⅛" = 1'-0" is common). Besides showing the overall picture of the exterior of the building, the elevations are mainly used to key specific areas to larger-scale details.

The elevations show the materials drawn to scale, basically indicating doors, window patterns, exterior grade, and mechanical penthouses, to name a few. The building elevations are a bit like the view seen from several hundred yards—an overall picture of the building rather than specific details. The materials seen in the elevation can be delineated if it makes the building read better. Brick can be shown by drawing the horizontal brick joints. Concrete can be drawn by dotting the wall, wood by showing the joints, and windows by showing the mullions. This treatment should not be overdone. The intent is to inform, not to confuse, the contractor. The elevations should not resemble a rendering for design development. In most cases, only a portion of the wall is delineated to show the material. The rest of the wall is left blank. Making a note of each material and running an arrow to its location on the elevation is a good practice.

Dimensions generally are not given on the elevations. These are given on the floor plan and larger-scale wall sections. The one exception is the elevation of every floor and roof deck. If the building has an established grid system, the grid spacing is shown and numbered on the elevation. Elevations are used to show proportions but also to indicate areas through which wall sections have been cut.

Two difficulties commonly arise in drawing elevations—labeling the elevation direction and showing door swings. Elevations are titled by labeling the compass side of the building view. The north elevation is on the north end of the building. The confusion is that the viewer is looking south to see the north elevation.

A door shown in elevation is generally delineated to show the side on which the hinges are placed. This is done by drawing a dotted line from the top and bottom corner of the door on one side to the center of the door on the opposite side. The side of the door that has the hinges is the center point where the two dotted lines intersect.

HINGE SIDE
OF DOOR

Start the elevations (after the sheet is laid out) by drawing the grids on the back of the sheet in blue. Since the floor plan was drawn before the elevations were started, a short cut would be to run a print of the plan, locate it under the sheet, and project all the corners, doors, and windows up into vertical lines in the elevation. If the plan was drawn accurately, this system eliminates scaling the elevations.

The next step is to scale the horizontal heights, such as the ground elevation, floor heights, and roof lines. It is generally wise to lay out the major horizontal and vertical lines lightly at first and then

to darken them after the length has been established.

The next step is to draw the remainder of the materials that are seen in the elevation, including doors, windows, control joints, mechanical penthouses, lights, and stairs, to name a few.

The building elevations are a two-dimensional view of the actual picture that could be seen by standing back and looking at the building, with one exception—the areas below grade are visible. Spaces that are below the ground level and outside the foundation wall, such as a stair to a basement door or a window well for basement light, are shown dotted. Some firms have adopted the practice of dotting a portion of the foundation wall and footings to indicate their presence. The actual dimensioning of the footings occurs on the structural drawings.

The final step in detailing the elevations is to key notes to larger details, specifying materials and giving floor elevations. Wall sections are indicated by drawing a dotted line through the wall with an arrow pointing to the direction in which the section is cut, with the detail and sheet number inside the arrow. A blow-up of a particular part of the elevation is indicated by drawing a dotted box around the area and keying it to the larger-scale detail number and sheet number.

Other details are shown by noting the area with the sheet and detail number where it may be found. All materials should be noted with an arrow pointing to the location. If the material occurs many times along the elevation, the arrow could contain several arrow heads to denote repetition, as follows:

The more commonly used term for heat-reducing glass is Solarbronze glass or Solargray glass. These, however, are trademarks.

The height of each floor and roof should be drawn to the side of the elevation. This specification consists of a dashed line from the floor or roof line with a ¼″ circle that has two opposite quadrants darkened. A note above the dashed line calls out the place the elevation is taken, while the dimension below the line gives the feet and inches above the bench mark.

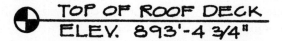

An important point in dimensioning the elevations is that the dimension should be to the highest structural material that has a known thickness. This is not necessarily the top of the floor or roof. If a concrete floor deck is to have a pad and carpet on top of it, the elevation dimension is to the top of the deck, not including the pad and the carpet. A common roof treatment is 1½″ metal deck, 1½″ rigid fiberglass insulation over the deck, and pitch and gravel on top of the insulation. The elevation is then given to the top of the metal deck.

BUILDING SECTIONS

The *building sections* are the next part of the working drawings. This part shows the cutting of sections through the entire building, typically at the same scale as the floor plans and exterior elevations (⅛″ = 1′-0″ is most common). As in the elevations, the building sections serve basically as a means of orientation and a key or directory to larger-scale details. Very few dimensions are given except the floor-to-floor and floor-to-ceiling heights and elevations of each floor above the bench mark.

The floor plans are seen only by cutting the building apart with a horizontal plane that is parallel to the floor. The building sections are seen by cutting the building apart at a vertical plane that is perpendicular to the floor. The draftsman has thousands of choices of where the section is to be cut, the only direction being that it should be through a space that will best describe what is happening in the building. An example would be an auditorium with a sloped floor and ceiling that is surrounded by one-story corridors and rooms with level floors and ceilings. Cutting a section through the building that would only show the one-story flat spaces without indicating the auditorium would not be very descriptive, although it certainly would be easier to draw.

A fairly sound rule of thumb for picking a place to cut a section is that it should be the most difficult area the draftsman can find in the building. It is a lot better to find difficulties while drawing the project than to wait for the contractor to find problems during construction. Cutting sections through the building is an excellent check for the architect to be certain that all systems in the project are compatible.

The number of sections drawn depends entirely on the complexity of the space, not on the size of the project. You could draw one section for a simple space or five or six for a difficult building.

Section cuts should be made at right angles to the major axes of the building. The long axis is referred to as the *longitudinal section*, and the short axis is the *transverse section*.

A place to start in building sections is at the floor plans, analyzing the best location or locations to cut a section through the building. A dashed line marks the location of a section on the plan.

The section line through the building doesn't necessarily have to be straight. It can jog back and forth one or several times to show spaces or interior elevations that would be missed with a straight line. After the plans have been marked, the fastest way to begin the section is to make a print of the plan, lay it under the drawing sheet, and project all walls up vertically where the section line cuts through them. The floor elevations and ceiling height should be scaled so that the termination of the walls can be located.

After each floor has been drawn lightly, the walls, ceiling, doors, and windows can be drawn darker. The wall sections are drawn by showing everything past the section line in elevation. The view shown in the section would be similar to the one seen by standing in the room facing the same direction when the project is completed.

The next step is to study the structural drawings so that the floor and roof supports can be accurately drawn to scale. This could include concrete double tees, prestressed concrete deck, poured-concrete slabs and beams, wood joists and plywood decking, glue-laminated wood beams with tongue-and-groove wood deck, steel beams with metal deck, and poured concrete.

The notes that should be included on the section range from general information to keys to other details. The name and number of each room shown in section should be given along with the letter of each stairway that is shown. Other notes should refer to items such as louvers, ceiling heights (feet and inches from the floor), fire-extinguisher cabinets, drinking fountains, built-in equipment, and air grills, to name a few. The detail key to larger-scale drawings includes wall sections and individual details of floor, window, and roof blow-ups. The detail indications are the same as the system used for exterior elevations. The building materials for walls and ceiling are not generally called out on the section. They are indicated in the room finish schedule.

Both elevations and sections have a tendency to be sparsely detailed rather than showing every nut and bolt. The reason is that the scale is too small to show much valuable information to the contractor. If a detail is complex, it could be drawn at 3″ = 1′-0″, 24 times larger than ⅛″ = 1′-0″.

LARGER-SCALE DETAILS

The floor plans, exterior elevations, and sections, all drawn at about the same scale, show almost every detail that will make up the remainder of the set. Exceptions to this are extremely few. The next part of the working drawings then becomes redrawing the details at a larger scale so that more can be shown. The first group in the larger details includes the blow-ups of the individual *wall sections* from the ⅛″ = 1′-0″ building section to a ¾″ = 1′-0″ scale, or six times larger. (½″ = 1′-0″ is also used for wall sections.) At the larger scale, an individual material can be drawn and hatched, even if it is just a 1″ strip of insulation.

The wall sections generally are drawn from the basement footings to the top of the roof material. If the detail does not fit on the sheet because of height, it can be cut in several nonstrategic places and squeezed together.

The first time that the components making up the wall are individually enlarged and hatched is during this stage. The majority of the enlarged wall sections are exterior wall conditions. The interior walls are generally much simpler and can be shown on the floor plan and room finish schedule. All conditions on the exterior walls, including windows, overhead door openings, curtain walls, and all different walls in the project should be drawn. In short, every wall condition unique to the project is detailed.

Although the wall section is basically a key to larger details, at the scale used (¾″ or ½″), the section begins to adequately define the intended construction techniques. The lack of detail in the overall building sections is now taken care of in the wall sections. Some of the items that should be enlarged and drawn accurately are windows (head, jambs, and sills), structural members, flashing, roof details, hatching of all materials, doors, wood members, insulation, and mechanical systems. Portions of the wall section that require further definition are then bubbled (keyed) to a larger detail. The wall-section dimensions included are mostly general, such as floor-to-floor heights, window openings, panel heights, fascias, and ceiling heights, as opposed to specific dimensions, such as the thickness of individual materials. The reason for including only general dimensions is that, without a doubt, a highly detailed condition will have to be drawn at a larger scale, and it is gener-

ally a good practice to save specific dimensioning for the largest scale at which it will be drawn. If a wall section at ¾″ = 1′-0″ is the largest scale at which the wall is to be shown, the individual materials and thicknesses should be shown. If a roof detail showing a portion of the wall below is to be drawn at a larger scale, the material dimensions should then be given on the enlarged roof detail. The same floor and roof elevations that are given on the exterior building elevations should be lettered on the wall sections.

The location at which a wall section is cut is limited to a necessary minimum. Several cases in point are

1. A building that has similar walls on all sides need only show detail on one wall section.
2. A wall that has a set-in window more than likely could have just one section of the wall through the window, eliminating the need for another section through the wall.
3. A wall section through a door is not necessary unless a door is unique.
4. On a two- or three-story building, a section from the lowest floor (or footings) to the roof not only eliminates confusion in the contractor's mind, but more than likely saves drafting time that would be needed to draw each floor individually.
5. If the two wall conditions are identical except for one or two minor details, such as interior wall finishes or different ceiling heights, it is only necessary to detail the more complicated wall section and provide adequate notes spelling out the differences.

The wall sections are the center link in the assembly process that occurs in the working drawing package. The package started with the small-scale drawings of the floor plans, exterior elevations, and building sections. It built up to the larger-scale wall sections, and will finally end with the large-scale building details. This is generally a stair-step process in which the detail is first shown at ⅛″, then at ¾″ in the section, and finally at 3″ in detail. It is very unusual to skip any of these steps in putting the working drawing package together.

The place to begin with the large-scale wall sections is to mark each condition to be shown on the floor plan and check it with the ⅛″ = 1′-0″ building section (if one has been drawn through the particular wall condition). The standard point of beginning is to make a scale drawing of the wall section on cedar paper to study the various components that must be assembled. When a proper solution has been reached on cedar paper, it can be used as an underlay to trace the final drawing. If the wall has a grid line running through it, this should be the first line of the detail and the base line from which other lines are measured. The major lines of the section should then be drawn in lightly, such as the thicknesses of the wall materials, floor locations, window head and sill heights, and structural members. After the detail has been laid out, the materials should be properly hatched or identified, and the dimensions shown.

If a priority can be established for degrees of importance in a set of drawings, the wall sections could be considered the second most valuable source of information to the contractor, the first being the floor plans. The wall composition and intersections of floors and the roof with the wall are extremely important details for the proper construction of the project.

The larger-scale architectural details ($1'' = 1'-0''$; $1\frac{1}{2}'' = 1'-0''$; $3'' = 1'-0''$, and, rarely, half-scale, or $6'' = 1'-0''$) are almost entirely larger-scale drawings of conditions that were shown in the wall sections. Increasing the size of the detail permits the architect to show all necessary material that makes up the section. This could not be done at a smaller scale. Items such as screws and bolts, metal flashing, anchoring devices for stone, and window frames that are too complicated to be shown adequately at the scale used for the wall sections should be drawn in the detail. Similarly, much of the material shown in the wall sections does not have to be drawn at a larger scale because of its straightforward construction technique. Selecting points in the wall section that require further definition then becomes necessary.

The details are typically increased two to four times from the scale at which the wall sections are drawn. At this size, very little, if any, material need be eliminated from the detail, certainly nothing that is to be in the actual construction. This is the last and largest scale in working drawings that the architect uses to inform the contractor of the intent of the drawing.

The details are basically the only group of drawings that deal with specific, unique construction conditions. Plans and sections show only the general concept of the project. The draftsman should take particular care to make the exact location of the detail known, since it does not necessarily apply to the entire building.

A broad range of materials can be included in the architectural details. A detail could be any item

from a floor drain to a roof flashing. Since each detail has already been presented at a smaller scale as part of a larger detail, the choice of what to present can be limited in this way:

1. Intersections of floors and walls should be drawn if the connection is difficult or not typical.
2. The connection of the head and sill (two details) of windows in the wall usually should be shown in large scale.
3. All curtain-wall details should be fully detailed.
4. Roof-flashing conditions are generally drawn.
5. The intersection of the roof and walls are necessary.

Although it is sometimes difficult to decide which details should be enlarged, it can be helpful to attempt to think the way a contractor might when bidding on or building the project. If any question exists about the drawing, a detail to the largest necessary scale should be done. If the scale of $\frac{3}{4}'' = 1'-0''$ adequately explains the material, then redrawing a portion of that detail at $3'' = 1'-0''$ is a waste of time and energy. The contractor knows what each detail involves to fabricate the condition at the job site, and skilled laborers do each task. Thus, showing a standard procedure in great detail is only a tribute to the amount of work done by the architect. Conversely, an insufficient amount of detail could lead to one of the following conditions:

1. The architect receives a telephone call from the contractor before the item is built to ascertain the intent of the detail.
2. The contractor performs the work, using discretion toward the intent of the drawing, possibly providing a substandard job. Court action (with questionable results) could result, requiring the contractor to redo the work to meet the standards that the architect originally wanted, but neglected to show.
3. The contractor calls the architect and, upon hearing what the architect wants, requires a cost-extra because the architect's intended detail is more expensive than the way the contractor bid the job.

An architectural detail starts with a sheet layout. This procedure varies in several ways from all other groups in the working drawing set. Very few details are larger than $4'' \times 5''$. Thus, the great majority of architectural details fit in a lined box of this size. An orderly method is to divide the drawing sheet into boxes 4″ × 5″. Most of the details fit these proportions, but if the detail requires a larger box, a double rectangle can be used. The reason for establishing a large grid is to create order on a sheet that is filled with fragmented details that have very little relation to each other.

The same basic steps as were used in previous drawings also apply to large-scale details. The first step is to locate the grid as a base, if a grid goes through the detail. The major lines of the drawing are located and drawn lightly at first and then darkened when the detail begins to take shape. All items, such as bolts and flashing, are necessarily included to show the total detail to the contractor. The final drawing step is to hatch the materials cut by the section.

The drafting techniques used to delineate details vary more in line thickness than any other group of drawings in the set. Insignificant materials, such as materials shown in elevation behind the detail or a nail holding a piece of roofing to a wood strip, are drawn with a thin, crisp line. Major items, such as through-wall flashing or window frames, are shown by drawing darker, wider lines. This is to give important items prominence—to make them "read" well. The drafting technique of emphasizing by line intensity and thickness can only be picked up with experience and knowledge.

The next steps in finishing the detail involve showing necessary dimensions and noting materials and conditions. Deciding which notes to include in the detail certainly comes from experience, but if you can place yourself in the position of assuming you are about to build the detail, any questions that come to mind can be noted. When showing dimensions, it is important to include a reference line and its dimension for orientation in the detail, whether it is a grid line, a floor-elevation bubble, or a wall.

The system used to key the larger details to the smaller drawings should be lettered. This is done by numbering the large details and placing that detail number on the next smaller detail of the same thing.

Windows, particularly on a job with complex patterns, are unique in that they are completely detailed on one sheet. This section is generally contained in the large-scale detail section and can include one or more sheets. The drawings included in this group are usually limited to two items—¼″ elevations of every window-frame condition and details cut through the head, jamb, and sill to show the window connection to the wall. Obviously, if only a few window sizes exist, this

technique is not necessary. It is primarily intended to organize a curtain wall or similar system on a large project.

Stairways in a project follow the same system used for windows. They are usually all grouped on the same sheet or sheets with all necessary details. The floor plan is the only group that shows every stair. At the usual scale for floor plans (¹/₁₆″ or ⅛″) the necessary degree of detail is very difficult to show. Most firms draw the final stair plan at ¼″ = 1′-0″. If this is not the scale of the floor plan, the stair is usually redrawn on the stair sheet at ¼″. Along with the plan of each stair, a section should be cut through the stairway, showing its full run. If a stairway starts on the first floor and goes up to the third floor, it is a good drafting procedure to show the entire stairway. The stair section should also be drawn at ¼″ = 1′-0″ to avoid the necessity of blowing up a great number of details.

The final step in showing the stairs is to draw the large-scale details of the treads, connections to the stringer, landings, and all other details necessary to the fabrication of the stairway. The scale is determined by the complexity of the detail, but, just as with the architectural details, the most common scales are 1½″ = 1′-0″ and 3″ = 1′-0″.

The vertical circulation systems are grouped together for several reasons. These details pertain only to specific parts of the building. They should be concentrated in one place for easy reference.

The stair sheet or sheets contain the information necessary to build every stair in the project. A job with several stairs probably has similar details so that some details may cover more than one stair. Stairs that are identical only have to be drawn once, but this should be noted. A similar procedure generally is followed for elevators, escalators, and moving ramps.

Except for the stairs, all other items in the vertical circulation group are done by a subcontractor. Assembling all details for an elevator on one sheet allows the elevator subcontractor to find the majority of the information in one spot.

TOILET DETAILS

The toilet details are the next step in the working drawings. The toilets require detail because of their complexity. This generally means drawing a floor plan of each toilet room and elevations of all the equipment to show the mounting height. The floor plan, drawn at ¼″ = 1′-0″, shows all wall finishes and dimensions the locations of the fixed toilet equipment in the room, including:

Toilet partitions
Handicapped partitions
Grab bars
Water closets
Lavatories
Counters
Urinals

Sanitary napkin dispensers and disposals
Towel dispensers and disposals
Mirrors
Floor drains

Ceiling grid patterns, established by acoustic ceiling tile
Light fixtures
Mechanical grills

Recessed door tracks
Changes in ceiling materials
Skylights
Speakers

Along with the items listed, the plan generally indicates floor finishes and door swings. Several options are available to show the mounting height of the toilet equipment. One is to draw an interior elevation of every wall that has equipment. Another system is to draw a key showing each fixture mounting height, which eliminates the need for wall elevations.

It is necessary to identify the toilet room or rooms both by dimensioning the walls to the closest grid line and by showing the room name and number.

INTERIOR WALL ELEVATIONS

It is not necessary to show *interior wall elevations* of every wall in the building, but some conditions make elevations extremely helpful. Elevations are generally drawn at the same scale as the floor plan and show a two-dimensional (height and width) picture of the wall from floor to finished ceiling. Interior elevations are chosen because complex items such as counters or elevator lobbies cannot be fully shown in plan. The dimension of height can be indicated only in elevation. The most common dimension string to show on the interior elevations is to give the mounting height off the floor of materials.

REFLECTED CEILING PLAN

The final group of drawings in the working drawing set is the *reflected ceiling plan*. This tells the contractor exactly how the ceiling is to be put together. The ceiling plan so closely resembles the effort put into the floor plan that most firms have a reprintable copy made of the floor plans for use in this group. The ideal time to make the prints of the floor plan is after the walls have been drawn but before any material hatching or dimension strings have been shown.

The best way to define the procedure involved in drawing the reflected ceiling plan is to assume the floor is a mirror and every item on the ceiling will be reflected onto the floor plan. This could include:

After the floor-plan print has been made, shade all walls in the building. (This is usually done with a blue pencil on the back of the sheet.) This makes the wall system stand out.

The room names and numbers to identify each area are drawn as the next step, followed by drawing the ceiling materials. In the case of plaster, a note calls the material out. If the ceiling is lay-in acoustic tile, the pattern of the tile (usually $2' \times 4'$) is drawn in each room in exactly the same proportions as it is to be built. The engineers supply the location of the light fixtures and the mechanical equipment in the ceiling, but the architectural drawings include all this information. This plan, along with every other, should have a north arrow and should have the same orientation as the floor-plan sheets. (North should be pointing the same direction on all sheets.)

The 12 categories that have been defined are not only a systematic method of assembling a set of working drawings but also prove quite versatile in covering almost every building project. A $15 million office building and a $100,000 medical office can follow the same working drawing pattern. The main difference is that the office building could require 100 sheets, while the medical office could be completed in 5.

Obviously, there is a great variety in the degree of complexity for individual projects. Some projects are too simple to require every step. A house does not generally demand a reflected ceiling plan because nothing is detailed on the ceiling. A theater couldn't possibly be done without a ceiling plan to show the necessary lighting, ventilating, and sound equipment.

The system, as explained, isn't the complete package in an architect's set of working drawings. Three other groups of drawings and specifications must be included with the architectural drawings to fully inform a contractor of the architect's intent. The structural, mechanical, and electrical engineers have coordinated their work with the architect, and their drawings are typically bound into the set behind the architectural working drawings. As was mentioned in Chapter 1, an architect may require the services of a special consultant on particular phases of the job. Occasionally, an architect has a consultant draw data on a sheet of the architect's paper so that it can be printed and included.

REGULATORY INFORMATION:

ADDRESS: 1719 HUMBOLDT AVE. SO
           MINNEAPOLIS, MINNESOTA
ZONING CLASSIFICATION: R2
OCCUPANCY: GROUP I
CONSTRUCTION: TYPE V

SURVEY INFORMATION:

SURVEY INFORMATION TAKEN FROM
A DRAWING TITLED "SURVEY FOR:
NORTHWESTERN NATIONAL BANK OF
MINNEAPOLIS" BY EGAN, FIELD & NOWAK,
SURVEYORS, DATED JUNE 20TH 1968.

PROPERTY DESCRIPTION:

THE SOUTH 37 FEET OF THE WEST
3.1 FEET OF LOT 9 AND ALL OF
LOT 13; EXCEPT THE NORTH 13 FEET
OF THE EAST 50 FEET THEREOF.

BENCHMARK:

TOP OF EXISTING RETAINING WALL
AT NORTHWEST CORNER OF SITE -
ELEVATION 209.8'

ELECTRICAL & TELEPHONE
ELECTRICAL & TELEPHONE SERVICES
TO BE UNDERGROUND

GENERAL SITE NOTE

ALL SODDING, SEE
ARE BY OWNER.

ALL CONCRETE WAL
BEAR ON UNDISTUR
COMPACTED FILL,

PROVIDE 4'-0" x 4'-0
FOR CONDENSING
BE DETERMINED I
BRICK PAVERS @ DRIV

SYMBOLS:

MASONRY
FRAME W
REINF. CO

DUPLEX CONVEN
WEATHERPROOF
SINGLE POLE SW
3 WAY SWITCH
4 WAY SWITCH
TELEPHONE OU
WALL FIXTURE
CEILING FIXTUR
EXHAUST FAN
RECESSED CE
BRICK PAVE

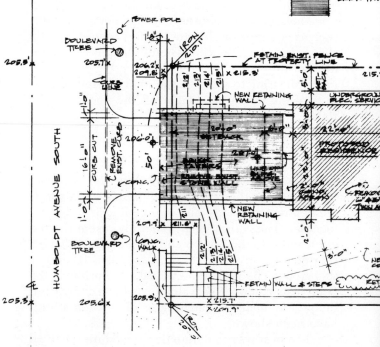

PLANTINGS

SLABS TO

C. SLAB
ATION TO
EE ALT.#3

ONSTRUCTION
STRUCTION
CONSTRUCTION

TLET
CE OUTLET

R

XTURE

WER POLE
100'

LINE OF BLDG.
ABOVE

24'-0"
REMOVE 10" ASH

REMOVE 8" ASH

REMOVE 4" & 6" TWIN
BOX ELDER

REMOVE 12" TREE

RETAIN 4" & 6"
TWIN BOX ELDER

RETAIN WALK

RETAIN EXIST. WALL

INDEX TO DRAWINGS:

SHEET 1 - SITE PLAN, INDEX TO DRAWINGS
2 - 1ST LEVEL PLAN, ROOM FINISH SCHEDULE
3 - 2ND LEVEL PLAN, INTERIOR ELEVATIONS
4 - 3RD LEVEL PLAN, INTERIOR ELEVATIONS
5 - EXTERIOR ELEVATIONS
6 - BUILDING SECTIONS &
SECOND FLOOR FRAMING PLAN
7 - BUILDING SECTIONS & DETAILS &
THIRD FLOOR & ROOF FRAMING
PLAN

comprehensive design, inc.

ARCHITECTS   DESIGNERS
6440 FLYING CLOUD DR.   EDEN PRAIRIE, MINN.
612-941-6244   55343

I hereby certify that this plan, specification, or
report was prepared by me or under my direct
supervision and that I am a duly Registered
Architect under the laws of the State of
MINNESOTA

Date 7-26-72   Reg. No. 10068

revisions
date 7-26-72
drwn RPJ
chkd ADG

project
RESIDENCE FOR
MR. & MRS. E. F. JOHNSON
1712 HUMBOLDT N. SO.
MPLS., MINN. 55405

SITE PLAN
INDEX TO DRAWINGS

contents
SITE PLAN
INDEX TO DRAWINGS

job no.
7210

1

of 7 sheets

50'

X 217.9'
220.3' X
IRON
220.8'

RETAIN EXIST. FENCE
AT PROPERTY LINE

216.2' X

8'-0"

LINE OF
BLDG. ABOVE

FUTURE
DECK

8" SPRUCE

216.9' X

IRON
217.8'

222.2'
222.5 X X 222.9'

STEPS
X 216.8

222'

221'

220'

219'

218'

217'

216'

RETAIN EXIST. FENCE AT
PROPERTY LINE

53.1'

EXIST. WALL

14" BOX ELDER
12" ELM
18" BOX ELDER

223.9' X   X 218.8'

216.2'

3.10'

14" TWIN BOX
ELDER

RETAIN EXIST.
WALK & STEPS

RETAIN LILAC BUSHES

RETAIN EXIST. WALLS

X 216.4

X 216.0'

X 211.6'

PROPERTY LINE

153.1'

215.4 X

215.9'

IRON
211.9'

IRON
222.7'

87'

X 216.4

SITE PLAN — 1/8" = 1'-0"

NORTH

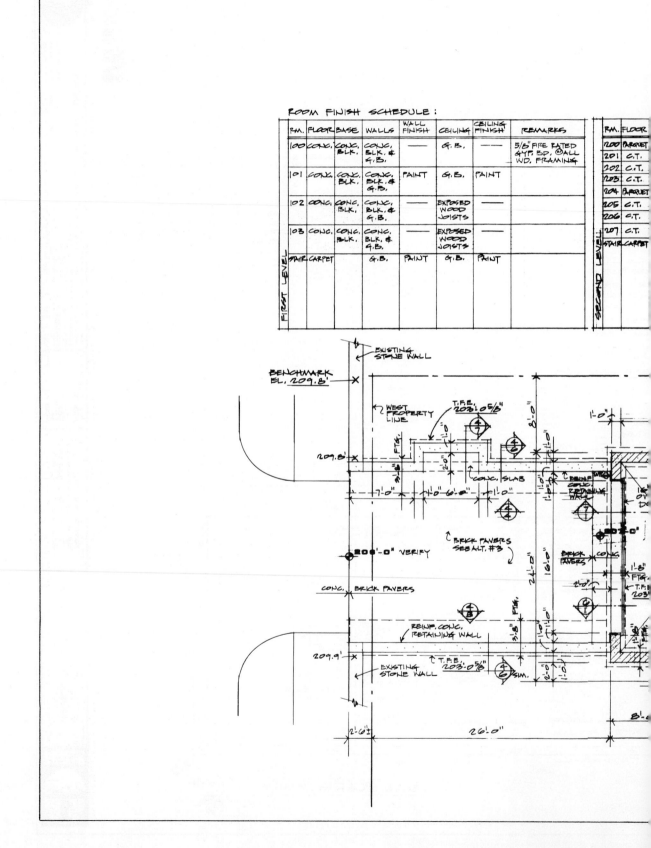

ROOM FINISH SCHEDULE:

RM.	FLOOR	BASE	WALLS	WALL FINISH	CEILING	CEILING FINISH	REMARKS
100	CONC.	CONC. BLK.	CONC. BLK. & G.B.	—	G.B.	—	5/8" FIRE RATED GYP. BD. @ALL WD. FRAMING
101	CONC.	CONC. BLK.	CONC. BLK. & G.B.	PAINT	G.B.	PAINT	
102	CONC.	CONC. BLK.	CONC. BLK. & G.B.	—	EXPOSED WOOD JOISTS	—	
103	CONC.	CONC. BLK.	CONC. BLK. & G.B.	—	EXPOSED WOOD JOISTS	—	
STAIR	CARPET		G.B.	PAINT	G.B.	PAINT	

FIRST LEVEL

RM.	FLOOR
200	PARQUET
201	C.T.
202	C.T.
203	C.T.
204	PARQUET
205	C.T.
206	C.T.
207	C.T.
STAIR	CARPET

SECOND LEVEL

EXISTING STONE WALL

BENCHMARK EL. 209.8'

WEST PROPERTY LINE

T.F.E. 203'-0 5/8"

209.8'

CONC. SLAB

REINF. CONC. RETAINING WALL

7'-0"   4'-0"   6'-0"   7'-0"

209'-0" VERIFY

BRICK PAVERS SEE ALT. #3

BRICK PAVERS   CONC.

CONC.   BRICK PAVERS

REINF. CONC. RETAINING WALL

209.9'

EXISTING STONE WALL

T.F.E. 203'-0 5/8"

SIM.

2'-0"±   26'-0"   8'-0"

8'-0"

1'-0"

24'-0"   16'-0"

2'-0"

LS	WALL FINISH	CEILING	CEILING FINISH	REMARKS
	PAINT	G.B.	PAINT	
	PAINT	G.B.	PAINT	THINSET C.T.
	PAINT	G.B.	PAINT	THINSET C.T.
	PAINT	G.B.	PAINT	THINSET C.T.
	PAINT	G.B.	PAINT	
	PAINT	G.B.	PAINT	THINSET C.T.
	PAINT	G.B.	PAINT	THINSET C.T.
	PAINT	OPEN	——	THINSET C.T.
	PAINT	G.B.	PAINT	

RM.	FLOOR	BASE	WALLS	WALL FINISH	CEILING	CEILING FINISH	REMARKS
300	CARPET	WOOD	G.B.	PAINT	G.B.	PAINT	
301	CARPET	WOOD	G.B.	PAINT	G.B.	PAINT	
302	CARPET	WOOD	G.B.	PAINT	G.B.	PAINT	
303	CARPET	WOOD	G.B.	PAINT	G.B.	PAINT	
304	C.T.	WOOD	G.B.	PAINT	WPGB	PAINT	
305	C.T.	WOOD	WPGB	C.T.	WPGB	PAINT	C.T. @ CURB
306	CARPET	WOOD	G.B.	PAINT	G.B.	PAINT	
307	C.T.	WOOD	G.B.	PAINT	WPGB	PAINT	WPGB & C.T. @ TUB ENCLOSURE
308	C.T.	WOOD	WOOD	OIL	WOOD	OIL	SAUNA - SEE ALT #1
309	CARPET	WOOD	G.B.	PAINT	G.B.	PAINT	
310	CARPET	WOOD	G.B.	PAINT	G.B.	PAINT	
311	CARPET	WOOD	G.B.	PAINT	G.B.	PAINT	
STAIR	CARPET		G.B.	PAINT	G.B.	PAINT	

THIRD LEVEL

NORTH PROPERTY LINE

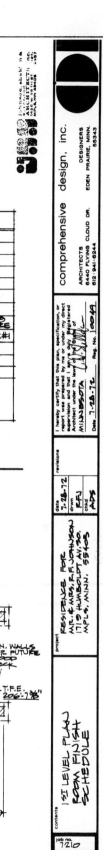

NOTE: SEE EXTERIOR ELEVATIONS FOR FOOTING STEPS

1ST LEVEL PLAN - 1/4"=1'-0"

NORTH

comprehensive design, inc.

ARCHITECTS
6440 FLYING CLOUD DR.
612-941-6244

DESIGNERS
EDEN PRAIRIE, MINN.
55343

I hereby certify that this plan, specification, or report was prepared by me or under my direct supervision and that I am a duly Registered Architect under the laws of the State of MINNESOTA

Date 7-28-72   Reg. No. 6048

revisions

date 7-28-72
drwn RFJ
chkd APS

project RESIDENCE FOR
MR. & MRS. R.F. JOHNSON
1719 HUMBOLDT AV. SO.
MPLS, MINN. 55405

contents 1ST LEVEL PLAN
ROOM FINISH
SCHEDULE

job no. 7210

of 7 sheets

2

84

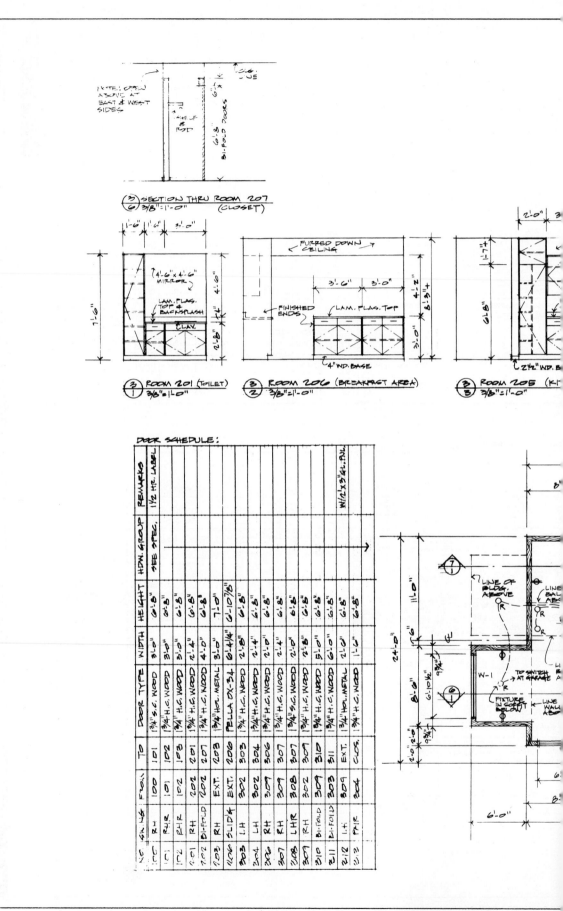

NOTE: OPEN ABOVE AT EAST & WEST SIDES

$\underbrace{5}_{6}$ SECTION THRU ROOM 207
3/8"=1'-0" (CLOSET)

1'-6" 1'-6" 3'-0"

4'-6" x 4'-6" MIRROR

LAM. PLAS. TOP & BACKSPLASH

LAV.

$\underbrace{3}_{1}$ ROOM 201 (TOILET)
3/8"=1'-0"

FURRED DOWN CEILING

3'-6" 3'-0"

FINISHED ENDS

LAM. PLAS. TOP

4" WD. BASE

$\underbrace{3}_{2}$ ROOM 206 (BREAKFAST AREA)
3/8"=1'-0"

2'-0"

$\underbrace{3}_{3}$ ROOM 205 (KI
3/8"=1'-0"

2½" WD. B

DOOR SCHEDULE:

NO	FROM	TO	DOOR TYPE	WIDTH	HEIGHT	HDW. GROUP SEE SPEC.	REMARKS
10	RH	101	1¾" S.C. WOOD	3'-0"	6'-8"		
101	RHR	101	1¾" S.C. WOOD	3'-0"	6'-8"		
102	RHR	102	1¾" H.C. WOOD	3'-0"	6'-8"		
2.01	RH	201	1¾" H.C. WOOD	2'-4"	6'-8"		
7.02	BI-FOLD	207	1¾" H.C. WOOD	4'-0"	7'-0"		
2.02	RH	203	1¾" HOL. METAL	3'-0"	7'-0"		1½ HR. LABEL
1.00	SLIDE	200	PELLA DX-54	6'-4¼"	6'-10⅞"		
303	LH	303	1¾" H.C. WOOD	2'-8"	6'-8"		
304	LH	304	1¾" H.C. WOOD	2'-4"	6'-8"		
307	RH	306	1¾" H.C. WOOD	2'-4"	6'-8"		
308	RH	307	1¾" S.C. WOOD	2'-0"	6'-8"		
307	LHR	308	1¾" H.C. WOOD	2'-8"	6'-8"		
310	RH	309	1¾" H.C. WOOD	3'-0"	6'-8"		
211	BI-FOLD	310	1¾" H.C. WOOD	6'-0"	6'-8"		
2.12	BI-FOLD	311	1¾" HOL. METAL	2'-0"	6'-8"		
2.13	L-H	EXT.	1¾" H.C. WOOD	1'-0"	6'-8"		
2.13	PAIR	CLOS.					W/2 x 5½ GL. PNL.

7/1

LINE OF BLDG. ABOVE

LINE BAL ABO

W-1

TOP SANITARY AT GARAGE A

FIXTURE IN CLOSET BELOW

LINE WALL ABO

11'-0"

24'-0"

8'-0"

6'-0"

2'-0"

6'-0"

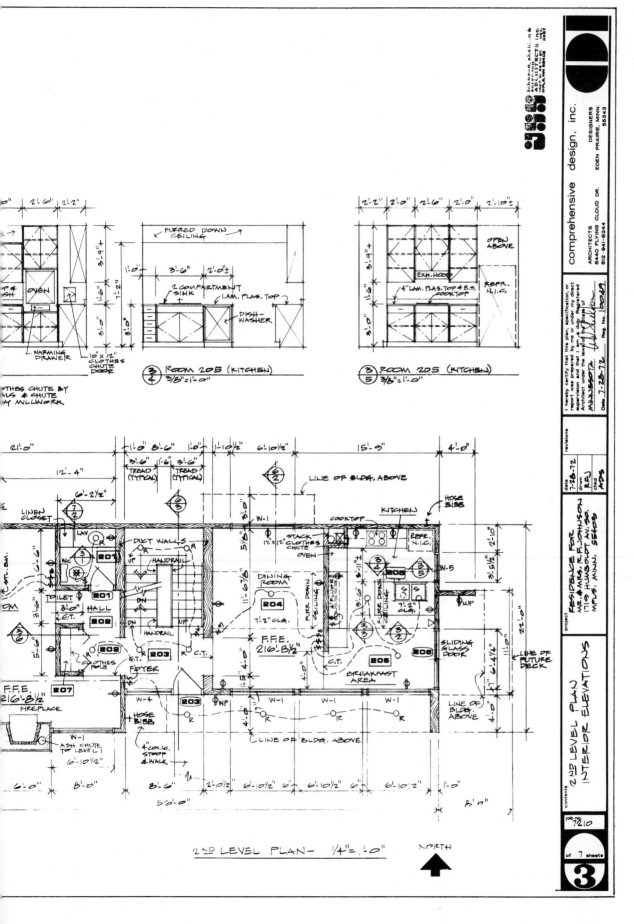

2'-6" 2'-2"

FURRED DOWN CEILING

3'-9"±

1'-0" 3'-6" 2'-0"±

OVEN

7'-2"

2 COMPARTMENT SINK

LAM. PLAS. TOP

3'-0" 3'-0"

DISH-WASHER

WARMING DRAWER

10" X 12" CLOTHES CHUTE DOOR

OTHES CHUTE BY
US & CHUTE
Y MILLWORK

③ ROOM 205 (KITCHEN)
④ 3/8"=1'-0"

2'-2" 2'-0" 2'-6" 2'-0" 2'-10"±

OPEN ABOVE

3'-9"±

EXH. HOOD

4" LAM. PLAS. TOP & B.S. COOKTOP

REFR. N.I.C.

3'-0"

③ ROOM 205 (KITCHEN)
⑤ 3/8"=1'-0"

21'-0"

1'-0" 8'-6" 1'-0" 1'-10½" 6'-10½" 15'-9" 4'-0"

12'-4"

3'-6" 1'-6" 3'-6"
TREAD (TYPICAL) TREAD (TYPICAL)

⑥
②

LINE OF BLDG. ABOVE

6'-2½"

⑦
②

⑥
③

KITCHEN

HOSE BIBB

LINEN CLOSET

LAV

COOKTOP

REFR. N.I.C.

DUCT WALLS

W-1

UP

HANDRAIL

12"X12" STACK CLOTHES CHUTE

OVEN

WC

③
③

201

R

R

201

DN

DINING ROOM

204

③
④

205

②
⑤

W-5

TOILET

3'-0" C.T.

HALL

202

DN

UP

HANDRAIL

R

7'-2" CLG.

③
②

③
②

W

⑥
②

202

203

R

C.T.

F.F.E. 216'-8½"

⑥
③

C.T.

③
②

208

205

SLIDING GLASS DOOR

WP

LINE OF FUTURE DECK

CLOTHES POLE

C.T.

FOYER

208

BREAKFAST AREA

LINE OF BLDG. ABOVE

F.F.E. 216'-8½"

207

FIREPLACE

W-4

203

WP

W-1

W-1

W-1

R

R

R

LINE OF BLDG. ABOVE

W-1

HOSE BIBB

ASH CHUTE TO LEVEL 1

4" CONC. STOOP & WALK

6'-10½"

6'-0" 8'-0" 8'-6" 2'-10½" 6'-10½" 6'-0" 6'-10½" 6'-0" 6'-10½" 1'-0"

56'-0" 8'-0"

2ND LEVEL PLAN - 1/4"=1'-0"

NORTH

jsa Johnson, sheldon & sorensen inc. ARCHITECTS

comprehensive design, inc.

ARCHITECTS
6440 FLYING CLOUD DR.
612-941-6244

DESIGNERS
EDEN PRAIRIE, MINN.
55343

I hereby certify that this plan, specification, or report was prepared by me or under my direct supervision and that I am a duly Registered Architect under the laws of the State of MINNESOTA

Date 7-28-72   Reg. No. 13042

revisions

date 7-28-72
drwn R.E.J.
chkd APS

project
RESIDENCE FOR
MR. & MRS. R. F. JOHNSON
1719 HUMBOLDT AV. SO.
MPLS. MINN. 55405

contents
2ND LEVEL PLAN
INTERIOR ELEVATIONS

job no.
7210

of 7 sheets

③

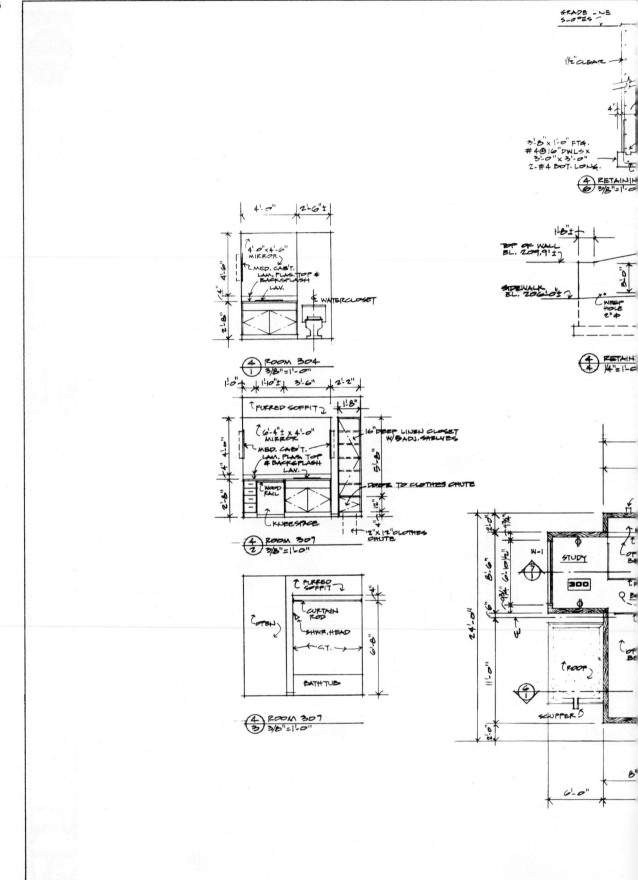

GRADE LINE
SLOPES

1½" CLEAR

3'-8" x 1'-0" FTG.
#4 @ 16" DWLS X
3'-0" x 3'-0"
2-#4 BOT. LONG.

④ RETAINING
⑥ 3/8"=1'-0"

4'-0"   2'-6"±

4'-0" x 4'-6"
MIRROR
MED. CAB'T.
LAM. PLAS. TOP &
BACKSPLASH
LAV.

4'-6"   4"   2'-8"

⅊ WATERCLOSET

④ ROOM 304
① 3/8"=1'-0"

1'-8"±

TOP OF WALL
EL. 209.9'±

SIDEWALK
EL. 206.0'±

2'-0"

WEEP
HOLE
2"∅

④ RETAIN
④ ¼"=1'-0"

1'-0"±   1'-10"±   3'-6"   2'-2"

FURRED SOFFIT

1'-8"

6'-4"± x 4'-0"
MIRROR
MED. CAB'T.
LAM. PLAS. TOP
& BACKSPLASH
LAV.

4'-0"   4"   2'-8"

16" DEEP LINEN CLOSET
W/5 ADJ. SHELVES

5'-8"

WOOD
RAIL

DOOR TO CLOTHES CHUTE

KNEESPACE

12"

12" x 12" CLOTHES
CHUTE

④ ROOM 307
② 3/8"=1'-0"

FURRED
SOFFIT

CURTAIN
ROD

OPEN

SHWR. HEAD

6'-8"

C.T.

BATH TUB

④ ROOM 307
③ 3/8"=1'-0"

STUDY

300

W-1

24'-0"   11'-0"   8'-6"

2'-0"   6'-10½"   1'-6"

ROOF

SCUPPER

2'-0"

6'-0"

8"

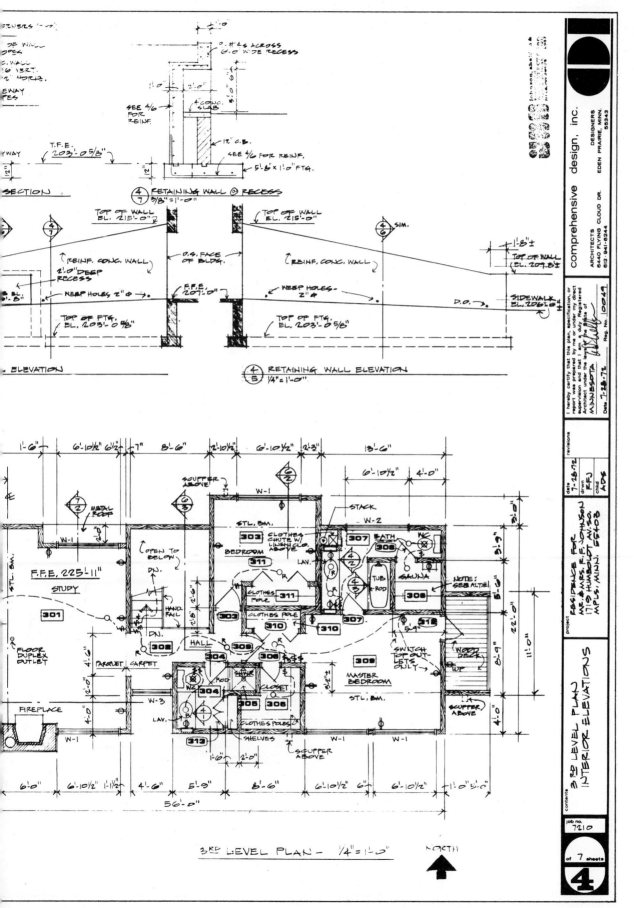

comprehensive design, inc.

ARCHITECTS • DESIGNERS
6440 FLYING CLOUD DR.
612-941-6244   EDEN PRAIRIE, MINN. 55343

I hereby certify that this plan, specification, or
report was prepared by me, or under my direct
supervision and that I am a duly Registered
Architect under the laws of the State of
MINNESOTA

Date 7-28-72   Reg. No. 10049

SECTION

4 RETAINING WALL @ RECESS
7 3/8" = 1'-0"

TOP OF WALL
EL. 215'-0"

TOP OF WALL
EL. 215'-0"

4 SIM.
6

REINF. CONC. WALL

O.S. FACE
OF BLDG.

REINF. CONC. WALL

1'-8"±
TOP OF WALL
(EL. 209.8'±

2'-0" DEEP
RECESS

F.F.E.
207'-0"

WEEP HOLES.
2" ∅

D.O.

SIDEWALK
EL. 206'.8'±

WEEP HOLES 2" ∅

TOP OF FTG.
EL. 203'-0 5/8"

TOP OF FTG.
EL. 203'-0 5/8"

ELEVATION

4 RETAINING WALL ELEVATION
5 1/4" = 1'-0"

SECTION:
T.F.E.
203'-0 5/8"

0 #4s ACROSS
6'-0 WIDE RECESS

4" CONC.
SLAB

SEE 4/6
FOR
REINF.

12" C.B.

SEE 4/6 FOR REINF.

5'-8" X 1'-0" FTG.

F.F.E. 225'-11"
STUDY

301

FLOOR
DUPLEX
OUTLET

PARQUET   CARPET

FIREPLACE

W-1

METAL
ROOF

W-1

SCUPPER
ABOVE

W-1

OPEN TO
BELOW

DN.

HAND
RAIL

DN.

302

HALL

308

304

W.C.

ROD

304

SHWR

305   308

LAV.

CLOTHES POLES

SHELVES

313

SCUPPER
ABOVE

STL. BM.

BEDROOM

311

CLOTHES
CHUTE W/
LINEN CLO.
ABOVE

LAV.

CLOTHES
POLE   311

303   CLOTHES POLE

310   310

304   308

W-1

STACK

W-2

307   BATH   308

WC

TUB
ROD

SAUNA

307

308

312

SWITCH
TOP OUTLETS
ONLY

MASTER
BEDROOM

308

CLOSET

STL. BM.

WOOD
DECK

WP

SCUPPER
ABOVE

NOTE:
SEE ALT #1

W-1   W-1   W-1

W-3

56'-0"

3RD LEVEL PLAN - 1/4" = 1'-0"

NORTH

date 7-28-72
drwn FPJ
ckd ADG

project RESIDENCE FOR
MR. & MRS. E. F. JOHNSON
1719 HUMBOLDT AV. SO.
MPLS. MINN. 55408

contents 3RD LEVEL PLAN
INTERIOR ELEVATIONS

job no.
7210

of 7 sheets

4

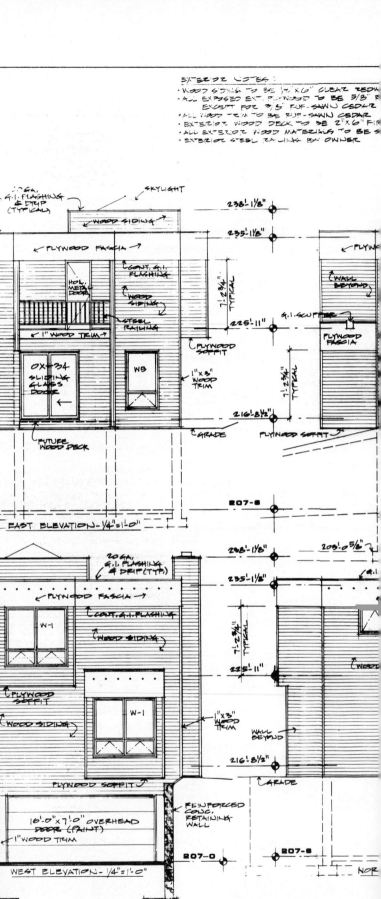

EXTERIOR NOTES:
· WOOD SIDING TO BE ¼" X 6" CLEAR REDW
· ALL EXPOSED EXT. PLYWOOD TO BE 5/8" R
    EXCEPT FOR ¾" RUF-SAWN CEDAR
· ALL WOOD TRIM TO BE RUF-SAWN CEDAR
· EXTERIOR WOOD DECK TO BE 2" X 6" FIR
· ALL EXTERIOR WOOD MATERIALS TO BE S
· EXTERIOR STEEL RAILING BY OWNER

EAST ELEVATION—¼"=1'-0"

WEST ELEVATION—¼"=1'-0"

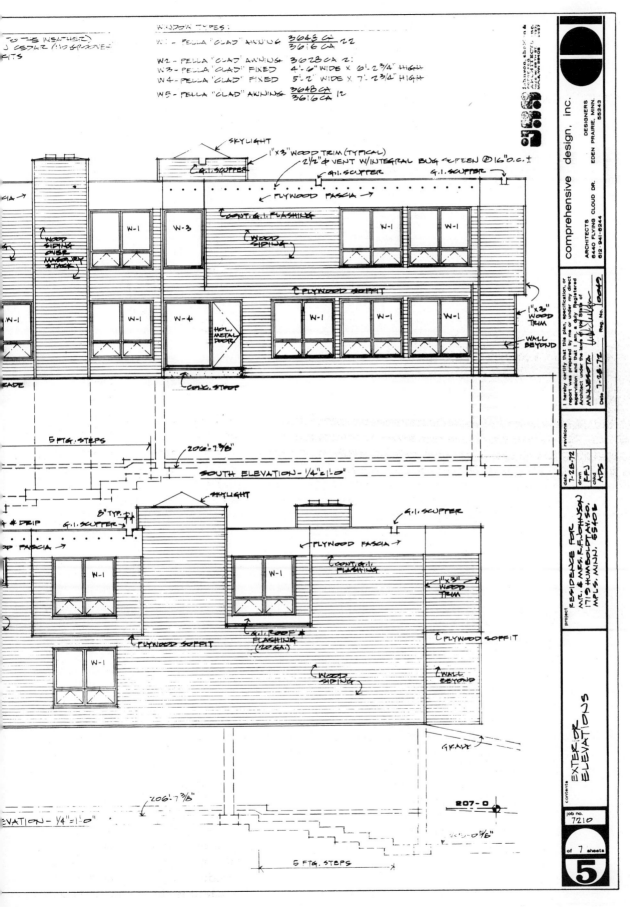

WINDOW TYPES:

W1 - PELLA "CLAD" AWNING 3648 GA 22 / 3616 GA 22

W2 - PELLA "CLAD" AWNING 3628 GA 2:
W3 - PELLA "CLAD" FIXED 4'-6" WIDE X 6'-2¾" HIGH
W4 - PELLA "CLAD" FIXED 5'-2" WIDE X 7'-2¾" HIGH
W5 - PELLA "CLAD" AWNING 3648 GA / 3616 GA 12

SOUTH ELEVATION - ¼"=1'-0"

EXTERIOR ELEVATIONS

comprehensive design, inc.

ARCHITECTS
6440 FLYING CLOUD DR.

DESIGNERS
EDEN PRAIRIE, MINN.
55343

612-941-6244

I hereby certify that this plan, specification, or report was prepared by me or under my direct supervision and that I am a duly Registered Architect under the laws of the State of MINNESOTA

Date 7-28-72 Reg. No. 10042

date 7-28-72
drwn R.P.J.
chkd K.P.S.

project
RESIDENCE FOR
MR. & MRS. R. F. JOHNSON
1715 HUMBOLDT AV. SO.
MPLS, MINN. 55403

contents
EXTERIOR ELEVATIONS

job no.
7210

of 7 sheets

5

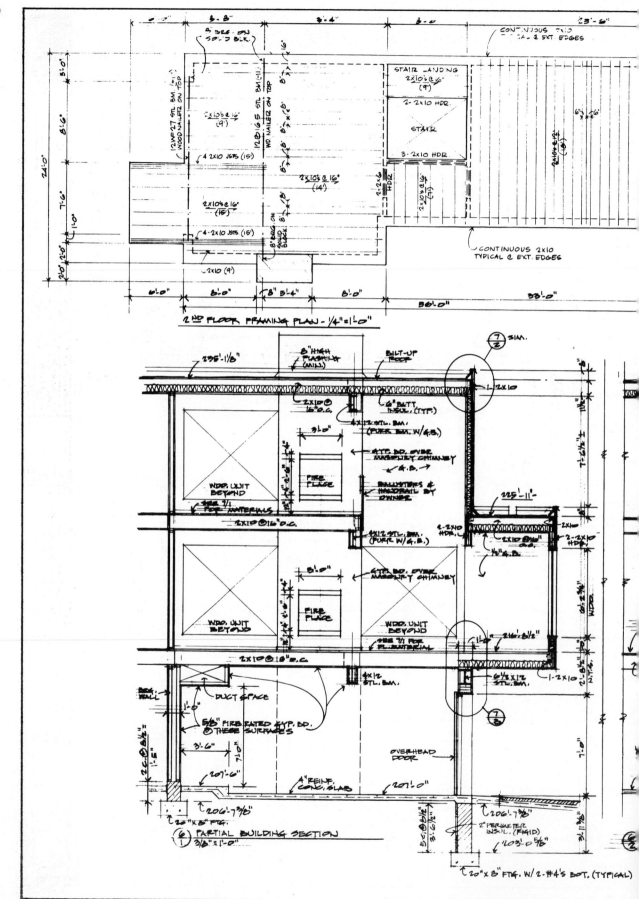

2ND FLOOR FRAMING PLAN - 1/4"=1'-0"

⑥ PARTIAL BUILDING SECTION
   3/8"=1'-0"

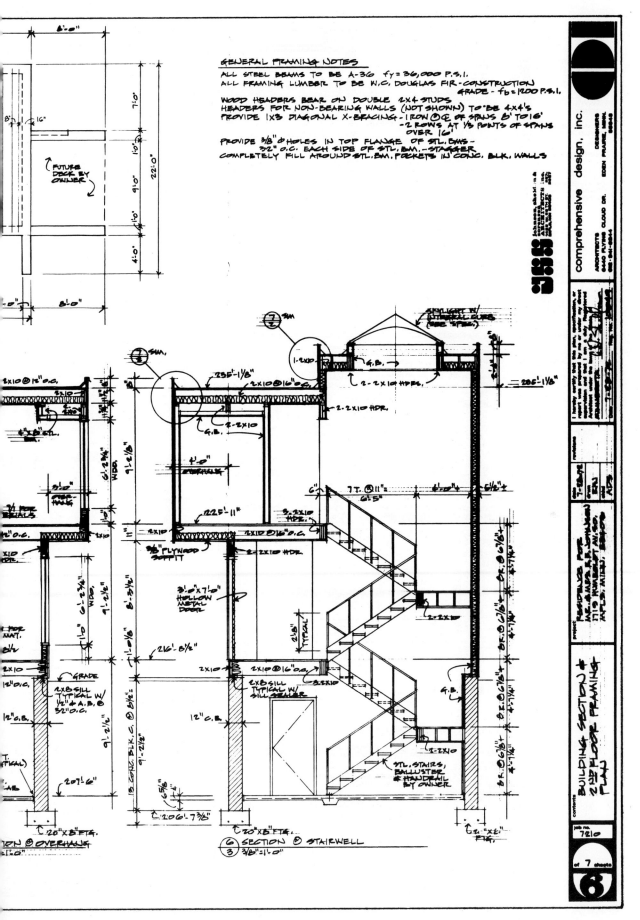

GENERAL FRAMING NOTES

ALL STEEL BEAMS TO BE A-36 fy=36,000 P.S.I.
ALL FRAMING LUMBER TO BE W.C. DOUGLAS FIR-CONSTRUCTION
GRADE - fb=1200 P.S.I.

WOOD HEADERS BEAR ON DOUBLE 2X4 STUDS
HEADERS FOR NON-BEARING WALLS (NOT SHOWN) TO BE 4X4's
PROVIDE 1X3 DIAGONAL X-BRACING - 1 ROW @ ℄ OF SPANS 8' TO 16'
-2 ROWS AT 1/3 POINTS OF SPANS OVER 16'

PROVIDE 3/8"∅ HOLES IN TOP FLANGE OF STL. BMS -
32" O.C. EACH SIDE OF STL. BM. - STAGGER
COMPLETELY FILL AROUND STL. BM. POCKETS IN CONC. BLK. WALLS

comprehensive design, inc.

ARCHITECTS
6440 FLYING CLOUD DR.   EDEN PRAIRIE, MINN.   55343
612-941-9444

BUILDING SECTION +
2ᴺᴰ FLOOR FRAMING
PLAN

project: RESIDENCE FOR
MR. & MRS. A.F. GRANDGE
1710 RIVERCREST AVE. SO.
MPLS., MINN. 55410

job no. 7210

6 of 7 sheets

③ SECTION @ STAIRWELL
3/8"=1'-0"

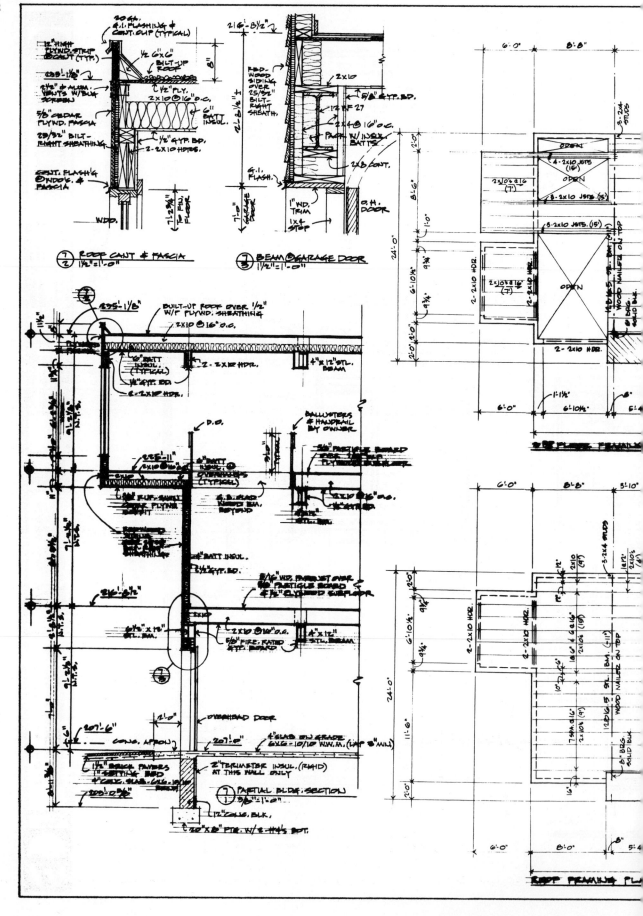

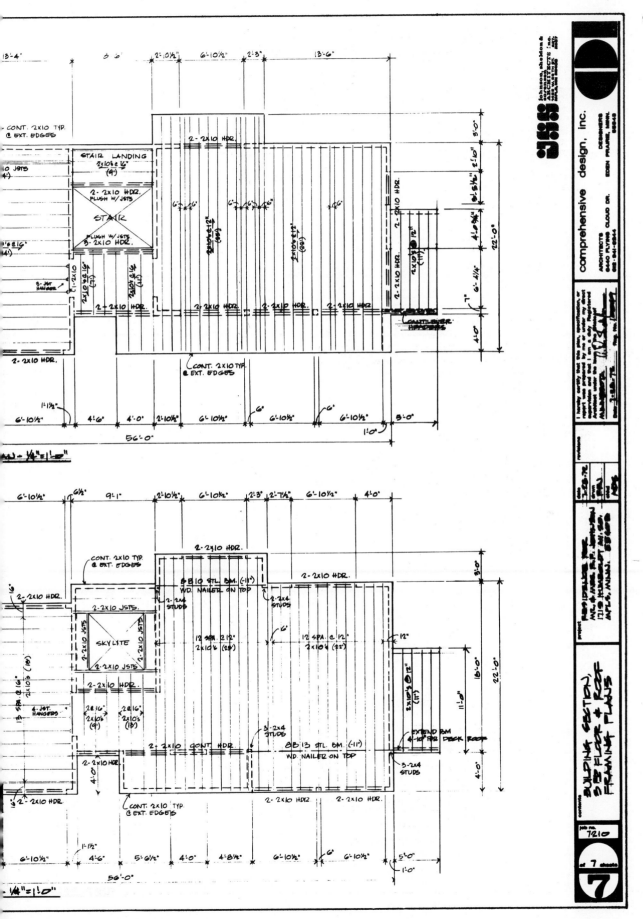

comprehensive design, inc.

ARCHITECTS DESIGNERS
6440 FLYING CLOUD DR. EDEN PRAIRIE, MINN.
612-941-8844 55343

Johnson shebeak
ARCHITECTS inc.
MILWAUKEE

job no.
7210

of 7 sheets
7

CONT. 2X10 TYP.
@ EXT. EDGES

STAIR LANDING
2x10 @ 16"
(4')

2- 2X10 HDR.
FLUSH W/ JSTS

STAIR

FLUSH W/ JSTS
3- 2X10 HDR.

3- JST
HANGER

2- 2X10 HDR.

2- 2X10 HDR.

2- 2X10 HDR.

2- 2X10 HDR.

2- 2X10 HDR.

2- 2X10 HDR.

CONT. 2X10 TYP.
@ EXT. EDGES

2- 2X10 HDR.

CANTILEVER
HEADERS

56'-0"

¼"=1'-0"

CONT. 2X10 TYP.
@ EXT. EDGES

2- 2X10 HDR.

8 B 10 STL. BM. (-11")
WD. NAILER ON TOP

2-2X4 STUDS

2-2X4 STUDS

2- 2X10 HDR.

2- 2X10 JSTS.

SKYLITE

2- 2X10 JSTS.

2- 2X10 HDR.

4- JST
HANGERS

2- 2X10 CONT. HDR.

3- 2X4 STUDS

8 B 13 STL. BM. (-11")
WD. NAILER ON TOP

3- 2X4 STUDS

EXTEND BM
4'-10" FOR DECK ROOF

2- 2X10 HDR.

2- 2X10 HDR.

CONT. 2X10 TYP.
@ EXT. EDGES

2- 2X10 HDR.

2- 2X10 HDR.

2- 2X10 HDR.

56'-0"

¼"=1'-0"

contents
BUILDING SECTION,
2ND FLOOR & ROOF
FRAMING PLANS

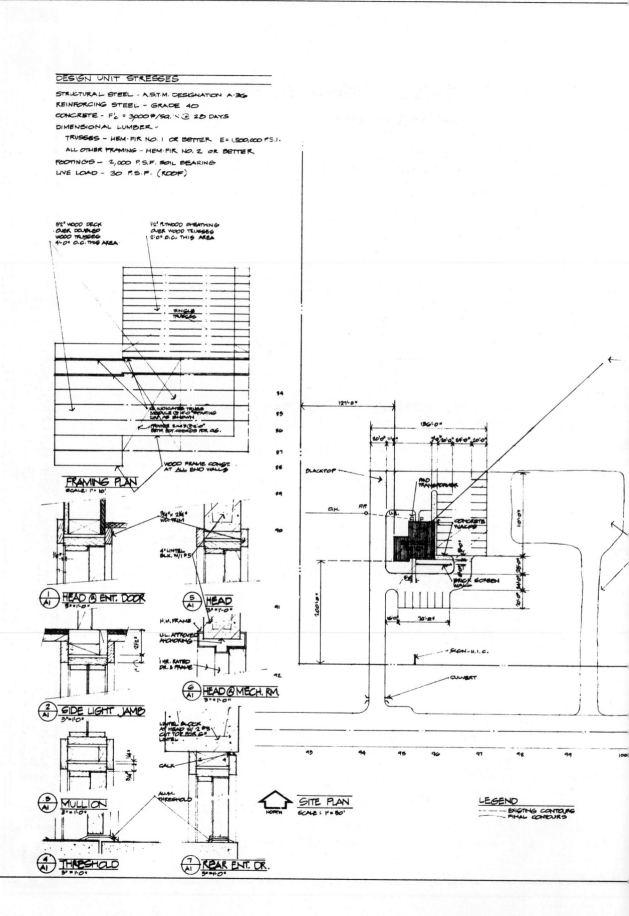

DESIGN UNIT STRESSES

STRUCTURAL STEEL - A.S.T.M. DESIGNATION A-36
REINFORCING STEEL - GRADE 40
CONCRETE - F'c = 3000#/SQ. X @ 28 DAYS
DIMENSIONAL LUMBER -
　TRUSSES - HEM-FIR NO. 1 OR BETTER E = 1,500,000 P.S.I.
　ALL OTHER FRAMING - HEM-FIR NO. 2 OR BETTER
FOOTINGS - 2,000 P.S.F. SOIL BEARING
LIVE LOAD - 30 P.S.F. (ROOF)

1½" WOOD DECK OVER DOUBLED WOOD TRUSSES 4'-0" O.C. THIS AREA

½" PLYWOOD SHEATHING OVER WOOD TRUSSES 2'-0" O.C. THIS AREA

SINGLE TRUSSES

X INDICATES TRUSS
MODULE @ 4'-0" SPACING LAP AS SHOWN.
PROVIDE 2x6 @ 2'-0" BETW. BOT. CHORDS FOR O.G.

WOOD FRAME CONST. AT ALL END WALLS

FRAMING PLAN
SCALE: 1" = 10'

HEAD @ ENT. DOOR 1/A1 3"=1'-0"

¾" x 2¼" WD. TRIM

4" LINTEL BLK. W/ 1#5

HEAD 5/A1 3"=1'-0"

SIDE LIGHT JAMB 2/A1 3"=1'-0"

H.M. FRAME
U.L. APPROVED ANCHORING
1 HR. RATED DR. & FRAME

HEAD @ MECH. RM. 6/A1 3"=1'-0"

MULLION 3/A1 3"=1'-0"

LINTEL BLOCK AT HEAD W/ 2#5 CUT TOP FOR 6" LINTEL

CALK

THRESHOLD 4/A1 3"=1'-0"

ALUM. THRESHOLD

REAR ENT. DR. 7/A1 3"=1'-0"

127'-0"
136'-0"
20'-0" 11'-0" 7'-0" 10'-0" 14'-0" 20'-0"

BLACKTOP
PAD TRANSFORMER
O.H. R.P.
W.S.
CONCRETE WALKS
BRICK SCREEN WALL

200'-0"
15'-0" 20'-0"

SIGN - H.I.C.
CULVERT

SITE PLAN
SCALE: 1" = 30'
NORTH

LEGEND
— — — EXISTING CONTOURS
——— FINAL CONTOURS

Matysik Restaurant

Fairchild, Wisconsin

SHEET SCHEDULE

A1 TITLE SHEET, SITE PLAN, DETAILS
A2 FLOOR PLANS, SCHEDULES
A3 ELEVATIONS, SECTION, DETAILS
A4 WALL SECTIONS, DETAILS
M1 MECHANICAL PLAN
E1 ELECTRICAL PLAN

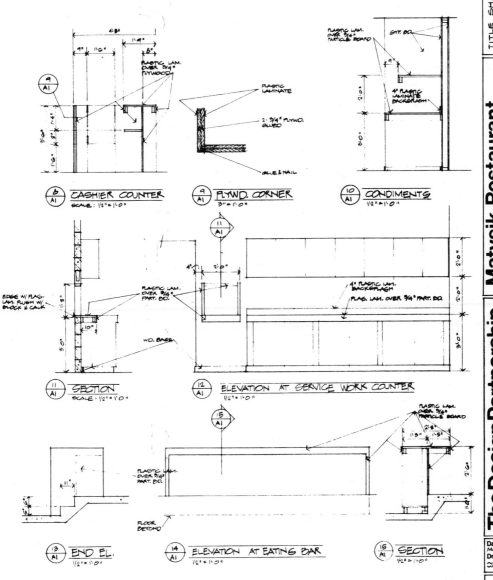

Matysik Restaurant
Fairchild, Wisconsin

TITLE SHEET
SITE PLAN
DETAILS

The Design Partnership
920 Nicollet Mall Suite 300
Minneapolis, Minnesota 55402

Date: MARCH 22, 1974
Dr: KWD
Ckd: WCA

A1

Room Finish Schedule

NO.	NAME	WALLS NORTH	EAST	SOUTH	WEST	CEILING	FLOOR	BASE	REMARKS
101	VESTIBULE	GLASS, GYP. BD.	GYP. BD.	GLASS, GYP. BD.	DIAG. SIDING	GYP. BD.	VINYL TILE	OAK	
102	FOYER	GYP. BD.	GYP. BD.	GLASS, GYP. BD.	—	GYP. BD.	CARPET	OAK	
103	DINING	GYP. BD.	CONC BLK, GYP. BD.	GYP. BD.	GLASS, GYP. BD.	EXP. DECK	CARPET	OAK	
104	HALL	WOOD, CONC. BLK.	—	GYP. BD.	—	GYP. BD.	VINYL TILE	OAK	
105	SERVING	CONC. BLK.	CONC. BLK.	—	—	EXP. DECK	VINYL TILE	OAK	
106	LUNCH ROOM	—	CONC. BLK.	GLASS, GYP. BD.	—	EXP. DECK	CARPET	OAK	
107	COATS	GYP. BD.	GYP. BD.	GYP. BD.	—	GYP. BD.	VINYL TILE	OAK	
108	MEN	CONC. BLK.	CONC. BLK.	CONC. BLK.	CONC. BLK.	GYP. BD.	CERAMIC TILE	C.T.	SEE NOTES 3
109	WOMEN	CONC. BLK.	CONC. BLK.	CONC. BLK.	CONC. BLK.	GYP. BD.	CERAMIC TILE	C.T.	SEE NOTES 3
110	STORAGE	CONC. BLK.	CONC. BLK.	CONC. BLK.	CONC. BLK.	GYP. BD.	CONCRETE	VINYL	SEE NOTES 2 & 3
111	MECHANICAL	CONC. BLK.	CONC. BLK.	CONC. BLK.	CONC. BLK.	GYP. BD.	CONCRETE	—	G.B. TO BE 5/8" TYPE X GYP. BD.
112	KITCHEN	CONC. BLK.	CONC. BLK.	CONC. BLK.	CONC. BLK.	GYP. BD.	CONCRETE	VINYL	SEE NOTES 2 & 3
113	DISHWASHING	CONC. BLK.	CONC. BLK.	CONC. BLK.	CONC. BLK.	GYP. BD.	CONCRETE	VINYL	SEE NOTES 2 & 3

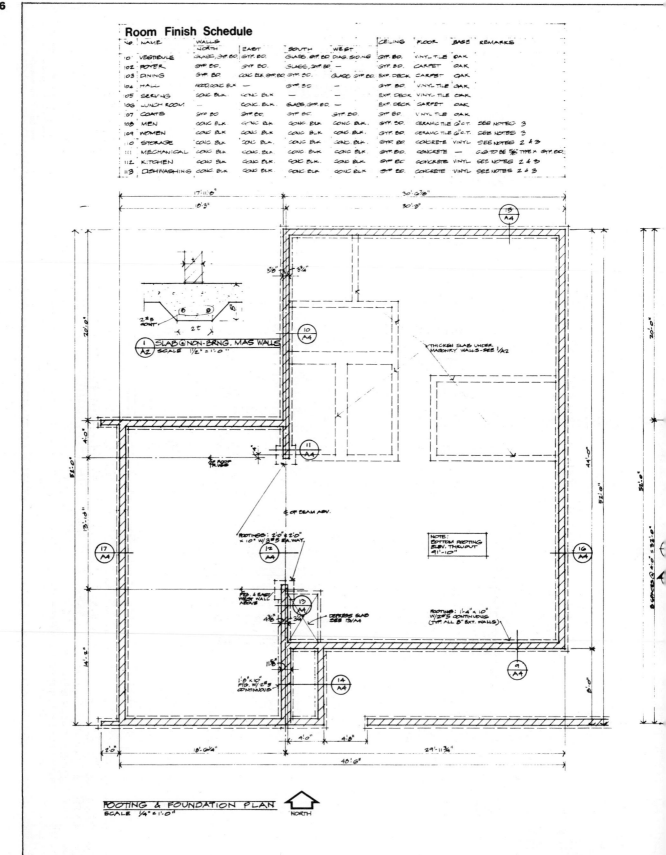

1/A2 — SLAB @ NON-BRNG. MAS. WALLS SCALE 1 1/2" = 1'-0"

THICKEN SLAB UNDER MASONRY WALLS—SEE 1/A2

€ OF BEAM ABV.

FOOTINGS: 2'-0" x 2'-0" x 10" W/ 3 #5 EA. WAY.

NOTE:
BOTTOM FOOTING
ELEV. THRUOUT
91'-10"

FTG. & EAST WEST WALL ABOVE

DEPRESS SLAB SEE 13/A4

FOOTING: 1'-4" x 10" W/ 2 #5 CONTINUOUS (TYP. ALL 8" EXT. WALLS)

1'-8" x 10" FTG. W/ 2 #5 CONTINUOUS

FOOTING & FOUNDATION PLAN
SCALE 1/4" = 1'-0"

NORTH

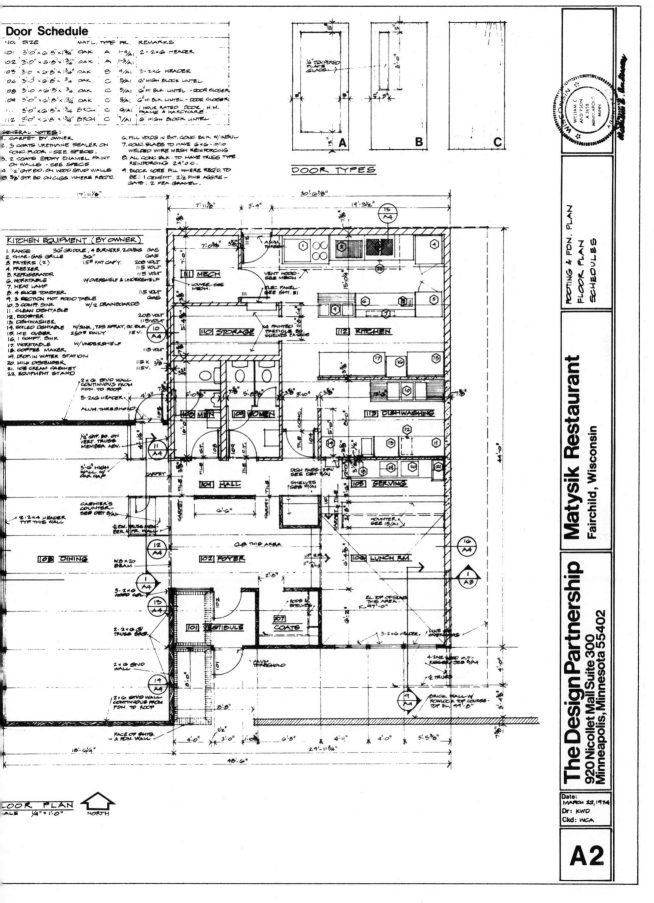

Door Schedule

NO.	SIZE	MAT'L.	TYPE	PR.	REMARKS
101	3'-0" x 6'-8" x 1¾"	OAK	A	1-4/A1	2-2x6 HEADER
102	3'-0" x 6'-8" x 1¾"	OAK	A	1-3/A1	
103	3'-0" x 6'-8" x 1¾"	OAK	B	4/A1	3-2x6 HEADER
104	3'-0" x 6'-8" x ¾"	OAK	C	5/A1	6" HIGH BLOCK LINTEL
108	3'-0" x 6'-8" x ¾"	OAK	C	5/A1	6" HI BLK LINTEL - DOOR CLOSER
109	3'-0" x 6'-8" x ¾"	OAK	C	5/A1	6" HI BLK LINTEL - DOOR CLOSER
111	3'-0" x 6'-8" x ¾"	BRCH	C	6/A1	1 HOUR RATED DOOR H.M. FRAME & HARDWARE
112	3'-0" x 6'-8" x 1¾"	BRCH	C	7/A1	6" HIGH BLOCK LINTEL

GENERAL NOTES:
1. CARPET BY OWNER
2. 3 COATS URETHANE SEALER ON CONC. FLOOR - SEE SPECS.
3. 2 COATS EPOXY ENAMEL PAINT ON WALLS - SEE SPECS.
4. ½" GYP. BD. ON WOOD STUD WALLS
5. ⅝" GYP. BD. ON C'LGS WHERE REQ'D.
6. FILL VOIDS IN EXT. CONC. BLK. W/INSUL.
7. CONC. SLABS TO HAVE 6x6-10/10 WELDED WIRE MESH REINFORCING
8. ALL CONC. BLK. TO HAVE TRUSS TYPE REINFORCING 24" O.C.
9. BLOCK CORE FILL WHERE REQ'D. TO BE: 1 CEMENT, 2½ FINE AGGREGATE, 2 PEA GRAVEL.

DOOR TYPES
A   B   C

KITCHEN EQUIPMENT (BY OWNER)
1. RANGE — 36" GRIDDLE, 4 BURNERS, 2 OVENS — GAS
2. CHAR-GAS GRILLE — 36" — GAS
3. FRYERS (2) — 15# FAT CAP'Y. — 208 VOLT
4. FREEZER — 115 VOLT
5. REFRIGERATOR — 115 VOLT
6. WORKTABLE — W/OVERSHELF & UNDERSHELF
7. HEAT LAMP — 115 VOLT
8. 4 SLICE TOASTER — 115 VOLT
9. 3 SECTION HOT FOOD TABLE — GAS
10. 3 COMP'T SINK — W/2 DRAINBOARDS
11. CLEAN DISHTABLE
12. BOOSTER — 208 VOLT
13. DISHWASHER — 115 VOLT
14. SOILED DISHTABLE — W/SINK, PRE-SPRAY, 2 COMP. BLK.
15. ICE CUBER — 250# DAILY — 115 V.
16. 1 COMP'T. SINK
17. WORKTABLE — W/UNDERSHELF
18. COFFEE MAKER — 115 VOLT
19. DROP-IN WATER STATION
20. MILK DISPENSER — 115 V.
21. ICE CREAM CABINET — 115 V.
22. EQUIPMENT STAND

MECH
STORAGE
KITCHEN
MEN   WOMEN
DISHWASHING
HALL
SERVING
DINING   FOYER   LUNCH RM.
VESTIBULE   COATS

FLOOR PLAN
SCALE ¼" = 1'-0"   NORTH

The Design Partnership
920 Nicollet Mall Suite 300
Minneapolis, Minnesota 55402

Matysik Restaurant
Fairchild, Wisconsin

FOOTING & FDN. PLAN
FLOOR PLAN
SCHEDULES

Date: MARCH 22, 1974
Dr: KWD
Ckd: WCA

A2

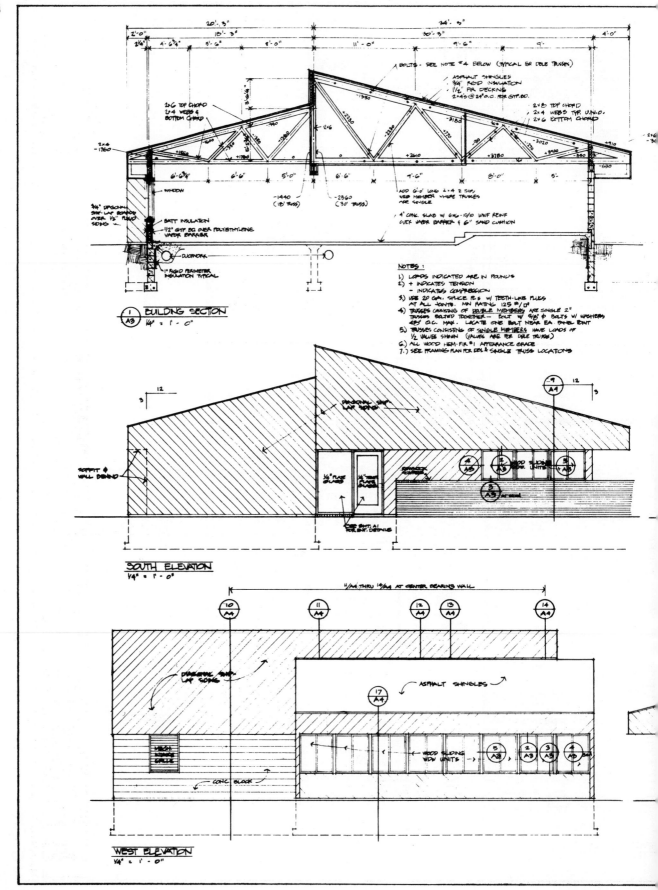

NOTES:

1) LOADS INDICATED ARE IN POUNDS
2) + INDICATES TENSION
   — INDICATES COMPRESSION
3) USE 20 GA. SPLICE PLS W/ TEETH-LIKE PLIES AT ALL JOINTS. MIN RATING 125 #/☐"
4) TRUSSES CONSISTING OF DOUBLE MEMBERS ARE SINGLE 2" TRUSSES BOLTED TOGETHER — BOLT W/ 5/8" ⌀ BOLTS W/ WASHERS 48" O.C. MAX. LOCATE ONE BOLT NEAR EA PANEL POINT
5) TRUSSES CONSISTING OF SINGLE MEMBERS HAVE LOADS OF 1/2 VALUES SHOWN (VALUES ARE FOR DBLE TRUSSES)
6) ALL WOOD HEM-FIR #1 APPEARANCE GRADE
7) SEE FRAMING PLAN FOR DBL & SINGLE TRUSS LOCATIONS

1/A3 BUILDING SECTION
1/4" = 1'-0"

SOUTH ELEVATION
1/4" = 1'-0"

WEST ELEVATION
1/4" = 1'-0"

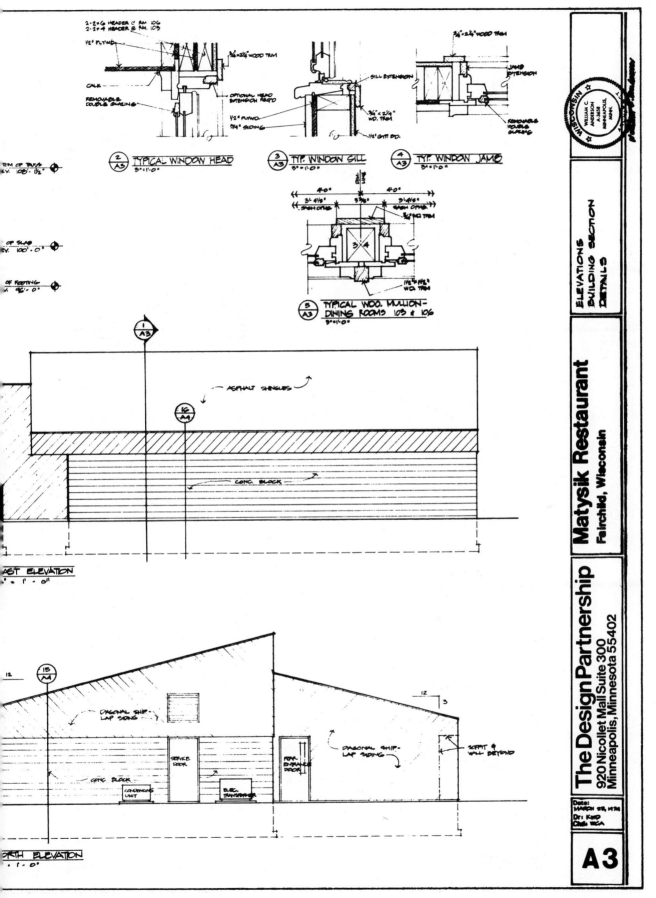

2-2×6 HEADER @ RM 106
2-2×4 HEADER @ RM. 103

½" PLYWD

¾"×3¼" WOOD TRIM

CALK

REMOVABLE
DOUBLE GLAZING

OPTIONAL HEAD
EXTENSION REQ'D

½" PLYWD

¾" SIDING

⌀ 2 / A3 TYPICAL WINDOW HEAD
3"=1'-0"

SILL EXTENSION

¾" × 2¼"
WD. TRIM

½" GYP. BD.

⌀ 3 / A3 TYP. WINDOW SILL
3"=1'-0"

¾"-2¼" WOOD TRIM

JAMB
EXTENSION

REMOVABLE
DOUBLE
GLAZING

⌀ 4 / A3 TYP. WINDOW JAMB
3"=1'-0"

4'-0" 4'-0"
3'-4⅛" 5⅜" 3'-4⅛"
SASH OPNG. SASH OPNG.

¾"×3 WD TRIM

3/4

1½"×1½"
WD TRIM

⌀ 5 / A3 TYPICAL WOO. MULLION-
DINING ROOMS 103 & 106
3"=1'-0"

TOM OF TRUSS
EV. 108'-1½"

OF SLAB
EV. 100'-0"

OF FOOTING
. 96'-0"

⌀ 1 / A3

ASPHALT SHINGLES

⌀ 16 / A-

CONC. BLOCK

AST ELEVATION
" = 1'-0"

⌀ 15 / A-

12

DIAGONAL SHIP-
LAP SIDING

12   3

DIAGONAL SHIP-
LAP SIDING

SOFFIT &
WALL BEYOND

CONC. BLOCK

SERVICE
DOOR

REAR
ENTRANCE
DOOR

CONDENSING
UNIT

ELEC.
TRANSFORMER

RTH ELEVATION
. 1'-0"

WISCONSIN
WILLIAM C.
ANDERSON
A-3658
MINNEAPOLIS
MINN.

ELEVATIONS
BUILDING SECTION
DETAILS

Matysik Restaurant
Fairchild, Wisconsin

The DesignPartnership
920 Nicollet Mall Suite 300
Minneapolis, Minnesota 55402

Date: MARCH 29, 1978
Dr: KMD
Chk: WCA

A3

100

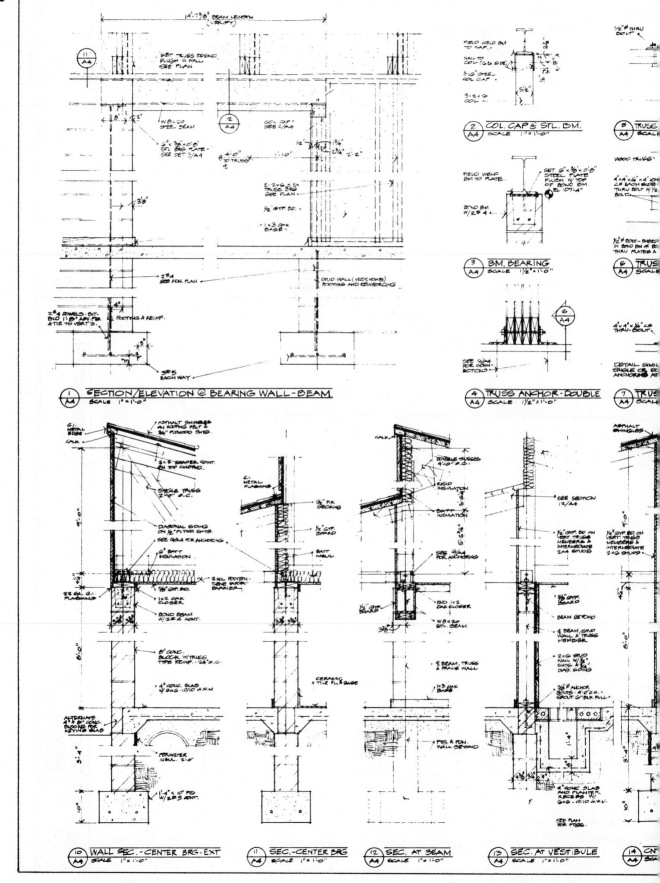

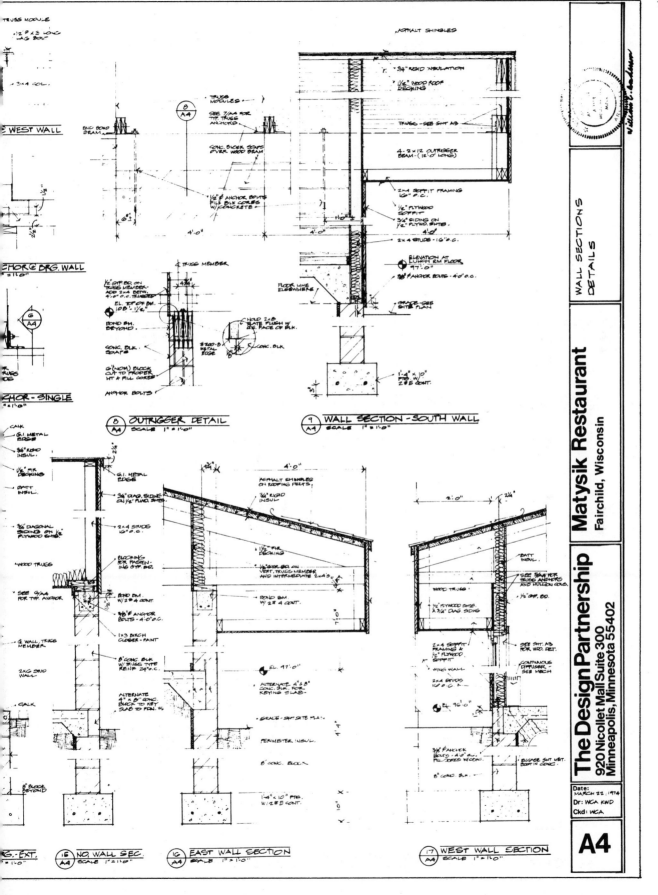

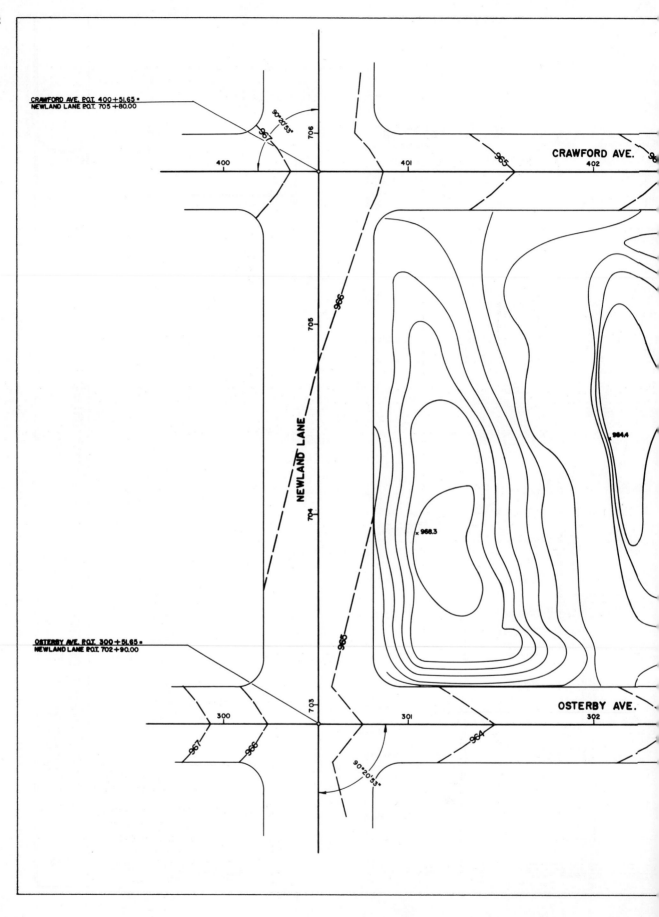

CRAWFORD AVE. P.O.T. 400+51.65 =
NEWLAND LANE P.O.T. 705+80.00

90°20'53"

706

CRAWFORD AVE.

400   401   965   402

705   966

NEWLAND LANE

704   × 968.3   968.4

OSTERBY AVE. P.O.T. 300+51.65 =
NEWLAND LANE P.O.T. 702+90.00

968

703   OSTERBY AVE.

300   301   302

967   966   964

90°20'53"

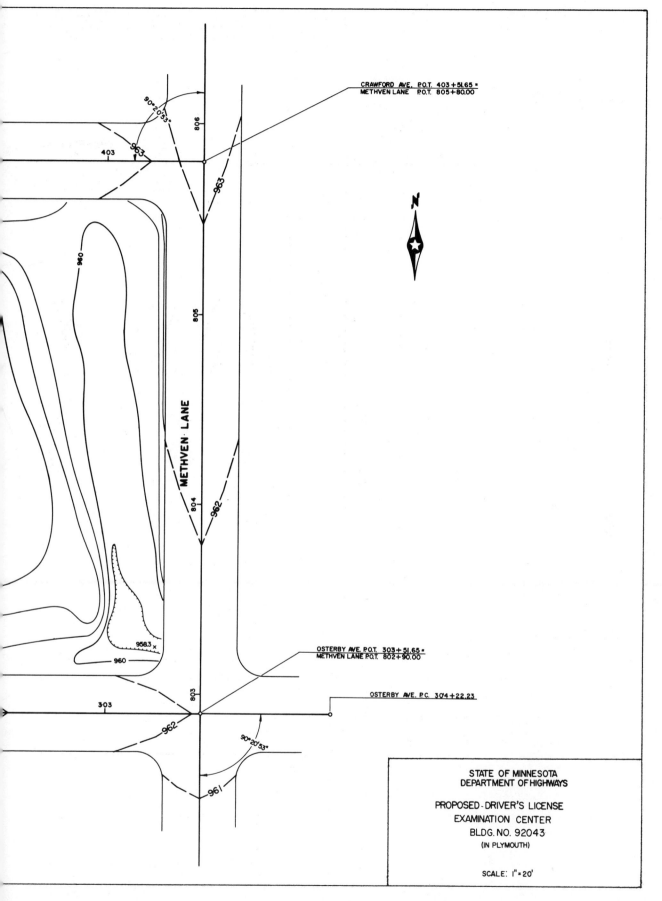

CRAWFORD AVE. P.O.T. 403+51.65 =
METHVEN LANE P.O.T. 805+80.00

90°20'53"

806

403

963

963

960

N

805

METHVEN LANE

804

962

958.3 x

960

OSTERBY AVE. P.O.T. 303+51.65 =
METHVEN LANE P.O.T. 802+90.00

OSTERBY AVE. P.C. 304+22.23

803

303

962

90°20'53"

961

STATE OF MINNESOTA
DEPARTMENT OF HIGHWAYS

PROPOSED - DRIVER'S LICENSE
EXAMINATION CENTER
BLDG. NO. 92043
(IN PLYMOUTH)

SCALE: 1" = 20'

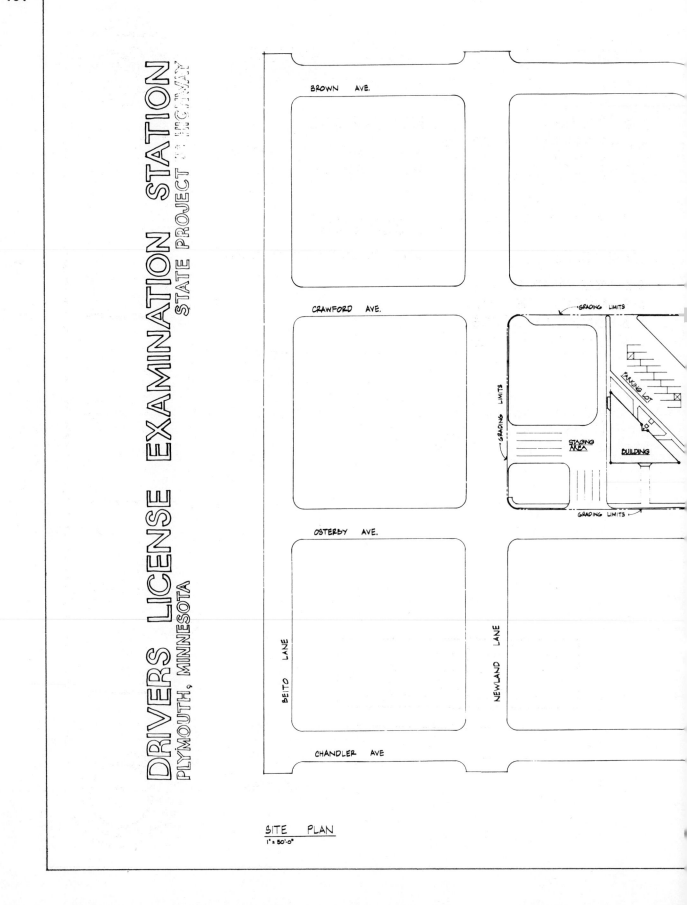

DRIVERS LICENSE EXAMINATION STATION
STATE PROJECT — HIGHWAY
PLYMOUTH, MINNESOTA

BROWN AVE.

CRAWFORD AVE.

OSTERBY AVE.

CHANDLER AVE

BEITO LANE

NEWLAND LANE

GRADING LIMITS

GRADING LIMITS

GRADING LIMITS

PARKING LOT

STAGING AREA

BUILDING

SITE PLAN

1" = 50'-0"

ARCHITECTURAL

A·1 TITLE SHEET & SITE MAP SURVEY
A·2 SITE PLAN
A·3 FLOOR PLAN & SCHEDULES
A·4 EXTERIOR ELEVATIONS
A·5 BUILDING DETAILS
A·6 MISCELLANEOUS DETAILS
A·7 REFLECTED CEILING PLAN

STRUCTURAL

S·1 FOUNDATION PLAN
S·2 ROOF FRAMING PLAN
S·3 STRUCTURAL DETAILS
S·4 STRUCTURAL DETAILS

MECHANICAL · ELEC.

ME·1 MECH/ELEC. SITE PLAN

MECHANICAL

M·2 FLOOR PLAN · PLUMBING
M·3 FLOOR PLAN · HVAC
M·4 MECHANICAL DETAILS

ELECTRICAL

E·2 FLOOR PLAN · ELECTRICAL

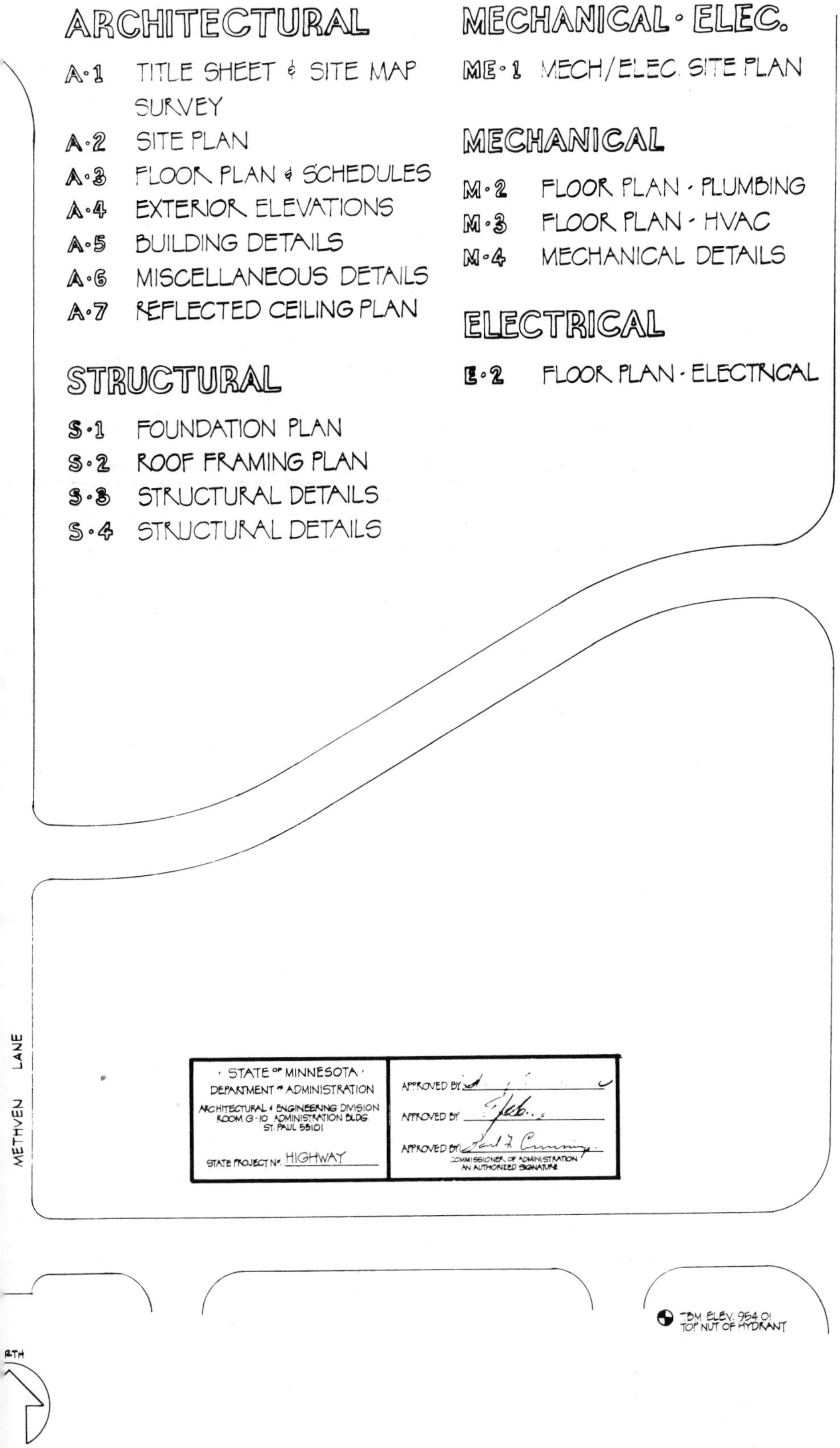

METHVEN LANE

FERNBROOK LANE

⊕ TBM ELEV. 964.01
TOP NUT OF HYDRANT

· STATE OF MINNESOTA ·
DEPARTMENT OF ADMINISTRATION
ARCHITECTURAL & ENGINEERING DIVISION
ROOM G·10 ADMINISTRATION BLDG.
ST. PAUL 55101

STATE PROJECT N° HIGHWAY

APPROVED BY
APPROVED BY
APPROVED BY
COMMISSIONER OF ADMINISTRATION
AN AUTHORIZED SIGNATURE

FREDERICK BENTZ / MILO THOMPSON & ASSOCIATES INC · ARCHITECTURE & URBAN DESIGN · 1234 DAIN TOWER, MINNEAPOLIS, MINNESOTA 55402 · TEL (612) 335-1207

DRIVERS LICENSE EXAMINATION STATION

PLYMOUTH, MINNESOTA

TITLE SHEET & SITE MAP

SCALE: 1" = 50'-0"

COMMISSION NUMBER 72.14
DATE 9/15/72
DRAWN KGR. SD
CHECKED KGR

I HEREBY CERTIFY THAT THIS PLAN, SPECIFICATION, OR REPORT WAS PREPARED BY ME OR UNDER MY DIRECT SUPERVISION AND THAT I AM A DULY REGISTERED ARCHITECT OR ENGINEER UNDER THE LAWS OF THE STATE OF MINNESOTA
DATE 4/18/74
REG NO 8108
REG NO
REG NO

A·1

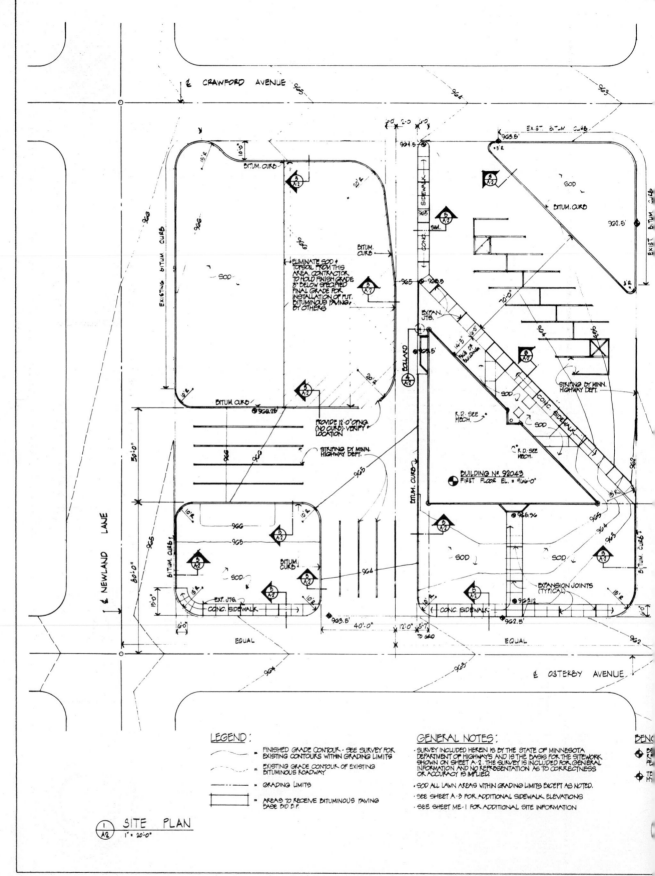

CRAWFORD AVENUE

BUILDING N° 92043
FIRST FLOOR EL. = 966-0"

① SITE PLAN
A2   1" = 20'-0"

LEGEND:
~~~~~~~ FINISHED GRADE CONTOUR · SEE SURVEY FOR EXISTING CONTOURS WITHIN GRADING LIMITS
~~~~~~~ EXISTING GRADE CONTOUR OF EXISTING BITUMINOUS ROADWAY
———————— GRADING LIMITS
▭▭▭▭ AREAS TO RECEIVE BITUMINOUS PAVING BASE BID D.P.

GENERAL NOTES:
· SURVEY INCLUDED HEREIN IS BY THE STATE OF MINNESOTA DEPARTMENT OF HIGHWAYS AND IS THE BASIS FOR THE SITEWORK SHOWN ON SHEET A·2. THE SURVEY IS INCLUDED FOR GENERAL INFORMATION AND NO REPRESENTATION AS TO CORRECTNESS OR ACCURACY IS IMPLIED.
· SOD ALL LAWN AREAS WITHIN GRADING LIMITS EXCEPT AS NOTED.
· SEE SHEET A·3 FOR ADDITIONAL SIDEWALK ELEVATIONS
· SEE SHEET ME·1 FOR ADDITIONAL SITE INFORMATION

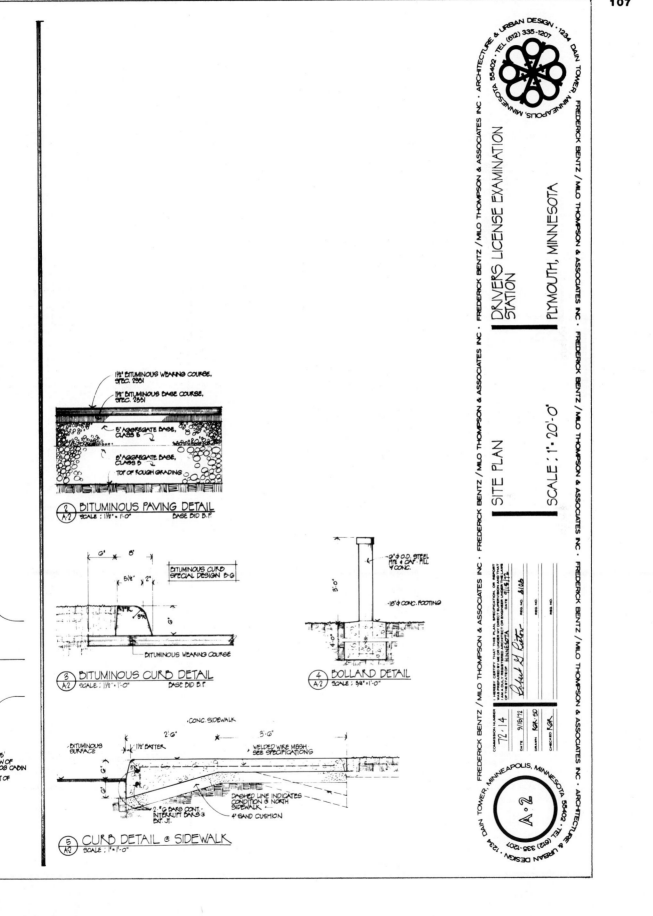

¢ METHVEN LANE

11½" BITUMINOUS WEARING COURSE, SPEC. 2331
1½" BITUMINOUS BASE COURSE, SPEC. 2331
5" AGGREGATE BASE, CLASS 5
6" AGGREGATE BASE, CLASS 5
TOP OF ROUGH GRADING

2 BITUMINOUS PAVING DETAIL
A-2 SCALE : 1½" = 1'-0"   BASE BID B.P.

BITUMINOUS CURB SPECIAL DESIGN B-6
BITUMINOUS WEARING COURSE

3 BITUMINOUS CURB DETAIL
A-2 SCALE : 1½" = 1'-0"   BASE BID B.P.

2"¢ O.D. STEEL PIPE ¢ CAP - FILL ¥ CONC.
18"¢ CONC. FOOTING

4 BOLLARD DETAIL
A-2 SCALE : ¾" = 1'-0"

CONC. SIDEWALK
BITUMINOUS SURFACE
1½" BATTER
WELDED WIRE MESH SEE SPECIFICATIONS
DASHED LINE INDICATES CONDITION @ NORTH SIDEWALK
2- ¾"¢ BARS CONT. INTERRUPT BARS @ EXP. JT.
4" SAND CUSHION

5 CURB DETAIL @ SIDEWALK
A-2 SCALE : 1" = 1'-0"

ARKS :
PARK ELEV. 970.85'
IN 24" ELM 100'W OF
K LANE S. OF LOG CABIN
984.01' TOP NUT OF
SEE SHEET A-1
TH

FREDERICK BENTZ / MILO THOMPSON & ASSOCIATES INC · ARCHITECTURE & URBAN DESIGN · 1234 DAIN TOWER · MINNEAPOLIS, MINNESOTA 55402 · TEL (612) 335-1207

FREDERICK BENTZ / MILO THOMPSON & ASSOCIATES INC · FREDERICK BENTZ / MILO THOMPSON & ASSOCIATES INC · FREDERICK BENTZ / MILO THOMPSON & ASSOCIATES INC · FREDERICK BENTZ / MILO THOMPSON & ASSOCIATES INC · FREDERICK BENTZ / MILO THOMPSON & ASSOCIATES INC

DAIN TOWER, MINNEAPOLIS, MINNESOTA 55402 · TEL (612) 335-1207 · ARCHITECTURE & URBAN DESIGN · 1234

DRIVERS LICENSE EXAMINATION STATION

PLYMOUTH, MINNESOTA

SITE PLAN

SCALE : 1" = 20'-0"

I HEREBY CERTIFY THAT THIS PLAN, SPECIFICATION OR REPORT WAS PREPARED BY ME OR UNDER MY DIRECT SUPERVISION AND THAT I AM A DULY REGISTERED ARCHITECT OR ENGINEER UNDER THE LAWS OF THE STATE OF MINNESOTA

Robert L. Rietow
DATE 9/18/72   REG. NO. 6106
REG. NO.
REG. NO.

COMMISSION NUMBER 72-14
DATE 9/18/72
DRAWN RGR-SD
CHECKED RGR

A-2

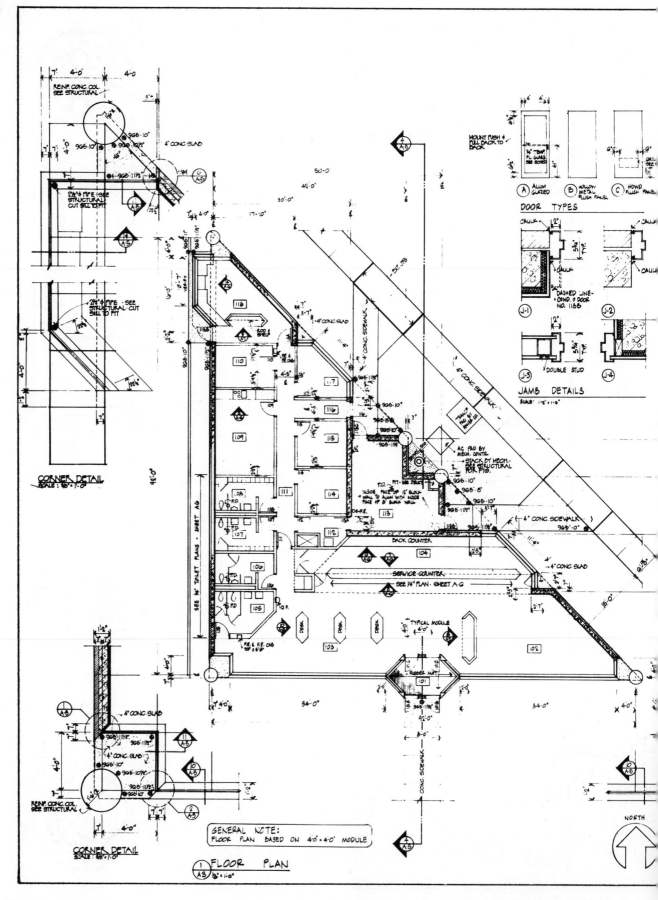

CORNER DETAIL
SCALE: 1/8" = 1'-0"

CORNER DETAIL
SCALE: 1/8" = 1'-0"

DOOR TYPES

Ⓐ ALUM. GLAZED   Ⓑ HOLLOW METAL FLUSH PANEL   Ⓒ HDWD. FLUSH PANEL

JAMB DETAILS
SCALE: 1 1/2" = 1'-0"

J-1   J-2   J-3 DOUBLE STUD   J-4

GENERAL NOTE:
FLOOR PLAN BASED ON 4'-0" × 4'-0" MODULE

① FLOOR PLAN
A-3 1/8" = 1'-0"

NORTH

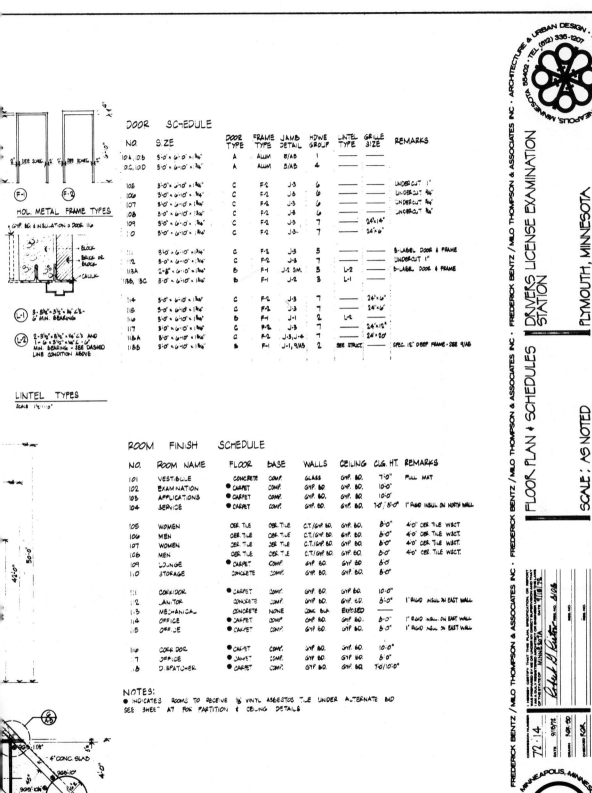

DOOR SCHEDULE

NO.	SIZE	DOOR TYPE	FRAME TYPE	JAMB DETAIL	HDWE GROUP	LINTEL TYPE	GRILLE SIZE	REMARKS
101A, 101B	3'-0" x 6'-0" x ¾"	A	ALUM	5/A5	1	—	—	
101C, 101D	3'-0" x 6'-10" x ¾"	A	ALUM	5/A5	4	—	—	
105	3'-0" x 6'-10" x 1¾"	C	F-2	J-3	6	—	—	UNDERCUT 1"
106	3'-0" x 6'-10" x 1¾"	C	F-2	J-3	6	—	—	UNDERCUT ¾"
107	3'-0" x 6'-10" x 1¾"	C	F-2	J-3	6	—	—	UNDERCUT ¾"
108	3'-0" x 6'-10" x 1¾"	C	F-2	J-3	6	—	—	UNDERCUT ¾"
109	3'-0" x 6'-10" x 1¾"	C	F-2	J-3	7	—	24"x14"	
110	3'-0" x 6'-10" x 1¾"	C	F-2	J-3	7	—	24"x6"	
111	3'-0" x 6'-10" x 1¾"	C	F-2	J-3	5	—	—	B-LABEL DOOR & FRAME
112	3'-0" x 6'-10" x 1¾"	C	F-2	J-3	7	—	—	UNDERCUT 1"
113A	2'-8" x 6'-10" x 1¾"	B	F-1	J-2 SIM.	5	L-2	—	B-LABEL DOOR & FRAME
113B, 13C	3'-0" x 6'-10" x 1¾"	B	F-1	J-2	3	L-1	—	
114	3'-0" x 6'-10" x 1¾"	C	F-2	J-3	7	—	24"x6"	
115	3'-0" x 6'-10" x 1¾"	C	F-2	J-3	7	—	24"x6"	
116	3'-0" x 6'-10" x 1¾"	B	F-1	J-1	2	L-2	—	
117	3'-0" x 6'-10" x 1¾"	C	F-2	J-3	7	—	24"x12"	
118A	3'-0" x 6'-10" x 1¾"	C	F-2	J-3, J-4	7	—	25"x20"	
118B	3'-0" x 6'-10" x 1¾"	B	F-1	J-1, 9/A5	2	SEE STRUCT.	—	SPEC. 12" DEEP FRAME - SEE 9/A5

HOL. METAL FRAME TYPES

(F-1) GYP. BD. & INSULATION @ DOOR 116

Block
Brick or block
Caulk

(L-1) 3 - 3½" x 3½" x ¼" ∠'s - 6" MIN. BEARING

(L-2) 2 - 3½" x 3½" x ¼" ∠'s AND 1 - 6" x 3½" x ⁵⁄₁₆" ∠ - 6' MIN. BEARING - SEE DASHED LINE CONDITION ABOVE

LINTEL TYPES
SCALE 1½"=1'-0"

ROOM FINISH SCHEDULE

NO.	ROOM NAME	FLOOR	BASE	WALLS	CEILING	CLG. HT.	REMARKS
101	VESTIBULE	CONCRETE	COMP.	GLASS	GYP. BD.	7'-0"	FULL MAT
102	EXAMINATION	●CARPET	COMP.	GYP. BD.	GYP. BD.	10'-0"	
103	APPLICATIONS	●CARPET	COMP.	GYP. BD.	GYP. BD.	10'-0"	
104	SERVICE	●CARPET	COMP.	GYP. BD.	GYP. BD.	7'-0"/8'-0"	1" RIGID INSUL. ON NORTH WALL
105	WOMEN	CER. TILE	CER. TILE	C.T./GYP. BD.	GYP. BD.	8'-0"	4'-0" CER. TILE WSCT.
106	MEN	CER. TILE	CER. TILE	C.T./GYP. BD.	GYP. BD.	8'-0"	4'-0" CER. TILE WSCT.
107	WOMEN	CER. TILE	CER. TILE	C.T./GYP. BD.	GYP. BD.	8'-0"	4'-0" CER. TILE WSCT.
108	MEN	CER. TILE	CER. TILE	C.T./GYP. BD.	GYP. BD.	8'-0"	4'-0" CER. TILE WSCT.
109	LOUNGE	●CARPET	COMP.	GYP. BD.	GYP. BD.	8'-0"	
110	STORAGE	CONCRETE	COMP.	GYP. BD.	GYP. BD.	8'-0"	
111	CORRIDOR	●CARPET	COMP.	GYP. BD.	GYP. BD.	10'-0"	
112	JANITOR	CONCRETE	COMP.	GYP. BD.	GYP. BD.	8'-0"	1" RIGID INSUL. ON EAST WALL
113	MECHANICAL	CONCRETE	NONE	CONC. BLK.	EXPOSED	—	
114	OFFICE	●CARPET	COMP.	GYP. BD.	GYP. BD.	8'-0"	1" RIGID INSUL. ON EAST WALL
115	OFFICE	●CARPET	COMP.	GYP. BD.	GYP. BD.	8'-0"	1" RIGID INSUL. ON EAST WALL
116	CORRIDOR	●CARPET	COMP.	GYP. BD.	GYP. BD.	10'-0"	
117	OFFICE	●CARPET	COMP.	GYP. BD.	GYP. BD.	8'-0"	
118	DISPATCHER	●CARPET	COMP.	GYP. BD.	GYP. BD.	7'-0"/10'-0"	

NOTES:
● INDICATES ROOMS TO RECEIVE ⅛" VINYL ASBESTOS TILE UNDER ALTERNATE BID
SEE SHEET A7 FOR PARTITION & CEILING DETAILS

CORNER DETAIL
SCALE: ⅜"=1'-0"

4" CONC. SLAB
REINF. CONC. COL. SEE STRUCTURAL

FREDERICK BENTZ / MILO THOMPSON & ASSOCIATES INC. · ARCHITECTURE & URBAN DESIGN · 1234 DAIN TOWER · MINNEAPOLIS, MINNESOTA 55402 · TEL (612) 335-1207

FREDERICK BENTZ / MILO THOMPSON & ASSOCIATES INC. · FREDERICK BENTZ / MILO THOMPSON & ASSOCIATES INC. · FREDERICK BENTZ / MILO THOMPSON & ASSOCIATES INC.

DRIVERS LICENSE EXAMINATION STATION

PLYMOUTH, MINNESOTA

FLOOR PLAN & SCHEDULES

SCALE: AS NOTED

COMMISSION NUMBER 72-14
DATE 9/15/72
DRAWN MR-50
CHECKED KGK
REG. NO. 4106

A·3

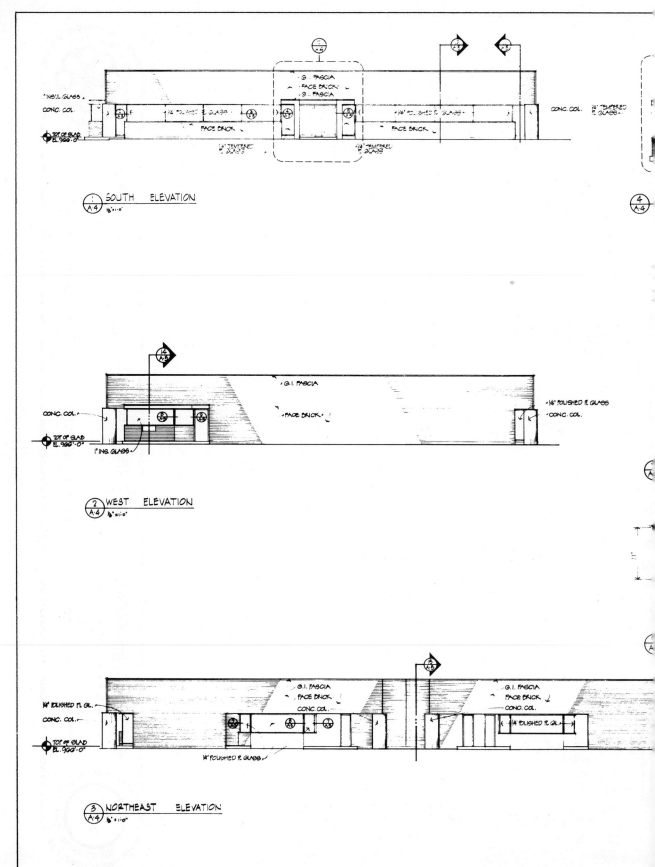

1"INSUL. GLASS

CONC. COL.

TOP OF SLAB
EL. 960'-0"

¼" POLISHED PL. GLASS

FACE BRICK

G.I. FASCIA
FACE BRICK
G.I. FASCIA

¼" POLISHED PL. GLASS

FACE BRICK

CONC. COL.

¼" TEMPERED
PL. GLASS

¼" TEMPERED
PL. GLASS

¼" TEMPERED
PL. GLASS

1/A·4 | SOUTH ELEVATION
⅛" = 1'-0"

CONC. COL.

TOP OF SLAB
EL. 960'-0"

1" INS. GLASS

G.I. FASCIA

FACE BRICK

¼" POLISHED PL. GLASS
CONC. COL.

2/A·4 | WEST ELEVATION
⅛" = 1'-0"

¼" POLISHED PL. GL.

CONC. COL.

TOP OF SLAB
EL. 960'-0"

¼" POLISHED PL. GLASS

G.I. FASCIA
FACE BRICK
CONC. COL.

G.I. FASCIA
FACE BRICK
CONC. COL.

¼" POLISHED PL. GL.

3/A·4 | NORTHEAST ELEVATION
⅛" = 1'-0"

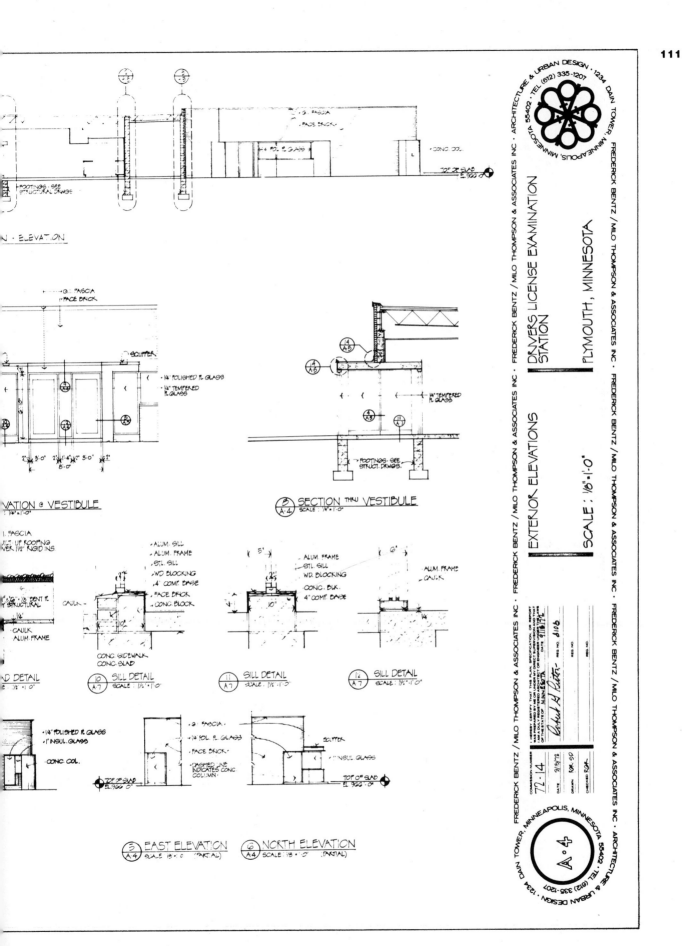

N · ELEVATION

·G· FASCIA
1"FACE BRICK

SCUTTER

1/4" POLISHED PL. GLASS

1/4" TEMPERED
PL GLASS

2" 3'-0" 1'-4" 2" 3'-0" 2"
8'-0"

VATION @ VESTIBULE

3 SECTION THRU VESTIBULE
A·4 SCALE : 1/4"·1'-0"

·1/4" TEMPERED
PL. GLASS

FOOTINGS· SEE
STRUCT. DRWGS.

1. FASCIA
BUILT UP ROOFING
OVER 1 1/2" RIGID INS.

·ALUM. SILL
·ALUM. FRAME
·STL. SILL
·WD BLOCKING
·4" COMP. BASE
·FACE BRICK
·CONC. BLOCK

CAULK

CAULK·
·ALUM. FRAME

CONC. SIDEWALK
CONC. SLAB

D DETAIL
A·7 SCALE : 1/2"·1'-0"

10 SILL DETAIL
A·7 SCALE : 1/2"·1'-0"

·ALUM. FRAME
·STL. SILL
WD. BLOCKING

CONC. BLK.
4" COMP. BASE

11 SILL DETAIL
A·7 SCALE : 1/2"·1'-0"

·ALUM. FRAME
·CAULK

12 SILL DETAIL
A·7 SCALE : 1/2"·1'-0"

·1/4" POLISHED PL. GLASS
·1" INSUL. GLASS

·CONC. COL.

·G· FASCIA
·1/4" POL. PL. GLASS
·FACE BRICK·
·DASHED LINE
INDICATES CONC.
COLUMN·

SCUTTER

1" INSUL. GLASS

TOP OF SLAB
EL. 966'-0"

TOP OF SLAB
EL. 966'-0"

5 EAST ELEVATION
A·4 SCALE 1/8"·1'-0" (PARTIAL)

6 NORTH ELEVATION
A·4 SCALE 1/8"·1'-0" (PARTIAL)

FREDERICK BENTZ / MILO THOMPSON & ASSOCIATES INC · ARCHITECTURE & URBAN DESIGN · 1234 DAIN TOWER, MINNEAPOLIS, MINNESOTA 55402 · TEL (612) 335-1207 · FREDERICK BENTZ / MILO THOMPSON & ASSOCIATES INC ·

DRIVERS LICENSE EXAMINATION
STATION

PLYMOUTH, MINNESOTA

EXTERIOR ELEVATIONS

SCALE : 1/8"·1'-0"

COMMISSION NUMBER 72·14
DATE 9/8/72
DRAWN RJK·SD
CHECKED RJK

A·4

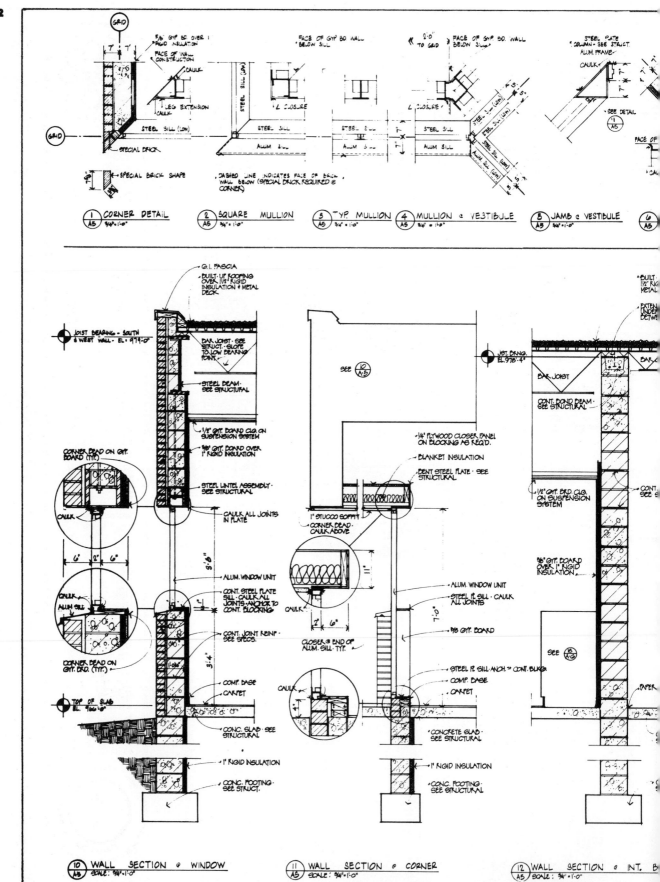

1 CORNER DETAIL A5 3/4"=1'-0"

2 SQUARE MULLION A5 3/4"=1'-0"

3 TYP. MULLION A5 3/4"=1'-0"

4 MULLION @ VESTIBULE A5 3/4"=1'-0"

5 JAMB @ VESTIBULE A5 3/16"=1'-0"

10 WALL SECTION @ WINDOW A5 SCALE: 3/4"=1'-0"

11 WALL SECTION @ CORNER A5 SCALE: 3/4"=1'-0"

12 WALL SECTION @ INT. B A5 SCALE: 3/4"=1'-0"

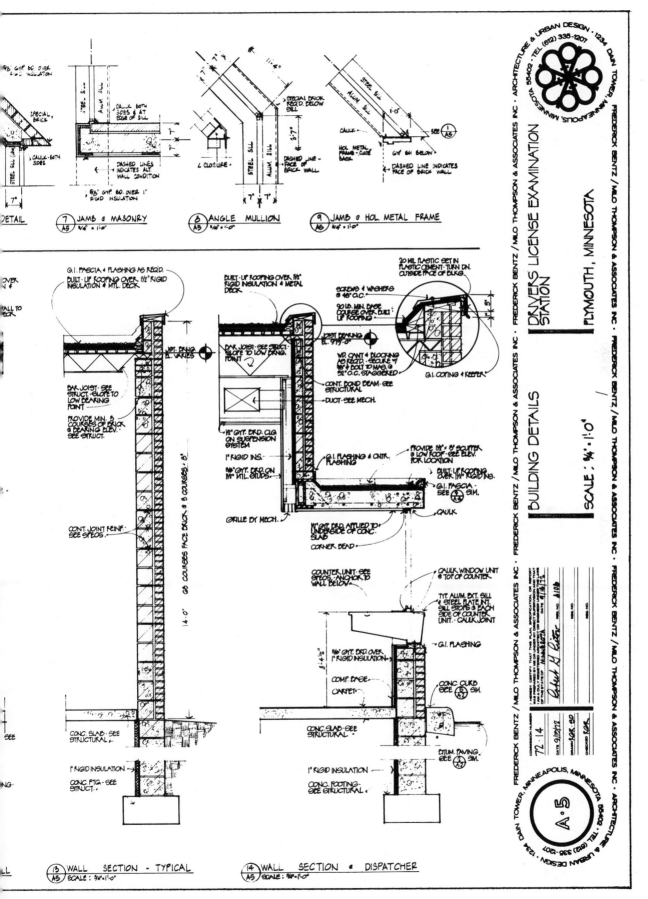

7 JAMB & MASONRY
A5 ¼" = 1'-0"

8 ANGLE MULLION
A5 ¼" = 1'-0"

9 JAMB & HOL. METAL FRAME
A5 ¾" = 1'-0"

13 WALL SECTION - TYPICAL
A5 ¾"=1'-0"

14 WALL SECTION & DISPATCHER
A5 ¾"=1'-0"

FREDERICK BENTZ / MILO THOMPSON & ASSOCIATES INC.

DRIVERS LICENSE EXAMINATION STATION

PLYMOUTH, MINNESOTA

BUILDING DETAILS

SCALE : ¾"·1'·0"

A·5

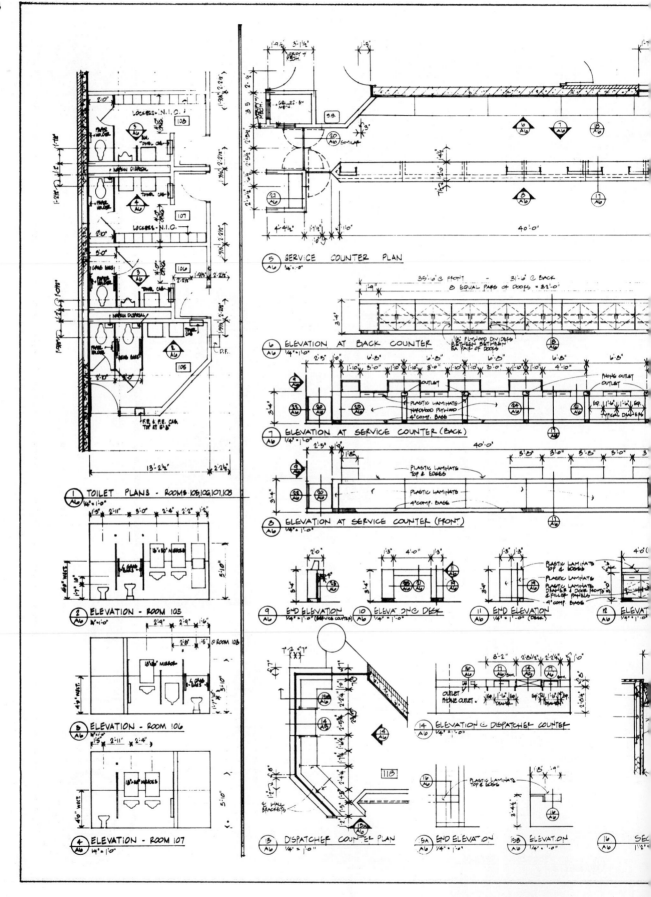

① TOILET PLANS - ROOMS 105,106,107,108
A16 1/4"=1'-0"

② ELEVATION - ROOM 105
A16 1/4"=1'-0"

③ ELEVATION - ROOM 106
A16 1/4"=1'-0"

④ ELEVATION - ROOM 107
A16 1/4"=1'-0"

⑤ SERVICE COUNTER PLAN
A16 1/4"=1'-0"

⑥ ELEVATION AT BACK COUNTER
A16 1/4"=1'-0"

⑦ ELEVATION AT SERVICE COUNTER (BACK)
A16 1/4"=1'-0"

⑧ ELEVATION AT SERVICE COUNTER (FRONT)
A16 1/4"=1'-0"

⑨ END ELEVATION
A16 1/4"=1'-0" (SERVICE COUNTER)

⑩ ELEVA'N @ DESK
A16 1/4"=1'-0"

⑪ END ELEVATION
A16 1/4"=1'-0" (DESK)

⑫ ELEVAT'N
A16

⑭ ELEVATION @ DISPATCHER COUNTER
A16 1/4"=1'-0"

⑬ DISPATCHER COUNTER PLAN
A16 1/4"=1'-0"

⑮A END ELEVATION
A16 1/4"=1'-0"

⑮B ELEVATION
A16 1/4"=1'-0"

⑯ SEC
A16 1/2"

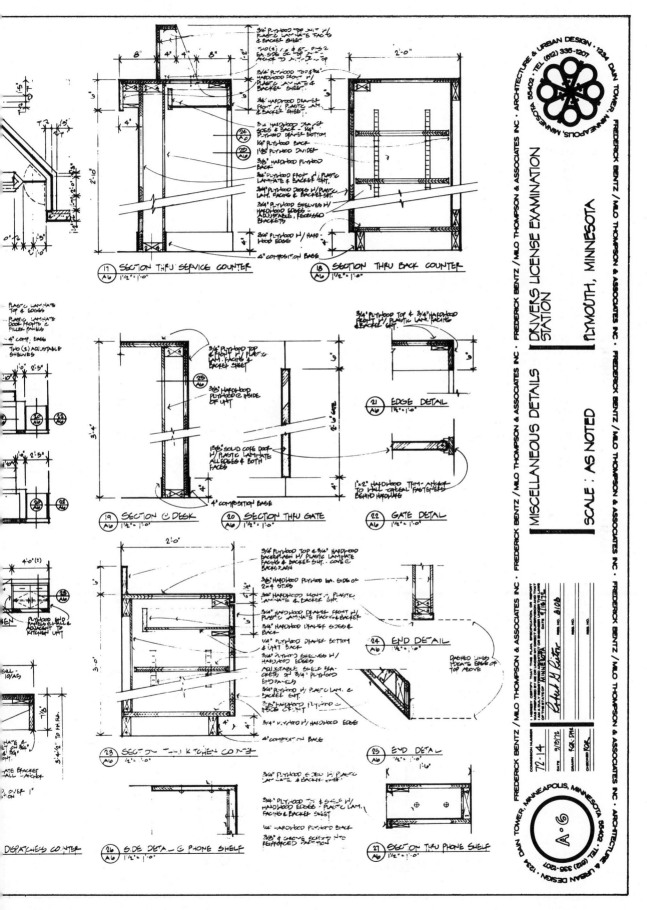

17 SECTION THRU SERVICE COUNTER
A6 1½"=1'-0"

18 SECTION THRU BACK COUNTER
A6 1½"=1'-0"

19 SECTION @ DESK
A6 1½"=1'-0"

20 SECTION THRU GATE
A6 1½"=1'-0"

21 EDGE DETAIL
A6 1½"=1'-0"

22 GATE DETAIL
A6 1½"=1'-0"

23 SECTION THRU KITCHEN COUNTER
A6 1½"=1'-0"

24 END DETAIL
A6 1½"=1'-0"

25 END DETAIL
A6 1½"=1'-0"

26 SIDE DETAIL @ PHONE SHELF
A6 1½"=1'-0"

27 SECTION THRU PHONE SHELF
A6 1½"=1'-0"

MISCELLANEOUS DETAILS

DRIVERS LICENSE EXAMINATION STATION

PLYMOUTH, MINNESOTA

SCALE : AS NOTED

FREDERICK BENTZ / MILO THOMPSON & ASSOCIATES INC.

A·6

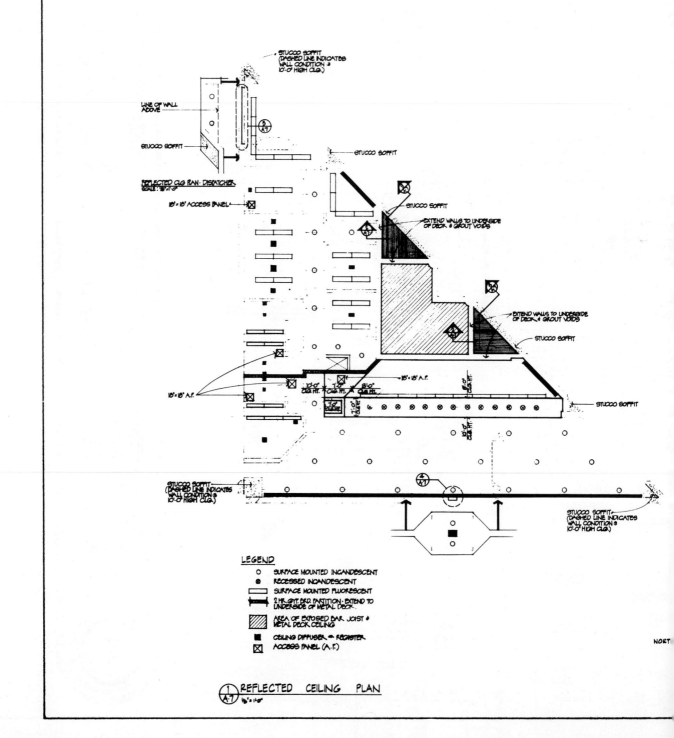

STUCCO SOFFIT
(DASHED LINE INDICATES
WALL CONDITION @
10'-0" HIGH CLG.)

LINE OF WALL
ABOVE

STUCCO SOFFIT

REFLECTED CLG PLAN · DISPATCHER
SCALE : 1/8"=1'-0"

18" x 18" ACCESS PANEL

STUCCO SOFFIT

STUCCO SOFFIT

EXTEND WALLS TO UNDERSIDE
OF DECK & GROUT VOIDS

EXTEND WALLS TO UNDERSIDE
OF DECK & GROUT VOIDS

STUCCO SOFFIT

18" x 18" A.P.

STUCCO SOFFIT

18" x 18" A.P.

STUCCO SOFFIT
(DASHED LINE INDICATES
WALL CONDITION @
10'-0" HIGH CLG.)

STUCCO SOFFIT
(DASHED LINE INDICATES
WALL CONDITION @
10'-0" HIGH CLG.)

NORT

LEGEND

○ SURFACE MOUNTED INCANDESCENT

⊙ RECESSED INCANDESCENT

▭ SURFACE MOUNTED FLUORESCENT

2 HR. GYP. BD. PARTITION · EXTEND TO
UNDERSIDE OF METAL DECK.

▨ AREA OF EXPOSED BAR JOIST &
METAL DECK CEILING

■ CEILING DIFFUSER & REGISTER

⊠ ACCESS PANEL (A.P.)

1 REFLECTED CEILING PLAN
A·7 1/8"=1'-0"

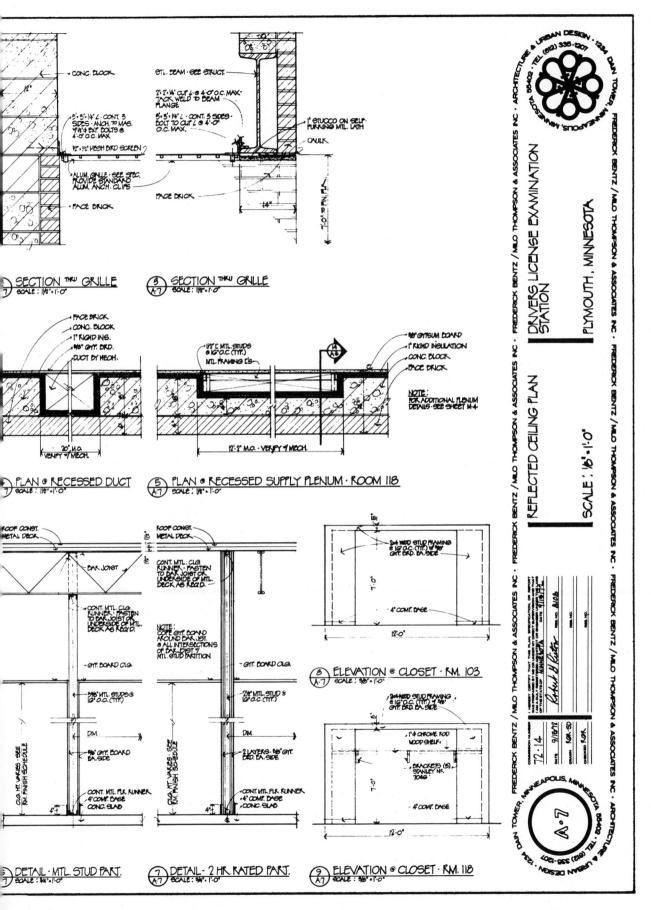

CONC. BLOCK

STL. BEAM - SEE STRUCT.

2" x 2" x 1/4" CLIP L @ 4'-0" O.C. MAX. - TACK WELD TO BEAM FLANGE

5" x 5" x 1/4" L - CONT. 3 SIDES - ANCH. TO MAS. W/1/2" ∅ EXP. BOLTS @ 4'-0" O.C. MAX

1" STUCCO ON SELF-FURRING MTL. LATH

5" x 5" x 1/4" L - CONT. 3 SIDES - BOLT TO CLIP L @ 4'-0" O.C. MAX.

1/2" x 1/2" MESH BIRD SCREEN

CAULK

ALUM. GRILLE - SEE SPEC. PROVIDE STANDARD ALUM. ANCH. CLIPS

FACE BRICK

FACE BRICK

SECTION THRU GRILLE
SCALE : 1 1/2" = 1'-0"

SECTION THRU GRILLE
SCALE : 1 1/2" = 1'-0"

FACE BRICK
CONC. BLOCK
1" RIGID INS.
5/8" GYP. BRD.
DUCT BY MECH.

1 1/2" C MTL. STUDS @ 16" O.C. (TYP.)
MTL. FRAMING L'S

5/8" GYPSUM BOARD
1" RIGID INSULATION
CONC. BLOCK
FACE BRICK

NOTE:
FOR ADDITIONAL PLENUM DETAILS - SEE SHEET M-4

20" M.O.
VERIFY W/ MECH.

12'-2" M.O. - VERIFY W/ MECH.

PLAN @ RECESSED DUCT
SCALE : 1 1/2" = 1'-0"

PLAN @ RECESSED SUPPLY PLENUM - ROOM 118
SCALE : 1 1/2" = 1'-0"

ROOF CONST.
METAL DECK

ROOF CONST.
METAL DECK

BAR JOIST

CONT. MTL. CLG. RUNNER - FASTEN TO BAR JOIST OR UNDERSIDE OF MTL. DECK AS REQ'D.

CONT. MTL. CLG. RUNNER - FASTEN TO BAR JOIST OR UNDERSIDE OF MTL. DECK AS REQ'D.

NOTE:
COPE GYP. BOARD AROUND BAR JST. @ ALL INTERSECTIONS OF BAR JOIST W/ MTL. STUD PARTITION

GYP. BOARD CLG.

GYP. BOARD CLG.

3 5/8" MTL. STUDS @ 16" O.C. (TYP.)

2 1/2" MTL. STUD @ 16" O.C. (TYP.)

DIM.

DIM.

5/8" GYP. BOARD EA. SIDE

2 LAYERS - 5/8" GYP. BRD. EA. SIDE

CONT. MTL. FLR. RUNNER
4" COMP. BASE
CONC. SLAB

CONT. MTL. FLR. RUNNER
4" COMP. BASE
CONC. SLAB

CLG. HT. VARIES - SEE RM. FINISH SCHEDULE

CLG. HT. VARIES - SEE RM. FINISH SCHEDULE

2x4 WOOD STUD FRAMING @ 16" O.C. (TYP.) W/ 5/8" GYP. BRD. EA. SIDE

4" COMP. BASE

7'-0"

12'-0"

ELEVATION @ CLOSET - RM. 103
SCALE : 3/8" = 1'-0"

2x4 WOOD STUD FRAMING @ 16" O.C. (TYP.) W/ 5/8" GYP. BRD. EA. SIDE

1" ∅ CHROME ROD

WOOD SHELF

BRACKETS (5) STANLEY Nº. 7046

4" COMP. BASE

7'-0"

12'-0"

DETAIL - MTL. STUD PART.
SCALE : 3/4" = 1'-0"

DETAIL - 2 HR. RATED PART.
SCALE : 3/4" = 1'-0"

ELEVATION @ CLOSET - RM. 118
SCALE : 3/8" = 1'-0"

DAIN TOWER, FREDERICK BENTZ / MILO THOMPSON & ASSOCIATES INC · ARCHITECTURE & URBAN DESIGN · 1234 DAIN TOWER, MINNEAPOLIS, MINNESOTA 55402 · TEL (612) 336-1207

FREDERICK BENTZ / MILO THOMPSON & ASSOCIATES INC · FREDERICK BENTZ / MILO THOMPSON & ASSOCIATES INC · FREDERICK BENTZ / MILO THOMPSON & ASSOCIATES INC · FREDERICK BENTZ / MILO THOMPSON & ASSOCIATES INC

DRIVERS LICENSE EXAMINATION STATION

PLYMOUTH, MINNESOTA

REFLECTED CEILING PLAN

SCALE : 1/8" = 1'-0"

COMMISSION NUMBER: 72-14
DATE: 9/18/72
DRAWN: KGR · SD
CHECKED: KGK

DWG. NO.
REV. NO.
REV. NO.

A·7

FOUR

BUILDING CONSTRUCTION AND TECHNOLOGY

MATERIALS

A drafting technician needs to understand the physical properties of the major materials used in construction in order to detail a building. Major materials include wood, ferrous metal, and concrete, plus a wide range of miscellaneous items.

Wood

Wood is a cellular organic material with fibers that are aligned in one direction. Thus, wood is considerably stronger when stressed perpendicular to the fiber rather than parallel.

Trees are divided into two classes: Hardwood (deciduous) are broadleaf trees that typically shed leaves annually; softwood (coniferous) are trees that generally retain needlelike leaves throughout the year. The terms *hardwood* and *softwood* are misleading because some softwoods are harder than some hardwoods. In general, softwoods are used for construction lumber, and hardwoods for finish material, such as floors and cabinets.

The softwood lumber species commonly used in construction are Douglas fir, hemlock, and southern pine. Each of the species is graded into many categories with varying structural characteristics and uses. Coast region Douglas fir graded "select structural" is recommended for use in light framing, while the same species graded "dense construction" is suggested for use as floor and roof joists.

Wood retains a percentage of moisture within its cell structure. As the moisture content increases, the wood expands; as it dries, the wood contracts. The percentage of moisture in wood (measured in the weight of the water content as compared to the overdry weight of the wood) can vary from nearly 0 to 200 percent for fresh-cut lumber. Critical shrinkage in wood occurs at moisture contents from 0 to about 30 percent, with the surrounding temperature and humidity affecting the range. It is desirable to obtain a moisture content in lumber compatible to the environment in which it will be placed rather than lumber that is kiln-dried to 0 percent moisture. The equilibrium moisture content is about 9 percent for wood at 70° with 50 percent air humidity. Shrinkage in wood takes place perpendicular to the grain of the wood.

Lumber is measured in units of board feet. A board foot is 1' long, 1' wide, and 1" thick. Similarly, a board 2" thick, 6" wide, and 1' long is also a board foot. The number designation is given to the nominal size of the lumber, not the actual size. Wood is dressed down to standards set by industry but still is referred to as the next larger whole number (the nominal dimension). Example: 2" × 4" is the nominal size of an actual piece of lumber 1½" × 3½"; 1" nominal lumber is actually ¾" thick, while larger-dimension lumber is ½" less than nominal size. Figure 4-1 shows board-foot measurement.

Wood has several weak points that can be remedied if properly handled. A large section of the United States has termite infestation which causes great damage to wood structure. This problem can be remedied by (1) chemically treating the soil; (2) chemically treating the exposed wood; (3) providing metal shields around all wood that termites can reach; or (4) using concrete foundations with protective caps.

Since wood rots if subjected to frequent water and air exposure, a paint or chemical preservative, such as creosote, acts as protection. Untreated wood burns, but several processes can qualify the material as fire retardant, such as impregnating the wood with chemicals or painting the wood with special paint, called *intumescent paint*.

Plywood is a manufactured wood product that makes good use of the structural characteristics of wood. Since wood is much stronger in one direction, the laminating of thin sheets of wood in alternating directions allows plywood to achieve strength in both directions. Figure 4-2 shows ways of cutting plywood. One way of making plywood is

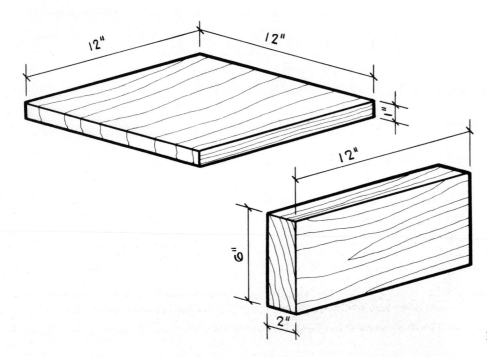

Figure 4-1. Board foot measurement.

to slowly turn a log (called a *flitch*) on a lathe while moving a cutting blade into the log. The result is a continuous sheet of wood, peeled from the log. The sheets are graded and glued together with either waterproof glue for exterior plywood or standard glue for interior plywood. In both cases, the glue joint is stronger than the wood. Plywood is glued in odd-numbered sheets (3, 5, 7) to form standard 4′ × 8′ or larger sheets, ranging from ¼″ to 1⅛″ in ⅛″ increments (see Figure 4-3).

Several designations must be called out when specifying plywood—interior or exterior (glue), thickness, species of wood, and the front and back veneer, rated from A to D. Grades A and B have neatly made patches, while C and D allow open knotholes—up to 2½″ in D grade.

Lumber core plywood and particle board are wood products similar to plywood in sheet size but different in composition and use. Lumber core plywood substitutes a solid core of lumber for the interior laminates of plywood. It generally has a thin veneer of finishable hardwood as the outside faces and is used for some cabinet work. Particle board is made from wood chips that are glued and pressed into sheets. The main uses for this product are for cabinet work and flooring under carpet. As with plywood, the standard sheet sizes range from 4′ × 8′ up to 4′ × 12′.

Another manufactured wood product is the glue-laminated structural member (Figure 4-4). A major problem with wood is the lack of uniformity in large sizes. Glue-laminated beams and columns are composed of relatively small wood members glued together to make a large structural unit. Glue-laminated timbers are available in depths of more than 40″ and can span over 100′ in an arch form. Glue-laminated timbers are available in three different appearance grades, ranging from low to high—industrial, architectural, and premium.

Ferrous Metal

Ferrous metal covers a wide variety of iron-base materials used in construction, the most common of which are cast iron, malleable iron, wrought iron, and steel. The first three types of iron products have quite similar production methods but differ slightly in characteristics.

The initial product in iron and steel production is the manufacture of *pig iron*, made by combining iron ore, coke, and limestone in a blast furnace. Many imperfections such as phosphorus, silicon, and sulfur are found in pig iron, plus 3 to 4.5 percent carbon, which makes the material extremely hard and brittle and virtually unusable in this form.

Cast iron is formed by remelting pig iron and pouring it into sand castings. The pig iron is generally melted with recycled scrap iron so that the product is not chemically changed but the carbon content is slightly lower (1.5 to 4 percent) than pig

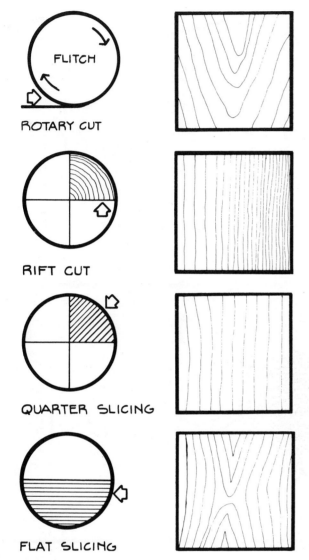

ROTARY CUT

RIFT CUT

QUARTER SLICING

FLAT SLICING

Figure 4-2.   Methods of cutting plywood.

iron. Cast iron is used for products that are not subjected to shock, such as plumbing pipe and shapes not easily produced by machining.

Malleable iron is made somewhat softer than cast iron by controlling the heating and cooling (called *annealing*). Malleable cast iron has a greater resistance to shock-impact breakage and is used for items such as builders' hardware.

Wrought iron is more than 97 percent pure iron. It has the physical properties of being tough and corrosion-resistant, and it can be rolled into thin sheets. Wrought iron is used as sheet material, gas and water piping, ornamental railings, and as a metal lath for plaster and stucco.

Steel differs from iron in that it has a lower carbon content, fewer natural impurities, and additional elements that alter the properties.

The carbon content in steel affects the strength and workability of the material. The higher the carbon percentage, the stronger but less workable the steel. The effective range of carbon in steel used in building is from 0.5 to 1.2 percent. Carbon steel without additional elements constitutes the majority of the steel used in construction.

Several strengths of steel are used for structural framing—A-36 is the most common; A-7 is slightly weaker; A-440, A-441, and A-242 are high strength and more expensive. The steel designation, such as A-36, is assigned by the American Society for Testing and Materials and is used by major steel manufacturers.

Beams used in construction are hot-rolled into the most common shapes and given I, W, B, JR, and M designations. Channels, H pilings, flat plates and angles, zees, and tees are other common

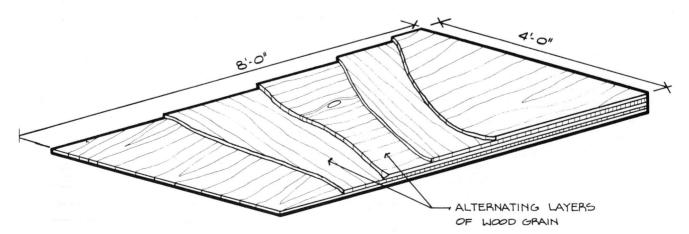

ALTERNATING LAYERS OF WOOD GRAIN

Figure 4-3.   Glued sheets are used for making plywood.

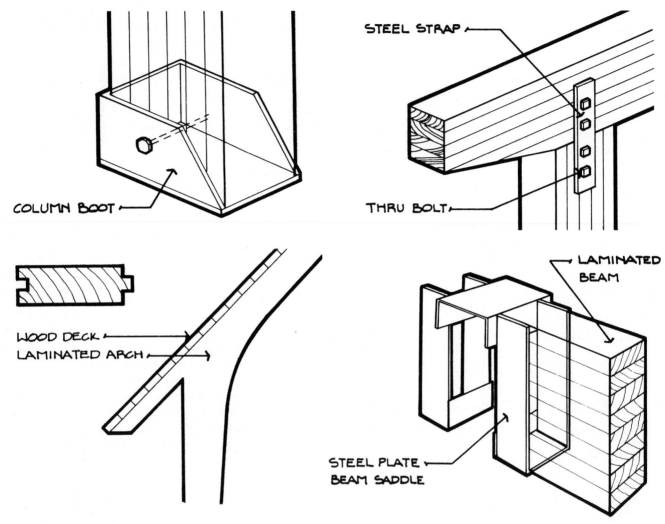

COLUMN BOOT

STEEL STRAP

THRU BOLT

LAMINATED BEAM

STEEL PLATE
BEAM SADDLE

WOOD DECK
LAMINATED ARCH

Figure 4-4. Various glue-laminated columns and beams.

shapes used in construction. Figure 4-5 shows some common shapes.

The methods of fastening steel shapes together at the job site are riveting, bolting, and welding. Riveting is seldom used anymore. Bolting and electric-arc welding are more common.

The addition of various alloy elements as well as a change in carbon content results in steel with different properties. A common architectural product, *stainless steel*, has a high chromium content (over 12 percent) and traces of nickel and manganese. Stainless steel has a high corrosion resistance and is excellent for exposed untreated surfaces.

Another alloy for exposed steel with entirely different properties is *weathering steel*, best known by its U.S. Steel trademark, Cor-ten. The exposed steel actually goes through a period of rusting when exposed to the atmosphere. This process stops in about a year and leaves all exposed steel a uniform dark gray.

Several surface applications are made to iron and steel to change the appearance or to protect it from oxidation (rust). This application can be a metallic coating, a plastic film, baked ceramic, or a paint finish.

The process of metal cladding iron or steel takes place either by dipping in molten metal or electroplating. The most common coating is galvanized zinc, although tin, aluminum, terne metal (a lead-tin alloy), chromium, and nickel are also bonded to iron. If galvanized zinc sheets are to be painted, they should also be *bonderized*, a process in which the sheet is dipped in a hot phosphate solution. The metal may also be primed with zinc chromate or red lead. Plastic film coatings on steel

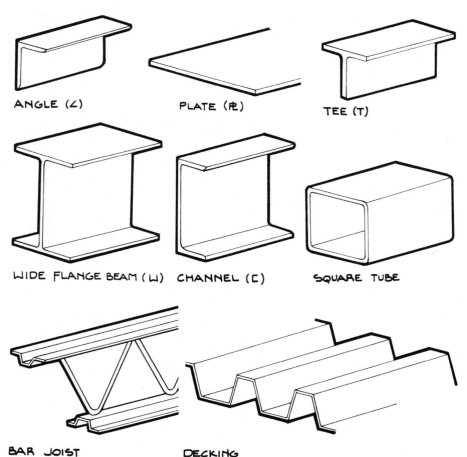

ANGLE (∠)   PLATE (℞)   TEE (T)

WIDE FLANGE BEAM (W)   CHANNEL (C)   SQUARE TUBE

BAR JOIST   DECKING

Figure 4-5. Some common shapes of steel used in construction.

are thin sheets ($^2/_{1000}''$ to $^{12}/_{1000}''$) that are heat-bonded to the metal. The plastic, typically poly-vinyl chloride, can be colored or clear. Porcelain enamel is baked ceramic (vitreous) finish applied to metal after it is formed, commonly found on iron and steel bathtubs and metal panels attached to the exterior of buildings.

Steel-measuring designations are confusing and must be defined carefully to be understood. Nonstructural sheet metal is measured in gauges that really relate to nothing. A standard gauge for a sheet metal galvanized gravel stop is 22 gauge, which is about $^1/_{32}''$ thick. The smaller the gauge number, the thicker the metal, ranging from less than $^1/_{64}''$ for 30 gauge to $^3/_8''$ for 000 gauge.

Structural plates are generally measured in fractions of an inch rather than in gauge. A plate welded to the bottom of a beam to act as a ledge for brick could be called out as a $^1/_4''$ plate.

Steel beams are rolled into various shapes and given letter designations, such as I, W, B, JR, and M. The most common beam is a wide flange, W.

Beams are called out with a three-part designation—the beam shape, the nominal depth of the beam in inches, and the weight of the beam in pounds per foot. A W12 × 53 beam is a 12″ deep wide-flange beam that weighs 53 lb/ft. Angles are called out by giving the length of each leg of the angle followed by the thickness: 6″ × 6″ × $^3/_8''$ ∠. Steel reinforcing bars (rebars) used in concrete are measured in $^1/_8''$ increments, but only the divisor of the fraction is given. A number 7 rebar is $^7/_8''$ in diameter.

An item generally found in the specifications is the thickness of galvanized metal plating on sheet metal, given in the number of ounces per square foot, on both sides. The standard for zinc galvanized sheet is 1.25 oz/sq ft.

Concrete

Concrete is the final product made by mixing cement, fine and coarse aggregate (sand and gravel or stone), and water in proper proportions (Figure

4-6). Although cement is often confused with the term concrete, it is not a structural material.

Portland cement, the only standard used in construction, is made by mixing crushed limestone with clay or shale and then burning it at 2700°F. The resulting clinker (hard residue) is ground to a consistency finer than flour, then mixed with gypsum and packaged in 94-lb sacks (1 cu ft).

Fine aggregate is specified as being clean, sharp sand, less than ¼″ in diameter and varying uniformly in size. Coarse aggregate is clean gravel or crushed rock, varying uniformly in size from ¼″ to 1½″ in diameter. This maximum size is reduced by code to be less than one-fifth the width of a wall or one-third the thickness of a floor slab or three-fourths the distance between reinforcing bars. The general requirements for water used in making concrete is that it be potable (drinkable) and free of high mineral concentrations.

The proper proportional mixing of the four materials yields a concrete with a specified compressive strength used in building. If structural concrete had a standard compressive strength, it would be 3000 P.S.I. It can, however, be mixed as low as 2000 P.S.I. for low-traffic drives or as high as 7000 P.S.I. and higher for special structural members. A design mix for 3000 P.S.I. concrete with a 20 percent safety factor would be 517 lb cement (5½ sacks), 1300 lb sand, 1800 lb gravel, and 34 gal water (6.2 gal per sack), which would yield 1 cu yd of concrete, the standard unit of measure.

The strength of concrete is greatly affected by the amount of water used in mixing (see Figure 4-7). This is referred to as the *water-cement ratio.*

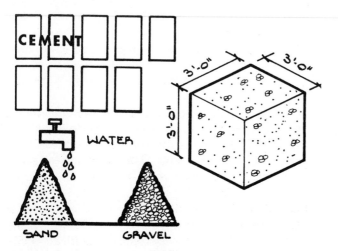

Figure 4-6. Materials for making concrete

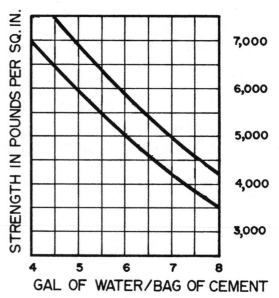

Figure 4-7. The water-cement ratio.

About 3½ gal water per sack of cement is required to complete the curing process of concrete. Even though this produces the strongest concrete, it is quite "stiff" to work with. As in the design mix above, the average water-cement ratio is around 6 gal per sack. If this were changed to 8 gal per sack, the strength of the concrete would be reduced nearly 1000 P.S.I.

When cement, aggregate, and water are mixed, a chemical reaction is started that is independent of drying. Concrete does not need air to cure. It can set underwater. The cement acts as a paste that bonds the fine and coarse aggregate into one. Water starts the reaction. Concrete sets or becomes firm within hours after it has been mixed, but curing, the process of attaining strength, takes considerably longer. Standard (type I) cement is assumed to achieve 100 percent of its compressive strength 28 days after mixing. The majority of the strength is achieved in the first days of curing. Approximately 50 percent of the total compressive strength is reached in 3 days—70 percent is reached in 7 days. The remaining 30 percent occurs in the last 21 days at a much slower rate, as shown in Figure 4-8.

Two physical properties have a very pronounced effect on the final compressive strength attained by concrete—temperature and the rate that the water used in mixing is allowed to leave the concrete. The optimum temperature for curing concrete is 73°F [22.8°C]. Any great variance from this mark reduces its compressive strength. Con-

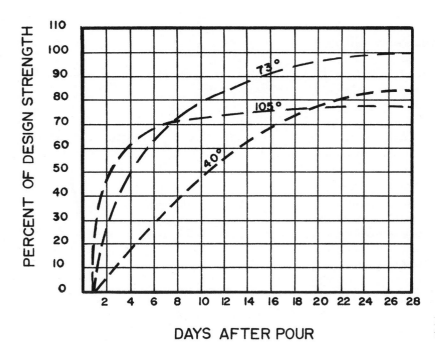

DAYS AFTER POUR

Figure 4-8. The effect of temperature on the curing of concrete.

crete cured at 90°F [32.2°C] has an approximate reduction in strength of 5 percent. Curing at 105°F [40.6°C] will cause greater than 20 percent reduction in compression. The other side of the 73°F [22.7°C] design temperature follows the same pattern until about 40°F [4.4°C], which causes a 15 percent reduction. Freezing concrete during curing not only affects the compressive strength but also greatly reduces the ability of the material to resist weathering.

The methods used to combat high temperature can range from shading the poured concrete to cooling the materials or adding ice in place of water. Freezing temperatures can be combatted by heating the materials to 70°F [21.1°C] before pouring and keeping the concrete at 45°F [7.2°C] for a period of seven days. This is usually accomplished by covering the concrete with plastic sheets and heating the interior space with a portable heater, called a *salamander*.

Hydration is a chemical reaction between the water and the lime in the cement when concrete is curing. The longer the water is present in the concrete, the longer the reaction takes place and, therefore, the stronger it becomes. Hydration can be sustained in concrete for over a year after it is poured if it is kept in contact with moisture. The amount of water used in mixing concrete is sufficient to complete the hydration, but unless the poured concrete is protected, much of it will evaporate. Several techniques are employed to assist in moisture retention:

1. A plastic vapor barrier is placed on the ground before the concrete slab is poured to prevent the water from seeping into the soil.
2. If a vapor barrier isn't used, the soil is thoroughly soaked before the concrete is placed.
3. Concrete placed in wood or metal forms retains much of its water if the forms are left in place for a long period of time.
4. Exposed concrete retains moisture if it is sprayed with water periodically or if the slab is flooded with water after it has set.
5. Materials such as wet burlap or plastic sheets can be placed over the exposed concrete.
6. An applied curing or sealing compound can be painted or sprayed over the concrete.

Several mixtures of portland cement are available for use in regular and special conditions. Type I cement is used in most standard applications.

If the heat generated during hydration causes problems, type II or IV cement can be used. Type III cement is called *high early strength* because it attains its initial strength much faster than type I, a characteristic extremely beneficial in freezing temperatures. Instead of supplying heat to the concrete for seven days to maintain a temperature above 45°F [7.2°C], three days is acceptable. Type V is used when a higher resistance to sulfate is desired.

Types I, II, and III cements also can contain an added ingredient, an air-entraining agent. The cement number is then preceded by the letter A. *Air entraining* is a process by which the microscopic voids in concrete are filled with millions of tiny bubbles. This add mixture has several important attributes—it makes the concrete easier to finish with a trowel, and more importantly, it protects the concrete from spalling due to freezing and thawing. The Portland Cement Association recommends the use of an air-entraining agent in most concrete that will be exposed to the weather. Several other add mixtures are available but are not as commonly accepted in building. A common add mixture is salt. It lowers the freezing point of water, permitting the placement of concrete at low temperatures. It is not allowed by the Portland Cement Association.

Many variables present when concrete is being mixed, placed, and cured can affect its final properties. Several tests have been devised to judge the properties of concrete as it is being placed on the job site. The first test is called a *slump test* (Figure 4-9), which is a rough test to determine the consistency of the concrete. A slump test mold is a funnel-shaped sheet metal form that is 12″ high, 8″ in diameter at the base, and 4″ in diameter at the top. The slump mold is filled from the top in three levels, each level being tamped 25 times with a ⅝″ diameter rod. After the top is smoothed evenly, the mold is slowly removed, causing the concrete to slump down from its original height. The metal mold is placed next to the slumped concrete, and the difference from the tops of each is measured in inches. A "right" slump consistency does not exist for all concrete work. It can vary from 1″ to 6″, depending on the specific requirements of the job. The design mix for the 1 cu yd of concrete cited in this discussion was made to have a 3″ slump.

Air entrainment can be determined at the site by using a portable testing device to submit a sample to pressure and water, having a direct reading scale to show the percentage of entrained air. In general terms, 6 percent air entrainment is usually specified for general construction.

A major problem with concrete tests is that the most important data, the compressive strength, cannot be determined until after curing has begun. This occasionally has caused the removal of defi-

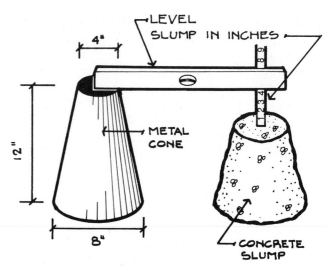

Figure 4-9.   A slump test.

cient concrete several weeks after it was placed. A compression test is made by placing three layers of concrete in a cardboard cylinder 6″ in diameter and 12″ high (Figure 4-10). Each layer is rodded 25 times with a ⅝″ diameter steel rod. The cylinder should be protected from damage but placed in the same temperature and humidity environment as the concrete from which the sample was obtained. At the end of the test curing time, usually determined to be 7 or 28 days, the outer cylinder is removed and placed in a press. The point at which the cylinder fails in compression is registered on a gauge in pounds, and the strength of the concrete is calculated in pounds per square inch. If the cylinder is tested in 28 days, it should fail at or above the specified compressive strength. A test done at 7 days should fail at approximately 70 percent of the compressive strength.

A sizable cost factor that must be figured with concrete construction is the form work involved in supporting the material while it is curing. Form

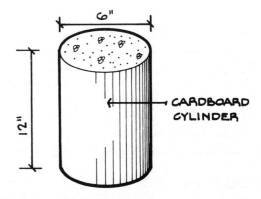

Figure 4-10.   A test cylinder for concrete.

work (Figure 4-11) is usually wood or steel that must be tied together with studs or tie rods that run through the concrete from the outside face of the form to the opposite outside face. The steel ties are broken off when the form is stripped (removed). The relatively high weight of concrete (approximately 150 lb/cu ft) necessitates an elaborate structural support system for the form work until the concrete has cured sufficiently to support itself.

Architects have been able to achieve strikingly esthetic results with poured-concrete walls by lining the inside of the form work with materials such as rough-sawn boards or vertically spaced wood strips. When the strips are removed, the concrete has the texture of the form material.

Several requirements have been established for placing concrete in the form work, designed to prevent damage to the material caused by separating the even mixture of large and fine aggregate. Specifications should not allow concrete to be dropped more than 4′, overvibrated with a mechanical vibrator, or overworked with a hand trowel, as in the case of a floor slab. Concrete can be placed at higher levels by using a crane with a special bucket or pneumatic guns or by pumping.

The compressive strength of concrete is approximately 3000 P.S.I. Concrete is assumed to fail as soon as it is placed in tension (a pull-apart force). This force occurs on the bottom part of a beam or footing as soon as it is loaded. Steel, on the other hand, takes a great deal of tension stress. Thus, the two materials are placed together to form a reinforced concrete member.

Steel and concrete have very similar coefficients of thermal expansion, a physical character-

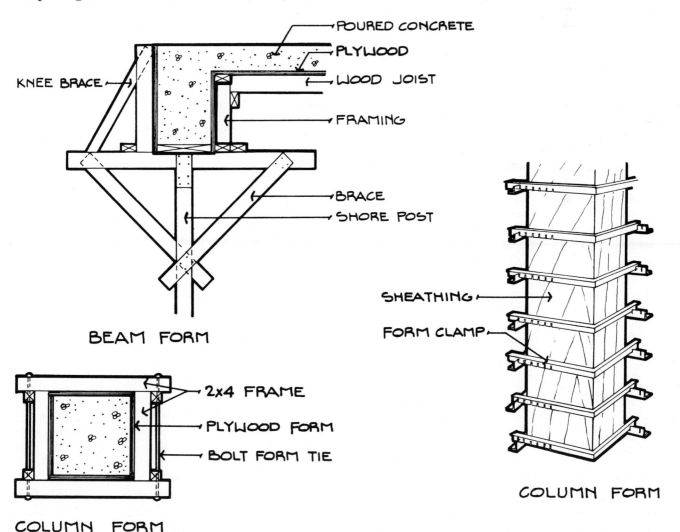

POURED CONCRETE
PLYWOOD
KNEE BRACE
WOOD JOIST
FRAMING
BRACE
SHORE POST

BEAM FORM

SHEATHING
FORM CLAMP

COLUMN FORM

2x4 FRAME
PLYWOOD FORM
BOLT FORM TIE

COLUMN FORM

Figure 4-11. Concrete form work.

istic that allows steel reinforcing. All materials expand and contract when exposed to temperature change. If steel and concrete had very dissimilar expansion rates, the bond between the two materials would be broken in extreme temperature conditions. To further the strength of the bond between steel and concrete, reinforcing bars generally have deformed surfaces (diamond-shaped ridges).

Prestressed and posttensioned concrete systems also utilize steel but in a different manner. The normal tensile stresses that build up in a loaded beam are counteracted by pulling the steel inside the beam to a very high stress point.

Prestressing (Figures 4-12 and 4-13) is usually done in a factory with the deformed steel bars being pulled to just under the elastic limit. The concrete is then poured into the form and allowed to cure completely. When the restraints on the outside of the form holding the steel are removed, the tension in the steel acts as compressive forces in the concrete.

Posttensioning has a similar result but can be done at the job site as well as in factory conditions. The steel is placed in hollow tubes so as to be nonbonding to concrete and stressed by pulling after the concrete has cured. The steel is then anchored at the ends. Both systems are considerably more costly than standard poured concrete but result in less bulky structural members that can span greater distances.

Several products are available that can be used as replacement for some of the mix in concrete. Products such as blast-furnace slag and pozzolan are used to replace up to about 50 percent of the

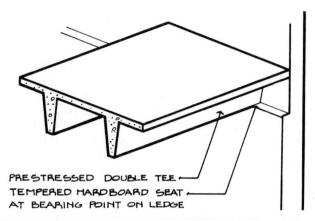

Figure 4-13. A prestressed double concrete tee.

cement. This allows a reduction in the water-cement ratio with the same consistency. Perlite and vermiculite are expanded minerals that can be used to replace some of the aggregate. The resulting concrete is lighter in weight and has a better insulation value, but it also has a reduced compressive strength.

Masonry

Masonry construction falls into two general categories—concrete masonry units and clay products.

Concrete masonry consists of units cast into many shapes, used in construction by binding together with mortar. Most concrete units are made according to modular dimensions that fit an 8″ increment. Modular block is given in nominal dimensions. For example, an 8″ × 8″ × 16″ block is actually 7⅝″ × 7⅝″ × 15⅝″. This is because a mortar joint ⅜″ thick makes each block 8″ high and 16″ long. Block called out with one number designation refers to the width: for example, 10″ block is 10″ wide, 8″ high, and 16″ long (see Figure 4-14).

Block is normally assumed to be hollow, which means it has 25 percent or more void space. A standard block has 40 to 50 percent of its gross cross-sectional area as a hollow core. The hollow core reduces the weight and also the load-bearing capabilities. However, the core can be poured with concrete and reinforced, if necessary. Some concrete shapes are cast solid, such as concrete brick or less than full-size block.

The standard weight of an 8″ × 8″ × 16″ block is between 40 and 50 lb. The standard block is made from portland cement, sand, and aggregate (not much larger than ⅜″). Lightweight block

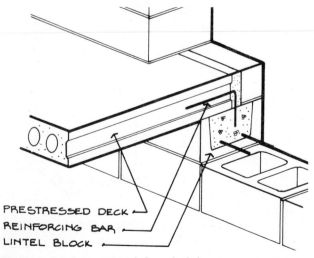

Figure 4-12. A prestressed floor deck bearing on a masonry wall.

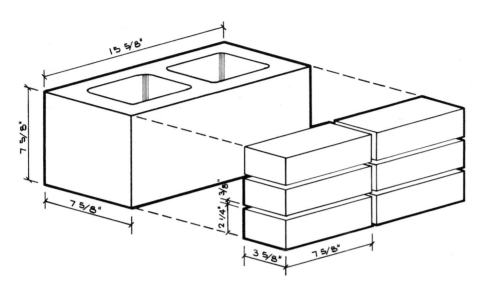

Figure 4-14.   Common masonry sizes.

weighing 25 to 35 lb can be made by substituting materials, such as coal cinders, clay, or pumice for standard-weight aggregate. The load-bearing properties of lightweight block, however, are less than for standard block (see Figure 4-15).

The properties of concrete block are naturally the same as concrete but can be altered to fit the need of concrete masonry units. The normal curing period of concrete is 28 days, but if concrete is subjected to high-pressure steam (150 lb), it will cure in approximately 6 hr. This process is called *autoclaving*; it allows block production to follow a 1-day cycle, and it produces a block that is less subject to dimensional shrinkage.

An inherent problem with concrete, and in particular with concrete masonry units, is that it is not waterproof. Exposed block that is subjected to water absorbs water and leaks through to the opposite side. To guard against this, block is commonly given a protective coating, such as masonry paint, clear silicone, or stucco.

Masonry units are typically bonded with mortar, a combination of portland cement, sand, hydrated lime, and water. Although not the only type of mortar, it does combine the compressive strength of portland cement and the plasticity of hydrated lime to form a durable joint. As with concrete, the mortar should not be allowed to freeze. Each horizontal layer of block is called a *course* upon which mortar is placed for another block course. The usual depth of a mortar joint is ⅜″, to allow modular coursing. Joints are made either by placing mortar along the outside edges of the block (face-shell mortar bedding) or by filling the edges of the cross-members as well as along the outside edges (full mortar bedding).

Masonry joints are tooled (finished) to various cross-sections in order to increase the watertightness of the joint as well as to accent or deemphasize the joint (Figure 4-16). The best and most common watertight joints are tooled to a concave or V profile. A raked joint is used to accent the mortar joint for interior block walls.

Rigidity is added to a block wall by placing reinforcing in the horizontal mortar joint every second or third course. Reinforcing can be wire welded to a ladder or truss form, or it can be chicken wire. Further support can be added to a wall by adding lateral support, or by adding a wall that intersects another wall at 90°, or by engaging a pilaster block in the wall.

Building codes dictate how high a masonry wall may be. A frequent situation allows a hollow masonry block to extend 18 times the nominal width of the wall without lateral support. A wall of 8″ blocks can be 12′ high without additional horizontal or vertical support.

In addition to the standard color and texture of concrete masonry units, several surface treatments can change the appearance of the face. Several companies manufacture a thin glazed title unit that is bonded to the exposed side of the block to give the wall a ceramic finish. This material is available in many colors and surface forms.

Another factory process involves grinding the exposed face of the block smooth to expose and polish the aggregate. A clear silicone finish is given to the face to add luster and produce a wall

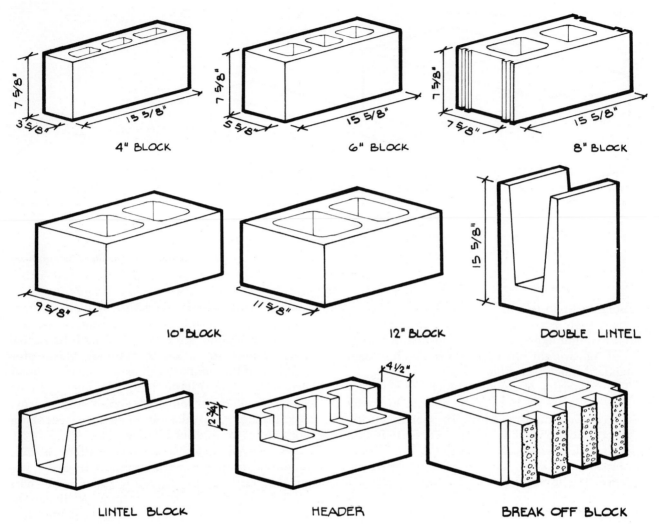

Figure 4-15. Standard concrete blocks.

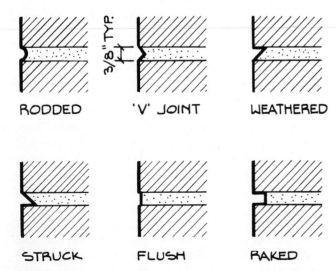

Figure 4-16. Masonry joints.

similar in appearance to terrazzo. Break-off block is produced by casting block into a blunt-toothed surface that projects several inches and forms a highly textured wall with shadowy patterns.

Two common methods of laying a block wall are stacked bond and running bond. *Stacked bond* is a vertical and horizontal pattern in which each block is stacked on top of another. This coursing method provides an attractive wall but is less strong than a running-bond wall. For this reason, stacked bond is more commonly used for interior walls.

Running bond is the standard method of laying a concrete block wall. The vertical mortar joints are staggered so that the vertical mortar joint in one course lines up with the middle of the block in the courses directly above and below.

Clay masonry products can be divided into two major categories—brick and structural clay tile. Both products are manufactured by mining clay, grinding it to a fine consistency, and mixing it with water.

The most common method of producing structural clay products involves mixing 12 to 15 percent water with clay and extruding the plasticlike material through a die to the proper shape. The extrusion is then wire-cut to the desired length and placed in a drying kiln at 100 to 300°F [37.8 to 148.9°C] for a period of one to two days. Preceding the drying period, clay products are "burned" in a kiln to produce a solid unit. The kiln time ranges from two to five days and has a maximum temperature range of from 1600 to 2400°F [871 to 1315°C], depending on the process and clay used.

Brick is made in a wide range of tones from white to black and in various reds and browns, depending on the clay, the minerals used, and the kiln process. By using various materials and different kiln temperatures and times, brick can be made to meet various conditions. Face brick, the standard on exposed walls, is fired to be hard, impervious to water, and even-colored. Common brick is not as hard as face brick, and color control is less even. Its main use is as a back-up material for other wall surfaces. Fire brick resists heat and is used for chimney liners. Brick pavers are fired very hard to resist wear, freezing, and thawing.

Brick is made in various sizes that have names like Roman, Norman, Norwegian, and Economy. The standard brick used in construction is called a *modular brick*. It is 2⅓″ high, 3⅝″ wide, and 7⅝″ long—a nominal dimension of 2⅔″ × 4″ × 8″ when a ⅜″ mortar joint is added. The modular brick has this unusual size to fit the modular dimensions of a concrete block, which is often used in conjunction with brick. Three brick courses plus two mortar joints equal the height of a block. Two horizontal bricks plus a mortar joint equal the width of a concrete block.

Brick is seldom used in construction without a back-up material to provide additional thickness, strength, and insulation (Figure 4-17). In residential construction this can be a wood wall, while in major building types the usual back-up is a masonry wall. In effect, this system involves two walls with a narrow air space between. Two systems are used to bond these walls together to make them act as one. A *masonry bond* (Figure 4-18) is accomplished by laying a running bond for five or eight courses and then turning the bricks

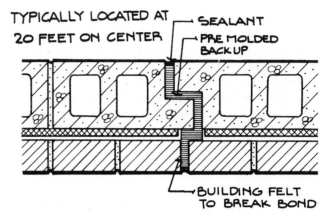

Figure 4-17.   Masonry wall expansion joint.

sideways and projecting that course into a concrete-block back-up, requiring an especially full-cut header block. The reason for five or eight courses of running bond is that the sixth brick course lines up with the second block course, while the ninth course corresponds with the third block course. Several other methods also involve

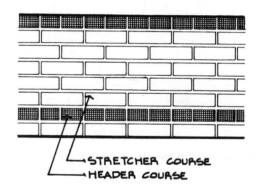

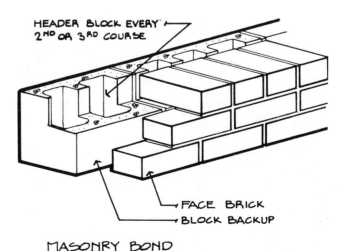

MASONRY BOND

Figure 4-18.   A masonry bond.

brick bonds and rely on projecting a course into the back-up.

The other type of bonding is a *mechanical bond* (Figure 4-19). This requires the placement of a metal tie, which is wire-welded in a truss or ladder-shape or corrugated metal, in the mortar beds of both the brick and the back-up. The walls usually are tied together at every second or third block course.

Structural clay tile units are produced in the same manner as brick and are available in a variety of shapes and finishes. The uses for clay tile closely parallel those described for concrete block. Standard units are used primarily as cores for finished walls, while structural facing tile can be used as the exposed wall treatment.

Brick patterns can be established by exposing different faces of the brick (Figure 4-20). The standard brick course exposes the *stretcher*. When a masonry bond is used, its header face is used. *Rowlock* and *soldier* coursing are used to accent areas of the wall. *Sailor* coursing is seldom used.

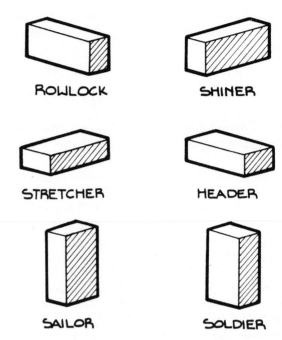

Figure 4-20. The names used for the different faces of brick.

Parging, a thin coat of mortar or plaster, is used to increase the weatherproof qualities of a brick wall. Cement mortar is applied to the back face of the brick or to the front face of the masonry back-up.

Powdery deposits, a problem peculiar to brick walls, are caused by the formation of water-soluble salts on the face of the wall. This problem is called *efflorescence*. The salts are combined in the clay of the brick and in the mortar and are brought to the surface by the presence of excess moisture penetrating the wall. A precaution against white efflorescent salt is to protect newly laid walls from heavy rain. If efflorescence occurs, a high-pressure stream of water washes it off. A 5 to 10 percent solution of muriatic acid (hydrochloric) also washes it off.

Stone

Stone, in most cases, is treated as a veneer material. Although it may be tied to a structural wall back-up, stone does not contribute to the load-bearing quality of the wall. Stone veneer can be handled by laying it similarly to masonry in either rubble or cut stone (ashlar) or by hanging stone slabs from the structure with steel supports. The three principle categories for stone, depending on how they were formed, are

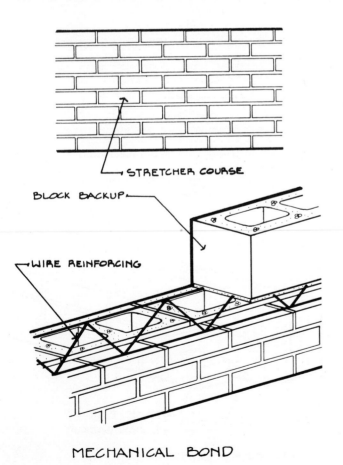

MECHANICAL BOND

Figure 4-19. A mechanical bond.

Group	Type Used in Construction
1. Igneous	Granite, lava stone
2. Sedimentary	Limestone, sandstone
3. Metamorphic	Marble, slate

Rough stone is generally broken down to workable dimensions at the quarry and occasionally sawed smooth on the back for dimensional stability. Stone cut in panels can range in thickness from 2″ to 8″, depending on the stone and the size of the panel. The square or rectangular panel can have a variety of finishes and is held in place with special corrosion-proof steel anchors (stainless steel, etc.; see Figure 4-21).

Stone is used for construction other than walls. Slate, limestone, and granite are used for floors and steps. Marble is used for decorative panels and window sills. A structural stone system that involves gluing stone columns and beams together is adaptable to small commercial systems.

Nonferrous Metal

Nonferrous metal categorizes all noniron base metals used in construction, including lead used for pads to silence mechanical equipment; special noncorrosive plumbing; sheets used to separate extreme acoustical problems; brass used for hardware and plumbing fittings; and cover plates for interior building joints. The two most common nonferrous metals, however, are aluminum and copper.

Aluminum   Aluminum is mined and refined electrically into a metal that is more than 99 percent pure. It is lightweight (not quite one-third the weight of steel) and extremely ductile. It carries electricity well enough to be used as a replacement for copper wire. Of its many attributes, aluminum has two qualities that qualify it as a major building material: its ability to resist corrosion and the ease with which it can be extruded or shaped.

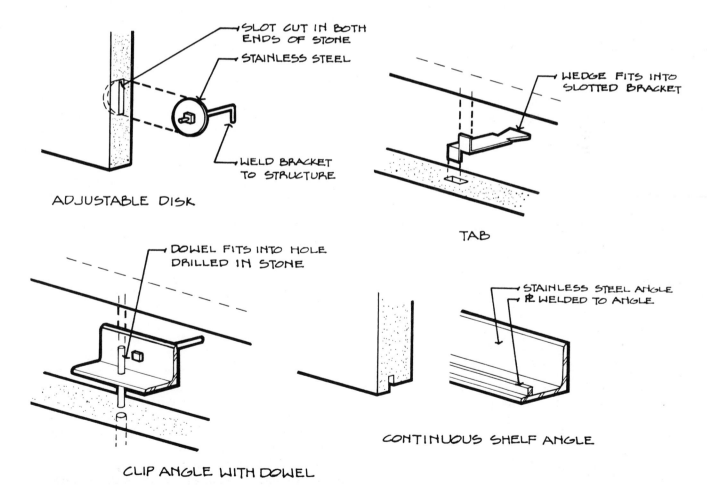

Figure 4-21.   Stone anchoring details.

Extruding is a technique in which a billet of aluminum is heated to a plastic state and squeezed by a hydraulic press through a steel die. The resulting extrusion conforms to the pattern of the die in lengths averaging 30′. This process is an excellent way to produce window frames, gravel stops, panel systems, and curtain-wall members (Figure 4-22).

When aluminum is exposed to air, a thin film of aluminum oxide forms on the exposed surface and protects against corrosion. If this surface is scratched, the area heals itself.

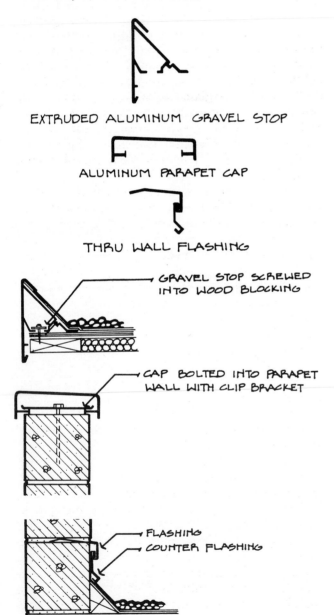

EXTRUDED ALUMINUM GRAVEL STOP

ALUMINUM PARAPET CAP

THRU WALL FLASHING

GRAVEL STOP SCREWED INTO WOOD BLOCKING

CAP BOLTED INTO PARAPET WALL WITH CLIP BRACKET

FLASHING
COUNTER FLASHING

Figure 4-22. Aluminum extrusions.

A precaution is taken to protect the finish of aluminum used in construction. Called *anodizing*, it involves electroplating a much thicker oxide coat than is natural to aluminum. The natural oxide is about $1/100,000''$ thick, while an anodized coating is from $4/1000''$ to $7/1000''$ thick. Coupled with anodized finishes, the aluminum can also be given a long-lasting color coating in the gray-black, brown-bronze color ranges.

In addition to extrusions, aluminum can be cast and rolled into shapes for building materials. By using the various alloys of aluminum and different forming methods, many building materials can be fabricated, such as window frames, flashing, gravel stops, and building panels. Aluminum thickness is measured in fractions of an inch or in thousandths of an inch. A gravel-stop thickness is typically $32/1000''$, which is $1/32+''$.

Since aluminum reacts chemically with concrete or dissimilar metals with which it comes in contact, it either should be protected with a coating of asphalt paint at the point of contact or should be separated from other metals with a plastic or lead shim.

Copper After it is refined, copper is typically rolled into sheets for use in construction. The metal weathers through a variety of colors when exposed to nature. This colored layer is called *patina;* it progresses from a natural copper color through shades of brown to a final green. A natural patina coat takes up to 10 years to reach the final green, and it provides a protective shield against corrosion. The process can be done much faster chemically; or if a clear plastic sheet is bonded to the copper, a "new penny" look can be achieved permanently.

The three types of copper are cold-rolled, soft, and lead-coated. Of the three, cold-rolled is the most frequently used. The thickness of copper is expressed in ounces per square foot—24-oz copper is copper that weighs 24 oz/sq ft, or about 20 ga (in sheet metal designation), which is about $1/32''$ thick. The most common copper sheet thicknesses are 32 oz, 24 oz, 20 oz, and 16 oz. Copper has a wide variety of uses, mainly in areas where durability, flexibility, and corrosion resistance is necessary, including roofing systems and building flashing (Figure 4-23).

As with aluminum, the galvanic activity of copper is such that it should be separated from many dissimilar metals. A battery process is started when certain metals touch in the presence of moisture (as when copper touches aluminum, zinc, steel, iron, or tin). The electrolysis process leads to deterioration of one of the metals. Given the presence of copper, the other metal breaks down. Aluminum deteriorates when it is allowed to come in contact with more active materials.

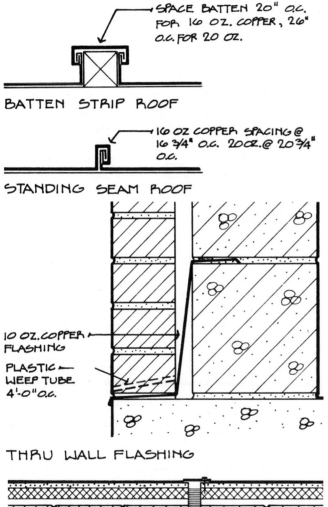

PLAN @ BRICK EXPANSION JOINT

Figure 4-23. Uses of copper in construction.

Glass

Glass is produced by fusing molten silica into a sheet. Float glass is formed on a pool of molten tin, and polished plate glass is made by grinding and polishing both faces of the sheet. These two processes produce a uniformly thick, distortion-free plate of glass. Another method of producing glass is the sheet method, in which molten glass is poured onto a smooth surface and cooled. This method, however, produces visual distortions and is generally unacceptable for architectural applications.

Glass is available in many sizes, ranging from ⅛″ to 3″ thick for bullet-resistant material. The thickness depends both on how the glass will be used and on how large a sheet is needed. The typical thickness found in construction is ¼″ to ⅜″. In addition to single-glass thickness, several units are produced that employ two sheets of glass, bonded together. Since the greatest area for heat loss in a building is at the glass, the two sheets of glass with a "dead" air space between them provide better insulation.

Two-sheet glass systems are manufactured by two methods. The first places two pieces of glass ³/₁₆″ apart by molding the glass together at the edges, with a combined thickness of ⅜″ or ⁷/₁₆″. This type of insulated glass is used in relatively small openings, those less than 3′ × 4′. The other insulated glass system spaces two plates of glass ¼″ or ½″ apart and seals the edges with a band of stainless steel. This unit comes in total thicknesses from ½″ to 1″ and can be used in openings 6′ × 8′ and larger (Figure 4-24). In both systems, the air space between the sheets of glass, a *wythe*, is sealed from the outer atmosphere and filled with dry air to prevent moisture condensation. Glass manufacturers have established a wide range of standard sizes for insulated glass, and large-order special sizes can be fabricated.

In addition to its various sizes, glass is available in different textures and colors. In general, textured glass is used infrequently in architecture, but the color range of glass is a major element in commercial design. Tinted glass can reduce light transmission, which, in turn, reduces the heat gain from the summer sun. Glass is tinted in gray, bronze, and blue-green color ranges and is available in insulated units (one sheet clear and one tinted); but the tinted sheet must be located closest to solar radiation to prevent heat from building up in the wythe.

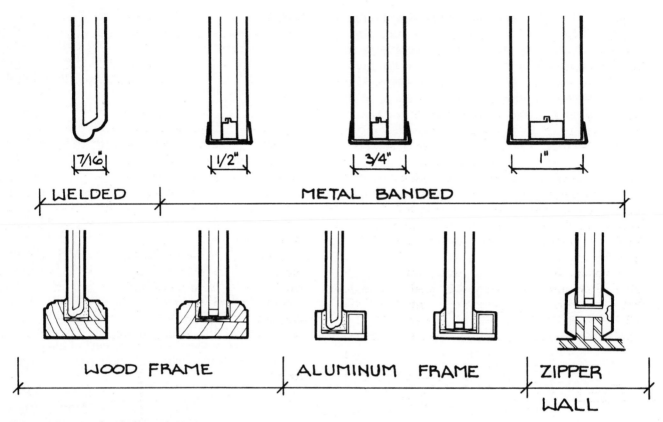

Figure 4-24.   Insulated glass sizes.

A different glass product is made by mirror-plating the interior side of an insulated glass panel. The result is a two-way mirror that reflects light on the brighter side of the glass yet is transparent when viewed through the other side. Mirrored glass is available in copper, bronze, gold, and gray tones.

A common commercial building system involves sheathing the complete exterior with glass walls. Transparent glass works in areas between each floor and ceiling, but an opaque material must be used from the ceiling to the floor above in order to hide the horizontal structure and mechanical systems. The material used is a sheet of glass backed with baked ceramic finish. The sheet, a *spandrel panel*, can be either a single panel of glass (¼" or ⅜") or two panels sandwiched together with Fiberglas or polyurethane foam to make a panel thickness of up to 2". Spandrel panels have standard finishes that match tinted or mirrored glass, as well as custom colors.

If glass is subjected to heat under special conditions, its strength and breakage properties can be changed. Heat-strengthened glass can be used in situations where twice the strength of standard

glass is desired. Tempered glass is four to five times stronger than standard glass and also has the properties of breaking into pellet-shaped pieces rather than sharp, jagged edges when fractured. Tempered glass is commonly used in doors. Glass must be cut to size before it is tempered, since any scratch on the surface causes the entire sheet to fracture.

Gypsum

Gypsum is mined in its natural form and then crushed and heated several hundred degrees to drive off some of its water. This material has the property of setting to smooth, hard consistency when it is mixed with water (plaster of paris is a form of gypsum). The setting time for gypsum can be adjusted greatly, but it usually is accomplished in several hours.

Gypsum either is processed as dry powder (plaster) or mixed with water and formed into sheets. Plaster is mixed commonly with lime to add plasticity and also with a variety of aggregates (sand and vermiculite are standard). Dry plaster is mixed with water at the job site and applied to a back-up in two or three coats. The back-up material, *lath*, can be wood, metal, gypsum board, or concrete block. One of the most common is expanded diamond mesh lath.

Plaster has no established thickness, but the norm is ¼″ for the first coat (*scratch* coat), ¼″ for the second coat (*brown* coat), and ⅛″ for the last coat (*finish* coat); the finished job ranges from ⅝″ to 1¼″. Several special plasters are available to compensate for the fact that plaster is not waterproof. Keene's cement plaster withstands high-humidity conditions, while exterior conditions call for portland cement plaster. Most plaster is applied with a steel trowel to provide a smooth, hard finish. A textured effect can be achieved by spraying.

Gypsum is mixed with water and a binder (glass fibers are common) and formed into boards that are uniformly thick (in increments from ⅜″ to ⅝″) and in various sheet sizes (the standard is 4′ × 8′). Gypsum board has a layer of paper applied to both faces to provide a painting surface. It can be nailed with an annular ring nail or screwed to wood or metal studs or glued to a solid back-up (Figure 4-25). Mechanical fasteners tend to pull away from studs, and so special nails or screws usually are used.

The joints between sheets of gypsum board are usually sealed by embedding a strip of perforated paper tape in joint cement and feathering out several other layers of cement to produce a smooth surface. Nails and screws are treated by depressing the surface around the nail and filling it with joint cement. The resulting wall system, referred to as *drywall*, has a 1-hour fireproof rating if ⅝″ thick.

Other gypsum products include a partition block (used for interior-wall back-up in a manner similar to concrete block and gypsum lath), a thin gypsum board used as a back-up for plaster. Gypsum has the advantages of being low in cost, easily erected, and permanent, together with the

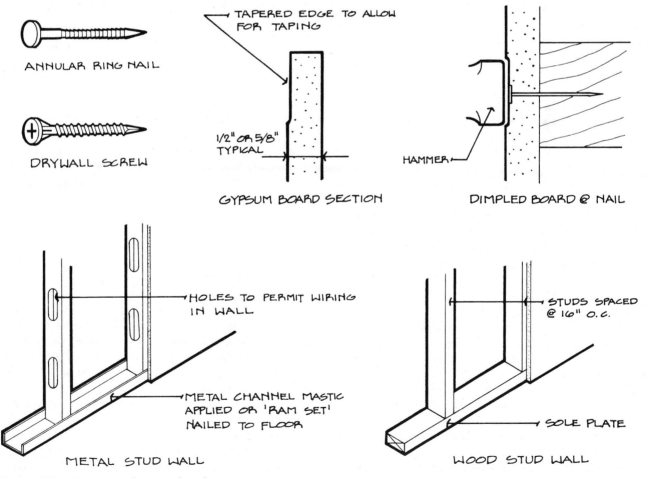

Figure 4-25.   Some uses of gypsum board.

strong advantage of being fireproof. Building codes require certain spaces to have fire ratings; that is, a fire must be contained within the space for a specified hourly rating. Gypsum products provide an excellent solution to many fire regulations.

Bitumen

Bituminous building products are used widely for roofing. Bitumen and asphalt are produced by a process of fractional distillation of crude oil, much as gasoline is refined. Bituminous products are waterproof, they function as preservatives, and they have a melting point that can be regulated at temperatures slightly higher than the heat generated on a roof by the sun.

Asphalt shingles are produced by impregnating felt (made from rags, wood fiber, or other cellulose fibers) with hot asphalt. The felt is then given additional coats of asphalt and coated with mineral chips (slate is common) and cut to size. The manufacture of roofing felt follows the same process but ends before the additional coat of asphalt is applied; roll roofing is finished before the mineral chips are applied. Applied roofing products are measured in the weight of the material per "square." A square equals a roof area 10' × 10', or 100 sq ft. Roofing felt weighs 15 or 30 lb. Roll roofing weighs 45, 55, or 65 lb. Roll roofing with a mineral surface weighs 90 lb, and asphalt shingles typically weigh 235 lb per square. Special shingles can exceed 600 lb.

Asphalt is a main ingredient in built-up roofing systems and can be made with different melting points to suit the conditions of the roof. Built-up roofing (Figure 4-26) is made by pouring hot molten asphalt over a prepared roofing deck and imbedding gravel chips into the material. The

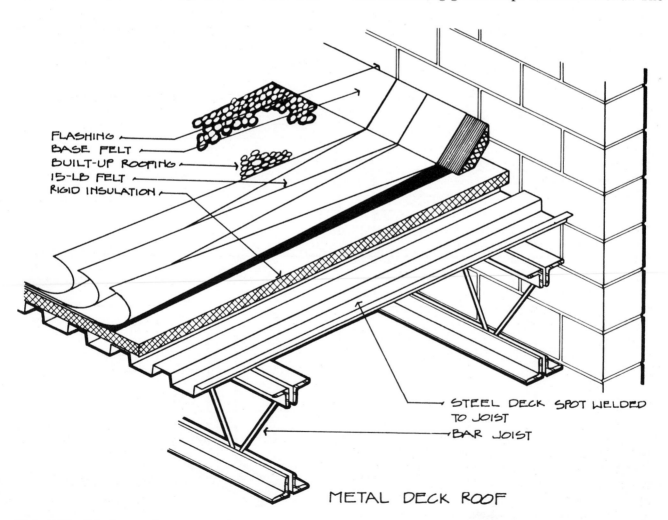

FLASHING
BASE FELT
BUILT-UP ROOFING
15-LB FELT
RIGID INSULATION

STEEL DECK SPOT WELDED TO JOIST
BAR JOIST

METAL DECK ROOF

Figure 4-26. A built-up roofing system.

higher the melting temperature of the asphalt, the steeper the slope of the roof to which it can be applied (up to 6″ rise to 12″ run). The melting temperature for asphalt ranges from 135 to 200°F [57.22 to 93.33°C].

Cement Asbestos

Cement asbestos, or *mineral fiber product*, is produced by mixing portland cement and asbestos fibers with water and forming the mixture into sheets or pipe. The resulting product is very hard, fireproof, dense, and resistant to water. It is also light in weight, since sheets can be made as thin as ⅛″. Products made with mineral fiber include interior and exterior wall panels, siding, shingles, and pipe used to distribute heat under a floor slab.

Mineral fiberboard is made in two grades—type F (flexible) and type U (utility). Sheet size is up to 4′ × 12′. The panels can range in thickness from ⅛″ to 2″ and can be fastened by corrosion-proof nails, metal fasteners, or mastic (glue).

Sealants

Sealants provide a weatherproof connection between dissimilar building materials or joints in a wall. Products of this type are categorized generally as either caulking compounds or sealants.

Caulking compounds are intended for application in conditions that have little, if any, movement and are not subjected to severe weather, such as interior spaces. Most caulking compounds, like window putty, have an oil base. They have the undesirable qualities of inflexibility, eventual breakdown due to loss of oil, and close temperature tolerances that must be achieved in application. While these disadvantages should limit caulking compounds to interior conditions, they also have a major advantage: They can cost as little as 5 percent of the price of some sealants.

Sealants encompass a wide range of products that are classified as *elastomers* (having the elastic quality of rubber). Sealants should have adhesive and cohesive strength, elasticity, durability under extreme temperature and weather conditions, an ability to return to their original shape after being extended or compressed, a wide range of temperature applications, short curing time, reasonable price; they should be nonstaining, colorfast, and easy to apply. These properties are not only de-

sirable but necessary in modern commercial construction. Products that fit these requirements in varying degrees are acrylics, silicones, polyurethane, and one- and two-part polysulfides. These sealants have unique properties, both in application and in final results. Unlike oil-based caulking compounds, they do not dry in the air to cure. Some use moisture in the air as a catalyst to cure, while others have added chemicals that start the curing process. Sealants are created to meet specific needs; it is possible that more than one would be used on a building project.

A properly sealed joint (Figure 4-27) consists of two parts, a compressible backup material and a sealant. The back-up—which can be polyethylene foam, neoprene, or butyl, all in a rope form—is pressed into the joint to approximately the same depth as the joint is wide. The sealant is then applied with a gun and tooled to a concave joint. To produce a bond, some sealants require that the joint be primed before sealant is applied. Sealants are available in a variety of colors that closely match the colors of anodized aluminum.

METHODS AND SYSTEMS OF DETAILING

One mark of a competent drafting technician is a fundamental knowledge of assembling building materials. First you must recognize the design conditions, and then you must devise a detail that applies to all conditions. This is seldom a totally inventive procedure. Most elements that make up a building detail are variations of conditions which have proven answers.

To define each building detail and system in this section is not possible or necessary. *Architectural Graphic Standards* and *Sweet's File* are de-

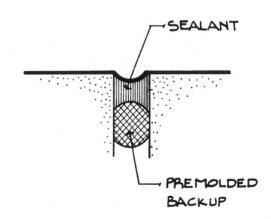

Figure 4-27. A sealed joint.

signed to do this. This section is intended to guide you through the important points of major building systems.

Footings and Foundations

A *footing* provides ground support for the weight of a building. The design of the footing is affected by the strength of the soil or the bearing capacity and the weight of the building.

Before a major building project is undertaken, the architect asks the owner for a soil investigation of the site. This study usually is performed by a professional soil engineer. It can determine the types of soil at various depths beneath the surface, the height of the water table or the depth at which water will settle in a hole dug in the ground, and the bearing capacity of the soil.

A common method of soil investigation is to bore into the soil with a hollow tube and study the extracted core at various points. Four borings, one located at each corner of the proposed building, are considered the minimum for necessary data. The depth of the boring depends on variables such as the type of building planned, the terrain, the soil, and the history of the soil in the vicinity. Generally, borings are extended 30' to 50' below grade, but this varies greatly. Often the final depth is left to the judgment of the soil engineer.

The soil engineer submits a report detailing the investigation to the architect and to the structural engineer. The soil-bearing pressure can range from 20 percent of the crushing strength for rock and 8000 lb/sq ft for compact sand to 1000 lb/sq ft for loose inorganic sand. This information is specified in the uniform building code. Table 4-1 shows a log of a test boring.

Soil conditions can have a pronounced effect not only on the footings used but also on the building's design. Clay is a difficult material on which to build, because its layers shrink and move. What initially is assumed to be a simple excavation could result in removing all the clay 15' below the entire building and replacing the material with acceptable soil.

A below-grade column, a *pile*, is used to support a structure when soil is extremely poor, such as peat or a swamp. Piles can be wood, steel, or concrete and can rely either on friction between the pile and soil or on the pile's extending through the soft material to hard strata. A common pile is an H-shaped steel beam that can be driven as much as

TABLE 4-1 LOG OF TEST BORING

DEPTH, FT	DESCRIPTION OF MATERIAL, SURFACE ELEVATION 1181.5'	WATER DEPTH, FT
1½	Lean clay, black, medium	
2½	Lean clay, grayish brown, medium	
4	Sandy clay, a little gravel, brown and some light-brown–gray mottled, stiff	
7½	Silty clay, brown mottled, medium	
9	Sandy clay, a little gravel, brown mottled	
14½	Sandy clay, a little gravel, gray, rather stiff	
19½	Silty clay, gray, rather stiff, a few lenses of silty sand	20½
24½	Sand, coarse-grained, some gravel, gray, waterbearing, dense	

200' down and hold a maximum of 200 tons. Piles can be spaced close together, about 3' on center for H pilings, to achieve the necessary loadbearing capacity. (See Figure 4-28.)

An alternative for poor soil conditions is to use a caisson support system. A *caisson* is a large, open-ended compartment, sunk into the ground by digging the soil out of the center. When the desired depth is achieved, the compartment is filled with concrete to support the building structure.

The most common footing used in small and medium construction is a standard poured-concrete footing with either a poured-concrete or a concrete-block foundation wall resting on top of the footing. The foundation wall acts as a barrier to prevent frost from getting under the floor slab and causing damage.

The climate, then, is one factor that determines the depth of a footing. Its effect can result in depth ranges from 5' or more below ground in Minnesota to only several inches in Texas. Engineers commonly require footing support for interior columns and block walls over 6" wide. Interior conditions do not require that the footing be dropped below the frost penetration.

Most building types demand a minimum of an 8" concrete-block foundation wall. The foundation wall usually is not connected to the first-floor slab; instead, it provides support for walls and columns. A good detail to follow for the ground-level slab is to provide 6" of gravel, then 6" of sand under the slab. The slab should be separated from the foun-

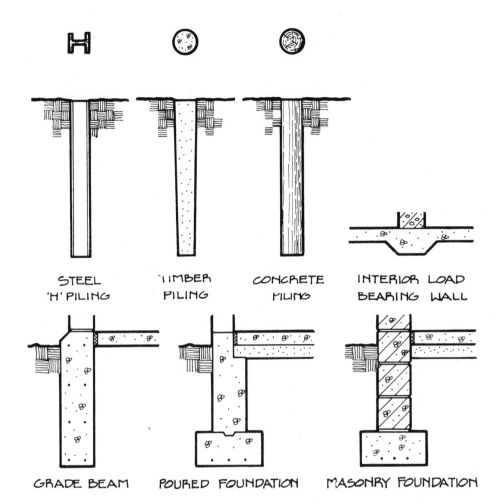

STEEL 'H' PILING TIMBER PILING CONCRETE PILING INTERIOR LOAD BEARING WALL

GRADE BEAM POURED FOUNDATION MASONRY FOUNDATION

Figure 4-28. Soil loadbearing conditions.

dation wall with a ½″ premolded joint filler and then sealed. In effect, this creates a floor slab that is free-floating from the foundation walls.

A grade beam is another building support in which the foundation wall and the floor slab are poured together, integrally. The foundation wall is usually reinforced with steel, like a structural concrete beam. A grade beam does not incorporate a continuous footing but instead spans the ground between supports. The supports can be piles, caissons, or pad footings.

Working drawings typically show the footings in wall section, but they do not dimension them or call out the steel reinforcement. This appears on the structural drawings. Some architects also show the footings as dotted lines on the exterior elevations. This is a good idea, particularly if the footings are not even but a step up in level. For example, a building on the side of a hill would have extremely deep footings at the top of the hill in order to be at the same elevation as the footing at the bottom of the hill. A pad footing is generally twice the width of the foundation wall and equal to the foundation wall in depth.

Waterproofing and Insulation

Two problems, water and cold penetration, can be averted by detailing materials on the outside face of the basement foundation wall (Figure 4-29). The usual practice is to coat the outside block foundation wall with two coats of portland cement plaster. The process is referred to as *parging*. Parging reduces the amount of water penetration and is used in ordinary soil conditions. Very wet soil conditions can warrant other solutions, such as dampproofing and waterproofing.

Dampproofing is done with a bituminous material that is applied in two coats over parged block or a poured-concrete foundation wall.

Waterproofing is the most extensive process for keeping moisture out of a basement. It consists

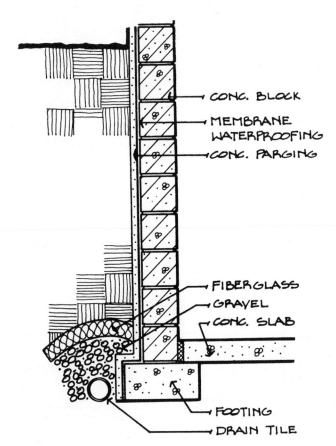

Figure 4-29.   Waterproof foundation wall.

of a waterproof membrane, perhaps a reinforced plastic sheet $^5/_{1000}''$ thick (5 mil), mastically applied (glued) to the outside foundation wall. The membrane is usually accompanied by a 10-mil polyethylene plastic waterproof barrier, placed directly under the floor slab.

The footing and foundation wall are not integral members, as the foundation only rests on its footing. The crack between the footing and foundation should also have a water barrier, a rubber dumbbell (Figure 4-30).

If water poses a problem in a basement, another common solution is to detail a perforated drain tile at the bottom of the footing on the outside. The tile carries off excess water to a storm sewer.

Concrete is a rather poor insulation material. When critical comfort is desired in a basement, insulation is added to the foundation wall. The detail includes the mastic application of rigid insulation, Styrofoam, to the foundation wall. The outside insulation is protected with a sheet of tempered hardboard which is mastically applied to the insulation.

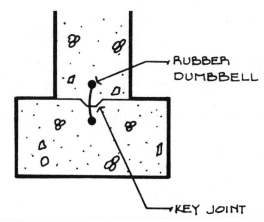

Figure 4-30.   Waterproof connection between footing and foundation.

In the case of a first-floor concrete slab that rests on the ground, a *slab on grade*, insulation may be placed directly under the slab to reduce cold transmission to the slab. It is also possible to place insulation on either side of the foundation wall.

Floors

A slab on grade is the most common floor found in the lowest level of a building. A concrete slab either can float independently of the foundation wall or be poured with it integrally. A common depth for a floating slab is 4″ with 6/6 × 10/10 wire mesh reinforcement. (The 6/6 × 10/10 designation indicates a 6″ square pattern of number 10 wire welded together.) Figure 4-31 shows some floor details.

A major problem with a slab on grade is that concrete is not a waterproof material. If the concrete is to be exposed, there are no problems; but if a floor material is to be applied to the slab, a vapor barrier should be placed under the slab, such as 10-mil polyethylene.

Many finish floor materials may be mastically applied directly to a concrete slab that has a vapor barrier. This process is called *thin set*. Materials such as slate, quarry and ceramic tile, wood, parquet, carpet, and vinyl asbestos tile may all be thin set to a concrete slab on grade.

Another system uses a concrete setting bed on top of the slab on which to apply the finish floor. Slate, quarry tile, ceramic tile, and terrazzo can be used for the finish floor.

A third system sets the finish floor up above the slab by resting it on supports, referred to as *sleepers*, usually wood. Wood floors, such as gym-

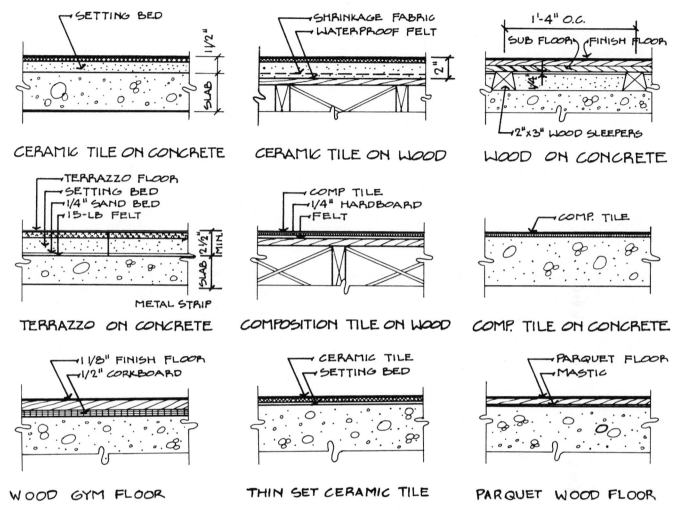

CERAMIC TILE ON CONCRETE — SETTING BED, 1/2″, SLAB

CERAMIC TILE ON WOOD — SHRINKAGE FABRIC, WATERPROOF FELT, 2″

WOOD ON CONCRETE — 1'-4″ O.C., SUB FLOOR, FINISH FLOOR, 2″×3″ WOOD SLEEPERS

TERRAZZO ON CONCRETE — TERRAZZO FLOOR, SETTING BED, 1/4″ SAND BED, 15-LB FELT, SLAB 2 1/2″ MIN., METAL STRIP

COMPOSITION TILE ON WOOD — COMP TILE, 1/4″ HARDBOARD, FELT

COMP. TILE ON CONCRETE — COMP. TILE

WOOD GYM FLOOR — 1 1/8″ FINISH FLOOR, 1/2″ CORKBOARD

THIN SET CERAMIC TILE — CERAMIC TILE, SETTING BED

PARQUET WOOD FLOOR — PARQUET FLOOR, MASTIC

Figure 4-31. Floor details.

nasium floors, use this technique. Computer rooms generally require a raised floor for wiring, and so the floor slab is depressed a minimum of 6″ and a special pedestal-supported floor is installed.

All the floor finishes mentioned can be used for floor systems above grade, but the means of structural support varies considerably. The structural systems can best be described if broken down into the following materials—wood, steel, and concrete. Figure 4-32 shows some base details.

Wood structure Wood structure is most typically used in residential and some small commercial projects. It is selected for its low cost, ease of assembly, accessability, and the fact that complex construction knowledge and equipment are not necessary. The disadvantages in wood floor framing are that it is not strong enough for major building types and it is not fireproof.

Wood structural floor members, *joists*, range from 2″ × 6″ to about 4″ × 10″. Two standard spacings are used for floor joists—16″ o.c. and 12″ o.c. (The abbreviation "o.c." is the *on center* distance.) In some conditions, wood joists can span distances of 30′, but the economical range is usually considered to be around 18′. Wood joists are supported by bearing the ends on a support or by hanging the joist from a beam. Plywood subflooring usually is used in conjunction with wood joists, either nailed or glued to the top of the joists to form a floor. Figures 4-33 and 4-34 show some wood-structure flooring.

A substitute for plywood is 1″ boards nailed diagonally to the joists. Generally, another material is applied to the top of subflooring, possibly another sheet of plywood or particle board. If the floor is to be carpeted or covered with vinyl tile, the additional material can be a thin layer of

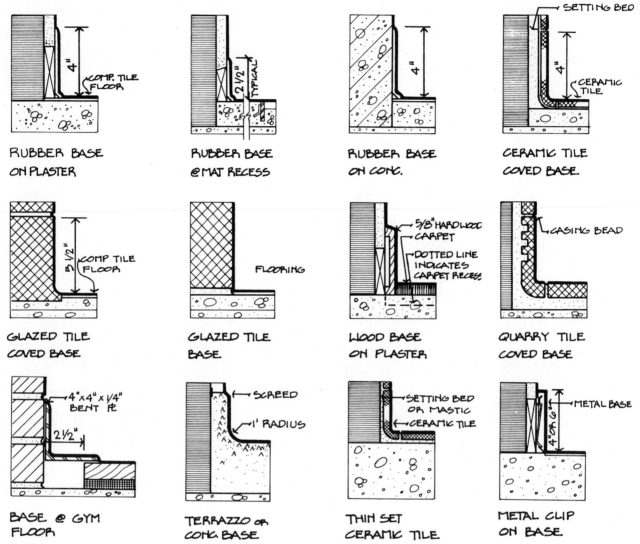

RUBBER BASE
ON PLASTER

RUBBER BASE
@ MAT RECESS

RUBBER BASE
ON CONC.

CERAMIC TILE
COVED BASE

GLAZED TILE
COVED BASE

GLAZED TILE
BASE

WOOD BASE
ON PLASTER

QUARRY TILE
COVED BASE

BASE @ GYM
FLOOR

TERRAZZO or
CONC. BASE

THIN SET
CERAMIC TILE

METAL CLIP
ON BASE

Figure 4-32. Base details.

poured concrete to lessen impact noise to the area below, or it can be hardwood flooring nailed to the subfloor.

Another type of wood-framing system uses thicker flooring materials that can span distances greater than 1'-4". The two materials commonly used are tongue-and-groove wood decking and tongue-and-groove plywood. The deck used is a nominal 2" material that can span 6' to 8' between supports. The plywood floor, called 2·4·1 T & G, is 1⅛" thick and can span 4'. The supports are either a wall or a continuous beam.

Steel structure Steel structure is possibly the most versatile of the three systems in that it can be adapted to most floor conditions from light-com-mercial to high-rise buildings. Steel frames (Figure 4-35) offer the advantages of being lightweight and easy to fabricate, and they span relatively long distances. The major disadvantage is that steel must be fireproofed, as it is less resistant to fire than large wood timbers are.

The most common system of steel support is the *open-web joist*, or *bar joist*, a truss shape built of steel angles or bars. The strength, and therefore spanning length, of an open-web joist depends on the depth of the joist, the shape and size of the structural members, and the type of steel used. (See Figures 4-36 and 4-37.) The most common depths for bar joists are from 8" to 24", with a usual spacing of 24" o.c. The span distance can be up to 40' for floors, making it one of the lightest struc-

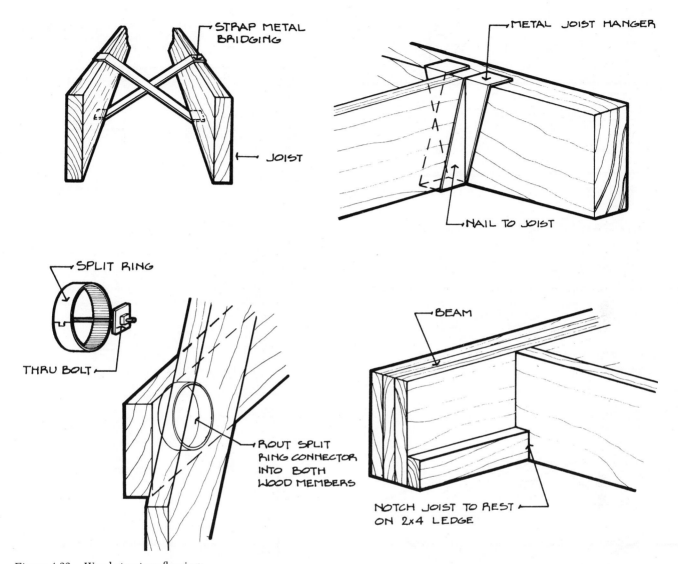

Figure 4-33. Wood-structure floorings.

tural systems for long spans. The end of a bar joist must bear on a wall or beam from 2½″ to 6″, depending on the size of the joist and end conditions.

The flooring used with metal joists is usually concrete or a combination of concrete and steel deck. A concrete slab can be as thin as 2½″ if it is reinforced and if it spans the 2′ between joists. Metal deck is corrugated into various depths from 1″ to 7½″ and has steel-reinforced concrete poured over the deck. The standard deck is 1½″ deep and has about 2″ of concrete topping.

Another system using metal deck and concrete is similar but uses thicker materials, allowing it to span between steel or concrete beams instead of bar joists. The economical spanning length for this flooring is from 6′ to 14′, with the deck bearing directly on the beams. The use of steel beams (Figure 4-38) and concrete slabs combines the advantages of solid, relatively lightweight flooring materials with the long spanning and lightweight characteristics of steel beams. The disadvantages lie in the comparatively narrow beam spacing and the necessity of fireproofing steel members. (See Figure 4-39.)

Concrete structure Concrete structure has many possibilities and is used extensively in medium and heavy construction. Its advantages lie in its plastic nature, or its ability to be shaped, its fireproof qualities, its poor sound transmission through the floor, and its ability to span up to 65′ economically in some systems. The disadvantages

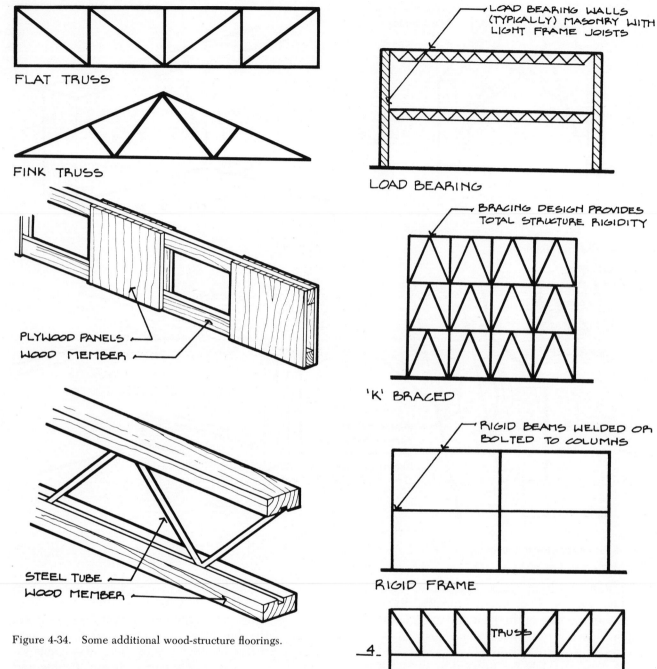

FLAT TRUSS

FINK TRUSS

PLYWOOD PANELS
WOOD MEMBER

STEEL TUBE
WOOD MEMBER

Figure 4-34.   Some additional wood-structure floorings.

LOAD BEARING WALLS
(TYPICALLY) MASONRY WITH
LIGHT FRAME JOISTS

LOAD BEARING

BRACING DESIGN PROVIDES
TOTAL STRUCTURE RIGIDITY

'K' BRACED

RIGID BEAMS WELDED OR
BOLTED TO COLUMNS

RIGID FRAME

TRUSS
4
COLUMN FREE FLOOR
3
2
COLUMN FREE FLOOR
1

STAGGERED TRUSS

Figure 4-35.   Steel frames.

are that poured-in-place floors require a complex system of secondary support while the material cures and that concrete structural framing adds weight to a building.

Concrete flooring can be precast or cast in place. *Precast concrete* is formed in a factory under controlled conditions and transported to the job site (Figure 4-40). *Cast-in-place concrete* indicates that the form work was built and supported at the final location of the floor and then poured with ready-mixed concrete.

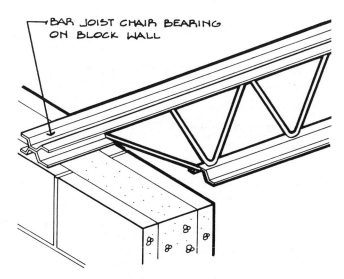

Figure 4-36. Bar joist bearing on a masonry wall.

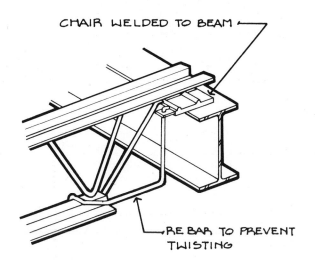

Figure 4-37. Bar joist bearing on a steel beam.

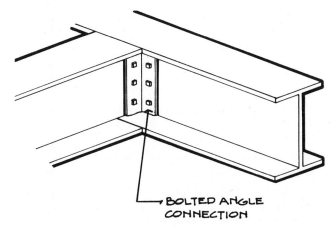

Figure 4-38. A beam-to-beam connection.

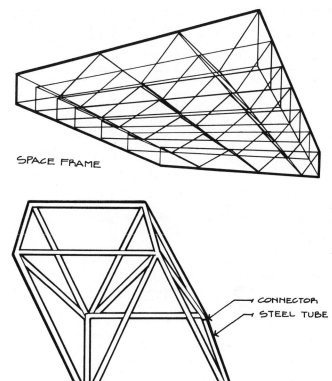

Figure 4-39. Steel space frames.

The typical precast floor materials are pre-stressed deck and tees and precast double tees. The deck and precast tee can span up to 36′, while the prestressed tee can be used to span up to 65′. In each case, the material can bear on a wall, beam (Figure 4-41), or ledge and has an additional 1½″ to 2″ of concrete topping poured over the precast member. Any finish floor material may be used with this system.

Cast-in-place concrete floor systems have many combinations that may be adapted to floor spans. Concrete pan-and-waffle slabs (Figure 4-42) are the placement of metal or Fiberglas pans on a temporary floor. The pans are placed with the open end down and are spaced 4″ to 7″ apart. When the entire floor area has been covered with pans, concrete is poured over the pans to a depth of several inches above the top of the pans. When the concrete has cured, the temporary floor below is taken down, and the exposed pans are removed. This structural system can span up to 50′. It is poured monolithically (together) with the beams and walls.

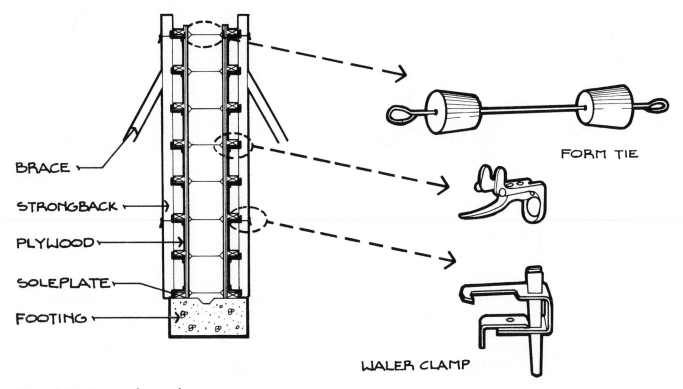

Figure 4-40. Concrete form work.

Other concrete methods include concrete or steel encased in concrete beams that support concrete slabs. Either the slab may be poured integrally with the beam, or it may rest on a beam that has been placed. The spanning system usually has limits of 30′, with slab depths of from 3½″ to 1′, depending on the slab used.

A unique concrete floor system is the *lift slab*, in which columns are erected to their final height and all floors are poured on top of each other. A collar is placed around the colums so that the floor can be hydraulically lifted into place. The lift-slab system allows most major construction to take place near ground level.

The choice of materials used for structural flooring is decided strongly by the building type. Many variables are brought into this decision, such as the span length, cost, size of the project, fire rating, sound-impact rating, weight of the material, and flexibility of the structure. In most cases, these parameters narrow the choice to several acceptable systems.

Walls

Exterior walls Exterior wall systems include an extremely wide range of materials, finishes, and support techniques. In some conditions, the exterior walls are load-bearing walls and support the weight of the floors and roof. Other wall conditions merely provide an exterior skin to protect against outside elements. This type is hung from the structural frame and is called a *curtain wall*. Columns provide support.

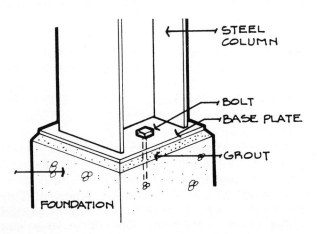

Figure 4-41. Steel column bearing on concrete footing.

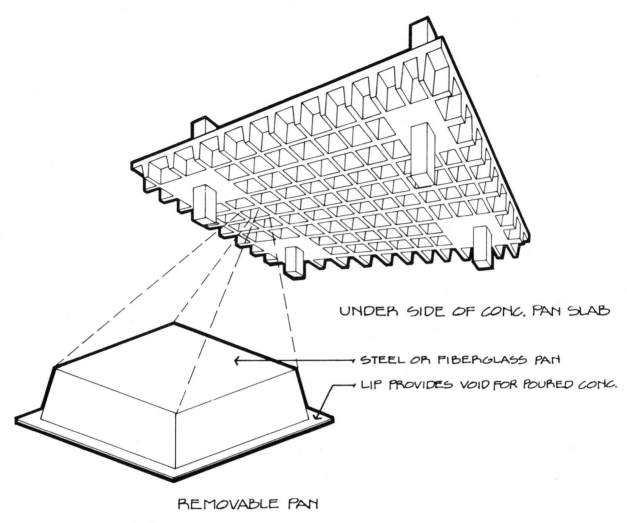

UNDER SIDE OF CONC. PAN SLAB

STEEL OR FIBERGLASS PAN

LIP PROVIDES VOID FOR POURED CONC.

REMOVABLE PAN

Figure 4-42. A waffle slab floor.

Wood wall systems offer the same advantages as wood floor framing: They are low in cost, easy to assemble, and readily accessible. Wood framing accounts for an overwhelming percentage of all residential and light commercial construction. (See Figure 4-43.)

The most common system for wood walls is the *western frame* (Figure 4-44). It consists of bolting a wood plate to the foundation wall, nailing joists to the plate, attaching subflooring to the joists, nailing a sole plate to the floor, and nailing studs at 16″ o.c. to the sole plate. Sheathing of ½″ plywood is nailed to the studs for a substructure for the siding. Usually 15-lb building felt is placed between the sheathing and siding.

An assortment of exterior finish materials may be applied directly to western frame, including: horizontal and vertical wood siding, either painted or stained (Figure 4-45); stucco, brick, or stone veneer; vinyl and aluminum siding; and wood shingles. Siding material and shingles are nailed to the sheathing. Galvanized or aluminum finish nails are used if the wood is to be left unfinished or stained, because regular nails rust. Stucco has an expanded metal lath nailed to the sheathing and building felt to anchor the stucco finish. The stucco finish usually is applied in three layers—scratch, brown, and finish coats.

Another type of stucco application uses a *self-furring lath* (an expanded metal lath with a paper back-up), which eliminates the need for sheathing. Brick and stone veneer is supported at the base or bottom by a shelf angle. It also can rest partially on the foundation wall. The veneer must be tied periodically to the wood frame; this is done by nailing a corrugated-galvanized tie to the sheathing. The

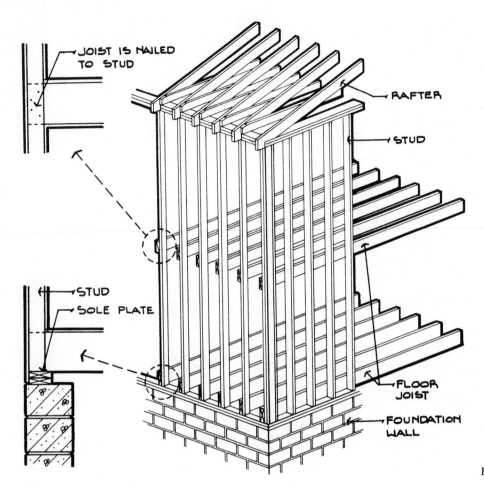

JOIST IS NAILED TO STUD

RAFTER

STUD

STUD

SOLE PLATE

FLOOR JOIST

FOUNDATION WALL

Figure 4-43.   A wood balloon frame.

tie is placed into the mortar bed of the brick to anchor it to the wood-frame construction, not to support it. (See Figure 4-46.)

The inside space between studs usually is insulated to reduce heating costs. Insulation can be sprayed foam or batt Fiberglas, which is cut to fit between the studs. The inside face of the Fiberglas can have a paper or aluminum sheet over the insulation to stop vapor moisture inside the space from penetrating the insulation and freezing.

Most wall systems other than wood frame act as a skin to protect the building from the elements rather than support it. Wall systems should be lightweight, weatherproof, easy to fabricate, and low in cost. Most systems use an independent structural framing unit to act as a skeleton. Several notable exceptions to this wall concept are masonry and poured concrete, although these walls can be used as nonloadbearing.

Metal wall systems are used in medium to major construction because of permanence and strength. Most metal walls are curtain walls rather than loadbearing walls. This means they are clipped to the structural frame.

One wall treatment uses metal panels that can be color-finished aluminum, weathering steel (Figure 4-47), stainless steel, or baked enamel on sheet metal. The panels are fabricated to various sizes and are attached to the frame according to details recommended by the manufacturer. A fairly standard application involves sandwiching an insulation material to the back side of the panel and attaching it to a metal mullion.

The most widely used metal wall system is extruded aluminum window mullions and glass; it easily accounts for most commercial construction. Aluminum is easily extruded into mullion shapes, permanently color-finished or anodized, lightweight, and easy to clip to a structural frame. These qualities make it an ideal choice for a curtain wall.

Aluminum curtain walls typically consist of a frame that is bolted to the steel or concrete structure. The frame has provisions for fixed or remov-

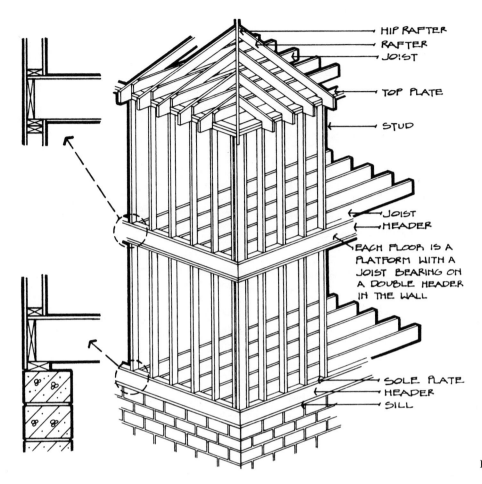

HIP RAFTER
RAFTER
JOIST
TOP PLATE
STUD
JOIST
HEADER
EACH FLOOR IS A
PLATFORM WITH A
JOIST BEARING ON
A DOUBLE HEADER
IN THE WALL
SOLE PLATE
HEADER
SILL

Figure 4-44.   A wood western frame.

able stops, allowing the windows to be glazed into the frame. The designer can use any of the available types of glass or insulated panels. Both fit in the window mullion frame.

An exterior elevation of the structural system used for a curtain wall is quite standard. It is a rectangular skeletal form with horizontal structural beams, *spandrel beams*, at each floor and vertical column. The structural frame and floor system derive no support from the curtain wall. It acts only as a protective skin. (See Figure 4-48.)

If the curtain wall is to be glazed, a combination of transparent and opaque glass is incorporated into the wall frame. The transparent glass is used in rooms, and the opaque panel—a spandrel panel—is used to cover the horizontal structure and mechanical space above the ceiling.

A unique system tying glazing or glass to a metal mullion is the *zipper wall*. It consists of a rubber or plastic gasket that accepts glass units and holds them in place by zipping an additional piece into the gasket. This system provides an all-glass

exterior curtain wall interrupted periodically by a 1½" gasket.

Concrete walls may be treated both as loadbearing and curtain-wall systems. Loadbearing concrete walls are poured in forms at the site and allowed to cure. The forms may be treated in many ways, giving the resulting wall a unique shape or texture. If heating requirements necessitate insulation in a poured-concrete wall, a lightweight insulation concrete or a rigid insulation sandwiched inside the form before the concrete is placed or rigid insulation mastic applied to the inside face of the wall can be used.

Precast curtain-wall concrete panels are applied similarly to metal panels, but the weight is considerably greater. Anchor supports are cast into the panel and then bolted to a metal clip attached to the building frame. The panel size and 2" minimum thickness varies according to the job, as does the finish, which can assume any texture compatible with concrete. Insulation can be treated by mastically applying insulation boards to the back

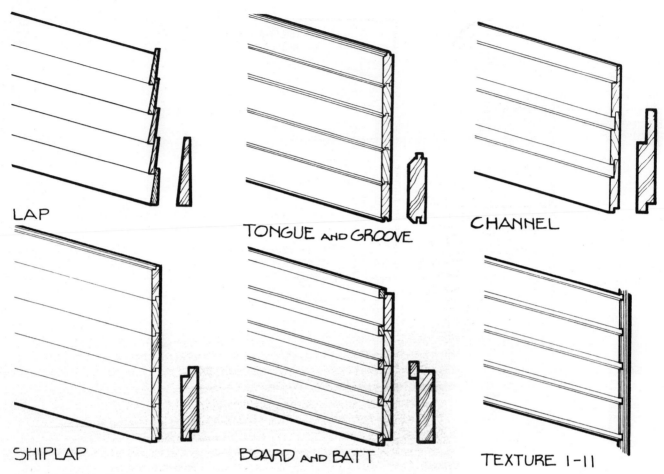

LAP

TONGUE and GROOVE

CHANNEL

SHIPLAP

BOARD and BATT

TEXTURE 1-11

Figure 4-45.   Wood siding.

side of the panel, by sandwiching rigid insulation between the layers of concrete, or by using lightweight insulation concrete. Similar details are followed when mineral fiberboard is used in place of precast panels.

Masonry wall systems include concrete masonry units and clay products. Concrete block can be used as a separate material or as a back-up

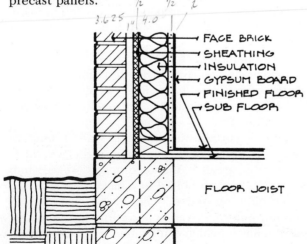

FACE BRICK
SHEATHING
INSULATION
GYPSUM BOARD
FINISHED FLOOR
SUB FLOOR

FLOOR JOIST

Figure 4-46.   Brick veneer on a wood frame.

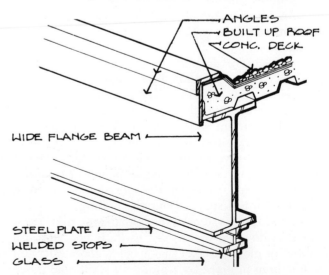

ANGLES
BUILT UP ROOF
CONC. DECK

WIDE FLANGE BEAM

STEEL PLATE
WELDED STOPS
GLASS

Figure 4-47.   A weathering steel roof condition.

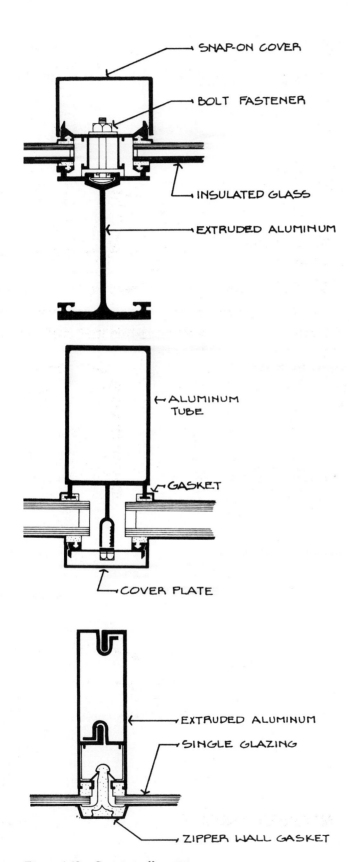

SNAP-ON COVER

BOLT FASTENER

INSULATED GLASS

EXTRUDED ALUMINUM

ALUMINUM TUBE

GASKET

COVER PLATE

EXTRUDED ALUMINUM

SINGLE GLAZING

ZIPPER WALL GASKET

Figure 4-48. Curtain wall sections.

for other products. The standard modular coursing for block is 8″. An economy is realized if these 8″ horizontal and vertical increments are followed in laying out masonry openings.

Doors, windows, and other openings must be supported with a structural lintel, either a steel angle or a lintel block that is reinforced with steel and poured with concrete (Figure 4-49). Block walls frequently require additional horizontal support to adequately tie the wall together. This is accomplished by incorporating metal reinforcing in the mortar joints. Concrete masonry units can be used either as loadbearing walls, usually on small structures, or as a filler wall material between columns and floor slabs. In the case of a filler wall, the structure is usually concrete, and the entire system is used as a back-up for another wall system.

Brick generally is used as a veneer wall and tied to a structural back-up, usually concrete block or clay tile. It is available in a wide range of earth colors and can be used in a variety of patterns by laying it with different sides exposed. Brick requires a steel lintel for support above masonry openings. The methods of tying brick to a back-up are mechanical bonding—such as welded wire, wire reinforcing, or corrugated metal—and brick bonds.

Stone walls can be used as a veneer with a back-up similar to brick. The process involves parging the back of the stone and using either a mechanical or a masonry bond. Stone panels can be hung from a building's skeletal structure with stainless steel or galvanized anchors that are tied into the building frame. This curtain-wall system usually has a back-up, such as masonry, to add rigidity and insulation value

Interior walls Interior walls fall into two general framing systems: *solid* and *stud. Solid walls* can achieve loadbearing qualities, have low sound transmission, and provide fire barriers. Solid walls include concrete masonry units, clay tile, gypsum lath block, and poured concrete. These wall types have a finish material applied over the wall, ranging from paint to plaster.

Stud walls are spaced structural members that support an outside skin. They are lightweight, easily fabricated, and can be made to be fireproof and reduce sound. Studs can be wood or steel and are generally spaced at 16″ o.c. Gypsum board or metal lath and plaster are the most usual facing materials

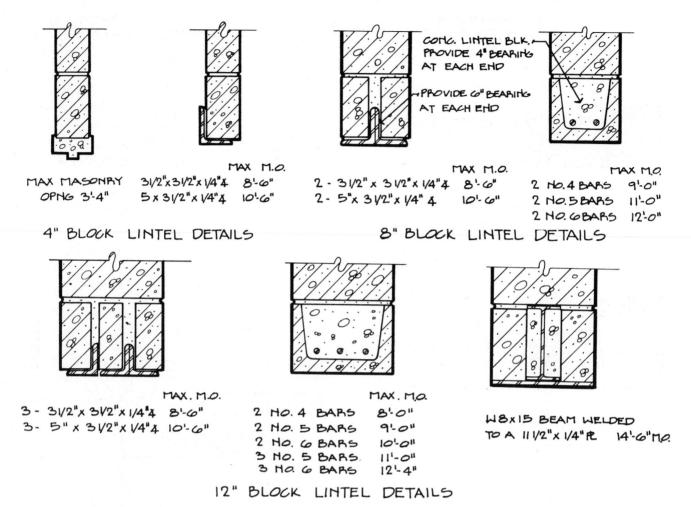

MAX MASONRY
OPNG 3'-4"

	MAX M.O.
3 1/2" x 3 1/2" x 1/4" 4	8'-6"
5 x 3 1/2" x 1/4" 4	10'-6"

4" BLOCK LINTEL DETAILS

CONC. LINTEL BLK.
PROVIDE 4" BEARING
AT EACH END

PROVIDE 6" BEARING
AT EACH END

	MAX M.O.
2 - 3 1/2" x 3 1/2" x 1/4" 4	8'-6"
2 - 5" x 3 1/2" x 1/4" 4	10'-6"

	MAX M.O.
2 NO. 4 BARS	9'-0"
2 NO. 5 BARS	11'-0"
2 NO. 6 BARS	12'-0"

8" BLOCK LINTEL DETAILS

	MAX. M.O.
3 - 3 1/2" x 3 1/2" x 1/4" 4	8'-6"
3 - 5" x 3 1/2" x 1/4" 4	10'-6"

	MAX. M.O.
2 NO. 4 BARS	8'-0"
2 NO. 5 BARS	9'-0"
2 NO. 6 BARS	10'-0"
3 NO. 5 BARS	11'-0"
3 NO. 6 BARS	12'-4"

W 8 x 15 BEAM WELDED
TO A 11 1/2" x 1/4" R   14'-6" M.O.

12" BLOCK LINTEL DETAILS

Figure 4-49. Masonry lintel sizes.

applied to studs. Paint, vinyl wall fabric, or wood paneling is applied over the hard surface.

Demountable wall systems have the unique feature of being removable and reusable. Metal plates are clipped to the floor and to the ceiling. Studs are then clipped into the plates. The wall panels are fastened to the studs.

Roofing

Structural designs for roofing are preferably similar to the selected floor framing or at least compatible. A wood-frame building does not normally have a concrete roof structure because the attachment details do not work together. Roof structures have slightly lower weight requirements than floor structures because snow loads are about the extent of imposed weight. For this reason, roof spans can be greater than floor spans.

Flat roofs or those with a gradual slope to a roof drain (1/8" pitch to the foot) are quite common in commercial roofing systems. In this condition, a built-up roof is the typical solution, consisting first of a layer of rigid insulation with hot asphalt applied to the roof deck, followed by several layers of building felt (usually 5-ply) fastened to each other with hot asphalt. A final coat of hot asphalt and imbedded pea-rock gravel is applied. This produces a roof that, with proper maintenance, can withstand the elements 20 years or longer. (See Figure 4-50.)

Common roof insulation materials are two 3/4" layers of either dense Fiberglas or Styrofoam, each with lapping joints or 1 1/2" of cellular glass or a low-density concrete insulation material. An increase in the thickness of the insulation material results in savings both in heating and in cooling.

Leaking, caused by a breakdown in the roofing system, is possibly the greatest single problem oc-

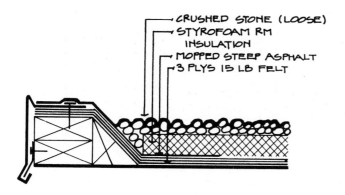

INSULATED ROOF MEMBRANE ASSEMBLY
(IRMA)

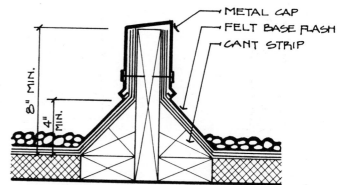

ROOF CONTRACTION JOINT

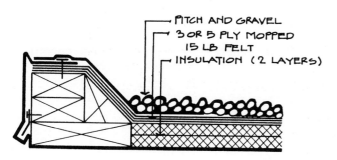

BUILT-UP PITCH AND GRAVEL ROOF

Figure 4-50. Roofing conditions.

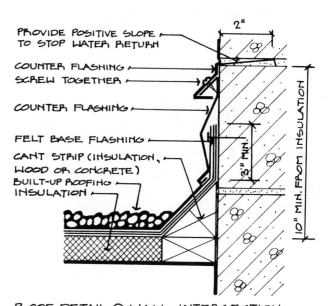

ROOF DETAIL @ WALL INTERSECTION

Figure 4-51. Roof contraction joint and flashing.

curring in a building after construction. Compounding the problem is the fact that a flat roof is generally more susceptible to damage than a sloped roof. It is quite possible for the exterior surface of a roof to experience a 200°F temperature change in varying weather conditions, meaning that the roof materials can expand and contract to the point of fracturing the roof composition. To combat this, a large roof surface is broken up into smaller areas with control joints, to reduce the extent of movement.

A *control joint*, or *contraction joint*, is the detail used to divide up a roof area. No requirement is set up for the exact distance between roof contraction joints, but an average is a square 100 feet on each side. Large buildings are divided further with expansion joints that run through the entire building from the footings to the roof. While contraction joints only compensate for the movement of the roof material, expansion joints allow for greater movement of the entire building, including the deck. (See Figures 4-51 and 4-52.)

Penetrations through the roof, such as plumbing pipes and support brackets, can be waterproofed with several details. Two of the more common waterproofing methods are flashing and pitch pockets. *Flashing* consists of bent pieces of metal that form a barrier at building joints to prevent water penetration. It is preferable to pitch pockets because pitch pockets tend to break up in time or to leak pitch through the penetration in the deck on hot days.

A 1″ rainfall on a roof 100′ square results in over 6000-gal of water, a sizable amount for disposal from a flat roof. A good detail to follow is to place a cast-iron roof drain on the roof and to run a 3″ to 6″ pipe through the interior of the building, if

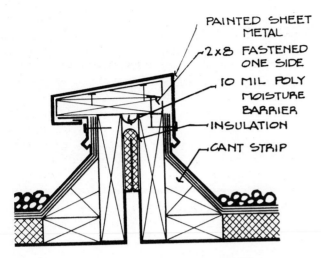

ROOF EXPANSION JOINT

- PAINTED SHEET METAL
- 2×8 FASTENED ONE SIDE
- 10 MIL POLY MOISTURE BARRIER
- INSULATION
- CANT STRIP

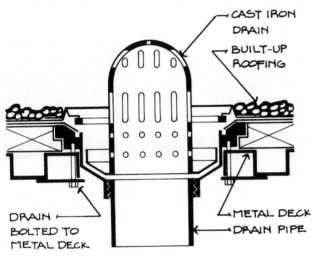

ROOF DRAIN

- CAST IRON DRAIN
- BUILT-UP ROOFING
- METAL DECK
- DRAIN PIPE
- DRAIN BOLTED TO METAL DECK

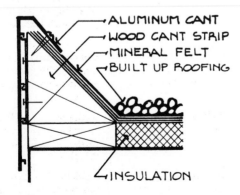

ALUMINUM ROOF CANT

- ALUMINUM CANT
- WOOD CANT STRIP
- MINERAL FELT
- BUILT UP ROOFING
- INSULATION

Figure 4-52. Roof expansion joint, cant, and drain.

it is heated. The pipe can be connected to a storm sewer or run directly outside.

An additional safeguard with roof drains is to place an overflow scupper in the outside gravel stop or parapet wall. The scupper does not function unless the drains become plugged.

When roof drains are used, two solutions are possible to achieve good drainage—a dead level roof or one that slopes to each drain. The level roof is easy to detail, but a sloped roof must be handled in one of two ways. The entire structure may be sloped slightly to accommodate drainage, or rigid insulation can be used that has a ⅛″/ft slope.

Two problem areas on a flat roof are encountered at the roof perimeter and at the intersection of the roof and a wall. Roof perimeters can be detailed either as copings or as cap flashing. A *coping*, also called a *parapet*, is an extension of the wall above the roof deck. The top of the coping is flashed with sheet metal such as 26-ga G.I., 16-oz copper, or .0299″ (or 1/32″) aluminum minimum, with the back side counterflashed over the roof felts. *Cap flashing*, or *gravel stop*, differs from a coping in that the wall material terminates at the height of the roof deck and a cap is attached to the perimeter. Cap flashing can be 24-ga G.I., 16-oz copper, or .0359″ (1/32″+) aluminum if it is attached to a rigid cant strip. Extruded aluminum .050 (1/16″−) thick can be used as a separate gravel stop.

The intersection of a roof with a building wall requires special protection to prevent leaks. The usual detail involves placing a 45° cant strip, either insulation or wood, at the corner and extending the roof felt over the cant and a minimum of 3″ vertically above the cant. Metal flashing is then lapped over the felt and extended into the wall. For brick, this means 2″ into the mortar joint. For concrete, the flashing is forced into a metal or plastic slot, called a *reglet*, that is cast into the concrete. Wood siding laps over the flashing and stops several inches above the cant.

The most common flat-roof system is built-up felts with hot asphalt and gravel. Several other systems are used occasionally. Silicone roofing can be applied in two coats over plywood or concrete decking. The most simple method of application is with a paint roller, resulting in a thin sheet of rubber that acts as a barrier.

A roll-roofing system has several layers of roof felts, cemented to each other with hot asphalt and given a final protective coat of a roll of 90-lb mineral surface felt.

Sloped roof systems pose less of a problem to roofing materials because the water runs off the surface naturally. The angle of the roof, or pitch, is a determining factor in the roofing materials selected. Roof pitch is measured in inches of rise per 12″ run. A 4/12 pitch means that for every horizontally measured 12″ increment of the roof, it rises 4″ vertically, at an 18° angle. Some materials used for pitched roofing are asphalt shingles, slate, clay tile, copper, terne metal, cedar shingles, built-up roofing, roll roofing, and mineral fiber shingles. All these materials have unique attachment requirements and minimum slopes and property characteristics. (See Table 4-2.)

Windows and Doors

Windows and doors provide no structural wall support but are placed in an opening and sealed to be weathertight. In most wall conditions, support must be placed above the opening to support the wall above. Wood framing usually solves support with a double header above the opening and support at the sides. Masonry openings are spanned with either a lintel block or a steel lintel. Concrete is typically spanned by adding additional reinforcing bars to the poured wall above the opening.

Windows, commonly made of wood and metal, are further classified by their operation, or how

TABLE 4-2 ROOFING MATERIALS

DETAIL	MATERIAL	MINIMUM PITCH	APPLICATION	UNDERLAYMENT	DESCRIPTION
1.	Asphalt shingles	3″ in 12″*	Nailed to wood deck	15-lb roof felt (1 layer nailed to deck)	Typical in residences, available in wide range of colors and textures
2.	Slate	4″ in 12″*	Nailed to deck (slate is predrilled)	15-lb felt over nailing concrete, gypsum tile, wood, or steel angles	Extremely durable, colors range from dark gray to dark red
3.	Clay tile	4½″ in 12″	Nailed to deck or nail strips (tile predrilled)	30-lb felt	Same color range as brick, available in a variety of shapes to produce many roof patterns
4.	Copper	1½″ in 12″ (batten) 3″ in 12″ (stand seam)	Seamed and soldered or seamed to wood batten strips	6-lb rosin paper over 15-lb roof felt	Will weather to a natural green if left uncoated, costly to install
5.	Terne metal	Same as copper	Same as copper	15-lb felt	Sheet metal with a coating of lead and tin, designed to be painted
6.	Cedar shingles	3″ in 12″ (shingles) 4″ in 12″ (shakes)	Nailed to wood deck or spaced sheathing	30-lb felt	Weathers to dark brown, available in smooth-sawn and rough textures
7.	Built-up roofing	6″ in 12″ max. to dead level	Felts applied with hot asphalt gravel set in hot asphalt	Layers of 15-lb over deck or rigid insulation	Common to level roofs, asphalt with higher melting point used as pitch increases
8.	Roll roofing	1″ in 12″	Nailed to deck with edges cemented with asphalt	Roll laps about 50%	Inexpensive installation, available in mineral surfaces similar to shingles
9.	Mineral fiber	4″ in 12″	Nailed to wood deck	30-lb felt	Available in natural gray cement or colors, more durable than asphalt shingles

* Special provisions will allow a lower minimum pitch.

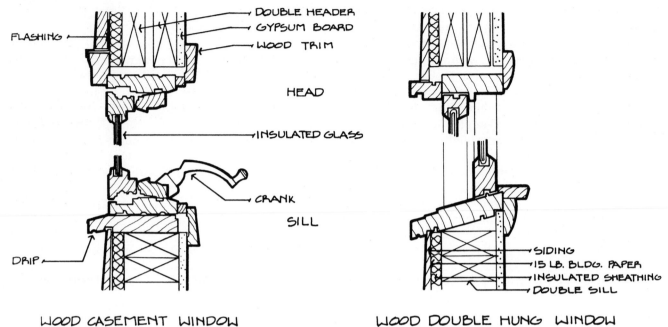

FLASHING

DOUBLE HEADER
GYPSUM BOARD
WOOD TRIM

HEAD

INSULATED GLASS

CRANK

SILL

DRIP

SIDING
15 LB. BLDG. PAPER
INSULATED SHEATHING
DOUBLE SILL

WOOD CASEMENT WINDOW

WOOD DOUBLE HUNG WINDOW

Figure 4-53.   Wood window details.

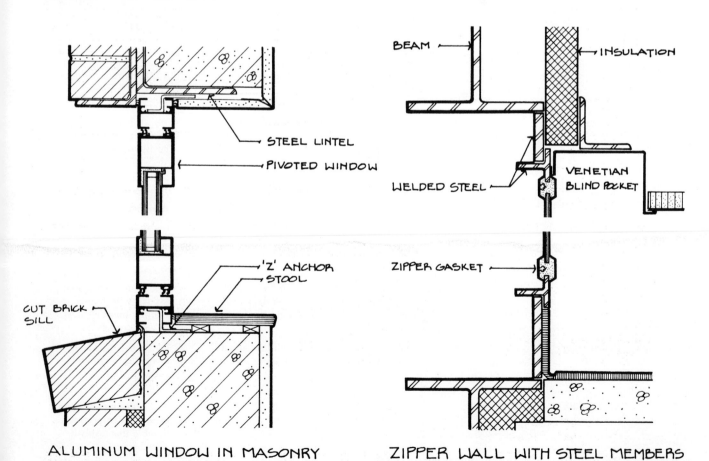

STEEL LINTEL
PIVOTED WINDOW

BEAM
INSULATION

VENETIAN
BLIND POCKET

WELDED STEEL

'Z' ANCHOR
STOOL

ZIPPER GASKET

CUT BRICK
SILL

ALUMINUM WINDOW IN MASONRY

ZIPPER WALL WITH STEEL MEMBERS

Figure 4-54.   Metal window details.

they open. Some common classifications are double-hung, casement, awning, hopper, sliding, jalousie, and fixed. The conditions in which the windows will be used determine the type to choose. Double-hung and casement windows are most common for residential use, while fixed and casement are frequently selected for commercial projects. (See Figures 4-53 and 4-54.)

Manufacturers' literature specifically details the installation procedure for a particular window. The detail is likely to include sections through the top of the window (*head*), side (*jamb*), and bottom (*sill*), along with the factory standard sizes (*sash size*). Unlike curtain-wall glass, window sizes conform to manufacturers' dimensions.

Window frames for residential use are commonly wood or extruded aluminum, while commercial construction almost totally uses extruded aluminum. An exception is the use of steel windows for industrial installations.

Manufacturers have made several adaptations to window designs to retain the good properties of the material but protect the weak points. Wood requires painting maintenance, and so one supplier covers the exposed frame with a thick, color-fast plastic extrusion. Another uses anodized aluminum as an outside surface. A third uses teak frames. (Teak is a yellow-orange wood with a high oil content that doesn't require a protective paint coat.)

Aluminum has the disadvantage of being too good a transmitter of temperature. Extreme cold passes through the frame from the exterior and causes frost to form on the inside. Several manufacturers improve the insulating properties of the aluminum by placing a plastic barrier between two

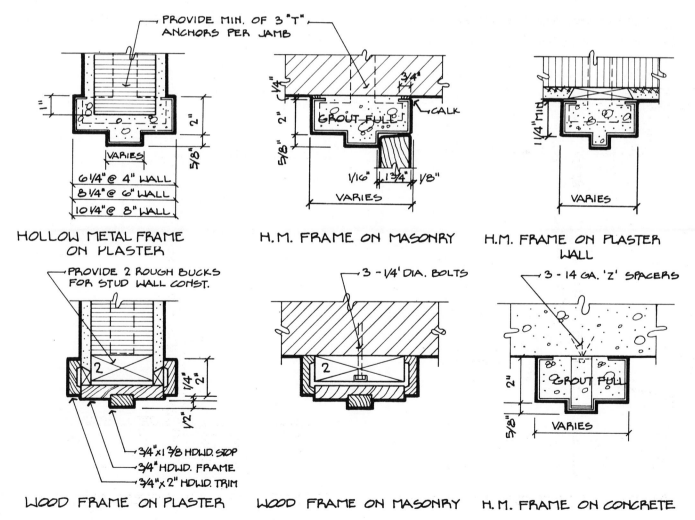

Figure 4-55. Door frame details.

extruded aluminum frames. In most instances, insulated welded glass units are available in place of a single sheet of glass.

The same terminology is used for door frames as for window frames—head, jamb, and sill. Frames are made of three materials, the choice of which is closely determined by the use. (See Figures 4-55 and 4-56.)

Wood frames are almost always used in residential projects, but seldom in commercial. Steel frames (hollow metal) are used commonly for commercial interior door frames as well as for some exterior frames. Major commercial entrances use anodized aluminum frames and, to a lesser extent, stainless steel. Cost, durability, finish, fireproof qualities, and ease of installation determine which material to use.

A door, called a *panel*, can be made from a variety of materials and fabricated in many ways. As in door frames, the common materials are wood, steel, and aluminum. Wood doors can be made with a void space in the center (a *hollow-core door*) or can be filled solid with a low-grade wood or gypsum. In general, wood doors have a stained or painted wood veneer or plastic laminate applied to the surface. Hollow-core wood doors are seldom used on commercial projects but are commonly found as residential interior doors. Steel doors are hollow-core frames covered with sheet steel. This core can be a simple brace frame or a honeycomb core. Hollow metal doors can have a painted or plastic laminate surface and are used in a variety of circumstances in interior and exterior commercial projects. Aluminum doors are commonly used as frames to accept glass for entrance doors. Most doors are 1¾″ thick, 2′-8″ wide (plus or minus 6″) and 6′-8″ high or more.

Door hardware includes closing devices, hinges, latches, doorknobs, and kick plates (Figure 4-57). Hardware has the following common designations for finish:

US3	brass, bright
US4	brass, dull
US10	bronze, dull
US10B	bronze, dull, oil-rubbed
US14	nickel-plated, bright
US26	chrome-plated, bright
US26D	chrome-plated, dull

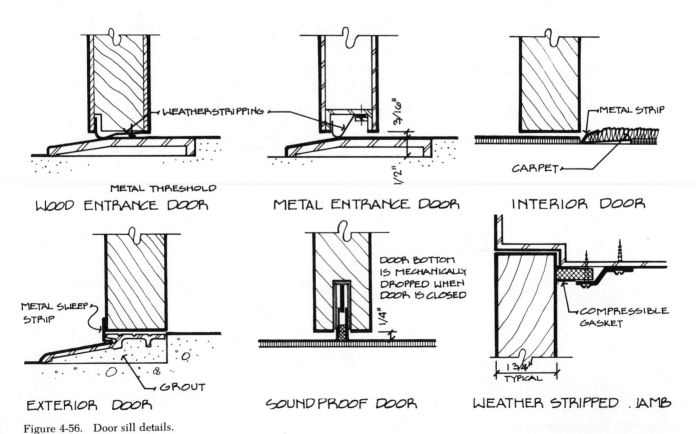

Figure 4-56. Door sill details.

US27	aluminum, satin
US28	aluminum, anodized
US32	stainless steel, polished
US32D	stainless steel, dull
USP	prime-coated for paint

Hinges, referred to as *butts*, are measured in pairs. Most commercial doors have 1½ pair of butts, or three hinges. Latching devices fall into three categories (See Figure 4-58):

Mortise—The locking device is recessed into a cavity cut into the door.

Unit—The lock is fastened into a notch cut out of the door.

Cylinder—The lock is fit into a hole drilled in the door.

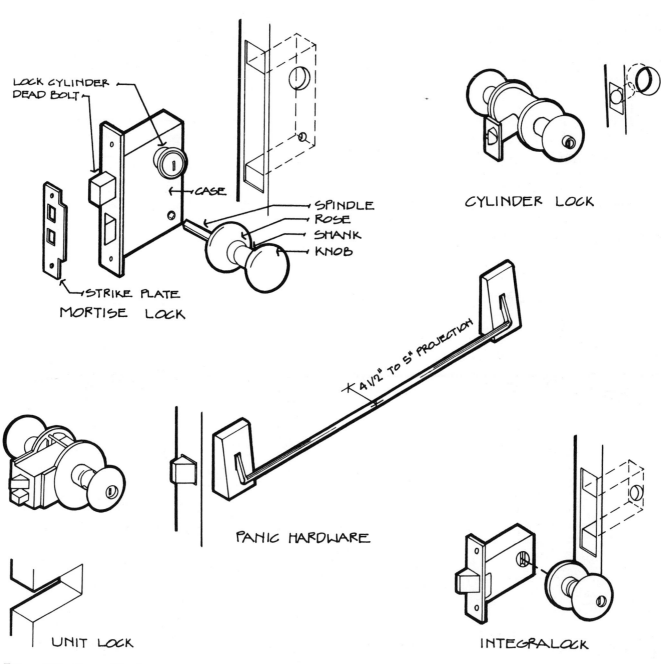

Figure 4-57. Types of hardware.

LABEL DOOR REQUIREMENTS

LABEL	TYPE OF DOOR	HOURLY RATING	MIN. DOOR THICKNESS	MAXIMUM GLASS AREA	DOOR OPERATION	FRAME TYPE	
							LABELED DOOR LOCATION
A	TIN CLAD 3-PLY	3 HR	3 PLY 2½"	NONE PERMITTED	AUTOMATIC OR SELF CLOSING	**A**	OPENINGS IN FIRE WALLS OR DIVISION WALLS BETWEEN BUILDINGS OR SECTIONS. OF BUILDINGS
	HOLLOW METAL	3 HR	1¾"			**B**	OPENINGS IN ENCLOSURES OF VERTICAL SHAFTS, SUCH AS STAIRS, ELEVATORS, PIPING, OR WIRING
B	TIN CLAD 3-PLY	1½ HR	3 PLY 2½"	100 SQ. IN. PER. OPENING. 12" MAX. HGT. & WIDTH ¼" WIRE GL.	SELF CLOSING IN REQUIRED MEANS OF EGRESS; OR AUTOMATIC CLOSING IN OTHER COND. SUBJECT TO CODE REG.	**C**	OPENINGS IN CORRIDOR AND ROOM PARTITIONS
	TIN CLAD 2-PLY	1½ HR	2 PLY 1¾"			**D**	OPENINGS IN EXTERIOR WALLS WHERE FIRE EXPOSURE IS SEVERE — NO GLASS PERMITTED.
	KALAMEIN	1½ HR	1¾"			**E**	OPENINGS IN EXTERIOR WALLS WHERE FIRE EXPOSURE IS MODERATE OR LIGHT. GLASS PERMITTED
	COMPOSITE	1½ HR	1¾"				
	HOLLOW METAL	1½ HR	1¾"				
C	TIN CLAD 3-PLY	45 MIN	3 PLY 2½"	ANY NUMBER OF LIGHTS NOT EXCEEDING 1296 SQ. FT. PER LIGHT; NEITHER WIDTH NOR HEIGHT TO EXCEED 54". GLASS MUST BE ¼" WIRE GLASS	SELF CLOSING IN REQUIRED MEANS OF EGRESS; OR AUTOMATIC CLOSING IN OTHER CONDITIONS SUBJECT TO CODE REG.		
	TIN CLAD 2-PLY	45 MIN.	2 PLY 1¾"				
	KALAMEIN	45 MIN.	1¾"				
	COMPOSITE	45 MIN.	1¾"				
	HOLLOW METAL	45 MIN	1¾"				
D AND E	TIN CLAD 3 PLY		3 PLY 2½"	NONE PERMITTED IN 'D' LABEL 'E' LABEL-ANY NUMBER OF LIGHTS NOT EXCEEDING 720 SQ. IN. PER LIGHT NEITHER WIDTH OR HEIGHT TO EXCEED 54"	SELF CLOSING IN REQUIRED MEANS OF EGRESS OR WHEN OPENING INTO FIRE ESCAPES		
	TIN CLAD 2 PLY		2 PLY 1¾"				
	KALAMEIN		1¾"				
	COMPOSITE		1¾"				
	HOLLOW METAL		1¾"				

LABELED FRAME TYPES

① STEEL CHANNEL FRAME 4" MIN. WIDTH

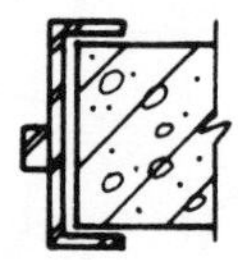

② MASONRY WALL WITH 'Z' STRAP ANCHOR (MIN 3 PER JAMB) GROUT FILL FRAME.

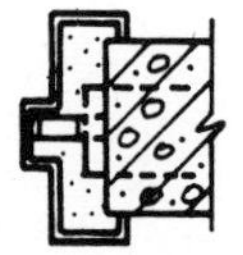

③ CONC. COL. WITH BENT STEEL CHANNEL AND EXPOSED BOLTS. GROUT FILL FRAME

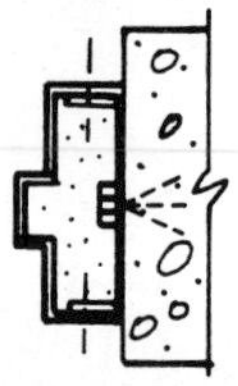

GENERAL NOTES

LABELED DOORS MUST BE FACTORY MORTISED FOR HARDWARE. DOUBLE ACTING DOORS AND DOORS WITH LOUVERS CANNOT BEAR LABLES. LATCHES OR LOCKS MUST BE PROVIDED FOR ALL LABEL DOORS; PUSH AND PULL BARS ONLY, ARE NOT ACCEPTABLE.

A   **B**   **C**   **D & E**

Figure 4-58.   Label door requirements.

FIVE

BUILDING EQUIPMENT AND SERVICES

A building necessarily must have a series of support facilities designed to meet its specific needs. The category of building equipment and services includes such broad items as heating, cooling, air conditioning, water supply and disposal, and lighting and electrical distribution. Each system requires engineering calculations that increase in complexity as the project's size increases. The technical complexity eventually reaches a point where architects can no longer rely on personal experience to locate and design building equipment and will retain the services of mechanical and electrical engineers. This section introduces the various categories of building equipment. It is not a workbook on mechanical design.

WATER DISTRIBUTION

Water distribution can include the purification process if the water is not potable (drinkable) as well as the piping of water to the building. Water is available either from surface sources such as rivers and lakes or from below-grade supplies such as wells. In general, above-grade water contains a low amount of dissolved minerals, but human and industrial waste contamination is a major problem. A subterranean water source can have dissolved minerals (hardness) from passing through layers of limestone, and it can be less polluted, since it passes through sand.

Water is obtained from lakes and rivers by pumping from the source into holding tanks for storage and treatment. Well water (Figure 5-1) also must be pumped to a holding tank. Three systems are commonly used:

1. A shallow well (25′ deep or less) can extract water by locating the pump at ground level and pumping to the surface. A surface pump cannot operate at a greater depth because of atmospheric pressure.

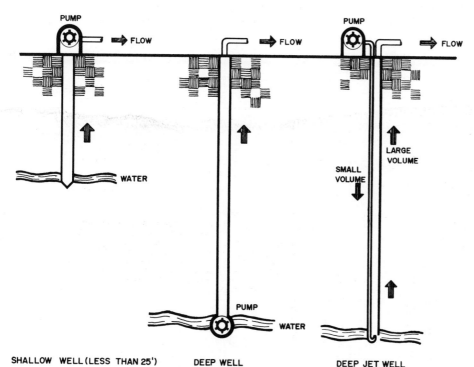

SHALLOW WELL (LESS THAN 25′)   DEEP WELL   DEEP JET WELL

Figure 5-1. Three systems for obtaining well water.

2. A deep well can operate if the pump is located below the ground water level. The pump and motor can be placed in a waterproof housing under water, or a submersed pump can be connected to a shaft with the motor at ground level.

3. Another system follows Venturi's principle, using a small pipe of high-pressure water forced into a jet and larger pipe below the water level to draw water into the larger pipe and up to the surface.

After the water has entered a storage tank, it is treated to make it potable if it is not already (Figure 5-2). A chlorine treatment reduces bacteria from sewage to below the danger point. *Turbidity* in water (suspended silt) is eliminated by filtration and coagulation of the silt with alum. Acidic water can be neutralized by adding sodium silicate or by filtering with calcium carbonate. Objectionable taste and odor can be reduced by passing the water through an activated charcoal filter.

Water containing dissolved magnesium and calcium salt is referred to as *hard water*. Water with more than 130 parts per million of this dis-solved salt reacts chemically with soap to form a curd and forms deposits on the walls of hot water pipes. Hard water can be reduced by passing it (Figure 5-3) through zeolite, which contains sodium ions to exchange with the dissolved magnesium and calcium until the process becomes "overloaded"; then the cylinder is either replaced or rejuvenated by passing a strong brine solution through the zeolite.

Water usually is not pumped directly from its source to a water tap in a building. Instead, it is stored in a drinkable state in a storage tank large enough to meet peak demands (Figure 5-4). These tanks can place the water under pressure or be elevated above the delivery point at atmospheric pressure. A pressure tank is frequently used for small applications such as residential wells; it consists of a tank with a cushion of air under pressure at the top of the tank. Water is pumped directly from the source. As the water is used, a pump replaces it, keeping the tank pressure within a range of about 40 pounds per square inch (P.S.I.).

Another method of supplying water involves pumping it into a water tower that is higher than any level it will supply. Water weighs 62.4 lb per

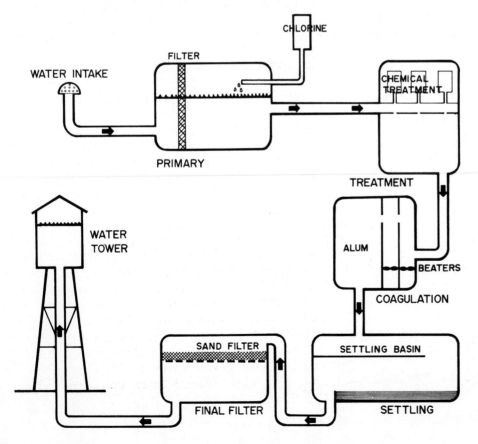

Figure 5-2. A water treatment system.

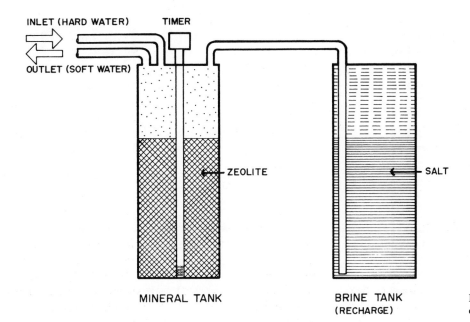

INLET (HARD WATER)   TIMER

OUTLET (SOFT WATER)

ZEOLITE

SALT

MINERAL TANK

BRINE TANK
(RECHARGE)

Figure 5-3. Hard water can be soft-ened by passing it through zeolite.

cu ft. Thus, a column of water 1″ square and 1′ high weighs 0.434 lb. A water tower 100′ above a faucet would exert a pressure of 100′ × 0.434 = 43.4 P.S.I. The standard pressure in a water main is about 40 P.S.I., but this can vary greatly. For low-rise buildings, 40 P.S.I. is sufficient, but the pressure will drop 1 P.S.I. for every 2.3′ in height. Distribution of water in high-rise buildings (Figure 5-5) can be accomplished either by pumping the

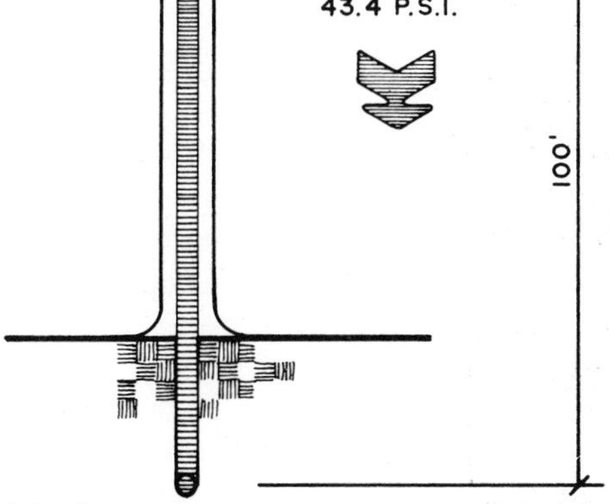

TOTAL DOWNWARD
PRESSURE
100′ X 0.434 =
43.4 P.S.I.

100′

Figure 5-4. A water tower.

water from the water main to storage tanks in various horizontal zones in the building or by putting the water from the main under a sufficient amount of pressure to force it to the top floor. To prevent damage in both cases, the pressure must be reduced periodically as it travels from top to bottom.

The piping (Figure 5-6) used to distribute water to a building is usually cast iron or steel in the street main and copper, iron, or a plastic (polyvinyl chloride) after it reaches the building. Usually, a shutoff valve in the street can cut all water flowing into the building.

The size of the pipe is determined by the volume of water used, by the fixture, and by how frequently it is used. The *National Plumbing Code* spells out the requirements for plumbing equipment in fixture units. A fixture unit equals 1 cu ft of water per min, or about 7.5 gal.

With charts indicating the number of fixture units and the average frequency of use for each plumbing unit, the mechanical designer can determine the pipe size and the storage requirements. Most plumbing fixtures require a working pressure of at least 8 P.S.I. with several exceptions, such as 15 P.S.I. for flush-valve water closets and urinals and 30 P.S.I. for a faucet connecting a hose. Several examples would be a lavatory (sink) that requires 1 fixture unit of water at 8 P.S.I, or a flush-valve water closet using 8 fixture units supplied at 15 P.S.I.

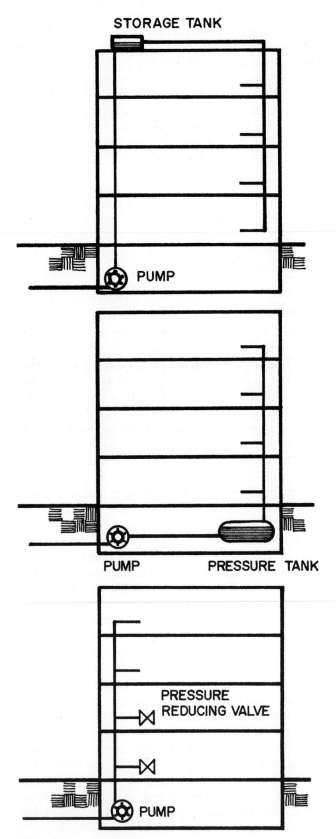

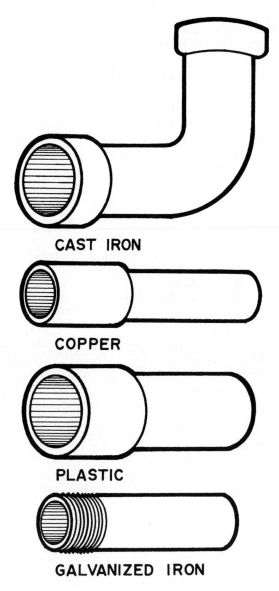

Figure 5-6.   Piping used for plumbing.

Valves control the flow of water, either by stopping and starting, throttling, or directing the flow. They can be manually or mechanically controlled.

Pipe connections differ with the material. Copper pipe uses copper or brass fittings that allow the pipe to slip snugly into a sleeve. The joint is then heated, and solder is applied to make a watertight joint. Plastic pipe uses similar fittings, but the connection is made by using a solvent or special heating equipment that fuses the joint. Iron pipe is threaded to permit connection with threaded fittings. A special compound is applied to the threads to prevent corrosion and make the connection watertight.

Figure 5-5.   Three methods of destributing water in high-rise buildings.

Water distribution in a building can be compared with water distribution in a tree: Both have a main supply that branches off into a fixture supply for each unit. Fixture-unit demand determines the size of each supply pipe, while the number of fixtures determines the diameter of the branch line. Most pipe dimensions are given as interior diameter (I.D.), although copper is an occasional exception when its outside diameter (O.D.) is used.

Water is distributed both at the temperature it is obtained from the source and at heated or cooled temperatures within the building and piped along with untempered water. Hot water is heated and stored in an insulated tank at 140°F [60°C] for residential use and 180°F [82.2°C] for public dishwashers. The heat loss due to long runs of pipe from the hot-water storage to the faucet can be reduced by insulating the pipe. Water held in the pipe naturally will lose heat, and so a "warm-up" period is required when the faucet is opened to evacuate water in the pipe. This inconvenience can be eliminated by providing a continuous loop back to the heater. Gravity will cause the cooler water in the pipe to flow back to the heater, or a circulating pump can be located on the return line.

Commercial buildings can also circulate chilled water to drinking fountains. This requires a circulating pump, because cold water is heavier than warm and will not circulate naturally. Cold-water and chilled-water pipes are insulated to prevent humidity from condensing on the pipe and dripping.

Plumbing fixtures are the equipment used for washing or disposal of waste. Fixtures must be impervious to moisture and are made of materials such as stainless steel, vitreous china or vitreous steel, Fiberglas, and ceramic tile.

PLUMBING DISPOSAL

Sewage

Waste water and solids are carried out of a building for sewage treatment in pipes at atmospheric pressure. This means that pipes must be sloped to flow. (See Figure 5–7.) Typical waste pipes are iron, plastic, and copper, but lead and glass may be used in conditions where the waste will react with the pipe, such as in a chemistry laboratory.

Each plumbing branch is connected to a main stack called a *soil pipe*, which at the lowest point in the building turns and slopes toward the sewer.

Cast iron is the typical soil-pipe material inside the building, but this generally changes to vitrified clay pipe outside the building.

The odor of sewer gas is stopped from entering a room by providing a water trap at each plumbing fixture. Some fixtures, such as a water closet, have built-in traps; the remainder must be provided with an external trap located on the waste line. A typical trap is a gooseneck pipe that contains enough water to prevent gas from leaking into the room.

A natural problem caused by using a water trap is that a siphon action is created, pulling the water out of the trap when water passes through the system. The siphon is eliminated by locating a vent pipe in the waste line; this prevents a vacuum from being formed. The vent stack connects to all fixture lines and penetrates through the roof of the building.

Venting is accomplished in three ways: (1) in *continuous venting* a vent pipe is connected to the waste line of each fixture; (2) in *loop venting* the last waste pipe on the branch is connected to the vent stack; and (3) in *sovent venting* a combination of vent and soil stack is used. The one pipe requires an aerator at each horizontal floor branch and a deaerator at the base of the stack.

A plumbing fixture such as a bathroom lavatory, then, must be provided with a hot-water and a cold-water supply, a waste line with a trap, and a vent stack.

Since each fixture has these requirements, a significant savings may be realized if plumbing systems are located in clusters. This is particularly important in multistory buildings with plumbing facilities stacked from floor to floor. Back-to-back mens' and womens' toilet fixtures usually have a hollow cavity between two walls. This space is called a *chase*; it allows connection room for supply, waste, and vent pipes to the plumbing fixtures.

Once sewage waste has left a building, it can be treated at a disposal plant run by the municipality in which the building is located. It also can be treated on the site if local sewage facilities are not available. Waste flows to a treatment plant by gravity, and so the lowest point of the sewer in the building must be higher than the sewer line. The flow level in a sewer tile is called the *invert elevation*, and is measured by giving its height in relation to a bench mark.

If this condition is not possible, a sump pump can be installed. A *sump* is a waste storage tank

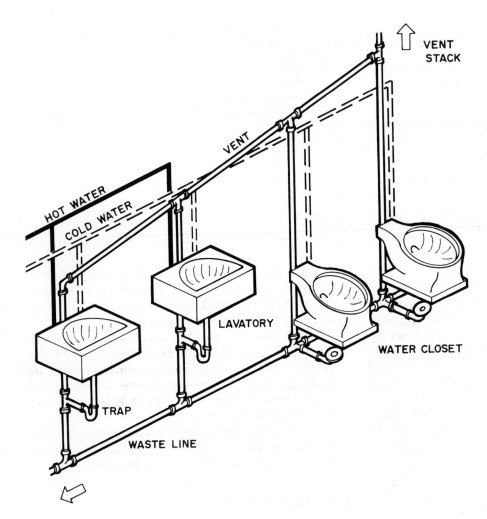

VENT
STACK

VENT

HOT WATER
COLD WATER

LAVATORY

WATER CLOSET

TRAP

WASTE LINE

Figure 5-7.   A typical plumbing system.

that collects sewage to a certain level, at which time a pump is started to evacuate it to a higher level. A similar setup is employed in a public sewer system to permit a flow of waste to the disposal plant, called a *sewage lift station.* Large-scale public sewage disposal generally means the separation of solids and liquids and the treatment of them by chemicals, aeration, ultraviolet rays, and filtration, to name several methods. Once harmful bacteria and other pollutants have been reduced, the liquid is discharged.

When municipal sewage disposal is unavailable, private sewage treatment is accomplished either by storage or by bacterial action and discharge. A storage tank is used to store building waste. When the tank becomes full, the waste is pumped into a truck and disposed. This system has obvious disadvantages and is seldom used, even if permitted by local code.

The alternative for private waste disposal is a septic tank (Figure 5-8), which is watertight and into which all building waste flows. Since 99 per-

cent of all waste is liquid, one function of a septic tank is to separate solid from liquid. The liquid sewage, called *effluent,* is permitted to flow out of the tank, while the solid settles to the bottom. A decomposition process then causes the solid waste to break down to dischargeable materials. The overflow effluent is evacuated into a *drain field,* a series of spaced pipes that allow the liquid to filter through the ground. The filtering process will purify the liquid sewage. Soil conditions determine the drain field. Sand or gravel give the best drainage, but solid rock is virtually unworkable. Restrictions require potable water wells to be at least 50' away from a septic tank and 100' away from a drain field.

Another, less-suitable means of disposing waste is a *cesspool,* which is a tank without a bottom that allows sewage to leach into the soil below. It lacks the decomposition qualities found in a septic tank and relies chiefly on percolation through the soil. Potable water wells must be located a minimum of 200' from a cesspool.

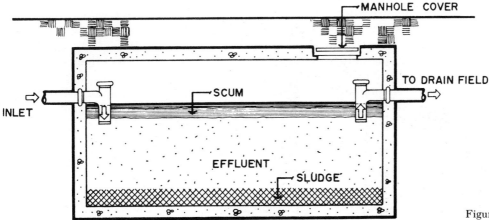

Figure 5-8. A septic tank.

Storm Water

In addition to building waste, another plumbing disposal product is the storm water that must be evacuated from the roof and the surrounding site. Like sewage waste, rain water typically flows by gravity through a storm sewer system. (See Figure 5-9.) But unlike sewage waste, it is not treated before it is discharged. Municipalities seldom allow storm-water pipes to be connected to the sanitary sewer. Instead, storm sewers are provided. The sewers bring the storm water to natural run-off lakes or streams, usually through concrete pipe.

Most commercial buildings have flat roofs, and water will not naturally run off the surface. A common solution is to locate roof drains that handle the rain water at intervals on the roof and run the metal drainpipe vertically through the building to connect to the storm sewer. This is particularly advisable in a cold climate where an outside drainpipe could freeze and become clogged. The warmth of the building will keep the pipe free. An alternative is to run a downspout along the outside face of the building; this is either connected to a storm sewer or allowed to run off onto the ground. An electric heating cable may be located in the pipe to prevent freezing.

The topography of the site is usually manipulated to prevent water from running toward the building and to slope parking areas to promote drainage. It is common to locate drains, called *catch basins*, at low points. These, in turn, are connected to the storm sewer.

The sizing of the pipe for storm water can only be determined by assuming a design load of rain and calculating it with the drainage area.

HEATING SYSTEMS

Heat is transmitted to an object or space by conduction, convection, or radiation. *Conduction* refers to the movement of heat through a solid. *Convection* heat is transferred by the motion of air or a liquid. *Radiation* is the movement of infrared heat through a space that heats up any solid in

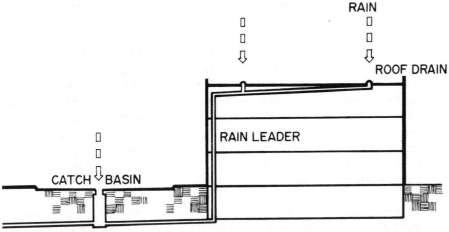

Figure 5-9. A storm sewer system.

sight, but not the space. Heating systems use one or more of these principles. Most conditions involve radiant units or forced conditioned air.

Heating systems must be compact, efficient, and flexible to fill the needs of the inhabitants. Several facilities that fill these requirements in varying degrees are available to the mechanical designer. *Hot-water* and *steam heating* are basically similar arrangements. In both, a heated fluid circulates through an enclosed pipe system to heat a space. *Circulating air* involves the movement of conditioned air through a space. In addition to heating, this system can also cool, clean, and deodorize air. Several *electric heating* units are available as furnaces, baseboard heaters, or panels that radiate heat.

In addition to this list of standard heating systems, many sophisticated systems are used in commercial buildings, ranging from a unit called a *heat pump* to an arrangement that uses the heat from the light fixtures to condition the space. Any heating system has advantages as well as shortcomings. The mechanical designer must choose the best system for the individual building's requirements.

Hot-Water Heating

A fairly common heating system is hot-water heating (Figure 5-10). The fuels most frequently used in hot-water heating are gas, oil, coal, or electricity. These fuels may be combined.

A thermostat device, an *aquastat*, keeps the water in the boiler at a constant temperature, around 200°F [93.3°C] with 30 P.S.I. A continuous-loop pipe runs from the boiler to radiators and back to the boiler. Radiators are usually either cast iron, which holds a fairly large volume of water, or fin tubes, a pipe with thin metal fins around the outside to rapidly dissipate heat. When the room temperature decreases, the thermostat in the room activates a pump on the return line of the radiators for the room. When the room reaches the set temperature, the thermostat turns off the pump. A necessary addition to an enclosed hot-water system is an *expansion tank*, which is an air cushion to provide for expansion of the water as it heats. A safety valve is placed on the boiler to relieve excessive boiler pressure.

The hot-water heating system has many variations, all of which offer uniform heat at a comfortable temperature level. The system can be zoned easily; that is, specific areas can be located on a separate branch line with a thermostat controlling the branch pump. Thus an apartment building can have each unit on a separately controlled branch.

A small disadvantage with hot-water heat is that as a vehicle for carrying heat to an area it cannot absorb as many calories of heat per volume as other methods, particularly steam. A greater drawback is that, in itself, the system can be used neither to cool a space nor to condition air (add fresh air, filter air, or control humidity). Hot water can be combined with other air systems to attain a total package.

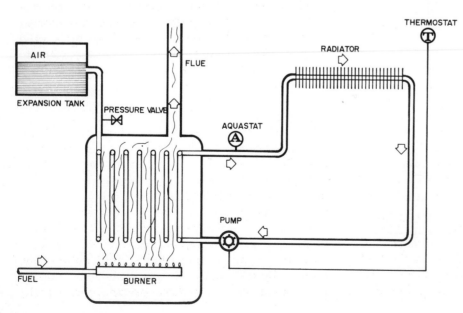

Figure 5-10. A hot-water heating system.

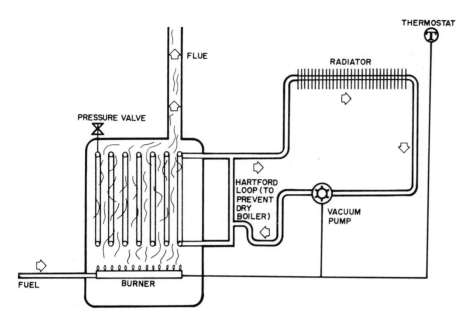

Figure 5-11.   A steam heating system.

Other hot-water heating systems vary in temperature and pressure and their methods of circulating water. A rather antiquated solution eliminates the circulating pump and allows the water to flow by gravity to the radiators. The hot water rises to the radiators and then "falls" back to the boiler as it cools. The sluggishness of the system and the need for bulky cast-iron radiators greatly reduce the advantages of this selection.

If hot water is under pressure, it can be heated much higher than 212°F [100°C] (400°F [204.4°C] is possible). This allows the circulation of superheated water to a radiator located in an air duct. As air passes through, it is heated and supplied to the living space.

Steam Heating

Steam heating systems (Figure 5-11) are quite similar to hot-water systems in that they are enclosed and involve circulation of heated water. Steam heating also uses a boiler, but the steam must be provided at a determined pressure—the higher the pressure, the more heat it can absorb. Circulation can be accomplished with two pipes, much like hot-water heating, or with one pipe that allows steam to pass in one direction and condensed water to return in the other.

Steam can be circulated through one type of system by providing a partial vacuum in the return line. Steam heating can vary in its method of piping and in its temperature-pressure relationship. A diagram of a steam system can be dis-

tinguished from hot-water heating because the steam system does not require an expansion tank. As with hot-water heating, steam heating cannot, in itself, be used for more than heating a space. That is, it cannot cool or condition the air.

Forced-Air Heating

Forced-air or circulating-air heating systems are versatile in that they can condition air (Figure 5-12). The usual operation involves drawing air from outside through a louver and initially filtering larger dust particles with Fiberglas or a similar material. The outside air is then mixed with a determined percentage of air already in the building and brought back through ducts. This percentage can vary from 0 percent in rooms with high odor potential, such as kitchens, to an accepted average of 60 to 75 percent. Air in the building is mixed with fresh outside air (*make-up air*) because of the economy involved in not having to heat or cool the entire volume of air at each air change.

After the air has been mixed, it passes through heating or cooling coils to reach the desired temperature. Humidity can be either increased or reduced by appropriately spraying water into the flow of air or by cooling it with coils, causing the water to precipitate. A further filtering removes unwanted airborne impurities. Unpleasant odors are eliminated by passing the air through activated charcoal. Small dust particles and pollen not trapped by the initial filter are removed by a device called an *electrostatic precipitator*, which,

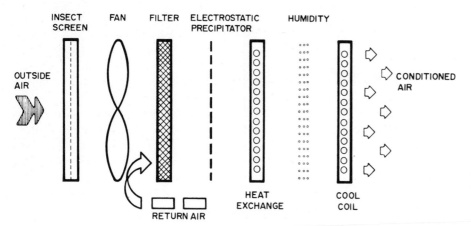

INSECT SCREEN   FAN   FILTER   ELECTROSTATIC PRECIPITATOR   HUMIDITY

OUTSIDE AIR

CONDITIONED AIR

RETURN AIR   HEAT EXCHANGE   COOL COIL

Figure 5-12. A forced-air heating system.

simply described, gives the particles an electric charge and pulls them to an oppositely charged plate.

This description gives a simple picture of most standard forced-air treatments. A disadvantage of this approach is the size of the required circulation network. The duct work generally is located in special chase openings between floors for vertical circulation and in a space provided between the floor slab and a recessed ceiling for horizontal distribution. The size of ducts can be reduced if the velocity of air is increased. But at some point the noise created by the rapid movement of air through the duct becomes more objectionable than the size. The maximum velocities considered in ducts is about 750' per min for residences, 1200' per min in schools and offices, and 1500' per min in industrial areas. Mechanical noise can be reduced by insulating the sides of the duct, by providing fins inside the duct at turns to reduce air turbulence, and by connecting ducts with flexible bellows rather than with metal to reduce vibration.

Each space to be conditioned should have an air supply and a separate return. The supply points can either be registers or diffusers, both of which block the unsightly appearance of an open duct. A *register* typically has an adjustable damper to regulate the amount of flow from the duct, while a *diffuser* directs the flow of air, slows the velocity, and mixes the supply air with existing room air. Diffusers can vary in shape from a round ceiling-mounted unit, to a special rectangular fluorescent light fixture that diffuses air through slits around the lens, to a ceiling with holes that turns the entire surface into a diffuser.

The greatest heat loss occurs at windows and along exterior walls, making this the logical location for heat diffusers and registers. Warm air rises because it is less dense, and so the best location is

to supply air low and situate the return-air grill high. The conditions most suitable for cooling a space are exactly the opposite. Diffusers should be located on side walls, supply grills near the ceiling, and return grills near the floor. A problem occurs in most cases because the same duct system is used for heating and cooling. Generally, heating takes precedence over cooling, and supply grills are located low around the perimeter of outside walls.

A common situation in building occurs when the architect does not know the placement of walls at the time the mechanical system is designed. Building types such as schools and offices are following a trend to have a majority of the space open, allowing the client to install movable walls to fit changing needs. This concept requires a mechanical system that can adapt to the changing floor plan, which can be accomplished by locating a package or zone of mechanical facilities within a determined module. If 12' × 12' is chosen, it means that the properly designed air supply and return diffusers could be located in the ceiling along with the light fixtures (possibly integral systems), and the electrical supply could be located under the floor in a special tunnel called a *raceway*. This allows the client to erect walls around this 12' square and have the room function properly with its own mechanical system

Solar Heat

Solar heating systems (Figure 5-13) use radiant energy from the sun. Solar systems generally use a lot of outside glass backed by large quantities of heat-absorbing material. The major advantage to this system is that it does not use fuel, which is costly and pollutes the environment. The prime drawback in solar heating lies in storing heat for sunless days and at night. Present systems such as heating rocks or tanks of water are inefficient and quite bulky.

The methods of distributing heat have been described briefly, from hot water to steam to forced air. Providing heat for these systems is not particularly complicated. The energy for heat commonly comes from gas, oil, and electricity. Coal is not used often because of its costly pollution-control equipment, the massive stockpile of fuel needed, and the problem of disposing of the burned ash. A building seldom has room for a coal-burning operation.

Coal is used as a heat source when an electric power company sells some of its heat, which is a by-product of making electricity, to nearby customers. This usually is transported to the site as high-pressure steam or water. Some large building complexes, such as a group of downtown buildings or a college campus, can realize a savings by providing a central energy center like that of a power company.

Hot water and steam generally are produced in a boiler, which has a jacket of water surrounding the source of heat. As the water is heated to the proper temperature, it is distributed to the radiation system. Large boilers commonly eliminate a continuous jacket of water and replace it with a series of tubes surrounding the flame. The water circulates through the tubes to be heated. Forced air is heated as it passes through a sealed metal box in the furnace, the flame heats the box to a design temperature on the opposite side so that the hot combustion gases will not contaminate the circulating air. If electrical energy is used, the circulating air passes through a coil that is heated electrically. Other electrical heating systems use panels or baseboard radiation units that heat when electricity passes through resistance.

COOLING SYSTEMS

Cooling air is a more complicated mechanical procedure than heating it. Two systems are available for refrigeration. The more common one uses a compressor, while the second, an absorption system, uses a flame. Both systems follow the physical principle that when a gas is allowed to expand rapidly, it absorbs heat and, therefore, cools.

A familiar example is the aerosol can that feels cool when the spray button is depressed. A *compression cooling cycle* works with a gas that has a very low boiling temperature, typically Freon-12 or Freon-22. The system contains five major components in a completely sealed circulating cycle (Figure 5-14). The compressor receives the Freon at a low temperature and compresses it to a high-pressure gas. As the gas is compressed, it

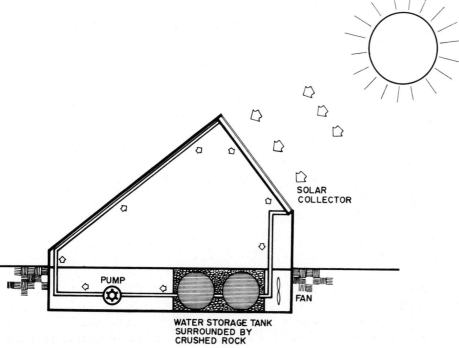

SOLAR
COLLECTOR

PUMP

FAN

WATER STORAGE TANK
SURROUNDED BY
CRUSHED ROCK

Figure 5-13. A solar heating system.

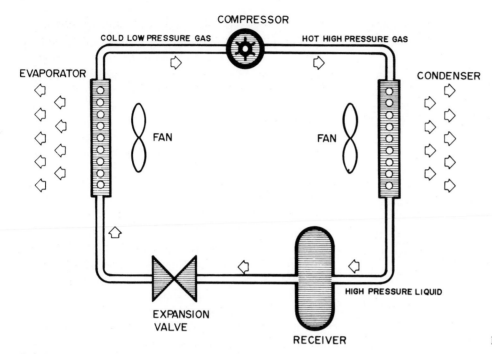

COMPRESSOR

COLD LOW PRESSURE GAS   HOT HIGH PRESSURE GAS

EVAPORATOR   CONDENSER

FAN   FAN

EXPANSION
VALVE

HIGH PRESSURE LIQUID

RECEIVER

Figure 5-14. A refrigeration cycle.

becomes hot. Then it passes through a condenser, which removes some heat, changing the Freon from high-pressure gas to high-pressure liquid. The heat exchange in the condenser is accomplished by blowing air past a radiator coil in small systems or by running water past the radiator coil in large systems. Warm air is forced through the condenser and wasted to the outside. A water system can be wasted to a sewer, but more commonly it is pumped to a tower on the roof. The water is sprayed into the air or allowed to fall through a series of baffles, and outside air is blown through the tower. This causes some of the water to evaporate, which cools it. Once the water is cool, it is returned to the condenser.

The liquid Freon, under high pressure and cool, passes from the condenser to the receiver, a storage tank for the system. The liquid Freon then travels to an expansion valve that changes it from liquid to gas and, therefore, greatly reduces its temperature (like an aerosol spray can). The gas then travels to an evaporator, which is another radiator in the cycle. This time the cool gas inside the evaporator absorbs heat from air or water forced past the coil, thus cooling the fluid. After the gas passes through the evaporator, it is at a low pressure and cool. It then circulates to the compressor to begin the cycle again. The evaporator is the only section of the refrigerant system that is located in the air stream.

An *absorption refrigeration cycle* is quite similar to a compression cycle, but heat in the form of a gas or oil flame is substituted for the compressor. An increase in temperature at this stage in the cycle causes the gas to increase in temperature and pressure, as it would with a compressor.

The size of the system has much to do with the method of heat exchange in both the condenser and the evaporator. Small units tend to use forced air for both because it is more economical. Larger installations use water to absorb heat in the condenser, as it is more efficient.

Some large air cooling systems also use water in the evaporator, where it is chilled. The water can then be circulated to radiators located in supply ducts at various points in the mechanical system; a volume of chilled water is easier to transport over a distance than conditioned air is.

The principle that warm air can hold more moisture than cool air is quite evident in summer, when moisture condenses on cold glass. The same technique is used to control humidity in a building with a refrigeration system. An extremely high humidity is unpleasant when coupled with an acceptable design temperature. A comfortable temperature and humidity for design purposes is 75°F [23.9°C] with 50 percent relative humidity. *Relative humidity* measures the percent of moisture air can hold at a particular temperature. The percentage can range from 0 to 100 percent. The design example above then indicates that at 75°F [23.9°C], 50 percent humidity is half the moisture the air could possibly hold. When the relative humidity reaches 100 percent, moisture in the air precipitates, a condition called the *dew point*. As the temperature drops, the dew point also drops. The volume of moisture held in air at 75°F [23.89°C] with a relative humidity of 50 percent reaches its dew point (100 percent saturation) if the air is chilled to 55°F [12.8°C].

To continue the example of the 75°F, 50 percent humidity design, a pound of air at this point contains approximately 65 grains of moisture. If the outside air is 85°F and has a 70 percent humidity, it contains approximately 125 grains of moisture per pound of air. This means that the temperature must be lowered 10°F, and 60 grains of moisture per pound of air must be removed. To reduce the amount of water in the air to 65 grains, the dew-point temperature of 55°F must be reached. At 55°F, 60 grains of moisture per pound of air will condense on the evaporator coil and be carried off as waste.

The problem now presents itself that air coming out of a diffuser at 55°F and 100 percent humidity will be extremely uncomfortable until it has mixed with the room air. The solution is to locate a reheat coil in the duct to heat the air to about 65°F [18.33°C] for supply into the room. To provide a comfortable environment, it then is necessary to heat air once it has been cooled.

Heating and cooling requirements are measured in British thermal units (Btu). A Btu is the amount of heat required to raise or lower 1 lb of water 1°F, or about the amount of heat given off when a wooden match is burned to the end. Air-conditioning loads are further measured in tons. A ton of air conditioning is equal to 12,000 Btu per hr, or the amount of heat necessary to melt 1 ton of ice in 24 hr. The term is seldom used by mechanical engineers.

It would not be possible to cover all the variations in mechanical systems designed by engineers. One rather innovative approach for a 20-story office tower involves the pumping of water from a deep water well which is at a constant 42°F [5.6°C]. Initially, this chilled water is pumped into heat exchangers in the ducts to absorb heat from the supply-air flow. This water, which has absorbed several degrees of heat, is pumped back to the main air cooling area, where it is circulated through the condensing coil to absorb more heat. The water is then pumped back to its source.

Another mechanical system is the heat pump. The system operates like a compressor air cooling system in the summer, but through a series of valves the condenser and evaporator switch functions in the winter. This allows the heat from the condenser to be discharged into the air duct, and the outdoor coil can act as the evaporator.

HEAT DESIGN

A definite and accurate method of design can be applied to the design for heating and cooling a space. Such things as the number of people in the space (a person at rest can radiate 450 Btu per hr, while strenuous exercise produces 1500 Btu per hr), the frequency at which exterior doors are opened, the amount of glass used in the design, the direction the building is facing, and the number and type of trees to be planted all have a bearing on the mechanical design.

The climate of the building site has an obvious effect on the mechanical size. Heating is formulated by using a minimum design temperature for the area. Fuel calculations can be done by using the average temperature below 65°F for each day for a year. This number is called *degree days*. If the average temperature for a day is 40°F, the number of degree days is 25 (65°F − 40°F). An average temperature above 65°F is not recorded. The design temperature for Duluth, Minnesota, is −25°F, and it has 9480 degree days per year; Dallas, Texas, has a design temperature of 0°F and 2256 degree days.

Major heat loss in a building is caused by the loss in temperature through the walls. The following formula is used to calculate this loss:

$$Q = UA(t_1 - t_2)$$

where Q = Btu transmitted per hour
U = overall coefficient of heat transfer through a wall design, expressed in Btu per hour per square feet per degrees Fahrenheit. (Mechanical engineers follow a guide that gives U factors for various wall conditions; see Figure 5-15.)
A = area of exposed wall to be studied, expressed in square feet
$(t_1 - t_2)$ = difference between the outdoor minimum design temperature and the indoor design temperature, in degrees Fahrenheit

For example, a wall composition consisting of brick veneer, 25/32″ insulation board, wood studs,

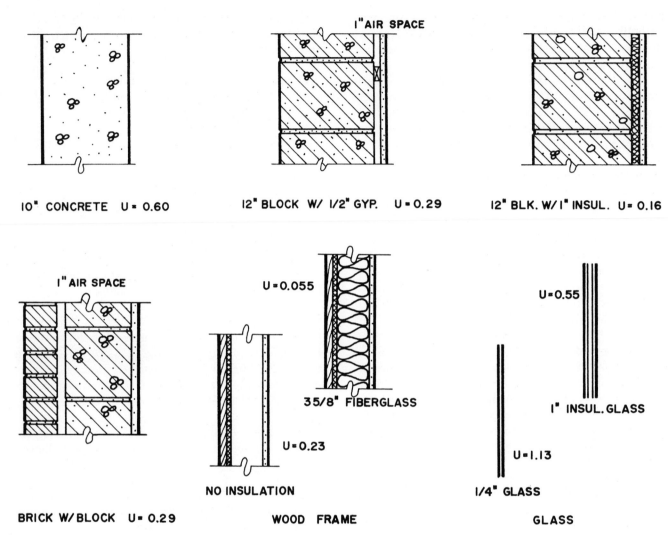

Figure 5-15.   The *U* factors for various wall conditions.

and a layer of 3/8″ gypsum board yields *U* factor of 0.21, obtained from the *ASHRAE Guide and Data Book*, by the American Society of Heating, Refrigerating and Air Conditioning Engineers (ASHRAE). A wall 20′ long and 10′ high with an outside design temperature of − 10°F and an inside design temperature of 75°F would have the following heat loss:

$$Q = UA(t_1 - t_2)$$
$$= .21 \times 200[75 - (-10)]$$
$$= 3570 \text{ Btu per hr}$$

This wall loses 3570 Btu per hr. Thus, the same amount must be supplied to keep the temperature at 75°F when it is −10°F outside.

The wall described above was not insulated between the studs. If it had been insulated with 3⅝″

mineral wool, the *U* factor would be reduced to 0.067. Substituting this into the formula,

$$Q = .067 \times 200[75 - (-10)]$$
$$= 1139 \text{ Btu per hr}$$

The addition of insulation to this particular wall condition reduced the amount of heat loss in the wall more than three times.

A mechanical engineer calculates the heat losses through all walls, roofs, ceilings, and floors; and the heat loss in glass and doors; and the amount of heat lost by air infiltrating into the building through cracks around doors and windows; and the make-up air mixed with the return air from the space. The total calculation yields the necessary size of the heating package as well as the heat loss of each room or area. The engineer must then select a heating system that will meet the design demand and properly locate the heat supply to comfortably distribute this heat load.

Cooling is designed in much the same way. The demand on a building's cooling system can have a pronounced effect on the architectural concept. Glass is a good example. In winter heating conditions, the greatest amount of solar radiation passes through a clear, colorless piece of glass. This radiant energy strikes objects in a room and causes them to heat up, actually aiding in the heating process. This condition is also present in summer cooling requirements, but then it acts as a detriment to the comfort in the space. In working with the architect, the mechanical engineer can recommend several glass types that can appreciably reduce the effect of solar radiation, but they also greatly change the exterior appearance of the building. Common glass selections include tinted glass (usually bronze or gray) and mirrored glass. In varying degrees, these glass choices reduce the heat buildup inside the space by reflecting some of the solar radiation back to the outside.

Deciduous trees, when properly placed, affect the heating and cooling requirements of a building. The heavy growth of leaves in the summer shades the building and reduces the heat gain. The loss of leaves in the winter allows the solar radiation to aid in heating the building.

Insulated glass also aids heating and, to some degree, cooling of a building space. It consists of two layers of glass with a sealed air space between them. The air space acts as an insulation barrier from the outside temperature, thus reducing the high U factor of glass.

Wall and roof insulation is an extremely economical addition since it appreciably reduces the U factor of the building section. Most insulation works by reducing the heat transfer through cellular air spaces. A greater thickness of insulation corresponds to a lower U factor of the wall condition.

Insulation reduces heat flow due to conduction, the movement of heat through solids. Radiant heat, the movement of heat by infrared radiation, can be reduced by placing a shiny surface in its path, thus reflecting the heat back into the space. The most common application of radiant heat insulation is foil-faced Fiberglas. The shiny foil side is placed in the wall toward the living space to reflect radiant heat back for winter heating conditions. Fiberglas insulation is also available with foil on both faces so

that the exterior face can reflect some infrared radiation from the sun to reduce summer heat gain. (See Figure 5-16.)

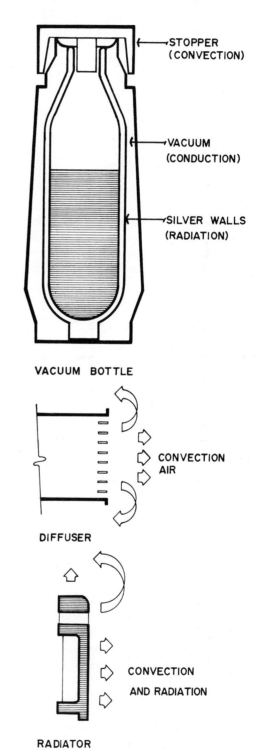

Figure 5-16. Heat transfer, conduction, connection, and radiation.

Convection heat, the movement of heat by the circulation of warmer particles of air, is reduced by placing a vapor barrier in the wall. It can be a thin sheet of plastic (4-mil polyethylene), placed on the room side of the insulation. Placement of the vapor barrier on the cold side (outside) of the insulation permits water vapor to penetrate the insulation and freeze inside the wall, causing many problems.

ELECTRICAL DESIGN

Electrical power is a vital factor in architecture, supplying a major portion of the energy consumed in a building. Most electricity is produced at power plants and brought to a building through insulated wires. Some electrical designs include gas turbines within the building that are sized sufficiently to provide heat and electricity for the complex; some building types, such as hospitals, have emergency power supplies that automatically tie into the system in a power failure.

Electrical energy consists of a flow of electrons through a copper or aluminum wire. In order for a circuit to be complete, one wire must be connected from the electrical source to the electrical device, and another wire must return from the device to the source.

Alternating current (AC) and direct current (DC) are the two types of electrical flow. The terms apply to the direction of flow of electrons in the conductor; *alternating current* reverses its flow continually, while *direct current* flows only in one direction. Direct current is seldom used or even available for architectural needs. It is produced either with chemical batteries or a special DC generator. Alternating current is produced at a constant rate of flow in each direction. In the United States, current flows in one direction 60 times per sec and in the reverse 60 times per sec. This is referred to as *60-cycle current.*

Four common terms are used in discussing electricity: voltage, ampere, ohm, and watt. *Voltage* refers to the force behind the electrons. It can be likened to the pressure in a water pipe. The symbol for voltage is E. The unit of measure for the flow of electrons past a point in a conductor is given in *amperes* (amp), or current. It is analogous to the gallons of water per minute that flow through a pipe. The symbol for amperage is I. The product of volts times amperes is equal to power, given in *watts.* (Watts are also referred to as *power:* 746 watts = 1 horsepower.) One watt is equal to 1 amp of current flowing under 1 volt of pressure. The symbol for watts is W. The amount of electrical resistance in a device is measured in *ohms,* symbolized by R. One ohm is the resistance that allows the passage of 1 amp of current under the pressure of 1 volt. The two resulting formulas are

$$W = EI$$

$$I = E/R$$

For example, a 10-amp unit air conditioner plugged into a 120-volt outlet uses

$$W = EI$$
$$= 120 \text{ volts} \times 10 \text{ amps}$$
$$= 1200 \text{ watts}$$

A graphical representation of direct current is a straight line indicating no change in the voltage within a time period. The graph of alternating current is a sine wave curve which indicates that the voltage goes from a plus high through 0 to a negative high. For 60-cycle electrical supply, this means that the high to low cycle occurs 60 times per sec. This example is called *single-phase current* and actually produces 0 power 60 times per sec. Single-phase current or voltage can prove undesirable for the operation of certain electrical equipment. Thus, power companies generate three-phase current. A graph of three-phase current would show three separate sine wave curves spaced at three points in time. The result is to level off the high and low peaks obtained with single-phase current. It is possible to separate a single phase from three-phase power if required.

A discussion of alternating current necessitates the introduction of the term *power factor.* Here is a brief definition: When electrical energy flows through a device, a magnetic field is established that resists the flow of electrons. This is known as *reactance.* The reactance in the field tends to cause the voltage and current to pull in diverse directions, causing a difference between true power and apparent power. The ratio between the two, called the *power factor,* is given as a percent figure between 0 and 100 percent. The calculation actually indicates the loss of efficiency in an electric device.

For example, find the real and apparent power produced by an electric motor running at 115 volts and drawing 12 amp with a power factor of 80 percent.

Apparent power $= W = EI$
$$= 115 \times 12$$
$$= 1380 \text{ watts}$$

Real power $= W = EI(PF)$
$$= 115 \times 12 \times 0.80$$
$$= 1104 \text{ watts}$$

or $= 1104/746$
$$= 1.48 \text{ hp}$$

Power factors can be corrected by using a device called a *capacitor*, which, when hooked into the electric equipment, brings the factor to nearly 1.

Alternating current has the definite advantage of having voltage increased or decreased without much loss in efficiency (0.5 to 3 percent is typical). A transformer simply consists of two windings insulated from each other but having a common iron core. The winding which receives the electrical energy is called the *primary*, and the winding that delivers the energy is called the *secondary*. Power companies step up voltages to facilitate the movement of large volumes of power which are then stepped down for distribution to consumers. Residential consumers have power stepped down to usable voltages before the electrical service enters their buildings, while larger buildings commonly have transformers located on the site or within the building to facilitate the larger electrical demand.

Dry and sealed liquid are the two basic transformers. Liquid transformers are usually more compact and more expensive. Both choices pose problems to architects. Building and electric codes must be followed to ensure safe installation in terms of potential hazards from fire or toxic fumes. If a transformer is located within a building, it is housed in a *transformer vault*, a special room which meets code requirements for floor, walls, ceilings, doors, and access panels. If the transformer is outside the building, it is placed on a raised concrete pad that must meet distance and protection requirements. (See Figure 5-17.)

In addition to these two types, transformers are built with various designs that determine the step-down voltage produced. Single-phase, delta-delta, delta-wye, and open-delta are some common transformer designs. Without explaining the intricacies of each, it should be noted that voltages of 120, 208, 240, 277, 480, and up are available from various transformer designs. A necessary preliminary step is to have an electrical engineer contact the local power company to confirm electrical service to the site.

Electric service enters a building either through above-grade wires strung from power poles or through wires buried underground in waterproof cable. The electric current is first metered by the utility company's watt-hour meter, which measures the use of electrical service in watts so that the customer can be billed properly. Since a watt is an extremely small unit of measure, power is measured in increments of 1000 watts (1 kilowatt, or 1 kW). The cost of electric power varies greatly, not only in different areas of the country but within the limits of each utility company, depending on the volume of electrical power consumed. A favorable electric rate could make mechanical features such as electric heat economically possible.

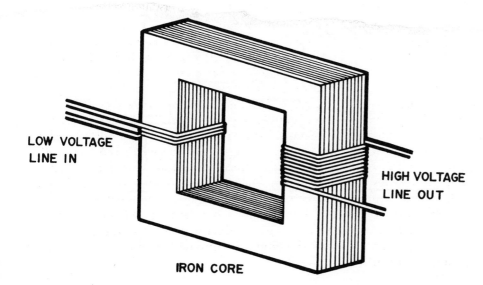

**LOW VOLTAGE
LINE IN**

**HIGH VOLTAGE
LINE OUT**

IRON CORE

Figure 5-17. A transformer.

Once the electric power has been metered, it is connected to the main distribution panel, first passing through the main disconnect switch. The disconnect switch allows the interruption of complete electric power in the event of an emergency, such as fire. Two special electric circuits—for emergency lighting such as exit signs and fire alarms—are connected to the service before it reaches the disconnect switch.

The main electric panel (Figure 5-18) serves as the distribution point for the building. Separate circuits branch out from the panel box to serve specific electrical requirements. Each circuit is protected from being overloaded by passing through a circuit-breaking device located within the panel box. The older system involves a fuse that melts if the circuit is overloaded. The more modern system employs a *circuit breaker,* a switch that trips off when overloaded. A circuit breaker can be reset when the electrical trouble is corrected. Fuses and circuit breakers are sized to carry a designed maximum amperage load, from 15 to 30 amp for glass screw-in fuses and much higher for cartridge fuses and circuit breakers.

For example, determine the number of 100-watt lights that may be placed in a 120-volt circuit protected by a 20-amp circuit breaker:

$$EI = W/100$$
$$120 \times 20 = 2400/100$$
$$= \text{twenty-four 100-watt lights}$$

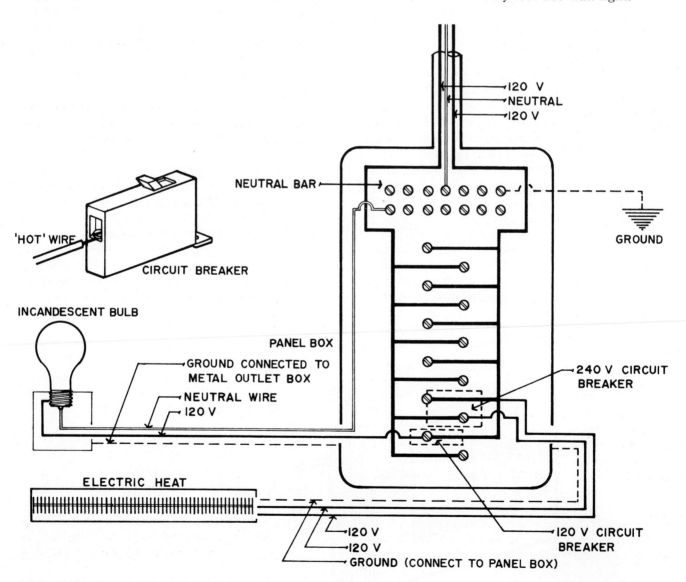

Figure 5-18. The main electric panel.

The explanation of a residential electric panel at this point should serve to clarify the methods of distribution for even larger building systems. Generally three wires are brought into the building, two wires at 120 volts each from the transformer secondary, and a third wire that is from the transformer center tap, called the *neutral*.

The two 120-volt lines are first connected to the main disconnect circuit breaker, rated to trip off at a maximum amperage draw for the entire service (60 amp is minimum; 100 amp is common; 150 or 200 amp is necessary for air conditioning).

The lines are then connected from the main disconnect to the service bars (v_1 and v_2). The neutral wire is connected to the neutral bar, consisting of a row of screws for wire connection. Even though the neutral wire from the transformer is grounded, the neutral bar is further grounded by being connected to a cold-water pipe in the house. The purpose is to dissipate any abnormal voltages that might occur on the transformer secondary.

It is possible to obtain 120 volts and 240 volts from this system. The larger voltage is required for major electric appliances such as ovens, water heaters, and dryers. The increased voltage results in a proportional reduction in amperage to produce the same power.

The connection of a 120-volt circuit involves hooking one wire to a circuit breaker, which in turn is attached to one of the service bars. This wire is referred to as the *hot wire* and is color-coded by using plastic-sheathed wire in any color except white or green. The second wire necessary to complete the electric circuit is connected to the neutral bar. The code demands that this wire must have white plastic insulation.

Connection of a 240-volt electric appliance to the distribution panel involves taking 120 volts from each of the two lines at the service bars. A 240-volt circuit breaker is snapped into the electric panel. This attaches to two poles (one each from v_1 and v_2). Two wires, each carrying 120 volts, run from the breaker to the appliance to complete the current flow. In this case, the neutral wire is not required.

Neither the 120-volt nor the 240-volt system described is grounded; that is, neither system is provided with an additional conductor that does not normally carry electric current. A *ground* is a safety wire that acts to carry power away from an electric device if a current-carrying wire should accidentally come in contact with the metal housing (a short

circuit). Just as with the neutral bar, the ground must be attached to a cold-water pipe.

Some types of electric distribution circuits enclose the wires in a metal conduit from the panel box to the outlet. With this system, the attachment of the panel box to a ground also grounds the outlet. A nonmetallic cable requires an additional ground wire which is connected to the grounded panel box and each outlet box. The code requires that this wire be identified with green plastic insulation. The fact that the outlet is grounded does not automatically ground the electric device. Portable electric equipment must have a third pole on the plug which connects the metal housing of the device to the grounded outlet. Permanent equipment has a screw attachment for the metallic conduit or the green ground wire.

The rated amperage in a circuit also determines the size of the wire that must be used. The minimum wire is #14, which can carry 15 amp; #12 carries 20 amp; #10 wire carries 30 amp—and on up to #00 wire, which can carry 150 amp. Copper and aluminum are commonly used for electric wire. Copper is a better conductor of electricity (aluminum has 40 percent less conductivity) and may be sized smaller, but the lower cost of aluminum makes the two competitive.

All wire is given a colored protective plastic coating to keep it from making contact with other wires. The coating usually is printed with the size of the wire, the maximum allowable voltage, the temperature in degrees Celsius that the coating will stand up to under heating of the wire, any special properties such as oil and gasoline resistance, and the Underwriters Laboratories seal. Wire can either be solid or several strands, whichever is more flexible.

Electric wires must be protected against contact with each other and causing a short circuit. They also must be shielded from other objects. Several methods have been devised to distribute electric power safely within a building. Local building codes dictate the systems that are acceptable at the site. Some common wiring systems (Figure 5-19) are

1. *Thinwall conduit* (electrical metallic tubing, or EMT) consists of galvanized steel tubing clamped together with special fittings. The system is completely grounded to the distribution panel to protect against short circuits. The usual procedure is to install the conduit first

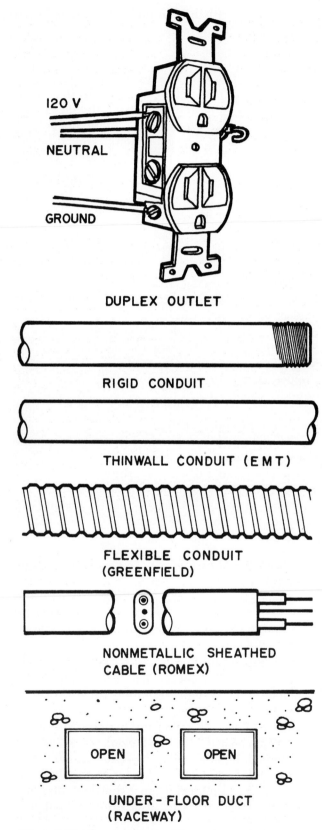

DUPLEX OUTLET

RIGID CONDUIT

THINWALL CONDUIT (EMT)

FLEXIBLE CONDUIT (GREENFIELD)

NONMETALLIC SHEATHED CABLE (ROMEX)

OPEN   OPEN

UNDER-FLOOR DUCT (RACEWAY)

Figure 5-19.   Some common wiring systems.

and then pull the wire through with a flexible steel "fish tape." In order that all bends in the conduit be gradual, a conduit bender, called a *hickey*, is used. Conduit comes in various diameters starting at ½". The size is determined by the size and number of wires it encloses.

2. *Flexible metal conduit* (Flex or Greenfield) is similar to thinwall in use, but it usually has more code restrictions. It consists of an empty spiral-wrapped armor cable that is flexible enough to turn corners. Like thinwall, it is grounded to the distribution panel and allows for the passage of loose wires through the conduit.

3. *Interlocked armor cable* (BX) is also a flexible armor-shielded cable, but it has two or more plastic-coated wires assembled within the casing. The common condition is to run a separate ground wire through the cable and then attach it to the outlet box. Since the wire is preinstalled in BX cable, its diameter is less than Greenfield. The armor must be cut back at each connection, and so a plastic sleeve is used to protect the wire.

4. *Nonmetallic sheathed cable* (Romex) consists of two or more wires enclosed in a flexible plastic case. Where Romex is allowed, it usually requires a separate ground wire bound in the cable of the same size as the electrical conductor wire.

5. *Knob and tube wiring* is never used in commercial construction and seldom allowed by residential codes. This old style of wiring consists of supporting each wire on nonmetallic knobs fastened to wall studs. The system has no potential for grounding and is not protected from accidental abuse.

6. *Rigid conduit* is similar to thinwall conduit except that the pipe is considerably heavier and is threaded. Its installation resembles plumbing connections, which makes it expensive to install. It is the most rugged wiring system but is seldom used unless a special need exists.

7. *Under-floor duct* (raceway) is commonly a metal-enclosed box that is placed on the floor deck prior to the placement of concrete flooring. Various outlets can be placed at the floor surface to provide flexibility in a space within walls.

8. *Busway* (bus duct) is a preassembled metal box system used to distribute high-current loads.

Its main use is to feed electric loads for further distribution at panels.

Electric current is seldom supplied on a constant basis to devices such as lights and heaters, as it is then necessary to interrupt the hot wire that supplies power. This is accomplished by using a variety of switches designed to meet the need. Lights may be turned off by using toggle switches. A single pole switch controls a light from one location, while a combination of 3- and 4-way switches can control lights from a number of points.

If more lights are to be operated by one switch than the single circuit load allows, a low-voltage relay can be used. This large switching device can control several circuits which, in turn, are switched by a single switch. Typically, the single switch has a low voltage (±24 volts) so that the wire leading to the relay can be doorbell wire, which needn't be enclosed in conduit. Incandescent and fluorescent lights can be reduced in intensity by using special dimmer switches called *rheostats* (fluorescent fixtures also require a special ballast). *Starters* and *contacters* are magnetic switches used chiefly for automatic control of large electric machinery.

A *receptacle* or *convenience outlet* is a contact device for connecting portable electric equipment. The common receptacle has two slots for the appliance connection and a third for a ground. Outlets are commonly rated at 15 or 20 amp, but special receptacles are available for higher-amperage devices. It is common to locate two outlets in the same grounded box, and so they are referred to as *duplex outlets*. A duplex outlet can be wired so that one outlet is controlled by a switch while the other is not.

LIGHTING

Light is a form of energy that falls in the same band as radio and infrared waves. Technically, the visible spectrum falls between 4000 and 7600 angstroms (Å), the area that produces the sensation of light in the eye.

Basically, light is produced with electrical energy in two ways: (1) by passing current through a wire, causing it to heat and give off light; or (2) by causing electrons to flow through a gas which subsequently glows.

The first example, *incandescent light*, is produced by enclosing a tungsten wire in a glass bulb filled with nitrogen and argon. The electrical resistance of the wire determines the wattage and the amount of light given off. The most common bulbs range from 25 to 1000 watts. Incandescent bulbs have a life of about 1000 hr, due to the gradual weakening of the tungsten as electric current passes through it. (See Figure 5-20.)

A marked increase in bulb life is realized if the rated voltage is slightly reduced, also reducing the light output. The reverse is true of increased voltage. A percent change in voltage proportionally changes the bulb life by 10 percent and the light output by 3 percent. This means that in an auditorium where bulbs are awkward to change, operating 120-volt lamps at 115 volts could prove economical by extending the bulb life. A special type of incandescent light, quartz-iodine, has an extended life and higher light output.

The second example, *gaseous discharge lamps*, have several distinct types, such as neon, sodium, mercury, and fluorescent. All operate by causing a gas to glow as electrons pass between two electrodes. The initial voltage must be increased above the normal operating level to start the electron flow. The most common gaseous discharge lamp is a fluorescent fixture. The glass tube is filled with mercury vapor which produces large amounts of ultraviolet radiation when an electric arc is passed through. This radiation is not within the visible spectrum, and so the walls of the tube are coated with phosphors that glow when struck by ultraviolet radiation. Fluorescent lights have several features that distinguish them from incandescent lights:

1. A *ballast*, or transformer (properly called an *auxiliary*) is required for the operation of fluorescent lamps. Usually one ballast is wired to supply two lamps. It draws approximately 20 percent additional power over the watt rating of the lamps.
2. The efficiency of a fluorescent lamp is greatly reduced if its temperature drops significantly below room temperature. A special lamp is available for low-temperature operation.
3. A flickering, stroboscopic effect occurs in fluorescent lamps due to the periodic cut in power—60 times per sec with 60-cycle AC. This effect can be compensated by attaching two lamps to the same ballast and hooking them out of phase so that when one is off the other is on.
4. The conversion of electrical energy to light is about 40 percent efficient for fluorescent lights,

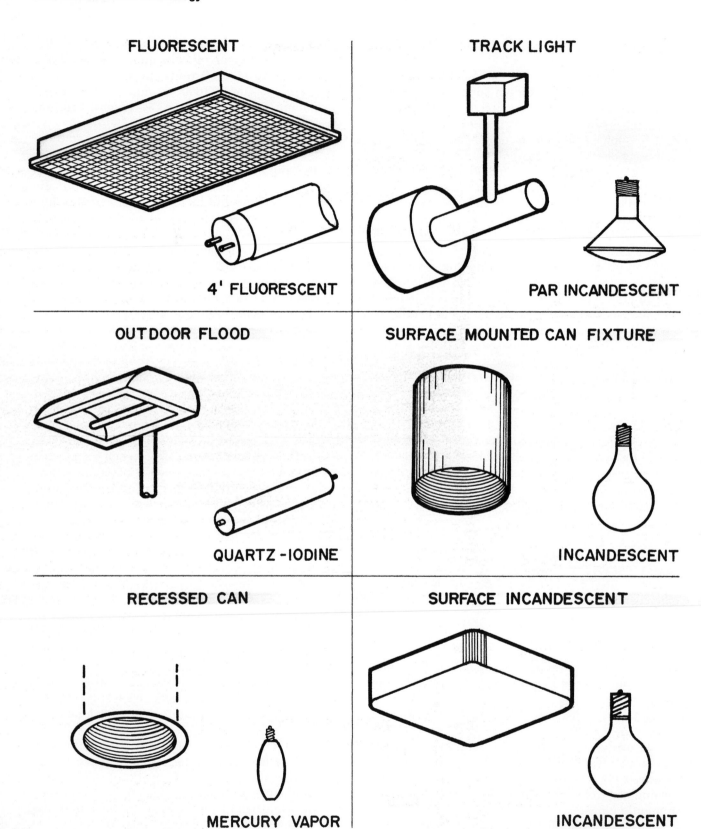

FLUORESCENT

4' FLUORESCENT

TRACK LIGHT

PAR INCANDESCENT

OUTDOOR FLOOD

QUARTZ-IODINE

SURFACE MOUNTED CAN FIXTURE

INCANDESCENT

RECESSED CAN

MERCURY VAPOR

SURFACE INCANDESCENT

INCANDESCENT

Figure 5-20. Electric fixtures.

while incandescent lamps are less than 10 percent efficient.

5. The life of a fluorescent light can be up to 10 times that of incandescent lights if the light is left on an average of 5 hr. Each time the lamp is turned on, a portion of the cathode burns off, until the lamp eventually fails to light.

6. The phosphor coating inside a fluorescent tube can be altered to give it a variety of color properties. Tubes are labeled according to the color they emit—cool white, white, daylight, softwhite, and so on.

Neon lamps are commonly used for advertising but seldom for commercial and residential lighting because of their low light level and poor color band. Sodium vapor lights produce a yellow-orange band of light which usually makes it unacceptable for interior use. Its chief application is for outdoor lighting. Mercury lights produce light in the blue-green color spectrum. Their use ranges from outdoor lighting to specialized interior light. The lamp life of a mercury vapor light, as with most other gaseous discharge lights, is many times longer than that of an incandescent bulb of the same intensity.

It is important for a technician to be familiar with the following terms used in lighting.

A *lumen* (lm) is the measure of total light output from a source; 1 lm is equal to the amount of light produced by a candle on a 1 sq ft surface at a distance of 1'. Each lamp is given a lumen output rating, such as:

40 watt	48″ rapid-start fluorescent white	3000 lm
40 watt	48″ rapid-start fluorescent softwhite	1900 lm
250 watt	Clear bulb, mercury vapor	11,000 lm
180 watt	Sodium vapor	19,000 lm
40 watt	Incandescent	470 lm
100 watt	Incandescent	1640 lm

In general, incadescent lights produce between 10 and 20 lm per watt, while fluorescent lights emit from 40 to 50 lm per watt of power consumed.

A *footcandle* (fc) is the unit of illumination when distance from the light source is taken into account. A more descriptive definition might be that footcandle illumination equals the number of lumens per square foot that reach the working surface. Typically, 2'-6″ is subtracted from the distance of the light source to the floor, accounting for usual table height. Some common surface footcandle requirements are

Classroom	70 fc
Library	70 fc
Drafting lab	100–200 fc
Auditoriums	5–15 fc
Residential work area	50 fc
Office	100 fc
Factory	50 fc

A *lamp* is the term used to describe the glass envelope enclosing the electric source of light. Incandescent lamps are usually referred to as *bulbs*, while fluorescent lamps are commonly called *tubes*.

The term *light fixture* includes the lamp, socket, housing, reflector, sometimes the wire connection box, and, in the case of gaseous discharge lamps, the auxiliary.

The *color spectrum* includes the band of visible light, ranging through red, orange, yellow, green, blue, indigo, and violet. (The colors are remembered easily with the name ROY G. BIV, the first initials of the colors being the letters in the name.) Sunlight contains the full spectrum band; incandescent and sodium lamps tend to give out warm orange-yellow colors; while mercury vapor and fluorescent lamps tend to produce light in the cool green-blue band.

Technical data published by each light-fixture manufacturer give lighting engineers sufficient information to design a fixture layout. These data include a chart, *the coefficient of utilization*, which accounts for the proportion of the room, the type of fixture, and the ceiling, floor, and wall materials with regard to the amount of light they reflect. (See Table 5-1.)

In Table 5-1, the reflection percentages need further clarification. To degrees, all surfaces absorb some light energy that strikes them. A light-colored, smooth surface absorbs less light—and thus reflects more—than a dark, rough area does. A ceiling generally is free of objects, whereas walls have doors, drapes, chalkboards, etc., and floors have furniture and carpet to absorb light. A lighting engineer must determine the percentage of reflection presented by each room condition.

Once the room's size, height, material finish, fixture choice, and footcandle levels have been decided, the engineer can determine the number of fixtures required. The formula is

ROOM RATIO
CEILING REFLECTION
WALL REFLECTION
FLOOR REFLECTION

Typical Distribution and Maximum Spacing	pcc →	80		70			50			30			10			0	Typical Luminaires and Luminaire Maintenance Category
	pw →	50	30	10	50	30	10	50	30	10	50	30	10	50	30	10	0	
	RCR ↓	Coefficients of Utilization for 20 Per Cent Effective Floor Cavity Reflectance, pFC																

7

0% 70%

Max. S/MH_wp = 1.3

RCR																		
1	.75	.72	.70	.73	.71	.69	.70	.68	.67	.68	.66	.65	.65	.64	.63	.62	
2	.67	.63	.59	.65	.62	.59	.63	.60	.57	.61	.58	.56	.59	.57	.55	.54	
3	.60	.55	.51	.59	.54	.51	.57	.53	.50	.55	.52	.49	.53	.50	.48	.47	
4	.54	.48	.44	.53	.48	.44	.51	.47	.43	.50	.46	.43	.48	.45	.42	.41	
5	.48	.42	.38	.47	.42	.38	.46	.41	.37	.44	.40	.37	.43	.39	.36	.35	
6	.43	.37	.33	.42	.37	.33	.41	.36	.33	.40	.36	.32	.39	.35	.32	.31	
7	.39	.33	.29	.38	.33	.29	.37	.32	.28	.36	.31	.28	.35	.31	.28	.27	2-lamp, 2'-wide white troffer with prismatic lens. (Multiply 0.9 for 4-lamp) LDD Maint. Category V
8	.35	.29	.25	.34	.29	.25	.33	.28	.25	.32	.28	.25	.32	.28	.24	.23	
9	.31	.25	.21	.31	.25	.21	.30	.24	.21	.29	.24	.21	.28	.24	.21	.20	
10	.28	.23	.19	.28	.22	.19	.27	.22	.19	.26	.22	.19	.26	.22	.19	.17	

8

0%

RCR																	
1	.69	.66	.64	.67	.65	.63	.65	.63	.61	.62	.61	.58	.59	.58	.57	.55
2	.61	.56	.53	.56	.55	.52	.56	.53	.51	.54	.52	.50	.52	.50	.49	.47
3	.53	.49	.44	.52	.48	.43	.50	.47	.43	.49	.44	.42	.46	.43	.41	.40

ISOLUS CURVE

TABLE 5-1

$$Fg = \frac{EA}{CU \times DF}$$

where Fg = total lumens
 E = footcandle level
 A = area in square feet
 CU = coefficient of utilization
 DF = depreciation factor

The depreciation factor takes into account the deterioration of the fixture, mainly the loss of lumens from the lamp and the buildup of dust and dirt on the fixture that can reduce its efficiency.

The room ratio must be determined before the coefficient of utilization can be found. A room that is wide in relationship to its height allows more light to reach the surface, while a square room is more efficient than a rectangular one. The formula is

$$\text{Room ratio} = \frac{W \times L}{H(W + L)}$$

where W = width
 L = length
 H = height (usually 2'-6" off the floor)

For example, find the number of two-lamp fixtures required to light a library's reading room to 70 fc. Assume the reflection factors are 80 percent for the ceiling, 30 percent for the walls, and 20 percent for the floor. The dimensions of the room are 40' wide, 60' long, and 9' high.

$$\text{Room ratio} = \frac{W \times L}{H(W + L)}$$
$$H - 2'\text{-}6" = 6\tfrac{1}{2}'$$
$$= \frac{40 \times 60}{6\tfrac{1}{2}(40 + 60)}$$
$$= 3.7$$

Following Table 5-1 for the fixture, a room ratio of 3.7 (rounded off to 4) with 80 percent ceiling reflectance, 30 percent wall reflectance, and 20 percent floor reflectance yields a factor of .48. Using the suggested depreciation factor of .70, the equation is

$$Fg = \frac{E \times A}{CU \times DF}$$
$$= \frac{70 \times (60 \times 40)}{.48 \times .70}$$
$$= 500{,}000 \text{ lm}$$

If 40-watt, 48", rapid-start white fluorescent lamps are used, each one produces 3000 lm, or 6000 lm per 2-lamp fixture. This yields 83 fixtures for the 40' × 60' space. The maximum allowable spacing between fixtures to provide a uniform light pattern is dependent upon the distance from the fixture to the working surface and upon the pattern of light thrown from the particular fixture. The diagram shown in Table 5-1 is called an *isolus curve*. It is an actual-scale elevation of the light pattern thrown. One-half to one-third of the fixture spacing should be used to determine side- and end-wall distances.

The necessity of a reflected ceiling plan can be realized when light fixtures, air diffusers, sprinkler heads, and structural members must all be coordinated. A common grid to follow, especially for offices and schools, is 2' × 4'. This is the general pattern established when a lay-in acoustic tile ceiling is used.

ACOUSTICS

Acoustics in architecture involves the treatment of sound in two basic ways: (1) transmission to other areas; and (2) control within a space. Sound is produced by a physical vibration that imparts a wave through the air or through another vehicle.

The *frequency,* or *pitch,* of sound is measured in the number of vibrations per second made by the wave. The range of human hearing spans from around 16 to 20,000 cycles per second (cps). Within this range, a male voice centers at 350 cps, a female voice at 700 cps, middle C at 261 cps, and high C at 4186 cps.

Sound waves are a form of energy, but their energy is so slight that it would take 250 people talking at once to produce 1 watt of power. Sound travels through different mediums at extremely diverse speeds. It passes through air at approximately 1130 ft per sec, through water at 5000 ft per sec, and through steel at over 15,000 ft per sec.

In addition to pitch, sound travels at an intensity measured in decibels (dB). The threshold of human hearing starts at 0 dB and ranges to around 140 dB, producing pain. Within this scale, the rustling of leaves is about 10 dB; a general office area produces about 50 dB; normal conversation, 60 dB; a symphony or stereo system, 90 dB; and jet aircraft, 140 dB. A reduction in sound level of 10 dB results in the subjective reaction of reducing the loudness by one-half, but a change of 2 or 3 dB is insignificant.

Sound transmission usually involves the reduction of sound intensity from its source to another space. The sound level in an apartment is generally not a concern from room to room, but it is a very definite problem when it transmits from one apartment to the next. Then it becomes noise, or unwanted sound. Sound vibrations are carried into adjacent spaces either by airborne sound waves that penetrate walls or by structure-borne transmissions such as vibrating mechanical equipment or footsteps.

Airborne sound energy can be reduced when it travels through a wall. The degree of reduction is dependent on the wall materials. Wall sections can be given a decibel rating to indicate efficiency in reducing sound. For example, sound rated at 60 dB striking a wall with a 35-dB rating is reduced to 25 dB after passing through the wall. The drawback with this system is that the rating fluctuates greatly as the pitch of the sound changes.

A more standard approach is to use assigned ratings of sound transmission class (STC). In effect, this is an average of the decibel reductions through a typical frequency range. Obviously, a higher STC rating results in a greater reduction in sound transmitted through the wall. Several useful recommended STC reductions are:

Adjacent doctors' consultation offices	STC 47
Adjacent offices in a normal office condition	STC 37
Adjacent bedrooms in a motel or apartment	STC 47
Adjacent classrooms	STC 37
School toilet areas	STC 42
School mechanical equipment rooms	STC 52

Common wall construction ranges from a low of STC 32 for 1/2″ gypsum board nailed to both sides of 2 × 4 wood studs to a high of STC 56 for a solid 12″ reinforced concrete. A more complete list is available in *Architectural Graphic Standards.* A 4″ concrete block provides an STC of 38, while doubling the thickness to 8″ increases the STC to 48.

In addition to standard wall construction, several techniques are used to increase the STC rating. Staggered wood studs (2 × 4 studs with a 2 × 6 plate) increase the STC rating of a 1/2″ gypsum board wall from 32 to 41. Adding an extra 1/2″ sheet of gypsum board to each side boosts the STC rating 5 points. Two other common solutions are to attach the wallboard to resilient metal clips which in turn are fastened to the studs (+10 STC if done on each side) and filling the wall cavity with absorptive material (+5 STC). (See Figure 5-21.)

All work done to provide an adequate sound reduction for walls is useless if other precautions are not taken. A common problem in offices and schools occurs with a lay-in ceiling. The sound passes from one room to the next through the ceiling tile. A crack under a door allows sound to escape unless a special soundproof door sill is used. Such things as doors that open to a common corridor, single-glazed windows between spaces, and electrical outlet boxes common to both spaces all can contribute to the reduction of effective airborne sound protection. Caulking around pipes that enter a party wall, special ducts to reduce sound transmission, and gaskets around door frames are common to commercial construction where sound is a concern.

Structure-borne sound transmission is caused when building materials are set in vibration by a direct mechanical contact, either in the form of impact such as footsteps or by mechanical equipment, including plumbing. This differs from airborne transmission in that the vibration sets up new sound waves on both sides of the surface.

The rating used for this type of transmission, called *impact noise rating* (INR), differs from STC in that it compares each floor and ceiling construction system against an accepted sound standard. An INR rating of 0 means that the floor construction is

1/2" GYP. BOARD

STC 32

DOUBLE 1/2" GYP. BD. EACH SIDE

STC 37

8" POURED CONCRETE

STC 51

3 COAT PLASTER ON LATH

STC 37

STAGGERED STUDS W/ DBL. GYP. BD.

STC 44

5/8" GYP. BD. W/ METAL STUDS

STC 39

2-4" CONC. BLK. W/ 4" SPACE

STC 53

6" BLOCK

STC 43

1 3/4" SOLID CORE DOOR W/GASKETS

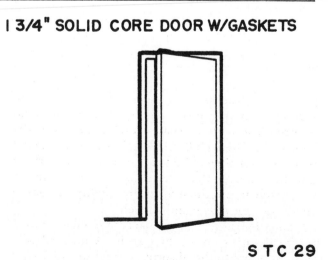

STC 29

Figure 5-21. Sound transmission ratings for common walls.

equal to the accepted standard. A minus INR indicates that the floor is below standard. The standard assumes a background noise level typical for an apartment in a quiet neighborhood. A condition in an atmosphere with less noise should have a +5 to +10 INR. Conversely, a more noisy area could have an INR of −5. Several common floor conditions are shown in Figure 5-22.

In general terms, impact noise can be treated by cushioning the impact with materials such as carpet or by insulating the floor system from the subfloor by using a resilient ceiling channel. Mechanical vibration can be treated by isolating mechanical equipment with springs or resilient pads. Since airborne sound and structure-borne sound are not the same, both STC and INR should be considered in the transmission of sound to adjoining areas.

The other concern of sound in architecture, *acoustics*, deals with the correction and reduction of sound within a space. Acoustical correction involves shaping the room for the best pattern of sound and selection of acoustical materials and possibly sound-amplification equipment. In practice, architects generally engage the services of an acoustical consultant for the design of complex acoustical problems, such as auditoriums. Sound reduction within a space involves lowering the level of sound reflected against walls, floors, and ceilings.

When sound is emitted from a source and strikes a surface such as a wall, a portion of the sound is absorbed by the material (by the change of sound energy to heat), and the remainder is reflected back into the room. A smooth, hard-surfaced wall can reflect up to 98 percent of the sound striking it.

The time it takes an emitted sound to decay to one-millionth (60 dB) of the original sound is referred to as *reverberation time*. This time can range from almost 0, when there is no reflection of sound, to possibly 25 seconds in a large space with very hard surfaces. Reverberation time is dependent on the volume, the shape, and the sound-absorbing properties of the space. Some reverberation of sound is good to have because it adds to the original sound, referred to as a "live" space. A room 80' wide, 100' long, and 20' high (160,000 cu ft) has a recommended reverberation time of 1.2 to 1.7 seconds. A reverberation time longer than the recommended standard will result in a reduction in the quality of hearing conditions for music and speech.

Sound-absorption materials are rated according to effectiveness on a 0 to 1 scale. A unit called a *sabin* is equal to the absorptive qualities of 1 sq ft of material when compared to 1 sq ft of total sound absorption. A totally absorptive material has a value of 1, while a totally reflective material has a rating of 0. A rating of .5 indicates that 50 percent of the sound that strikes the surface is absorbed. Acoustical materials are tested with sound at pitches of 250, 500, 1000, and 2000 cps and are averaged to yield the noise reduction coefficient. The absorption coefficients per square foot for materials are

Concrete floor	.02
Heavy carpet on a pad	.55
Gypsum board (wall and ceiling)	.07
Acoustic ceiling tile	.70

The formula for calculating reverberation time is

$$T = \frac{.05\, V}{a}$$

where T = reverberation time in seconds
V = volume in cubic feet
a = absorption units

Find the reverberation time in a room 80' wide, 100' long, and 20' high with a concrete floor and gypsum board walls and ceiling.

Floor—8000 sq ft concrete @ .02
= 160 sabins
Walls—7200 sq ft gypsum board @ .07
= 504 sabins
Ceiling—8000 sq ft gypsum board @ .07
= 560 sabins
1224 sabins

$$T = \frac{.05(160,000 \text{ cu ft})}{1224}$$
$$= 6.5 \text{ sec}$$

The text indicated that a reverberation time between 1.2 and 1.7 sec is recommended for a room this size—far less than 6.5 sec. Substituting acoustic tile for gypsum board on the ceiling, the total absorption units would change to 6264 sabins.

$$T = \frac{.05(160,000 \text{ cu ft})}{6264}$$
$$= 1.3 \text{ sec}$$

The addition of acoustic tile increases the absorption 5½ times and reduces the loudness by over 40 percent.

Acoustical treatment does not suck up sound. It only can prevent some of the sound striking a surface

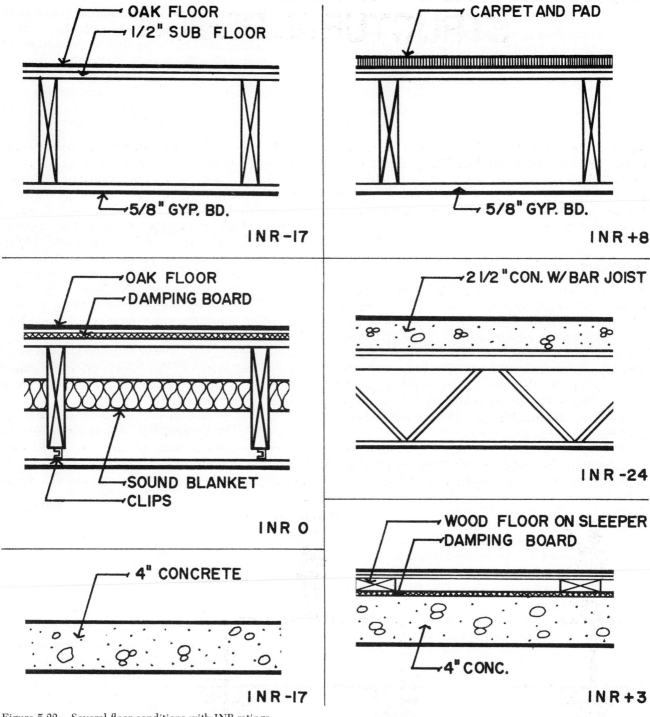

OAK FLOOR
1/2" SUB FLOOR

5/8" GYP. BD.

INR -17

CARPET AND PAD

5/8" GYP. BD.

INR +8

OAK FLOOR
DAMPING BOARD

SOUND BLANKET
CLIPS

INR 0

2 1/2" CON. W/ BAR JOIST

INR -24

4" CONCRETE

INR -17

WOOD FLOOR ON SLEEPER
DAMPING BOARD

4" CONC.

INR +3

Figure 5-22.   Several floor conditions with INR ratings.

from being reflected back into the room. This frequently is referred to as *sound attenuation*.

Another point to realize is that a good sound-absorption material does not necessarily reduce sound travel through walls (commonly the reverse is true). Sound-attenuating material has an indirect effect on sound transmission in that it can significantly reduce the loudness of reverberated sound.

SIX

STRUCTURAL DESIGN

Structural design is basically the selection of materials that support a building. They are like the skeleton that supports the body. Wood, steel, and concrete are used most often for structural support because of their strength, ease of fabrication, cost, and availability.

MECHANICS

A general pattern for choosing a structural design is first to analyze all forces that are assumed to act on a building and then to design a framing system with known structural properties that can adequately resist those forces. Force has both direction and magnitude, or a vector quality. Building structures involve only forces that are in static equilibrium. All external forces (loads) are counteracted by the resisting force of a structure (reaction), which causes a building to remain stationary.

The greatest force acting on a building is in a straight-down direction, a result of the weight of the building, the *dead load;* another great force is the weight of movable objects such as people and furniture, the *live load.* Other forces acting on a building include wind loads, seismic (earthquake) forces, and snow loads. Typically, live loads and dead loads are accumulated along horizontal members' called *beams,* which in turn are supported by vertical columns that are supported by footings and, finally, the earth. Structural design involves determining the loads on a building and using the properties of the materials to size the structural member.

To maintain equilibrium, each force must be resisted by an equal reaction (Figure 6-1). When a load on a beam is located a distance away from the supporting column, an additional force is introduced into the calculations. The force, called a *moment* (*M*), tends to cause the point of load to rotate about the column connection (Figure 6-2).

The magnitude of the moment is dependent upon the load (in pounds) and the distance from the load to the support (in feet). The units are in foot-pounds. For algebraic purposes, assume that forces tending to rotate about a point in a clockwise direc-

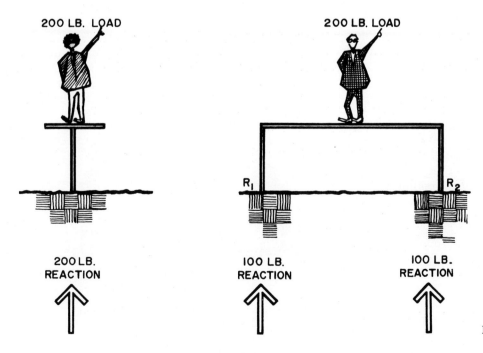

200 LB. LOAD

200 LB. LOAD

R₁   R₂

200 LB. REACTION

100 LB. REACTION

100 LB. REACTION

Figure 6-1. Forces and reactions.

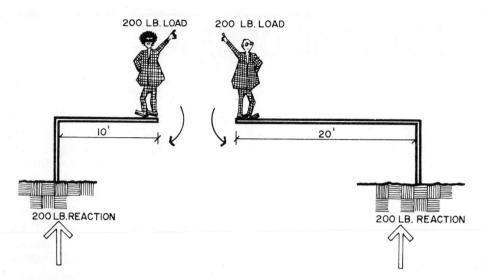

Figure 6-2. Moments.

tion are positive, while those rotating about a point in a counterclockwise direction are negative. Example (a) in Figure 6-2 produces a clockwise moment of +2000 ft-lb about point A. Example (b) produces a counterclockwise moment of −4000 ft-lb about point B. For a structure to maintain equilibrium, the algebraic sum of all moments must equal 0. The sum of all forces must also equal 0 (Figure 6-3).

For example, a 50-lb boy standing 12′ away from pivot point R will produce −600 ft-lb about point R. To resist this moment, the 150 lb man also must exert a moment of 600 ft-lb about point R. To do this, he must stand 4′ from point R. The equation would read:

$$\Sigma MR^* = -(12' \times 50 \text{ lb}) + (150 \text{ lb} \times D)$$
$$150D = 600 \text{ ft-lb}$$
$$D = 4'$$

In addition to a 600 ft-lb balancing moment, a 200-lb reaction (upward force) at point R must be exerted to counter the 200-lb load (150 lb + 50 lb).

The most common structural framing system is a beam supported by two columns. If the load along the beam is not equally distributed, the columns will carry different loads. It is necessary to solve the moments at both end conditions to determine their reactions (Figure 6-4):

$$\Sigma MR_1 = 4'(3000 \text{ lb}) + 10'(5000 \text{ lb}) - 13'R_2$$
$$13R_2 = 62,000 \text{ ft-lb}$$
$$R_2 = 4769 \text{ lb}$$

*The term ΣMR is read: the summation of moments about point R.

Note that in this example moments are all taken about point R_1. The 3000-lb load is 4′ away; the 5000-lb load is 10′ away; and the resisting force R_2 is 13′ from R_1. The 3000-lb and 5000-lb forces would, if they were allowed to rotate freely about point R_1, go in a clockwise direction and thus have plus signs. The resulting upward force of R_2 would rotate in a counterclockwise direction, and so the moment is negative:

$$\Sigma MR_2 = -3'(5000 \text{ lb}) - 9'(3000 \text{ lb}) + 13R_1$$
$$13R_1 = 42,000 \text{ ft-lb}$$
$$R_1 = 3231 \text{ lb}$$

The calculations can be checked by comparing the total load with the computed reactions. If the figures are equal, the design is in equilibrium. In the example above, downward loads of 3000 lb + 5000 lb are equal to upward reactions of 3231 lb + 4769 lb.

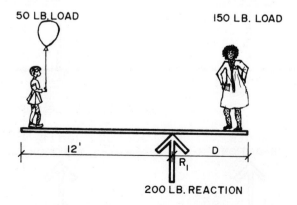

Figure 6-3. Equilibrium.

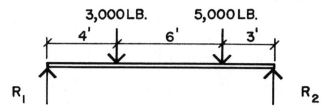

Figure 6-4.   Point loading.

The above example indicates point loadings on a beam. This is like the loads encountered when secondary beams rest on another beam. The other common loading condition involves uniformly distributed loads. These can be caused by floor decks that rest directly on a beam. A uniform load is treated as a concentration of the total load at a point in the center of the load. The diagram is better understood if it is redrawn with the uniform loads indicated as point loads (Figure 6-5):

$$\Sigma MR_1 = 3'(1200 \text{ lb}) + 12'(1000 \text{ lb}) - 16R_2$$
$$16R_2 = 15,600 \text{ ft-lb}$$
$$= 975 \text{ lb}$$
$$\Sigma MR_2 = 4'(1000 \text{ lb}) - 13'(1200 \text{ lb}) + 16R_2$$
$$= 1225 \text{ lb}$$

A check of the calculations prove they are correct.

$$975 + 1225 = 1200 + 1000$$

Example (Figure 6-6):

$$\Sigma MR_1 = 2'(500 \text{ lb}) + 12'(1000 \text{ lb}) - 16R_2$$
$$+ 22'(700 \text{ lb})$$
$$16R_2 = 1775 \text{ lb}$$
$$\Sigma MR_2 = 16R_1 - 14'(500 \text{ lb}) - 4'(1000 \text{ lb})$$
$$+ 6'(700 \text{ lb})$$
$$16R_1 = 425 \text{ lb}$$

The above example shows two point-loading conditions between columns and a third load canti-

levered past one of the supports. Study the diagram carefully to understand the reason for assigning the + and − signs.

Shear and Bending Moments

A beam with a uniformly distributed load is subject to three separate conditions which can cause it to fail. It is necessary to examine each condition with the beam that is selected to be sure that all are satisfied. (See Figure 6-7.)

1. *Vertical shear* is a downward force at or near the support that tends to cut or shear the beam off at the supports.
2. *Horizontal shear* causes a beam to fail by pulling the fibers apart parallel to the beam.
3. *Bending* is a force due to moments in the beam which tend to bend the beam past failure.

Shear (V)

Shear is dependent on the reactions at supports and the magnitude of the loads and their locations. A graphical indication of the shear force along a beam is called a shear diagram.

The reactions in Figure 6-8 were calculated to be 2735 lb at R_1 and 2565 lb at R_2. Drawing a shear diagram involves choosing a vertical scale for the load magnitudes and projecting the load directly down to the shear diagram. Shear must start and end at 0 to be in equilibrium with downward loads considered to be negative and reactions considered to be positive.

The procedure of drawing a shear diagram could be likened to walking along the beam from left to right and recording graphically any load or reaction that is encountered. The reaction at R_1 places +2735 lb above the 0 line, which continues at the same magnitude for 3' until the 1800-lb load. At this point the shear is reduced to +935 (2735 lb − 1800 lb), which carries along straight on the

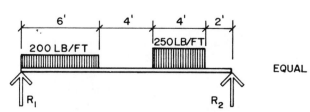

Figure 6-5.   A uniformly distributed load.

EQUAL

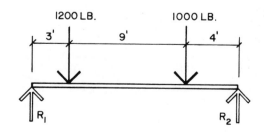

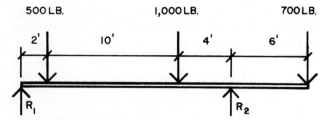

Figure 6-6.   Point loading with cantilever.

graph until the 2000-lb load. Subtracting 2000 lb from 935 lb places the shear at -1035 lb, which continues for 4' until the 1500-lb load. This further reduces the shear to -2565 lb, which continues until the end reaction of $+2565$ lb causes the diagram to close at 0. This diagram indicates that the greatest shearing force on the beam occurs along a 3' length from R_1, and its force is 2735 lb. (The + or − sign is ignored for this; thus only the larger number is of concern.) This figure will be used to check the chosen beam to determine if the design is adequate.

The shear diagram of a uniformly distributed load (Figure 6-9) differs in that the increasing load for every foot you "walk" along the beam causes the shear to decrease at a constant angle. An easy way to calculate the diagram is to determine the shear at the beginning of the uniform load, and again at the end of the load, and then connect the points. The reaction at R_1 of 1212 lb is located, but it is immediately subjected to a load of 200 lb/ft. A

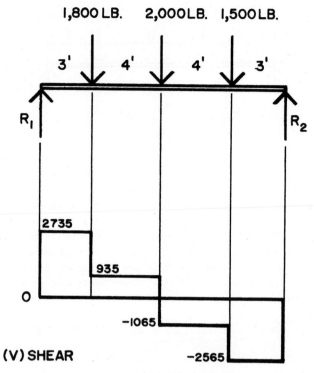

Figure 6-8.   Shear of a point loading condition.

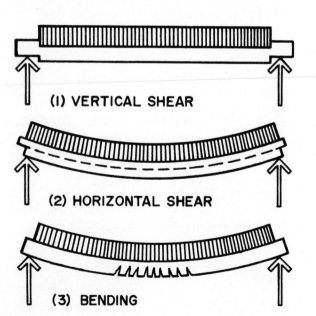

Figure 6-7.   Causes of beam failure.

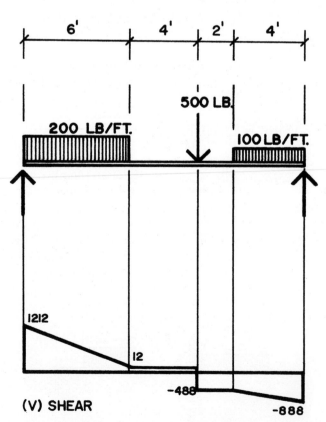

Figure 6-9.   Shear of a uniform load.

point 6′ to the right of R_1 reduces the shear by 1200 lb (6′ × 200 lb/ft), which is subtracted from 1212 lb. The completed diagram indicates that the maximum shear is 1212 lb at point R_1.

Bending Moments (M)

The force that tends to cause beam failure due to bending is determined by the algebraic sum of the moments acting on the beam. The moment at any point along a beam can be calculated by extending the shear diagram one step further. The unit of measure for shear is in pounds, while bending moments are given in pounds times feet, or foot-pounds.

The beam diagram (Figure 6-10) is calculated to have reactions of 2500 lb at R_1 and 3500 lb at R_2. The resulting shear diagram starts out with the 2500-lb reaction at R_1, then drops down to +500 lb

4′ from R_1, due to the 2000-lb load, and further drops to −3500 lb at 12′ from R_1 because of the 4000-lb load. Finally it closes to 0 due to the reaction at R_2.

The moment diagram is drawn with the data determined from the shear diagram. Each point of change on the shear diagram is located on the moment diagram, and a proper horizontal scale in foot-pounds is chosen. The next step is to calculate the area between the shear diagram and the 0 shear line (hatched in on Figure 6-10). This is the same as taking the algebraic sum of the moments. From R_1 to the first point of change on the shear diagram 4′ out is a rectangle with 2500-lb magnitude horizontally and 4′ vertically which produces an area of +10,000 ft-lb. The moment is positive because the 2500-lb shear force is positive.

The next rectangle along the shear diagram is 4′ from R_1 to 12′ at a magnitude of 500 lb. The 8′ length and the +500-lb shear produces a positive moment of 4000 ft-lb. Since the moment has a plus sign, it is added to the moment of force at the beginning of the calculation (4000 ft-lb + 10,000 ft-lb = 14,000 ft-lb at a point on the beam 12′ from R_1).

Perhaps the most important point in shear and moment diagram calculations occurs when the shear is 0 because that point also yields the maximum moment on the beam. In the example, the shear diagram passes through 0 at a distance of 12′ from R_1. Thus, the maximum moment is 14,000 ft-lb. The next rectangle created by the shear diagram is 4′ long and −3500 lb in magnitude. The negative 14,000 ft-lb moment causes the moment diagram to close to 0 at R_2.

Most beams are uniform in cross section between supports. This means that the beam must be designed to meet the maximum conditions even though the shear and moment diagrams indicate the maximum occurs only along a short length. In the above example, the beam would have to withstand a 3500-lb shear force and a 14,000 ft-lb moment.

The moment diagram for a uniformly distributed load (Figure 6-11) is a curve because of the varying magnitude of the shear diagram. A simple way to calculate the moment is to divide the shear diagram into a rectangle and triangle and figure their area separately. The moment at a point 4′ right of R_1 is the area of the rectangle (1343 lb × 4′ = 5372 ft-lb) plus the area of the remaining triangle*

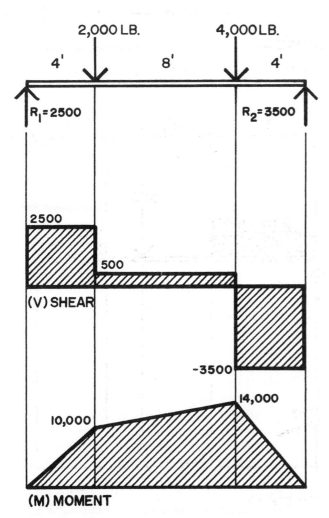

Figure 6-10.   Moment of a point loading condition.

* The area of a triangle is $\frac{bh}{2}$.

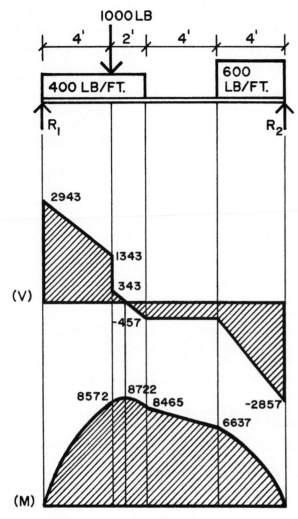

Figure 6-11. Moment of a uniform load.

Formulas for shear and moment and for some common beam conditions (Figure 6-12) are given in *The Manual of Steel Construction,* published by the American Institute of Steel Construction, Inc.

Framing

Structural framing generally consists of a rigid subflooring or roofing material that transmits its load to beams that rest on other beams or columns. The most common system for wood framing is plywood flooring resting on wood joists and then on beams or walls. Steel framing commonly includes steel decking with a concrete topping that rests on open-web steel joists or steel beams, which in turn are supported by major steel beams. A common concrete framing design is to pour a relatively thin slab $(2\frac{1}{2}''+)$ integrally with concrete beams.

The design of a framing system begins with the selection of materials. In many cases, the building type dictates the structural choice. Wood is the obvious choice for a residence, while it would probably be a poor selection for an office building in a downtown area with a high population density. Some factors determining materials selection are strength, weight, appearance, ease of fabrication, cost, available labor, and fire resistance.

Once the framing material has been selected, the load bearing on the structure must be determined. As mentioned, this is broken into two categories—live load and dead load.

Live loads are commonly assigned by local code according to the building occupancy and use. A residence commonly has a 60 lb/sq ft live load; a school assembly room has a 100 lb/sq ft load; and library book stacks must withstand live loading of 250 lb/sq ft. Obviously, these loading requirements are arbitrary for each particular spot in the room when movable objects are involved, but they generally prove adequate for structural calculations.

Dead-load calculations involve the load per square foot of all building materials being supported by the structure, including the weight of the structure itself. The ambiguity of this for the beginning designer is that it is necessary to estimate the weight of a structure before the structure has been determined. Dead loads, particularly in concrete, can be a very sizable percentage of the total load. The weight of some building materials are shown in Table 6-1.

A dead load is determined by cutting a cross section through the floor to add up the total load.

$\left(\dfrac{1600\text{ lb} \times 4'}{2} = 3200\text{ ft-lb}\right)$, which totals 8572 ft-lb.

The remaining area above the 0 shear line is a bit more difficult to calculate. The shear force past the 1000-lb point load on the beam is 343 lb, which is decreasing at a rate of 400 lb/ft. This means that the base of the triangle is approximately $\frac{7}{8}'$ or 0.875' long before it crosses the 0 shear line. A triangle 0.875' by 343 lb has a moment of 150 ft-lb. Added to the positive 8572 ft-lb moment, the maximum along the beam is 8722 ft-lb at a point approximately 4.875' right of R_1. A check by adding the negative moments will close the moment diagram at R_2 to less than 10 ft-lb of 0. The reason the moment does not exactly equal 0 is the approximate location of where the shear diagram crosses 0.

It should be noted that a proficiency in figuring moments is very necessary for structural design.

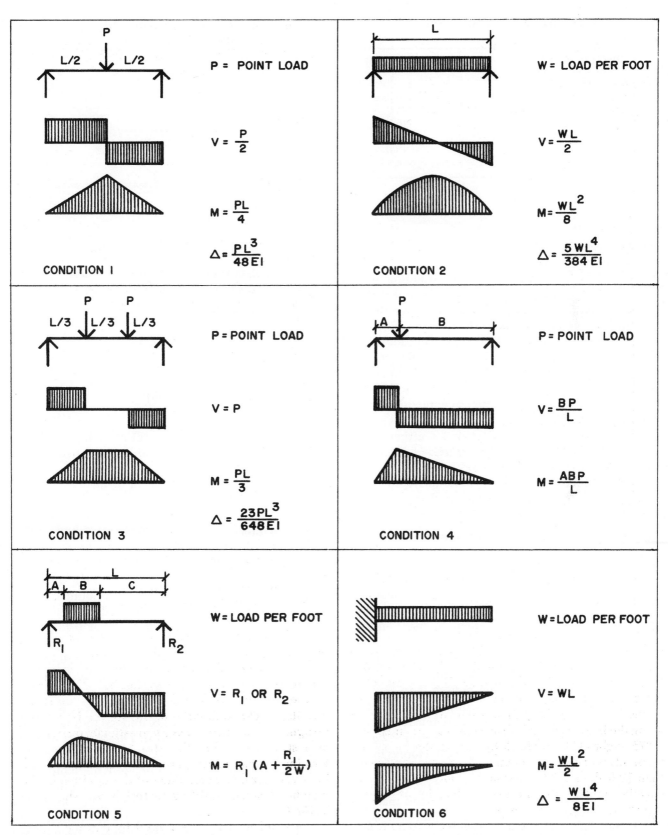

Figure 6-12. Beam conditions.

TABLE 6-1 WEIGHTS OF COMMON BUILDING
MATERIALS

BUILDING MATERIAL	WEIGHT
Structural steel	490 lb/cu ft
Structural concrete	150 lb/cu ft
Wood	40 lb/cu ft
Quarry tile flooring	10 lb/sq ft
Timber deck per inch of thickness	3 lb/sq ft
Suspended plaster	10 lb/sq ft
5-ply pitch-and-gravel roofing	6.5 lb/sq ft

Using the data in Table 6-1, a 6″ concrete slab (Figure 6-13) with a tile floor and a plaster ceiling suspended from the slab would have a dead-load weight of 95 lb/sq ft.

In effect, framing is a pattern of structural members designed to consolidate the loads so that they may efficiently be reacted against by walls or columns. A concrete slab with a dead load of 95 lb/sq ft and a live load of 100 lb/sq ft spanning 14′-0″ between two 20′-0″ beams would produce the following loading conditions: Every linear foot along the slab between beams A and B weighs 2730 lb (14 × 195 lb) with the combined live and dead loads. This load is divided equally between beams A and B. Thus, the beam-loading diagram for either beam would be a uniformly distributed load of 1365 lb/ft. (See Figure 6-14.) This same analysis would be used if the spanning material were wood joists, steel bar joists, or whatever. The two factors that do change would be the dead-load weight per square foot and the structural properties of the material.

Bending

A beam in static equilibrium—one that has balanced loads and reactions, has a resisting moment in the cross section of the beam equal to the bending moment.

Figure 6-15 shows a section of a loaded beam, the top portion of which is in compressive stress (pushing together), while the bottom is in tension (pulling apart). A horizontal section at a point in the beam where the compression and tension forces balance out to be 0 is referred to as the *neutral axis*. The sum of all tension and compression forces in the beam, called the *resisting moment*, is equal to the bending moment imposed on the beam. It is then necessary to select a beam with size and material properties adequate to resist the bending moment caused by the live and dead loads.

An extremely important formula resulting from the properties of resisting moments is *flexure:*

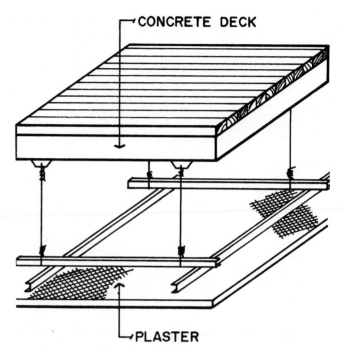

CONCRETE DECK

PLASTER

Figure 6-13.   A dead load on a floor.

$$S = \frac{M}{f}$$

where M = maximum moment in inch-pounds
f = maximum allowable fiber stress of material
S = section modulus of beam

This formula is for beams of one material, say wood or steel, not for reinforced concrete. The moment is dependent on exterior loads. One common error in plugging this into the formula is the failure to multiply the maximum moment by 12 to convert from foot-pounds to inch-pounds. *Fiber stress* is a property of the material measuring its maximum allowable fiber strength at the farthest point from the neutral axis. The units are given in pounds per square inch. A common value of f for wood is 1200 P.S.I., and for steel, 20,000 P.S.I.; but these vary greatly with the species of wood or strength of steel. The *section modulus, S*, is determined by rather complex understanding, the result of which can be found in *The Manual of Steel Construction* for steel and *Architectural Graphic Standards* for wood. It is dependent upon the cross-sectional shape and size of the beam, not the structural characteristics of the material. The unit of S is in inches to the third power (in.³). For example: The load in Figure 6-11 produced a maximum moment of 8722 ft-lb. Find the proper beam size in wood and steel to resist the load.

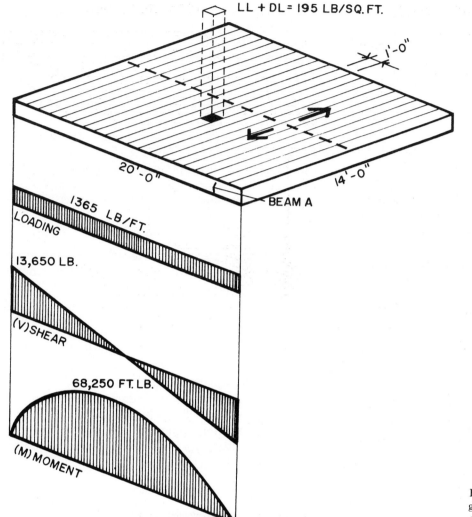

LL + DL = 195 LB/SQ. FT.

1'-0"

20'-0"

14'-0"

BEAM A

1365 LB/FT.

LOADING

13,650 LB.

(V) SHEAR

68,250 FT. LB.

(M) MOMENT

Figure 6-14. The beam loading diagram for a uniformly distributed load of 1365 lb/ft.

Wood*

$$S = \frac{M}{f}$$

(Multiply moment by 12 to convert to in. − lb.)

* Choose Douglas fir construction grade from *Architectural Graphic Standards* which has a fiber stress of 1500 P.S.I.

$$= \frac{8722 \times 12}{1500}$$

$$= 69.77 \text{ in.}^3$$

Checking *Architectural Graphic Standards*, a 3 × 14 wood beam has a section modulus of 79.73 in.³, which is slightly larger than the design requirements and thus adequate.

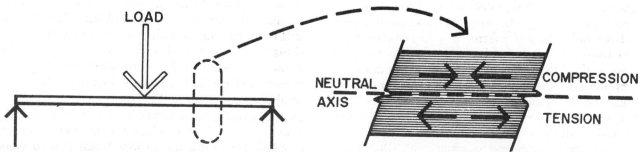

LOAD

NEUTRAL AXIS

COMPRESSION

TENSION

Figure 6-15. Bending.

Steel†

$$S = \frac{M}{f}$$

$$= \frac{8722 \times 12}{20,000}$$

$$= 5.23 \text{ in.}^3$$

Checking *The Manual of Steel Construction*, an M6 × 12 steel beam has a section modulus of 7.24 in.³ An M10 × 9 beam has a section modulus of 7.8 in.³ The letter in the beam indicates the rolled shape, in this case, miscellaneous (*M*). The first number in the beam designation is the height of the beam, and the second number is the weight in pounds per foot. Both beams will work, but the 10″ beam weighs 3 lb/ft less and therefore costs less.

The formula for finding the section modulus of a rectangular cross-section beam (Figure 6-16) is

$$S = \frac{bd^2}{6}$$

where b = width of beam
      d = depth of beam

Substituting a 3 × 14 beam into the formula,

$$S = \frac{3 \times 14^2}{6}$$

$$= 98 \text{ in.}^3$$

The reason for the discrepancy between the calculated figure of 98 in.³ and the 79.73 in.³ that was found in the table is that the actual wood-beam dimensions were used to determine the table.

$$S = \frac{2\frac{5}{8} \times 13\frac{1}{2}^2}{6}$$

$$= 79.73 \text{ in.}^3$$

† Choose A-7 steel which has a bending fiber stress of 20,000 P.S.I.

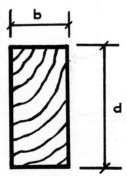

Figure 6-16. A rectangular beam.

A quantity developed from the section modulus is the *moment of inertia (I)*, which again is dependent on the physical size and shape of a cross-section through the beam rather than on its structural properties. The moment of inertia is taken about the neutral axis of the beam. In the steel manual, a figure is given for both the X-X axis and Y-Y axis for I and S (Figure 6-17).

If the beam is used in the normal way, with the flanges horizontal, the quantities for the X-X axis should be used. It is not necessary to calculate I for steel beams because they are given in the steel manual. Rectangular wood beams would use the formula

$$I = \frac{bd^3}{12}$$

In the formula, b and d are actual rather than nominal dimensions; I is given in units of in.⁴ The moment of inertia determines mainly the allowable deflection in a beam or slenderness in a column.

Modulus of elasticity defines the rate of deformation of a material as stress is applied to it. The quantity is shown by the letter E and is given in units of pounds per square inch. Since the factor measures the degree of stiffness of the material, it is commonly used to determine the deflection in a beam. The modulus of elasticity is not dependent upon the physical size of the beam but instead is determined by the material. The values of E are

Wood	1,760,000	P.S.I. (dependent on species)
Steel	29,000,000	P.S.I. (constant for structural steel)
Concrete	2,500,000	P.S.I. (dependent on the compressive strength of the concrete)

WOOD CONSTRUCTION

The properties of wood are discussed in Chapter 4. Two common softwood species used as structural materials are Douglas fir and southern pine. Within the species, the wood is graded according to structural properties and physical appearance. The modulus of elasticity of both southern pine and Douglas fir is 1,760,000 P.S.I., but the fiber stress ranges from 3000 P.S.I. to 1200 P.S.I.

Beams

The steps commonly used to design wood beams are

1. Determine the maximum shear and moment on the beam.

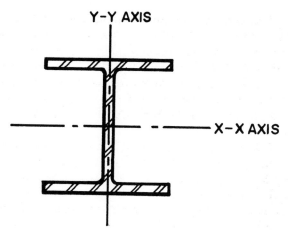

Figure 6-17. A steel section.

2. Choose the species and grade of lumber.
3. Calculate the minimum allowable section modulus with the formula $S = M/f$. Once this has been figured, a beam size with a slightly larger section modulus should be selected. Many choices will work but the most efficient beams usually have a width (b) from one-half to one-third their depth (d) when used in the formula $S = bd^2/6$.
4. Once a beam has been selected, it should be checked for horizontal shear. A strong failure possibility exists for a wood beam when the parallel fibers slide past each other. See example (c) in Figure 6-7.

   The section in Figure 6-15 indicates that the greatest tendency for horizontal shear occurs along the neutral axis. A direct relationship exists between the vertical shear calculated in the shear diagram and horizontal shear. Horizontal shear is $3/2$ times vertical shear for wood.

   To determine the amount of unit vertical shear in a rectangular beam, divide the maximum shear by the area of the beam: V/bd. The formula is then extended for horizontal shear: $H = 3V/2bd$. The maximum allowable horizontal shear is given for each grade of lumber in *Architectural Graphic Standards*, ranging between 165 P.S.I. and 95 P.S.I. for the two common wood species (the typical is 120 P.S.I.). If the calculated horizontal shear exceeds the maximum allowable, a larger beam must be selected.
5. If the beam selected in step 3 has adequate resistance to horizontal shear in step 4, it then must be checked for deflection. Deflection (Δ) is the "sag" produced when the design-loading conditions are imposed on a beam. Deflection is

measured in inches from the neutral position of the beam to its final deflected point when loaded.

Building codes have generally established the maximum allowable deflection in a beam to be the length (l) of span in inches divided by 360 for plaster. Certain conditions permit an increased deflection of $1/240$, but $1/360$ is more common.

Beam deflection is dependent upon the beam condition, the load, the length of span, the modulus of elasticity of the beam material, and the moment of inertia of the beam section. Figure 6-12 gives deflection formulas for several common beam conditions. If the deflection of the beam exceeds $1/360$, a beam with a larger moment of inertia should be selected.

As an example, design beam B using Douglas fir select structural lumber with a total load of 50 lb/sq ft. The allowable bending fiber (f) for the wood selected is 1900 P.S.I. (Table 6-2). The allowable horizontal shear (H) for the wood selected is 120 P.S.I. (See Figure 6-18.) Here are the steps you would follow:

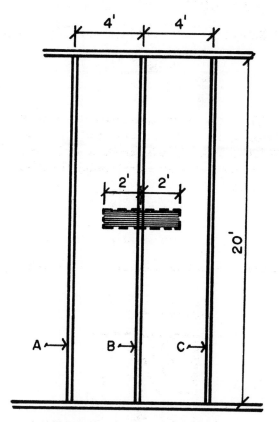

LIVE LOAD = 40 LB./SQ. FT.
DEAD LOAD = 10 LB./SQ. FT.

Figure 6-18. Loading conditions.

TABLE 6-2 LUMBER GRADES AND ALLOWABLE STRESSES*

ALLOWABLE UNIT STRESSES FOR STRESS GRADE LUMBER

Species & Commercial Grade	AVAILABLE FOR FOLLOWING USES					ALLOWABLE UNIT STRESSES IN PSI				
	Light Framing	Joists & Planks	Beams & Stringers	Posts & Timbers	Decking	Extreme Fiber in Bending f	Horizontal Shear H	Compression Perpendicular to Grain C⊥	Compression Parallel to Grain C	Modulus of Elasticity E
Cedar, Western Red										
Select Dex					X	900		240		1,100,000
Commercial Dex					X	700		240		,,
Douglas Fir, Coast Reg'n										
Dense Select Structural	X		X			2050	120	455	1500	1,760,000
Select Structural	X		X			1900	120	415	1400	,,
1750f Industrial	X					1750	120	415	1400	,,
1500f Industrial	X					1500	120	390	1200	,,
1200f Industrial	X					1200	95	390	1000	,,
Dense Construction		X	X			1750	120	455	1400	,,
Construction		X	X			1500	120	390	1200	,,
Standard		X				1200	95	390	1000	,,
Dense Select Structural		X				2050	120	455	1650	,,
Select Structural		X				1900	120	415	1500	,,
Dense Construction				X		1500	120	455	1400	,,
Construction				X		1200	120	390	1200	,,
Select Dex					X	1500		390		,,
Commercial Dex					X	1200		390		,,
Douglas Fir										
Dense Select Structural	X		X			2050	120	455	1500	1,760,000
Dense Select Structural MC 15	X					2300	125	455	1700	,,
Select Structural	**X**		**X**			**1900**	**120**	**415**	**1400**	,,
Select Structural MC 15	X					2100	125	415	1550	,,
1500f Industrial	X					1500	120	390	1200	,,
1500f Industrial MC 15	X					1750	125	390	1400	,,
1200f Industrial	X					1200	95	390	1000	,,
1200f Industrial MC 15	X					1500	110	390	1200	,,
Dense Select Structural		X				2050	120	455	1650	,,
Dense Select Structural MC 15		X				2300	125	455	1850	,,
Select Structural		X				1900	120	415	1500	,,
Select Structural MC 15		X				2100	125	415	1650	,,
Dense Construction		X				1750	120	455	1400	,,
Dense Construction MC 15		X				2050	125	455	1600	,,
Construction		X				1500	120	390	1200	,,
Construction MC 15		X				1750	125	390	1400	,,
Standard		X				1200	95	390	1000	,,
Standard MC 15		X				1500	110	390	1200	,,
Dense Construction			X			1750	120	455	1200	,,
Construction—Decking			X			1500	120	390	1000	,,
Dense Select Structural				X		1900	120	455	1650	,,
Select Structural				X		1750	120	415	1500	,,
Dense Construction				X		1500	120	455	1400	,,
Construction—Decking				X		1200	120	390	1200	,,

* Joseph A. Wilkes, AIA; Wilkes and Faulkner; Washington, D. C. *Architectural Graphic Standards,* Reser and Ferman, Wiley Publishing Company, N. Y.

TABLE 6-2   (continued)

	ALLOWABLE UNIT STRESS GRADE LUMBER									
	AVAILABLE FOR USES					ALLOWABLE UNIT STRESSES IN PSI				
Species & Commercial Grade	Light Framing	Joists & Planks	Beams & Stringers	Posts & Timbers	Decking	Extreme Fiber in Bending f	Horizontal Shear H	Compression Perpendicular to Grain C⊥	Compression Parallel to Grain C	Modulus of Elasticity E
Hemlock, Eastern										
Select Structural	X		X			1300	85	360		1,210,000
Prime Structural		X				1200	60	360		,,
Common Structural		X				1100	60	360		,,
Utility Structural		X				950	60	360		,,
Select Structural				X				360		,,
Fir, White										
Selected Decking					X	1100		365		1,210,000
Commercial Decking					X	850		365		,,
Hemlock, West Coast										
Select Structural	X					1600	100	365		1,540,000
1500f Industrial	X					1500	100	365		,,
1200f Industrial	X					1200	80	365	1900	,,
Select Structural		X				1600	100	365	1200	,,
Construction		X				1500	100	365	1100	,,
Standard		X				1200	80	365	1000	,,
Construction			X			1500	100	365	1000	,,
Construction				X		1200	100	365	1100	,,
Select Dex					X	1300		365		,,
Commercial Dex					X	1000		365		,,
Hemlock, Western										
Select Structural	X					1600	100	365	1100	1,540,000
Select Structural MC 15	X					1800	105	365	1200	,,
1500f Industrial	X					1500	100	365	1000	,,
1500f Industrial MC 15	X					1650	105	365	1150	,,
1200f Industrial	X					1200	80	365	900	,,

1. Beam B will carry half the load between span A–B and half the load between span B–C. This means every linear foot along beam B will support 4 sq ft of floor surface (4 sq ft × 50 lb = 200 lb per linear ft). Figure 6-12 (condition 2) indicates that the maximum moment formula is

$$M = \frac{wl^2}{8}$$

$$M = \frac{200 \text{ lb } (20')^2}{8}$$

$$= 10,000 \text{ ft-lb, or } 120,000 \text{ in.-lb}$$

The shear formula is

$$V = \frac{wl}{2}$$

$$V = \frac{200 \text{ lb } (20')}{2}$$

$$= 2000 \text{ lb}$$

2. The lumber grade was stated as a condition in the problem.
3. Determine the section modulus:

$$S = \frac{M}{f}$$

$$= \frac{120,000}{1900}$$

$$= 63.16 \text{ in.}^3$$

Checking this figure against the section modulus of several beams, the following will work:

3 × 14	S = 79.73 in.³	I = 538.21 in.⁴
4 × 12	S = 79.90 in.³	I = 459.42 in.⁴
6 × 10	S = 82.73 in.³	I = 392.96 in.⁴
6 × 12	S = 121.23 in.³	I = 697.06 in.⁴

Try a 4 × 12 because it is closest to the one-third to one-half ratio of b to d.

4. Check the beam choice for horizontal shear:

$$H = \frac{3V}{2bd}$$

$$= \frac{3(2000)}{2(3.5 \times 11.5)}$$

$$= 74 \text{ P.S.I.}$$

Douglas fir select structural has an allowable horizontal shear of 120 P.S.I., and so the beam will work.

5. Check the beam choice for deflection: Figure 6-12 (condition 2) indicates the formula for deflection is

$$\Delta = \frac{5Wl^3}{348 \, EI}$$

where W = 4000 ft-lb
E = 1,760,000 P.S.I., Douglas fir
l = 20', or 240"
I = 459.42 in.⁴ (for a 4" × 12" timber)

$$\Delta = \frac{5 \times 4000(240)^3}{384 \times 1,760,000 \times 459.42}$$

$$\Delta = .89 \text{ in.}$$

Checking against the code, maximum = $l/360$

$$\frac{20 \times 12}{360} = .66 \text{ in.}$$

The deflection in the beam is greater than is allowable, and so a 4 × 12 beam will not work. The procedure is to choose a different beam with an acceptable section modulus (step 3) but a larger moment of inertia (I) so that the deflection is less. A 6 × 12 beam will obviously satisfy steps 3 and 4, and when its moment of inertia is plugged into the deflection formula, the maximum Δ equals 0.58 in. This is less than the 0.66

in. allowable, and so a 6 × 12 wood beam can be used for beam B.

Other general items must be checked in beam design. A beam with a relatively light load and long span should be checked for deflection. The only deciding factor for deflection, depending on the beam's size, is the moment of inertia. This formula, $I = bd^3/12$, is obviously much more dependent on the depth of the beam than on the width (since the depth is cubed). Therefore a beam with greater depth in proportion to its width will possibly be more efficient in satisfying deflection. A beam with a relatively short span or a large load located near the supports should be checked for horizontal shear. Vertical shear is seldom a problem, since wood is considerably stronger perpendicular to its fiber. Shear stress in a beam is dependent only on the size of the beam, $V = V/bd$; a beam with a larger cross-sectional area will proportionally reduce unit shear.

Joists and Rafters

Wood floor *joists* and roof *rafters* are simply small beams typically placed 12" or 16" on center. Instead of calculating each joist like a beam, a table has been established to determine the maximum span. The rafter and joist tables found in *Architectural Graphic Standards* require only two limiting factors to determine the span. One of the joist tables is first chosen by the live-load design covering conditions of 30, 40, 50, and 60 lb/sq ft. These tables take into account certain dead-load condi-

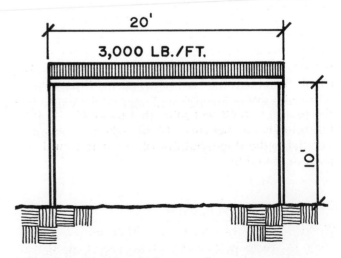

Figure 6-19. A uniform load.

tions such as the weight of the joists, flooring, and possibly plaster.

Once the table has been selected, it is necessary to know the limitations placed on timber design by local building codes. This is usually done by defining either the allowable deflection or by bending in the joist. If deflection is limited, the modulus of elasticity is the only indeterminate factor that must be substituted into the deflection formula for a uniform load to provide the maximum span. The range is from $E = 1,000,000$ P.S.I. to 1,600,000 P.S.I. The other case limits the bending fiber, therefore determining the section modulus when it is substituted into a formula with a known moment. The table ranges from an f of 900 to 1800 P.S.I. Once the live-load and code limitations have been determined, the maximum allowable span is given for 12″ and 16″ joist spacing.

Using Table 6-3 (example 1), find the joist size for a 17′-6″ span with a 60 lb/sq ft live-load floor which also supports a plaster ceiling. The local code limits design to $f = 1500$ P.S.I. in bending. Checking in the 60 lb/sq ft live-load table down the $f = 1500$ P.S.I. column, a 2 × 10 will span 17′-7″ with 12″ spacing, or a 2 × 12 will span 18′-5″ with 16″ spacing. It is a good idea to cross-check the selected joist with the other limiting factor in the table (in this case deflection) to be sure the properties of the lumber grade are not exceeded.

A southern pine #2 joist (example 2) has a maximum f of 1200 P.S.I.; if the code is limited by deflection to $E = 1,600,000$ P.S.I., a 2 × 12 joist at 16″ o.c. can span 17′-5″. Cross-checking the joists for bending where $f = 1200$ P.S.I., Table 6-3 indicates 16′-6″ is the maximum allowable span. The lower span would limit the joist.

The roof-rafter tables are laid out in the same way with one difference. There are two groups for roof covering, the difference being the pound per square foot dead load of the roofing materials. It should be noted that the tables figure rafter span in horizontal distance rather than the actual length of the roof. A 6 in 12 roof pitch that measures 12′-0″ horizontally is actually 13′-5″ when measured parallel to the slope, but the 12′-0″ span would be used in the table.

Columns

Wood columns can be made either from a solid piece of wood or from several pieces of wood laminated together. They are designed to react against the loads along the beam connected to the column. The force the column must be designed to resist is equal to the end reactions of the beam calculated by the summation of moments.

In addition to the requirement that the column must resist the downward force, it must also resist the tendency to buckle. Short columns are not subject to this failure, but buckling becomes a greater problem as the column becomes proportionally longer in relation to its least dimension. The ratio of the laterally unbraced length of the column in inches (l) to the least dimension of the column in inches (d) is called the *slenderness ratio*. By code, l/d cannot exceed 50.

A common formula for column design is

$$\frac{P}{A} = \frac{0.3E}{(l/d)^2}$$

where P = total load in pounds
A = cross-sectional area of column in square inches
E = modulus of elasticity of material in pounds per square inch
l = unbraced length of column in inches
d = least dimension of column in inches

The steps commonly used to design wood columns are

1. Determine the load on the column. This is the minimum acceptable value of P.
2. Select a species and grade of lumber.
3. Select a column size, generally square, and check it to be certain l/d does not exceed 50.
4. With the selected column size, substitute the figures into the column formula $P/A = 0.3E/(l/d)^2$. *Architectural Graphic Standards* gives the values for E and C (compression parallel to the grain). Substitute E, l, and d into the equation to determine P/A (the allowable compressive strength). Then choose one of the following alternatives: (1) If $0.3E/(l/d)^2$ does not exceed the value of C for the wood choice, the figure is multiplied by the cross-sectional area of the beam to determine the load the column will support; (2) if $0.3E/(l/d)^2$ exceeds the value of C, multiply the value of C by the cross-sectional area to determine the load the column will support.

As an example, design a column 10′ long capable of supporting 30,000 lbs using Douglas fir dense construction. $E = 1,760,000$; $C = 1200$.

TABLE 6-3 WOOD JOIST SIZES—60 LB LIVE LOAD*

FLOOR JOISTS   LIVE LOAD = 60 POUNDS PER SQUARE FOOT

MAXIMUM ALLOWABLE LENGTHS "L" BETWEEN SUPPORTS

From building code or other authority determine the allowable modulus of elasticity "E" (if span is to be limited by deflection) or the allowable extreme fiber stress in bending "f" (if span is to be determined by bending) for the species and grade of lumber used. Refer to the column below with corresponding value to determine the safe span for size and spacing of rafter and roof joist desired. Check span selected for deflection with spans for bending to see it does not exceed length permitted for bending stress "f" of material used.

Size (Nominal) in Inches	Spacing (C to C) in Inches	E= / f=	Span "L" Limited by Deflection								Span "L" Determined by Bending														
			1,000,000		1,200,000		1,400,000		1,600,000		900		1,000		1,100		1,200		1,300		1,400		1,500	
			Ft	In	Ft	In	Ft	In	Ft	In	Ft	In	Ft	In	Ft	In	Ft	In	Ft	In	Ft	In	Ft	In
2 × 6	12	L=	8-	1	8-	7	9-	1	9-	6	8-	2	8-	7	9-	0	9-	5	9-	9	10-	2	10-	6
		H=		45		49		52		54		46		49		51		54		56		59		61
	16	L=	7-	4	7-	10	8-	3	8-	7	7-	1	7-	6	7-	10	8-	2	8-	6	8-	10	9-	2
		H=		54		58		61		64		52		55		58		61		64		66		69
2 × 8	12	L=	10-	9	11-	5	12-	0	12-	7	10-	10	11-	5	11-	11	12-	6	13-	0	13-	6	13-	11
		H=		46		49		52		55		46		49		52		54		57		59		61
	16	L=	9-	9	10-	5	11-	0	11-	5	9-	5	9-	11	10-	5	10-	10	11-	4	11-	9	12-	2
		H=		54		58		62		65		52		55		58		61		64		67		69
2 × 10	12	L=	13-	6	14-	5	15-	2	15-	10	13-	7	14-	4	15-	0	15-	8	16-	4	17-	0	17-	7
		H=		46		49		52		55		46		49		52		54		57		59		62
	16	L=	12-	4	13-	2	13-	10	14-	6	11-	10	12-	6	13-	1	13-	8	14-	3	14-	9	15-	4
		H=		55		59		62		65		52		55		58		61		64		67		70
2 × 12	12	L=	16-	4	17-	4	18-	3	19-	1	16-	4	17-	3	18-	1	18-	11	19-	8	20-	5	21-	2
		H=		47		50		53		55		47		50		52		55		57		60		62
	16	L=	14-	11	15-	10	16-	8	17-	5	14-	3	15-	1	15-	10	16-	6	17-	2	17-	10	18-	5
		H=		55		59		62		66		52		56		59		62		65		67		70
2 × 14	12	L=	19-	1	20-	3	21-	4	22-	4	19-	1	20-	2	21-	2	22-	1	23-	0	23-	10	24-	8
		H=		47		50		53		56		47		50		53		55		58		60		62
	16	L=	17-	6	18-	7	19-	6	20-	5	16-	9	17-	7	18-	6	19-	3	20-	1	20-	10	21-	2
		H=		55		59		62		66		53		56		59		62		65		68		70

NOTES: (For span length limited by deflection):
1. Maximum allowable deflection = l_{360} of the span length.
2. Modulus of elasticity as noted for "E".
3. Dead load:
   A. Weight of joist.
   B. Double thickness of flooring (5 lbs).
   C. Weight of plaster ceiling ignored.
4. Weight of plaster ceiling was included in computing horizontal shear "H" induced by load.

NOTES: (For span length determined by bending):
1. Allowable stress in extreme fiber in bending as noted for "F".
2. Dead load:
   A. Weight of joist.
   B. Double thickness of flooring (5 lbs).
   C. Plastered ceiling (10 lbs).
3. Live load = 60 lbs per sq ft with plastered ceilings.
           = 70 lbs per sq ft with unplastered ceiling.
4. Total load was considered in computing horizontal shear "H" induced by load.
* Architectural Graphic Standards, Reser and Ferman, Wiley Publishing Company, New York, 1900, p. 223.

1. $P = W/2 = 60,000/2 = 30,000$ lb.
2. The species and grade of lumber is given in the problem.
3. Select a 6 × 6 column, checking l/d. 10′ × 12″/5.5 × 22. Since this is less than 50, it is acceptable for the slenderness ratio.
4. Substitute the figures into $P/A \times 0.3E/(l/d)^2$

$$\frac{P}{A} = \frac{0.3(1,760,000)}{(10 \times 12/5.5)^2}$$

$$= 1110 \text{ P.S.I.}$$

This is less than the 1200 P.S.I. value of C for Douglas fir dense construction (follow condition 1 in the text). $1110(5.5 \times 5.5) = 33,577$ lb. The design requirement was for 30,000 lb, and so a 6 × 6 column works.

The column-design formula has been further abbreviated in *Architectural Graphic Standards*. By substituting the values for the cross-sectional area, the length of the column, and the least dimension: $Y = A\ 0.3/(l/d)^2$. Values for Y are given for common column sizes for 6′ to 14′. The only value necessary for the determination of a column-bearing capacity is to select a wood species to obtain its modulus of elasticity. The formula is $P = YE$.

For example, determine the axial load capacity of a 10 × 10 southern pine column 13′-0″ high. For southern pine, $E = 1,760,000$ P.S.I. The value of Y for a 10 × 10 column 13′-0″ high is 0.101.

$$\begin{aligned} P &= YE \\ &= 0.101 \times 1,760,000 \\ &= 177,760 \text{ lb} \end{aligned}$$

Laminated Products

Laminated beams, columns, and arches have a major advantage over solid timber—their quality can be controlled. Natural imperfections can be "worked around" when lumber is being cut into relatively small cross-sectional areas and lengths, but a beam spanning 60′ requiring a depth of 40″ seldom could be found in nature. Laminated beams are typically built up from 1″ and 2″ members that, when glued together, have properties for f, H, C, and E similar to solid wood. The glue joint is sufficiently stronger in horizontal shear than the wood fiber, and so beam tolerances may be designed according to the properties of the wood. Much of the data needed for design can be found in the manufacturers' literature

in *Sweet's File*. This material commonly includes spanning tables for typical loads, along with the engineering properties of the product. Most manufacturers are flexible enough in their fabrication to make custom sizes and shapes.

Timber Deck

One possible treatment of a roof supported by wood beams is to use a roof deck made of tongue-and-groove lumber. It is possible to eliminate the ceiling with this treatment and finish the exposed underside of the deck. Timber decking is commonly available in nominal thicknesses of 2″, 3″, 4″, and 5″ and in widths ranging to 10″. Manufacturers' data in *Sweet's File* should be consulted for the allowable span of the deck. Just as in the joist tables, the span is either limited by deflection (E) or bending (f). Plaster ceilings are seldom used in conjunction with timber deck, and so the deflection limitation of $^1/_{360}$ is commonly dropped to $^1/_{240}$. It is possible to span lengths of 20′ with 5″ timber deck.

STEEL CONSTRUCTION

Steel is rolled into many structural shapes and is available in a variety of strengths to meet the requirements of frame construction. Steel offers the advantages of being considerably stronger for its weight than other materials and of being easily connected at the job site with bolts or welds.

Beams

The principal shapes rolled for structural beams are wide flange (W), American Standard (S),* and miscellaneous shapes (M). Standards have been established so that most steel companies can supply the shapes shown in the *Manual of Steel Construction*, published by the American Institute of Steel Construction, Inc. (AISC). References to properties of steel and tables will be found in this manual. Steel beams are given a three-numeral designation to indicate their shape, height in inches, and weight in pounds per foot. An S15 × 50 beam is 15″ high, rolled into an American Standard shape, and weighs 50 lb/ft. A steel beam (Figure 6-20) has two parts—the web (a) and the flange (b). The size of each is given in the AISC manual under the particular beam size.

The nomenclature used in steel design is quite similar to wood design. The minimum yield point

---

* This shape previously was called an *I beam*.

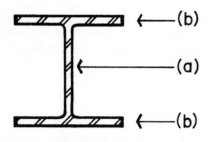

WIDE FLANGE BEAM

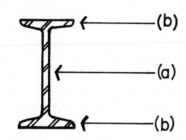

AMERICAN STANDARD BEAM

Figure 6-20.   A steel beam.

for the particular steel (F_y) is measured in P.S.I. and ranges from a low of 32,000 for A373 to a high of 50,000 for high-strength steels. A common structural steel is A36, which has an F_y of 36,000 P.S.I. The AISC manual allows certain percentages of the yield point for various conditions steel encounters. For A36, tension (f_t) = 0.60 F_y, or 22,000 P.S.I.; shear (F_v) = 0.40 F_y, or 14,500 P.S.I.; and bending (F_b) = 0.66 F_y, or 24,000 P.S.I. The last figure for bending corresponds to the bending fiber for wood (but for wood the figure is around 1200 P.S.I.). The modulus of elasticity (E) remains at a constant 29,000,000 P.S.I. for the various strengths of steel.

The steps commonly used to design steel beams are as follows

1. Determine the maximum shear and moment on the beam.
2. Choose the strength of steel for the design.
3. Calculate the minimum allowable section modulus with the formula $S = M/f$. Once this has been figured, consult the AISC manual for a section modulus slightly larger. The value for S should be taken about the X-X axis.

    Several beams will meet the requirement, but two points are generally considered: (1) If clearance under the beam for duct work or

ceilings is critical, a shallow beam might be chosen; and (2) steel is priced according to weight. Thus, the beam having the lightest weight per foot is most economical. These two points are generally opposite—the lightest beam is typically also the deepest.

4. Once the beam has been selected, it should be checked for shear. As with wood, steel is critical in horizontal shear rather than vertical shear. Unlike wood, steel has the same horizontal resistance to shear as for vertical shear.

    It is assumed that only the web of a steel beam will resist the horizontal shear imposed on the beam by the loads. The unit shear limits for structural steels range from 13,000 to 20,000 P.S.I., with A36 having an allowable shear stress of 14,500 P.S.I. The check for shear then becomes a matter of dividing the maximum shear in the beam by the area of the web of the beam. If it exceeds the allowable F_v of the steel, it will fail. The obvious step then is to select a different beam with a greater web cross-sectional area. The formula for maximum allowable shear is

$$f_v = V/dt$$

where V = maximum shear
d = total depth of beam
t = thickness of web

5. If the beam selected in step 3 has adequate resistance to the horizontal shear in step 4, it must then be checked for deflection. The deflection formulas given in Figure 6-12 should be used with the value of E = 29,000,000 P.S.I. and the value of I obtained from the AISC manual for the beam selected. (I should be about the X-X axis.) The amount of deflection in inches should not exceed the maximum code limitations of $^1/_{360}$. If the deflection in the beam exceeds the maximum, a beam with a large moment of inertia should be selected.

For example, design a beam using A36 steel. The total load on beam A is a load of 60,000 lb from beam B, which is equally distributed between beams A and C. (See Figure 6-21.) Here are the steps to follow in designing the beam:

1. The load of beam A is 30,000 lb, halfway between supports. Checking Figure 6-12, condition 1, the formula for maximum shear is

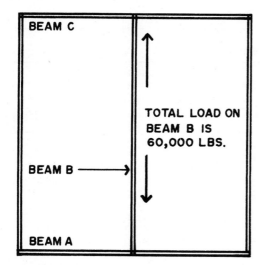

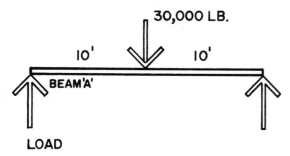

PLAN

LOAD

Figure 6-21. Steel loading conditions.

$$V = \frac{P}{2}$$

$$= \frac{30,000}{2}$$

$$= 15,000 \text{ lb}$$

Maximum moment is

$$M = \frac{PL}{4}$$

$$= \frac{30,000 \times 20}{4}$$

$$= 150,000 \text{ ft-lb, or } 1,800,000 \text{ in.-lb}$$

2. The strength of steel was stated in the problem as A36.

3. Determine the section modulus:

$$S = \frac{M}{f}$$

$$= \frac{1,800,000}{24,000}$$

$$= 75 \text{ in.}^3$$

Checking this figure against the section modulus in the AISC manual, the following beams will work:

W12 × 58	$S = 78.1 \text{ in.}^3$	$I = 476 \text{ in.}^4$
W14 × 53	$S = 77.8 \text{ in.}^3$	$I = 542 \text{ in.}^4$
W16 × 50	$S = 80.8 \text{ in.}^3$	$I = 657 \text{ in.}^4$
W18 × 45	$S = 79 \text{ in.}^3$	$I = 706 \text{ in.}^4$

A shortcut in selecting the beam is to consult the elastic section modulus table in the AISC manual. This table lists beams according to increasing values of I; the most economical beams in each group appear in bold type.

No mention is made of beam depth in the problem. Therefore, select the W18 × 45, the lightest per foot with the greatest moment of inertia and therefore the least deflection. (See Table 6-4, example 1.)

4. Check the beam choice for horizontal shear:

$$f_v = \frac{V}{dt}$$

where $d = 18$ in.
  $t = 0.335$ in.

$$f_v = \frac{15,000}{18 \times 0.335}$$

$$= 2487 \text{ P.S.I.}$$

The acceptable shear for A36 steel is 14,500 P.S.I., which far exceeds the calculated shear; and so the beam will work.

5. Check the beam choice for deflection. Figure 6-12, condition 1, indicates that the formula for deflection is

$$\Delta = \frac{Pl^3}{48\,EI}$$

where $W = 30,000$ lb
  $l = 240''$
  $E = 29,000,000$ P.S.I.
  $I = 706 \text{ in.}^4$, for a W18 × 45 beam

$$\Delta = \frac{30,000(240)^3}{48 \times 29,000,000 \times 706}$$
$$= 0.42 \text{ in.}$$

The allowable deflection is $l/360 = \dfrac{240}{360} = 0.66$

in. The calculated deflection is less than the allowable, and so the beam is acceptable for deflection.

TABLE 6-4 ELASTIC SECTION MODULUS*

W SHAPES
PROPERTIES FOR DESIGNING

			FLANGE		Web Thickness t_w	ELASTIC PROPERTIES					
						Axis X-X			Axis Y-Y		
	Area A	Depth d	Width b_f	Thickness t_f		I	S	r	I	S	r
DESIGNATION	In.²	In.	In.	In.	In.	In.⁴	In.³	In.	In.⁴	In.³	In.
W18 × 114	33.5	18.48	11.833	0.991	0.595	2040	220	7.79	274	46.3	2.86
× 105	30.9	18.32	11.792	0.911	0.554	1850	202	7.75	249	42.3	2.84
× 96	28.2	18.16	11.750	0.831	0.512	1680	185	7.70	225	38.3	2.82
W18 × 85	25.0	18.32	8.838	0.911	0.526	1440	157	7.57	105	23.8	2.05
× 77	22.7	18.16	8.787	0.831	0.475	1290	142	7.54	94.1	21.4	2.04
× 70	20.6	18.00	8.750	0.751	0.438	1160	129	7.50	84.0	19.2	2.02
× 64	18.9	17.87	8.715	0.686	0.403	1050	118	7.46	75.8	17.4	2.00
W18 × 60	17.7	18.25	7.558	0.695	0.416	986	108	7.47	50.1	13.3	1.68
① × 55	16.2	18.12	7.532	0.630	0.390	891	98.4	7.42	45.0	11.9	1.67
× 50	14.7	18.00	7.500	0.570	0.358	802	89.1	7.38	40.2	10.7	1.65
→ × 45	13.2	17.86	7.477	0.499	(0.335)	(706)	(79.0)	7.30	34.8	9.32	1.62
W18 × 40	11.8	17.90	6.018	0.524	0.316	612	68.4	7.21	19.1	6.34	1.27
× 35	10.3	17.71	6.000	0.429	0.298	513	57.9	7.05	15.5	5.16	1.23
W16 × 96	28.2	16.32	11.533	0.875	0.535	1360	166	6.93	224	38.8	2.82
× 88	25.9	16.16	11.502	0.795	0.504	1220	151	6.87	202	35.1	2.79
W16 × 78	23.0	16.32	8.586	0.875	0.529	1050	128	6.75	92.5	21.6	2.01
× 71	20.9	16.16	8.543	0.795	0.486	941	116	6.71	82.8	19.4	1.99
× 64	18.8	16.00	8.500	0.715	0.443	836	104	6.66	73.3	17.3	1.97
× 58	17.1	15.86	8.464	0.645	0.407	748	94.4	6.62	65.3	15.4	1.96
W16 × 50	14.7	16.25	7.073	0.628	0.380	657	80.8	6.68	37.1	10.5	1.59
② × 45	13.3	16.12	7.039	0.563	0.346	584	72.5	6.64	32.8	9.32	1.57
× 40	11.8	16.00	7.000	0.503	0.307	517	64.6	6.62	28.8	8.23	1.56
→ × 36	(10.6)	15.85	6.992	0.428	0.299	447	56.5	(6.50)	24.4	6.99	(1.52)
W16 × 31	9.13	15.84	5.525	0.442	0.275	374	47.2	6.40	12.5	4.51	1.17
× 26	7.67	15.65	5.500	0.345	0.250	300	38.3	6.25	9.59	3.49	1.12

* Manual of Steel Construction, American Institute of Steel Construction, Inc., New York, 7th edition, p. 1-32.

A buckling effect similar to that in a column could occur in a beam if the top flange member is not adequately supported. This type of lateral support can come from a floor deck that is attached to the top flange in which the unbraced length is zero; or from cross-beam supports, in which case the unbraced length is the distance between supports. The lateral support should be checked if a length along the beam is unbraced. To do this, consult the table in the AISC manual ("Allowable Moments in Beams") for A36 steel and shown here in Figure 6-22. First, compute the maximum moment in kip-feet. (A kip is equal to 1000 lb.) Next, enter the table with the moment along the left side and the unbraced length along the bottom. Travel horizontally along the moment line and vertically

with the unbraced length until they intersect. Any beam above and to the right of this point will work. If the first beam encountered is a dashed line, it will be the least acceptable in depth but not the most economical in weight. Keep reading to the right until the first solid line is intersected: This is the lightest acceptable beam.

Using Figure 6-22, check to see if the W18 × 45 beam selected in the problem will be acceptable with the unbraced length of 10'. Follow these steps:

1. The moment was calculated to be 150,000 ft-lb, which is 150 ft-kip.
2. Entering the table at 150 ft-kip and reading up, then over, and at an unbraced length of 10' and

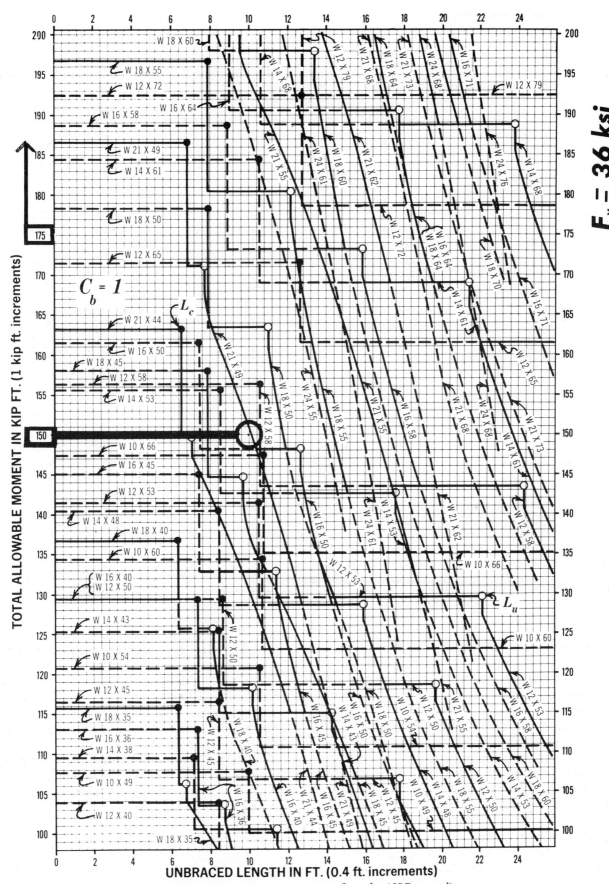

Figure 6-22. Allowable Moments in Beams (Reproduced with permission from the AISC manual).

reading up, the points intersect at point 1 in Figure 6-22. Reading to the right and above the 150 ft-kip line, the first line encountered is the solid W21 × 49 beam. Since it is solid, it is the lightest choice.

If 21 in. is too deep for the beam choice, read further along the 150 ft-kip line, which then intersects a W12 × 58 beam followed by a W18 × 50. The W18 × 50 beam is 3″ smaller and only 1 lb/ft heavier.

It should be noted that the first beam chosen, a W18 × 45, falls short of being acceptable when checked in the table. The W18 × 45 will only withstand a 150 ft-kip moment with an unbraced length of 8′. The W21 × 49 beam should be re-checked again for shear and deflection. It has larger values for I and for the thickness of the web, and so both will be acceptable.

A majority of the beam conditions encountered have a floor deck attached to the upper flange, which makes the unbraced length of the beam equal zero. A shortcut to beam calculations then becomes choosing the first beam above the calculated moment along the left side of the table.

For example, a uniformly distributed load along a beam that is adequately braced is calculated to have a maximum moment of 175 ft-kip. Select the appropriate beam in A36 steel.

Checking the table in Figure 6-22, the first beam above 175 ft-kip, point 2, is a W18 × 50. Since this choice and the next, a W14 × 61, are both dotted, the most economical choice is a W21 × 49. Even though it will withstand a maximum moment of over 186 ft-kip, it is the lightest acceptable choice. This method of selection does not check shear and deflection, which should then be calculated.

Columns

A column is dependent upon three major points that determine its loadbearing capacity:

1. The compressive strength of the steel used (pounds per square inch)
2. The area of the column (square inches)
3. The slenderness ratio of the column

The slenderness ratio corresponds to l/d ratio in wood, but for steel it is the l/r ratio; l is the height of the column in inches, and r is the radius of gyration of the column in inches. The radius of gyration is a figure dependent on the size and shape of a cross section of the column. A value for r is given for both the X-X axis and the Y-Y axis in the AISC manual. Since a column generally can buckle in either direction, the smaller value for r is used. The most common choice for a column is a wide flange shape, as the more square shape of the column will bring the radius of gyration about each axis closer.

A further refinement of the slenderness ratio is necessary to compensate for the type of restraint at each end condition of the column. The common end conditions result in the factor of k equalling 1, and so the slenderness ratio $kl/r = l/r$.

The steps commonly used to design steel columns are

1. Determine the load on the column.
2. Select a trial column size to determine the loadbearing potential. Data for r and A also are available for pipes and tubes in the AISC manual.
3. Calculate the kl/r ratio with the l being the column height in inches and r being the least radius of gyration of the column selected. Assume that the conditions for k equal 1.
4. Once the l/r ratio has been determined, it should be located in the AISC table "Allowable Unit Stress for Columns" for the particular strength of steel. This table directly relates the slenderness ratio value to the allowable unit compression stress (F_a) in units of kips per square inch.
5. Substitute into the formula $P = F_a \times A$, where A = area of trial column; F_a was found in step 4. If the value for P exceeds step 1, the column is acceptable. If the value for P is less than step 1, a column with a larger A and r should be tried.

For example, design a column 15′-0″ high with A36 steel capable of supporting an axial load of 110,000 lb. Follow these steps:

1. The total concentrated load is equal to 110,000 lb.
2. Select a W16 × 36 beam. (See Table 6-4, example 2.) The value of r about the X-X axis is 6.50 in. The value of r about the Y-Y axis is 1.52 in. The value of A is 10.6 sq in.
3. Calculate the slenderness ratio.

$$\frac{l}{r} = \frac{15 \times 12}{1.52} = 118.4$$

value for F_a for 119 is 10.43 ksi. The value of 118.4 is interpolated to be 10.51 ksi.

4. Check the table "Allowable Unit Stress for Columns" for A36 steel (See Table 6-5). The value for F_a for 118 is 10.57 kip/sq in. (ksi). The

5.
$$P = F_a \times A$$
$$= 10{,}510 \times 10.6$$
$$= 111{,}406 \text{ lb}$$

TABLE 6-5 ALLOWABLE STRESS (KSI) FOR COMPRESSION MEMBERS OF 36 KSI SPECIFIED YIELD STRESS STEEL*

MAIN AND SECONDARY MEMBERS Kl/r NOT OVER 120						MAIN MEMBERS Kl/r 121 TO 200				SECONDARY MEMBERS † l/r 121 TO 200			
$\frac{Kl}{r}$	F_a (ksi)	$\frac{Kl}{r}$	F_a (ksi)	$\frac{Kl}{r}$	F_a (ksi)	$\frac{Kl}{r}$	F_a (ksi)	$\frac{Kl}{r}$	F_a (ksi)	$\frac{l}{r}$	F_{as} (ksi)	$\frac{l}{r}$	F_{as} (ksi)
1	21.56	41	19.11	81	15.24	121	10.14	161	5.76	121	10.19	161	7.25
2	21.52	42	19.03	82	15.13	122	9.99	162	5.69	122	10.09	162	7.20
3	21.48	43	18.95	83	15.02	123	9.85	163	5.62	123	10.00	163	7.16
4	21.44	44	18.86	84	14.90	124	9.70	164	5.55	124	9.90	164	7.12
5	21.39	45	18.78	85	14.79	125	9.55	165	5.49	125	9.80	165	7.08
6	21.35	46	18.70	86	14.67	126	9.41	166	5.42	126	9.70	166	7.04
7	21.30	47	18.61	87	14.56	127	9.26	167	5.35	127	9.59	167	7.00
8	21.25	48	18.53	88	14.44	128	9.11	168	5.29	128	9.49	168	6.96
9	21.21	49	18.44	89	14.32	129	8.97	169	5.23	129	9.40	169	6.93
10	21.16	50	18.35	90	14.20	130	8.84	170	5.17	130	9.30	170	6.89
11	21.10	51	18.26	91	14.09	131	8.70	171	5.11	131	9.21	171	6.85
12	21.05	52	18.17	92	13.97	132	8.57	172	5.05	132	9.12	172	6.82
13	21.00	53	18.08	93	13.84	133	8.44	173	4.99	133	9.03	173	6.79
14	20.95	54	17.99	94	13.72	134	8.32	174	4.93	134	8.94	174	6.76
15	20.89	55	17.90	95	13.60	135	8.19	175	4.88	135	8.86	175	6.73
16	20.83	56	17.81	96	13.48	136	8.07	176	4.82	136	8.78	176	6.70
17	20.78	57	17.71	97	13.35	137	7.96	177	4.77	137	8.70	177	6.67
18	20.72	58	17.62	98	13.23	138	7.84	178	4.71	138	8.62	178	6.64
19	20.66	59	17.53	99	13.10	139	7.73	179	4.66	139	8.54	179	6.61
20	20.60	60	17.43	100	12.98	140	7.62	180	4.61	140	8.47	180	6.58
21	20.54	61	17.33	101	12.85	141	7.51	181	4.56	141	8.39	181	6.56
22	20.48	62	17.24	102	12.72	142	7.41	182	4.51	142	8.32	182	6.53
23	20.41	63	17.14	103	12.59	143	7.30	183	4.46	143	8.25	183	6.51
24	20.35	64	17.04	104	12.47	144	7.20	184	4.41	144	8.18	184	6.49
25	20.28	65	16.94	105	12.33	145	7.10	185	4.36	145	8.12	185	6.46
26	20.22	66	16.84	106	12.20	146	7.01	186	4.32	146	8.05	186	6.44
27	20.15	67	16.74	107	12.07	147	6.91	187	4.27	147	7.99	187	6.42
28	20.08	68	16.64	108	11.94	148	6.82	188	4.23	148	7.93	188	6.40
29	20.01	69	16.53	109	11.81	149	6.73	189	4.18	149	7.87	189	6.38
30	19.94	70	16.43	110	11.67	150	6.64	190	4.14	150	7.81	190	6.36
31	19.87	71	16.33	111	11.54	151	6.55	191	4.09	151	7.75	191	6.35
32	19.80	72	16.22	112	11.40	152	6.46	192	4.05	152	7.69	192	6.33
33	19.73	73	16.12	113	11.26	153	6.38	193	4.01	153	7.64	193	6.31
34	19.65	74	16.01	114	11.13	154	6.30	194	3.97	154	7.59	194	6.30
35	19.58	75	15.90	115	10.99	155	6.22	195	3.93	155	7.53	195	6.28
36	19.50	76	15.79	116	10.85	156	6.14	196	3.89	156	7.48	196	6.27
37	19.42	77	15.69	117	10.71	157	6.06	197	3.85	157	7.43	197	6.26
38	19.35	78	15.58	118	10.57	158	5.98	198	3.81	158	7.39	198	6.24
39	19.27	79	15.47	119	10.43	159	5.91	199	3.77	159	7.34	199	6.23
40	19.19	80	15.36	120	10.28	160	5.83	200	3.73	160	7.29	200	6.22

* *Manual of Steel Construction*, American Institute of Steel Construction, Inc., New York, 7th edition, p. 5-84.
† K taken as 1.0 for secondary members.
Note: $C_c = 126$.

The column is acceptable.

A short cut to column design involves entering the column safe loading tables, found in the AISC manual, with the height of the column in feet. The selection simply involves reading across the table at the column height until the column load in kips is found.

Open-Web Steel Joists

Open-web steel joists, commonly called *bar joists,* are truss-shaped structural members fabricated from light structural members, such as bars, angles, and channels. They have the advantage of being able to span relatively long distances (150′) with much less dead-load weight than a solid beam has. Bar joists are commonly spaced up to 5′ apart with decking attached to the top cord member to provide lateral bracing. Bridging is quite common to prevent buckling of the joist.

Open-web joists are classed in several categories according to the strength of steel and the shapes used for fabrication: DLJ and DLH series (deep long span), with depths of up to 72″; LJ and LH series (long span), with depths of up to 48″; and J and H series, with depths of up to 24″. The proper designation for open-web joists is to give first the depth in inches, then the series of the joist, and then the particular joist designation within the series—an example is 20J6.

The procedure to be followed for the selection of open-web joists is

1. Calculate the weight per linear foot that will be bearing on the joist. This includes live-load plus dead-load weight of the joist.
2. Consult the open-web steel joist tables in the AISC manual. The span in feet should be read along one side of the table until it intersects with the closest value for the pounds per linear foot calculated in step 1. Each division of the table contains two numbers—the bold-faced value is the maximum allowable load, while the number beneath it is the allowable load that will limit deflection to $^1/_{360}$. Once an acceptable value has been found, the corresponding joist size is read in the table.

Using Table 6-6, select an open-web joist that will support a roof system with a 40 lb/sq ft live load and a 10 lb/sq ft total dead load. The joists will be spaced at 4′-0″ o.c. and will span 35′-0″. Deflection should be limited to $^1/_{360}$.

1. The total load is 50 lb/sq ft. A joist spacing of 4′-0″ o.c. means each linear foot of the joist will support 2′-0″ on each side, or a total of 4 sq ft. The total load per foot of joist will be 4 sq ft. × 50 lb/sq ft = 200 lb/ft.
2. Referring to the open-web joist table in the AISC manual, we see that at a span of 35′ a 22H7 steel joist will hold a load of 209 lb/ft with a deflection of $^1/_{360}$.

CONCRETE CONSTRUCTION

The properties of concrete, discussed in Chapter 4, should be reviewed. The ratio of cement, sand, coarse aggregate, and water plays an extremely important role in the final compressive strength of concrete. This strength, f'_c, is specified to meet certain minimum standards, generally within a range of 3000 to 5000 P.S.I. for structural use.

Concrete is assumed to be a compression material and will fail in tension. As in Figure 6-15, a simple beam-loading condition will produce compression in the top section of the beam and tension in the lower portion. It then becomes necessary in designing a homogeneous (one-material) concrete beam to oversize the beam to a point where the loads are resisted in compression only. This is seldom done because of the gross inefficiency of the design.

Because of their great similarity in coefficients of temperature expansion, steel and concrete are combined. Concrete provides all the resistance to compressive forces, and steel provides all the resistance to forces in tension.

The design of concrete beams, columns, and slabs is considerably more complex than wood or steel, in part because there is an infinite combination of sizes and ratios of concrete to steel. To further confuse this fundamental observation of concrete design, two different theories are commonly used by structural designers. The more conservative approach called *working-stress design,* involves setting certain stress standards for steel and concrete and designing the beam so that it will not exceed the allowable factor. Technically, this method relies on the fact that concrete acts elastically (its unit stress compared with unit strain is almost proportional) until it reaches approximately 45 percent of the compressive strength of concrete. Working-stress design is similar in concept to the method used in wood and steel design.

The second method of concrete design is called *ultimate-strength design.* It has become increasingly popular with structural engineers in the design of contemporary buildings. Ultimate strength

TABLE 6-6 STANDARD LOAD TABLE OPEN WEB STEEL JOISTS, H-SERIES*

ALLOWABLE TOTAL SAFE LOADS IN POUNDS PER LINEAR FOOT BASED ON ALLOWABLE STRESS OF 30,000 PSI

Joist Designation	22H6	22H7	22H8	24H6	24H7	24H8
Depth in Inches	22	22	22	24	24	24
Resisting Moment in Inch Kips	422	526	653	462	576	716
Maximum End Reaction in Pounds	5400	5600	5800	5600	5800	6000
Approximate Weight in Pounds per Foot	9.7	10.7	12.0	10.3	11.5	12.7
Span in Feet						
22	491	509	527			
23	470	487	504			
24	450	467	483	467	483	500
25	432	448	464	448	464	480
26	415	431	446	431	446	462
27	386	415	430	415	430	444
28	359 351	400	414	393	414	429
29	335 316	386 368	400	366	400	414
30	313 286	373 332	387 382	342 342	387	400
31	293 259	361 301	374 346	320 310	374 361	387
32	275 235	342 274	363 315	301 282	363 329	375
33	258 214	322 250	352 287	283 257	352 300	364 344
34	243 196	303 228	341 263	266 235	332 274	353 315
35 →	230 180	286 209	331 241	251 215	313 251	343 288
36	217 165	271 192	322 221	238 198	296 231	333 265
37	206 152	256 177	314 204	225 182	280 212	324 244
38	195 140	243 163	301 188	213 168	266 196	316 225
39	185 130	231 151	286 174	202 155	252 181	308 208
40	176 120	219 140	272 161	193 144	240 168	298 193
41	167 112	209 130	259 149	183 134	228 156	284 179
42	159 104	199 121	247 139	175 124	218 145	271 167
43	152 97	190 113	235 130	167 116	208 135	258 155
44	145 90	181 105	225 121	159 108	198 126	247 145
45				152 101	190 118	236 135
46				146 94	181 110	226 127
47				139 89	174 103	216 119
48				134 83	167 97	207 111

* *Manual of Steel Construction*, American Institute of Steel Construction, Inc., New York, 7th Edition, p. 5-297.

is determined by using factors just prior to the failure of the material. The cross-sectional members are designed so that the full strengths of the materials are used when the design is fully loaded. Any technical references to both methods of design can be obtained from the American Concrete Institute (ACI) publications.

Working-Stress Design

Working-stress design of beams involves assuming a certain stress factor for concrete and then designing around it. The factor for the allowable compressive stress for concrete is 0.45 f'_c, which for 3000 P.S.I. concrete is 1350 P.S.I. and for 4000 P.S.I. concrete is 1800 P.S.I. Several other necessary factors linked to the compressive strength of concrete are shown in Table 6-7. A ratio is established between the modulus of elasticity of steel and concrete which is expressed in a whole number term (N). It is computed by dividing various factors of p, k, j, and R into groups of tables found in the ACI specifications.

Two final terms that should be defined are b and d. The width of the beam is designated b, but only a portion of the beam is calculated for the depth d. The effective depth of the beam for calculations

TABLE 6-7   FACTORS NECESSARY FOR CONCRETE DESIGN

FACTOR	SYMBOL	$f_c' = 3000$	$f_c' = 4000$
Allowable compressive stress	f_c	1350 P.S.I.	1800 P.S.I.
Modulus of elasticity	E_c	3,200,000 P.S.I.	3,700,000 P.S.I.
Allowable shear	v_c	60 P.S.I.	70 P.S.I.
Allowable shear with stirrups	v	274 P.S.I.	316 P.S.I.
Ratio E_sE_c	n	9 $\downarrow$	8 $\downarrow$
Constant values for steel with a tensile strength of 20,000 P.S.I.	p	0.01293	0.01884
	k	0.3831	0.4186
	j	0.8723	0.8605
	R	225.6	324.3

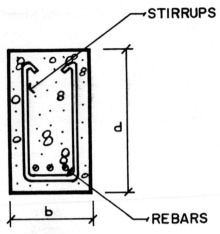

Figure 6-23.   A concrete beam.

is from the center of the steel reinforcing to the top of the beam. (See Figure 6-23.) Generally 2½″ are added to the bottom of the beam, ½″ for the other half of the reinforcing bar, and 2″ for fire protection.

The procedures used to design a concrete beam in the working-stress method are

1. Determine the loading conditions, including the weight of the beam. This can be done by assuming the depth of the beam to be 1″ for each foot of span and by assuming the depth to be 1½ times the width. The weight of a beam per foot can be estimated to be 1 lb/sq in. of cross-sectional area.

2. Estimate the width of the beam (b).

3. Determine the beam depth with the formula

$$d = \sqrt{\frac{M}{Rb}}$$

4. Once the beam size has been calculated for concrete, it is necessary to determine the area of reinforcing steel (A_s) to resist tension. Use either of the following formulas:

$$A_s = pbd$$

or

$$A_s = \frac{M}{f_s j d}$$

The resulting value for A_s is in square inches and can be divided many ways. The area of reforcing bars is found in *Architectural Graphic Standards*. The steel is called *longitudinal reinforcing*, which resists tension. The next step indicates the need for additional steel to resist shear.

5. The allowable unit shear (V_c) in concrete is 60 P.S.I. for 3000 P.S.I. concrete. An excess of this amount could cause diagonal cracking in the beam. Steel reinforcing bars, called *stirrups* (web reinforcement), are placed vertically at the points of greatest shear. The formula to determine the necessity for shear reinforcing is $v = V/bd$.

The result is unit shear per square inch, which cannot exceed the allowable of 60 P.S.I. for f_c' 3000.

6. The location of web reinforcement or stirrups involves calculating the distance where the shear on the beam exceeds the allowable shear for concrete (V_c).

Figure 6-24 shows a uniformly distributed load producing a maximum shear force at the end reactions of 30,000 lb. The beam design for such a moment is 14″ × 24″, or 336 sq in. The code will allow a shear value of 60 P.S.I. for f_c' 3000 P.S.I. concrete, which, when taken times the area of the beam, produces a total shear resistance of 20,160 lb. The code reduces the maximum shear by permitting the calculation to be made the distance (d, or the depth of the beam) away from the end reaction. The depth of the beam is 24″, and the shear is dropping at 3000 lb/ft; thus, 24″ from the end reaction, the shear will be 6000 lb less, or 24,000 lb.

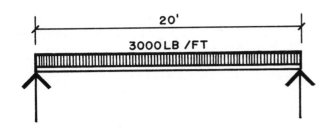

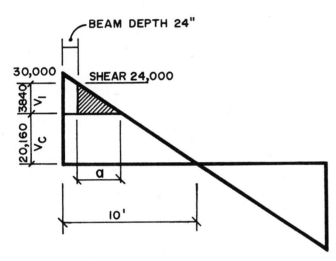

Figure 6-24.   Shear conditions in a concrete beam.

This is indicated on the shear diagram (Figure 6-24) as the hatched section, meaning that web reinforcement must resist the difference between the maximum shear at the distance (d) away from the support and the shear resisted by the concrete (given the factor V'). In the example the difference is 3840 lb when the shear drops below the value that is resisted by the concrete (V_c). It is no longer necessary to provide web reinforcement.

This length (a) can be found by calculating the distance it will take the uniform load to place the value v' below the shear resistance of the concrete. In the example, a 3000 lb/ft force would also be a force of 250 lb/in. The value of v' = 3840 would be reduced to 0 in 15+" (3840/250 = 15.4"). This can be rounded off to 16". The code requires that stirrups should also be located in the space (d) between the face of the support and a distance (d) past (a)—(d + a + d). In this example, stirrups are required (24" + 16" + 24") = 64" out from the support.

It is necessary to calculate the spacing required between stirrups (S). The code establishes the limit to

$$S = \frac{d}{2}$$

or

$$S = \frac{A_v f_v d}{V'}$$

whichever is less. A_v is the cross-sectional area of the stirrup. The common sizes are #3 reinforcing bars = 0.11 sq in. and #4 = 0.20 sq in. This is taken times 2 because a horizontal section through a beam will intersect the U-shaped stirrup twice. In the example:

$$S = \frac{d}{2}$$

$$= \frac{24}{2}$$

$$= 12''$$

Trying #4 bars:

$$S = \frac{A_v f_v d}{V'}$$

$$= \frac{2(0.20) \times 20,000 \times 24}{3840}$$

$$= 50''$$

The spacing for stirrups is 12" o.c. and is usually started a distance S/2 from the face of the support. In the example, five stirrups are required.

There is one further step involved in checking the design that concerns the bond between the reinforcing bars and the concrete. This is commonly a formality since the bar selected usually will have an adequate bond. Without the values shown in the ACI manual, the calculation for bond is quite complex.

The formula for unit bond stress is

$$U = \frac{V}{E_o jd}$$

where U = bond stress in pounds per square inch
  V = maximum shear
  E_o = sum of perimeters of reinforcing bars
  j = constant depending on values of f'_c and f_s
  d = depth of beam

The value of U, which the design cannot exceed, is determined by the compressive strength of the concrete, the diameter of the bar, and where it is used in the beam. Without the bond-stress tables found in the ACI manual, the check is

$$U = \frac{3.4\sqrt{f_c'}}{\text{diameter of bar}}$$
(Not over 350 P.S.I. for bars with more than 12″ below the bar to the bottom of the beam)

$$U = \frac{4.8\sqrt{f_c'}}{\text{diameter of bar}}$$
(Not over 500 P.S.I. for other conditions)

Using Figure 6-25, design a beam spanning 18′ and supporting a combined live load and dead load of 2500 in./ft. Use $f_c' = 3000$ P.S.I. concrete and $f_s = 20,000$ P.S.I. steel. Here are the steps to follow:

1. Estimate the depth of the beam at 18″ and the width at 12″. The area is 216 sq in., and therefore the weight is 216 lb/ft. This can be rounded off to 200 lb/ft when added to the live load.

$$V = \frac{W}{2}$$

$$= \frac{48,600}{2}$$

$$= 24,300 \text{ lb}$$

$$M = \frac{Wl}{8}$$

$$\doteq 109,350 \text{ ft-lb, or } 1,312,200$$

2. Estimate the width of the beam if b = 14″.

3. $d = \sqrt{\dfrac{M}{Rb}}$ Table 6-6 indicates R = 225.6.

$$d = \sqrt{\frac{1,312,200}{225.6 \times 14}}$$

$$= 20.4 \text{ in.}$$

To this, add 2.5 in. for fireproofing and the other half of the reinforcing bar. The total beam is 14″ × 23″.

4. Calculate the area of steel required:

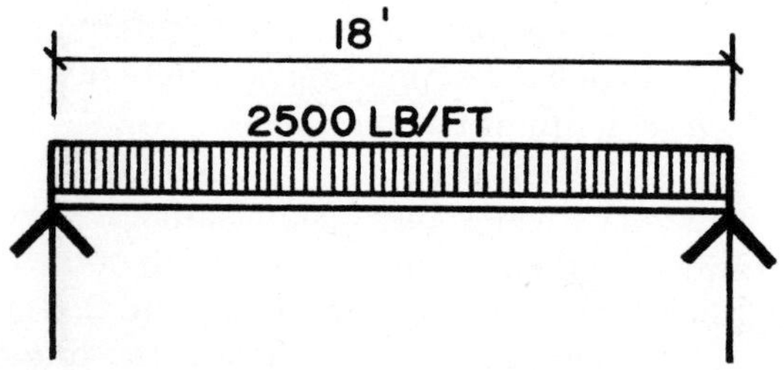

Figure 6-25. A uniform load.

$A_s = pbd$
$= 0.01293 \times 14 \times 20.4$ (p is from Table 6-6)
$= 3.69$ sq in.

A #9 reinforcing bar has a cross-sectional area of 1 sq in. Use four #9 bars.

5. Determine the amount of unit shear:

$$v = \frac{V}{bd}$$

$$= \frac{24,300}{14 \times 20.4}$$

$$= 85 \text{ P.S.I.}$$

This exceeds the allowable of 60 P.S.I.; investigate for web reinforcement.

6. Referring to Figure 6-26, find the magnitude of $V_c = bdv_c = 14 \times 20.4 \times 60 = 17,136$ lb. Find the magnitude of V'.

Shear is decreasing at a rate of 2700 lb/ft, or 225 lb/in. At a point d from the support, the shear is reduced $20.4 \times 225 = 4580$ lb. The value of shear at this point is $24,300 \times 4580 = 19,720$ lb. This value minus the shear accounted for by the concrete equals $V' = 19,720 - 17,136 = 2584$ lb. With shear reducing at a rate of 225 lb/ft, $a = \dfrac{2584}{225} = 11.5$ in. The total length of stirrup reinforcement is $20.4 + 11.5 + 20.4 = 52$ in.

$$S = \frac{d}{2}$$

$$= \frac{20.4}{2}$$

$$= 10.2 \text{ in.}$$

$$S = \frac{A_v f_v d}{V'}$$

$$= \frac{2(0.11)20,000 \times 20.4}{2584}$$

$$= 35 \text{ in.}$$

Try #3 rebars. The 10.2 in. o.c. spacing is critical. Figure 6-27 shows the end condition of the beam as it was designed.

Ultimate-Strength Design

Ultimate-strength design of a concrete beam follows the premise that live-load factors imposed by code

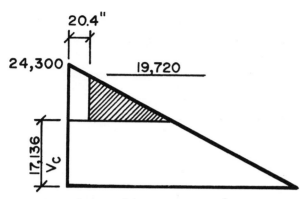

Figure 6-26.   Shear conditions in a concrete beam.

and dead loads can be given a safety factor for an unexpected load which will satisfy any circumstance. The ultimate loading condition is calculated by providing a 50 percent safety factor for dead loads and an 80 percent safety factor for live loads:

$$U - 1.5\,DL + 1.8\,LL$$

This satisfies the safety factors necessary for loading so that the materials can be designed for their maximum strength. Theoretically, any loading condition over this amount would cause the material to fail.

Ultimate-strength design works on the principle that the relation between the stress placed on concrete (in pounds per square inch) and the strain caused within the material changes greatly as the stress reaches the yield point. Figures 6-28 and 6-29 show the behavior of both ultimate strength and working stress when they are stressed.

One-way slab   A *one-way slab* is simply a thin, wide concrete beam spanning between supports. The same calculations are used for a slab as were used for a beam using a 12″ wide section as the width of the beam (*b*). The major difference between using slabs or beams appears in shear calculations due to the impracticability of providing web reinforcement. It then becomes necessary to limit shear to v_c.

For example, design a slab spanning 15′ which supports a live load of 150 lb/sq ft and the dead load of the slab. Use 3000 P.S.I. concrete and 20,000 P.S.I. steel. (Refer to the steps under concrete beam design.)

1.   Estimate the depth of the slab to be ½″ per foot of span. (½″ × 15′ = 7.5 in.) The weight of a section of the slab with b = 12″ and d = 7.5″ equals 12 × 7.5 × 1 lb/sq in = 90 lb. The total load per foot = 240 lb/sq ft. V for a 1′ width = $\frac{W}{2} = \frac{3600}{2}$ = 1800 lb. M for a 1′ width = $\frac{Wl}{8}$ = 6750 ft-lb, or 81,000 in.-lb.
2.   The width of the slab is set as 12″.

3. $d = \sqrt{\dfrac{M}{Rb}} = \sqrt{\dfrac{81,000}{225.6 \times 12}} = 5.6$ in.

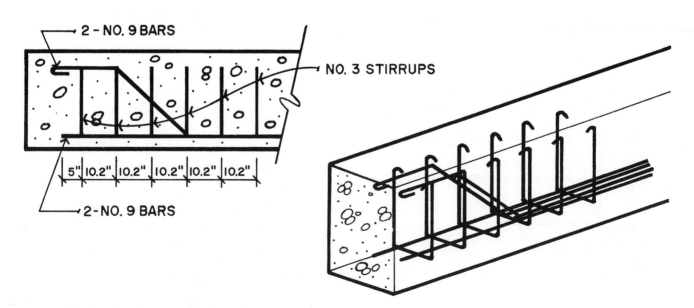

Figure 6-27.   The end condition of the designed beam.

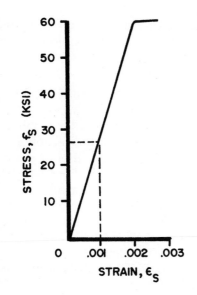

STEEL

Figure 6-28. Stress and strain in steel.

To this add 1″ for fireproofing and the width of half of the reinforcing bar. The total slab depth is 6.6 in.

4. Determine the cross-sectional area of steel required:

$$A_s = pbd$$
$$= 0.01293 \times 12 \times 5.6$$
$$= 0.87 \text{ sq in.}$$

There are an unlimited number of possible choices; #6 bars ($A = 0.44$ sq in.) spaced at 6″ o.c. will work.

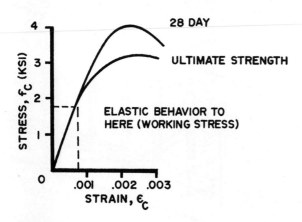

CONCRETE

Figure 6-29. Stress and strain in concrete.

5. Referring to Figure 6-30, check for shear. The maximum shear minus the distance (d) from the support is

$$V_d = 1800 - (5.6 \text{ in.} \times 20 \text{ lb/in.})$$
$$= 1688 \text{ lb}$$

$$v = \frac{V_d}{bd} = \frac{1688}{12 \times 5.6} = 25 \text{ P.S.I.}$$

The unit shear does not exceed 60 P.S.I., and so it is acceptable.

A second type of floor slab is called a *two-way slab*. Instead of receiving its support from two opposite sides, four sides support the slab. Two-way slabs can be considerably thinner than one-way systems.

Columns   The two major types of reinforced concrete columns are tied and spiral. (See Figure 6-31.)
• **Tied columns**   Tied columns have longitudinal bars to assist in carrying some of the downward force with the horizontal ties acting to prevent the bars from buckling. The vertical bars must account for from 1 to 8 percent of the gross cross-sectional area of the column. The minimum number of bars shall be 6. They shall not be smaller than #5 bars. The most common concrete column is a short column, so labeled because its height is not more than 10 times its least dimension. The load allowed for a short tied column is

$$P = 0.85 \, Ag(0.25f'_c + f_s p_g)$$

where P = load in pounds
  Ag = area in square inches
  f'_c = compressive strength of concrete
  f_s = compressive strength of steel to be at 40 percent of the minimum yield but not greater than 30,000 P.S.I.
  p_g = ratio of steel reinforcing to area of column

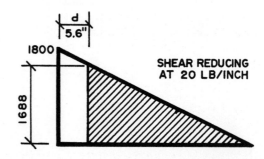

Figure 6-30. Shear in a concrete slab.

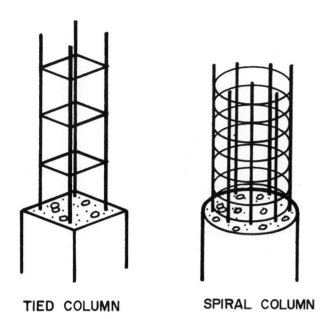

TIED COLUMN   SPIRAL COLUMN

Figure 6-31. Column reinforcement.

Determine the load a 20″ × 20″ column 10′ high (short) can carry. Use f'_c = 3000 P.S.I. and steel with a yield point of 50,000 P.S.I. (f_s = 40% × 50,000 = 20,000). Use ten #9 bars which make the area of steel = 10 sq in. The ratio p_g = $^{10}/_{400}$ = 0.025.

$$P = 0.85Ag(0.25f'_c + f_sp_g)$$
$$= 0.85 \times 400[0.25 \times 3000 + (20,000 \times 0.025)]$$
$$= 425,000 \text{ lb}$$

• **Spiral columns** Spiral columns consist of vertical bars to assist in carrying some of the downward force with closely spaced spiral ties acting to prevent the bars from buckling. This system is more efficient than a tied column. The typical spiral column is a cylinder and has many of the same restrictions as to number and size of bars as a tied column. The formula for a tied column is

$$P = Ag(0.25f'_c + f_sp_g)$$

For example, determine the load a 20″ diameter spirally reinforced column 10′ high (short) can carry. Use the same data as given in the previous example. (p_g will change to 0.032.)

$$P = Ag(0.25f'_c + f_sp_g)$$
$$= 314[0.25 \times 3000 + (20,000 \times 0.032)]$$
$$= 436,460 \text{ lb}$$

Rather than calculate the many possibilities between the area of steel and concrete, it is much easier to consult the column load tables in the ACI manual.

• **Footings** A footing is designed to distribute the weight of a building uniformly to the soil it is resting on. The soil conditions will determine its bearing capacity, which in turn limits the size of the footing. Gravel that has a bearing capacity of 12,000 lb/sq ft will support a building footing only to that point. This means the footing should be made of a sufficient size to distribute the load at 12,000 lb/ft. A footing is designed in much the same way as a beam, only in an inverted position:

1. Determine the load on the foundation wall per linear foot and design a 1′ section of the footing. Calculate the size of the footing so that it will equal the bearing capacity of the soil.
2. Calculate the moment using the length (*l*) of the beam as the total width of the footing minus the width of the foundation wall.
3. Calculate the minimum depth of the footing:

$$d = \sqrt{\frac{M}{Rb}}$$

This depth proves to be a minimum and usually is inadequate when the bond between the reinforcing bars and concrete is checked. The design approach is to arbitrarily increase the depth of the footing for a trial section.
4. Check for shear the distance (*d*) from the face of the wall $v = V/bd$. The code allows the maximum unit shear in footings to be 110 P.S.I. for f'_c = 3000 P.S.I. concrete and 126 P.S.I. for f'_c 4000 P.S.I. concrete.
5. Determine the area of tension steel required:

$$A_s = \frac{M}{f_sjd}$$

6. Check the bond stress of the bars selected in step 5.

Referring to Figure 6-32, design a reinforced-concrete footing that will support a 1′-0″ concrete wall with a load of 15,000 lb/linear ft. Use f'_c = 3000 P.S.I. and f_s = 20,000 P.S.I. Use a soil-bearing capacity of 4000 lb/sq ft.

1. Estimate the weight of the footing to be 1000 lb/ft so that the total load of the footing plus the wall load is 16,000 lb/ft. The bearing capacity of

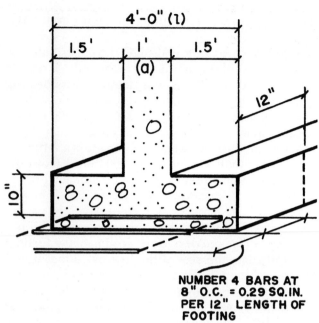

4'-0" (1)

1.5'   1'   1.5'

(a)

12"

10"

**NUMBER 4 BARS AT
8" O.C. = 0.29 SQ.IN.
PER 12" LENGTH OF
FOOTING**

Figure 6-32.   Footing.

the soil is 4000 lb/sq ft, and so a 1' cross section of the footing must be 4' wide to be adequately supported by the soil (4 sq ft × 4000 lb/sq ft = 16,000 lb).

2. Determine the moment. The load used for the moment calculation is not affected by the weight of the footing, and so only the foundation wall load is used: 15,000/4 = 3750 lb/ft.

$$M = \frac{w(l - a)^2}{8}$$

$$= \frac{3750(4 - 1)^2}{8}$$

$$= 4219 \text{ ft-lb, or } 50,628 \text{ in.-lb}$$

3. To get the minimum footing depth:

$$d = \sqrt{\frac{M}{Rd}}$$

$$= \sqrt{\frac{50,628}{225.6 \times 12}}$$

$$= 4.4 \text{ in.}$$

This is minimal. Try a 10" slab for the trial.

4. Compute unit shear. The shear at the distance (d) from the face of the footing is calculated by determining that the maximum shear at the face of the foundation wall is 1.5' × 3750 = 5625 lb, or 312 lb/in. A point 10" from the wall will reduce the shear to 2505 lb [5625 − (312 × 10)]. The unit shear formula is

$$v = \frac{V}{bd}$$

$$= \frac{2505}{12 \times 10}$$

$$= 20.9 \text{ P.S.I.}$$

This is acceptable, since the maximum allowable is 110 P.S.I.

5. Determine the area of steel required:

$$A_s = \frac{M}{f_s jd}$$

$$= \frac{50,628}{20,000 \times 0.8723 \times 10}$$

$$= 0.29 \text{ sq in.}$$

Spacing #4 bars at 8" o.c. will work.

SEVEN

PROFESSIONAL PRACTICE

THE ARCHITECT'S CONTRACT

When an architect receives a commission for a building project, he or she first signs the owner-architect agreement. This contract establishes the obligations of the two parties. In effect, it stipulates the services the architect provides, the response the owner gives to the architect, and the monetary compensation due the architect. When this procedure is completed, the architect's accounting department budgets the amount of time to be allotted to the project. Table 7-1 presents the percent of the total effort, in terms of time and money, that an architectural firm allocates to each phase of the job.

The following is an example of how an actual job is handled in an architectural office. Assume a school has a $2.5 million budget. (See Table 7-2.)

At this early stage, the only realistic cost estimate that the architect can apply is a cost per square foot. Assuming $25/sq ft (this cost is not an accurate figure for current school construction; it is intended to give a base for the example rather than to establish a cost for building), this gives an adequate 100,000 sq ft school that has reasonable finishes. The owner-architect agreement stipulates the architectural fee as 7 percent of the construction costs, or $175,000. Initially, the architect's accounting department allocates the fee for the complete production of the job. Usually, the engineering consultant receives about one-third of the fee for structural, mechanical, and electrical calculations and drawings. This leaves roughly $116,000

for the production of architectural drawings. Through calculations, the accounting office determines the average hourly salary of the people working on the project. On this particular project the figure is about $6/hr.

The average salary figure is multiplied by 2½ to obtain the cost of the job. The 2½ multiple is a fairly standard calculation for the following: the cost of a person's salary (one part); the cost of overhead (one part); and the profit for the firm (one-half of one part). In this case, 2½ times the average hourly salary is $15/hr, which allows 7733 work hours to be budgeted to the project. Broken down into phases within the office, it allows 1160 hr for schematics; 1546 hr for design development; 3093 hr for construction documents; 386 hr for bidding; and 1546 hr for construction. This is not the only method to determine the time needed to produce a job in an office, but it is a common procedure.

After the amount of time is allocated for a particular job, the definition of the services is apparent. The services vary from job to job, but an order can be defined for general encounters.

TABLE 7-1 THE PHASES OF ARCHITECTURAL PRACTICE

PHASE	PERCENT OF TOTAL EFFORT
Schematic design	15
Design development	20
Construction document	40
Bidding or negotiation	5
Construction	20

TABLE 7-2 ARCHITECTURAL FEE BREAKDOWN

ITEM	CALCULATION
Square footage of school	100,000 sq ft
Cost per square foot	$25
School budget	$2,500,000
Percent of architect's fee	.07
Architect's fee	$175,000
Percent of engineering consultant's fee	.33
Engineering consultant's fee	$58,300
Architect's fee	$175,000
Minus engineering fee	$58,300
Budget for architectural drafting	$116,700
Average hourly salary	$6
2½ multiple {one part salary, one part overhead, one-half part profit}	2½
Office charge per work hour	$15
Work hours allotted to project	7,733

THE AMERICAN INSTITUTE OF ARCHITECTS

AIA Document B141

Standard Form of Agreement Between Owner and Architect

THIS DOCUMENT HAS IMPORTANT LEGAL CONSEQUENCES; CONSULTATION WITH AN ATTORNEY IS ENCOURAGED WITH RESPECT TO ITS COMPLETION OR MODIFICATION

AGREEMENT

made this   second   day of   August   in the year of Nineteen Hundred and   seventy-seven

BETWEEN the Owner:
       General Restaurants, Inc.
       Bloomington, Indiana

and the Architect:
       Design Partnership, Inc., A.I.A.
       Chicago, Illinois

For the following Project:
(Include detailed description of Project location and scope)

       Architectural services for the Beef and Burgundy Restaurant

       located at 2617 Anderson Parkway, Bloomington, Indiana.

       The project scope includes building construction and site work.

The Owner and the Architect agree as set forth below.

Figure 7-1. Owner-architect agreement.

PERCENTAGE OF CONSTRUCTION COST

I. THE ARCHITECT shall provide professional services for the Project in accordance with the Terms and Conditions of this Agreement.

II. THE OWNER shall compensate the Architect, in accordance with the Terms and Conditions of this Agreement.

A. *FOR BASIC SERVICES,* as described in Paragraph 1.1, Basic Compensation shall be computed on the basis of one of the following PERCENTAGES OF CONSTRUCTION COST, as defined in Article 3, for portions of the Project to be awarded under

A Single Stipulated Sum Construction Contract

percent (8 %)

~~Separate Stipulated Sum Construction Contracts~~

~~percent (%)~~

~~A Single Cost-Plus-Fee Construction Contract~~

~~percent (%)~~

~~Separate Cost-Plus-Fee Construction Contracts~~

~~percent (%)~~

B. *FOR ADDITIONAL SERVICES,* as described in Paragraph 1.3, compensation computed as follows:

1. Principals' time at the fixed rate of   dollars ($ 50   ) per hour.
For the purpose of this Agreement, the Principals are:

    James R. Williams
    Bruce M. Kennedy

2. Employees' time (other than Principals) at a multiple of   two and one-half
(2.5   ) times the employees' Direct Personnel Expense as defined in Article 4.

3. Services of Professional consultants at a multiple of   one and one-third
(1.33   ) times the amount billed to the Architect for such services.

C. *AN INITIAL PAYMENT* of fifteen thousand

dollars ($ 15,000.00   )

shall be made upon the execution of this Agreement and credited to the Owner's account.

D. *FOR REIMBURSABLE EXPENSES,* amounts expended as defined in Article 5.

III. THE OWNER AND ARCHITECT agree in accordance with the Terms and Conditions of this Agreement that:

A. *IF SCOPE* of the Project is changed materially, compensation shall be subject to renegotiation.

B. *IF THE SERVICES* covered by this Agreement have not been completed within
(24   ) months of the date hereof, the amounts of compensation, rates and multiples set forth in Paragraph II shall be subject to renegotiation.

AIA DOCUMENT B141 • OWNER-ARCHITECT AGREEMENT • JANUARY 1974 EDITION • AIA® • ©1974
THE AMERICAN INSTITUTE OF ARCHITECTS, 1735 NEW YORK AVE., N.W., WASHINGTON, D. C. 20006   **2**

Figure 7-1 (continued).

TERMS AND CONDITIONS OF AGREEMENT BETWEEN OWNER AND ARCHITECT

ARTICLE 1

ARCHITECT'S SERVICES

1.1 BASIC SERVICES

The Architect's Basic Services consist of the five phases described below and include normal structural, mechanical and electrical engineering services and any other services included in Article 14 as Basic Services.

SCHEMATIC DESIGN PHASE

1.1.1 The Architect shall review the program furnished by the Owner to ascertain the requirements of the Project and shall confirm such requirements to the Owner.

1.1.2 Based on the mutually agreed upon program, the Architect shall prepare Schematic Design Studies consisting of drawings and other documents illustrating the scale and relationship of Project components for approval by the Owner.

1.1.3 The Architect shall submit to the Owner a Statement of Probable Construction Cost based on current area, volume or other unit costs.

DESIGN DEVELOPMENT PHASE

1.1.4 The Architect shall prepare from the approved Schematic Design Studies, for approval by the Owner, the Design Development Documents consisting of drawings and other documents to fix and describe the size and character of the entire Project as to structural, mechanical and electrical systems, materials and such other essentials as may be appropriate.

1.1.5 The Architect shall submit to the Owner a further Statement of Probable Construction Cost.

CONSTRUCTION DOCUMENTS PHASE

1.1.6 The Architect shall prepare from the approved Design Development Documents, for approval by the Owner, Drawings and Specifications setting forth in detail the requirements for the construction of the entire Project including the necessary bidding information, and shall assist in the preparation of bidding forms, the Conditions of the Contract, and the form of Agreement between the Owner and the Contractor.

1.1.7 The Architect shall advise the Owner of any adjustments to previous Statements of Probable Construction Cost indicated by changes in requirements or general market conditions.

1.1.8 The Architect shall assist the Owner in filing the required documents for the approval of governmental authorities having jurisdiction over the Project.

BIDDING OR NEGOTIATION PHASE

1.1.9 The Architect, following the Owner's approval of the Construction Documents and of the latest Statement of Probable Construction Cost, shall assist the Owner in obtaining bids or negotiated proposals, and in awarding and preparing construction contracts.

CONSTRUCTION PHASE — ADMINISTRATION OF THE CONSTRUCTION CONTRACT

1.1.10 The Construction Phase will commence with the award of the Construction Contract and will terminate when the final Certificate for Payment is issued to the Owner.

1.1.11 The Architect shall provide Administration of the Construction Contract as set forth in AIA Document A201, General Conditions of the Contract for Construction, and the extent of his duties and responsibilities and the limitations of his authority as assigned thereunder shall not be modified without his written consent.

1.1.12 The Architect, as the representative of the Owner during the Construction Phase, shall advise and consult with the Owner and all of the Owner's instructions to the Contractor shall be issued through the Architect. The Architect shall have authority to act on behalf of the Owner to the extent provided in the General Conditions unless otherwise modified in writing.

1.1.13 The Architect shall at all times have access to the Work wherever it is in preparation or progress.

1.1.14 The Architect shall make periodic visits to the site to familiarize himself generally with the progress and quality of the Work and to determine in general if the Work is proceeding in accordance with the Contract Documents. On the basis of his on-site observations as an architect, he shall endeavor to guard the Owner against defects and deficiencies in the Work of the Contractor. The Architect shall not be required to make exhaustive or continuous on-site inspections to check the quality or quantity of the Work. The Architect shall not be responsible for construction means, methods, techniques, sequences or procedures, or for safety precautions and programs in connection with the Work, and he shall not be responsible for the Contractor's failure to carry out the Work in accordance with the Contract Documents.

1.1.15 Based on such observations at the site and on the Contractor's Applications for Payment, the Architect shall determine the amount owing to the Contractor and shall issue Certificates for Payment in such amounts. The issuance of a Certificate for Payment shall constitute a representation by the Architect to the Owner, based on the Architect's observations at the site as provided in Subparagraph 1.1.14 and the data comprising the Application for Payment, that the Work has progressed to the point indicated; that to the best of the Architect's knowledge, information and belief, the quality of the Work is in accordance with the Contract Documents (subject to an evaluation of the Work for conformance with the Contract Documents upon Substantial Completion, to the results of any subsequent tests required by the Contract

Figure 7-1 (continued).

Documents, to minor deviations from the Contract Documents correctable prior to completion, and to any specific qualifications stated in the Certificate for Payment); and that the Contractor is entitled to payment in the amount certified. By issuing a Certificate for Payment, the Architect shall not be deemed to represent that he has made any examination to ascertain how and for what purpose the Contractor has used the moneys paid on account of the Contract Sum.

1.1.16 The Architect shall be, in the first instance, the interpreter of the requirements of the Contract Documents and the impartial judge of the performance thereunder by both the Owner and Contractor. The Architect shall make decisions on all claims of the Owner or Contractor relating to the execution and progress of the Work and on all other matters or questions related thereto. The Architect's decisions in matters relating to artistic effect shall be final if consistent with the intent of the Contract Documents.

1.1.17 The Architect shall have authority to reject Work which does not conform to the Contract Documents. Whenever, in his reasonable opinion, he considers it necessary or advisable to insure the proper implementation of the intent of the Contract Documents, he will have authority to require special inspection or testing of any Work in accordance with the provisions of the Contract Documents whether or not such Work be then fabricated, installed or completed.

1.1.18 The Architect shall review and approve shop drawings, samples, and other submissions of the Contractor only for conformance with the design concept of the Project and for compliance with the information given in the Contract Documents.

1.1.19 The Architect shall prepare Change Orders.

1.1.20 The Architect shall conduct inspections to determine the Dates of Substantial Completion and final completion, shall receive and review written guarantees and related documents assembled by the Contractor, and shall issue a final Certificate for Payment.

1.1.21 The Architect shall not be responsible for the acts or omissions of the Contractor, or any Subcontractors, or any of the Contractor's or Subcontractors' agents or employees, or any other persons performing any of the Work.

1.2 PROJECT REPRESENTATION BEYOND BASIC SERVICES

1.2.1 If more extensive representation at the site than is described under Subparagraphs 1.1.10 through 1.1.21 inclusive is required, and if the Owner and Architect agree, the Architect shall provide one or more Full-Time Project Representatives to assist the Architect.

1.2.2 Such Full-Time Project Representatives shall be selected, employed and directed by the Architect, and the Architect shall be compensated therefor as mutually agreed between the Owner and the Architect as set forth in an exhibit appended to this Agreement.

1.2.3 The duties, responsibilities and limitations of authority of such Full-Time Project Representatives shall be set forth in an exhibit appended to this Agreement.

1.2.4 Through the on-site observations by Full-Time Project Representatives of the Work in progress, the Architect shall endeavor to provide further protection for the Owner against defects in the Work, but the furnishing of such project representation shall not make the Architect responsible for construction means, methods, techniques, sequences or procedures, or for safety precautions and programs, or for the Contractor's failure to perform the Work in accordance with the Contract Documents.

1.3 ADDITIONAL SERVICES

The following Services shall be provided when authorized in writing by the Owner, and they shall be paid for by the Owner as hereinbefore provided.

1.3.1 Providing analyses of the Owner's needs, and programming the requirements of the Project.

1.3.2 Providing financial feasibility or other special studies.

1.3.3 Providing planning surveys, site evaluations, environmental studies or comparative studies of prospective sites.

1.3.4 Providing design services relative to future facilities, systems and equipment which are not intended to be constructed as part of the Project.

1.3.5 Providing services to investigate existing conditions or facilities or to make measured drawings thereof, or to verify the accuracy of drawings or other information furnished by the Owner.

1.3.6 Preparing documents for alternate bids or out-of-sequence services requested by the Owner.

1.3.7 Providing Detailed Estimates of Construction Cost or detailed quantity surveys or inventories of material, equipment and labor.

1.3.8 Providing interior design and other services required for or in connection with the selection of furniture and furnishings.

1.3.9 Providing services for planning tenant or rental spaces.

1.3.10 Making revisions in Drawings, Specifications or other documents when such revisions are inconsistent with written approvals or instructions previously given and are due to causes beyond the control of the Architect.

1.3.11 Preparing supporting data and other services in connection with Change Orders if the change in the Basic Compensation resulting from the adjusted Contract Sum is not commensurate with the services required of the Architect.

1.3.12 Making investigations involving detailed appraisals and valuations of existing facilities, and surveys or inventories required in connection with construction performed by the Owner.

1.3.13 Providing consultation concerning replacement of any Work damaged by fire or other cause during construction, and furnishing professional services of the type

AIA DOCUMENT B141 • OWNER-ARCHITECT AGREEMENT • JANUARY 1974 EDITION • AIA® • ©1974
THE AMERICAN INSTITUTE OF ARCHITECTS, 1735 NEW YORK AVE., N.W., WASHINGTON, D. C. 20006

Figure 7-1 (continued).

set forth in Paragraph 1.1 as may be required in connection with the replacement of such Work.

1.3.14 Providing professional services made necessary by the default of the Contractor or by major defects in the Work of the Contractor in the performance of the Construction Contract.

1.3.15 Preparing a set of reproducible record prints of drawings showing significant changes in the Work made during the construction process, based on marked-up prints, drawings and other data furnished by the Contractor to the Architect.

1.3.16 Providing extensive assistance in the utilization of any equipment or system such as initial start-up or testing, adjusting and balancing, preparation of operation and maintenance manuals, training personnel for operation and maintenance, and consultation during operation.

1.3.17 Providing services after issuance to the Owner of the final Certificate for Payment.

1.3.18 Preparing to serve or serving as an expert witness in connection with any public hearing, arbitration proceeding or legal proceeding.

1.3.19 Providing services of professional consultants for other than the normal structural, mechanical and electrical engineering services for the Project.

1.3.20 Providing any other services not otherwise included in this Agreement or not customarily furnished in accordance with generally accepted architectural practice.

ARTICLE 2
THE OWNER'S RESPONSIBILITIES

2.1 The Owner shall provide full information, including a complete program, regarding his requirements for the Project.

2.2 The Owner shall designate, when necessary, a representative authorized to act in his behalf with respect to the Project. The Owner shall examine documents submitted by the Architect and shall render decisions pertaining thereto promptly, to avoid unreasonable delay in the progress of the Architect's services.

2.3 The Owner shall furnish a certified land survey of the site giving, as applicable, grades and lines of streets, alleys, pavements and adjoining property; rights-of-way, restrictions, easements, encroachments, zoning, deed restrictions, boundaries and contours of the site; locations, dimensions and complete data pertaining to existing buildings, other improvements and trees; and full information concerning available service and utility lines both public and private, above and below grade, including inverts and depths.

2.4 The Owner shall furnish the services of a soils engineer or other consultant when such services are deemed necessary by the Architect, including reports, test borings, test pits, soil bearing values, percolation tests, air and water pollution tests, ground corrosion and resistivity tests and other necessary operations for determining subsoil, air and water conditions, with appropriate professional recommendations.

2.5 The Owner shall furnish structural, mechanical, chemical and other laboratory tests, inspections and reports as required by law or the Contract Documents.

2.6 The Owner shall furnish such legal, accounting, and insurance counseling services as may be necessary for the Project, and such auditing services as he may require to ascertain how or for what purposes the Contractor has used the moneys paid to him under the Construction Contract.

2.7 The services, information, surveys and reports required by Paragraphs 2.3 through 2.6 inclusive shall be furnished at the Owner's expense, and the Architect shall be entitled to rely upon the accuracy and completeness thereof.

2.8 If the Owner becomes aware of any fault or defect in the Project or non-conformance with the Contract Documents, he shall give prompt written notice thereof to the Architect.

2.9 The Owner shall furnish information required of him as expeditiously as necessary for the orderly progress of the Work.

ARTICLE 3
CONSTRUCTION COST

3.1 If the Construction Cost is to be used as the basis for determining the Architect's Compensation for Basic Services, it shall be the total cost or estimated cost to the Owner of all Work designed or specified by the Architect. The Construction Cost shall be determined as follows, with precedence in the order listed:

3.1.1 For completed construction, the cost of all such Work, including costs of managing construction;

3.1.2 For Work not constructed, (1) the lowest bona fide bid received from a qualified bidder for any or all of such Work, or (2) if the Work is not bid, the bona fide negotiated proposal submitted for any or all of such Work; or

3.1.3 For Work for which no such bid or proposal is received, (1) the latest Detailed Estimate of Construction Cost if one is available, or (2) the latest Statement of Probable Construction Cost.

3.2 Construction Cost does not include the compensation of the Architect and his consultants, the cost of the land, rights-of-way, or other costs which are the responsibility of the Owner as provided in Paragraphs 2.3 through 2.6 inclusive.

3.3 The cost of labor, materials and equipment furnished by the Owner for the Project shall be included in the Construction Cost at current market rates including a reasonable allowance for overhead and profit.

3.4 Statements of Probable Construction Cost and Detailed Cost Estimates prepared by the Architect represent his best judgment as a design professional familiar with the construction industry. It is recognized, however, that neither the Architect nor the Owner has any control over the cost of labor, materials or equipment, over the contractors' methods of determining bid prices, or over competitive bidding or market conditions. Accordingly, the

Figure 7-1 (continued).

Architect cannot and does not guarantee that bids will not vary from any Statement of Probable Construction Cost or other cost estimate prepared by him.

3.5 When a fixed limit of Construction Cost is established as a condition of this Agreement, it shall be in writing signed by the parties and shall include a bidding contingency of ten percent unless another amount is agreed upon in writing. When such a fixed limit is established, the Architect shall be permitted to determine what materials, equipment, component systems and types of construction are to be included in the Contract Documents, and to make reasonable adjustments in the scope of the Project to bring it within the fixed limit. The architect may also include in the Contract Documents alternate bids to adjust the Construction Cost to the fixed limit.

3.5.1 If the Bidding or Negotiating Phase has not commenced within six months after the Architect submits the Construction Documents to the Owner, any fixed limit of Construction Cost established as a condition of this Agreement shall be adjusted to reflect any change in the general level of prices which may have occurred in the construction industry for the area in which the Project is located. The adjustment shall reflect changes between the date of submission of the Construction Documents to the Owner and the date on which proposals are sought.

3.5.2 When a fixed limit of Construction Cost, including the Bidding contingency (adjusted as provided in Subparagraph 3.5.1, if applicable), is established as a condition of this Agreement and is exceeded by the lowest bona fide bid or negotiated proposal, the Detailed Estimate of Construction Cost or the Statement of Probable Construction cost, the Owner shall (1) give written approval of an increase in such fixed limit, (2) authorize rebidding the Project within a reasonable time, or (3) cooperate in revising the Project scope and quality as required to reduce the Probable Construction Cost. In the case of (3) the Architect, without additional charge, shall modify the Drawings and Specifications as necessary to bring the Construction Cost within the fixed limit. The providing of such service shall be the limit of the Architect's responsibility in this regard, and having done so, the Architect shall be entitled to compensation in accordance with this Agreement.

ARTICLE 4
DIRECT PERSONNEL EXPENSE

Direct Personnel Expense is defined as the salaries of professional, technical and clerical employees engaged on the Project by the Architect, and the cost of their mandatory and customary benefits such as statutory employee benefits, insurance, sick leave, holidays, vacations, pensions and similar benefits.

ARTICLE 5
REIMBURSABLE EXPENSES

5.1 Reimbursable Expenses are in addition to the Compensation for Basic and Additional Services and include actual expenditures made by the Architect, his employ-

ees, or his professional consultants in the interest of the Project for the expenses listed in the following Subparagraphs:

5.1.1 Expense of transportation and living when traveling in connection with the Project; long distance calls and telegrams; and fees paid for securing approval of authorities having jurisdiction over the Project.

5.1.2 Expense of reproductions, postage and handling of Drawings and Specifications excluding duplicate sets at the completion of each Phase for the Owner's review and approval.

5.1.3 If authorized in advance by the Owner, expense of overtime work requiring higher than regular rates and expense of renderings or models for the Owner's use.

5.1.4 Expense of computer time for professional services when included in Paragraph II.

5.1.5 Expense of computer time when used in connection with Additional Services.

ARTICLE 6
PAYMENTS TO THE ARCHITECT

6.1 Payments on account of the Architect's Basic Services shall be made as follows:

6.1.1 An initial payment as set forth in Paragraph II is the minimum payment under this Agreement.

6.1.2 Subsequent payments for Basic Services shall be made monthly in proportion to services performed so that the compensation at the completion of each Phase, except when the compensation is on the basis of a Multiple of Direct Personnel Expense, shall equal the following percentages of the total Basic Compensation:

Schematic Design Phase	15%
Design Development Phase	35%
Construction Documents Phase	75%
Bidding or Negotiation Phase	80%
Construction Phase	100%

6.1.3 If the Contract Time initially established in the Construction Contract is exceeded by more than thirty days through no fault of the Architect, compensation for Basic Services performed by Principals, employees and professional consultants required to complete the Administration of the Construction Contract beyond the thirtieth day shall be computed as set forth in Paragraph II for Additional Services.

6.2 Payments for Additional Services of the Architect as defined in Paragraph 1.3, and for Reimbursable Expenses as defined in Article 5, shall be made monthly upon presentation of the Architect's statement of services rendered.

6.3 No deductions shall be made from the Architect's compensation on account of penalty, liquidated damages, or other sums withheld from payments to contractors.

6.4 If the Project is suspended for more than three months or abandoned in whole or in part, the Architect

6

Figure 7-1 (continued).

shall be paid his compensation for services performed prior to receipt of written notice from the Owner of such suspension or abandonment, together with Reimbursable Expenses then due and all termination expenses as defined in Paragraph 8.3 resulting from such suspension or abandonment. If the Project is resumed after being suspended for more than three months, the Architect's compensation shall be subject to renegotiation.

6.5 Payments due the Architect under this Agreement shall bear interest at the legal rate commencing sixty days after the date of billing.

ARTICLE 7
ARCHITECT'S ACCOUNTING RECORDS

Records of Reimbursable Expenses and expenses pertaining to Additional Services on the Project and for services performed on the basis of a Multiple of Direct Personnel Expense shall be kept on a generally recognized accounting basis and shall be available to the Owner or his authorized representative at mutually convenient times.

ARTICLE 8
TERMINATION OF AGREEMENT

8.1 This Agreement may be terminated by either party upon seven days' written notice should the other party fail substantially to perform in accordance with its terms through no fault of the party initiating the termination.

8.2 In the event of termination due to the fault of parties other than the Architect, the Architect shall be paid his compensation for services performed to termination date, including Reimbursable Expenses then due and all termination' expenses.

8.3 Termination Expenses are defined as Reimbursable Expenses directly attributable to termination, plus an amount computed as a percentage of the total compensation earned to the time of termination, as follows:

    20 percent if termination occurs during the Schematic Design Phase; or

    10 percent if termination occurs during the Design Development Phase; or

    5 percent if termination occurs during any subsequent phase.

ARTICLE 9
OWNERSHIP OF DOCUMENTS

Drawings and Specifications as instruments of service are and shall remain the property of the Architect whether the Project for which they are made is executed or not. They are not to be used by the Owner on other projects or extensions to this Project except by agreement in writing and with appropriate compensation to the Architect.

ARTICLE 10
SUCCESSORS AND ASSIGNS

The Owner and the Architect each binds himself, his partners, successors, assigns and legal representatives to the other party to this Agreement and to the partners, successors, assigns and legal representatives of such other party with respect to all covenants of this Agreement. Neither the Owner nor the Architect shall assign, sublet or transfer his interest in this Agreement without the written consent of the other.

ARTICLE 11
ARBITRATION

11.1 All claims, disputes and other matters in question between the parties to this Agreement, arising out of, or relating to this Agreement or the breach thereof, shall be decided by arbitration in accordance with the Construction Industry Arbitration Rules of the American Arbitration Association then obtaining unless the parties mutually agree otherwise. No arbitration, arising out of, or relating to this Agreement, shall include, by consolidation, joinder or in any other manner, any additional party not a party to this Agreement except by written consent containing a specific reference to this Agreement and signed by all the parties hereto. Any consent to arbitration involving an additional party or parties shall not constitute consent to arbitration of any dispute not described therein or with any party not named or described therein. This Agreement to arbitrate and any agreement to arbitrate with an additional party or parties duly consented to by the parties hereto shall be specifically enforceable under the prevailing arbitration law.

11.2 Notice of the demand for arbitration shall be filed in writing with the other party to this Agreement and with the American Arbitration Association. The demand shall be made within a reasonable time after the claim, dispute or other matter in question has arisen. In no event shall the demand for arbitration be made after the date when institution of legal or equitable proceedings based on such claim, dispute or other matter in question would be barred by the applicable statute of limitations.

11.3 The award rendered by the arbitrators shall be final, and judgment may be entered upon it in accordance with applicable law in any court having jurisdiction thereof.

ARTICLE 12
EXTENT OF AGREEMENT

This Agreement represents the entire and integrated agreement between the Owner and the Architect and supersedes all prior negotiations, representations or agreements, either written or oral. This Agreement may be amended only by written instrument signed by both Owner and Architect.

ARTICLE 13
GOVERNING LAW

Unless otherwise specified, this Agreement shall be governed by the law of the principal place of business of the Architect.

AIA DOCUMENT B141 • OWNER-ARCHITECT AGREEMENT • JANUARY 1974 EDITION • AIA® • ©1974
THE AMERICAN INSTITUTE OF ARCHITECTS, 1735 NEW YORK AVE., N.W., WASHINGTON, D. C. 20006   7

Figure 7-1 (continued).

ARTICLE 14
OTHER CONDITIONS OR SERVICES

None

This Agreement executed the day and year first written above.

OWNER

[signature]

_____
Partner, General Restaurants, Inc.

ARCHITECT

[signature]

_____
Design Partnership, Inc., A.I.A.

AIA DOCUMENT B141 • OWNER-ARCHITECT AGREEMENT • JANUARY 1974 EDITION • AIA® • ©1974
THE AMERICAN INSTITUTE OF ARCHITECTS, 1735 NEW YORK AVE., N.W., WASHINGTON, D. C. 20006

Figure 7-1 (continued).

Schematic Design Phase

The purpose of the *schematic design phase* is to allow an architect to work with a client on an approach to the concept of a building. Generally, a program is written to define all the spaces and their relationships within the proposed building. In writing the program, the architect will suggest possible alternative solutions within the guidelines of cost, time to construct, and function. This, in turn, assists the owner in determining the feasibility of the project. The schematic design studies may include:

1. A diagram of the site, showing the building as it could be situated on the client's property and its relation to other buildings and traffic
2. Floor plans, showing the relationship of spaces and the general concept of the architect
3. A statement of why the architect arrived at various conclusions and the overall design concept
4. An estimate from the architect of the possible construction costs

As the term *schematic* implies, this is the beginning stage for a building. It is a scheme with many loose ends. The architect is not going to storm out of the room if the client totally rejects the concept. Usually the scheme is presented with sketches and models, along with the architect's commentary. The architect then, in effect, presents enough information to the client to describe the building concept but does not invest too much time (and fee) because the ideas may not be received favorably.

No magic is involved in arriving at an acceptable solution for schematics. The architect takes all the factors into account that affect the design and mixes them with his or her professional ability to reach a design solution. Some points affecting this decision are obtained by meeting with the client and the people who will actually use the space. This is extremely important, because it takes individual requirements into account. When a client loses the need for specific and singular demands in building, the need for an architect greatly diminishes.

The surrounding physical environment is a factor that must be placed in proper perspective to arrive at a solution. The physical environment can include water, streets, the topography, climate, sun orientation, pedestrian access, and relation to other buildings, to mention a few.

Engineering demands also affect the schematic design solution. These might include considering soil conditions, structurally supporting the building, heating and lighting the space, and acoustically conditioning the area. The consulting engineers are included in this preliminary design stage to the extent that their professional knowledge may point out a faulty engineering concept before the project is pursued further.

Cost is another extremely important aspect. The architect must use his or her professional ability to weigh design decisions against the client's budget.

A final point in schematics is difficult to define because it involves the architect's design philosophy. This individuality is the reason that two architects never arrive independently at exactly the same design solution, given the same program and site limits.

Following the example of the school, the schematic phase has 1160 work hours available. First, the architect meets with the school board to determine if their educational needs can be programmed into 100,000 sq ft. The type of required facilities is established, as dictated by the following: the number of students, the number and types of classrooms, cafeteria and dining areas, library, administrative offices, and other variables. To expand further on the schematic plan, the faculty and students are consulted to obtain their specific needs. These data are recorded and usually bound into a program that states the educational concept and the individual needs of each space. At the same time, the site plan is provided by the owner so that the building mass can be located in relation to parking, athletic facilities, the topography, and the many other necessary physical requirements.

The design department filters through all the many parameters and arrives at a building concept. The actual presentation to the client probably will occur in stages. When enough of an idea is on paper, the client and architect meet to discuss the scheme. In this stage ideas are culled out for a final solution. Not until the design-development phase are these ideas refined.

The final point of presentation of schematics is readied. The clients (in this case, the school board) can see the building's location on the site, line drawings of the floor plans, perhaps sections through the building, and a scale model or perspective sketch of the exterior. This, in effect, becomes a preview of coming attractions for the school. The clients now decide whether they would like this to be the new school.

Along with the presentation, the architect in the case we are discussing supplies a statement of probable construction cost, based on the $25/sq ft estimate. At this time, the architect receives written approval from the clients as to their general acceptance of the scheme. This, more than anything, protects the architect from the clients' later changing their minds after too much time has been invested in the project to absorb a major revision.

The schematic phase took four people in the office over seven weeks of research and design to complete, just making the budget. An architectural firm is willing to spend this amount of time on preliminary drawings because if the original concept is not valid, they cannot possibly end up with a well-designed, workable school the day the ribbon is cut at the front door. At the completion of this phase, the client owes the firm over $26,000 (15 percent of the fee).

Design-Development Phase

During the *design-development phase* in an architect's office, the schematics phase is refined in preparation for the construction documents. The client has given written approval of the schematics, and now it is a process of refining the idea. The client now is approving the more finished proposal rather than acting as a consultant. Generally, the design-development package includes the same basic material as did the schematics, but in much greater detail. It includes, but is not necessarily limited to:

1. Line-drawing floor plans (to scale), showing all rooms, wall thicknesses, and openings
2. Exterior building elevations, showing materials
3. The site plan, indicating the building location, roads, and parking, as well as any major landmarks
4. Sections through the building, describing the interior spaces
5. A decision by the structural, mechanical, and electrical engineers indicating how their respective systems function and how they affect the operation of the building
6. An outline specification, indicating materials
7. A refined cost analysis based on the more complete drawings

Because the architectural concept has been approved, the architectural firm now tries to make the design function in the best possible way.

Although the schematic approval certainly does not lock all walls and materials into a mold that is beyond change, it does give the architect an indication that the owner approves of the concept, and at this point the architect is concerned with seeing that everything works. Such things as plumbing requirements or pedestrian traffic flow might still cause walls to be moved.

Many hundreds of major as well as minor changes occur during this phase. The only static element involved is the design concept reached in schematics. Certainly, these items are so numerous and totally unique to a specific project that dwelling on what they might include is impossible. Generally, all the design points that were loose in schematics have to be tied together in design development to provide a smooth transition into the next phase—*contract documents*.

Just as in schematics, the architect is dealing with the client and must bear in mind that the presentation must be clear and easy enough for a layperson to understand. In effect, an architect speaks two different languages. During the first two phases, the architect provides the client with the information necessary to approve a building scheme without ever fully seeing the project in full scale. The architect's job in schematics and design development is to fully inform the client, who probably is not familiar with building, what he or she is getting for the money. To achieve this, the architect uses "flashy" visual aids—color perspective, models, and presentation drawings. These aids put the building scheme in a dimension that the client can understand. When the client accepts the design-development drawings, the architect changes hats and is now in the position of telling a skilled contractor exactly how the project should be built.

On the school project, the design-development phase includes refining the approved schematic drawings. The matters of building elevations, parking, access, and a more specific building location are resolved on the site plan. Details, such as the turning radius of a school bus on the drive to the entrance or storage of maintenance equipment, are discussed also. Window and door placement and how they fit into walls are determined. The floor plans receive a great deal of refinement, not only in the relationship of one department to another but also within each space. It is not enough, as in schematics, to allocate 1500 sq ft to one chemistry lab and locate it near the math, biology, and physics classrooms. The layout in design development includes the lab tables, fume hoods, and chemical storage facilities within the lab. This means researching as well as meeting with the science faculty and possibly a science equipment representative to arrive at a layout for the space. How exterior walls will be constructed is detailed preliminarily, and the materials are selected. The school board now has made most of the major decisions and given written approval that cannot be changed.

With this degree of detail completed in design development, the building cost is updated to reflect the school design. This can be done by estimating the materials incorporated in the building to give the school board a more accurate idea of the cost.

Another extremely important aspect in the design-development phase is the updating of engineering data. The engineers have completed the column locations (not necessarily the exact sizes), the air-duct sizes, the locations for electrical-transformer rooms, and other items that affect the final design.

Roughly, 1546 work hours have been invested so far to obtain final acceptance of the design. Much of this time was spent in researching and organizing the specific points and transferring them into presentation drawings in an effort to inform the client of how the building will look.

Construction Document Phase

Three terms used in the *construction document phase* of an architect's contract are applied to approximately the same item: *working drawings, contract documents,* and *construction documents.*

The *working drawings* are the set of drawings produced by the architect to indicate the quantity of material on the job. The *contract documents* or *construction documents* are composed of the working drawings and the specifications. All three are used interchangeably in an office: *Working drawings* is the most common phrase; *construction documents* is the most correct term to refer to the total phase within the office; and *contract documents* refers to the completed package of drawings, specifications (with preface material and all addenda). As the term implies, the *contract document package* constitutes a major portion of the legal contract between the owner and the contractor.

The key to a smooth operation within an architectural firm is an even transition among the pro-

duction phases. This is particularly important in changing gears from design development to construction documents. At this point, the architect begins to produce detailed and complex working drawings for a skilled contractor from the schematic and design-development drawings previously shown to the client. The architect actually changes to a technical language when he or she begins the working drawings. The architect is producing an extremely complex package, intended to tell a contractor exactly how to build the project and what to charge. In the previous phase, the drawings were intended to give the client a general idea of the entire project. The working drawing package is so detailed that it would be almost as impossible for a person not trained in construction to understand the drawings as it would be for the contractor to construct a building from a schematic or design-development set of drawings.

The construction document phase is the most time consuming and exacting of the five phases. Since the design has been locked in, all the materials must be detailed to provide an efficient, watertight structure carefully patterned after the final design of the design-development package. All items must be coordinated so that at the completion of working drawings a package is prepared indicating the exact location, types of material, and assembly directions of every item in the building on site. The architectural drawings not only must be complete but also must be coordinated with structural, mechanical, and electrical drawings. The client acts in a rather passive capacity in that he or she is approving the progress rather than making major changes.

The construction details must accomplish two things: (1) The type, quality, and quantity of the materials required must be accurately described to contractors so that they can submit a bid; and (2) every material must be detailed so that the contractor can properly assemble the building. The final package that is put together for the contractor, referred to as the *construction documents,* consists of the working drawings and specifications. The drawings indicate quantity, and the specifications define quality. The working drawings completely cover the construction requirements efficiently and economically. Once the scope and intent of the work are defined clearly, any further laboring on the detail wastes time and money.

In the production of a set of construction documents the primary factor is coordination. The structural engineers have all beams, walls, and columns sized so that the architectural details will work. The mechanical drawings indicate the duct sizes and locations, the mechanical equipment, and all plumbing piping. Electrical drawings indicate outlets, fans, speakers, lights, and telephones. Generally, the size of a commercial job dictates that a separate complete set of structural, mechanical, and electrical drawings be completed and bound into the working drawings.

The specifications constitute the other portion of the construction document package that demands a total degree of coordination. The specification writer must be aware of every material used in the project so that he or she can prepare written information on the following:

1. The scope of the work
2. Whether shop drawings should be submitted
3. The quality of the material or the products that may be used (trade names)
4. The way the finished material should appear or react
5. How the material should be applied
6. When the material may be applied (weather permitting)
7. How the finished material is to be protected during construction
8. If there is to be any special guarantee on the work

The package of drawings and specifications is assembled for the purpose of telling a contractor precisely how to build and what materials to use. The construction document set is the only source of information the contractor has to follow. If a contractor varies from them in any way, he or she runs the risk either of being required to replace the work or of facing legal action.

Now that the school board has approved the design-development drawings, the task of assembling the construction drawings begins. The number of people assigned to work on the project jumps from the three or four who completed design development to possibly six during this phase. The architects and technicians need approximately three months to coordinate and complete the working drawings. At the same time, the engineers and consultants are working to complete their phase so that as many as twenty professionals are working to complete this project. Coordination usually is handled by exchanging copies of the latest drawings

between the architect and the various consultants. These copies are referred to as *check sets.*

The obvious way to start working drawings is to refine further the design-development floor plans and site plans. Along with dimensioning every wall on the plan, the materials are indicated graphically. During this time the architect continues to meet with the board and school officials to keep them informed of the progress and have them make decisions on specific details.

At the completion of construction documents, all data pertaining to the scope and intent of the project are formulated into a package. The data package must have absolutely no loose ends and is set up as follows:

1. The soil-boring data provided by the owner have been bound into the specification for the bidders' reference.
2. The existing site-data survey—showing topography, trees, power poles, and so on—is in the working drawings.
3. The specifications contain specific information varying from the types and amounts of insurance the owner and contractor must carry to whether the contractor is to provide outdoor toilet facilities for the workers during construction.
4. The specifications also give information to the bidders on where the bids are to be submitted, if a cash deposit for the construction is necessary, if the bidder is allowed to substitute materials for those specified, and so on.
5. A bid form on which the bidder submits the exact dollars and cents amount of the bid to complete the work and the length of time needed for construction.
6. The architectural working drawings and specifications.
7. The structural, mechanical, and electrical drawings and specifications.
8. Special consultant drawings and specifications, such as kitchen equipment and acoustical considerations.

With this completed data package, the architect is in the best position to update and revise the cost estimate. Obviously, it is too late to make major changes that would mean a higher cost than planned. However, several procedures that will affect the contract amount are open, even at this late point. The most common practice is to receive the

THE AMERICAN INSTITUTE OF ARCHITECTS

AIA Document A701

Instructions to Bidders

Use only with the latest Edition of AIA Document A201, General Conditions of the Contract for Construction

TABLE OF ARTICLES

1. DEFINITIONS

2. BIDDER'S REPRESENTATION

3. BIDDING DOCUMENTS

4. BIDDING PROCEDURES

5. CONSIDERATION OF BIDS

6. QUALIFICATION OF CONTRACTORS

7. POST-BID INFORMATION

8. PERFORMANCE BOND AND
   LABOR AND MATERIAL PAYMENT BOND

9. FORM OF AGREEMENT BETWEEN OWNER
   AND CONTRACTOR

Figure 7-2.   The American Institute of Architecture's guidelines for instructions to bidders.

THE AMERICAN INSTITUTE OF ARCHITECTS

AIA DOCUMENT A701

INSTRUCTIONS TO BIDDERS

Table of Articles

1. DEFINITIONS
2. BIDDER'S REPRESENTATION
3. BIDDING DOCUMENTS
4. BIDDING PROCEDURES

5. CONSIDERATION OF BIDS
6. QUALIFICATION OF CONTRAC–TORS
7. POST–BID INFORMATION

8. PERFORMANCE BOND AND LABOR AND MATERIAL BOND
9. FORM OF AGREEMENT BETWEEN OWNER AND CONTRACTORS.

ARTICLE 1

DEFINITIONS

1.1 Bidding Documents include the Advertisement or Invitation to Bid, Instructions to Bidders, the bid form, other sample bidding and contract forms and the proposed Contract Documents including any Addenda issued prior to receipt of bids.

1.2 All definitions set forth in the General Conditions of the Contract for Construction, AIA Document A201, or in other Contract Documents are applicable to the Bidding Documents.

1.3 Addenda are written or graphic instruments issued by the Architect prior to the execution of the Contract which modify or interpret the bidding documents by addition, deletions, clarifications or corrections.

1.4 A Bid is a complete and properly signed proposal to do the Work or designated portion thereof for the sums stiplated therein supported by data called for by the Bidding Documents.

1.5 Base Bid is the sum stated in the Bid for which the Bidder offers to perform the Work described as the base, to which Work may be added or deducted for sums stated in Alternate Bids.

1.6 An Alternate Bid (or Alternate) is an amount stated in the Bid to be added to or deducted from the amount of the Base Bid if the corresponding change in project scope or materials or methods of construction described in the Bidding Documents is accepted.

1.7 A Unit Price is an amount stated in the Bid as a price per unit of measurement for materials or services as described in the Contract Documents.

1.8 A Bidder is one who submits a Bid for a prime contract with the Owner for the Work described in the proposed Contract Documents.

1.9 A Sub-bidder is one who submits a bid to a Bidder for materials or labor for a portion of the Work.

ARTICLE 2

BIDDER'S REPRESENTATION

2.1 Each Bidder by making his bid represents that:

2.1.1 He has read and understands the Bidding Documents and his Bid is made in accordance therewith.

2.1.2 He has visited the site and has familiarized himself with the local conditions under which the Work is to be performed.

2.1.3 His Bid is based upon the materials, systems and equipment described in the Bidding Documents without exceptions.

ARTICLE 3

BIDDING DOCUMENTS

3.1   COPIES

3.1.1 Bidders may obtain from the Architect (unless another issuing office is designated in the Advertisement or Invitation to Bid) complete sets of the Bidding Documents in the number and for the deposit sum, if any, stated in the Advertisement or Invitation. The deposit will be refunded to Bidders who submit a bonafide Bid and return the Bidding Documents in good condition within 10 days after receipt of Bids. The cost of replacement of any missing or damaged documents will be deducted from the deposit. A Bidder receiving a contract award may retain the Bidding Documents and his deposit will be refunded.

3.1.2 Bidding Documents will not be issued to Sub-bidders or others unless specifically offered in the Advertisement or Invitation to Bid.

3.1.3 Complete sets of Bidding Documents shall be used in preparing bids; neither the Owner nor the Architect assume any responsibility for errors or misinterpretations resulting from the use of incomplete sets of Bidding Documents.

3.1.4 The Owner or Architect in making copies of the Bidding Documents available on the above terms, do so only for the purpose of obtaining bids on the Work and do not confer a license or grant for any other use.

3.2   INTERPRETATION OR CORRECTION OF BIDDING DOCUMENTS

3.2.1 Bidders shall promptly notify the Architect of any ambiguity, inconsistency or error which they may discover upon examination of the Bidding Documents or of the site and local conditions.

3.2.2 Bidders requiring clarification or interpretation of the Bidding Documents shall make a written

AIA DOCUMENT A701 • INSTRUCTIONS TO BIDDERS • JANUARY 1974 EDITION • AIA® • ©1974
THE AMERICAN INSTITUTE OF ARCHITECTS, 1735 NEW YORK AVE., N.W., WASHINGTON, D. C. 20006   **1**

Figure 7-2 (continued).

request to the Architect, to reach him at least seven days prior to the date for receipt of bids.

3.2.3 Any interpretation, correction or change of the Bidding Documents will be made by Addendum. Interpretations, corrections or changes of the Bidding Documents made in any other manner will not be binding, and bidders shall not rely upon such interpretations, corrections and changes.

3.3 SUBSTITUTIONS

3.3.1 The materials, products and equipment described in the Bidding Documents establish a standard of required function, dimension, appearance and quality to be met by any proposed substitution.

3.3.2 No substitution will be considered unless written request for approval has been submitted by the Bidder and has been received by the Architect at least ten days prior to the date for receipt of bids. Each such request shall include the name of the material or equipment for which it is to be substituted and a complete description of the proposed substitute including drawings, cuts, performance and test data and any other information necessary for an evaluation. A statement setting forth any changes in other materials, equipment or work that incorporation of the substitute would require shall be included. The burden of proof of the merit of the proposed substitute is upon the proposer. The Architect's decision of approval or disapproval of a proposed substitution shall be final.

3.3.3 If the Architect approves any proposed substitution, such approval will be set forth in an Addendum. Bidders shall not rely upon approvals made in any other manner.

3.4 ADDENDA

3.4.1 Addenda will be mailed or delivered to all who are known by the Architect to have received a complete set of Bidding Documents.

3.4.2 Copies of Addenda will be made available for inspection wherever Bidding Documents are on file for that purpose.

3.4.3 No Addenda will be issued later than four days prior to the date for receipt of bids except an Addendum, if necessary, postponing the date for receipt of bids or withdrawing the request for bids.

3.4.4 Each Bidder shall ascertain prior to submitting his bid that he has received all Addenda issued, and he shall acknowledge their receipt in his bid.

ARTICLE 4

BIDDING PROCEDURE

4.1 FORM AND STYLE OF BIDS

4.1.1 Bids shall be submitted in duplicate on the forms provided by the Architect.

4.1.2 All blanks on the bid form shall be filled in by typewriter or manually in ink.

4.1.3 Where so indicated by the makeup of the bid form, sums shall be expressed in both words and figures, and in case of discrepancy between the two, the written amount shall govern.

4.1.4 Any interlineation, alteration or erasure must be initialed by the signer of the Bid.

4.1.5 All requested alternates shall be bid.

4.1.6 Where there are two or more major items of work for which separate quotations have been requested, Bidder may state his refusal to accept less than whatever combination of the items he stipulates.

4.1.7 Bidder shall make no additional stipulations on the bid form nor qualify his bid in any other manner.

4.1.8 Each copy of Bid shall include the legal name of Bidder and a statement whether Bidder is a sole proprietor, a partnership, a corporation, or any other legal entity, and each copy shall be signed by the person or persons legally authorized to bind the Bidder to a contract. A Bid by a corporation shall further give the State of incorporation and have the corporate seal affixed. A Bid submitted by an agent shall have a current Power of Attorney attached certifying agent's authority to bind Bidder.

4.2 BID SECURITY

4.2.1 If so stipulated in the Advertisement or Invitation to Bid, each Bid shall be accompanied by a bid security in the required form and amount pledging that the Bidder will enter into a contract with the Owner on the terms stated in his Bid and will, if required, furnish bonds as described hereunder in Article 8 covering the faithful performance of the Contract and the payment of all obligations arising thereunder. Should the Bidder refuse to enter into such Contract or fail to furnish such bonds, if required, the amount of the bid security shall be forfeited to the Owner as liquidated damages, not as penalty.

4.2.2 If a surety bond is required it shall be written in the form of AIA Document A310, Bid Bond, and the Attorney-In-Fact who executes the bond on behalf of the surety shall affix to the bond a certified and current copy of his Power of Attorney.

4.2.3 The Owner will have the right to retain the bid security of Bidders until either (a), the Contract has been executed and bonds, if required, have been furnished or (b), the specified time has elapsed so that Bids may be withdrawn, or (c), all Bids have been rejected.

4.3 SUBMISSION OF BIDS

4.3.1 All copies of the Bid, the bid security, if any, and any other documents required to be submitted with the Bid shall be enclosed in a sealed opaque envelope. The envelope shall be addressed to the party receiving the Bids and shall be identified with the Project name, the Bidder's name and address, and the portion of the project or category of work for which the Bid is submitted. If the Bid is sent by mail the sealed envelope shall be enclosed in a separate mailing envelope with the notation "BID ENCLOSED" on the face thereof.

2   AIA DOCUMENT A701 • INSTRUCTIONS TO BIDDERS • JANUARY 1974 EDITION • AIA® • ©1974
THE AMERICAN INSTITUTE OF ARCHITECTS, 1735 NEW YORK AVE., N.W., WASHINGTON, D. C. 20006

Figure 7-2 (continued).

4.3.2 Bids shall be deposited at the designated location prior to the time and date for receipt of bids indicated in the Advertisement or Invitation to Bid, or any extension thereof made by Addendum. Bids received after the time and date for receipt of bids will be returned unopened.

4.3.3 Bidder shall assume full responsibility for timely delivery at location designated for receipt of Bids.

4.3.4 Oral, telephonic or telegraphic Bids are invalid and will not receive consideration.

4.4 MODIFICATION OR WITHDRAWAL OF BID

4.4.1 A Bid may not be modified, withdrawn or canceled by the Bidder during the stipulated time period following the time and date designated for the receipt of Bids, and Bidder so agrees in submitting his Bid.

4.4.2 Prior to the time and date designated for receipt of Bids, Bids submitted early may be modified or withdrawn only by notice to the party receiving Bids at the place and prior to the time designated for receipt of Bids.

  .1 Such notice shall be in writing over the signature of the Bidder or be by telegram; if by telegram, written confirmation over the signature of Bidder must have been mailed and postmarked on or before the date and time set for receipt of Bids; it shall be so worded as not to reveal the amount of the original Bid.

4.4.3 Withdrawn Bids may be resubmitted up to the time designated for the receipt of Bids provided that they are then fully in conformance with these Instructions to Bidders.

4.4.4 Bid security, if any is required, shall be in an amount sufficient for the Bid as modified or resubmitted.

ARTICLE 5

CONSIDERATION OF BIDS

5.1 OPENING OF BIDS

5.1.1 Unless stated otherwise in the Advertisement or Invitation to Bid the properly identified Bids received on time will be opened publicly and will be read aloud, and an abstract of the amounts of the Base Bids and major Alternates, if any, will be made available to Bidders. When it has been stated that Bids will be opened privately, an abstract of the same information may be made available to the Bidders within a reasonable time.

5.2 REJECTION OF BIDS

5.2.1 The Owner shall have the right to reject any or all Bids and in particular to reject a Bid not accompanied by any required bid security or data required by the Bidding Documents or a Bid in any way incomplete or irregular.

5.3 ACCEPTANCE OF BID (AWARD)

5.3.1 The Owner shall have the right to waive any informality or irregularity in any Bid received.

5.3.2 It is the intent of the Owner, if he accepts any Alternates, to accept them in the order in which they are listed in the bid form, but the Owner shall have the right to accept alternates in any order or combination and to determine the low Bidder on the basis of the sum of the Base Bid and the Alternates accepted.

5.3.3 It is the intent of the Owner to award a contract to the lowest responsible Bidder provided the Bid has been submitted in accordance with the requirements of the Bidding Documents, is judged to be reasonable, and does not exceed the funds available.

ARTICLE 6

QUALIFICATION OF CONTRACTORS

6.1 SUBMISSION OF QUALIFICATION STATEMENT

6.1.1 Bidders to whom award of a contract is under consideration shall submit to the Architect upon his request a properly executed Contractor's Qualification Statement, A.I.A. Document A305, unless such a Statement has been previously required and submitted as a prerequisite to the issuance of Bidding Documents.

ARTICLE 7

POST–BID INFORMATION

7.1 SUBMISSIONS

7.1.1 Unless waived by the Architect, the Bidder shall, within seven days of notification of selection for the award of a contract for the Work, submit the following information to the Architect:

  .1 A designation of the Work to be performed by the Bidder with his own forces.

  .2 The proprietary names and the suppliers of principal items or systems of material and equipment proposed for the Work.

  .3 A list of names of the Subcontractors or other persons or organizations (including those who are to furnish materials or equipment fabricated to a special design) proposed for the principal portions of the Work.

7.1.2 The Bidder will be required to establish to the satisfaction of the Architect and the Owner the reliability and responsibility of the proposed Subcontractors to furnish and perform the Work described in the Sections of the Specifications pertaining to such proposed Subcontractors' respective trades.

7.1.3 Prior to the award of the Contract, the Architect will notify the Bidder in writing if either the Owner or the Architect, after due investigation, has reasonable and substantial objection to any person or organization on such list. If the Owner or Architect has a reasonable and substantial objection to any person or organization on such list, and refuses in writing to accept such person or organization, the Bidder may, at his option, (1) withdraw his bid,

Figure 7-2 (continued).

or (2) submit an acceptable substitute Subcontractor with an increase in his bid price to cover the difference in cost occasioned by such substitution. The Owner may, at his discretion, accept the increased bid price or he may disqualify the Bidder. In the event of either withdrawal or disqualification under this Subparagraph, bid security will not be forfeited, notwithstanding anything to the contrary in Paragraph 4.4.1.

7.1.4 Subcontractors and other persons and organizations proposed by the Bidder and accepted by the Owner and the Architect must be used on the Work for which they were proposed and accepted and shall not be changed except with the written approval of the Owner and the Architect.

ARTICLE 8

PERFORMANCE BOND AND LABOR AND MATERIAL PAYMENT BOND

8.1   OWNER'S RIGHT TO REQUIRE BONDS

8.1.1 The Owner shall have the right, prior to the execution of the Contract, to require the Bidder to furnish bonds covering the faithful performance of the Contract and the payment of all obligations arising thereunder in such form and amount as the Owner may prescribe and with such sureties secured through the Bidder's usual sources as may be agreeable to the parties. If the furnishing of such bonds is stipulated in the Bidding Documents, the premiums shall be paid by the Bidder; if required

by the Owner subsequent to the submission of bids, the cost shall be reimbursed by the Owner.

8.2   TIME OF DELIVERY AND FORM OF BONDS

8.2.1 The Bidder shall deliver the required bonds to the Owner not later than the date of execution of the Contract, or if the Work is commenced prior thereto in response to a letter of intent, the Bidder shall, prior to commencement of the Work, submit evidence satisfactory to the Owner that such bonds will be furnished.

8.2.2 Unless otherwise specified in the Bidding Documents, the bonds shall be written in the form of AIA Document A311, Performance Bond and Labor and Material Payment Bond.

8.2.3 The Bidder shall require the Attorney-In-Fact who executes the required bonds on behalf of the surety to affix thereto a certified and current copy of his Power of Attorney.

ARTICLE 9

FORM OF AGREEMENT BETWEEN OWNER AND CONTRACTOR

9.1   FORM TO BE USED

9.1.1 Unless otherwise provided in the Bidding Documents the Agreement for the Work will be written on the Standard Form of Agreement between Owner and Contractor where the basis of payment is a Stipulated Sum, AIA Document A101.

AIA DOCUMENT A701 • INSTRUCTIONS TO BIDDERS • JANUARY 1974 EDITION • AIA® • ©1974
THE AMERICAN INSTITUTE OF ARCHITECTS, 1735 NEW YORK AVE., N.W., WASHINGTON, D. C. 20006

Figure 7-2 (continued).

owner's approval to accept separate bids, referred to as *add alternates*, on items that could be eliminated, such as carpeting. This gives the owner the option of accepting the base bid or of varying the total contract amount to fit the budget, by approving or rejecting alternatives.

After a rather extensive series of checks within the office and a final approval by the owner, the project is now ready to go out for bids.

Bidding Phase

Negotiating or obtaining bids for a project can be done in several ways. All bidding methods have a common goal—securing the best price for competent construction of the project. The architect's responsibility is to assist the owner in obtaining competitive bids on the project. The three most common means of sending a project out for bid are (1) negotiated sum, (2) invitational bid, and (3) competitive bid. Although the three methods accomplish the same goal—a signed contract for a specified sum—they differ in how the contractor is selected. The scope and type of project dictate, to a certain extent, how the contractor is chosen.

The first method, a *negotiated sum*, has some definite limitations. The system involves choosing one contractor without securing costs from any other source. Generally, the owner is familiar with the contractor and perhaps previously has worked with her or him and knows the quality of the work. With this system it is possible for the owner to retain the contractor during the contract document stage (or even in the design stages in some cases) and have the contractor work with the architect to make sure that the owner's budget will be met.

A rather dangerous (for the owner's pocketbook) branch of this method is called *cost-plus*, which refers to a contract signed between the owner and contractor that does not contain a stipulated sum. Rather, it directs the contractor to enter into the project with a guarantee that he or she will be paid for all materials and labor plus a percentage of profit. This can prove dangerous, as the owner does not know the final cost of construction until the project is completed. This method of bidding generally is used when the owner is concerned mostly with occupying the building as fast as possible. A very large office building might be constructed according to such an agreement. The months that can be shaved off the construction drawing and design time could more than make up for the added financing necessary at the final billing. The reason is that the contractor does not

have to wait until the completion of the architect's construction document package to start the job.

The advantages of a negotiated sum is that no question exists as to who the contractor is, and the owner has the option of using an architect together with the contractor to ascertain the construction costs. The disadvantage of this system is that the owner has no point of comparison with the price obtained. Because of this drawback, most owners elect (or may be required by law on a public project) not to use this form of bidding.

The term *invitational bid* is self-descriptive. The owner, wishing quality construction, asks certain contractors who are familiar to her or him or to the architect to submit bids on the completed drawings and specifications. If a contractor is not on the list, he or she is not allowed to bid.

The advantage of this system is obvious: The owner chooses from among quality contractors, just as in a negotiated bid, except that he or she is afforded the choice of a low bidder. The disadvantage of this system is that most state laws disallow the method on public projects on the grounds that it is discriminatory. It still is used widely on private building projects.

Competitive bidding is another bidding procedure. Any contractor that can provide bid security or obtain a bid bond is allowed to submit a cost. A *bid bond* is, in a sense, an insurance policy guaranteeing the owner that if a contractor bids on the project, and is the low bidder, he or she will enter into a contractual agreement with the owner to build the project. The specifications define the bonding requirements for the project. Generally, it is 5 percent of the contractor's bid. This means that if the general contractor's bid on the school is $1.5 million, he or she must provide a $75,000 bond or a certified check for that amount, agreeing to sign a contract under penalty of forfeiture on the bond. Obviously, with that amount of money on the table, most contractors practicing questionable construction techniques will be dissuaded from submitting a bid. In the case of a bid bond, the forfeiture of the bond by the contractor must be paid by the bonding company. Thus, the company makes certain the contractor has every intention of entering into a contract if he or she is the successful bidder before they issue the bond.

Most laws that apply to the method of how public bids may be received have two requirements: (1) they are to be competitive; (2) the lowest responsible bidder is to be accepted. The phrase *lowest responsible bidder* generally is accepted to mean that if the low bidder has an

THE AMERICAN INSTITUTE OF ARCHITECTS

AIA Document A310

Bid Bond

KNOW ALL MEN BY THESE PRESENTS, that we
_(Here insert full name and address or legal title of Contractor)

Standard Building Co., Bloomington, Indiana

as Principal, hereinafter called the Principal, and
New York Casualty Co., Buffalo, New York _(Here insert full name and address or legal title of Surety)

a corporation duly organized under the laws of the State of
as Surety, hereinafter called the Surety, are held and firmly bound unto
_(Here insert full name and address or legal title of Owner)

General Restaurants, Inc., Bloomington, Indiana

as Obligee, hereinafter called the Obligee, in the sum of

Four Hundred Fifty Seven Thousand Three Hundred Eighteen

Dollars ($ 457,318   ),

for the payment of which sum well and truly to be made, the said Principal and the said Surety, bind ourselves, our heirs, executors, administrators, successors and assigns, jointly and severally, firmly by these presents.

WHEREAS, the Principal has submitted a bid for
The Beef and Burgundy Restaurant _(Here insert full name, address and description of project)
2617 Anderson Parkway
Bloomington, Indiana

NOW, THEREFORE, if the Obligee shall accept the bid of the Principal and the Principal shall enter into a Contract with the Obligee in accordance with the terms of such bid, and give such bond or bonds as may be specified in the bidding or Contract Documents with good and sufficient surety for the faithful performance of such Contract and for the prompt payment of labor and material furnished in the prosecution thereof, or in the event of the failure of the Principal to enter such Contract and give such bond or bonds, if the Principal shall pay to the Obligee the difference not to exceed the penalty hereof between the amount specified in said bid and such larger amount for which the Obligee may in good faith contract with another party to perform the Work covered by said bid, then this obligation shall be null and void, otherwise to remain in full force and effect.

Signed and sealed this   tenth   day of   December   19 77

Mark Wolfgram	*Adam Anderson*	
(Witness)	(Principal)	(Seal)
	Senior Vice President	
	(Title)	
Susan McGuire	*Rick S Robinson*	
(Witness)	(Surety)	(Seal)
	Corporate Officer	
	(Title)	

AIA DOCUMENT A310 • BID BOND • AIA ® • FEBRUARY 1970 ED • THE AMERICAN
INSTITUTE OF ARCHITECTS, 1735 N.Y. AVE., N.W., WASHINGTON, D.C. 20006   1

Figure 7-3. A bid bond.

THE AMERICAN INSTITUTE OF ARCHITECTS

AIA Document A101

Standard Form of Agreement Between Owner and Contractor

where the basis of payment is a

STIPULATED SUM

*THIS DOCUMENT HAS IMPORTANT LEGAL CONSEQUENCES; CONSULTATION WITH
AN ATTORNEY IS ENCOURAGED WITH RESPECT TO ITS COMPLETION OR MODIFICATION*

Use only with the latest Edition of AIA Document A201, General Conditions of the Contract for Construction.

This document has been approved and endorsed by The Associated General Contractors of America.

AGREEMENT

made this   fifteenth   day of   December   in the year of Nineteen
Hundred and   seventy-seven

BETWEEN the Owner: General Restaurants, Inc.
                          Bloomington, Indiana

and the Contractor: Standard Building Co.
                          Bloomington, Indiana

the Project: The Beef and Burgundy Restaurant
                          2617 Anderson Parkway
                          Bloomington, Indiana

the Architect: Design Partnership, Inc., A.I.A.
                          Chicago, Illinois

The Owner and the Contractor agree as set forth below.

Figure 7-4.   An agreement between an owner and contractor.

ARTICLE 1

THE CONTRACT DOCUMENTS

The Contract Documents consist of this Agreement, Conditions of the Contract (General, Supplementary and other Conditions), Drawings, Specifications, all Addenda issued prior to execution of this Agreement and all Modifications issued subsequent thereto. These form the Contract, and all are as fully a part of the Contract as if attached to this Agreement or repeated herein. An enumeration of the Contract Documents appears in Article 7.

ARTICLE 2

THE WORK

The Contractor shall perform all the Work required by the Contract Documents for
(Here insert the caption descriptive of the Work as used on other Contract Documents.)

        The Beef and Burgundy Restaurant
        2617 Anderson Parkway
        Bloomington, Indiana

ARTICLE 3

TIME OF COMMENCEMENT AND COMPLETION

The Work to be performed under this Contract shall be commenced   March 15, 1978

and completed   November 15, 1978
(Here insert any special provisions for liquidated damages relating to failure to complete on time.)

        The contractor will pay liquidated damages of five-hundred dollars
        ($500) each calendar day past the completion date that the project
        is unfinished. Completion is defined in Section 8.1.3 of the
        General Conditions. The owner will pay the contractor a bonus of
        two-hundred dollars ($200) for each prior to the completion date
        that the project is finished.

Figure 7-4 (continued).

ARTICLE 4

CONTRACT SUM

The Owner shall pay the Contractor for the performance of the Work, subject to additions and deductions by Change Order as provided in the Conditions of the Contract, in current funds, the Contract Sum of

(State here the lump sum amount, unit prices, or both, as desired.)

Four Hundred Fifty Seven Thousand Three Hundred Eighteen Dollars ($457,318.00)

ARTICLE 5

PROGRESS PAYMENTS

Based upon Applications for Payment submitted to the Architect by the Contractor and Certificates for Payment issued by the Architect, the Owner shall make progress payments on account of the Contract Sum to the Contractor as provided in the Conditions of the Contract as follows:

On or about the   fifteenth   day of each month   ten   per cent of the proportion of the Contract Sum properly allocable to labor, materials and equipment incorporated in the Work and   ten   per cent of the portion of the Contract Sum properly allocable to materials and equipment suitably stored at the site or at some other location agreed upon in writing by the parties, up to the   five   days prior to the date on which the Application for Payment is submitted, less the aggregate of previous payments in each case; and upon Substantial Completion of the entire Work, a sum sufficient to increase the total payments to   one-hundred   per cent of the Contract Sum, less such retainages as the Architect shall determine for all incomplete Work and unsettled claims.

(If not covered elsewhere in the Contract Documents, here insert any provision for limiting or reducing the amount retained after the Work reaches a certain stage of completion.)

Any moneys not paid when due to either party under this Contract shall bear interest at the legal rate in force at the place of the Project.

AIA DOCUMENT A101 • OWNER-CONTRACTOR AGREEMENT • JANUARY 1974 EDITION • AIA® • ©1974
THE AMERICAN INSTITUTE OF ARCHITECTS, 1735 NEW YORK AVE., N.W., WASHINGTON, D. C. 20006   3

Figure 7-4 (continued).

ARTICLE 6

FINAL PAYMENT

Final payment, constituting the entire unpaid balance of the Contract Sum, shall be paid by the Owner to the Contractor   *thirty*   days after Substantial Completion of the Work unless otherwise stipulated in the Certificate of Substantial Completion, provided the Work has then been completed, the Contract fully performed, and a final Certificate for Payment has been issued by the Architect.

ARTICLE 7

MISCELLANEOUS PROVISIONS

7.1   Terms used in this Agreement which are defined in the Conditions of the Contract shall have the meanings designated in those Conditions.

7.2   The Contract Documents, which constitute the entire agreement between the Owner and the Contractor, are listed in Article 1 and, except for Modifications issued after execution of this Agreement, are enumerated as follows:

(List below the Agreement, Conditions of the Contract (General, Supplementary, and other Conditions), Drawings, Specifications, Addenda and accepted Alternates, showing page or sheet numbers in all cases and dates where applicable.)

```
Specification Document titled "The Beef and Burgundy Restaurant"

Job Number 77-36

Architectural Drawings A-1, A-2, A-3, A-4, and A-5

Mechanical Drawings M-1, M-2, M-3

Structural Drawings S-1, S-2, S-3, S-4

Electrical Drawings E-1, E-2, E-3

Addenda 1, 2, and 3 issued by the architect
```

This Agreement executed the day and year first written above.

OWNER _Rick Schroeder_   CONTRACTOR _Allan Anderson_

AIA DOCUMENT A101 • OWNER-CONTRACTOR AGREEMENT • JANUARY 1974 EDITION • AIA® • ©1974
THE AMERICAN INSTITUTE OF ARCHITECTS, 1735 NEW YORK AVE., N.W., WASHINGTON, D. C. 20006   **4**

Figure 7-4 (continued).

extremely poor record on past projects, the public body has the option of signing a contract with the next in line. In this case the unsuccessful low bidder would not be required to forfeit the bid bond. There usually is a 30-day period between the date when bids are accepted and when the contract between the owner and contractor must be signed. This period allows the owner to check such things as the reputation of the low bidder.

In competitive bidding, as in invitational bidding, an exact time and location is established in the specification as to when and where the bids will be opened. This is the final step in the bidding phase. It helps to know the events that took place prior to the bid opening. Once the contract documents have been completed by the architect, he or she makes it known in the construction trade that the project is out for bids. This can be done by advertising the job in local and regional newspapers, by listing in *Dodge Reports,* a publication especially for contractors, or by calling the contractors to see if they are interested.

Once the contractor checks out a set of contract documents from the architect's office, he or she begins to compile a bid for the project. This is the first true test of the competency and completeness of the construction documents. Using only the working drawings and specifications as reference materials, the contractors must figure the exact cost of the materials, workers' wages, and the amount of profit they need without exceeding the bids submitted by other contractors. They must make calculations on the amount of work the general contractor will do as well as accumulating bids from subcontractors on items that will be performed by another company. The project could take three years for completion, and a contractor must anticipate rises in labor costs and materials because the submitted bid is not subject to change.

During the bidding phase the architect assumes the role of interpreter. If contractors have questions about the drawings or the materials (the specific manufacturer), they are allowed to use only the architect as a source of information. To ensure a fair and impartial service to all contractors, the architect documents any changes in the drawings or specifications that might affect the contract amount. These changes are referred to as *addenda* and are sent to every person who has checked out a set of plans. Addenda are considered legal changes, having precedence over the original contract documents. Typically, contractors acknowledge in their bids the receipt of all addenda.

The bid submitted by a contractor is not a legal contract between the owner and the contractor, nor does it imply any obligation on the owner's part to even accept it. In a sense, the bidding procedure is rather one-sided. The owner can accept or reject any or all bids, while contractors face the possibility of forfeiting their bid bonds if they are selected and do not enter into a contractual agreement to build the project. After the bids have been opened, the specification usually states that the owner and architect have 30 days to review the bids before a contract must be signed. Usually, the low bidder is selected on public projects, but cases have arisen in which the past work of the low bidder has been so unacceptable that the owner has rejected the bid.

The division of responsibility on a building project is specified as follows:

1. The owner and architect have a contract stating respective responsibilities.
2. The owner-contractor contract basically stipulates that if the contractor faithfully follows the contract documents prepared by the architect, the owner will compensate her or him with the bid sum.
3. The architect and contractor do not have a contract.
4. The contractor and subcontractors have contracts that state that if a subcontractor performs a particular job on the building, in accordance with the construction documents, he or she is entitled to compensation by the contractor in the amount of the bid to the contractor.
5. Neither the owner nor the architect has any contractual responsibility to subcontractors.

An important point now arises: With the potluck approach of competitive bidding, how can an owner be assured that he or she will receive quality construction on the project? An owner is most likely to get a conscientious contractor that has every intention of doing good work; however, the low bidder may plan to substitute poor work for quality construction. The only protection an owner has is the architect. The architect's construction document package indicates all construction details and the quality and quantity of work to be performed. If the specifications and drawings are complete, it should leave the contractor only one path for construction, the way the architect intended it to be built.

The bidding phase on the school or any project still poses questions unique to the particular project. Situations might include a contractor's request to substitute an auditorium seat to replace the one specified or the correction of an error in the plan. In the case of the auditorium seat, the architect would examine the replacement seat (and possibly ask for the owner's opinion), and if the quality matched the previously specified seat, the contractor might be allowed to bid it. This approval is included in an addendum that is distributed to all persons having plans. A similar addendum would be used to correct an error in the plan.

The bidding period on a $2.5 million school can typically last five weeks, giving the contractors enough time to compile bids. At the bid opening, the architect certainly anticipates that cost estimates made during the phases of schematics, design development, and construction documents will prove accurate.

Two types of contracts are used for building projects—a single contract and a separate contract. A *single contract* has a single contractor responsible for all of the work (referred to as *turnkey*). A *separate contract* has a separate prime contractor in charge of each major division of construction (general construction, electrical, plumbing, heating, ventilating, and air conditioning). Pros and cons for the single-contract system can be proposed. The coordination of the project may be smoother because one contractor is in charge of the entire project. However, the added responsibility may cause the single contractor to charge more. Since the separate-contract system is the more orthodox pattern on public bidding, assume that the school will accept three prime bids—general, mechanical, and electrical.

If the low bid for general construction on the school is $1.5 million (including the architectural and structural part of the project), the low mechanical bid is $650,000 (including plumbing and air conditioning), and the electrical low bid is $350,000, the architect's estimate was accurate. If the job follows a standard pattern, possibly five contractors bid on each phase, with about a 10 percent spread between the low and high bidders.

The architect is involved financially in the outcome of the bidding. If the architect's initial estimate of the school building was just 10 percent high, certainly the owner will be pleased, because the bid saves $250,000. However, the architect's fee is reduced by $17,500. (The architect's fee is based on the cost estimate at the start of the project, but the final fee is based on the contract construction sum.) Since 80 percent of the architectural fee is collected and spent by the completion of

the bidding phase, a reduction of this magnitude can only mean that the architect loses money on the job. If he or she had known the accurate bid early, the job might have been budgeted accordingly; but with only 20 percent of the architect's project remaining, the only alternatives are to cut the inspection service by one-half or to make up the time from money designated as profit. The answer is obvious. The architect loses money.

A bid substantially higher than the estimate would also cause problems for the architect. The owner has no obligation to accept any of the bids and very likely will reject the high bids. Although usually not written into the owner-architect agreement, an understanding generally exists that if the costs exceed the estimate by more than 10 percent, the architect makes the changes necessary to reduce the building cost at no additional fee. This means redrawing and voiding items and sending the project out for bids again. The firm loses money if the bids come in either high or low, very graphically pointing out the necessity of obtaining an accurate cost estimate. A project the size of a $2.5 million school might cause an architect to use part of the fees to obtain the services of a professional cost estimator, thus ensuring the meeting of costs during the design and working drawing phases.

Assuming the bids are favorable, the owner enters into a contractual agreement with the lowest responsible bidder within 30 days after the bid opening. Before the project is begun, the contractors supply the materials necessary for the job. The materials can include a package of insurance, a list of subcontractors, permits, a schedule of values and a progress schedule. The package of insurance is required by the specifications and is submitted to the owner before work can be started. Before the project is begun, the prime contractors submit a list of the subcontractors they intend to use on the job. During bidding only the prime contractor was known to the owner. The contractor usually is responsible for obtaining and paying for any permits required by local or state regulations. These must be secured before the project is begun. The schedule of values is submitted to the architect, who breaks the lump sum into unit prices for specific items such as poured concrete or painting. The progress schedule gives the time schedule the contractors anticipate with three prime contractors on the job. A progress schedule is mandatory for coordination. With the architect's advice, the owner issues a notice to proceed.

CERTIFICATE OF INSURANCE

AIA DOCUMENT G705

This certifies to the Addressee shown below that the following described policies, subject to their terms, conditions and exclusions, have been issued to:

NAME & ADDRESS OF INSURED

Standard Building Co.
203 Bond Street, Bloomington, Indiana

COVERING (SHOW PROJECT NAME AND/OR NUMBER AND LOCATION)

Beef and Burgundy Restaurant

Addressee:
(Owner)

⌐General Restaurants, Inc.⌐
802 Boyd Street
Bloomington, Indiana
                          January 4, 1978
⌐   ⌐   Date

KIND OF INSURANCE	POLICY NUMBER	Inception/Expiration Date	LIMITS OF LIABILITY		
1. (a) Workmen's Comp.	AC 21675	6/1/77 6/1/79	$ ////////// Statutory Workmen's Compensation		
(b) Employers' Liability	AC 24050	6/1/77 6/1/79	$ 75,000 One Accident and Aggregate Disease		
2. Comprehensive General Liability	AC 10020	6/1/77 6/1/79	$ 100,000 Each Occurrence—Premises and Operations		
			$ 100,000 Each Occurrence—Independent Contractors		
			$ 75,000 Each Occurrence—COMPLETED OPERATIONS AND PRODUCTS		
(a) Bodily Injury			$ 100,000 Each Occurrence—Contractual		
			$ 300,000 Aggregate—COMPLETED OPERATIONS AND PRODUCTS		
(b) Personal Injury	AC 27172	6/1/77 6/1/79	$ 100,000 Each Person Aggregate		
			$ 500,000 General Aggregate		
			$ 200,000 Each Occurrence—Premises—Operations		
			$ 200,000 Each Occurrence—INDEPENDENT CONTRACTOR		
(c) Property Damage	AC 1922P	6/1/77 6/1/79	$ 500,000 Each Occurrence—COMPLETED OPERATIONS AND PRODUCTS		
			$ 100,000 Each Occurrence—Contractual		
			$ 1,000,000 Aggregate—		
			$ Aggregate—OPERATIONS, INDEPENDENT CONTRACTOR, PRODUCTS AND CONTRACTUAL		
3. Comprehensive Automobile Liability	AC 17142	6/1/77 6/1/79			
(a) Bodily Injury			$ 100,000 Each Person—		
			$ 500,000 Each Occurrence—		
(b) Property Damage			$ 100,000 Each Occurrence—		
4. (Other)	None				

UNDER GENERAL LIABILITY POLICY OR POLICIES

	Yes	No
1. Does Property Damage Liability Insurance shown include coverage for XC and U hazards?	X	
2. Is Occurrence Basis Coverage provided under Property Damage Liability?	X	
3. Is Broad Form Property Damage Coverage provided for this Project?	X	
4. Does Personal Injury Liability Insurance include coverage for personal injury sustained by any person as a result of an offense directly or indirectly related to the employment of such person by the Insured?	X	
5. Is coverage provided for Contractual Liability (including indemnification provision) assumed by Insured?	X	

UNDER AUTOMOBILE LIABILITY POLICY OR POLICIES

	Yes	No
1. Does coverage above apply to non-owned and hired automobiles?	X	
2. Is Occurrence Basis Coverage provided under Property Damage Liability?	X	

CANCELLATION OR NON-RENEWAL
In the event of cancellation or non-renewal of any of the foregoing, fifteen (15) days written notice shall be given to the party to whom this certificate is addressed.

EXTENT OF CERTIFICATION
This certificate is issued as a matter of information only and confers no rights upon the holder. By its issuance the company does not alter, change, modify or extend any of the provisions of the above policies.

Associated Construction Insurance Co.
NAME OF INSURANCE COMPANY
417 Chautauqua, Norman, Oklahoma
ADDRESS

Kenneth Berg
SIGNATURE OF AUTHORIZED REPRESENTATIVE

AIA DOCUMENT G705 • CERTIFICATE OF INSURANCE • FEBRUARY 1973 EDITION • AIA® • ©1973
THE AMERICAN INSTITUTE OF ARCHITECTS, 1735 NEW YORK AVE., NW, WASHINGTON, D.C. 20006

ONE PAGE

Figure 7-5. A certificate of insurance.

THE AMERICAN INSTITUTE OF ARCHITECTS

AIA Document A311

Performance Bond

KNOW ALL MEN BY THESE PRESENTS: that

    Standard Building, Co.
    203 Bond Street
    Bloomington, Indiana

(Here insert full name and address or legal title of Contractor)

as Principal, hereinafter called Contractor, and,

    New York Casualty Company
    Buffalo, New York

(Here insert full name and address or legal title of Surety)

as Surety, hereinafter called Surety, are held and firmly bound unto

    General Restaurants, Inc.
    802 Boyd Street
    Bloomington, Indiana

(Here insert full name and address or legal title of Owner)

as Obligee, hereinafter called Owner, in the amount of

    Four Fundred Fifty Seven Thousand Three
    Hundred Eighteen Dollars   Dollars ($ 457,318.00   ),

for the payment whereof Contractor and Surety bind themselves, their heirs, executors, administrators, successors and assigns, jointly and severally, firmly by these presents.

WHEREAS,

Contractor has by written agreement dated December 1519 77, entered into a contract with Owner for
(Here insert full name, address and description of project)

    Beef and Burgundy Restaurant
    2617 Anderson Parkway, Bloomington, Indiana

in accordance with Drawings and Specifications prepared by

    Design Partnership, Inc., A.I.A.
    1622 Sullivan Street, Chicago, Illinois

(Here insert full name and address or legal title of Architect)

which contract is by reference made a part hereof, and is hereinafter referred to as the Contract.

AIA DOCUMENT A311 • PERFORMANCE BOND AND LABOR AND MATERIAL PAYMENT BOND • AIA ®
FEBRUARY 1970 ED. • THE AMERICAN INSTITUTE OF ARCHITECTS, 1735 N.Y. AVE., N.W., WASHINGTON, D. C. 20006

1

Figure 7-6. A performance bond.

PERFORMANCE BOND

NOW, THEREFORE, THE CONDITION OF THIS OBLIGATION is such that, if Contractor shall promptly and faithfully perform said Contract, then this obligation shall be null and void; otherwise it shall remain in full force and effect.

The Surety hereby waives notice of any alteration or extension of time made by the Owner.

Whenever Contractor shall be, and declared by Owner to be in default under the Contract, the Owner having performed Owner's obligations thereunder, the Surety may promptly remedy the default, or shall promptly

1) Complete the Contract in accordance with its terms and conditions, or

2) Obtain a bid or bids for completing the Contract in accordance with its terms and conditions, and upon determination by Surety of the lowest responsible bidder, or, if the Owner elects, upon determination by the Owner and the Surety jointly of the lowest responsible bidder, arrange for a contract between such bidder and Owner, and make available as Work progresses (even though there should be a default or a succession of defaults under the contract or contracts of completion arranged under this paragraph) sufficient funds to pay the cost of completion less the balance of the contract price; but not exceeding, including other costs and damages for which the Surety may be liable hereunder, the amount set forth in the first paragraph hereof. The term "balance of the contract price," as used in this paragraph, shall mean the total amount payable by Owner to Contractor under the Contract and any amendments thereto, less the amount properly paid by Owner to Contractor.

Any suit under this bond must be instituted before the expiration of two (2) years from the date on which final payment under the Contract falls due.

No right of action shall accrue on this bond to or for the use of any person or corporation other than the Owner named herein or the heirs, executors, administrators or successors of the Owner.

Signed and sealed this   second   day of   January   19 78

Mark Wolfgram
(Witness)

Alan Anderson
(Principal)   (Seal)

Senior Vice President
(Title)

Susan McGuire
(Witness)

Rick S. Robinson
(Surety)   (Seal)

Corporate Officer
(Title)

Figure 7-6 (continued).

THE AMERICAN INSTITUTE OF ARCHITECTS

AIA Document A311

Labor and Material Payment Bond

THIS BOND IS ISSUED SIMULTANEOUSLY WITH PERFORMANCE BOND IN FAVOR OF THE
OWNER CONDITIONED ON THE FULL AND FAITHFUL PERFORMANCE OF THE CONTRACT

KNOW ALL MEN BY THESE PRESENTS: that

    Standard Building Co.
    203 Bond Street
    Bloomington, Indiana

(Here insert full name and address or legal title of Contractor)

as Principal, hereinafter called Principal, and,

    New York Casualty Co.
    Buffalo, New York

(Here insert full name and address or legal title of Surety)

as Surety, hereinafter called Surety, are held and firmly bound unto

    General Restaurants, Inc.
    802 Boyd Street
    Bloomington, Indiana

(Here insert full name and address or legal title of Owner)

as Obligee, hereinafter called Owner, for the use and benefit of claimants as hereinbelow defined, in the

amount of **Three Hundred Thousand**

    (Here insert a sum equal to at least one-half of the contract price)   Dollars (**$ 300,000.00**   ),

for the payment whereof Principal and Surety bind themselves, their heirs, executors, administrators, successors and assigns, jointly and severally, firmly by these presents.

WHEREAS,

Principal has by written agreement dated **December 15 19 77**, entered into a contract with Owner for
(Here insert full name, address and description of project)

    Beef and Burgundy Restaurant
    2617 Anderson Parkway, Bloomington, Indiana

in accordance with Drawings and Specifications prepared by

    Design Partnership, Inc., A.I.A.
    1622 Sullivan Street
    Chicago, Illinois

(Here insert full name and address or legal title of Architect)

which contract is by reference made a part hereof, and is hereinafter referred to as the Contract.

AIA DOCUMENT A311 · PERFORMANCE BOND AND LABOR AND MATERIAL PAYMENT BOND · AIA ®
FEBRUARY 1970 ED. · THE AMERICAN INSTITUTE OF ARCHITECTS, 1735 N.Y. AVE., N.W., WASHINGTON, D. C. 20006

3

Figure 7-7.   A labor and material payment bond.

LABOR AND MATERIAL PAYMENT BOND

NOW, THEREFORE, THE CONDITION OF THIS OBLIGATION is such that, if Principal shall promptly make payment to all claimants as hereinafter defined, for all labor and material used or reasonably required for use in the performance of the Contract, then this obligation shall be void; otherwise it shall remain in full force and effect, subject, however, to the following conditions:

1. A claimant is defined as one having a direct contract with the Principal or with a Subcontractor of the Principal for labor, material, or both, used or reasonably required for use in the performance of the Contract, labor and material being construed to include that part of water, gas, power, light, heat, oil, gasoline, telephone service or rental of equipment directly applicable to the Contract.

2. The above named Principal and Surety hereby jointly and severally agree with the Owner that every claimant as herein defined, who has not been paid in full before the expiration of a period of ninety (90) days after the date on which the last of such claimant's work or labor was done or performed, or materials were furnished by such claimant, may sue on this bond for the use of such claimant, prosecute the suit to final judgment for such sum or sums as may be justly due claimant, and have execution thereon. The Owner shall not be liable for the payment of any costs or expenses of any such suit.

3. No suit or action shall be commenced hereunder by any claimant:

a) Unless claimant, other than one having a direct contract with the Principal, shall have given written notice to any two of the following: the Principal, the Owner, or the Surety above named, within ninety (90) days after such claimant did or performed the last of the work or labor, or furnished the last of the materials for which said claim is made, stating with substantial

accuracy the amount claimed and the name of the party to whom the materials were furnished, or for whom the work or labor was done or performed. Such notice shall be served by mailing the same by registered mail or certified mail, postage prepaid, in an envelope addressed to the Principal, Owner or Surety, at any place where an office is regularly maintained for the transaction of business, or served in any manner in which legal process may be served in the state in which the aforesaid project is located, save that such service need not be made by a public officer.

b) After the expiration of one (1) year following the date on which Principal ceased Work on said Contract, it being understood, however, that if any limitation embodied in this bond is prohibited by any law controlling the construction hereof such limitation shall be deemed to be amended so as to be equal to the minimum period of limitation permitted by such law.

c) Other than in a state court of competent jurisdiction in and for the county or other political subdivision of the state in which the Project, or any part thereof, is situated, or in the United States District Court for the district in which the Project, or any part thereof, is situated, and not elsewhere.

4. The amount of this bond shall be reduced by and to the extent of any payment or payments made in good faith hereunder, inclusive of the payment by Surety of mechanics' liens which may be filed of record against said improvement, whether or not claim for the amount of such lien be presented under and against this bond.

Signed and sealed this   **second**   day of   January   19 78

Mark Wolfgram
(Witness)

Allan Anderson
(Principal)   (Seal)

Senior Vice President
(Title)

Susan Mc Guire
(Witness)

Rick S. Robinson
(Surety)   (Seal)

Corporate Officer
(Title)

AIA DOCUMENT A311 · PERFORMANCE BOND AND LABOR AND MATERIAL PAYMENT BOND · AIA ®
FEBRUARY 1970 ED. · THE AMERICAN INSTITUTE OF ARCHITECTS, 1735 N.Y. AVE., N.W., WASHINGTON, D. C. 20006   **4**

Figure 7-7 (continued).

Construction Phase

Well-defined areas of responsibility exist during the construction phase; the architect acts as the contract administrator, and the contractor acts as the construction superintendent. During this phase the architect's duty is to see that the construction documents are followed, not to tell the contractor *how* to do the job.

The responsibility of the architect during construction is to act as the owner's agent in administration of the contract. In general terms this involves:

1. Interpreting the contract documents
2. Establishing acceptable standards of quality
3. Judging the performance of the contractor
4. Authorizing monthly payments to the contractor
5. Informing the owner about the status of the project
6. Making an inspection at the completion of the project to see that all items have been completed and that the work was done in accordance with the contract

The architect has the power to reject work only if it is not in accordance with the drawings and specifications. Even then, the only items not subject to arbitration are architectural decisions that affect artistic considerations.

The contractor has the responsibility to supervise the acquisition of materials and their installation. He or she has a free hand as to the method of installation but must make certain that all the architect's details are followed and that the quality conforms to the specifications. The contractor's duties during the construction phase include:

1. Knowing the intent of the drawings and specifications
2. Cooperating fully with the other contractors on the job and with the architect
3. Directing the construction of the job, using proper construction techniques in the correct sequence
4. Providing an adequate safety program on the site

A project representative from the architect's office who is knowledgeable in building techniques is assigned to the project when construction begins. The project representative serves full time on the project only when it is extremely large ($10 million or more) or when it has unique problems. The project representative's job is to coordinate and relate the findings and problems encountered at the site back to the proper person in the architect's office. He or she observes construction and acts as the architect's interpreter when the intent of the drawings and specifications needs defining. He or she works closely with the architect relating an opinion given to the contractor or any discrepancy noticed between the drawings and the actual construction. This is done in the form of a memorandum or field report written by the representative to the architect (and possibly to the owner and contractor). The observation of a project has no set pattern as to the number of visits required; the complexity of the work dictates this. The field reports should contain specific information relating the contractor's activities on all phases of construction.

Another major service performed by the architect during construction is approving the contractor's monthly request for payment. One document requested from the contractor prior to the commencement of the project was a schedule of values. In the schedule, the contractor breaks the bid into various subelements used to compile the bid, such as the costs for excavation, concrete forming, or roofing. All these subelements must add up to the contractor's bid. The architect watches to see that the contractor does not "front load" the schedule, that is, place a higher value on items finished early in the project, such as excavation, while lowering the charges for work at the end of the project, such as roofing. The contractor is entitled to monthly payment for work completed and materials stored for use on the project, minus 10 percent of the amount requested that month. This 10 percent will be paid when the project is determined to be substantially complete by the architect.

The method of determining the amount to be paid by the owner is to relate the amount of labor and materials completed on the job back to the schedule of values the contractor submitted. If the schedule indicates that concrete work is valued at $50,000 and the monthly estimate claims that 80 percent of the concrete work is complete, the contractor should receive $40,000. However, if the contractor "front loaded" the schedule of values to read that concrete work should cost $90,000, 80 percent of that amount would mean an overpayment for the work done. Similarly, if the contractor claims to be 80 percent complete but in

CHANGE ORDER

AIA DOCUMENT G701

OWNER	☒
ARCHITECT	☒
CONTRACTOR	☒
FIELD	☐
OTHER	

PROJECT: The Beef and Burgundy Restaurant
(name, address) 2617 Anderson Parkway
            Bloomington, Indiana

CHANGE ORDER NUMBER: 4

TO (Contractor)

Standard Building Co.
203 Bond Street
Bloomington, Indiana

ARCHITECT'S PROJECT NO: 77-36

CONTRACT FOR: Beef and Burgundy
               Restaurant

CONTRACT DATE:

You are directed to make the following changes in this Contract:

Substitute Number 1 Grade K.D. red oak in lieu of the painted pine
hand rail as shown on Architectural Plan 1/A-2 and detailed on
Sheet 5/A-4.
The rail shall be hand-sanded smooth and painted with two coats of
Pratt Lambert high-gloss 38 clear varnish, steel wool rubbed smooth,
and painted with one coat of Pratt Lambert dull varnish.

The original Contract Sum was . . . . $ 457,318.00
Net change by previous Change Orders . . . . $ 5,140.00
The Contract Sum prior to this Change Order was . . . . $ 462,458.00
The Contract Sum will be (increased) (decreased) (unchanged) by this Change Order . . . $ 925.00
The new Contract Sum including this Change Order will be . . . . $ 463,383.00
The Contract Time will be (increased) (decreased) (unchanged) by   (0) Days.
The Date of Completion as of the date of this Change Order therefore is   .

Design Partnership, Inc.,   Standard Building Co.   General Restaurants, Inc.
ARCHITECT   A.I.A. CONTRACTOR   OWNER
1622 Sullivan Street   203 Bond Street   802 Boyd Street
Address   Address   Address
Chicago, Illinois `   Bloomington Indiana   Bloomington, Indiana

BY _Thomas Hovel_   BY _Allan Anderson_   BY _Dick Schroeder_

DATE August 16, 1978   DATE August 21, 1978   DATE August 29, 1978

Figure 7-8. A change order.

ARCHITECT'S FIELD ORDER

AIA DOCUMENT G708

OWNER	☒
ARCHITECT	☒
CONSULTANTS	☐
CONTRACTOR	☒
FIELD	☒
OTHER	☐

PROJECT: Beef and Burgundy Restaurant
(name, address) 2617 Anderson Parkway
Bloomington, Indiana
OWNER: General Restaurants, Inc.

FIELD ORDER NO: 2

DATE: August 2, 1978

TO (Contractor)

Standard Building Co.
203 Bond Street
Bloomington, Indiana

ARCHITECT'S PROJECT NO: 77-36
CONTRACT FOR: Beef and Burgundy
Restaurant

CONTRACT DATE: December 15, 1977

You are hereby directed to execute promptly this Field Order which interprets the Contract Documents or orders minor changes in the Work without change in Contract Sum or Contract Time.

If you consider that a change in Contract Sum or Contract Time is required, please submit your itemized proposal to the Architect immediately and before proceeding with this Work. If your proposal is found to be satisfactory and in proper order, this Field Order will in that event be superseded by a Change Order.

Description: (Here insert a written description of the interpretation or change)

Change Door 112 B from right-hand swing to left-hand swing

as shown on architectural Sheet A-2

Attachments: (Here insert listing of attached documents that support description)

None

ARCHITECT:

BY: *Thomas Flood*

Figure 7-9. An architect's field order.

APPLICATION AND CERTIFICATE FOR PAYMENT   AIA DOCUMENT G702

PAGE ONE OF 2 PAGES

PROJECT: Beef and Burgundy Restaurant
(name, address)   2617 Anderson Parkway
Bloomington, Indiana

TO (Owner)   General Restaurants, Inc.
802 Boyd Street
Bloomington, Indiana

ARCHITECT: Design Partnership, Inc., A.I.A.

ARCHITECT'S PROJECT NO: 77-36

CONTRACTOR: Standard Building Co.

CONTRACT FOR: Beef and Burgundy Restaurant

APPLICATION DATE: June 1, 1978   APPLICATION NO: 3

PERIOD FROM: May 1, 1978   TO   June 1, 1978

Application is made for Payment, as shown below, in connection with the Contract.
Continuation Sheet, AIA Document G702A, is attached.
The present status of the account for this Contract is as follows:

ORIGINAL CONTRACT SUM .... $ 457,318.00

Net change by Change Orders .... $ 657.00

CONTRACT SUM TO DATE .... $ 457,975.00

TOTAL COMPLETED & STORED TO DATE .... $ 190,063.00
(Column G on G702A)

RETAINAGE   10   % .... $ 19,005.00
or as noted in Column I on G702A

TOTAL EARNED LESS RETAINAGE .... $ 171,058.00

LESS PREVIOUS CERTIFICATES FOR PAYMENT .... $ 69,800.00

CURRENT PAYMENT DUE .... $ 101,258.00

Subscribed and sworn to before me this   first   day of   June   , 19 78
Notary Public:
My Commission expires: April 1, 1979

ATTN: Richard Fox

CHANGE ORDER SUMMARY

Change Orders approved in previous months by Owner— 2 TOTAL	ADDITIONS $	DEDUCTIONS $

Subsequent Change Orders		
Number	Approved (date)	
1	3/20/78	200.00	
2	4/12/78	457.00	

TOTALS	657.00	

Net change by Change Orders $ Add $657.00

State of: Indiana   County of: Jackson

The undersigned Contractor certifies that the Work covered by this Application for Payment has been completed in accordance with the Contract Documents, that all amounts have been paid by him for Work for which previous Certificates for Payment were issued and payments received from the Owner, and that the current payment shown herein is now due.

Contractor: Standard Building Co.

By: Date: June 1, 1978

In accordance with the Contract and this Application for Payment the Contractor is entitled to payment in the amount shown above.

Architect: Design Partnership, Inc., A.I.A.

By:

☒ OWNER
☒ ARCHITECT
☒ CONTRACTOR   ☐☐

This Certificate is not negotiable. It is payable only to the payee named herein and its issuance, payment and acceptance are without prejudice to any rights of the Owner or Contractor under their Contract.

Figure 7-10.   A certificate for payment.

CONTINUATION SHEET   *AIA DOCUMENT G702A*

AIA Document G702, APPLICATION AND CERTIFICATE FOR PAYMENT, containing CONTRACTOR'S signed Certification is attached.

In tabulations below, amounts are stated to the nearest dollar.

Use Column I on Contracts where variable retainage for line items may apply.

PAGE 2 OF 2 PAGES

APPLICATION NUMBER: 3

ARCHITECT'S PROJECT NO: 77-36

ITEM NO. A	DESCRIPTION OF WORK B	SCHEDULED VALUE C	WORK COMPLETED Previous Applications D	This Application E	STORED MATERIALS F	TOTAL COMPLETED AND STORED TO DATE G(D+E+F)	%	BALANCE TO FINISH H(C-G)	RETAINAGE I
1	General Conditions	44,850	20,000	20,365	—	40,365	90	4,485	4,036
2	Earth Work	20,120	9,200	10,920	—	20,120	100	0	2,012
3	Concrete & Forms	93,200	27,650	48,774	—	76,424	82	16,776	7,642
3	Reinforcing Steel	26,550	4,100	14,485	—	18,585	70	7,965	1,858
4	Masonry	19,550	1,600	5,242	—	6,842	35	12,708	684
5	Structural Steel	41,400	7,250	8,450	—	15,700	38	25,700	1,570
5	Metal & Orn. Metal	2,100	0	1,470	—	1,470	70	630	147
6	Carpentry	15,290	0	0	529	529	10	14,761	53
6	Mill Work	29,200	0	0	2,300	2,300	25	6,900	230
7	Damp Proofing	17,000	0	0	—	—	—	17,000	0
7	Roofing Sheet Met.	22,100	0	0	—	—	—	22,100	0
7	Calk/Weatherstrip	1,450	0	0	—	—	—	1,450	0
8	Hollow Metal	2,900	0	0	—	—	—	2,900	0
8	Finish Hardware	7,130	0	0	—	—	—	7,130	0
8	Alum. Windows	17,000	0	0	—	—	—	17,000	0
8	Glass & Glazing	16,560	0	0	—	—	—	16,560	0
9	Acoustical Trmt.	1,020	0	0	—	—	—	1,020	0
9	Special Coating & Paint	19,450	0	0	—	—	—	19,450	0
9	Ceramic Tile	14,600	0	0	—	—	—	14,600	0
9	Lath & Plaster	11,400	0	0	—	—	—	11,400	0
10	Misc. Specialties	6,605	0	0	—	—	—	6,605	0
10	Toilet Accessories	900	0	0	—	—	—	900	0
11	Kitchen Equipment	27,600	0	0	7,728	7,728	28	19,872	773
	SUB-TOTAL or TOTAL	457,975				190,063		247,912	19,005

AIA DOCUMENT G702A • CONTINUATION SHEET • MARCH 1971 EDITION • AIA® • © 1971
THE AMERICAN INSTITUTE OF ARCHITECTS, 1735 NEW YORK AVE., N.W., WASHINGTON, D. C. 20006

Figure 7-10 (continued).

reality is only 50 percent finished, it will also result in an overpayment. Tactics like these result in the same final payment at the end of the project, but if the contractor should file bankruptcy halfway through, the owner has paid for more of the project than has been built at that point. To afford some protection to the owner, the monthly requests for payment from the contractor are submitted first to the architect for approval. The architect's field representative usually studies and approves the payment request because of his or her close first-hand knowledge of the project. Upon the architect's approval, the request for payment is signed and forwarded to the owner for payment within seven days.

A responsibility of the architect during construction is to approve shop drawings submitted by the contractor. A *shop drawing* is a drawing, diagram, illustration, schedule, performance chart, brochure, or other information that is prepared by the contractor or any subcontractor, manufacturer, supplier, or distributor to illustrate how specific portions of the work shall be fabricated or installed. The working drawings are general in that the architect does not yet know which manufacturer the contractor will use and thus cannot detail the installation instructions that are unique to each product. Therefore when the contractor submits shop drawings, he or she is informing the architect of the exact manner in which the product chosen will work in the project. This choice by the contractor is not a random selection because the specifications written by the architect spell out the choice of products or quality of materials which must be used. Consider the windows in a project, for example. When the job is drawn and specified, the architect may have three or four manufacturers in mind that would each be compatible with the building concept. Every window manufacturer produces a unique detail, and so it is not possible for the architect's drawings to reflect the exact way in which a specific window will be installed. The working drawings then are intended to show the architect's concept. Several similar brands of window might fulfill the concept. The purpose of a shop drawing is for the window manufacturer who has a contract with the general contractor for installation to give specific details to the contractor and architect on how the window will follow the working drawing detail.

All shop drawings are submitted first to the prime contractor for approval. After this, the architect stamps approval or changes the detail. Actu-

ally, the two parties are approving different aspects of the drawings. The prime contractor is responsible for the work done by the subcontractors so that the approval affirms that the shop drawings do not deviate from the construction documents. The architect is certifying that the material detailed follows the intent of the design. The specifications indicate the phases of construction that require shop drawings. They also state that these phases cannot be started by the contractor until he or she has received written approval of the shop drawings from the architect.

Upon substantial completion of the project, the architect schedules a meeting with the prime contractors and the owner to determine which items must be finished before the project can be termed complete. With the notes taken during this meeting the architect writes a memorandum called a *punch list* that contains a room-by-room list of specific items to be completed. The punch list is circulated to all concerned parties so that the loose ends of construction may be tied together.

During the last phase of the contract on the school, all the items discussed in general under the construction section are applied to specific points encountered. The size and organization of the firm dictates whether the field representative will work specifically in construction observation or will be a member (or members) of the team involved in the working drawings. The size of the school probably will not dictate that the field representative be involved on a full-time basis. Visits to the site will occur at least once a week but are not scheduled regularly. Construction speed and complexity will vary greatly from the start to the finish of the school, and so the greatest efficiency lies in having the architect's representative at the site when it is most important. The representative will send a written field report to the architect each time he or she visits the site, covering such diverse items as the temperature and weather conditions to the progress each trade has made since the last visit. If the field representative encounters a condition at the site that requires a change from the drawings without changing the contract amount, such as moving a door 10 in. to miss a structural column, he or she will issue a field order. This report then is coordinated with the architectural office to make sure that the change will not affect any other aspects of the job.

The size of the project discussed here means that the contractor probably needs 12 to 15 months for construction. It also means that the job file in

CONTRACTOR'S AFFIDAVIT OF RELEASE OF LIENS

AIA DOCUMENT G706A

OWNER ☒
ARCHITECT ☒
CONTRACTOR ☒
SURETY ☐
OTHER

TO (Owner)

⌐ General Restaurants, Inc.
802 Boyd Street
Bloomington, Indiana ⌐

└ ┘

PROJECT:
(name, address) Beef and Burgundy Restaurant
2617 Anderson Parkway

ARCHITECT'S PROJECT NO: 77-36

CONTRACT FOR:
Beef and Burgundy Restaurant

CONTRACT DATE: December 15, 1977

State of: Indiana

County of: Jackson

The undersigned, pursuant to Article 9 of the General Conditions of the Contract for Construction, AIA Document A201, hereby certifies that to the best of his knowledge, information and belief, except as listed below, the Releases or Waivers of Lien attached hereto include the Contractor, all Subcontractors, all suppliers of materials and equipment, and all performers of Work, labor or services who have or may have liens against any property of the Owner arising in any manner out of the performance of the Contract referenced above.

EXCEPTIONS: (If none, write "None". If required by the Owner, the Contractor shall furnish bond satisfactory to the Owner for each exception.)

    None

SUPPORTING DOCUMENTS ATTACHED HERETO:

1. Contractor's Release or Waiver of Liens, conditional upon receipt of final payment.

2. Separate Releases or Waivers of Liens from Subcontractors and material and equipment suppliers, to the extent required by the Owner, accompanied by a list thereof.

CONTRACTOR: Standard Building Co.

Address: 203 Bond Street
Bloomington, Indiana

BY: *Allen Anderson*

Subscribed and sworn to before me this
tenth day of November 19 78

Notary Public: *Mary Pinta*

My Commission Expires: April 1979

Figure 7-11. The contractor's affidavit of release of liens.

CONTRACTOR'S AFFIDAVIT OF PAYMENT OF DEBTS AND CLAIMS

AIA Document G706

OWNER ☒
ARCHITECT ☒
CONTRACTOR ☒
SURETY ☐
OTHER

TO (Owner)

General Restaurants, Inc.
802 Boyd Street
Bloomington, Indiana

ARCHITECT'S PROJECT NO: 77-36

CONTRACT FOR:
Beef and Burgundy Restaurant

CONTRACT DATE: December 15, 1977

PROJECT: (name, address) Beef and Burgundy Restaurant
2617 Anderson Parkway, Bloomington, Indiana

State of: Indiana
County of: Jackson

The undersigned, pursuant to Article 9 of the General Conditions of the Contract for Construction, AIA Document A201, hereby certifies that, except as listed below, he has paid in full or has otherwise satisfied all obligations for all materials and equipment furnished, for all work, labor, and services performed, and for all known indebtedness and claims against the Contractor for damages arising in any manner in connection with the performance of the Contract referenced above for which the Owner or his property might in any way be held responsible.

EXCEPTIONS: (If none, write "None". If required by the Owner, the Contractor shall furnish bond satisfactory to the Owner for each exception.)

None

SUPPORTING DOCUMENTS ATTACHED HERETO:

1. Consent of Surety to Final Payment. Whenever Surety is involved, Consent of Surety is required. AIA DOCUMENT G707, CONSENT OF SURETY, may be used for this purpose.
   Indicate attachment: (yes) (no).

The following supporting documents should be attached hereto if required by the Owner:

1. Contractor's Release or Waiver of Liens, conditional upon receipt of final payment.
2. Separate Releases or Waivers of Liens from Subcontractors and material and equipment suppliers, to the extent required by the Owner, accompanied by a list thereof.
3. Contractor's Affidavit of Release of Liens (AIA DOCUMENT G706A).

CONTRACTOR: Standard Building Co.

Address: 203 Bond Street
Bloomington, Indiana

BY: Allan Anderson

Subscribed and sworn to before me this tenth day of November 19 78

Notary Public: [signature]

My Commission Expires: April 1979

AIA DOCUMENT G706 • CONTRACTOR'S AFFIDAVIT OF PAYMENT OF DEBTS AND CLAIMS • APRIL 1970 EDITION

ONE PAGE

Figure 7-12. A contractor's affidavit of payment.

CERTIFICATE OF SUBSTANTIAL COMPLETION

OWNER ☒
ARCHITECT ☒
CONTRACTOR ☒
FIELD ☐
OTHER

AIA DOCUMENT G704

PROJECT: Beef and Burgundy Restaurant
(name, address) 2617 Anderson Parkway
Bloomington, Indiana

ARCHITECT: Design Partnership, Inc., AIA

ARCHITECT'S PROJECT NUMBER: 77-36

TO (Owner)

General Restaurants, Inc.
802 Boyd Street
Bloomington, Indiana

CONTRACTOR: Standard Building Co.
CONTRACT FOR: Beef and Burgundy
Restaurant

CONTRACT DATE: December 15, 1977

DATE OF ISSUANCE: November 15, 1978

PROJECT OR DESIGNATED AREA SHALL INCLUDE:

Complete building project and site work

The Work performed under this Contract has been reviewed and found to be substantially complete. The Date of Substantial Completion is hereby established as November 15, 1978
which is also the date of commencement of all warranties and guarantees required by the Contract Documents.

DEFINITION OF DATE OF SUBSTANTIAL COMPLETION

The Date of Substantial Completion of the Work or designated portion thereof is the Date certified by the Architect when construction is sufficiently complete, in accordance with the Contract Documents, so the Owner may occupy the Work or designated portion thereof for the use for which it is intended.

A list of items to be completed or corrected, prepared by the Contractor and verified and amended by the Architect, is appended hereto. The failure to include any items on such list does not alter the responsibility of the Contractor to complete all Work in accordance with the Contract Documents.

Design Partnership, Inc., A.I.A
ARCHITECT
BY _[signature]_
11/15/78
DATE

The Contractor will complete or correct the Work on the list of items appended hereto within fifteen days from the above Date of Substantial Completion.

Standard Building Co.
CONTRACTOR
BY _[signature]_
11/17/78
DATE

The Owner accepts the Work or designated portion thereof as substantially complete and will assume full possession thereof at _____ (time) on _[signature: Rick Schroeder]_ (date).

General Restaurants, Inc.
OWNER
BY _[signature]_
11/21/78
DATE

The responsibilities of the Owner and the Contractor for maintenance, heat, utilities and insurance shall be as follows:
(NOTE — Owner's and Contractor's legal and insurance counsel should determine and review insurance requirements and coverage)

Heat, maintenance, utilities, and insurance to be the owner's responsibility after November 15, 1978.

AIA DOCUMENT G704 • CERTIFICATE OF SUBSTANTIAL COMPLETION • APRIL 1970 EDITION • AIA®
© 1970 • THE AMERICAN INSTITUTE OF ARCHITECTS, 1735 NEW YORK AVE., NW, WASHINGTON, D.C. 20006

ONE PAGE

Figure 7-13. A certificate of completion.

the office more than likely fills a file cabinet. It includes memos on construction meetings, shop drawings, field orders, and samples of products. Although the architect's official capacity ends when the building is finally turned over to the client, his or her liability and obligation to the owner never end.

The procedures involved in processing an architectural project are complex. The discussion in this section is obviously too short to afford anything but a surface view of an architect's practice. The best possible avenue for further study is to become involved with a job in an architectural firm. There is an advantage to working on and learning the project procedures, as they change very little from job to job. When the framework of architectural practice is understood, the administration of individual projects follows. The problems unique to a particular job generally fit within this skeletal form.

Many problems encountered in an architect's practice are incurred during construction. It would not be fair to say that all the problems stem from faults in the drawings and specifications, but an accurate, well-drawn set certainly minimizes these conditions. Keep in mind that it is going to be much easier to correct a mistake on a wall when it is in the drawing stage than to wait until the wall is built and must be moved.

CONSTRUCTION MANAGEMENT

One rather important deviation from the usual pattern of construction just described is a system called *construction management*, or *fast track*. Instead of retaining a general contractor, the owner uses the services of a construction management company. In this system, every trade on the job acts as a subcontractor, and coordination between trades is handled by the construction manager. The construction manager receives a fee for this service from the owner and acts as the owner's representative. The great benefit of this system is that separate contracts are signed for each major parcel of construction (excavation, footings, steel framework, and so on), affording two benefits: (1) The lowest bid for each parcel of construction can be accepted, rather than the lowest composite bid; and (2) the project can be started in phases, allowing a considerable time savings. The time factor is shortened because drawings for work to be completed early in the project can be finished and sent out for bid while the rest of the job is still on the drawing board. With construction costs rising a sizable percentage each month, the faster a project can be started, the less it will cost.

Many architectural firms have assumed the role of construction administrator as an extension of their services.

SPECIFICATIONS

The specifications included in the contract document package should give contractors sufficient data to bid the project and determine the quality of all materials shown in the working drawings. The Construction Specifications Institute, Inc. (CSI), has established a format that subdivides the areas of building construction into 16 major areas and further divides each area into various building trades. While it is not mandatory that the major divisions be memorized, three important sources have adopted this format: (1) *Architectural Graphic Standards*, (2) most architect's specifications and product data, and (3) *Sweet's File*. In addition, a system for cost accounting closely follows the CSI format. Both are compatible with computer programming. Finding material in these publications becomes much easier if an architectural technician at least is familiar with the numerical outline system. (See Table 7-3.)

Section 0 in the CSI format contains instructional material necessary for the contractor to bid the project. Most of this material is standard and, unfortunately, probably is most often unread by the contractor or by the architectural staff. Some subdivisions and their major points in Section 0 from a typical architect's specification are discussed below. Exact procedures may differ from one firm to another as does the numbering system.

Section 00001

Section 00001 includes the title of the project, the location, the name and address of the architectural firm, and the signature of the registered architect legally responsible for the project.

Section 00010

Section 00010 lists the table of contents for the specifications.

Section 00015

Section 00015 lists the table of contents for all drawings in the construction document package, including architectural, structural, mechanical, and electrical drawings.

TABLE 7-3 CSI FORMAT*

DIVISION 1—GENERAL REQUIREMENTS
Reference
Numbers †
01010   SUMMARY OF THE WORK
01100   ALTERNATIVES
01200   PROGRESS AND PAYMENT
01300   SUBMITTALS
01400   TESTING LABORATORY SERVICES
01500   TEMPORARY FACILITIES AND
            CONTROLS
01600   MATERIAL AND EQUIPMENT
01700   PROJECT CLOSEOUT

DIVISION 2—SITE WORK
Reference
Numbers †
02010   SUBSURFACE EXPLORATION
02100   CLEARING
02110   DEMOLITION
02200   EARTHWORK
02250   SOIL POISONING
02300   PILE FOUNDATIONS
02350   CAISSONS
02400   SHEETING, SHORING AND BRACING
02500   SITE DRAINAGE
02550   SITE UTILITIES
02600   PAVEMENTS AND WALKS
02700   SITE IMPROVEMENTS
02800   LANDSCAPING
02850   RAILROAD WORK
02900   MARINE WORK
02950   TUNNELING

DIVISION 3—CONCRETE
Reference
Numbers †
03100   CONCRETE FORMWORK
03150   EXPANSION AND CONTRACTION
            JOINTS
03200   CONCRETE REINFORCEMENT
03300   CAST-IN-PLACE CONCRETE
03350   SPECIALLY FINISHED CONCRETE
03360   SPECIALLY PLACED CONCRETE
03400   PRECAST CONCRETE
03500   CEMENTITIOUS DECKS

DIVISION 4—MASONRY
Reference
Numbers †
04100   MORTAR
04150   ACCESSORIES
04200   UNIT MASONRY
04400   STONE
04500   MASONRY RESTORATION AND
            CLEANING
04550   REFRACTORIES

DIVISION 5—METALS
Reference
Numbers †
05100   STRUCTURAL METAL
05200   STEEL JOISTS
05300   METAL DECKING
05400   LIGHTGAGE FRAMING
05500   MISCELLANEOUS METAL
05700   ORNAMENTAL METAL

DIVISION 6—WOOD AND PLASTICS
Reference
Numbers †
06100   ROUGH CARPENTRY
06130   HEAVY TIMBER CONSTRUCTION
06150   TRESTLES
06170   PREFABRICATED STRUCTURAL WOOD
06200   FINISH CARPENTRY
06300   WOOD TREATMENT
06400   ARCHITECTURAL WOODWORK
06500   PREFABRICATED STRUCTURAL
            PLASTICS
06600   PLASTIC FABRICATIONS

DIVISION 7—THERMAL AND MOISTURE PROTECTION
Reference
Numbers †
07100   WATERPROOFING
07150   DAMPPROOFING
07200   INSULATION
07300   SHINGLES AND ROOFING TILES
07400   PREFORMED ROOFING AND SIDING
07500   MEMBRANE ROOFING
07600   FLASHING AND SHEET METAL
07800   ROOF ACCESSORIES
07900   CALKING AND SEALANTS

DIVISION 8—DOORS AND WINDOWS
Reference
Numbers †
08100   METAL DOORS AND FRAMES
08200   WOOD AND PLASTIC DOORS
08300   SPECIAL DOORS
08500   METAL WINDOWS
08600   WOOD AND PLASTIC WINDOWS
08700   HARDWARE AND SPECIALTIES
08800   GLAZING
08900   CURTAINWALL SYSTEM
08950   STOREFRONT SYSTEM

DIVISION 9—FINISHES
Reference
Numbers †
09100   LATH AND PLASTER
09250   GYPSUM DRYWALL
09300   TILE
09400   TERRAZZO
09450   VENEER STONE
09500   ACOUSTICAL TREATMENT
09550   WOOD FLOORING
09650   RESILIENT FLOORING
09680   CARPETING
09700   SPECIAL FLOORING
09800   SPECIAL COATINGS
09900   PAINTING
09950   WALL COVERING

DIVISION 10—SPECIALTIES
Reference
Numbers †
10100   CHALKBOARDS AND TACKBOARDS
10130   CHUTES
10150   COMPARTMENTS AND CUBICLES
10230   DISAPPEARING STAIRS
10240   DOCK FACILITIES
10250   FIREFIGHTING DEVICES
10300   FIREPLACES
10350   FLAGPOLES
10400   IDENTIFYING DEVICES
10500   LOCKERS
10530   PLASTIC SPECIALTIES
10550   POSTAL SPECIALTIES
10600   PARTITIONS
10650   SCALES
10670   STORAGE SHELVING
10700   SUN CONTROL DEVICES (EXTERIOR)
10750   TELEPHONE ENCLOSURES
10800   TOILET AND BATH ACCESSORIES
10900   WARDROBE SPECIALTIES
10950   WASTE DISPOSAL UNITS

DIVISION 11—EQUIPMENT
Reference
Numbers †
11100   BANK EQUIPMENT
11150   COMMERCIAL EQUIPMENT
11170   CHECKROOM EQUIPMENT
11180   DARKROOM EQUIPMENT
11200   ECCLESIASTICAL EQUIPMENT
11300   EDUCATIONAL EQUIPMENT
11400   FOOD SERVICE EQUIPMENT
11500   ATHLETIC EQUIPMENT
11550   INDUSTRIAL EQUIPMENT
11600   LABORATORY EQUIPMENT
11630   LAUNDRY EQUIPMENT
11650   LIBRARY EQUIPMENT
11700   MEDICAL EQUIPMENT

11800   MORTUARY EQUIPMENT
11830   MUSICAL EQUIPMENT
11850   PARKING EQUIPMENT
11880   PRISON EQUIPMENT
11900   RESIDENTIAL EQUIPMENT
11960   SHIPYARD EQUIPMENT
11970   THEATER EQUIPMENT

DIVISION 12—FURNISHINGS
Reference
Numbers †
12100   ARTWORK
12200   BLINDS AND SHADES
12300   CABINETS AND FIXTURES
12500   DRAPERY AND CURTAINS
12600   FURNITURE
12670   RUGS AND MATS
12700   SEATING

DIVISION 13—SPECIAL CONSTRUCTION
Reference
Numbers †
13010   AIR SUPPORTED STRUCTURES
13050   ACCESS FLOORING
13100   AUDIOMETRIC ROOM
13250   CLEAN ROOM
13300   GREENHOUSE
13350   HYPERBARIC ROOM
13400   INCINERATORS
13440   INSTRUMENTATION
13450   INSULATED ROOM
13500   INTEGRATED CEILING
13540   NUCLEAR REACTORS
13550   OBSERVATORY
13650   PREFABRICATED STRUCTURES
13700   RADIATION PROTECTION
13750   CHIMNEYS
13770   SOUND ISOLATION
13800   STORAGE VAULTS
13850   SWIMMING POOL

DIVISION 14—CONVEYING SYSTEMS
Reference
Numbers †
14100   DUMBWAITERS
14200   ELEVATORS
14300   HOISTS AND CRANES
14400   LIFTS
14500   MATERIAL HANDLING SYSTEMS
14600   MOVING STAIRS AND WALKS
14700   PNEUMATIC TUBE SYSTEMS

DIVISION 15—MECHANICAL
Reference
Numbers †
15010   GENERAL PROVISIONS
15100   BASIC MATERIALS AND METHODS
15180   INSULATION
15200   WATER SUPPLY AND TREATMENT
15300   WASTE WATER DISPOSAL AND
            TREATMENT
15400   PLUMBING
15550   FIRE PROTECTION
15600   POWER OR HEAT GENERATION
15650   REFRIGERATION
15700   LIQUID HEAT TRANSFER
15800   AIR DISTRIBUTION
15900   CONTROLS AND INSTRUMENTATION

DIVISION 16—ELECTRICAL
Reference
Numbers †
16010   GENERAL PROVISIONS
16100   BASIC MATERIALS AND METHODS
16200   POWER GENERATION
16300   OUTSIDE POWER TRANSMISSION
            AND DISTRIBUTION
15400   SERVICE AND DISTRIBUTION
16500   LIGHTING
16600   SPECIAL SYSTEMS
16700   COMMUNICATIONS
16850   HEATING AND COOLING
16900   CONTROLS AND INSTRUMENTATION

* Courtesy of the Construction Specifications Institute.
† *Note:* The reference numbers shown relate, insofar as possible, to the *Uniform System* cost accounting numbers and the current document identifying system of the Institute.

Section 00030

Section 00030 is a *notice of call for bids*. This informs the contractor who the owner is, his or her address, and when bids are due. It also states where contract documents may be obtained and whether the contractor must leave a cash deposit when checking out a set of contract documents.

This section also stipulates any preconditions to bidding. Two common preconditions are that the contractor must provide a bid bond (discussed previously in the chapter) and that the procedure is laid out for obtaining approval of building materials not specified.

Section 00035

Section 00035 is the *instruction to bidders*. This is a more complete definition of what is expected of the contractor. An important statement in this section requires that the bidder be familiar with the drawings, the specifications, and the site. It also states that the contractor cannot make a legitimate claim for additional compensation due to information he or she might have overlooked in the three sources. This means that if the contractor missed seeing a wall shown in the plans, no extra fees for building the wall are allowed. It does not mean that the contractor must bear the additional cost of putting in special footings due to poor soil conditions which were not known (from soil borings) at the time of bidding.

This subdivision covers information necessary to the contractor in filling out the legal bid form. It covers such data as which spaces are to be filled in; whether the bid is to be sealed in an envelope; whether the contractor is to include all material, labor, and transportation costs in the bid; who may legally sign the bid; and what bid security is to be submitted with the bid.

Section 00035 can also contain statements pertaining to the following:

1. The contractor may find an error or request an interpretation of the contract documents. The contractor must bring this to the attention of the architect ten days prior to the bid opening. The architect only gives an interpretation in writing in the form of an addendum which is sent by registered mail to all bidders.
2. The allowance of substitutions in the specified materials is generally spelled out. Several practices are accepted by architectural firms, all of which are intended to guarantee the quality of construction materials.
3. A way of ensuring that the owner and architect will get the material wanted is to allow only one manufacturer's product. All others are unacceptable. This is called a *proprietary specification*. It has obvious drawbacks because of its restrictive nature. It is usually disallowed on public bids because it eliminates competitive bidding. A more acceptable variation of this procedure is for the specifications to allow three manufacturers' products, giving the contractors some latitude for choice.

   A further widening of the choice of material selection is allowed in an architect's specification that merely defines quality or material standards that the product must meet. Any manufacturer that can comply with the specified requirements is allowed to bid. This is called a *performance specification*.

   Another form of specification is called a *base bid with prior approval*. This starts out the same way as a proprietary specification does in that one manufacturer's product is specified but the contractor is allowed to request approval of other materials subject to the review of the owner and the architect. If approval is given, the architect sends a list of these products to all bidders in the form of an addendum.

   The final common form of specification is again similar to a proprietary specification but this time allows the contractor to propose a cash difference between the specified product and the one he or she wants to use. The owner and architect then have the option of accepting the specified product or paying more or less than the bid amount by letting the contractor use the preferred material.
4. Section 00035 also contains information on who is allowed to bid. If bidding is restricted to one or several contractors, it is stated. If competitive bidding is allowed, a statement as to the qualifications of bidders is given. "The owner reserves the right to reject any bid if evidence submitted by, or investigation of, such bidder fails to satisfy the owner that such bidder is properly qualified to carry out the obligations of the contract and to complete the work contemplated therein."
5. A further statement in the instructions to bidders informs the contractor that seven days

after he or she has been selected and has signed a contract, he or she is to supply the architect with the following:

a. A cost breakdown of each major item in the specifications
b. A list of all subcontractors that the general contractor intends to use (for the architect's approval)
c. A list of all proposed materials
d. Certificates indicating proper insurance
e. Certificates indicating the contractor has obtained a bond guaranteeing performance and payment for labor and materials
f. A time schedule

6. If the owner wants the project completed by a certain date, it is stated in the instruction to bidders. A few projects go a step further and penalize the contractor a cash sum per day for each day the job runs past the designated completion date. Some courts have ruled that a penalty clause is not valid unless the owner is willing also to pay a bonus if the job is completed early.

Section 00040

Section 00040 is a *proposal form.* This is the legal bid form used by the contractor to indicate the amount he or she will charge the owner to complete the work detailed in the contract documents. The proposal form includes the base bid sum plus a figure for all alternates in the proposal. Alternates are defined in the specifications (Section 01100). They are items the owner has the option of selecting or deleting beyond the base bid. An example could be carpeting in a school library. If carpet is an add alternate, the contractor will include a cost in the proposal for the installation. The owner then has the choice of accepting the carpet for that sum above the base bid. A deduct alternate works in much the same way, only the cost of the carpet already would be included in the base bid, and the alternate would indicate the amount the owner would save if he or she opts not to carpet the library.

Section 00031

Section 00031 is an *agreement form.* This is a sample of the contract between the owner and contractor, usually an AIA document.

Section 00080

Section 00080 states the *general conditions.* This is an extremely important AIA document that defines many common legal requirements necessary to ensure the proper operation of the project. The first article defines the contract documents, what they consist of, and the intent of the drawings and specifications. The next four articles in the general conditions define the architect, owner, contractor, and subcontractor. It establishes legal limits about the obligations of the four parties involved and their responsibilities to each other. Some major requirements spelled out in the general conditions for each position are listed below.

1. The architect

    a. Provides administration of the contract documents.
    b. Is the owner's representative during construction.
    c. Is given access to the project.
    d. Determines whether work is progressing according to the contract documents and so informs the owner.
    e. Approves the contractor's application for payment.
    f. Interprets the contract documents.
    g. Provides the final decision on aesthetic questions.
    h. Rejects work that does not comply with the contract documents.
    i. Reviews shop drawings for compliance with design.
    j. Prepares change orders.

2. The owner

    a. Furnishes all necessary surveys.
    b. Pays for easements.
    c. Orders a stoppage of work if the contractor fails to properly complete the work.
    d. Has deficiencies in work corrected and deducts cost from the bid amount on seven days' notice.

3. The contractor

    a. Reports any errors in the drawings to the architect.
    b. Works with drawings.
    c. Supervises and directs work.

d. Provides and pays for all labor, material, equipment, heat, water, and utilities.

e. Enforces strict discipline and order among employees.

f. Warrants that all materials are new and of good quality.

g. Pays all sales tax and necessary permit fees.

h. Complies with all local laws.

i. Employs a competent supervisor for the job.

j. Is responsible for the acts and omissions of employees and subcontractors.

k. Submits a progress schedule to the architect.

l. Maintains a set of contract documents, with any changes, on the site.

m. Approves and verifies dimensions on shop drawings before forwarding to the architect.

n. Resubmits shop drawings which are not acceptable.

o. Starts any portion of work only with approved shop drawings.

p. Keeps the site clean during construction and sees that it is "broom clean" at completion.

The subcontractors

a. The contractor shall furnish a list of all subcontractors.

b. The contractor will not use any subcontractor unacceptable to the owner and architect. If a substitution causes a change in the contract amount, the owner will pay or be refunded the difference.

c. All work will be performed in accordance with the contract documents.

d. Payment requests will be submitted to the contractor.

e. All claims for additional cost or completion time will be made to the contractor.

f. The contractor will pay all subcontractors proportionally to the work done and to payment received from the owner.

g. Nonpayment to the contractor because he or she did not comply with the contract documents, through no fault of the subcontractor, does not eliminate payment to the subcontractor.

h. The contractor will justly share insurance money with subcontractors.

i. The owner and architect are not responsible for payment to subcontractors.

Article Six in Section 00080, *general conditions*, covers the right of the owner to retain separate contracts for various phases of work on the same job. Commonly, this includes general, mechanical, plumbing, and electrical contractors on the project. The article stipulates that the contractors coordinate their work and provide reasonable storage space for each other. If any part of the contractor's work depends on another contractor, he or she is responsible for the inspection of the other's work and is to report any defect to the architect. Any damage done to work resulting from the acts of two contractors is to be settled between them either by agreement or by arbitration.

Article Seven in Section 00080 deals with miscellaneous provisions such as laws, royalties, tests, and arbitration. The contractor agrees to abide by all laws in effect at the building site. Both the owner and contractor are liable for damage caused by the other. The owner can require the contractor to furnish bonds ensuring performance according to the contract documents and payment of materials and labor costs. If the contractor uses a patented material or process, he or she will pay the royalties unless it was indicated in the contract documents, in which case the owner will pay. It is the responsibility of the contractor to inform the architect when the work has progressed to a point where tests or inspections called for in the specifications should be made. It is also required of the contractor to pay for these items. If either party in the contract fails to pay money when it is due, it will accrue interest at the legal rate.

The final point covered in Article Seven deals with disputes related to interpreting the contract document. As was previously indicated, the architect has the final decision on matters relating to design. All other disputes are subject to binding arbitration. This involves setting up a panel with three members, one appointed by each party and a third member mutually agreeable to both sides. An arbitration board acts much as a jury does in that it hears testimony from both sides and renders an opinion. Article Seven specifies that the decision of the arbitration board is final and is admissible in a court of law. The contractor is to continue working during arbitration unless it is agreeable to both contractor and owner that work may be suspended.

Article Eight of the general conditions deals with definitions of time in the contract. The project is to be considered legally started on the date established in the architect's notice to proceed, a form the architect sends to the contractor when the preconditions in the contract have been met, and the contract is signed, and the bonds and insurance are paid. The project is considered substantially complete on a date certified by the architect.

Days in the contract are defined as calendar days, not working days. If the contract stipulates a number of days for completion of the work, the time will be from the notice to proceed to the date of substantial completion. The contractor will be granted an extension in the time to finish the project by a change order for delays caused by

1. Neglect of the owner or architect
2. Changes ordered in the work
3. Fire
4. Transportation delays
5. Labor disputes
6. Unavoidable casualties or events beyond the control of the contractor

Article Nine of Section 00080 covers the payment procedures to the contractor. Prior to the first monthly application for payment, the contractor is to submit a schedule of values dividing the total bid sum into the actual costs for material and labor for each area of work. Once the architect has approved the schedule of values, it becomes the base for the contractor's monthly application for payment. An example would be if the contractor's schedule of values indicates concrete work to cost $100,000 and the request for payment indicates that he or she is 60 percent complete with concrete work. The contractor is due $60,000.

The contractor submits an itemized application for payment to the architect ten days prior to the date due. The architect then has seven days to issue a certificate for payment for work he or she determines is properly due. The contractor is entitled to submit an application for payment for material, labor, and profit incorporated in the project and material stored and paid for but not yet used on the job. The architect may refuse to issue a certificate for payment for the following reasons:

1. If defective work is not remedied
2. If a third party has filed claim against the job
3. If the contractor fails to pay subcontractors
4. If the architect reasonably doubts that the job can be finished with the unpaid balance of

the contractor's bid or according to the time schedule
5. If the contractor has caused damage to another contractor
6. If the contractor has failed to do the work satisfactorily

If the architect fails to issue a certificate for payment in seven days after the contractor's request or the owner fails to make payment within seven days after the date established in the contract, the contractor may upon seven days' additional notice, stop work until he or she is paid. When the contractor considers the job to be substantially complete, he or she will submit a list of items necessary for completion of the project to the architect. Upon inspection the architect will prepare a certificate of substantial completion fixing the date at which all items on the list will be complete.

On final inspection, if all the items shown in the contract documents have been determined to be acceptable, the architect will issue a certificate of payment to the owner. The contractor is to then submit evidence to the owner and architect that all bills for labor and material have been paid as well as a consent from the surety for final payment. Once all requirements in the general conditions have been met, the owner will make final payment including any retained percentage. It is common for the contract to stipulate that progressive payments to the contractor will have a percentage retained, typically 10 percent, until final completion and acceptance of the work. The owner retains the right to make claims against the contractor for unsettled liens, defective work, failure of the work to comply with the contract documents, or special guarantees.

Article Ten of Section 00080 pertains to safety on the job site. The contractor is responsible for instituting safety precautions and shall designate a staff member to be in charge of accident prevention. The contractor agrees to comply with all local laws dealing with safety.

Article Eleven deals with the types of insurance that should be provided by both the contractor and the owner. The contractor is responsible for the following:

1. Workmen's compensation
2. Bodily injury, occupational sickness, damage claims, and death for both employees and nonemployees
3. Property damage

All these policies shall have limits not less than the legal requirements. The contractor must file certificates of insurance acceptable to the owner prior to when the notice to proceed is issued by the architect. The owner is responsible for the following:

1. Owner's liability insurance
2. Property insurance with fire and extended coverage covering the interests of the owner, contractor, and all subcontractors
3. Steam-boiler insurance

Article Twelve of Section 00080 covers any changes made in the contract documents after the owner and contractor have signed a contract. The article stipulates that the owner has the right to make changes in the job without invalidating the contract. Additions, deletions, changes in the contract, or time are items handled by the change order. A *change order* is a document that, when signed by the owner, contractor, and architect, legally changes the contract documents in cost, scope of work, or time. The cost to the owner is handled either as lump sums, unit prices, or cost plus a percentage profit for the contractor. A change order is generally instituted by the architect in the form of a written document or drawing detailing the proposed change. The contractor then surveys the change, includes proposed changes in price, and signs the agreement. The architect is next to sign the order if he or she agrees with the price; it then is forwarded to the owner, whose signature will execute the change. The article indicates that any below-grade conditions unknown at the time of bidding that could alter the project cost will allow the contractor to request an adjustment in the contract sum. It also is stated that the architect has the right to order minor changes not affecting the contract sum or completion time by issuing a field order.

Article Thirteen of Section 00080 deals with correction of work already completed by the contractor. The architect has the right to inspect all work in the project. If the contractor covers up work contrary to the architect's specific directive, the architect may require the uncovering of the work at the contractor's expense. The architect also may request the uncovering of any work he or she suspects to be faulty. If it is, the contractor will pay for the cost of uncovering and replacing. If it is not faulty, the owner will pay the additional expense. The contractor will correct promptly all work rejected by the architect that does not conform to the contract documents. Any work found to be defective within one year from the date of substantial completion is to be replaced by the contractor. Failure of the contractor to fulfill this obligation allows the owner to have the work corrected and charge it to the contractor.

The final article of Section 00080, Article Fourteen, deals with the means of terminating the contract between the owner and contractor. The contractor may void the contract if

1. The work is stopped for 30 days because of a court order.
2. An emergency makes building materials unavailable, through no fault of the contractor or his or her agents.
3. The architect fails to issue a certificate for payment or the owner fails to make payment.

Under the above conditions, the contractor is due the full amount for materials, labor, and profit expended on the job at that point. The owner is entitled to terminate the contract if

1. The contractor is bankrupt.
2. The contractor refuses to supply enough skilled workers or proper materials.
3. The contractor refuses to pay subcontractors.
4. The contractor disregards laws.
5. The contractor is guilty of a substantial violation in the contract documents.

Under these conditions, the owner can take possession of the site, materials, and construction equipment to finish the project. If the cost of completing the project, including additional architectural fees, exceeds the unpaid balance of the bid amount, the contractor shall pay the difference.

Section 00090

Section 00090 lists *supplementary conditions*. This involves necessary changes in the preceding general conditions to custom fit them to the job or to meet the preferences of the architect. As the heading implies, this section is intended as a supplement to the main body of information in the general conditions.

End of Architect's Specification, Section 0

The main body of the specifications covers the quality of all materials used in the job. A typical section in the specification covers the following points:

1. General—work included, related work specified elsewhere, testing, submittals (samples, shop drawings, and test reports), product delivery, storage and handling, job conditions
2. Products—materials, mix ratio, manufacturer, fabrication
3. Execution—site work, inspection by contractor,

installation, quality control, site protection, cleaning, required schedules, or manuals

The following specification for open-web steel joists is for a specific architectural project and is intended primarily to indicate the degree of completeness necessary in a specification. Every product from glass to roofing must be defined to this extent.

Section 0520—Steel Joists

PART 1—GENERAL

01 CONDITIONS OF THE CONTRACT
The Conditions of the Contract (General, Supplementary and other Conditions) and the General Requirements (Sections of Division 1) are hereby made a part of this Section.

02 SCOPE
This Section includes all labor, material, equipment and related services necessary to furnish and install all steel joists indicated on the Drawings or specified herein.

The following work is specified under other Sections:

01) Building in anchors in masonry walls—Section 0420, UNIT MASONRY.
02) Loose structural angles for support and anchorage of steel joists at masonry walls and structural steel frames for roof openings—Section 0510, STRUCTURAL METAL.

03 STANDARDS
Work shall conform to the following standards, unless otherwise specified herein.

American Institute of Steel Construction (AISC) and Steel Joist Institute (SJI) "Standard Specifications for Open Web Steel Joists, J-Series and H-Series," March 1, 1965.
AISC and SJI "Standard Specifications for Longspan Steel Joists, LJ-Series and LH-Series," November 1, 1969.
AISC and SJI "Standard Specifications for Deep Longspan Steel Joists, DLJ-Series and DLH-Series," February 1, 1970.

AISC "Specification for the Design, Fabrication and Erection of Structural Steel for Buildings," February 12, 1969.

04 QUALIFICATION OF MANUFACTURERS
Open web steel joists shall be manufactured by a member of the SJI or AISC. Other manufacturers must obtain prior approval as provided in Substitution of Materials, Section 0090, SUPPLEMENTARY CONDITIONS.

05 SUBMITTALS
Submit shop drawings for approval in the form of a reproducible transparency (see Section 0130, SUBMITTALS). Shop Drawings shall indicate field welding requirements.

06 PRODUCT DELIVERY, STORAGE AND HANDLING
Transport, store and handle steel joists and accessories in a manner that will prevent damage or deformation. Replace damaged material. Store joists clear of the ground and protect from dirt, water and the elements. Protect shop finish from scratching, staining and damage.

PART 2—PRODUCTS

07 STANDARD STEEL JOISTS
Standard steel joists shall be H-Series open web steel joists, LH-Series longspan steel joists and DLH-Series steel joists conforming to SJI Standard Specifications. Fabrication shall conform to the requirements of AISC "Specification for the Design, Fabrication and Erection of Structural Steel for Buildings."
Longspan joists shall be underslung with parallel chords unless otherwise indicated on the Drawings. Deep longspan joists shall be underslung with level bottom chords and sloped top chords.

End bearing plates on joists installed with a slope greater than ¼″ per foot shall be accurately pitched in fabrication to provide a level, full bearing surface when erected. Fabricated non-standard bearing plates and end conditions where indicated on the Drawings. Provide end anchors.

Extended ends shall be designed to support the loads indicated on the Drawings.

Bridging for H-Series joists shall consist of rigid horizontal bracing welded or bolted to joist chords, and bridging for LH-Series joists shall consist of rigid diagonal cross bracing bolted to joist chords. Bridging for DLH-Series joists shall be rigid diagonal cross bracing composed of steel angles welded or bolted to joist chords. Provide bridging anchors to anchor ends of bridging lines.

Provide ceiling extensions for joists in areas to have finished ceilings.

08 SHOP FINISH

Joists and accessories shall be thoroughly cleaned after fabrication and shop primed. Joists exposed to view in the finished work shall be given one spray coat of gray rust inhibitive primer containing at least 50% rust inhibitive pigments. Paint shall be carefully applied to provide a smooth and even surface. Concealed joists shall be given one coat of shop paint conforming to the SJI Standard Specifications.

The fabricator shall furnish sufficient (one gallon minimum) paint of each type to the erector for field touch up of connections and abrasions.

Part 3—Execution

09 ERECTION

Set joists accurately to lines and dimensions indicated on the approved shop drawings. Install joists so that required bearing is obtained.

H-Series joists shall have a minimum bearing of 2½″ on steel and 4″ on solid masonry and concrete, and LH-Series joists shall have a minimum bearing of 4″ on steel and 6″ on solid masonry and concrete. DLH-Series joists shall have the minimum bearing indicated on the Drawings.

Temporarily brace joists during erection, and install bridging immediately as joists are set. Securely fasten bridging to top and bottom chords in a manner that will not damage joists members. Where joists are exposed to view in finished work, bridging shall be carefully aligned and neatly installed. Securely anchor ends of bridging lines to walls and beams at both top and bottom chords.

Securely weld joists to supporting steel, and anchor joists to masonry and concrete according to SJI Standard Specifications unless otherwise indicated on the Drawings.

Keep construction loads off joists until they are permanently anchored and bridged. Avoid excessive concentrated loads during construction by distributing loads to insure that the load carrying capacity of the joists is not exceeded.

Immediately after erection, clean welds, scratches or other abraded spots on joists and touch up with the same paint used for the prime coat.

Writing a specification is a very exacting job. It is seldom done from scratch but instead is patterned after a master specification for all material. The specification writer then goes through the master, deletes the material that does not pertain to the job, and possibly custom writes sections to exactly fit the needs of the project. The high percentage of repetitive materials found in a specification permits the use of such equipment as a magnetic-tape automatic typewriter, a computer printer that will identify with the master specification, or an optical scanner with a computer that permits the technician to write a portion of the specification. The computer specification also can have built-in safety checks to eliminate the fabrication of incompatible materials.

THE ARCHITECT'S OFFICE

Three separate methods of forming an architect's office are commonly used: proprietorship, partnership, and corporation. The first, a *proprietorship*, is an office owned solely by one person. This is not necessarily a one-person office; rather, one individual owns the company and usually participates totally in the profits and losses. This approach has the positive features of allowing an architect to be very much involved in all activities within the office. The drawback comes with the limited size an office can attain when one person leads all major activities. As the size of an office increases, a common setup is to have several architects with like or compatible talents form a *part-*

nership. The sharing of responsibilities and tasks allows this office form to grow and diversify. Frequently, each partner becomes involved in diverse phases such as design, client contact, or production. Partnerships also can be formed on an unequal basis—a senior partner might derive a greater portion of the profits and losses than a junior partner. Some states allow architectural firms to form *corporations.* The operation of such an office is quite similar to a partnership; key members in the firm are major stockholders.

Really, in office policies and in work produced, there is no such thing as a typical architect's office. Some firms specialize in building types such as hospitals, houses, or schools. Most offices accept a diversified practice. A few firms may turn down a potential project because the philosophy of the client or the project does not meet that of the firm. Some firms have adopted a four-day work week, while others frequently work seven, usually on a voluntary basis. Some firms are design-oriented and pride themselves in unique approaches to a design problem and allocate an appropriate portion of the total fee to the design budget. Other firms are more concerned with the production of a job, meeting a minimal budget or just producing the working drawings for a project and letting another firm do the design.

The benefits to employees vary greatly in offices. Aside from a salary, firms can provide hospitalization, transportation costs, profit sharing, retirement benefits, and fees for employees to attend seminars or conferences, to name a few. In addition to the tangible benefits, each office has a personality all its own. This can take the form of the relationships between principals of the firm and its employees, and it certainly includes friendships formed among employees. The office sometimes encourages its employees to participate in various architectural competitions or expresses appreciation when a team of employees completes a project. It also may encourage professional registration and may share in the cost of attaining it. Sometimes it encourages membership in the AIA. Some offices even sponsor unusual competitions between firms, such as kite design and flying or snowman building. If an office does assume such a posture with its employees, it certainly goes a long way toward developing a sense of pride in the firm.

An architect usually receives a fee in one of three ways. The most common is to receive a percentage of the construction costs at the completion of the project, depending on the building type. A typical schedule* states that the percentage fee is based on the complexity of the building by type and on the construction cost. The building types range from a low fee for utilitarian buildings (such as a warehouse) to a high fee for commercial buildings designed for special use (such as a church, auditorium, bandshell, and so on) or to an even higher percentage fee for custom residences. The reasoning behind the variety of schedules is that it does not take the same amount of time per dollar for an office to produce each building type. The fee schedule for each specific type is generally a curve that relates percentage of fee to total construction costs. This starts off at a higher-percentage fee for lower-priced projects and gradually lowers to a lower level for a larger project. An example could be a 10 percent architectural commission for a $100,000 library, which would lower to 8 percent for a $2 million library. The reason for a reduced fee as the project increases is that it requires less architectural time per dollar of construction cost.

Another contract commonly signed between the owner and the architect involves compensation to the architect as a multiple of his or her direct personal expenses. This means that the architect's fee is based on a percentage above the actual cost to the office to produce the job. In addition to the charge for all hourly architectural personnel time, it covers transportation, drawing reproduction, postage, overtime, and computer time.

The final common method of compensation for the architect is to receive a lump sum payment plus direct personal expenses. This is commonly used when only one partner is involved in the project.

The liability involved in construction of a building is very complex. In short, an architect is legally responsible for the design when it comes to the health and safety of its occupants. An example could be the design of a balcony handrail in an apartment building. If the architect's drawings detailed the vertical support pickets to be spaced 2'-0" apart, the architect could be held liable if a child climbed between the pickets and fell. All architectural firms strive for conditions that eliminate dangerous situations in their design. Most do this by implementing a series of checks and standard details that reduce the possibility for error.

* The state schedule refers to a minimum recommended fee schedule adopted by the state chapter of the AIA.

With the extremely high monetary judgments handed down by courts, most architects take the additional precaution of carrying professional liability insurance.

Each state protects its people by requiring anyone involved in the design of most public and private buildings to prove competency. Once this has been proved, he or she is legally entitled to the title of an architect. While each state is responsible for licensing its own architects, a national organization has developed a uniform testing system used by most states. The National Council of Architectural Registration Boards, NCARB, provides a uniform test to all states, which means that while an architect is registered in the state in which he or she passed the exams, he or she may make application in another state, citing successful completion of the exam. Most states recognize the NCARB exam without requiring additional testing. It is illegal for an architect to build in a state in which he or she is not registered. Not every person in a firm that is working on a project need be licensed. Rather, one member of the firm, usually a partner, must sign each sheet of the working drawings and the title page in the specification. This makes her or him legally responsible for all data in the construction documents. A typical state requirement follows:

I hereby certify that this plan, specification, or report was prepared by me or under my direct supervision and I am a duly registered architect under the laws of the state of Minnesota Reg. No.

———

Architectural registration is a two-part requirement for an individual without a degree from an accredited school of architecture, which is a five-year college degree. It is reduced to one requirement with a degree. An equivalency examination must be taken by anyone not holding a Bachelor of Architecture degree. The prerequirements are as follows: be of good character, have the equivalent of a high school diploma; and have a minimum of 12 years of practical experience in offices of practicing registered architects or a combination of experience and acceptable architectural education totalling 12 years. The equivalency examination consists of three parts: history, design, and construction theory and practice. The tests are given once a year and take 10 hours a day for two days—architectural history (2 hours), design (8 hours covering design and site planning), and con-

struction theory and practice (10 hours covering structures, building construction, mechanical equipment, and professional administration). The applicant may take these tests as many times as is necessary to pass them and retains credit for any part passed in previous attempts. Once all three parts are passed, the applicant is eligible to take the professional examination.

The professional examination is required of all applicants. The prerequirements are as follows: be of good character; be at least 21 years old; and have a Bachelor of Architecture degree from an accredited school and three years of practical experience or have passed the equivalency examination. The professional examination is a four-part test consisting of environmental analysis, programming, design and technology, and construction. The test is given once a year and takes two days. The examination is graded entirely by machine and is on a pass-fail basis—an applicant who passes only three parts must retake the entire test. The professional examination is drawn from a real architectural problem encountered by an architectural firm somewhere in the United States. A packet containing information relating to the project is mailed to the candidate several months prior to the exam. At the examination, the candidate is provided with four additional packets of information to be used in each of the tests.

This test supersedes the previously administered seven-part, four-day examination given by NCARB which all applicants were required to take.

Functions within an Office

A definite pecking order has been established in an architect's office as to who does what and when. The larger an office, the more departmentalized it becomes out of necessity. Some offices have gone so far in forming departments that it gives credence to the standing professional joke that if you go to work for a certain large architectural firm they will have you detailing toilet partitions for the full length of your employment. Although it never gets quite that compartmentalized, many firms do have separate departments for design, promotion, production, specifications, and contract administration. Each of these departments closely follows the phases of an architect's contract. A small to medium-sized firm undoubtedly will move personnel from one department to another, depending on the workload. This is where the pecking order starts, but it doesn't reach the final definition until each member within the department is also given a title. The department an employee is put in depends on his or her educational background and talent. Therefore, a new employee with a vocational drafting degree would likely work on the production of working drawings. A graduate of a school of architecture probably would work in the design department. An employee with experience in construction could be made a field representative in the contract administration department.

The position in which an employee is placed within the department is guided by experience and talent. The two variable points between the department an employee is placed in and the position within that department is education for department and experience for position. The common element in both is the talent he or she displays in each case.

The purpose of this section is to define the exact duties for each position in an architectural firm. It requires no particular insight into the profession to realize that the first position a new graduate can expect is near the bottom. The first position could possibly be that of a working drawing technician. A *technician* is responsible for drawing the details in a set of working drawings in a neat, orderly, and correct manner. He or she must display an aptitude in these areas so that his or her drafting techniques coincide with the approved standards established by the office. The process of assembling a building is difficult. The technician can expect as much help as needed to produce the working drawings. This help can come from many quarters, which brings up one of the key points to advancement in this profession. *If the source is valuable, learn all you can from it.* Receiving personal criticism is difficult to accept, but if the source can be objectively considered more knowledgeable, learn from it. If a more experienced technician tells you that your lettering is bad, do not sulk for an hour. Ask why it's bad and how it can be improved.

Most architectural offices have adopted a drafting manual that establishes its preferred techniques. This is one document the technician should be thoroughly familiar with, since it tells how things are to be done in that architectural firm. Perhaps a better way to understand the workings of an office is to study a set of prints of a project recently completed by the firm. The knowledge a technician can gain by comprehending a full set of drawings is probably the most valuable source of reference. Past objects also are an important way of acquiring details for a present project in working drawings.

A great percentage of the preliminary material a technician is expected to draw will be quite clear already. The design-development drawings include a site plan, floor plans, exterior elevations, and wall details. With this package in a well-refined condition, the technician's task is one of further refining the material, not starting from scratch. A set of working drawings is, in actuality, a building project in itself. The general rule is to start drawing the building at a very small scale and progressively increase the scale to indicate more detail. The technician's immediate superior, the job captain, spells out most major items.

Every job has a job captain at the head of a production staff. The job captain provides everyone with a layout of the sheets to work on, including, roughly, the location of the drawing on the sheet and an idea about how the detail should be drawn. The job captain is always available for consultation on items that might prove difficult to technicians, and so the job captain becomes the best source of information on the job.

While technicians are told in broad terms what to draw, it is taken for granted that they know how to draw. This certainly covers the fundamental points of good line quality and printing, but it assumes also the necessary knowledge and common sense to think out a detail. With the use of all source materials within reach, this is not so difficult as it may seem. Some attributes and responsibilities that an architectural technician should possess are

1. A good drafting ability
2. An ability to work well as a team member
3. A good attitude toward work
4. An ability to accept constructive criticism
5. A workable knowledge of drafting techniques

The technician's position cannot be considered substandard. Many individuals in an office find this workload so acceptable to their capabilities that they have no desire to advance further. As the experience of a technician increases, assuming the aptitude and desire are there, the next position is job captain on a relatively small job.

A *job captain* assumes a much greater role in the production of the job than a technician. One responsibility is to coordinate the activities of technicians assigned to the job. This means assigning work, correcting drawings by red-lining prints, and seeing that all drafting meets office standards. To meet this need requires that a job captain be more skilled in drafting and more knowledgeable in construction techniques than the technicians working under his or her supervision.

Another duty of the job captain is to act as liaison between the immediate superior (the project manager) and the technicians on the project. The data collected by the project manager in client meetings and discussions with consultants are transmitted to the job captain for inclusion into the working drawings. The job captain is in charge of the supervision of the working drawings, while the project manager directs the overall production. If the actual intent of this breakdown of command is followed, all data put into the working drawings are given first to the job captain for coordination and distribution to the technicians.

The job captain has the strongest ties to production of the project and, therefore, to the technicians. This individual seldom meets with the client but receives the necessary information from dialog (memos or conference) with the project manager.

Generally, a job captain is selected for a project on the basis of merit and experience. When a technician has gained sufficient experience in all areas of working drawings, he or she will be considered for a position as job captain. The first job will, without doubt, be fairly small and simple. This offers the employee a chance to prove his or her worth and lets the employer see if the individual can handle the responsibility. The criteria for judging a job captain's performance are simple. If he or she meets the office budget and the client's building budget and has the technicians produce a well-drawn set of working drawings, and the contractor had little—if any—problems building the project from the drawings, the job captain wins. Many variables are involved in this formula, some of which are out of the job captain's control. However, fair or not, this is the general test for a job captain. If he or she is relatively successful in the first venture, the next project will be larger and more complex.

Given this long list of duties, a job captain has less time to spend drafting. It is the job captain's duty to see that the project work is done efficiently and in accordance with established firm standards. Time spent managing and overseeing the work of team members may be more valuable to the firm than the time devoted to drafting.

When the job captain has gained sufficient experience on various types of construction and displays an aptitude and personality that meet the requirements of the position, the next step in office authority is to *project manager*. The responsibility for management of the project in an architect's office usually will be carried completely by a principal of a small firm. When a number of partners exist, the projects may be distributed among them. In large firms, project authority may be assigned to an associate. The project manager may or may not be the designer, but he or she will direct the project from start to finish. The project manager (and the principal responsible for the project, if not the project manager) maintains contact with the owner. He or she may be assisted in this operation by the job captain. In some circumstances (usually on a small job), the project manager and the job captain will be the same person.

The project manager is in charge of the project's coordination, including all information from the client, engineers, consultants, and public officials. He or she is the main link between data gathered outside the office and the production of the job from schematics through construction. Much of the project manager's time is spent in conference, coordinating the various staff members making up the project team. The client will be most familiar with the project manager since he or she attends most, if not all, meetings defining the program requirements. The manager makes the presentations of design material to the owner and transmits the reaction to the proper staff members. As the title indicates, the project manager directs the total operation of the job, including the design department, the engineers, the job captain and technicians, the consultants, and the field representatives.

The attributes a project manager must possess should increase proportionally with his or her advanced position above that of a job captain. The manager must have a good temperament and personality to get along well with the client, as well as the intelligence to command the client's respect. He or she must possess the poise necessary to present the project to an audience of several hundred citizens or the board of a multimillion-dollar corporation. He or she must have the leadership talent to direct all professional staff members who would be involved in a project. This means that he or she must be knowledgeable enough in all fields to direct the jobs of architectural design, production, specifications and construction, engineering data, consulting reports, and client relations. The best project manager will be one who has had experience in drafting and as a job captain because these roles give the insight necessary to assemble a building properly. In the position, the project manager has assumed the role of an administrator and seldom, if ever, participates in actually drawing the building. His or her opinion is valued on design decisions. In some firms, the project designer is also the project manager, but, for the most part, the manager does not physically produce design drawings.

Another of the project manager's activities is that of promotion. Few jobs walk in the front door of an architect's office, and so office members must actively go out and solicit work. Generally, these potential jobs will be sought by staff members with experience in design and construction who can intelligently answer questions about the proposed building and the services their particular firm can provide. This generally is done by a project manager.

The position of a project manager varies from firm to firm, depending on its size. A small firm with one or several architects in partnership probably will have a partner take the position of project manager on a job. This means that the project manager holds the highest position in the firm. A larger office that receives possibly 25 commissions or more a year would more than likely have partners in the firm, just as the smaller office, but there are too many commissions to assign a partner the full-time position of project manager on each job. This means that each partner can control only his or her jobs if there is a project manager on every job. The project then will have a partner-in-charge and a project manager assigned to it, the only difference being that a partner-in-charge will have several projects at the same time. Depending on the office, the project manager also might be an associate in the firm.

A position within the office that usually is assigned to a staff member with the experience of a project manager is *office manager*. This job involves coordinating everything to provide an efficient operation. For most purposes, the office manager is the boss of technicians and job captains and the person who seeks help from the project managers. He or she is counsel for design decisions and technical matters and makes certain that all jobs are properly staffed and supplied.

The era has passed of the long drafting room with row after row of desks and an elevated platform at one end where the master technician sits to view all that is happening. A well-run modern office, however, does need strict control to efficiently produce good buildings and well-executed sets of drawings. For this reason there is an office manager. His or her experience and knowledge is probably the most important factor in providing a smooth office operation.

For efficiency, many larger architectural firms have a separate design department with highly skilled staff members. This department receives initial data from the client and hands over the schematic and design-development drawings when they are completed by the production staff. The design department is composed of staff members with a talent for design in the same categories that were spelled out in the production department.

The overall coordination of the project is the job of the project manager. Working with her or him in design will be the *senior designer*. Design staff members report to the senior designer. The main job of this department is to provide an efficient, workable design that fits the needs of the client's program. Several other necessary jobs are performed by this department, such as making presentation drawings or models of the project for the client's information, or designing and laying out promotional material of the office's past work for the purpose of gaining future work.

A specialty job within an architect's office is that of the *specification writer*. This extremely important position gives the bidder the information needed to determine the quality of materials to be used. A small firm could dispense with this position by having the project manager or job captain prepare the specifications, but this exacting and time-consuming position is more easily handled by a specialist.

The specification writer has other jobs that are not related to the production of a specific project: He or she must (1) interview salespeople, manufacturers' representatives, and so on, and see that pertinent information is distributed to the staff; and (2) secure catalogs, literature, data specifications, and samples of materials and equipment.

Another specialized job in an architectural firm is that of a *field representative*. Unlike all other positions, for this job formal education in architecture is secondary to practical experience with construction techniques. Some firms refer to this position as an *inspector*, which is a misnomer, since the only inspection of a job is done by a local building inspector to see that all governing codes and laws are observed. The basic job of the field representative is to observe construction to make certain the project is being built in accordance with the construction documents.

All these people in an architectural practice must have one fundamental common denominator—the ability to comprehend and draw architectural details. For this reason, a job captain must be a technician first; and when sufficient experience is attained, he or she is qualified to be a project manager. This is also the reason why most architectural firms schedule members of their design staff to work on construction documents for several jobs. Without this first experience of putting a building together, a member of the architectural profession loses some of the most valuable experience to be gained in an office.

EIGHT

ARCHITECTURAL HISTORY

To establish when architecture began is difficult. The first step evolved when people moved from caves and fabricated shelters. Little remains of prehistoric architecture because of the nonpermanent materials used, but the first attempts were probably houses and places of worship. One mysterious remnant of very early architecture is a stone edifice, Stonehenge, in England (Figure 8-1). It has been identified as a place of worship, but it is still undetermined which culture built it and for what purpose.

EGYPTIAN ARCHITECTURE (3000 B.C. to A.D. 100)

The Egyptian culture was the first to produce a significant architectural style and also had the longest duration of any style in history. The First through the Tenth Dynasties, the Old Kingdom, lasted almost 1000 years, from 3200 B.C. to 2160 B.C. The Eleventh and Twelfth Dynasties, the Middle Kingdom, lasted until 1680 B.C. The following dynasties managed to survive with varying degrees of importance until the Greek civilization of Alexander the Great.

The Egyptian civilization was formed along and nurtured by the Nile River. The Nile most certainly had a profound impact on Egypt. Its yearly floods would supply the necessary topsoil along the banks to sustain an agrarian culture. Besides being a source of water, the Nile also provided transportation. Its banks supplied the stone necessary for the gigantic building style. The Egyptians formed cities linearly along the east side of the Nile and reserved the west bank for burial tombs.

Egyptian building can be divided into three types: tombs, temples, and domestic buildings. The religion of Egypt basically involved two thoughts: a cult of the dead, in which life after death was considered a reality, coupled with a belief that the gods took on the dual role of being part animal and part human. The concept of human immortality included the theory that the dead should be provided with the material objects found in life.

The practice of providing a house for deceased rulers (and to a much lesser degree, Egyptian noble classes) started in the Old Kingdom with a stone tomb, the mastaba (Figure 8-2). A *mastaba* is essentially a flat-topped building with *battered* (sloped) walls containing rooms for burial and worship, both above and below grade. This style evolved into a series of stepped mastabas and finally the familiar pyramid in the late Third Dynasty. A complex located at Gizeh (near Cairo) contains three massive pyramids, the largest of which was built for Cheops, the second ruler of the Fourth Dynasty (Figure 8-3). The Pyramid of Cheops covers 13 acres and is 480' high. It has a burial chamber approximately 19' high and 17' wide located in the center of the mass.

Figure 8-1. Stonehenge.

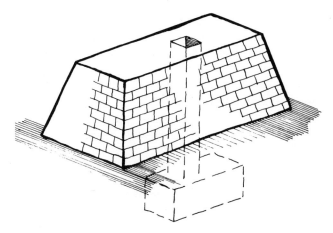

Figure 8-2. A mastaba.

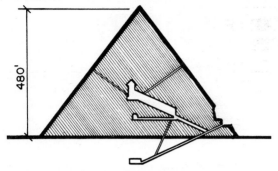

Figure 8-3. The Pyramid of Cheops.

The work force required to construct a project of this magnitude was drawn from prisoners of Egyptian conquests and from farm laborers out of work because of the yearly flooding of the Nile. Crude construction techniques and a knowledge of the lever were the only technologies possessed by the Egyptian builder. Construction of a tomb usually began very early in the life of the ruler to enable completion of the tomb within the ruler's lifetime (30 years was considered a typical life span).

Middle Kingdom tomb design gravitated away from pyramids toward a design of cutting the burial vault into "live" rock in the cliffs along the Nile.

Egyptian temple architecture usually consisted of stone post-and-beam construction. The design typically follows an axial plan with a hall surrounded by closely spaced columns. The roof is commonly formed by continuous slabs of stone lintels. Light is introduced into the space by means of a *clearstory,* a space made by raising the central portion of the roof and leaving the space between the two roof heights open for windows. The temple entrance and a majority of the walls are battered.

Residential design usually was accomplished with sun-dried brick, vertical wood boards that were sewn together, or reeds and mud. Home design followed a broad pattern of entering into a small enclosed courtyard, surrounded by a large central living room and several smaller rooms for food preparation and sleeping. The roof was generally flat and had a stair leading to it for access.

Egyptians formulated an architectural style that prevailed with little change for most of their 2500-year influence. Nearly every form in Egyptian stone architecture was an adaptation from earlier reed and mud designs. Stone walls were battered to echo the older mud-brick form. Stone pylons (engaged columns in walls) had circular lines painted around them to symbolize an earlier column form consisting of bundles of reeds bound together. Even columns were made to look like bundles of reeds with a capital (top of the column) carved like a papyrus or lotus bud (Figure 8-4).

The architecture of Egypt is unique in that it failed to carry over to another culture. Although history repeatedly shows older architectural styles strongly influencing newer forms, this did not happen with Egyptian design. The massive stone monuments and unique style had very little effect on any other architectural style.

Egyptian Architectural Examples

The following are Egyptian architectural examples:

1. The *pyramid group at Gizeh* consists of three large pyramids from the Fourth Dynasty: Cheops (480' high), Chephren (471' high), and Mykerinos (218' high).
2. The *Great Sphinx at Gizeh* is a stone sculpture 240' long and 66' high of a lion's body and the head of Chephren.
3. The *Pyramid of Zoser at Sakkara* is the first large pyramid in the Third Dynasty, designed by architect Imhotep. Through a series of changes the building evolved into a six-stepped pyramid 200' high.
4. The *temple group at Thebes* is a major religious center of the Middle and New Dynasties. In the vicinity of Thebes is *Khons at Karnak* (1198 B.C.), a typical temple with an open courtyard, columned hall, and sanctuary (Figure 8-5). Approximately 250' long and 90'

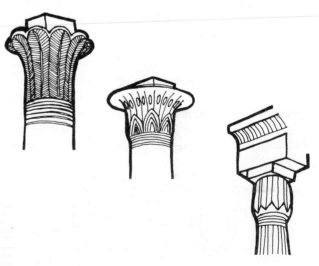

Figure 8-4. Capitals of columns.

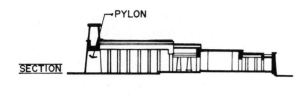

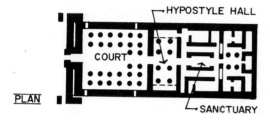

Figure 8-5. The Temple Khons at Karnak.

wide, its entrance consisted of a long avenue faced by small sphinxes. *Ammon at Karnak* (1530 to 323 B.C.) was the largest Egyptian temple. Its 10-acre court is surrounded by a wall 30′ thick, while the temple itself is 1100′ × 300′.

5. *Hatshepsut at Deir el Bahri* (1520 B.C.) is a mortuary temple to a powerful queen of the New Kingdom. The building is a three-level 300′ long terrace connected by ramps which abut high cliffs behind. *Ramesseum at Thebes* (1301 B.C.) is a typical New Kingdom mortuary temple built by one of Egypt's prolific builders, Rameses II. The temple is on an axial plan 530′ long and consists of a series of stair-stepped courts within the temple.

6. *Tutankhamen Tomb*, at Thebes, is the tomb of King Tut, who was an Eighteenth Dynasty king who gained prominence in A.D. 1922, when his undisturbed burial tomb was discovered. This was one of the few tombs that had not previously been robbed.

7. The *Temple of Rameses II*, at Abu Simbel, is carved into rock along the Nile. On the exterior were four seated statues of Rameses II over 65′ high and an interior temple with ceilings 30′ high. The temple was cut apart from the rock and moved to safety when it was in danger of being flooded by the recently completed Aswan Dam.

WESTERN ASIAN ARCHITECTURE (3000 B.C. TO 331 B.C.)

Occurring at about the same period as Egyptian culture (3200 B.C. to the time of the Greeks), a completely separate architectural style was formed in the area that is now Iraq, Iran, Syria, and Turkey. The area was called *Mesopotamia*, a Greek word meaning "middle-river." The area was bounded by two rivers, the Tigris and Euphrates, which provided a highly productive farming condition. The entire area was called the *Fertile Crescent*.

The western Asiatic empires did not have the natural protection of deserts, as did Egypt. They were vulnerable to attack and frequently changed governing powers. The four main periods in the history of this area are (1) Babylonian, 3000 to 1250 B.C.; (2) Assyrian, 1250 to 612 B.C.; (3) Neo-Babylonian, 612 to 539 B.C.; and (4) Persian, 539 to 331 B.C.

Wood and stone were not common to Mesopotamia. Thus, the most frequently used material was brick that was dried and fired by the sun. The Babylonian and Assyrian architectural style commonly used stepped platforms on which to place temples, palaces, and towns, primarily to avoid flooding. A stepped temple form was called a *ziggurat* (Figure 8-6).

Babylonian and Assyrian architecture revolved mainly around a temple and palace design that was contained within fortified walls. Brick walls of temples and palaces were usually faced with glazed brick or alabaster slabs (a gypsum material).

Both cultures had developed the arch as a means of spanning areas with brick. The Assyrians went on to use the dome to cover square areas. Characteristic of the Assyrian style were a man-headed, winged bull found at gateways, wainscots carved in stone, and vividly colored baked-enamel brick friezes.

The Persian civilization was located southeast of the Mesopotamian cultures of Babylon and Assyria. Unlike the northern area, stone was available, allowing columns to be widely used. The

Figure 8-6. A ziggurat.

Persians developed a relatively slender column that was more widely spaced than the Egyptian counterpart because it held light-weight timber roofs instead of stone. The Persians imitated the platform style of building and faced the walls with carved stone reliefs of figures. They borrowed much of their architectural style from the Assyrians and Egyptians but managed to develop a light, graceful form that departed from earlier Mesopotamian design.

The most characteristic Persian building type was the palace, usually consisting of a large square hall surrounded by equally spaced columns supporting the roof. The walls were usually sun-dried brick with stone frames around doors and windows.

The fragmented rulership of the western Asian area did not lead to the consistent architectural form achieved by the Egyptians. While the Babylonians were involved principally with trade, the war-waging qualities of the Assyrians and Persians meant that many of their architectural forms included fortifications. Like the Egyptians, the dominant religion involved the worship of many gods, coupled with a belief in life after death. In contrast to Egyptian belief, preservation of the body was not necessary to achieve eternal life. Many developments from the western Asiatic area are still used. Among them are (1) our numerical system; (2) cuneiform writing, which developed into the Western world's alphabet; (3) astronomy; and (4) three religions—Mohammedanism, Judaism, and Christianity.

Western Asian Building Examples

The following are examples of the architectural style of western Asia.

1. The *ziggurat near Susa* is a thirteenth-century B.C. Babylonian temple structure. It consists of five tiered buildings set on top of each other. It is 350' square and 174' high. Some Assyrian ziggurats went up to seven levels.
2. The *City of Babylon* was rebuilt by King Nebuchadnezzar II in the sixth century B.C., after it was destroyed by the Assyrians. The fortified inner city was nearly 1 mile square and contained a 10-acre palace with the Hanging Gardens, the Tower of Babel (a seven-tiered ziggurat to the god of the city), the Ishtar Gate, and many dwellings and businesses.
3. The *City of Khorsabad* was built in the seventh century B.C. by the Assyrian King Sargon II. The 1-mile-square fortified city contained most of the important buildings, including the *palace of Sargon*. This structure covered 23 acres and was raised on a terrace accessible by ramps wide enough for chariots. It contained temples, residences, and state chambers with entrances that were guarded by 12'-6"-high stone winged bulls with a man's head.
4. The *Palace of Persepolis* is a fifth- and fourth-century B.C. Persian stone palace, 1500' × 900'. A most impressive feature was a 225' square hall with a 37' ceiling supported by 100 columns.

GREEK ARCHITECTURE (650 B.C. TO 30 B.C.)

The roots of the civilization that founded Greece started at about the same time as Egypt and Mesopotamia, 3000 B.C. This new Aegean culture, so named because of its boundary with the Aegean Sea, originally started on the island of Crete from an Asiatic race that migrated to the area. Crete was structured primarily as a series of separately ruled cities with Knossos and Phaestos among the more powerful and with the sea playing a very important role in the culture.

The architectural character of Crete was generally a carryover from their western Asian background with flat-roofed buildings several stories high. Palace and tomb walls were of Cyclopean masonry (boulder-sized rubble stones) and cut stone without mortar. Technology had progressed to the point where flushing water closets and a central drainage system were used in palaces. The ruling power on Crete was King Minos, who gives this culture its name—the Minoan culture. This culture lasted until about 1400 B.C., when it was destroyed, possibly by an earthquake.

Mainland Greek civilization stemmed from Minoan colonization as well as from the incursion of several northern tribes. The Achaean and Dorian Greeks took over much of the holdings of the Minoans on both the Greek Peninsula and on Crete. The most important cities prior to the invasions were Tiryns and Mycenae. The architectural style was quite similar to that of Crete with minor exceptions, such as slightly sloped roofs, a carryover from the northern style.

The Mycenean civilization, as this mainland culture was called, along with the Minoan, was able to achieve large stone building forms, usually of tombs and palaces. The architectural character was not as refined as the styles of Egypt and Mesopotamia, but such techniques as stucco, gypsum floors, corbeled arches, and domes (a spanning technique of placing each course farther than the one below to form a triangular opening) were all used. The two cultures were, for the most part, destroyed at the time of the Dorian invasion, 1100 B.C. A nonproductive dark age occurred for the next 500 years.

The birth of the Greek state had a most profound influence on the Western world. Not only did their eventual conquerors, the Romans, have great admiration for Greek architecture, but it reoccurred in the fifteenth-century Renaissance style and still later in the classical style, used so frequently in the first half of the twentieth century. Greece opened up many avenues of thought in the medical, legal, astronomical, and geographical fields that were accepted for almost 2000 years. The new philosophy of Greece was one of free individual thought rather than the subservient attitude adopted by the Egyptian pharaohs or Babylonian kings. This new thought process definitely passed into the architectural style of the Greeks.

To say that a dark age started at the time of the Dorian invasion of Greece is slightly misleading, because some crafts and arts remained. However, the actual beginning of Greek culture started on the mainland about 650 B.C. Many factors had a hand in formulating the Greek architectural character. The climate allowed outdoor activity in both summer and winter and permitted the grand outdoor entrances and theaters. The mountains provided access to deposits of limestone and marble, called *Pentelic marble* because of Mt. Pentelicus, while the rough terrain established a natural barrier for the individual city-states. Most important was the philosophy of Greek life, which had a profound effect on their building form; for the first time architecture involved all people.

The period of Greek history is divided into two parts—Hellenic (650 to 323 B.C., the date of the death of Alexander the Great) and Hellenistic (to about 30 B.C.). Prior to this, the Romans had taken Greece as a province in 146 B.C. The high point of the culture, referred to as the Golden Age of Greece, goes from the final defeat of a Persian invasion, 480 B.C., to the death of Alexander the Great, 323 B.C.

Hellenic architecture began with features common to the earlier Aegean style, particularly in

plan. The temple, with a great deal of outside colonnade emphasis, was the most common building type of the period. Early structures were probably made of wood, but about 600 B.C. the Greeks made a transformation to stone, using many of the same details. The typical structural support system of column and beam, called a *trabeated* system, necessitated a relatively short span. This meant that Greek architecture seldom was daring in engineering feats or massive in size. Rather, it was one of uncompromising refinement and beauty. Stone temple design began to take on a certain number of characteristics that formulated the main style:

1. The floor plan was usually rectangular, with the length in a 2:1 ratio to the width.
2. The exterior had a row of closely spaced columns on all four elevations; larger temples had a second row of interior columns that lined up with the exterior row. A rectangular room (or rooms) was located within the perimeter of the column row. This room, the *naos*, had solid walls without windows or roof openings and housed the statue of the god for whom the temple was built. Entrance to the temple was always on the width elevation and faced east.
3. Roofs were a low-pitched gable usually structured with timber and sheathed with thin sheets of marble.
4. Marble was the chief material used for temples. If limestone was used in its place, it commonly was covered with a finely ground marble plaster.
5. Worship did not take place within the temple but around its exterior. The naos area was for viewing the statue of the god. This concept led to several characteristics in temple treatment. The exterior emphasis was very important. Buildings were placed on stepped pedestals, *crepidoma*, for better vision. Building sizes were kept relatively small because mass interior worship was not common.
6. Classical orders were established. In effect this determined the exterior elevations. An *order* is a combined foundation, column, and top member, or entablature. The Greeks used three separate orders in their buildings; in several examples the orders were intermixed in the same building.

   a. The first, simplest, and most widely used order was called *Doric*. The base or crepidoma was usually three steps high with the column resting directly on it (Figure 8-7). Hellenic columns were usually four to six times as high as the base diameter and had a smaller diameter at the top than at the bottom, usually three-quarters smaller. Columns were not one piece of stone but instead were cylindrical stone drums placed on top of each other and keyed together with metal clips. Fluting was carved into the stone after it was assembled. The main body of the column is called the *shaft*, with the most characteristic part of the order, the *capital*, at the top of the shaft. The Doric capital is a very simple transitional means of going from a cylindrical column to a square support (Figure 8-8). A beam, commonly without

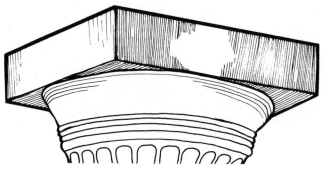

Figure 8-8. A Doric capital.

any decoration, called the *architrave*, rested on the capital and was the first portion of the entablature. There were three other entablature sections. The *frieze* was a band around the building above and about the same depth as the architrave which was carved with figures and a decorative fluted pattern, called the *triglyph*. The *cornice* was a narrow band acting as a transition between the horizontal lines below to the low pitched roof on the pediment. The *pediment*, a triangular-shaped piece, was usually carved with figures at both ends.

b. The second order, *Ionic*, was developed in the Greek colonies in Asia Minor and transported to Greece. The Ionic differed from the Doric mainly in proportions and the capital treatment. The ratio of column height to diameter changed from the rather stubby proportion of Doric to about nine times as high as the base diameter, producing a more slender shaft. Doric columns rested directly on the crepidoma, while Ionic columns added a base consisting of several circular rings slightly larger than the column. This had the function of spreading the axial load on the column to a greater area of the crepidoma. The most obvious change occurred in the capital design, which took the appearance of a ram's horn or scroll, called the *volute* (Figure 8-9). The entablature frequently had no frieze, which gave it a lighter appearance.

c. The *Corinthian* order was the last order in Greek architecture and was used sparingly. It was closely patterned after the Ionic order, with the exception of the capital. The shaft on the Corinthian order was slightly more slender and the height was

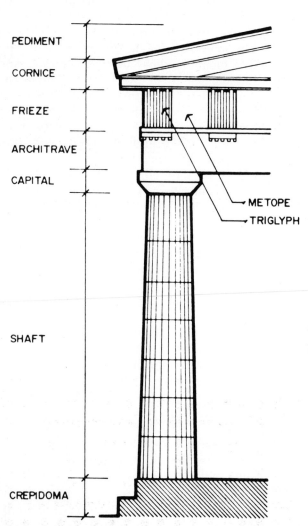

PEDIMENT

CORNICE

FRIEZE

ARCHITRAVE

CAPITAL

METOPE

TRIGLYPH

SHAFT

CREPIDOMA

Figure 8-7. A Doric column.

Figure 8-9.   An Ionic capital.

Figure 8-10.   A Corinthian capital.

10 times the diameter. The capital treatment was proportionally much wider than Doric and Ionic and contained a combination of an Ionic volute with carved acanthus leaves under the scroll (Figure 8-10). The style, however, was too decorative for the Greeks to accept fully. Later, the Romans adopted it as their predominant order.

The Parthenon in Athens (Figure 8-11) is the most perfect example of Greek temple architecture. It was built in the fourth century B.C. of Pentelic marble. The optical refinements used in this temple show the extent of thought placed in design. Columns were canted slightly inward to correct the optical illusion that vertical lines (columns) appear to fan out at the top if they are exactly parallel. This inclination was so slight that if all the columns were projected they would meet at a point 1½ miles up. Optically, corner columns as they appeared against the sky as a background looked to be spaced further apart and thinner than the columns in front of the dark-colored naos wall. To correct for this, the corner column was spaced closer to the next one and was slightly more squat.

Again, optically, the profile of a column appears to be slightly concave along the shaft. Thus, the column was corrected to be $^{11}/_{16}''$ convex. This type of refinement is known as *entasis*.

The horizontal lines of the stylobate and entablature also appear to be concave even though they are straight. Thus, the Parthenon had the hori-

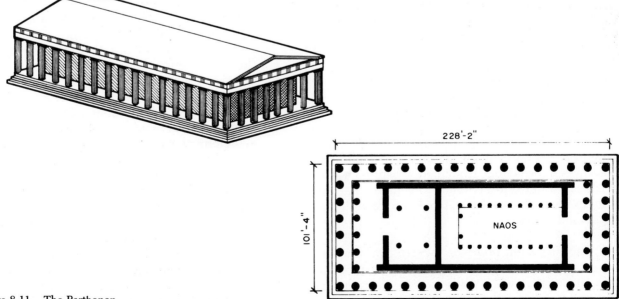

Figure 8-11.   The Parthenon.

zontal lines convex by slightly over 2½″ in the center to compensate for the illusion. Optical perfection even got to the point that the top row in letters of inscriptions on a building was made slightly larger than the next lower line so that they would appear to be the same height when viewed from the ground.

Greece was ruled by a fragmented governmental system in which cities ruled themselves. A great deal of jealousy existed between the city-states. Athens emerged as the leading power after the defeat of the Persians in 479 B.C., beginning 50 years of the most impressive building in Greek architectural history. When Athens was ruled by Pericles (444 to 429 B.C.), many major public buildings were begun, and an attempt to unify the city-states was made in the formation of the Delian League.

The end of Pericles' leadership marks the beginning of a power struggle that first placed Sparta as the most powerful city-state, followed by Thebes, which was replaced by Macedonia. The high point in Greek conquest began in 336 B.C., when 20-year-old Alexander the Great assumed leadership. He set out to conquer the Persians and in six years, after never having lost a battle, he controlled most of the civilized world. Alexander extended the sphere of Greek influence as far west as India and as far south as Egypt. He died of fever at 33 in Babylon, which allowed his generals to split the empire into separate states. All attempts at unification failed and eventually allowed Greece to be taken by Rome.

Aegean and Greek Building Examples

One of the greatest Minoan architectural examples is the *Palace of King Minos*, at Knossos, Crete. Knossos was chief among the cities in the Minoan empire. The palace was a vast two-story building of cut stone and brick. It had a complex of rooms and was built in approximately 2000 B.C. The building was about 400′ square and was arranged around a central court the size of a football field. The queen's chamber contained a bathroom with flushing water closets and a central drainage system. Two Mycenaean architectural examples are described below.

1. The *Citadel at Mycenae, Greece*, was a walled city in southern Greece built around 1250 B.C. The walls were constructed of cyclopean masonry (large rubble stone). The most famous feature was the lion gate entrance to the citadel. It spanned an opening of over 10′ and had two 10′ lions carved into the lintel.

2. The *Treasury of Atreus at Mycenae, Greece*, also called the Tomb of Agamemnon, the King of Trojan Wars, was built in 1325 B.C. The single beehive-shaped room, 48′ in diameter and 44′ high, was set into the side of a hill. The dome was made of corbeled stone that was dressed smooth after it was in place. A rather grand open entrance, over 100′ long and constructed of stone walls 10′ thick, led to the tomb.

The Acropolis in Athens is a hill that is the site of one of the most impressive building projects in history. It is a complex of several temples and theatres built during the fourth century B.C. The following examples are all found on the Acropolis:

1. The *Parthenon* (447 to 432 B.C.). The optical refinements of the Parthenon, the most perfect example of Greek architecture, have been discussed. The temple is approximately 100′ by 230′, with 8 columns across the front and 17 across the side (counting the end columns twice). It was designed in the Doric order using Pentelic marble. The naos of the temple housed a 42′ statue of Athena made of gold plates (designed to be removed in case of invasion), ivory, and precious stones.

   The Parthenon was not entirely a Doric temple, since several interior columns were Ionic to allow a greater ceiling height with a single column. The temple was in a good state of repair and was converted to use as a Christian church until it was used to store gunpowder and was struck by a Turkish shell in the seventeenth century.

2. *Erechtheion* (421 to 405 B.C.). A Pentelic marble, Ionic-order temple just north of the Parthenon, the Erechtheion had the unusual characteristics of having windows and a non-symmetrical floor plan, both of which are not typical of Greek architecture. In plan, the temple had three attached porches and was built on two levels. The probable reason for the asymmetrical plan was that it was necessary to dodge the old temple of Athena and several sacred spots of ground on the Acropolis. The north and east porches are good examples of Ionic order, while the south porch contains the most well-known feature, the Porch of the Maidens. The porch is supported by six col-

umn statues of 7' stone female figures, called *caryatids*.

3. The *Temple of Niké* (427 B.C.) was an extremely small (18' × 27') Ionic-order temple just south of the entrance to the Acropolis, dedicated to the "Winged Victory." The front had four columns, and the naos room was only 12' × 13'. The temple was dismantled by the Turks in the seventeenth century but was reconstructed 150 years later.

4. *Propylaea* (437 to 432 B.C.) was the grand entrance to the Parthenon. It included a steep flight of steps and a covered hall with Doric-order columns at the front and rear and Ionic columns in the central hall to permit a higher interior space. The plan was asymmetrical, indicating that it was never finished.

5. The *Theater of Dionysus* (500 to 330 B.C.) was an 18,000-spectator theater carved out of the side of the Acropolis. In plan, the seats formed a half circle around the stage and were stepped in three tiers.

The following are examples of Greek architecture in other areas:

1. The *Temple of Poseidon* (The God of the Sea), Paestum, is an extremely well-preserved example of an early Doric-order temple, built in 460 B.C. The building has six columns across the front and is 14 columns deep. The columns in the naos are intact and show the method used to support the roof. One row of columns the same height as the exterior columns was used to support a stone architrave upon which a shorter tier of columns was placed.

2. The *Temple of Zeus* (The Supreme God), Agrigentum, was from 510 to 409 B.C. A large Doric-order temple, 361' × 173' and 120' high, it had columns engaged with exterior walls rather than the typical free-standing column. The naos formed a central room the entire length of the temple with smaller aisle rooms at the side. Coarse stone was used as the building material. It was covered with a thin coat of ground marble plaster.

3. The *Tower of the Winds*, Athens, 48 B.C., was an example of late Hellenistic architecture. The building varies from the standard rectangular-temple floor plan, as did many monuments. In this case, the tower had an octagonal plan about 25' across. A combination of Corinthian and Doric orders, the building contained a water clock and had a statue on the roof peak that rotated with the wind to act as a weather vane.

4. The *Tomb of King Mausolus*, Halicarnassus, was built in 350 B.C. The word *mausoleum* is derived from this monumental tomb, which was one of the Seven Wonders of the ancient world. Erected by the king's widow, the building is theorized to be an Ionic temple with a pyramidal roof set on a 65' high pedestal. The tomb was over 140' high, including a chariot with four horses at the roof peak.

Although the most common building type was the temple, the Greeks built many other building forms that suited their lifestyle. In general terms, the sense of proportion and order found in temples carried over, to a lesser extent, to the other buildings. Some of these building types follow:

1. The *theater* was an open-air structure usually hollowed out of the side of a hill for seating, called the *cavea*. Commonly the cavea was wrapped around the place of performance, called the *orchestra*, in a one-half to two-thirds circle. Seating ranged to as high as 20,000 people.

2. The *odeion* was similar to a theater in concept but was specifically for musical presentations.

3. The *agora* was the town square, which was the hub for business and social activities.

4. The *stoa* was a long, colonnaded building serving many purposes, such as public meetings, religious shrines, and shelters. The stoa built into the side of the Acropolis was over 500' long.

5. The *stadium* is a rectangular field up to 600' long with sloped seats on either side for Olympic field events. The stadium at Athens seated 50,000 spectators.

6. The *hippodrome* was similar to a stadium only longer, for horse racing.

7. The *palaestra* was a wrestling school.

8. The *gymnasium* was for physical exercise.

ROMAN ARCHITECTURE (300 B.C. TO A.D. 365)

Roman history actually started with the Etruscans. It is believed that they migrated to the Italian peninsula from Asia Minor around the eighth century B.C. Little is known of the Etruscans before they landed north of the Tiber River, but it is quite evident that they had a highly developed civilization. Eventually they dominated most of Italy from the Alps on the north to the Greek colonies along the southern coast. Their culture was sophisticated to the point of having interests in seamanship, music, and building. The Etruscans are credited with developing an arch form that later played an extremely important role in Roman architecture.

Like the Greeks, the Etruscan kingdom was a loosely fabricated network of individual cities, of which Rome was one. Rome was founded in 753 B.C. and was under Etruscan rule until 509 B.C., when it broke away. Rome established a republic and gradually proceeded to overpower its neighbors. The established pattern was to conquer, protect, and absorb—which allowed the empire to grow and prosper with very little unrest. While Rome exacted tribute from the new conquests, the people also participated in trade, received protection from the Roman army, and were made to feel a part of a strong nationalist group that owed allegiance to Rome.

Rome's architectural, cultural, and religious habits reflected an attitude toward life. Much less philosophical than the Greeks', it was rather one of practicality, coupled with a strong sense of obligation to the state. If the Greeks were a group of philosophers and poets, the Romans were more engineers and statesmen. With this as a national fiber, the Romans had no qualms about lifting architectural styles, religion, or just about anything else they admired from areas they won.

The Greek culture must have dazzled the Romans when it became a Roman state in 146 B.C., as it took very little time for the Romans to adopt the Greek concept of architecture. Prior to this, the Roman armies had taken all of Italy in 273 B.C. and extended the empire to Sicily and Africa with the defeat of Carthage in the Punic Wars, over 100 years of war that included the defeat of the Roman armies in northern Italy when Hannibal crossed the Alps. The final Roman victory was won in 146 B.C.

Roman expansion was not a planned world conquest. It was instead a procedure of finding that the best method of protecting against invading neighbors was to rule them. With this done, it began again with new neighbors. The Roman empire finally extended from the Atlantic on the east, to the Euphrates on the west, Britain on the north, and Egypt on the south.

It was mentioned that Greek architecture strongly influenced Roman design. They adopted the Greek orders—Doric, Ionic, and Corinthian—and added two of their own, Tuscan and Composite. *Tuscan* order was derived from the Etruscans and was simpler than the Doric order. It employed an unfluted column shaft and a simple capital. This order was seldom used by the Romans. The other order added by the Romans went one step beyond the Greeks: *Composite* order was a combination of Corinthian and Ionic capitals. The order was not developed until the first century A.D. and, together with the Corinthian capital, was the most popular with Roman architects. The Romans frequently used columns in ways the Greeks would not have attempted. This included engaging columns in walls, using a half column in a pier wall, and using the orders as a means of decoration rather than structure.

While similarities between Greek and Roman styles can be found easily, the advances made by the Romans are much more noteworthy in a discussion of their architecture. The Greeks were largely occupied with temple building—not so with the Romans. Temples, theaters, legal buildings, buildings for sporting events, and public gathering and buying were all necessary facets of their lives, and all needed suitable enclosures. Their practical nature extended to the construction of bridges, roads, and aqueducts, some of which could still function today.

The greatest difference between the two styles was the Roman talent for engineering. The Greeks stayed mainly with the conservative post-and-beam approach in structuring buildings of closely spaced columns with relatively short spans. In contrast, the Romans employed arch, vault, and dome forms that allowed them to free the play of columns greatly.

The use of one material, concrete, allowed the Romans to achieve their engineering advances. Roman concrete was similar to the material we use today. Their method of placement differed in that the aggregate and mortar were placed in alternate layers rather than mixed. Cement was used primarily as a back-up and structural material and usually, was faced with cut stone fastened with iron or brass ties. The Romans seldom used solid stone in their structures, preferring the economies of concrete. The introduction of manufactured concrete into the empire meant that architecture was no longer dependent on local materials and could achieve uniformity. It also meant that relatively unskilled labor could be employed in the work force.

If the Romans inherited the vault form from the Etruscans, it was totally their own ingenuity that refined it to the point it reached in their building form. The Greeks were contained within limits of about 10′ with stone post-and-beam lintel construction, while the Romans vaulted 80′ to 90′ and, in the case of the Pantheon, built a dome spanning 142′. During construction, vaults were supported by a wooden formwork built under the span, a procedure called *centering*. Concrete and occasionally brick ribs then were placed on the form. Since concrete was seldom exposed, it usually was given a finish coat of plaster or stucco.

The simplest vault form is the *barrel vault*, a half-circular span that can be extended to any length. The next progression in vaulting is the *cross vault*, or *groin vault*, which involves the in-

tersection of two vaults at 90° and opens up a large center space. Instead of transmitting the forces directly downward, as with post and beam, the forces of a vault are directed downward and outward. The additional thrust required very thick side walls or a system commonly used by the Romans called *buttressing*, a method of resolving the forces into the side walls. Frequently the force of one vault was counteracted by another vault. The dome was one of the Romans' greatest engineering achievements. A case in point is the hemispherical dome of the Pantheon in Rome with walls 4′ thick, the largest stone span of its type ever built. (See Figure 8-12.)

The republic formed in Rome consisted of two elected bodies that established the legal system. It prospered until the time of Julius Caesar's death in 44 B.C. The ensuing power struggle allowed the winner, Caius Octavius, to assume the title of emperor in 27 B.C. Following rulers added the

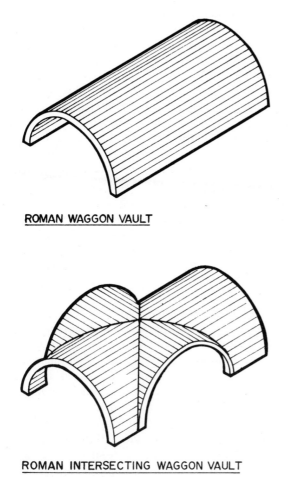

ROMAN WAGGON VAULT

ROMAN INTERSECTING WAGGON VAULT

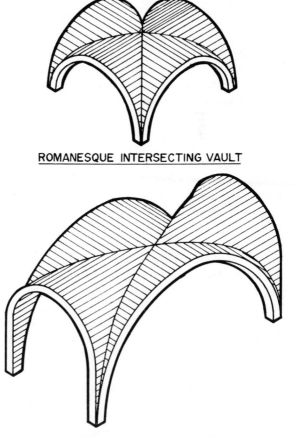

ROMANESQUE INTERSECTING VAULT

ROMANESQUE INTERSECTING WAGGON VAULT

Figure 8-12. Various Roman vaults.

name Augustus to their name giving the title *Augustan Age* to this period of history. The rule of Rome, up to around 300 A.D., was truly a great period of architectural history.

The Roman empire slowly began to decay, both from internal forces and from barbarian attacks. One contributing factor came when Constantine divided the empire into two parts in 330 A.D. by moving the capital to Byzantium, or Istanbul in present-day Turkey. The western Roman empire ended in 476 A.D., when Italy elected a king.

Roman Building Examples

The many good examples of Roman architectural types are described below.

Forum The *forum* in Rome was the hub of the city; all the facilities necessary for the culture of Rome radiated from the forum. It was similar in concept to the Greek agora but much grander in scale. The oldest and most prominent forum in Rome was the *Forum Romanum*, built before Christ. It acted as a central court for many of the legal buildings and temples in Roman life. As the Roman empire grew in power the Forum Romanum proved too small, starting a competition among the emperors to see who could build the grandest forum. Starting with the *Forum of Caesar*, the contest was finally won with the *Forum of Trajan* in 113 A.D. The resulting appendages to the Forum Romanum left a rather cluttered plan totally lacking in a central theme.

Temples The Roman concept of religion was quite different from the Greek ideals of veneration of the gods. Roman religion was primarily a state policy in which it was felt that something done for one of the gods would be returned by a favor.

Most Roman gods were borrowed from the Greeks (with different names), and so their temple design was similar, too. Roman temples were frequently less rectangular than the 2:1 ratio used by the Greeks. Their engineering knowledge also permitted them to have a larger open space. This usually meant moving the side *cella* walls (the chief room in the Roman temple, corresponding to the Greek naos) out to where they engage with the columns, leaving half of the column exposed.

The other primary difference in Roman temple architecture was the common practice of placing the building on a high platform accessible by a long flight of steps in the front. While Greek temples always faced east, the Romans sited their temples toward the forum of which they were part. Here are some famous Roman temples:

1. The *Temple of Mars Ultor*, Rome, 14 to 2 B.C., was located in the Forum of Augustus, adjacent to the Forum Romanum. This temple was dedicated to the avengement of the death of Caesar by his great-nephew, Caius Octavius. The Corinthian building had an almost square plan slightly over 100' on a side. The marble-sheathed building is one of the finest examples of Augustan architecture.

2. The *Temple of Vesta*, Rome, A.D. 205, was in the Forum Romanum. A round Corinthian-order temple with 18 columns and an interior cella room 18' in diameter, this was the most sacred temple in Rome. It housed the eternal flame tended by the Vestal Virgins. The building was raised 10' on a podium.

3. The *Pantheon*, Rome, A.D. 120, is one of the most significant buildings in the history of architecture (Figure 8-13). The Pantheon is a 142' hemispherical dome resting on cylinder walls 20' thick. The round floor plan has a rectangular portico attached at one side with eight 46' Corinthian-order columns. The interior of the dome is a coffered-waffle pattern structured of concrete and covered with stucco. Light is brought into the Pantheon by a 27' diameter opening at the top of the dome. The exterior of the building was originally sheathed in marble with Egyptian granite column shafts. The building was dedicated as a Christian church in the seventh century, which assisted in its remarkable preservation. The grand facing materials were stripped to adorn other structures, but the Pantheon remains as a classic example of Roman engineering.

Basilica The Roman *basilica* functioned as a hall of justice and a central place for business. The basilica form closely met the requirements of the Christian religion (more so than Roman temples did) and was adopted several centuries later as a prototype church design. The plan was commonly rectangular, about twice as long as wide, with two or four rows of columns running along the length, forming side aisles. The *nave* (the center space) roof was raised above the side-aisle roof, which allowed windows into the area, a design approach that was almost the rule for later church architecture. The *Basilica of Trajan*, A.D. 98, was located

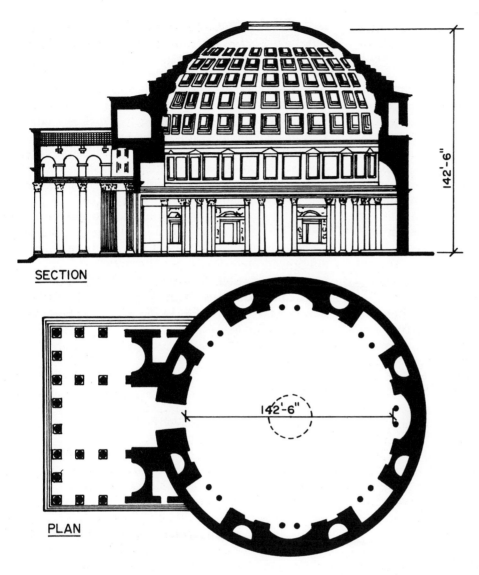

SECTION

PLAN

142'-6"

142'-6"

Figure 8-13.   The Pantheon.

in the Forum of Trajan in Rome. The nave and side aisles were larger than a football field, and the nave had a ceiling height of 120'. The interior columns were red granite with white marble Corinthian capitals.

Thermae   An example of the Roman lifestyle can be found in their *thermae*, or public baths. They acted as the social and recreational (almost ritualistic) centers for the empire and grandly depicted the luxuries of Rome. In addition to containing pools with water at various temperatures (cold, warm, hot), the complex included dressing rooms, enclosed parks suitable for athletic events with spectator seating, apartments for lectures, theaters, libraries, and shops. Water was brought into the complex by aqueduct, and it was heated and

stored in reservoirs for pools. The building was heated radiantly with hot air circulating through ducts cast in the concrete floor.

• *Caracalla*   This public bath in Rome was built in A.D. 211. The enclosing courtyard was 1200 sq ft and could accommodate 1600 bathers. The main building, 750' × 380', was symmetrical along both transverse and longitudinal axes with three cross-vaults supported with Corinthian columns in the center. The design and scale of Caracalla was reproduced in 1906 by Stanford White in the Pennsylvania Railroad Station, New York.

• *Diocletian*   Built in Rome in A.D. 302, Diocletian was similar in plan to Caracalla but larger. The structure had accommodations for 3000 bathers with a 90' high central hall spanned with three groin vaults supported by composite columns. The building attained additional prominence in the sixteenth century, when Michelangelo converted the central hall into a church (S. Maria degli Angeli).

Amphitheaters   Two strong Roman traits, engineering talent and harsh savagery, are best exemplified in their amphitheaters. The closest counterpart in modern buildings would be a football stadium. The Roman design is still considered a prototype in crowd control and architectural style. The design concept simply involved placing two semicircular theaters together forming bowl-shaped seating around an arena. Large segments of the population amused themselves with Christian martyrdom, gladiatorial battles, combat with wild beasts, and even naval encounters as several amphitheaters had provisions to flood the arena floor to a depth to permit boats.

• **The Colosseum**   The Colosseum, built in Rome in A.D. 70, is also called the *Flavian Amphitheater* (Figure 8-14). It is located several hundred yards east of the Forum Romanum. This elliptical stadium, 620' × 513', had a seating capacity for 50,000 spectators. The oval-shaped arena, the size of a football field, has a complete basement to provide rooms for gladiators and animals. A series of masts were provided around the 157' high exterior walls so that ropes could be strung to provide a fabric roof in inclement weather. The exterior facade has 80 arched openings on each of the first three levels. The fourth and final level consists of a wall engaged with Corinthian columns. The first-floor arches are supported by Doric-order columns, the second-floor arches are Ionic, and Corinthian columns are found on the third level. Once again, the complex engineering feats displayed in the Colosseum could not have been attempted without concrete.

• **The Circus Maximus**   Built in Rome in 46 B.C, the Circus Maximus is akin to the arenas and was established for horse and chariot racing. Patterned after the Greek hippodromes, the open-air circus in

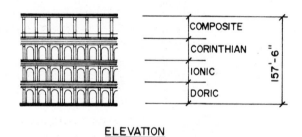

ELEVATION

PLAN

Figure 8-14. The Colosseum.

Rome was of gigantic proportions, seating over a quarter of a million people and almost half a mile long. The complex was brought to prominence by Julius Caesar and flourished until the sixth century.

Monuments The series of conquests made by Rome led to a competition of sorts in erecting columns and arches (Figure 8-15) lauding the achievements of Roman generals. One way of acclaiming triumphs was to erect an arch with bas-reliefs indicating the heroic deeds of the emperor or general. Most arches had a center passage archway with possibly a smaller arch on either side. The *Arch of Titus* (Figure 8-16), Rome, A.D. 82, was a single arched opening with a total height of 47'. The *Arch of Constantine*, Rome, A.D. 312, 67' × 82', had three arches with eight free-standing Corinthian columns supporting an entablature and *attic* (the rectangular block above) that made up approximately half the total height.

Another favorite method of showing heroic deeds was to erect a column, usually in a forum, with battle scenes carved into the stone. *Trajan's Column*, Rome, A.D. 113, adjacent to Trajan's Basillica, was a 115' Doric-order column. The column consisted of a spiral band wrapped around the shaft containing over 2500 carved figures. If unwrapped, the band would be over 800' long. A spiral stair inside the column ascends to the top.

Aqueducts A final note of triumph to Roman engineering can be seen in the aqueduct system. It is estimated that Rome consumed 350 million gallons of water per day, which was brought into the city by means of 11 raised concrete-lined ducts. The most famous section in the *Pont du Gard*, Nîmes, France, A.D. 14 (Figure 8-17). Its span over the Gard River is 156' high in three arched tiers. The lowest level also has a roadway incorporated into the water duct.

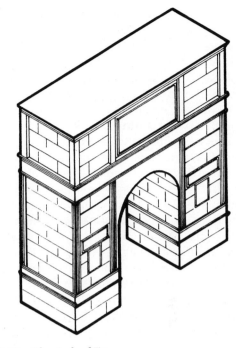

Figure 8-16.   The Arch of Titus.

EARLY CHRISTIAN ARCHITECTURE (A.D. 313 TO 800)

It is ironic that the force which originally set out to eliminate Christianity eventually caused it to spread throughout Europe. The amphitheaters attest to the fact that Christianity was an extremely unpopular belief during Roman times. The reason for Rome's marked resistance was not primarily due to theological disputes. The brief study of Roman character in the previous section indicates that they probably would have assimilated Christianity easily into the Roman lifestyle; rather it was

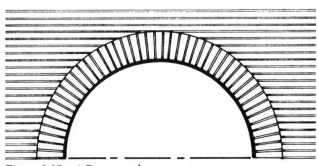

Figure 8-15.   A Roman arch

Figure 8-17.   The Pont du Gard.

due to the unbending Christian demands of total acceptance and insistence that all other religions are wrong and that subservience even to government is wrong. This Rome could not tolerate.

In A.D. 313, Roman Emperor Constantine declared in the Edict of Milan that the Christian religion had as much right to exist as any other. Constantine went further in 326 by establishing Christianity as the official religion of the empire. Prior to this time, Christianity was basically a secret fraternity, which meant that no building was done. This thrust a whole new class and spirit of the population into light with only one architectural heritage to rely upon—pagan Rome.

The only logical option was then to choose a Roman building type that would suit the communal theme of worship. This was a drastic change from the Greek and Roman tradition in which temples were erected primarily as a shelter for a statue of a particular god. For this reason, the Roman temple form was not highly adaptable to Christianity. Compared with the grandeur of Roman design, the new church architectural style started on a very modest scale.

The time attributed to this period of architecture, A.D. 313 to 800, saw the Roman empire in its final stage of decay. The Emperor Diocletian determined that the administration of Rome could be more efficiently handled if the city of Byzantium was established as the capital of the western empire. In 330, 50 years later, Constantine moved the seat of the empire to Byzantium and changed its name to Constantinople.

While this position hastened the decline of the Roman empire, it was not the cause. Actually, the split went further than governmental ideologies. Eventually, Christianity divided into the Roman influence and the Eastern Orthodox religion of Constantinople. Architectural styles were divided along the political split, too. While Christian Rome chose the basilica plan, the Byzantine empire chose to expand the traditional eastern dome as a central theme. The architectural character, called Byzantine because of the previous capital, was perpetuated for many years, as is witnessed by such familiar buildings as St. Mark's in Venice and the Kremlin in Moscow.

Several attempts were made at reunification of the empire by predecessors of Constantine, but the spark that once fired Rome seemed to be gone. Rome finally succumbed to warring tribes with the invasion of the Huns in the fourth century and the sacking of the city in 410 by the Goths. The eastern Byzantine empire fared much better than her western counterpart, lasting until the Ottoman Turk invasion in 1453.

With the power of Rome gone, Western Europe was thrust into a vacuum that allowed any strong faction to assume leadership within a limited area. The elimination of a centralized government caused the uniform Latin language to break up into French, Spanish, and Italian. The once-grand architectural character of the empire now was reduced to communities with little need or technical skill or funds for major buildings. The communication and commerce networks formed by Rome had little reason for existence.

The period of history from the fifth to the ninth centuries is commonly referred to as the *Dark Ages*. The social structure that formed in these chaotic times was the feudal system. It was organized so that the working class, the serfs, were granted the right to farm land by swearing allegiance and a portion of their crops to a noble. In return, the serf was offered protection. The noble, in turn, was granted land holdings by a king who demanded loyalty. The pattern that evolved was a largely fractionalized governing body with anything but subsistence buildings being reserved for the social elite. Towns were designed like fortresses with high walls and narrow, winding streets. Sanitation facilities were lacking, and rampant disease was the rule rather than the exception.

The void that was created with the fall of Rome was filled by Christianity, which provided solace and an escape from the feudal lifestyle. The church gained power not only on a religious basis but also in governmental authority. Eventually the unified Church of Rome spread throughout Europe to the point where baptism was required for social acceptance. Excommunication meant loss not only of religious rights but also of political and legal rights. The church became the dynamic influence in culture, politics, and education, with local bishops acting as feudal lords.

The power of the church obviously made all other forms of building subservient to religious architecture. The character of early Christian architecture in Europe is an adaptation and modification of Roman ideas. This went so far that a majority of the materials used in churches were taken from Roman buildings.

This was particularly true of columns. The typical rectangular basilican church plan had three or five aisles separated by closely spaced columns that supported the entablature. Other plans placed the nave columns farther apart and spanned between them with arched supports. The central-nave wood-truss roof was higher than the side-aisle roofs to allow a penetration of windows in the wall above the nave row of columns. With very few exceptions, this was the plan of the Roman legal halls. The major facilities in a Christian church were labeled from the outside in as follows: *court-yard; narthex*, or enclosed entrance porch; *nave*, or *central aisle* for the congregation; *side aisles; bema* (and high altar), a raised stage in front of the nave; and *apse*, a circular projection at the end of the main body of the church, also included in the Roman basilica. (See Figure 8-18.)

The procession of columns down the nave added to the perspective effect of a long, linear approach toward the altar at the apse end, the focal point of the church. In all cases, the apse end faced east (toward Jerusalem), with the narthex entrance facing west.

In many respects early Christian architecture was plain, both in interior and exterior treatment. This probably was dictated in part by economics, by lack of skilled labor, and quite possibly by the loss of the flashy, outgoing spirit of the Romans.

The Byzantine Christian church did not follow the style of its western counterpart. Instead the dome was adapted as the dominant architectural element. The Roman use of the dome involved placement of loadbearing columns or walls directly under the dome. In effect, this was a cylinder the same diameter as the dome. Byzantine style differed in that a circular plan was less acceptable because it placed the focal point of the building in the center, and this was inconsistent with the Christian liturgy which required the entire congregation to be in front of the altar. For this reason the *pendentive* was developed. A simplistic description of the pendentive is a warped triangle with its base wrapped around the dome and the opposite point transferring the load down to one of four columns. In this way, the circular plan of the dome is translated to a square floor plan. This plan was a step better than circular but still not the desired rectangular plan considered ideal for worship. A rectangular plan was achieved with a domed basilica, which involved engaging partial domes, opposite each other, at a lower level with the center dome. The combination of main and two half-domes created a rectangular, column-free space in St. Sophia in Constantinople nearly 220' long and over 100' wide.

In most cases the Byzantine dome was built of manufactured brick with mortar joints. It is quite possible that these domes were constructed

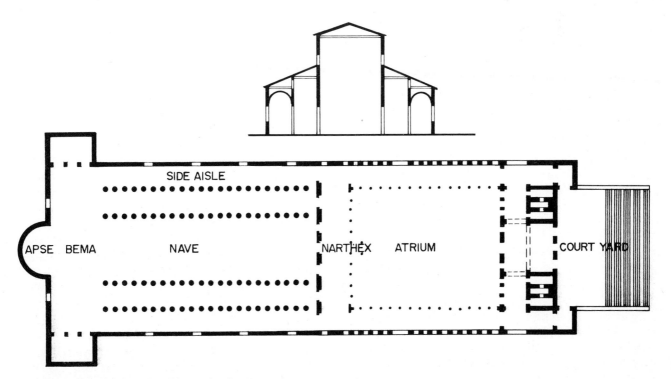

Figure 8-18.   The plan of an early Christian church—St. Peter's in Rome.

without wood centering, a temporary support, but rather corbeled in slightly with each course. After the dome was finished, the interior commonly was finished in marble slabs, mosaic, or *fresco* (paint and wet plaster). The Byzantine church forbade the use of statues in the church, and so brightly colored paintings and mosaics were used as a means of expression.

Byzantine architecture departed from the Greek and Roman system of column orders and established a separate column called a *basket capital*. This was a slightly tapered square form that rested on the shaft. The capital was carved with geometric forms resembling a basket; hence, its name. A common addition above the Byzantine capital was a stone block, called a *dosseret*. The purpose of a dosseret block was to combine, both visually and structurally, the forces of two intersecting arches at a column.

To summarize the two varying Christian styles:

1. Early Christian (European)—basilican plan; followed Roman orders; horizontal space; plain ornamentation
2. Byzantine—domed rectangular plan; separate, decorative column orders; high, open space; colorful ornamentation

Early Christian Building Examples

Some early Christian building examples are

1. The *Church of the Nativity*, Bethlehem, A.D. 330, was built by Constantine over the reported birthplace of Christ. It was a typical five-aisle basilica plan with a wood-truss gable roof. The combined nave and apse was 185′ × 88′.
2. *St. Peter*, Rome, A.D. 330, was built by Constantine. The church was later razed for the construction of the St. Peter's of Renaissance time. Again, it had a typical five-aisle basilica plan, this time with a nave nearly 300′ × 200′.
3. *St. Paul Outside the Wall*, Rome, A.D. 380, was the largest and possibly the most impressive example of early Christian architecture. The church burned in the nineteenth century and was rebuilt along the original design. The five-aisle basilica plan had a timber truss roof supported by 20 columns in each row. The columns supported a series of arches upon which an entablature rested.

Byzantine Building Examples

Some Byzantine building examples are

1. *Hagia Sophia* (St. Sophia), Constantinople, A.D. 532 to 537, was the largest and most impressive Byzantine church (Figure 8-19). One of the great buildings in architectural history, it ranks with Cheops, the Parthenon, and the Pantheon. The central interior worship space was an oval that covered a column-free area 220′ × 107′, with an overall building dimension of over 300′ × 220′. The nave was spanned with one main dome 107′ in diameter which was 180′ above the floor. The dome was supported on four pendentives that transmitted the vertical forces to four massive columns. A great deal of lateral force (forces other than vertical) that was developed had to be resolved. This was accomplished on the east and west sides by engaging half-domes to act as buttresses. The north and south sides of the dome were supported by massive buttresses that reacted against the dome force in stair-stepped levels. The dome was the main feature of the space with 40 windows around its base.

    Surrounding the dome with lower ceilings accented the height, giving the viewer the feeling that the dome was suspended. The interior of the Hagia Sophia was done in richly carved marble with ornately carved basket-capital columns. Its exterior was less impressive, with plastered brick and a lead-sheathed dome. The Turks took over the church in the fifteenth century and turned it into a mosque, adding four exterior towers, called *minarets*.
2. *St. Vitale* was built in Ravenna, Italy, from A.D. 526 to 547. The Byzantine influence was not contained to the eastern empire but spread even to the Italian peninsula. The church was patterned after a Roman building done in the third century. The plan consisted of an internal octagonal plan bounded by columns which supported a dome 54′ in diameter, around which an exterior octagonal plan, 115′ in diameter, bounded the building. The dome is somewhat unique in that 2′ long hollow clay pots were assembled to produce a much lighter structure than brick or concrete. This was protected with a wood-frame roof over the dome. The interior treatment is an example of beautifully carved column capitals and mosaics.
3. *St. Mark's*, Venice, was built in from A.D. 1042 to 1085. The plan of St. Mark's is referred to as

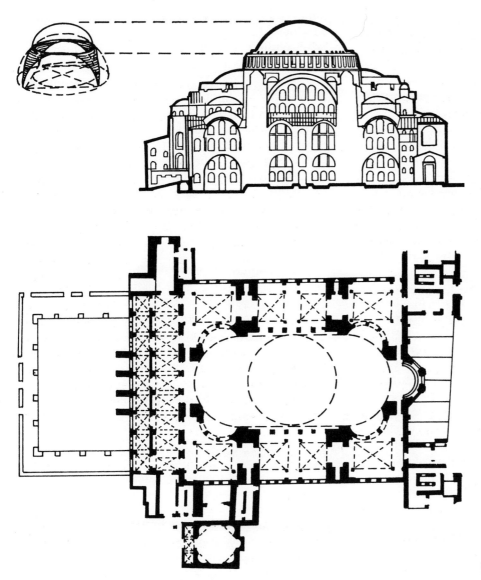

Figure 8-19. The Hagia Sophia.

a *Greek cross*, because it is plus shaped with four equal legs. Each leg of the cross has a dome over, and there is one in the center, making five in all. The church faced the piazza of San Marco, spectacular open courtyard similar in concept to the Roman forum. Both in the interior and exterior are magnificent examples of colored marble and mosaics. Later Gothic additions included the gold-gilded exterior domes.

ROMANESQUE ARCHITECTURE (A.D. 800 TO 1100)

The period of history after the demise of the Roman empire, the Romanesque era, resulted in a general and immediate decline in art and architecture. The building done in the early Christian era was certainly not as massive, imaginative, or numerous as the earlier Roman attempts. The loss of the common bond of Roman power left Europe in a fragmented and confused state, a condition certainly not conducive to architectural greatness. Gradually a ruling structure was established and the countries in Europe, as we know them today, began to evolve. The transition of architectural styles have been, to this point, basically caused by one civilization that assumed power and asserted influence—not so with Romanesque. The changeover came because of different needs and tastes.

One of the only bright factors in the Dark Ages was the Christian church. Christianity became a sanctuary for many people attempting to escape from the harsh conditions of life. The many monastic orders became the seat of learning for intellectual pursuits, including architecture. Obviously the main building type that evolved from this system was for religious use, namely cathedrals, baptistries, campaniles, and monasteries.

The necessary catalyst to establish social unity (and thus architectural unity) came in the person of the Frankish king, Charlemagne. In 800 he embarked on a crusade to reunite the holdings of Rome and establish the Holy Roman Empire. The grand scheme lasted only until Charlemagne's death in 814, but it accomplished two strong concepts: a break between church and state and a strong assist in tying Europe into a unified civilization.

During this brief period, art and knowledge were bolstered, and a different attitude in architecture was assumed. This time in architecture was given the name *Carolingian Renaissance* (rebirth), which later gave way to Romanesque and then to Gothic architecture.

As the name *Romanesque* implies, the style was derived from Roman building forms. The previous section showed that early Christian buildings used the basilica form. The Romanesque architect also relied on the old Roman legal building design, but more importantly he became aware of space by using Roman vaulting techniques. In plan, Romanesque buildings differed slightly from early Christian in that a cross-shaped plan was often adapted. (This was called a *Latin cross*. It differed from a Greek cross in that one leg, the nave, was longer than the other three.)

The choir was raised and a detached *campanile* (bell tower) was commonly included. The lack of a common governmental system was possibly the greatest contributing factor for the differences in styles. Italy, France, Germany, and England did not experience the same Romanesque architecture at the same time.

Generally, the ninth through twelfth centuries is the period of time attributed to Romanesque architecture. This time of Robin Hood and the Crusades was the awakening of Europe from the Dark Ages. The architectural style that evolved was crude in some respects. It certainly reflected the sober and dignified character commonly found in the beginning of a period of art.

Many characteristics are common to both Romanesque and Gothic architecture. It often proves difficult for the novice to tell the two apart. One

rather tell tale sign lies in the treatment above windows. Romanesque has rounded arches at the head, while Gothic has pointed window heads.

This is possibly one of the most exciting pivotal points in architecture, in that people became profoundly aware of interior space and the limits of their material, stone. Not only did Roman architecture serve as the foundation for the style, but in many cases existing Roman buildings in the area provided materials for new construction.

The first attempts to span roof areas was done with the Roman barrel and cross vaults. This method proved difficult to construct and very heavy, and so it was eventually abandoned for a *rib-vaulting system,* which simply involved the construction of a dressed-stone skeletal rib between column supports. After this was completed, lightweight nonstructural panels were placed between the ribs to fill in the space. Rib-vaulting techniques progressed to a means of running ribs to four points (quadripartite) and six points (sexpartite), as well as terminating the ribs at different levels in the case of cross-vaulting. Other innovations made in church design included simple yet magnificent sculpture and stained-glass rose windows at the nave (west) end.

Romanesque Building Examples

Some Italian Romanesque architectural examples follow.

1. *Pisa Cathedral,* 1063 to 1092, was one of the most famous building groups in the world, consisting of a cathedral, campanile, baptistry, and a rectangular Gothic building, the *Campo Santo.* The *cathedral* is a Latin-cross basilican plan nearly 300' long with an elliptical dome over the intersection of the legs of the cross, called the *crossing.* The exterior has bands of horizontal red and white marble with a series of arches spanning between columns. The west entrance has five tiers of columns. The *campanile,* better known as the Leaning Tower of Pisa, is 52' in diameter and over 175' tall (Figure 8-20). Three of the eight tiers were started when it was determined that due to insufficient soil conditions the tower was tipping. The remaining levels were erected to compensate for the tilt but it kept sinking. Pisa is now almost 14' out of plumb and still tipping. The *baptistry* has a circular plan nearly 130' in diameter, with a series of half-columns en-

Figure 8-20. The Leaning Tower of Pisa.

gaged in the outside wall that are connecting semicircular arches. The roof consists of a rounded cone surrounded by a hemispherical dome. Many later alterations make this principally a Gothic building.

2. *St. Michele*, Pavia, 1117, had a Latin-cross plan 158′ long in which the nave was divided into two square bays using ribbed vaulting. The side aisles were also vaulted, with two bays equalling one of the nave vaults.

Here are some examples of French Romanesque architectural style:

1. *Abbey Church*, Cluny, 1089 to 1131, was part of a famous monastic group in Burgundy, now destroyed. The church was 443′ long with five aisles and a barrel vault spanning the nave.

2. *Abbaye-aux-Hommes*, Caen, 1066 to 1080, was a large basilican-plan church that had many features common to the later Gothic style (Figure 8-21). The west entrance had engaged-spired towers on either side, a Gothic characteristic. The nave, over 200′ long, was spanned with a series of sexpartite vaults that were buttressed by a semibarrel vault at the side aisle. This counteracting technique is called a *flying buttress*. Although the Abbaye-aux-Hommes was covered with a timber roof, it was a prototype to the typical exposed Gothic flying buttress. The church is also distinctive because of its nine pointed spires.

3. *Abbey St. Denis*, Paris, 1137 to 1144, was built by Abbé Suger, a prolific French builder. It is noteworthy because it was the burial place for French kings and is a definite prototype of the Gothic style.

Some German Romanesque architectural examples are:

1. The *Church of the Apostles*, Cologne, 1035 to 1220. The plan is an adaptation of a Latin cross with rounded transepts and apse, over 280′ × 88′. The nave is spanned with a series of ribbed sexpartite vaults covered with a timber gable roof and a vaulted dome at the crossing.

2. *Worms Cathedral*, Worms, 1110 to 1181. This is a classic Romanesque example constructed of brick. Both the east and west ends have octagonal apses with engaged-spired towers on either side of the apse. The nave and side aisle on either side are spanned with cross vaults and an octagonal tower at the crossing.

English Romanesque is more commonly referred to as *Norman architecture* since the French Normans conquered the Saxons in 1066. The Normans introduced England to many innovations including the feudal system and Romanesque architecture.

Durham Cathedral, Durham, 1093 to 1133, is an example of Norman architecture. It has a monumental Latin-cross plan over 450′ long. The nave is made up of massive carved piers that are spanned with ribbed cross vaults. The Anglo-Norman style is most impressive because of size and detail, and Durham is the best example.

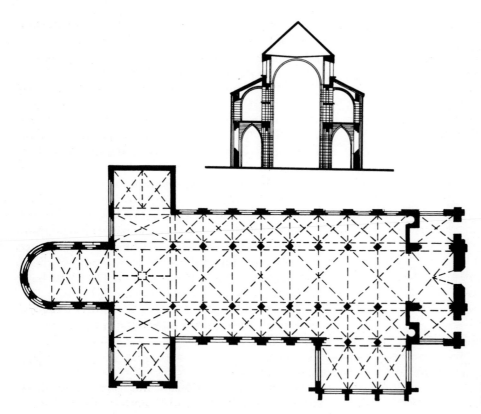

Figure 8-21. The Abbaye-aux-Hommes.

GOTHIC ARCHITECTURE (A.D. 1100 TO 1500)

Europe was finally beginning to roll after the fall of the Roman empire almost a thousand years before. Unlike the eastern Byzantine style which lasted until the fifteenth century, European architecture continuously strove for a more impressive architectural expression. Early Christian architecture lasted 500 years, Romanesque another 300 years, and Gothic for the 400 years from 1100 to 1500. These three times in history are lumped together and called the *medieval period,* the time between the decline of Rome and the Renaissance.

There was not a pronounced change or exact date when one form progressed to the next. Rather, it was a transition of ideas. The Renaissance labeled the final medieval style *Gothic,* a term stemming from the name of the barbaric Goth tribe. The name was intended to show contempt for the style that the Renaissance period considered a contributing factor in the decline of the Roman empire. The word *vandalism* also comes from a barbaric tribe, the Vandals. In both cases, the connotation is clearly derogatory. The achievements made in Gothic architecture, however, make this attitude of Renaissance designers very wrong. The Gothic period is possibly the greatest human endeavor to express religious belief through architecture.

As was noted, Romanesque architecture was not a unified style throughout Europe, due primarily to the fragmented governmental structure. The Continent had politically progressed greatly by the thirteenth century. The Hundred Years War ended in the defeat of England and the unification of France into a central kingdom. Germany was reduced to a series of independent but powerful states. The central-city form of government in Italy established Venice, Florence, Milan, and Genoa as individual spheres of influence.

The feudal system was still in operation in Europe, but it was becoming outmoded because it did not meet social change. In many respects the architectural sophistication found in Gothic times reflected new concepts in democracy, international trade, and technical skill in general.

One strong unifying factor in the Gothic style was the formation of trade guilds, which took some of the building influence away from the church. Each cathedral building trade became an elite profession with members moving between projects, thus creating a link from one project to the next. In this system, the master builder (architect) and mason were considered to have status positions, usually being granted free housing and tax exemptions.

Church architecture had again such a high priority that it overshadowed all other building forms. The church acted not only as a point of communication with God, but the square in front of the church served as the community meeting place, the center of commerce, and the stage for dramatic performances.

A definite rivalry began between French towns to see which could erect the loftiest and most impressive cathedral. The limits of the material and the ingenuity of engineering capabilities raised the nave vault at Notre Dame in Paris to 114′. This later was surpassed by the Cathedral at Chartres with a 123′ vault, then by Rheims with 124′, to be challenged by Amiens with 138′. The final bidder was the small northern French community of Beauvais, which attempted a vault height of 158′. This exceeded the structural limitations and part of the vault fell and had to be rebuilt. Beauvais also attempted a 500′ spire over the crossing; this also collapsed.

Gothic architecture was not a totally new style. It was a refinement of several forms, primarily Romanesque. The marked difference between the two lies in the spatial treatment and structural daring found in the Gothic style. The most familiar features in Gothic design—a ribbed vault, the pointed arch, twin towers at the west end, and the buttress—were all known to Romanesque designers but it took Gothic architectural expression to blend these elements into a cohesive form.

Gothic architecture originated, or more precisely, evolved, in northern France, and there it experienced its greatest and most bold expression. France also displayed the most prolific Gothic building boom, having constructed over 500 cathedrals in the style. England followed suit 50 years after the style's inception in France with a similar building type that was not quite as lofty (longer, narrower, and lower), but just as impressive. About the only European country that did not follow France's lead was Italy, one reason being that a strong Roman influence still existed. Gothic architecture existed in Italy, but it never reached the expression attained on the rest of the Continent. German Gothic was imported directly from France rather than being evolved from its own Romanesque style. Perhaps for this reason, Germany seemed to prefer the heavier Romanesque form.

Vaulting techniques had been in existence over 1000 years before thirteenth-century Gothic architects began to use them in cathedrals. Then it was primarily the Romanesque rib vault that was used. This system was simply a skeletal rib pattern that spanned between supports with thin nonstructural panels filling the void. The difference in the styles lies in the spider-web effect achieved in the ribbing in Gothic. This lacelike treatment established a spatial concept that far surpassed the earthbound feeling created with previous vaults.

This structural idea was carried over into wall systems in which a nonloadbearing curtain-wall stone panel was used. This meant that the wall between piers could be penetrated with windows without affecting the structure. The resulting building was a magnificent skeletal structure with panels of stone and stained glass.

A very familiar Gothic treatment was to engage towers on either side of the west entrance to the church. The great majority of Gothic cathedrals were symmetrical about an east-west axis except when it came to the towers on the west end. In the case of this singular feature, the towers and spires were occasionally dissimilar. Perhaps the strongest factor dictating this unorthodox feature was the length of time it took to build a church. The century-or-longer construction took place while styles changed or the congregation lacked funds.

The pointed arch, the most traditional Gothic feature, was developed as a functional approach to a problem rather than decoration. The half-round Romanesque arch had the disadvantage of being fixed in height. Depending on the width of span, it could go no higher nor lower and still be circular. The difficulty develops when an arch spans between two unequal levels, thus producing a lopsided arch. The Gothic answer was to combine two circular segments together with separate centers forming a point in the center. The obvious result is an arch that can span any area starting at uneven heights simply by varying the height of the point in the arch. A less obvious result is that the arch transmits more of its thrust downward to piers than outward to walls. Pointed arches were used most at window heads but were employed throughout Gothic buildings.

A great deal of time and construction knowledge had passed from when Egyptian builders stacked stone blocks on top of each other to the thirteenth century. The outstanding trait displayed by Gothic builders was that they definitely understood their building materials. While the pyramids are impressive in scale, their structural display is hardly complicated. Not so with Gothic architects' work; their lacelike structures seem to defy gravity on their slender supports.

In order to construct cathedrals with the sophistication displayed, Gothic builders had to be knowledgeable in the actions caused by thrusts. A study in structures reveals that a building cannot stand unless the vector forces are counteracted by equal and opposite forces. As the height of cathedrals rose, the forces projected outward became considerably more difficult to handle. The obvious solution of making the nave and side aisle walls more massive was incongruous to the Gothic style.

The solution came with a bridgelike arch that stands free on the outside of the building, the *flying buttress*. This served the purpose of transmitting the lateral force in the nave vault away from the building to pier buttresses and then to the ground. The curious exterior elevation showing a series of arched bridges (flying buttresses) along both sides of the nave and at the apse end was a common Gothic characteristic. The size of cathedrals and the required flexibility meant that the structure had to be constructed of small stone coursing with large mortar joints. This was an apparent departure from the previous technique of setting large stones in thin beds of mortar.

A discussion of Gothic characteristics must certainly go beyond the vaulting techniques and pointed arches incorporated in the building. Along with the astounding engineering accomplishments came a beautifully refined treatment of both interior and exterior spaces. The structural "freeing-up" of walls allowed them to act as panels protecting against weather rather than loadbearing piers. This, in turn, permitted the walls to be penetrated with light through magnificent stained-glass windows. This produced an awe-inspiring interior treatment of space that meshed perfectly with the weblike structural form. Gothic architecture is perhaps the best example studied thus far in concerning itself with a combination of internal and external spaces.

Gothic Building Examples

In France, these are famous Gothic building examples:

1. *Notre Dame,* Paris, 1163 to 1250, was built on an island in the Seine River. The cathedral (Figure 8-22) is one of the earliest and most classic Gothic examples. In plan, the double-side-aisle church is nearly 450' long and 150' high with a slight bend along its axis. The west-end entrance, including twin towers without spires and a most impressive rose window, is the finest example of French Gothic architecture. The weblike articulation on the exterior is achieved in part with the more than 25 arched flying buttresses running along the nave sides and the rounded apse.

2. The *Cathedral at Chartres,* 1194 to 1260, was rebuilt from an earlier Romanesque church. This truly remarkable cathedral is over 400' long and 200' wide. The west-end towers have different-style spires and the flying buttresses are in three tiers. The character of this church is best expressed in its 160 magnificent stained-glass windows and many carved figures set into niches on the exterior.

3. The *Cathedral at Rheims,* 1211 to 1290, was the coronation place for French kings. The highly ornate west facade with a 40' rose window and over 500 carved statues took on the late Gothic appearance of a wedding cake. It was Rheims that served as a pattern for Westminster Abbey in London.

4. The *Cathedral at Amiens,* 1220 to 1288, along with Notre Dame and Rheims, is among the greatest French Gothic cathedrals. Amiens is noted for its carved woodwork in the choir stalls. In plan, the cathedral is 450' long and 150' wide with seven rounded chapels at the apse end, called the *chervet.*

5. The *Cathedral at Beauvais,* 1247 to 1568, is the largest attempt at Gothic building, but its nave was never completed. As was mentioned, Beauvais had difficulty in engineering the structure. Both a portion of the 160' high central vaulting and a 500' central spire collapsed after erection. Even though this cathedral was only half completed, it stands as the boldest accomplishment in Gothic design.

In England, some Gothic building examples are

1. The *Cathedral at Canterbury,* 1071 to 1500. The English architectural character went through a far greater series of changes than the rest of Europe. Canterbury is a prime example of the combination of styles resulting from 400 years of building. In plan, the cathedral is

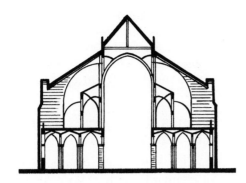

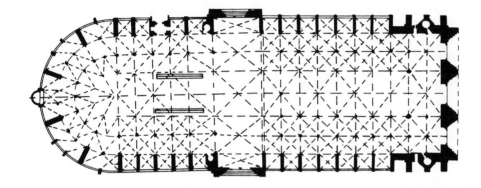

Figure 8-22. Notre Dame.

more than 500′ long with many attached appendages resulting from the time it served as a Benedictine monastery. The nave crossing has a central tower, which was typical of English Gothic, and flying buttresses which were not.

2. The *Cathedral at Salisbury*, 1220 to 1284, is the best example of English Gothic, partly because it is one of the few built entirely in one style. In plan, the church is 450′ long with a 400′ spire over one of the crossing transepts.

3. The *Cathedral at Winchester*, 1079 to 1250, has a rather dull west-end elevation with small engaged spires on either side of the entrance. The claim to fame of Winchester Cathedral is that it is the longest (560′) Gothic cathedral.

In Germany, some famous examples of Gothic architecture are:

1. The *Cathedral at Cologne*, 1248 through the nineteenth century, is the largest Gothic church in northern Europe, 468′ long, 275′ wide, with a nave vault 150′ high and twin west-end spires 500′ high. While the cathedral certainly attained the scale of French Gothic, its proportions lack the finesse of the style.

2. The *Cathedral at Ulm*, 1377 to 1492, is a flying-buttressed church with the outstanding

characteristic of a single, centrally located west-end spire 530′ high.

Here are some Gothic architecture examples to be found in Italy:

1. The *Cathedral at Milan*, 1385 to 1485, next to the Cathedral at Seville, Spain, it is the largest medieval church in Europe, 500′ long and 200′ wide. Called the *Church of 100 Spires*, the highly ornate white marble facade is a lacework of statues, buttresses, and pinnacles. The nave vault is 150′ high with side-aisle vaults of 100′, which meant that a triforium was not possible. The elimination of this change in level as a means of admitting light permitted only clearstory windows as a way to bring daylight into the church. The result is a very dimly lit space.

2. The *Cathedral at Florence*, 1296 to 1462, also called *S. Maria del Fiore*. The cathedral was done in many stages with its most famous feature, the dome, being the first transitional step from Gothic to Renaissance. It is an example of how little the French Gothic influenced southern Italian buildings. While the form goes through the paces of being Gothic, its spirit is still reminiscent of the Roman basilica. In plan,

the cathedral is 500' long and 130' wide in a Latin cross with rounded legs on all but the nave length. The exterior is distinguished by a treatment of colored marble panels. In addition to the cathedral, a campanile and baptistry make this complex as famous as the Pisa group. Of particular note are the magnificent bronze doors on the baptistry; they took Lorenzo Ghiberti 21 years to complete.

3. *Italian civic buildings.* In addition to the many fine cathedrals built in Italy in the Middle Ages, the powerful city-states constructed a number of excellent public buildings. The *Doges Palace,* Venice, 1309 to 1424, is perhaps the best example of medieval civic planning. Built next to St. Mark's Cathedral, the complex is over 500' long and has a two-leveled arched facade with a third level paneled in red and white marble. The *Palazzo Vecchio,* Florence, 1298 to 1314, was the fortified seat of Florentine government; it has a tower extending above the block-shaped building (Figure 8-23).

In Spain, the most important Gothic architectural example is the *Cathedral at Seville,* 1402 to 1520. This church is the largest medieval church built—second in size only to St. Peter's in Rome, which was built during the Renaissance. Seville is hardly a classic example of pure Gothic architecture. The fact that it was erected on the site of an

existing mosque and underwent many changes until it was considered complete left the exterior in a rather confused state. The interior is impressively ornate with a 130' nave vault and a plan that covers nearly 200,000 sq ft.

RENAISSANCE ARCHITECTURE (A.D. 1420 TO 1800)

The fifteenth century found Europe again prime for change in both philosophy of life and architectural style. During the 1000 years prior, medieval culture, although hardly dead, did gravitate toward the subservience of the individual to a feudal lord or king. Rather than make the obvious transition of altering or improving on the existing Gothic, an abrupt about-face was made.

Italy never quite accepted the accomplishment of the foreign Gothic form. Rather, the Italians preferred to look 10 centuries back to when Rome was the greatest power on earth. It was here that they found the ideals in justice, architecture, and culture that they wished to echo. The movement away from Gothic actually started with the legal profession when it began to study briefs prepared in Roman times rather than medieval judgments. The logic displayed in Roman law very much impressed fifteenth-century scholars, and they began to study further. An eventual result was the revival not only of Roman justice but, of prime concern to this discussion, of Roman architectural style.

The resulting form was called *Renaissance,* which literally means "rebirth." This movement started in the country where the style had flourished so many years before. The Italian peninsula was a living museum of Roman greatness.

The style that started in the fifteenth century was to have a pronounced effect on all of Europe and the United States up to the twentieth century. Any disbelief in this can be dispelled by looking at a great majority of the public buildings done in this country through the 1930s, starting with the Capitol in Washington, D.C.

The Renaissance period cannot be studied properly if the discussion is limited strictly to architecture. The time is one of the most unique in history and has been labeled the *Age of Discovery.* The invention of the movable-type printing press by Gutenberg spread books and knowledge rapidly throughout Europe. One work of particular interest to architecture is the publishing of the *Treatise on Architecture* by Vitruvius, a Roman from the time of Augustus. The book attempted to establish the

Figure 8-23.   The Palazzo Vecchio.

rules for classical Roman orders and very obviously influenced Renaissance design when it was reprinted in the fifteenth century. The invention of the mariner's compass paved the way for exploration by Magellan, Vasco de Gama, Columbus, and many others. A third dramatic invention was the introduction of gunpowder into warfare, which radically changed many facets of life.

Not since the Greek culture had people made such a conscious effort to understand life and their surroundings. Not only were the sciences of medicine, anatomy, and astronomy highly esteemed, but art and architecture were recognized as unique individual talents. In many instances Renaissance artists participated in art, architecture, and sculpture simply by changing the medium in which they worked. Except for a few isolated examples in architectural history, this was the first period that gave the individual architect credit for accomplishments.

The new attitude assumed in Italy which dealt with the individualistic and critical human spirit was labeled *humanism*. The very nature of the movement dealt with reform in science, art, and even the solidity of the church. When taken in the context of the spirit of the time, the reformation proposed by Luther in the attitude of the church was a very natural step. The quest for knowledge became so broad that people actually became learned in all fields—Renaissance Man.

The movement produced so many masters in arts and science that it seems to eclipse all earlier endeavors. Men like Brunelleschi, Michelangelo, Bramante, and Borromini quite possibly could never have achieved their masterful contribution in any other time.

If one individual can exemplify the Renaissance time it had to be Leonardo da Vinci. Not only was his talent in art and architecture widely renowned, but he also mastered astronomy, anatomy, implements of warfare, and machines with advanced design such as the submarine, helicopter, airplane, and machine gun.

The characteristic style of the Renaissance definitely reverted to Rome. The actual step began in Florence with a competition for the baptistry doors on the cathedral group. Lorenzo Ghiberti spent 21 years casting the scenes in bronze. Of perhaps greater historical importance is one of the other contestants, Filippo Brunelleschi, who, after losing the competition in 1401, traveled to Rome to study architecture. Brunelleschi returned to Florence more than 15 years later to again enter a competi-

tion, this time for the dome on the cathedral. His winning submittal was a departure from the Italian Gothic style in which the rest of the cathedral was done. The egg-shaped dome was raised on a cylindrical drum with a capped element called a *lantern*. This was the first break in the medieval tradition of the progressive evolution of style, from Roman to early Christian to Romanesque to Gothic. Rather, a typical Roman and Byzantine architectural character was chosen. The following year, Brunelleschi designed the first total Renaissance building, the Foundling Hospital in Florence. This was the opening volley in an architectural character that started in the 1400s and lasted nearly 500 years.

Renaissance architecture superficially adopted the Roman exterior building treatment, including the five column orders, but engineering technology had progressed in 1000 years. Rather than adopt the Roman structural techniques, the Renaissance period adapted the style as a "skin" treatment. The high-vaulting structural buttressing systems, pointed arches, and windows of the Gothic style were all abandoned, but the techniques used in supporting medieval buildings were retained. In addition to structural changes, the function of buildings became more highly diverse than in Roman times, ranging from palaces to libraries.

Several architectural factions within the period should be mentioned. The straight Roman pursuit, the Renaissance, was the main approach, and it became more highly stylized with time and evolved into the High Renaissance form. A strong departure from Renaissance, *Baroque* began as a reaction against the firm adherence to classical style. While Renaissance architecture followed almost a cookbook approach to exterior design, Baroque was definitely a dissident form. The rule of the style was a curved line rather than a straight one, typically accomplished with stucco; the style was asymmetrical, rather than balanced; and it was unpredictable instead of orderly. The champion of the Renaissance was an architect, Andrea Palladio (1508–1580), while one leader of the Baroque was Michelangelo.

Characteristics of the Renaissance style included large ashlar stone walls, compared with the rubble and mortar of Gothic. Walls were commonly left rough-exposed to the outside. Windows were similar to Roman treatment in that they were small with semicircular arches or decoration at the head. Columns followed the Roman orders and like their predecessors were used both for decoration and for structural loadbearing. Roofing techniques reverted back to the classical nonribbed barrel vault. Along with this, the purely Gothic technique of buttressing was eliminated, making it necessary to resolve roof forces in massive side walls.

The emphasis on the vertical line, so apparent in Gothic, changed in the Renaissance to a building form that was largely horizontal. In fact, a characterization of the style would be largely a rectangular box appearance on the exterior with Roman decoration. The dome became an extremely important feature, with both Roman and Byzantine architecture contributing to its form. The usual approach was to set an elliptically shaped dome up on a cylindrical drum, which in turn transmitted the load to pendentives supported by columns.

The Renaissance style started and reached its highest form in the city-state system in Italy. Principally, Florence, Rome, Venice, and the surrounding northern Italian area led the architectural reform. One particular Florentine family, the Medici, acted as patrons of the arts. Without their assistance, both financial and influencial, Renaissance art quite probably would never have reached its full potential. The architecture that started at Florence in the fifteenth century gradually took over the rest of Western Europe and remained for nearly 500 years. The importation of Italian architects and the publication of several works of the Renaissance served to spread the style throughout Western civilization. The form was introduced, rather artificially, in the United States during the nineteenth century.

Renaissance Building Examples

Some important examples of Italian Renaissance architecture are described below.

1. The *Florence Cathedral Dome,* Florence, 1420 to 1434, was the result of the dome competition won by Brunelleschi. It was the first example of the Renaissance. Built on an existing Italian Gothic church, the brick dome spans an octagonal space 138′ in diameter (Figure 8-24). The egg-shaped dome was set up on a cylindrical drum to avoid the squat appearance of a hemispherical shape. Built according to Gothic structural techniques, it consists of an inner and outer shell with eight main ribs. Buttressing the outside walls was eliminated with the introduction of a hoop made of iron and wood at the base of the dome. This tied the forces of the dome together to prevent it from breaking apart. Michelangelo used this same principle by wrapping iron chains around the dome of St. Peter's Cathedral in Rome.

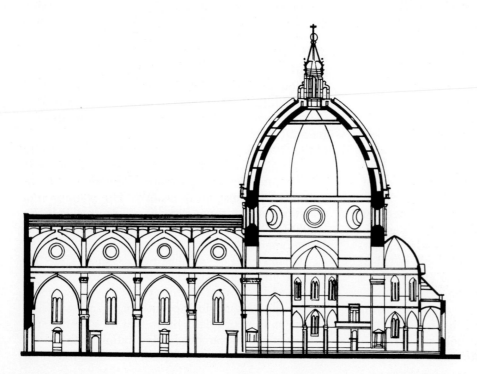

Figure 8-24. The Florence Cathedral dome.

2. The *Foundling Hospital,* Florence, 1421 to 1445, was the first building in Europe with this particular function. Brunelleschi's design included an attached porch with semicircular arches supported by Corinthian columns, the most recognizable feature, and definitely Roman.

3. The *Pitti Palace,* Florence, 1458 to 1780, was second in size only to the Vatican in Italy. The palace looks over the famous Boboli Gardens. Brunelleschi designed the three-story, rough-masonry building with a symmetrical window treatment and a half-arch at the head.

4. The *Riccardi Palace,* Florence, 1444 to 1460, was designed by Michelozzo Michelozzi. The palace was originally built for the Medici family and later acquired by the Riccardi family. With a width of 80' and over three stories high, the rectangular front elevation is capped with a 10' high cornice. The first floor was finished with coarse ashlar stone with the remaining two floors being finished in progressively finer stonework.

5. The *Tempietto,* Rome, 1502 to 1510, designed by well-known Renaissance architect Donato Bramante, was a small circular chapel, 30' in diameter, built at the place where St. Peter was martyred. In plan the hemispherical dome set up on a drum is supported by 16 Doric-order columns.

6. The *Gesu Church,* Rome, 1568 to 1584, was designed by Giacomo Vignola. Vignola was known both for his architecture and for his book *The Five Orders of Architecture,* which greatly influenced the French Renaissance. The Gesu Church is a Latin-cross plan, 225' long and 115' wide, with a dome raised on a drum at the crossing. The Baroque design is quite familiar because it served as a pattern for many later churches.

7. The *Farnese Palace,* Rome, 1530 to 1546, was designed initially by Antonio Sangallo and later by Michelangelo. A three-story rectangular plan, 180' × 230', with an 81' square enclosed courtyard, the palace is perhaps the finest example of Renaissance palace design. The exterior elevation is again a three-story rectangular front with rows of Baroque windows on each level. It is capped by an 8' cornice.

8. The *Laurentian Library,* Florence, 1521 to 1534, has a chapel designed by Michelangelo. The chapel is part of St. Lorenzo, designed a century before by Brunelleschi. The space is 40' square and treated in a Baroque style. The chapel serves as a tomb for two Medicis and is best known for Michelangelo's sculpture on each casket.

9. The *Capitol,* Rome, was designed by Michelangelo in 1546. The central building is flanked on either side by a palace and museum that form a piazza (square). A dominant feature in the complex is the double stair on the exterior.

10. *St. Peter's Cathedral,* Rome, 1506 to 1626, is the largest church in the world and not the work of any one architect (Figure 8-25). It initially was designed by Bramante to replace an early Christian church and to provide a burial place for Pope Julius II. The building originally was designed to have a Greek-cross plan (a plus shape with four equal legs) but later was changed to a Latin cross 600' long. Through the death of architects and popes involved with the project and periods of lack of funding, the cathedral went through many phases of change. At 72, Michelangelo became the guiding force behind the most prominent building in Renaissance architecture. His design included a 138' diameter dome, 9' thick at the base and over 450' high. Ten chains have been placed around the base of the dome to prevent it from spreading. The nave is spanned by a barrel vault 84' wide. The last major addition came in the middle of the seventeenth century, when Giovanni Bernini designed a 650' front oval court surrounded by 284 columns. The scale of St. Peter's is so gigantic, it is difficult to comprehend.

England finally was expelled from France in 1453, forming a new spirit of French nationalism. In the first half of the sixteenth century, French kings in turn invaded the Italian city-states of Venice, Naples, and Milan. While not faring at all well on the battlefield, the encounter did have the side effect of introducing France to the Italian Renaissance. France moved into the new building style with great vigor, placing a strong emphasis on elaborate living facilities for the noble class. France had overbuilt their number of churches during the Gothic period, and so not many were constructed in the Renaissance. The following 200 years found the country engaged in a very elaborate and extravagant building program, ending

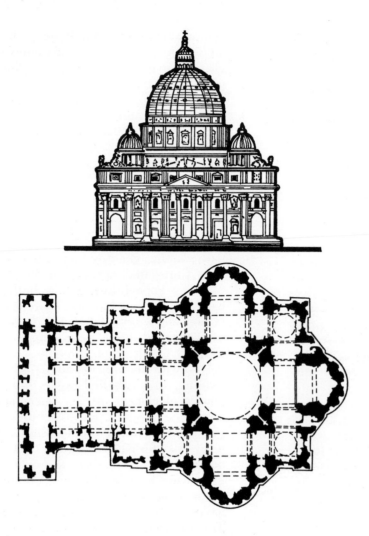

Figure 8-25.   St. Peter's Cathedral.

with the French Revolution in 1789. Napoleon Bonaparte assumed leadership in 1804 and continued the Renaissance building style, most notably in the city plan of Paris under the design of Baron Hausmann.

Some important French Renaissance building examples are described here:

1. The *Chateau de Blois*, 1498 to 1524, was actually begun during the Gothic period with major additions completed in a 300-year span. Its most famous feature is the stair tower of Francis I, a very elaborate spiral projecting out into a central courtyard.

2. The *Louvre*, Paris, 1546 to 1878. The 300 years of construction from Francis I to Napoleon III resulted in a building reflecting the full range of the French Renaissance. It was originally a palace for French kings and in conjunction with the Tuileries Palace, destroyed in 1871, covers 45 acres along the River Seine. The general pattern of the Louvre is a three-story square building with an open central courtyard. The exterior facade consists of engaged and free-standing Roman-order columns and window treatments with rounded arched heads. The Louvre now contains some of the world's most valued art treasures.

3. The *Palace of Versailles*, 1661 to 1756, was built for Louis XIV as the most extravagant expression of the Renaissance. The complex was designed by Louis le Vau and Jules Mansart; the main palace is over one-quarter mile long. Versailles contains many acres of magnificent gardens, fountains, and smaller buildings. The most significant structure, aside from the palace, is the *Petit Trianon*, 1762, a small, square building with engaged Corinthian columns, a favorite of Marie Antoinette. The hall of mirrors at Versailles served as the place for the signing of the World War I peace treaty.

4. The design of the *Dome of the Invalides*, Paris,

1680 to 1691, was completed by Mansart. The 90′ triple dome, one of the most impressive in the Renaissance, is supported by four piers at the crossing of the Greek-cross church plan. The outer lead-sheathed, egg-shaped dome is capped with a lantern 350′ high. The building is the burial place of Napoleon Bonaparte.

5. The *Pantheon*, Paris, 1757 to 1790, is not the same as the Pantheon in Rome; it was a Greek-cross plan, 264′ long with a triple-shelled dome at the crossing. The building has very definite Roman ties with free-standing Corinthian columns at the west entrance. The area below the Pantheon provides burial crypts for many French artists, including the building's architect, Jacques Soufflot.

England's geographic distance from Italy meant that it was the last European nation to come under the influence of the Renaissance. The governmental structure proved ready for the new and innovative period, and the style flourished. This was the time of Elizabeth I, Sir Walter Raleigh, Shakespeare, and Ben Johnson. England was emerging as a powerful trading nation with the resultant change from a feudal to a democratic state. Two architects, Christopher Wren and Inigo Jones, were the dynamic force behind the building form. Their contribution accounted for much of the English Renaissance. Wren's list of buildings was lengthened considerably when a disastrous fire swept London in 1666. The following period saw Wren develop a master plan of London and design 52 churches in a 40-year period. Some important English Renaissance buildings are described below.

1. *Whitehall Palace*, London, 1619 to 1622, was the most important building designed by Inigo Jones. It was built as a banqueting house. The rather modest plan, 120′ × 70′, was later intended to be a portion of Whitehall Palace, a complex nearly one-quarter mile square, but it was never built. The front facade is of very strict classical order, showing the influence of the Italian Renaissance (Palladio) on Jones's work.

2. *St. Paul's*, London, 1675 to 1710, was the finest work of Christopher Wren. It was built over the site of a medieval church which was destroyed in the Great Fire of 1666. The Latin-cross plan is over 500′ long, 120′ wide, and 366′ high to the top of the dome lantern. The

dome over the crossing consists of three shells and spans 112′. The west front is of classical proportions with an engaged 212′ tower at either side of the entrance. Of some interest is the comparison between this cathedral and St. Peter's in Rome. St. Paul's was built over 35 years under one architect, one mason, and one bishop, while St. Peter's was completed over 100 years by 13 architects and 20 popes.

MODERN ARCHITECTURE (NINETEENTH AND TWENTIETH CENTURIES)

In a strict sense, the term *modern architecture* does not convey a style, such as Greek or early Christian. It is unique in that it is more a product of technology than previously studied styles. In early building, stone was almost the only material used in architecture. The Romans introduced concrete but continued to use it in much the same manner as stone. It took the technology of the nineteenth and twentieth centuries to develop an economical way to produce iron and to incorporate its use in architecture. This meant that the structure took on characteristics of flexibility rather than the dominant massive element of loadbearing stone.

The core of Renaissance architecture was based on Roman design, which meant that a building was considered successful if it was patterned after principles 1000 years old. Originally this concept proved an excellent expression for the Renaissance artist to mold highly sophisticated design with technology. But without new input the style became stereotyped, and the works of Palladio acted as a text for new design. Architecture became more an applied surface treatment than an approach to solve the needs of the times. Further research into the past supplied an endless store of architectural styles for nineteenth-century designers. Greek architecture provided the necessary elements for the Neoclassical style, while Gothic designs were the pattern for Romanticism. The adaptation of past styles is given the term *eclecticism*. For architecture, eclectic design is not particularly wrong, but it definitely spurns advance. The period of eclecticism in the eighteenth and nineteenth centuries was so widely accepted that it eclipsed nearly all new design.

The new thinking of the Renaissance was largely responsible for the advances bringing about the *industrial revolution*. What once demanded the efforts of people could be performed by machine. A Scotsman, James Watt, invented the steam engine in the mid-1700s, and within 50 years it was being used to power factories. Along with the factory system came living conditions that closely paralleled the Middle Ages. People were forced to work long hours and live in grossly inadequate housing with little or no sanitation facilities. In some respects, the eclecticism in architectural design proved an escape from real life.

One reaction against European eclecticism was a movement begun in Belgium in the 1890s, *art nouveau.* This "new art" is best described as a free-flowing sinuous decoration with both iron and reinforced concrete meeting the requirements of the form. Two architects, Henri Van de Velde and Victor Horta, were best known for their contribution to the decorative art. While art nouveau was probably the first significant step toward modern architecture, the form rapidly lost "steam" and was obsolete by World War I.

At about the same period in history, America was beginning to emerge as a nation. Its natural ties to Western Europe continued over into architecture and most of her building attempts followed closely the pattern in Europe. The exceptions were the early houses, commonly two-story units with a central fireplace. The structure was made of rough logs covered with horizontal clapboard siding. Roofing was usually a steep sloped gable with small casement windows that provided interior light.

The simplicity and functionalism of this style was an excellent solution to the housing problem. As America began to prosper, its taste in architecture tended toward something a bit more extravagant. England was going through a design style called *Georgian,* which was brought across the Atlantic during the eighteenth century. While the style was done in stone in England, it was reproduced in wood in America. Georgian design was a late Renaissance form typically with symmetrical features and a Palladian motif.

The Federal style, which paralleled the classic revival in Europe, was the next form to be adapted by the United States. This was the design used for the Capitol and White House in Washington, D.C. Among the many talents displayed by Thomas Jefferson was his architectural expertise. He was so impressed by the writings of Palladio and the classic revival that his designs for the Richmond state capitol, Monticello, and the University of Virginia were all directly influenced by his studies in Europe.

Up until the time of the Civil War, America was very content to derive its architectural character from the European past. One of the first American architects to break away from European eclecticism was Henry Hobson Richardson. His pioneering design qualifies him as an architect highly responsible for modern architecture in America. Richardson's early buildings just after the Civil War were actually an eclectic form of Romanesque. His use of the rounded arch in the Trinity Church in Boston and the Marshall Field warehouse in Chicago was much more than copying twelfth-century architecture.

Individual designers began to emerge as the influencing force that caused the trend toward modern building. The first major use of iron in construction was in England in 1775, when Abraham Darby designed a cast-iron arch bridge to span 100′ across the Severn River. Another milestone in building came in 1851 with a competition for the hall at the London Great Exhibition. The winning entry by Joseph Paxton was a truly revolutionary piece of architecture. The design consisted of prefabricated steel members that held glass panels; it was demountable (actually moved to a different site two years after it was erected); the building covered nearly a million square feet, was designed in nine days, and was erected in five months (Figure 8-26). While the building materials were incombustible, the contents caught fire in 1937, and the entire structure was consumed in 20 minutes.

The Paris Exhibition in 1889 provided the proving ground for two very unique structures. Gustave Eiffel designed a 1000′ observation tower that bears his name and has become the symbol of Paris (Figure 8-27). Unlike the acclaim given Paxton, Eiffel received considerable opposition to his steel-frame monument.

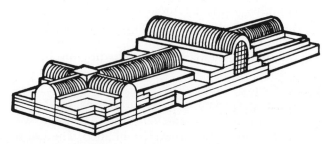

Figure 8-26.   The London Exhibition Hall.

Figure 8-27.   The Eiffel Tower.

The same exhibition had a structure designed by Dutert for the display of machines. It was a steel-hinged arch structural form 1400' long and spanning 375'. At about the same time an American engineer, John Roebling, perfected systems of weaving steel cable and the design of suspending bridges. His most impressive structure, the Brooklyn Bridge, was begun just after the Civil War.

These five men—John Roebling, Gustave Eiffel, Joseph Paxton, Abraham Darby, and F. Du-

tert—displayed unique principles of modern design by using the advanced nineteenth-century technology in an honest expression of the material. Their contribution is so notable because the vast majority of design was concerned with concealing a steel skeletal form behind an eclectic facade or casting Corinthian columns out of iron.

At the end of the Civil War, Chicago had emerged as a financial and cultural center that provided an environment for new architecture. The Great Fire of 1871, which destroyed the central city, provided a means for allowing many new buildings to be built. The design was labeled the "Chicago School of Architecture" and was accomplished by many talented designers, all of whom displayed a vigorous spirit toward modern building. Men such as John Root, William Le Baron Jenney, William Holabird, and Martin Roche made an indelible impression on modern architectural design.

An oversimplification of the concept of the Chicago School would be as follows: Roman orders as well as other unnecessary ornamentation were eliminated, the vertical nature of tall buildings was stressed, windows were used widely and their design was incorporated in the vertical approach to commercial building, and new concepts in iron structure were incorporated honestly in architecture (rather than being covered with false ornamentation).

Several factors contributed to the evolution of modern commercial architecture in Chicago. Land costs in the central city made tall office buildings the most economical way to build, while the invention of the passenger elevator made it possible. Of the architectural masters assembled in Chicago in the 1880s and 1890s, Louis Sullivan was considered the giant. His firm of Adler and Sullivan was responsible for some of the most noteworthy projects. A statement attributed to Sullivan, "Form follows function," very briefly sums up the philosophy of the Chicago style.

The year 1893 marked the four-hundredth anniversary of the discovery of America, and it was decided to stage a Columbian Exhibition in Chicago to commemorate the event. The Chicago firm of Burnham and Root was given the overall design responsibility, and architects such as Louis Sullivan were given individual building designs. The unexpected death of Root, the designer in the firm, and the presence of the highly successful New York architect Charles McKim left Daniel Burnham at the helm of a ship he had little chance of controlling. Under a great deal of influence from McKim, the eventual theme of the fair was an unfortunate blend of classical Rome with modern technology. Sullivan's transportation building was the only Chicago School entry in the exposition, with all others imitating designs 2000 years old. The resulting eclectic theme became an immediate hit with the American public and marked the beginning of the end of the Chicago School of architecture. The crowds that came to the Columbian Exposition returned home and duplicated what they had seen, a pattern that continued for the next 40 years.

Eclecticism was displayed particularly in public architecture, with many courthouses and state capital buildings following the classical form. Several buildings broke with tradition while staying in the guidelines of eclecticism. The Woolworth Building in New York was done in Gothic, while the Nebraska state capital followed such a simplified form of classical design that it actually started a new eclectic style.

The increasing population in urban centers contributed to spiraling land costs and therefore the necessity for taller and taller buildings. The 1930s produced the Chrysler Building, Rockefeller Center, and the Empire State Building.

It would be a gross error to depict the period of architectural history from 1890 to beyond World War II as a total waste in eclecticism. But instead of a movement, most notable modern design was being done by individual architects in America and Europe. Perhaps the top of the list should be headed by Frank Lloyd Wright. While his early significant training came when he worked with Louis Sullivan and much of his early work was done in Chicago, he was not truly a member of the Chicago School of architecture. His definite genius for design coupled with the fact that he practiced

architecture for 70 years made his contribution to architecture unsurpassed. Wright's concept of organic architecture involved making a building seem part of the site. This in part was accomplished by using large projecting roof overhangs and low roofs to accent the horizontal nature of the building. Wright found acceptance with his individual residential design (Figure 8-28) more rapidly than with his public and commercial endeavors, but his Johnson's Wax Headquarters, Guggenheim Art Gallery, and a 528-story, mile-high office tower that was never built are some of his more imaginative designs.

Walter Gropius was a German architect who had a major hand in shaping modern architecture. His design for the Fagus Shoe Factory in 1911 marks one of the most significant curtain-wall buildings prior to World War II. Gropius established a most productive design-oriented school, the Bauhaus, in 1919. The intent of the school was to incorporate design with much of the new technology of the twentieth century. The Bauhaus was responsible for design functions in such diverse fields as print type, tubular steel, furniture, and architecture (Figure 8-29).

Prior to World War II, Gropius came to the United States to practice and teach architecture at Harvard. Marcel Breuer, an associate of Gropius, also came to the United States to establish one of the most imaginative firms in the country. Ludwig Mies van der Rohe, also a German architect who eventually practiced in the United States, was considered one of the first masters of the modern steel curtain wall.

Mies worked under a famous German architect, Peter Behrens (as did Gropius and Le Corbusier), where he learned the discipline and use of iron and glass, materials that played such an important part in his architecture. His design for the German Pavilion in Barcelona, Spain, in 1929, is a

Figure 8-28.   The Robie House by Frank Lloyd Wright.

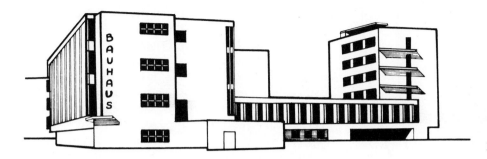

Figure 8-29. The Bauhaus.

prime example of the simplicity in design used by Mies. The statement "Less is more" capsulizes his architectural philosophy. His design for the Seagram Building in New York City, Crown Hall at Illinois Institute of Technology (Figure 8-30), and 860 Lake Shore Drive apartments in Chicago in the 1950s led the way to a realistic expression in architecture between America's commercial needs and its industrial technology.

Charles Edward Jeanneret, better known as Le Corbusier, started practicing architecture in France before World War I. He is best known for his use of reinforced concrete as a plastic, moldable material. Le Corbusier's 60-year contribution to architecture ranged in scope from an apartment complex in Marseilles and the Chapel of Ronchamp , both in France, to the city of Chandigarh, India.

Several other architects were major contributors to twentieth-century design. Finnish architect Alvar Aalto designed a tuberculosis hospital in Paimio, Finland, and Baker Dormitory at Massachusetts Institute of Technology. Erich Mendelsohn, a German architect who eventually practiced in the United States, is well known for his Einstein Tower Observatory near Berlin. An Italian designer, Pier Luigi Nervi, displayed his talent basically in concrete. His thin-shell rib design for the sports centers at the 1960 Rome Olympics became a prototype project. Swiss engineer Robert Maillart was responsible for perhaps one of the most unique and expressive forms of design, bridges. His spans through the Swiss Alps merge sculpture and engineering.

Finnish architect Eliel Saarinen entered a competition for the Chicago Tribune Tower in the 1920s. While his submittal was not chosen, it proved extremely imaginative. Saarinen later moved to the United States and, together with his son Eero, completed several impressive projects, including the General Motors Technical Institute in Warren, Michigan. Eero Saarinen went on to

achieve one of the most highly productive careers in architecture. His designs for Dulles Airport, the TWA Terminal at Kennedy Airport (Figure 8-31), CBS headquarters, the John Deere Headquarters, and the Jefferson Memorial Arch in St. Louis are all among some of the most significant structures in the country.

Modern architecture of the 1950s began with the United Nations Secretariat by Wallace Harrison and Le Corbusier in 1950. The tinted green glass curtain wall provided an image on which large corporations rapidly capitalized. The architectural firm of Skidmore, Owings and Merrill de-

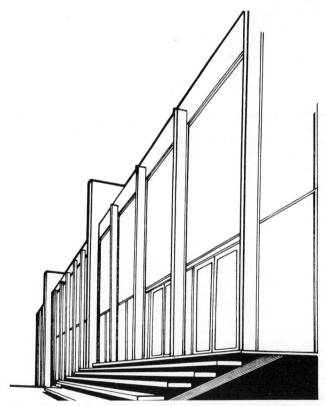

Figure 8-30. Crown Hall at Illinois Institute of Technology.

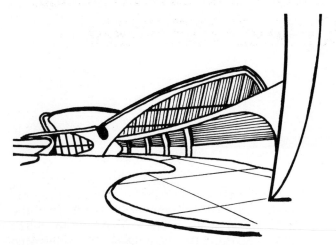

Figure 8-31. The TWA Terminal at Kennedy Airport.

signed the Lever House in 1952, which continued the pace of sheathing a building in glass and providing an open public lobby. Rather than the necessary 6' thick masonry walls to support the 16-story Monadnock Building in Chicago (done by Burnham and Root in 1891), the curtain-wall office buildings after the 1950s were structural skeletons with a thin skin. Many factors have been instrumental in dictating the evolution of the highrise curtain-wall building—economics, corporate image, flexibility, and concentration of services are a few. Today every section of the country can boast architectural talent. The credit for new, esthetically pleasing design is due not only to architects' imaginations. Clients must be equally daring to accept and finance a unique approach to their building needs.

Current architecture is certainly not a topic for a section on architectural history. Each issue of *Architectural Record* or *Progressive Architecture* brings to light new and inventive forms designed by architects. Yet, just as in architectural history, there are present masters of architecture. A partial list might include the following: Harry Weese, successful Chicago architect; Ralph Rapson, Chairman of the School of Architecture, University of Minnesota, also in private practice; Minoru Yamasaki, architect expressing vertical lines and multiarched tracery; Benjamin Thompson, one of the founders of The Architects' Collaborative (TAC) with Walter Gropius; Hugh Stubbins, one-time chairman of the Department of Architecture at Harvard, now in private practice; José Sert, worked with Le Corbusier, teaches at Harvard and in private practice; Philip Johnson, prodigy of Mies van der Rohe, highly successful east coast practice; Paul Rudolph, one-time chairman of the Department of Architecture at Yale, presently in private practice, introduced bush-hammered concrete to American architecture; I. M. Pei, worked with Hugh Stubbins, now in private practice; Edward Larabee Barnes, worked with Gropius and Breuer in private practice on the east coast; Kevin Roche, one of the partners in Eero Saarinen's firm after his death; Skidmore, Owings and Merrill (SOM), one of the largest and most successful architectural firms in the country; Louis Kahn, professor at Yale with private practice; John Andrews, partnership firm with innovative design; and Gunnar Birkerts, architect with a diverse, exciting practice.

NINE

SITE PLANNING AND DESIGN

SITE PLANNING

Site planning is a logical manipulation of buildings, vehicles, and people with reference to topography, climate, and functional needs to create a useful complex. A planner performs the task of moving people, buildings, and cars into a functional order.

Every building project undertaken by an architectural firm involves site planning to varying degrees. Planning is usually such an important aspect of building design that it can drastically affect the outcome of the architecture. Even a well-designed building should be considered less that successful if such functions as automobile and pedestrian traffic are not solved or if the best building location is not selected. A tie between site planning and architecture is so necessary that the two should not be considered separately. Rather, planning the site use should be the first step in the design of a building.

History

Historically, planning has always been an integral part of architecture. Up until the Renaissance, town plans were typically developed in nongeometric patterns. This tight, walled-city arrangement served as a means of defense as well as a means of tightly grouping people and buildings.

Renaissance planners preferred the more "intellectual" approach of a rigidly imposed geometric pattern with streets radiating from a center like bicycle spokes, as is seen in the plans of Paris and Washington, D.C. The relaxation of tensions among European powers in the 1800s, plus the mass movement of the population into the cities caused by the industrial revolution, started a grouping of people into congested areas that has never stopped. Several divergent systems of establishing a city plan have been developed:

1. A superimposed grid pattern placed over the site is perhaps the most prevalent planning technique in the United States today. Many cities have been developed by establishing north-south and east-west streets at 90° to each other, generally with a 300′ block-to-block separation.

   By its rigid nature, the system offers the strong advantage of being able to extend forever and make orientation to the center of the city quite easy (145th Street is probably parallel to 1st Street and a recognizable distance away). The shortcomings should also be quite evident: A grid fails to take all but major topographic and physical features into account; a grid is usually an uninspired way to lay out a site; and a rigid grid easily fails to establish major traffic corridors and commercial areas.

2. Another method of working within a geometric grid pattern is to plan a neighborhood inside the boundaries of major traffic corridors, allowing a less rigid treatment to design recreation, schools, and neighborhood shopping areas. This approach is best applied to established communities that attempt neighborhood redevelopment.

3. A more natural approach to planning is to design a network of streets according to the natural surroundings. Having a road follow the natural curve of a hill produces a totally different design than a road that runs straight over a hill. If design is bettered by the natural approach, the ability to orient a stranger to the surroundings is a weak feature of such design.

4. A further step in planning a nongridded community is to isolate transportation from dwelling. Such a design allows roads to go only slightly into the neighborhood. The remainder of the community is designated for walking, bicycling, and recreation. This plan is called *planned unit development (PUD)*.

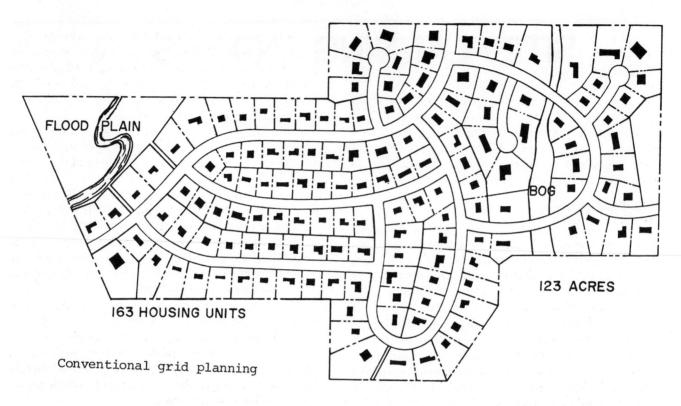

FLOOD PLAIN

BOG

123 ACRES

163 HOUSING UNITS

Conventional grid planning

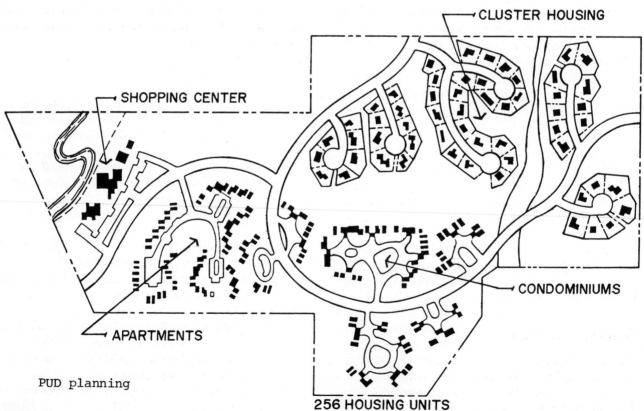

CLUSTER HOUSING

SHOPPING CENTER

CONDOMINIUMS

APARTMENTS

256 HOUSING UNITS

PUD planning

Figure 9-1. A comparison of conventional grid planning and PUD planning.

Modern dependence on usable forms of transportation has altered the course of planning more than any other point. Automobiles require a sizable percentage of the city to permit the flexibility required by our society. Freeway corridors have typically cut into the core of cities with little regard for the existing cityscape. No matter what the scope of the project, from single-family dwellings to a new university complex, the first duty of planners is to provide acceptable access.

Researching the Site

Before planners can begin to place the various elements on the site, they must assemble data about the site. Good site planning reflects research about the physical features of the area, such as existing landscape, utilities (water, sewer, gas), topography, views, and traffic patterns. A marked contrast of good and poor planning can be seen in housing projects throughout the country. One developer will take trees, climate, and topography into the overall design scope, while another will bulldoze the site and landscape flat before attempting to build. Both solutions manage to meet the broad requirement of providing housing, but one is compatible with and complements the site, while the other totally disregards the surroundings.

The limits of planning any area should be fully understood by the designer before he or she begins. The term *neighborhood* could be defined as the urban land area served by an elementary school. If a designer had such an assignment, he or she would consider corridors to a school along with local shopping centers, avenues to work, and recreational areas.

Access to streets and roads adjoining the site must be planned for vehicles. Each car in the program is assigned a size and path to get into and out of a parking space. After vehicular traffic, physical features of the site, climate, and all other demands have been considered, the planners are ready to begin their design with the proper tools.

Assembling the Plan

The next progression is to assign an order and function to the various elements in the design so that the plan begins to follow a logical pattern. This simply means that items which are compatible should be grouped, while nonrelated facilities should be treated in a way which will not reduce the effectiveness of the total plan. A recreation camp obviously should have the riding stable adjacent to the riding trails but not upwind (the prevailing wind) of the residence cabins. A good site solution, then, takes into account all physical problems or assets of the land.

No precise equation can be stated to direct the design of a site. A site plan is not as systematically solved as is a structural beam condition. Two prime factors in site planning are the concept of design and deciding how an area might be used now and in the future. Thus, no single, unique approach exists for laying out a site. It would be unlikely that two planners would come up with the same scheme. Two solutions could differ greatly in concept and still meet the logical requirements of the program and be successful.

Many assumptions must be made to determine how an area will be used, both now and in the future. Many assumptions can be guided by research, such as future traffic corridors and location of high-density housing. Typically, several factors must be referred to the professional experience of planners for a proper answer.

If planning could be broken down into a pattern for analysis, the following points should be taken into account:

1. Physical land features
   a. Will the site meet the program requirements?
   b. Is the cost of the land compatible with the cost of the proposed building?
   c. Will the site contribute to the esthetics of the building? Consider noise, pollution, view, and water.
   d. Can pedestrians, vehicles, and services circulate adequately within the site?
   e. Are the building and road systems feasible with respect to the topography?
   f. Will the site provide the necessary flexibility to allow future expansion?
2. Climate
   a. General weather, including the most severe, should be taken into account.
   b. Prevailing winds could be reduced partially with landscaping.
   c. The building should be oriented in relation to the sun.
   d. Proper drainage should be provided for the maximum anticipated rainfall.

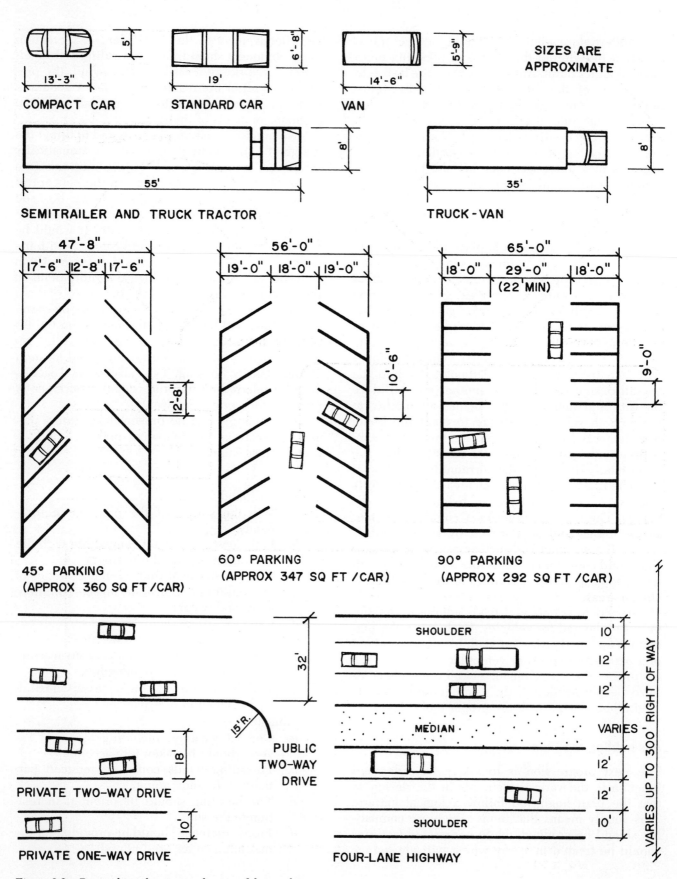

Figure 9-2. Researching the site involves careful size planning.

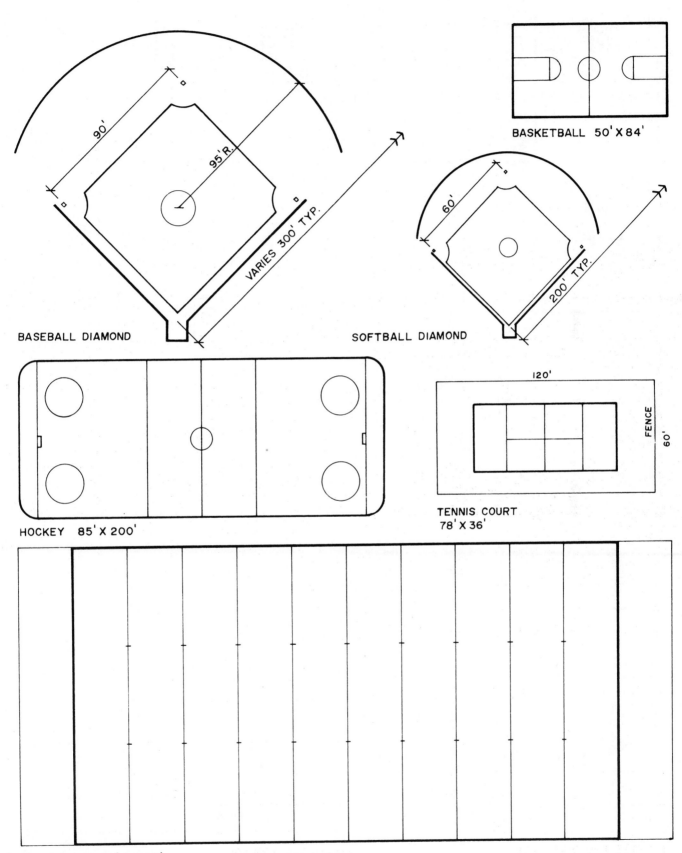

BASKETBALL 50' X 84'

BASEBALL DIAMOND

90'

95' R.

VARIES 300' TYP.

SOFTBALL DIAMOND

60'

200' TYP.

HOCKEY   85' X 200'

120'

FENCE

60'

TENNIS COURT
78' X 36'

FOOTBALL   160' X 300'

Figure 9-2 (continued).

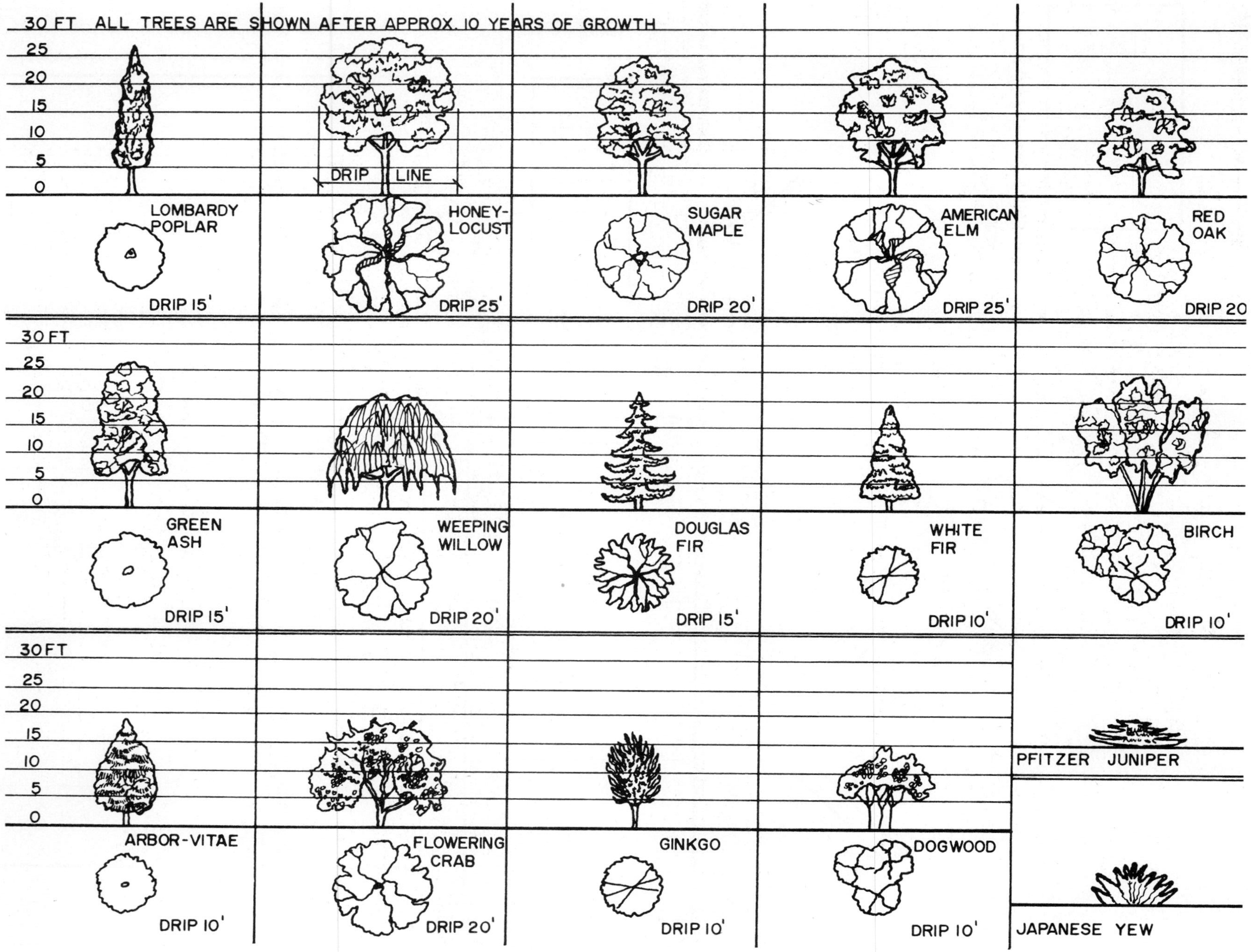

30 FT ALL TREES ARE SHOWN AFTER APPROX. 10 YEARS OF GROWTH
25
20
15
10
5
0
DRIP LINE
LOMBARDY POPLAR
DRIP 15'
HONEY-LOCUST
DRIP 25'
SUGAR MAPLE
DRIP 20'
AMERICAN ELM
DRIP 25'
RED OAK
DRIP 20
30 FT
25
20
15
10
5
0
GREEN ASH
DRIP 15'
WEEPING WILLOW
DRIP 20'
DOUGLAS FIR
DRIP 15'
WHITE FIR
DRIP 10'
BIRCH
DRIP 10'
30 FT
25
20
15
10
5
0
ARBOR-VITAE
DRIP 10'
FLOWERING CRAB
DRIP 20'
GINKGO
DRIP 10'
DOGWOOD
DRIP 10'
PFITZER JUNIPER
JAPANESE YEW

Figure 9-2 (continued).

3. Traffic flow
   a. Does pedestrian movement between buildings and from parking areas work well?
   b. Are major walking patterns such as corridors to schools, recreation, and shopping included?
   c. Although vehicular traffic certainly must be considered, it is better to channel this flow rather than to let it dominate the entire site.
   d. An excessive amount of service vehicles (as for a restaurant) could warrant additional roads to separate types of traffic.

Examples of Site Plans

The best way to discuss site planning is to point out some logical steps that should be assumed in determining a specific plan. The first example is a relatively flat site located along a metropolitan freeway with a busy street bounding the east, a service road along the north, and residential streets on the other two sides. The plan involves locating a hospital complete with emergency treatment on the site. The beginning step is to assign an area for each item required on the site to determine the proportions. The building size can be roughly estimated from the schematic design drawings, while

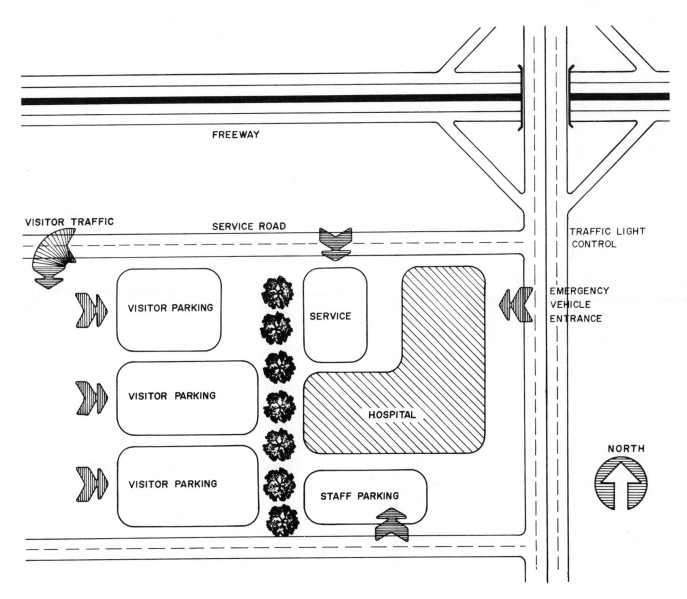

Figure 9-3. A site plan.

the number of vehicles planned can be taken by 350 sq ft/car (a figure used to estimate the stall size plus driveway requirements).

Parking can be further broken down into four separate classifications: emergency, staff, service, and visitor.

Emergency access should be divorced from all other vehicle traffic and should be most accessible to probable entry points along the eastern and northeastern corners. The necessity for rapid entry and exit from the emergency entry could warrant an entry along the busy east street with control of traffic signals at intersections.

Staff parking should be located convenient to the building in a separate lot, possibly with controlled access. If a staff entrance is provided, parking should obviously be adjacent. The around-the-clock work of the hospital staff and the unscheduled nature of doctors' time probably means that not many cars will be entering or exiting from this lot at the same time, and so that entry could be located along the service road to the north or possibly on the residential street to the south, if entry into the lot was not too far along the street.

Services for the building, ranging from laundry to food, is the third form of vehicle access. This again could require a separate building entrance and probably a separate entry from the street. The nature of service facilities would indicate that it should be shielded from the public but certainly accessible by medium-sized trucks. Possibly, it could be located along the service road toward the western edge of the site.

Public parking is the last and largest form of vehicle traffic for which provision must be made. Nearly all public parking will follow the pattern of visitors' hours, meaning that a sufficient number of entrances should be provided along the street to prevent congestion in the lot. Rather than inject this amount onto the uncontrolled busy street to the east or the residential streets, it would be best to locate parking lots along the northern service road. In this way the traffic would pass onto a relatively noncongested street, and it could be controlled at the northeastern corner of the site. In addition, the parking area, if broken into smaller lots with landscaping, could act as a barrier between the freeway noise and the hospital.

The flat site means that no initial concern involving topography would be assumed unless a multileveled entry was designed. The hospital design would then go hand in hand with the site plan in determining the best layout for the plot. In addition to parking, considerations such as the location of utilities, the view from patients' windows, the angle of the sun, the contouring of the site, and the landscape design should all be determined. It is the job of the planners to solve all conditions in the site and produce a logical esthetic solution.

Given the same site and a building with the same square footage, a housing project for the elderly obviously would take on a completely different site design. To be acceptable, the design of the site plan should be dictated by the function of the facility.

Planning the *building location* becomes a matter of establishing priorities between the units. The initial design input should include the function of each facility and how it relates to the total complex. Once the physical size of each unit has been determined and a logical order of the relationship of spaces has been established, a pattern of layout should begin to appear. This becomes as much a design problem as the location of interior spaces in a building.

One rather effective method that can be used in designing a site layout is to graphically manipulate "cut-out" areas around the site plan until an acceptable scheme is reached. The first step is to cut and label construction-paper squares or rectangles that correspond to the area of each facility to be located on the site. The area of the square should be laid out at the same scale as the site plan. To further assist the design, facilities which relate to each other should be cut from paper of the same color. An example would be a junior college project where the athletic building and the practice fields would be the same color paper so that it could be seen that they should relate. Special parking for this building should also be cut out and labeled. Once each space on the plan has been cut out of colored paper and labeled, the procedure becomes one of moving the squares around the plan until an acceptable layout has been reached.

Items such as topography, access to public roads, view, prevailing winds, and solar angles can all be marked on the plan as a reminder for design input. The purpose of assembling spaces with necessary ties in the same color becomes evident when the planner begins to move the areas into a possible design. One color isolated from the rest should indicate a flaw in the plan. Once an acceptable plan has been reached, a cedar-paper overlay of the scheme should be traced to retain a possible solution. This process should be repeated two or three times so that the designer can choose the best solution or take the best parts from several designs.

This is by no means the only way to establish a site layout, but it does have the advantages of speed and simplicity. It allows an inexperienced site planner the possibility of instantly changing the design simply by moving the paper cut-outs. Once an acceptable solution has been reached using this method, a great deal of refinement must be exercised to produce a finished product. Roads must be drawn to scale, landscape and tree locations should be considered, and walks should be indicated, to name several refinements.

Contours, or *topography,* present the most difficult elements in site planning. The general topographic demands include providing drainage away from the building; limiting the ramp slope for vehicle and pedestrian access; making logical grade changes that will better the function of the site without diminishing the existing topographic strong points; returning the contours to their existing elevation at the boundary line so that the adjacent land is not altered; and not disturbing the existing water shed from surrounding land so that water flowing through the site is not changed.

An architect generally makes observations through visits to the site and from photographs, along with a topographic survey of the land. Such a survey, provided by the owner, is produced by taking elevations or an aerial photograph of the site and extending the data into contours. The finished product is a three-dimensional plan of the site shown in two dimensions. The length and width of the site are indicated, and the height of the land is shown in a series of topographic lines. Each line has a specified elevation, and every point along that line is at the same elevation. Generally topographic contours are given at 1′, 2′, 5′, or 10′ intervals and are marked with their elevation above sea level.

A topographic plan is, at first, difficult to visualize because it is actually a three-dimensional drawing with each contour showing height. Most architectural site models display the contour by layering each level with cardboard or similar material. This becomes more realistic if the thickness of the cardboard corresponds with the scale of the model; that is, at a 1″ = 50′ scale, 2″ contours should be made from cardboard that scales 2′ thick.

The fastest way to comprehend topography is to construct a site model from a topographic plan. The lowest elevation on the plan will be the first sheet of cardboard and cut to the same size as the site boundary. The next topographic increment would again have the entire site cut out of cardboard, this time minus the area lower than the contour line. With each successive contour stacked and glued to the next, the resulting finished product is an exact scale replica of the site as shown on the topographic survey.

ARCHITECTURAL DESIGN

"Form follows function"; "less is more"; and "organic architecture" are a few simplistic architectural concepts that show a design philosophy. History has shown that certain periods of architecture—such as Greek, Roman, and Renaissance—actually developed formulas or guidelines to evolve building design. But it is only necessary to study a recent issue of *Architectural Record* to conclude that modern architecture neither can be capsulized in a statement nor written in an equation.

Building has always been one of the best mediums for expressing greatness. Egyptians immortalized their dead rulers with pyramids. Christians built lofty Gothic churches. Public buildings achieved great importance in Roman and Renaissance periods. Large corporations realized the potential of promoting their corporate image, as with the construction of the Seagram Building and Lever House in the 1950s. Contemporary program needs have become too complex, and architects, along with clients, have become too sophisticated to accept a preconceived design philosophy. However, it is only necessary to go back to the first third of the twentieth century to find hospitals that are designed like Egyptian temples and banks that look like something from a movie set.

It simply is not possible to comprehensively discuss the fundamentals of architectural design in the span of one chapter. Many books have been written on the subject, but the resulting passage of knowledge to readers is difficult to determine even when each passage is savored and comprehended. It is like discussing the development of imagination.

It might be beneficial to examine some of the academic courses considered valuable, with respect to design, in training an architect. Color, texture, dimensional perception, and form are all beneficial in learning design. Perhaps most of these skills could be summarized into what architects call *massing,* a process of projecting a functional floor plan into a three-dimensional form.

Good pieces of architecture attain a three-dimensional, sculptural quality. Massing becomes just as arduous a task for an accomplished designer as for a novice. We are primarily concerned with the quality in the final object. Architects use two basic tools to study massing—freehand sketching and study models. Both provide a rapid medium to analyze and refine a design.

The most important element in learning design is a good critic to review progress and point out inconsistencies. A design lab in a school of architecture thrives on the competition among students just as positively as it does on criticism from instructors. A common course of action is to receive periodic criticism from instructors, almost continual reaction from fellow classmates, and a final review in the form of a jury comprising professional designers. Coupled with self-evaluation, this process allows students to develop their design philosophies.

The final result in an architectural design can vary widely, even given the same basic requirements. The variety found in the designs of three-

bedroom homes is an example. Every design must follow a series of logical steps to fulfill the requirements of good design.

First, familiarize yourself with the *physical features of the site*. (Review the first section of this chapter.)

Next, determine the *space needs* of the client. This can be accomplished best in a real design with the architect and client meeting to discuss building requirements. A hypothetical design, like the ones encountered by students, is handled in much the same way; the designer has to answer many of his or her own questions. In either case, data should be compiled in a written document, a program. A completed program should spell out each room as to size, function, furniture, and special requirements, such as preferred view or built-in equipment.

Once the program has been prepared and approved, the business of assembling a functional arrangement of spaces or a *schematic design* can be started. Several techniques can be used, but the final outcome of each is to produce a floor plan

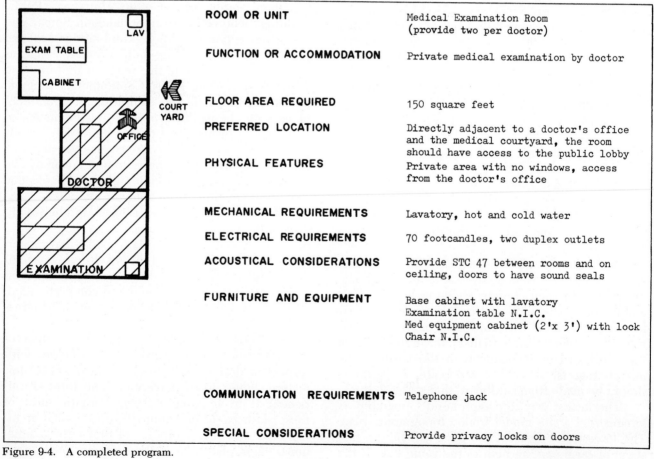

ROOM OR UNIT	Medical Examination Room (provide two per doctor)
FUNCTION OR ACCOMMODATION	Private medical examination by doctor
FLOOR AREA REQUIRED	150 square feet
PREFERRED LOCATION	Directly adjacent to a doctor's office and the medical courtyard, the room should have access to the public lobby
PHYSICAL FEATURES	Private area with no windows, access from the doctor's office
MECHANICAL REQUIREMENTS	Lavatory, hot and cold water
ELECTRICAL REQUIREMENTS	70 footcandles, two duplex outlets
ACOUSTICAL CONSIDERATIONS	Provide STC 47 between rooms and on ceiling, doors to have sound seals
FURNITURE AND EQUIPMENT	Base cabinet with lavatory Examination table N.I.C. Med equipment cabinet (2'x 3') with lock Chair N.I.C.
COMMUNICATION REQUIREMENTS	Telephone jack
SPECIAL CONSIDERATIONS	Provide privacy locks on doors

Figure 9-4. A completed program.

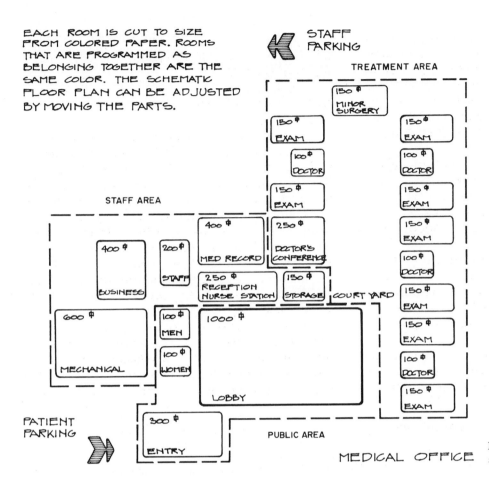

EACH ROOM IS CUT TO SIZE FROM COLORED PAPER. ROOMS THAT ARE PROGRAMMED AS BELONGING TOGETHER ARE THE SAME COLOR. THE SCHEMATIC FLOOR PLAN CAN BE ADJUSTED BY MOVING THE PARTS.

Figure 9-5. A program layout for a small medical center.

with a logical orientation of areas. Perhaps the easiest technique for students to grasp is an adaptation of an architect's flow or "bubble" diagram. A *bubble diagram* is a rough-sketch floor plan, approximately to scale, with arrows to indicate the relationship of one space to another.

The system we will discuss begins with each room being cut to scale (⅛″ or ¼″ = 1′-0″ is best) from colored construction paper. The room sizes are obtained from the program and should generally be square or rectangular. Spaces with similar functions or areas that should be logically grouped can be cut from paper of the same color. The color contrasts show up any errors, such as the isolation of one room from the others in its group. A small medical clinic would have the doctors' offices and the examining rooms all cut from the same color. Each square should be identified with the room name, area, and any unique program requirements. The design process involves manipulating all the room pieces into a logical pattern with reference to entrances, circulation between spaces, corridors, views, and the many other necessary points. Once an acceptable solution has been reached, a cedar-

paper tracing of the plan should be made, and the process should be tried several more times. The success of this effort lies mainly in the designer's ability to properly determine the problems and come up with logical solutions. The distinct advantage of this technique is that it allows the designer complete flexibility, for the plan permits any number of modifications simply by moving the rooms. A further addition to this system is to draw the site plan at the same scale and use it as a boundary for the floor plan.

Once a schematic plan has been approved, it must be refined into a workable building with structural, mechanical, and electrical facilities. The process of design development is one of taking the rough jigsaw puzzle produced in the schematic phase and making it a hard-line drawing. When a plan has been selected, the designer should begin to project it into the third dimension. Probably the easiest way is to construct a cardboard mockup. Building a model at this early stage is more for the education of the designer than for the interest of the client. This is the point at which the floor plan is combined with the massing of a model to provide a building. Neither the plan nor the model should be considered so rigid that it is not subject to change. The final result of this process is to produce floor plans, elevations, and sections through major areas in the building.

A talent in architectural design is acquired from a variety of sources. One of the most obvious can be found in monthly professional publications—*Architectural Record and Progressive Architecture*. Architects and students alike find reading several of these magazines the best way to keep current with the best design in the profession.

TEN

LAWS AND PRACTICES

BUILDING CODES

Building codes are written sets of rules adapted by local, regional, or state governments. Codes affect all buildings within their jurisdiction. The purpose of a building code is to indicate a minimum safety and health standard allowable in a building. Virtually every building project an architect comes in contact with is affected by a building code.

Several national codes have been written for adoption by local governments, rather than writing a new code for every city. The most common national codes are BOCA (Building Officials' Conference of America) Building Code; National Building Code; Southern Standard Building Code; and the Uniform Building Code. Local governmental bodies commonly draft additional code provisions to add to the main code to customize the national code to local needs. Nonconformance with a code once it has been adopted by a governmental body means that the building cannot be occupied.

Early in the schematic phase of a building, an architect runs a preliminary code check. He or she determines the code that is enforced at the building site and makes notes on all sections which apply to the particular building. Most codes fall into several classifications: type of occupancy (school, hospital, or other); type of construction (wood frame, reinforced concrete); or location within the fire zones in the area. The architect must combine all code items that apply to the particular building, in its particular location, with the construction materials intended, to come up with the code requirements. To further confuse the issue, most codes are written in a legally correct style that is difficult to comprehend.

A building code is not intended to limit design or the use of materials but instead to channel the safe use of materials and building design. In most code requirements, provisions are aimed at protecting people in emergency conditions, such as

fire, smoke, and earthquake. Many are designed to get people out of a burning building.

An architect prepares an initial code review while the building design is still fluid so that the code can guide certain design decisions. Most firms prepare a written code review and keep it up to date throughout the working drawing stage to maintain absolute compliance with the code.

The task of enforcing code requirements lies with local building officials. A building inspector reviews a set of architectural plans before the department issues a building permit. Any code violation is usually detected at this point, and the plan must be corrected before construction is started. A city building inspector is also assigned to the project while it is under construction to make certain the code is being followed.

Each building code has unique requirements, and each building poses unique situations within that code. Thus a simple summary is impossible. Some general demands of the Uniform Building Code (UBC) are listed here to give an idea of what code requirements are and how they apply to design. Only a complete check of the code enforced at the building site is considered adequate, however.

Type of Building Materials

The method of classifying construction according to the fire-resistant nature of the material is as follows. The "Hourly Rating" column refers to a building-code designation for fire protection. A 4-hr rating for structural steel means that the material will retain its structural integrity for 4 hr in the presence of fire. The code spells out many acceptable conditions from which the architect may choose. A steel column encased in 2½" of grade A concrete (if it is 6" × 6" or greater) will give the column a 4-hr fire insulative protection; 2" will give

3-hr protection; 1½″ will give 2 hr; and 1″ will give 1-hr protection.

TYPE I AND II BUILDINGS (noncombustible construction materials)

BUILDING CONDITION	HOURLY RATING
Exterior bearing wall	4 hr
Interior bearing wall	3 hr (Type II is 2 hr)
Structural frame	3 hr (Type II is 2 hr)

The materials may be steel, iron, concrete, or masonry. Loadbearing walls must be made of non-combustible, fire-resistant material. Stairs must be noncombustible (reinforced concrete, iron, or steel). Roof materials, including the structural frame, must have protective fire covering if the floor to ceiling dimension is less than 25′.

TYPE III BUILDING (combustible construction materials)

BUILDING CONDITION	HOURLY RATING
Exterior bearing wall	4 hr
Interior bearing wall	1 hr
Structural frame	1 hr of heavy timber

Structural materials may be heavy timber (minimum of 8″ × 8″ column, 6″ × 8″ floor framing), steel, or concrete. Exterior walls must be noncombustible fire-resistant materials. The minimum wood deck can be 2″ thick or any other approved material. Stairs can be any material allowed in the code except minimum 2″ wood risers in a timber-frame structure.

TYPE IV BUILDING (noncombustible structural materials)

BUILDING CONDITION	HOURLY RATING
Exterior bearing wall	1 hr
Interior bearing wall	1 hr
Structural frame	1 hr

Structural materials may be iron, steel, concrete, or masonry. Floor construction must be non-combustible except for wood flooring, which may be added as a surface treatment. Stairs may be of any type permitted by the code. Roof decking and the structure must be of noncombustible material.

TYPE V BUILDING (combustible construction materials)

BUILDING CONDITION	HOURLY RATING
Exterior bearing wall	1 hr
Interior bearing wall	1 hr
Structural frame	1 hr

Structural materials may be wood, iron, steel, concrete, or masonry. Stairs, floors, and roof decks can be any material permitted by the code.

Building Occupancy Types

In addition to code classification by materials, buildings are broken down into occupancy types. Through 10 occupancy groups, the code provides the minimum allowable standards for buildings ranging from auditoriums to warehouses. The following is an abbreviated version of Uniform Building Code occupancy classification system:

Group A   Assembly building with a stage seating over 1000

Group B   Assembly building with an occupant load less than 1000 (such as school auditorium or gymnasium)

Group C   Educational building through twelfth grade; day-care facilities when used by more than six children

Group D   Mental hospitals, jails, nurseries for full-time care of prekindergarten children, hospitals, and nursing homes

Group E   Storage buildings for highly inflammable materials such as dry cleaning plants, paint-spray rooms, woodworking establishments, and repair garages

Group F   Service stations, stores, office buildings, restaurants (with less than 100 people), educational buildings past the twelfth grade, and factories not using highly inflammable products

Group G   Storage buildings for noncombustible materials and cold-storage facilities

Group H   Hotels and apartment houses

Group I   Residential

Group J   Private garages

A first step in determining the code requirements is to check the occupancy requirements. It is possible for a multiple structure, such as a school, to have several classifications defining individual areas. The main body of the school would be Group C, a 1200 seat auditorium would be Group A, and the gymnasium would be Group B.

Building Dimensions and Other Common Guidelines

Once the construction materials and occupancy requirements have been defined, the code establishes rules for the maximum allowable area and height at which the building may be designed. For example, a Group C educational building built with Type II construction cannot exceed 34,000 sq ft, while the code will not even allow the construction of a Group D hospital with Type III, IV, and V materials. The limiting factor also applies to building height. The maximum height of a Group D school with Type II construction is four stories.

The Uniform Building Code affects many factors of design that are too numerous to mention. It again should be noted that failure to follow the code to the exact letter means that the building does not meet the law and can be closed by the inspector ("red-tagged") until the code infraction has been corrected. Some of the more obvious UBC requirements are listed below:

1. *Stairs*—Stairs with an occupant load of more than 50 people must be 44″ or more wide. A load of 50 or less can be 36″ wide, and 10 or less can be 30″ wide. Handrails cannot extend more than 3½″ into the required minimum width of the stairs. The maximum rise for a stair is 7½″, while the minimum tread dimension can be 10″. The only exception is that an 8″ rise and a 9″ run is allowed for a private stair. Stair landings must be at least as long as the stairs are wide. A stair is required to have a landing every 12 vertical feet. Handrails cannot be less than 30″ or more than 34″ high.
2. *Ramps*—Exit ramps must be a minimum of 44″ wide. The maximum slope of a ramp cannot be greater than 1′ rise in 8′ of run.
3. *Corridors*—The minimum width of a corridor with an occupant load of more than 10 is 44″, except in a school through twelfth grade, where the minimum corridor width is 6′ if the occupant load is over 100. A dead-end corridor (one that does not lead to an exit) cannot be over 20′ long.
4. *Exits*—Every usable portion of a building must have at least one exit. Buildings with more than 10 people must have two exits per floor. Occupant loads from 500 to 999 per floor are required to have three exits, while occupant loads of 1000 or more per floor need four exits. Exit width is determined by dividing the occupancy by 50. An auditorium with 1000 occupants, divided by 50, has a total width requirement of 20′; this, divided into the four necessary exits, means that each exit is a minimum of 5′ wide, probably two 3′ doors. The

UBC also stipulates that certain rooms must have two exits even if they fall into the guidelines called out above. The most common include

a. Assembly areas (bars, conference rooms, gymnasiums, dining rooms, auditoriums, churches) for over 50 people
b. Homes for the aged, hospitals for over 5 people
c. Classrooms for over 50 people
d. Dormitories, dwellings, hotels for over 10 people
e. Offices for over 30 people

If two exits are required in a room, the exits must be separated from each other by at least one-fifth of the perimeter distance of the room. No point in a building without sprinklers shall be more than 150′ from an enclosed exit, measured along the path an occupant would travel. If the building is equipped with an automatic fire-extinguishing system, the distance is increased to 200′.

5. *Doors*—Exit doors shall swing in the direction of travel when the occupant load is over 50. Exit doors must be able to open from the inside without a key. The minimum size of an exit door is 3′-0″ × 6′-8″ and cannot exceed 4′ in width. Revolving, sliding, and overhead doors cannot be used as exits. A floor or landing must be located on each side of a door, eliminating the possibility of a door at the end of a stair (except for Group I and H occupancies).
6. *Exit enclosures*—Most public stairs in a building are required to be enclosed with a fire-resistant construction. An enclosed usable space may not be located under a stair.

Special Requirements for the Particular Type of Occupancy

Group A   The auditorium must be provided with a main exit capable of exiting half the total occupant load. Stairs must be enclosed. One lavatory, two water closets for each sex, and one drinking fountain for each floor must be provided.

Group C   Kindergarten, day-care, first- and second-grade students must be located on the ground floor. One water closet per 100 boys, one per 35 girls in elementary, and one per 45 girls in secondary schools must be provided, as must one urinal for every 30 boys. One lavatory for every two water closets or urinals and one drinking fountain per floor shall be provided in elementary and secondary schools. In an open-plan school, the maximum travel distance to an exit cannot exceed 100′.

Group D Every room in Group D shall have two approved means of egress (not the same as exit doors). The minimum size of wheelchair exits is 44″.

Group E Storage areas with a size greater than 200 sq ft must have two separate exits. In areas where highly flammable or explosive materials are stored, the maximum distance to an exit is 75′.

Boiler rooms Two exits must be provided when a boiler room is larger than 500 sq ft and when the fuel-fed boiler exceeds 1 million Btu/hr. This applies to all but residential occupancy.

PERSPECTIVE

Drawing in perspective is an accurate method of showing a building with three-dimensional character. A common example is the way railroad tracks appear to converge at a distance when they actually are parallel. The simpler method of drawing, *isometric*, was probably learned in mechanical drafting and is not used frequently in architecture because of its distortion. In *perspective* drawing, parallel lines converge to a point.

The mechanical process of drawing in perspective was discovered in the Renaissance, although people before that time attempted a variety of ways to draw height, width, and depth. An architect seldom draws a finished perspective for his or her own study. The process is time consuming and serves little purpose beyond a quick sketch. The need for a perspective usually is generated by the client. It is a most helpful tool for the owner to sell the proposed building to a church board, school district, or business.

The steps to follow in drawing a perspective are

1. Establish a picture plane. This is simply a horizontal line drawn across the sheet roughly one-third from the top. Instead of a line, the picture plane should be thought of as a piece of glass with the horizontal line being the top edge. If the picture plane is envisioned as a pane of glass, then the perspective drawing is accomplished by drawing the three-dimensional objects viewed through the glass directly on the glass.

2. Determine the best view of the building by cutting out a scale drawing of the floor plan and rotating it. Locating the front corner of the plan so that it touches the picture plane is common but not necessary. The angle between the picture plane and the walls of the building has an obvious effect on the finished product. Thus, care should be taken in choosing the orientation.

3. Locate the *station point*, the point from which the building is viewed with respect to the floor plan. The least amount of distortion is achieved if the angle formed from the station point to the outside corners of the building lies between 30° and 60°. This is referred to as the *cone of vision*. A 30° cone will place the station point a distance away from the building, making the finished perspective longer and less massive; a 60° cone achieves the opposite. To find the station point, set an adjustable triangle at half the desired cone of vision. Starting from the two extreme corners of the floor plan, draw lines down until they cross. This is the station point.

4. The next step is to find the *vanishing points*. Vanishing points are two points located on the picture plane that act as points of divergence for parallel lines. Set an adjustable triangle to the angle of the walls on the right side of the floor plan. Using the same angle, project a line from the station point through the picture plane. The intersection of the two lines is the right vanishing point. The same procedure is followed to locate the left vanishing point. The only lines that diverge at these two vanishing points are the ones parallel to the walls on the floor plan, which originally were used to find the points. All other lines must be found by locating the two end points on the line and connecting them.

5. Once the vanishing points have been located, the third dimension, *height*, is introduced into the perspective. Tape an elevation (at the same scale as the plan) to one side of the vanishing points in the lower third of the sheet. A decision must be made on the height from which the perspective is to be viewed. Located at

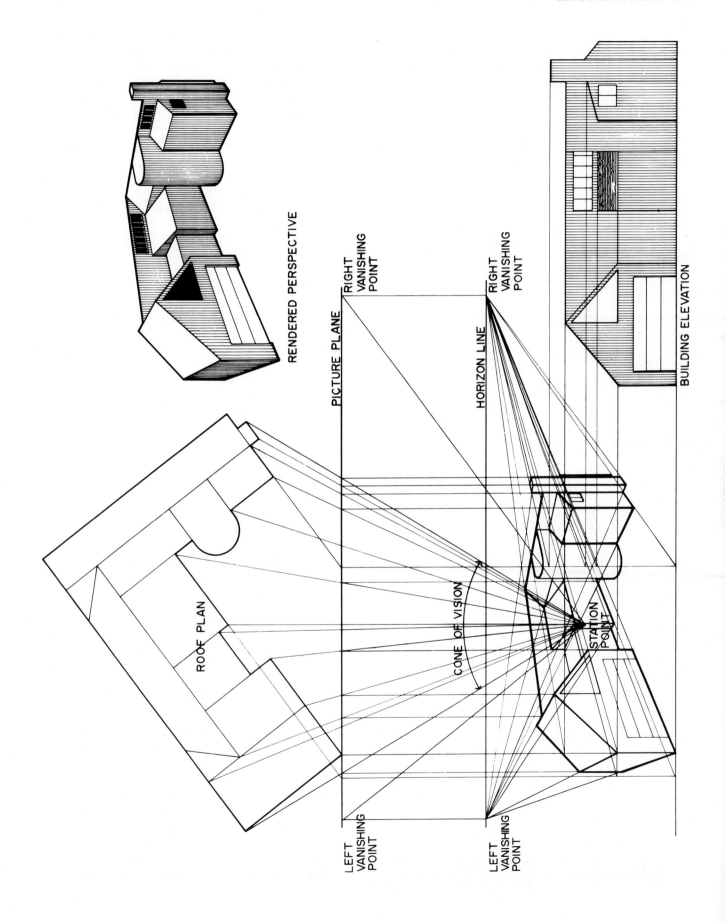

RENDERED PERSPECTIVE

PICTURE PLANE

RIGHT VANISHING POINT

HORIZON LINE

RIGHT VANISHING POINT

BUILDING ELEVATION

ROOF PLAN

CONE OF VISION

STATION POINT

LEFT VANISHING POINT

LEFT VANISHING POINT

ground level, the perspective will appear monumental and much higher. If the level chosen is 5′ above grade, the building will be seen the same as it would be to people walking up to it. A level above the roof line will produce an aerial view. Once a level has been selected, it should be located to scale on the elevation. This point is drawn horizontally across the sheet. It is referred to as the *horizon* and is the horizontal plane at which lines vanish. The final step is to vertically drop the vanishing points from the picture plane to the horizon line.

6. The actual business of drawing a perspective involves projecting a line from the station point to every corner of the floor plan. The point where this line passes through the picture plane is where it will appear in perspective. Each point is projected down vertically from the picture plane to the elevation. The only lines that can be measured in a perspective are ones that lie on the picture plane. Lines behind the picture plane will appear smaller, and those in front will appear larger. For this discussion of perspective, we located one corner of the floor plan on the picture plane, and so this is the only one in true height. To find this line, project the corner down from the picture plane and project the ground level and top of the line over from the elevation on the side. The intersection of these lines will give the first line of the perspective. The remainder of the perspective is drawn by projecting lines to the two vanishing points and darkening the actual drawing.

Several points should be remembered when drawing a perspective:

1. The perspective will have less distortion if the cone of vision is between 30° and 60°.
2. The vanishing points are found by drawing lines parallel to the outside walls from the station point.
3. The only lines that vanish at the vanishing points are those parallel to the outside walls.
4. The only lines that can actually be measured in the perspective are those on the picture plane.

In addition to these points, several "tricks" should be understood about the ways to manipulate a perspective.

The following four figures are of a simple mass which has not been changed in relation to the pic-ture plane. By changing one condition in each example, each perspective takes on an entirely different look. Figure 10-1 shows a perspective with a 40° cone of vision and a horizon line 5′ above the ground line. The building would be seen from this angle if the observer were entering the building.

Figure 10-2 has all conditions the same as the first example, except the horizon line is 15′ above the roof. This vantage point allows more of the form to be seen and the roofs to be exposed.

Figure 10-3 retains the same conditions as Figure 10-1, except the station point is moved to one side. This moves the perspective beyond the recommended cone of vision. The result is a distorted view of the building which can be used to emphasize one plane.

Figure 10-4 is again the same as Figure 10-1, except the picture plane has been moved behind the plan. The result resembles a photographic enlargement of the first example.

RENDERING

Rendering, or architectural delineation, could be considered beyond the scope of this text. A section on rendering is included to acquaint you with styles and techniques. A rendering is used to present a design to a client, to an instructor, or to the general public. The following figures are examples of pencil and ink renderings. Rendering mediums also include watercolor, opaque paint, an air brush (a small pen-sized spray gun), colored chalk, and felt-tipped pens.

Most architects have their renderings done by professional renderers. Do not be intimidated by the quality of the work. Start with very simple techniques and do them well.

If you are going to include a tree, locate it in the perspective drawing so that it is drawn to scale. Trees, people, and cars make the rendering more realistic and keep it in scale. An easy way to draw cars is to trace them from a new car brochure, which usually provides a variety of sizes and perspectives. The architectural publications are a good source of people illustrations.

MODEL BUILDING

The two forms of architectural models are those used for presentation and those used for study. The only real differences lie in the time spent in assembly and the materials used. A *study model* is rapidly assembled from inexpensive materials. A

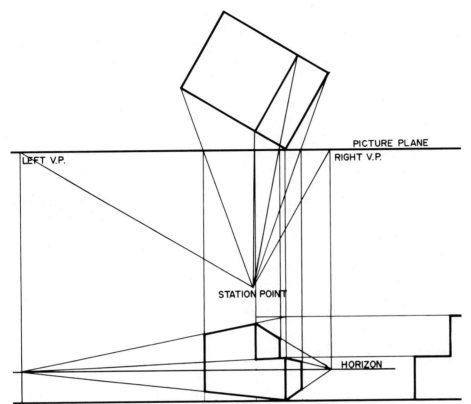

Figure 10-1.

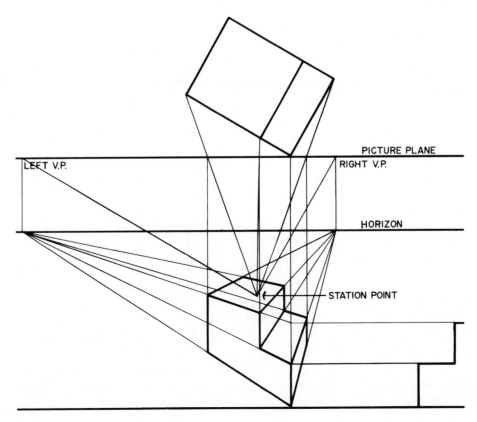

Figure 10-2.

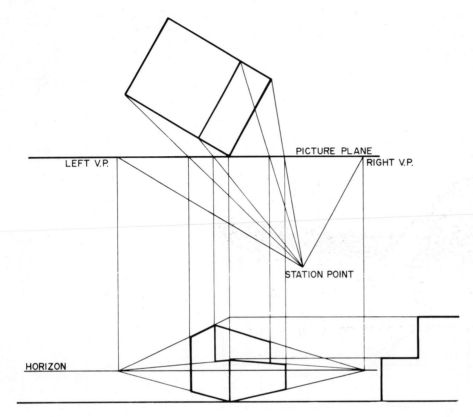

PICTURE PLANE

LEFT V.P.   RIGHT V.P.

STATION POINT

HORIZON

Figure 10-3.

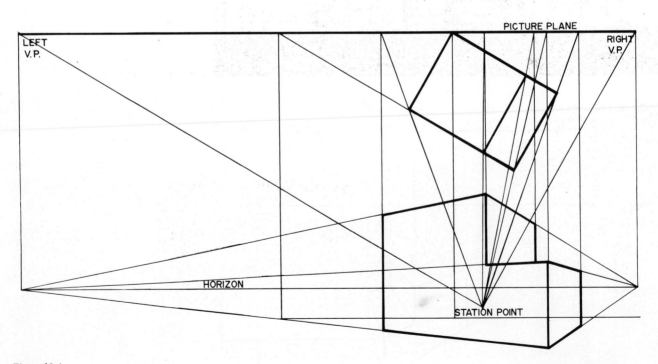

PICTURE PLANE

LEFT V.P.   RIGHT V.P.

HORIZON

STATION POINT

Figure 10-4.

Figure 10-5.   Ink renderings.

Figure 10-5 (continued).

Figure 10-5 (continued).

north elevation   **east elevation**

Figure 10-6.   Pencil renderings.

Figure 10-6 (continued).

Figure 10-6 (continued).

presentation model is a product of great care and choice materials.

Study models are invaluable in determining the massing and design. By necessity this form should be built rapidly and altered easily. The best materials are thin gray cardboard called *chipboard;* or a better buff-colored material, *Kraft board;* a metal straightedge; white glue; and a sharp mat knife.

Cut the proposed elevations and plan out of chipboard and assemble the pieces into a form. The chipboard should be cut accurately to produce a finished model with square corners and scalable dimensions. Choose an architectural scale that provides a model large enough to study but not so large that it consumes great amounts of time and material (try ⅛" = 1'-0"). The resulting model becomes a starting point to "play around" with the form. If a flat roof does not seem to work over an area, simply cut a chisel roof out of chipboard and try it on the model. The great flexibility of a cardboard study model allows the designer to rapidly test a variety of ideas in a short time.

An even faster way of producing a massing model is to stack pieces of corrugated cardboard into the building form. This works well if flat roofs and geometric forms are incorporated. The resulting form is quite crude but good for study purposes.

A study model can be used for simple presentations by gluing prints of the exterior elevations to the model. This provides an easy way to show door and window openings and material finishes on the building massing. A better model can be assembled by using 1/32" white cardboard and very carefully cutting out the windows and filling the openings with bronze or gray 1/16" plexiglas.

A *presentation model* has a very different purpose. Like the rendered perspective, it is used by the architect to accurately depict the design to the client. A study model of a building can be assembled in less than an hour, while a presentation model of the same building could take several hundred hours. Quality materials and exacting assembly techniques must be used to fabricate a model that looks very much like the finished building. Some of those materials are basswood, bass plywood, plexiglas, Fiberglas, strips of brass and aluminum, and various grades of cardboard. The figures that follow show some finished models.

INDEX

Abbreviations, standard, 19-20
Acoustics, 186-190
Aggregate, 124
Agreement form, 266
Air entraining, 126
Aluminum, 133
American Institute of Architects (AIA), 22
  (*See also* specific document)
American Society for Testing and Materials (ASTM), 22
Anodizing, 134
Application and Certificate for Payment (AIA), 257-258
Architectural Graphic Standards (John Wiley), 21
Architectural technician, responsibilities of, 274
Athletic fields; sizes of, 319
Autoclaving, 129

Balloon frame, 151
Bar joist; design of, 214
Beam design:
  concrete, 215-218
  steel, 207-212
  wood, 200-204
Bench mark, 65
Bending, 198
Bending moments, 195
Bid Bond (AIA), 242
Bidders, Instructions to (AIA), 236-240
Bidding, 241, 247-248, 265-266
Bitumen, 138
Block (*see* Masonry)
Brick (*see* Masonry)
Bubble diagram, 325
Building codes, 23, 327-330
Building construction, definition of, 1
Building equipment, definition of, 2
Building sections, 75-75
Building technology, definition of, 1

Caisson, 140
Catch basin, 169
Caulking compounds, 139
Ceiling plan, reflected, 79-80
Cement, 124
Cement asbestos, 139
Certificate of Insurance (AIA), 249
Certificate of Substantial Completion (AIA), 262
Change Order (AIA), 255, 269
Check set, 9
Circuit breaker, 180
Client, coordination of, 9
Columns:
  design of: concrete, 220-222
    steel, 212-214
    wood, 205
  orders of, Greek, 283-284
Commission, phases of a, 7
Completion, Certificate of Substantial (AIA), 262

Concrete:
  block, sizes of, 130
  compressive strength of, 126
  form work, 127
  one-way slab design, 219
  pan construction, 149
  prestressed, 128
  properties of, 123-128
  structural design of, 214-222
  temperature, effect of, 125
Concrete structure, 145-148
Concrete walls, 151
Construction documents, 234-235, 269
Construction management, 263
Construction phase, 254
Construction Specifications Institute, Inc.
  (CSI), format of, table, 264
Consultants, 11
Contours (*see* Topographic lines)
Contract, architect's, 223-231
Contract documents (*see* Construction documents)
Contractor Agreement, Owner-(AIA), 243-246
Contractor's Affidavit of Payment of
  Debts and Claims (AIA), 261
Contractor's Affidavit of Release of Liens (AIA), 260
Cooling design, 177
Cooling systems, 173-175
Coordination (*see* Client; Consultants; Engineers; Specification
  writer; Staff, architectural)
Copper, 134
Curtain wall, 148, 151

Dampproofing, 141
Dead load, 191
Debts and Claims, Contractor's
  Affidavit of Payment of (AIA), 261
Degree days, 175
Design, 4, 323-326
  beam (*see* Beam design)
  definition of, 4
  layout, 325
  one-way slab, concrete, 219
  of open-web steel joist, 214
  schematic, 232
Design-development phase, 233-234
Detail index, 38-62
Detailing:
  definition of, 1
  methods and systems of, 139-162
Details, 63
  larger-scale, 76-79
Dimensions, 24, 68
Doors, 157-162
  hardware for, 72, 160-161
  labeled, requirements for, 162
  numbers for, 67
  schedule for, 70
Drafting board, 15
Drafting equipment, 13-19

Drafting procedures, 23-37
Drawing:
  in perspective, 330-333
  to scale, 23
  survey, 64
Drawings, working, 63-80
    detail, 25, 63
    notes on, 33
    shop, 10, 259

Efflorescence, 132
Elasticity, modulus of, 200
Electric panel, 180
Electric wiring, 180-182
Electrical design, 178-183
Elevation(s), 63, 75
  exterior, 73-75
  interior, 79
  layout of, 28
Engineers, 11
Extruding, 134

Fast track (see Construction management)
Fee breakdown, 223
Ferrous metal, 120-123
Fiber stress, 198
Field Order, Architect's (AIA), 256
Field representative, 276
Flashing, 155
Floor-plan layout, 27, 67-70
Floors, 142-143
Fluorescent light, 183
Footcandle, 185
Footings, 140
  design of, 221
Foundations, 140
Framing, structural, 196
French curve, 30

General conditions, 266-269
Glass, 135-136
Grid, 26, 68
Grid planning, 316
Gypsum, 136-138

Hardware, door, 72, 160-161
Heat design, 175-176
Heating systems, 169-173
  forced-air, 171-172
  hot-water, 170
  solar, 172
  steam, 171
History, architectural, 3, 279-314
    Byzantine, 296
    definition of, 3
    early Christian, 293-296
    Egyptian, 279-281
    Gothic, 300-304
    Greek, 282-287
    modern, 309-314
    Renaissance, 304-309
    Roman, 287-293
    Romanesque, 297-299
    Western Asian, 281-282
Humidity, control of, 174

Impact noise rating (INR), 187, 189
Incandescent light, 183
Instructions to Bidders (AIA), 236-240
Insulated glass, 135
Insulation, 142, 177
Insurance, Certificate of (AIA), 249
Interior elevations, 79

Job captain, 274, 275
Joists, design of: open-web steel, 214, 270
  wood, 204, 206

Key plan, 69

Labor and Material Payment Bond (AIA), 252-253
Laminated beams, columns, and arches, 207
Lath, 137
Lettering, 30
Liens, Contractor's Affidavit of Release of (AIA), 260
Lift-slab construction, 148
Lift station, 168
Light fixtures, 184
Lighting design, 183-186
Line quality, 34
Lintel sizes, 154
Live load, 191
Loading, conditions of, 197
Lumber grades, unit stresses, for, table, 202

Masonry, 128-132
  (See also Concrete)
Masonry bond, 131
Masonry dimensions, 24
Mastaba, 279
Material, hatching of, 21
Mechanical bond, 132
Models, building of, 332, 334
Modulus of elasticity, 200
Moment, 191
  total allowable, in beams, 211
Mortar joints, 130

National Council of Architectural Registration Boards
    (NCARB), 273
National Plumbing Code, 165
Neatness, importance of, in drafting, 23
Nonferrous metal, 133-135
Notes on working drawings, 33

Office manager, 276
Office personnel, 273-277
Office practice, 271-277
One-way slab design, concrete, 219
Open-web steel joists, 214, 270
Owner-Architect Agreement (AIA), 224-231
Owner-Contractor Agreement (AIA); 243-246

Panels, spandrel, 136
Parging, 132
Parking space, 318
Patina, 134
Payment, Application and Certificate for (AIA), 257-258
Payment procedures, 268

Performance Bond (AIA), 250-251
Perspective drawing, 330-333
Piles, 140
Planned unit development (PUD), 315
Plans:
    architectural, 63, 67-70
        exterior, 63-67
    site (*see* Site plans)
Plaster, 137
Plot plan (*see* Site plans)
Plumbing disposal, 167-169
Plywood, 120
Presentation model, 334
Print machine, 17
Professional practice, definition of, 2
Programming, 324
Project manager, 275
Projects, types of, 5-8
        commercial construction, 7-8
        residences, 5-7
Proportioning lines, 30
Proposal form, 266
Punch list, 259
Pyramid, 280

Rafters, roof, 204
Reference materials, 21-23
References and cross-references in drafting, 25-27
Reflected ceiling plan, 79-80
Refrigeration cycle:
    absorption, 174
    compression, 173
Registration, National Council of Architectural
    Registration Boards (NCARB), 273
Rendering, 332
Reverberation time, 189
Roofing, 154-157
    built-up, 138
    materials for, table, 157
Roofs:
    built-up, 155
    contraction joints for, 155
    drains for, 156
    expansion joints for, 156
    plans for, 66
Room finish schedule, 70, 73
Room numbers, 67
Running bond, 130

Safety on job site, 268
Salamander, 125
Schematic design, 232
Sealants, 139
Section modulus, 198-200
Section(s), 21, 63, 75-76
    layout of, 28
Septic tank, 168
Sewage, disposal of, 167-168
Shear, 193
Sheet, layout of, 36
Shop drawings, 10, 259
Site planning, 3-4, 315-323
    definition of, 3
    history of, 315
    researching and, 317
    survey drawings, 64
Site plans, 64-67
    assembly of, 317
    examples of, 321-323
    layout of, 322

Skills, basic, 1
Slump test, 126
Soil, borings of, 140
Soil pipe, 167
Sound attenuation, 190
Sound transmission class (STC), 187, 189
Spandrel panels, 136
Specification writer, 12, 276
Specifications, 263-271
    sample, 270
Stacked bond, 130
Staff, architectural, coordination of, 9-11
Stairways, 67
Steel:
    properties of, 121-123
    structural design of, 207-214
        allowable stress for, table, 213
Steel structure, 144-145
Stone, 132-133
Storm water, 169
Structural design, 191-222
    concrete construction, 214-222
    mechanics of, 191-200
    steel construction, 207-214
    wood construction, 200-207
Structures, definition of, 2
Study model, 332
Sump, 167
Sweet's File (F.W. Dodge), 21
Symbols, 19, 21

Technician, architectural, responsibilities of, 274
Thinwall conduit, 181
Timber decking, 207
Time Savers Standards (McGraw-Hill), 21
Toilet rooms, 68
Toilets, details of, 79
Topographic lines, 65
Trade associations, 22
Trade publications, 22
Transformers, 179
Trees, growth of, 320

U factors, 176
Ultimate-strength design in concrete construction,
    214, 218-222
Underwriters' Laboratories, Inc. (UL), 22

Vanishing point, 330
Vault forms, 289
Vehicles, sizes of, 318
Venting, plumbing of, 167

Wall systems:
    exterior, 148-153
    interior, 153
Water:
    distribution of, 163, 164
    pressure of, 165
    purification of, 164
    softening, 164
    storm, 169
    well, 163-164
Water-cement ratio, 124
Waterproofing, 141-142
Well water, 163-164

Western frame, 149
Windows, 157-159
  dimensioning, 68
Wiring systems, 181-183
Wood:
  properties of, 119
  structural design of, 200-207
Wood frame, 143-144
  dimensions of, 24

Working drawings (*see* Drawings, working)
Working-stress design of beams, 215-218
Wythe, 135

Ziggurat, 281, 282
Zipper wall, 151